With kindest personal
regards of the author
Earl L. Core

Confederate troops under General William E. Jones set fire to the suspension bridge at Morgantown but are ordered to desist by Lieutenant William L. Wilson, April 28, 1863. The heat of discord between eastern and western Virginia was about to split the state in two. (From a painting by Diane Lenhart.)

# The Monongalia Story

## A Bicentennial History

## III. Discord

### By Earl L. Core

West Virginia University
and
Morgantown Public Library

McClain Printing Company
Parsons, West Virginia
1979

Standard Book Number 87012-309-2
Library of Congress Card Number 78-62434
Printed in the United States of America
Copyright © 1979 by Earl L. Core
Morgantown, West Virginia
All Rights Reserved

*To*
*FREDA*

*and our children*
*Ruth*
*Merle*
*Harry*
*David*

*and our grandchildren*
*Kathleen*
*Arden*
*Harry*
*Michael*
*Kevin*
*Brian*

*and our great-grandchildren*
*Jenifer*
*Micah*

# Preface

This is the third volume of a projected five-volume work designed to constitute a bicentennial history of Monongalia County, West Virginia. The first volume, published in 1974, is a prelude to the history, including a general description of the land, with an account of the exploration and early settlements, ending with the political establishment of the county in 1776. The second volume, bearing the date 1976, deals with the history of the pioneer period, from 1776 to 1826.

The present volume deals with the next fifty-year period, from 1826 to 1876. The subtitle is Discord, and the bitterness of the Civil War period is the central feature. Not only was there a steadily widening gap between North and South in the years before the war, but in Virginia there was also a gulf developing between East and West that complicated the political situation and added to the agony.

Acknowledgments of assistance are due hundreds of persons who have provided materials of value and most of these are recognized in footnote and other citations. Special appreciation is expressed to the staff of the West Virginia University Library, the Morgantown Public Library, and the Monongalia County Courthouse, as well as to members of the Monongalia Historical Society.

I am especially indebted to Miss Diane Lenhart for the numerous sketches and maps which she designed especially for this work. The map of Monongalia County in 1826 used on the back endpaper was also drawn by Miss Lenhart from source materials of that period.

It is a pleasure to recognize also the unusually careful work of Miss Doris Geiler, who prepared the manuscript for the printer.

Very special thanks are also due Norman Shively, whose posthumously published "Index" to Wiley's *History of Monongalia County* has saved the present author countless hours of time in consulting that work.

A substantial portion of the material in this volume has been included in weekly columns in the *Sunday Dominion-Post (Panorama Magazine)* and appreciation is expressed to the publishers of that newspaper.

July 1, 1978                                    EARL L. CORE

# Contents

# Introduction

By 1826 the pioneer period of Monongalia County's history had come to an end and the citizens were seriously involved in the building of a new society in the Monongahela Valley. A letter written November 25, 1822, by John Steen, a carpenter who had come to Morgantown from Washington, D.C., to a friend, Louis Marceron, in Washington, helps to provide some notion of what the county was like as it began the second half century of its story.[1]

"This country is very hilly, or I may say all hills, but very healthy as I myself am an instance of it, for I have not had pain, ache or illness since I came here, and am so very fat that I never was fatter in my life. It is not a very rich country, as money is very scarce and we have not a good market for our produce unless we would send it to New Orleans, which we could do by water; but the distance is so very great that the farmers only send it to Pittsburgh, which is 90 miles from here by water, and then the Pittsburgh market is generally overstocked and they get very little for it.

"The land is only middling good, producing about 20 bushels of wheat and rye, 50 of oats, and 35 to 50 of corn to the acre. This country abounds with stone-coal, limestone, and iron ore and is timbered with oak of all kinds, particularly white oak, black and white walnut, ash, hickory, beech, poplar, some yellow pine,[2] dogwood, and other kinds too tedious to mention. It is well watered with good springs, but the creeks have so much descent that they are nearly dry in the summer, and the river is also so low in warm weather that it can be waded or indeed you may jump from stone to stone and so cross it without wetting

1. This letter, preserved by a grandson of Marceron, was published in full in the *New Dominion*, October 22, 1926.
2. He probably meant white pine (*Pinus strobus*).

your feet. We have saw mills, grist mills, iron furnaces, &c., in abundance near us.

"Our farmers are generally very lazy and are not possessed of much perseverance. Some of them are very great cheats, alias rascals, that is, they will do anything to get a little hard money as they never had a cent since they were born. Some are very rich in land. They make all their clothing, sugar, &c. The farmers that attend to their work live very comfortably and can save something every year.

"Wheat sells at present for 50 cents a bushel, rye for 45 cents, corn 34 cents, potatoes 34 cents, oats 25 cents per bushel; beef 2½ cents, pork 3 cents, bacon 8 cents, butter 8, country sugar 10, candles 12½ cents per pound. There is plenty of carpenter's work to do, and a carpenter can earn about $1 per day and found, and receive grain or other things in payment, but cash is out of the question. Country linen sells for 18 to 37½ cents per yard, lindsey woolsey from 50 to 75 cents per yard; shoes and imported dry goods, about the same price as in Washington when I left it. Ironmongery very little higher.

"I must now tell you something about Morgantown. It is three-eighths of a mile square. The streets are laid out east & west & north & south, crossing each other at right angles. It contains about 600 inhabitants. There are a great many tolerably good brick houses and frames in it, a market house about half as large as Capitol Hill market, a brick courthouse with two wings, a cupola on it and a bell in it, a two-story frame jail, Lord keep me out of it, and a publick school house built of brick &c.

"The inhabitants comes next. They are generally sober, generous and obliging, and all live easy and comfortable, and are very friendly to strangers. There are seven carpenters and cabinet-makers in this town. They all get enough to do. Mary teaches school and is doing very well in this county. . . . Eliza teaches school in the country about five miles from this town, and is doing tolerable well. . . . Sarah is assisting Mary to teach, and I am in a notion of turning school-master myself. It is the best business going."

# CHAPTER FIFTY-ONE

# 1827

As Monongalia County began its second half century, one of the problems weighing most heavily on the minds of its citizens was that of transportation. The principal markets were largely on or near the Atlantic seaboard, separated from the Monongahela Valley by a rugged mountain complex. Roads were difficult to build; at best, they often had long, steep grades.

The rivers were more promising but the promises often proved empty. In the first place, the Monongahela and the Cheat flowed north, while most early traffic moved west or east. The ease of water transport justified a long detour to reach the Ohio, where a westward trend was restored, but unfortunately the water level much of the time was either too low for boats to travel regularly or too high for them to travel safely.

**Building Roads.** Work on the roads was mostly done by citizens, who were required to put in a given number of days' work annually, or to pay for someone to work in their stead. A newspaper editor, who signed himself as "Bernard," outlined the problems:

"There is scarcely anything of a public nature which should interest more, the Citizens of Monongalia, than the improvement of their roads; they are essential to the prosperity of our County, and it is with pleasure I observe, a laudable spirit prevailing throughout our County, having in view, the formation, not only of passable, but of good and substantial highways. Notwithstanding this prevailing spirit, many years must elapse, under the present system of things, before we can expect any important or general improvement to be made. The present mode of road-working is considered, not only inefficacious, but highly unjust and partial in its effects—he whose estate is worth

1

ten thousand dollars contributes no more labour toward the making of roads, than he, whose property is worth but ten; although we would suppose the interest of the former, to be an hundred times greater, than that, of the latter. For years this has been a loud subject of complaint, especially among the poorer classes of the community. . . . Some other means must be adopted by which to make our roads . . . that hereafter in Winter, as well as in Summer our roads may be traversed without endangering the neck, either of horse or rider."[1]

"Bernard" later suggested that state aid might be sought, similar to that granted for the Staunton and Parkersburg road: "thus we might have $800 to expend annually which would add much to the facility of travel, and comfort of trade."[2]

Citizens were still incensed and disappointed that the National Road had missed Monongalia County. "Had our representatives in Congress or in the General Assembly been alert," they complained, "the road would have come through Morgantown." An editorial writer who signed himself "Hamilton," stated the case:

"Had Virginia pursued the course adopted by Pennsylvania, enacting that the National road must pass through Morgantown (not a mile from a straight line from Cumberland to the mouth of Fishing creek) the inevitable consequence would have been, that the National road would have passed through Monongalia a distance of more than fifty miles—would to God she had done so, as we neither had in Congress or our Assembly, a single voice willing or able to advocate our claims."[3]

**The Railroad.** Meanwhile, a fantastic and almost incredible new form of transportation was being discussed in Baltimore and elsewhere. The completion of the Erie Canal in 1825, around the northern flank of the Alleghenies, resulted in the diversion of trade and emigration from the National Road and threatened the doom of the city of Baltimore. For centuries, cars in English mines had been running on rails made of wood. By 1800 cast iron rails had come into use. Horses, ponies, or mules provided the motive power. Richard Trevithick, in England, invented the

1. *Monongalia Chronicle*, February 3, 1827.
2. *Monongalia Chronicle*, February 17, 1827.
3. *Monongalia Chronicle*, February 10, 1827.

first steam locomotive in 1804. It was not a great success, but in 1814 George Stephenson made the first practical model. It ran on rails about nine miles from a coal mine to the sea, at a speed about that of a walking horse.

Baltimore businessmen had already begun to realize that the cost of completion of the Chesapeake and Ohio canal[4] would prove inexpedient as a measure to counteract New York's advantage. How about building a railroad across the mountains?

So on April 2, 1827, the Baltimore and Ohio Railroad Company was incorporated, the first railway in North America. The company was organized with a capital of $3 million.

The directors asked Virginia for permission to construct its lines along the Shenandoah, thence to the headwaters of the Kanawha and down that stream to the Ohio River. The general assembly, however, feared that this route to the sea might be injurious to the commonwealth, so the request was denied unless the western terminus was at some point north of the mouth of the Little Kanawha.

This set off a great flurry of exploration and the promotion of numerous competitive routes. Morgantown newspapers during the summer and fall had column after column suggesting the advantages or disadvantages of various routes. One proposal, presented at great length, would bring the railroad up the Potomac, thence from the headwaters of that stream to the Cheat near Dunkard Bottom, thence down the Cheat and across the mountain to Deckers Creek and the Monongahela at Morgantown. From here one route would be up the river to the mouth of Buffalo Creek, thence up that stream to its head, across to Fishing Creek and down to its mouth. Another possible route was down the river to Scotts Run, up that stream and across to Dolls Run, down Dolls Run to Dunkard Creek and up Dunkard to its head and across to the head of Fishing Creek.

A party exploring the adjacent country, assisting the "Engineers of the contemplated Rail Road" returned to Morgantown on August 10, "after a tour of ten or twelve days hard duty. They report the finding of a route from Morgantown to the Maryland line, in the direction of the Bear Creek route, much better than was expected; indeed they have no doubt of its

4. See Earl L. Core, *The Monongalia Story*, vol. 2 (1976), pp. 438, 486, 519.

being a much easier route, for a road than the one selected for the National road."[5]

"C. D.," who said he had traveled with the party of engineers, after describing the advantages of the Morgantown route, concluded by saying:

"The only difficulty to be surmounted between Cheat and the Ohio river, would then be encountered, with a single stationary Engine to let down and draw up waggons out of the valley of Deckers creek."[6] It was felt that the grade between Cheat River and Deckers Creek would be too great for a locomotive to traverse, but it could be replaced by a stationary engine.

Early in October it was reported:

"The Engineers returned to this place, on Wednesday evening from the Ohio river. We understand that they went up Buffalo and down Fishing Creeks and returned up Fishing and down Dunkard Creeks. They will remain here some time examining the surrounding country."[7]

**The Monongalia Chronicle.** The county's one newspaper was the *Monongalia Chronicle.* Volume 1, No. 2, of this weekly paper, in the Library of West Virginia University, is dated May 21, 1825. It was started by Henry and Carpenter, priced at two dollars a year in advance. David S. Carpenter continued the paper, despite the obstacles experienced by most papers of the time, and despite his own poor health. Almost anything was accepted in payment of subscriptions, including "wheat, rye, corn, oats, flour, linen, lincy [*sic*], flax, wool, bees-wax, candles, tallow, beef, pork, butter, lard, wood, feathers, chickens, eggs, sugar, bacon, flaxseed, nails, iron, rags, & *cash* [italics added]."[8]

For several weeks each issue carried an ad for "An apprentice to the Printing Business. . . . A boy from 13 to 14 years of age would be preferred, who can read and write." Evidently help was hard to find.

At about midyear of 1827 he had to miss several issues. He commented later:

5. *Monongalia Chronicle,* August 11, 1827.
6. *Monongalia Chronicle,* October 27, 1827.
7. *Monongalia Chronicle,* October 6, 1827.
8. *Monongalia Chronicle,* February 3, 1827.

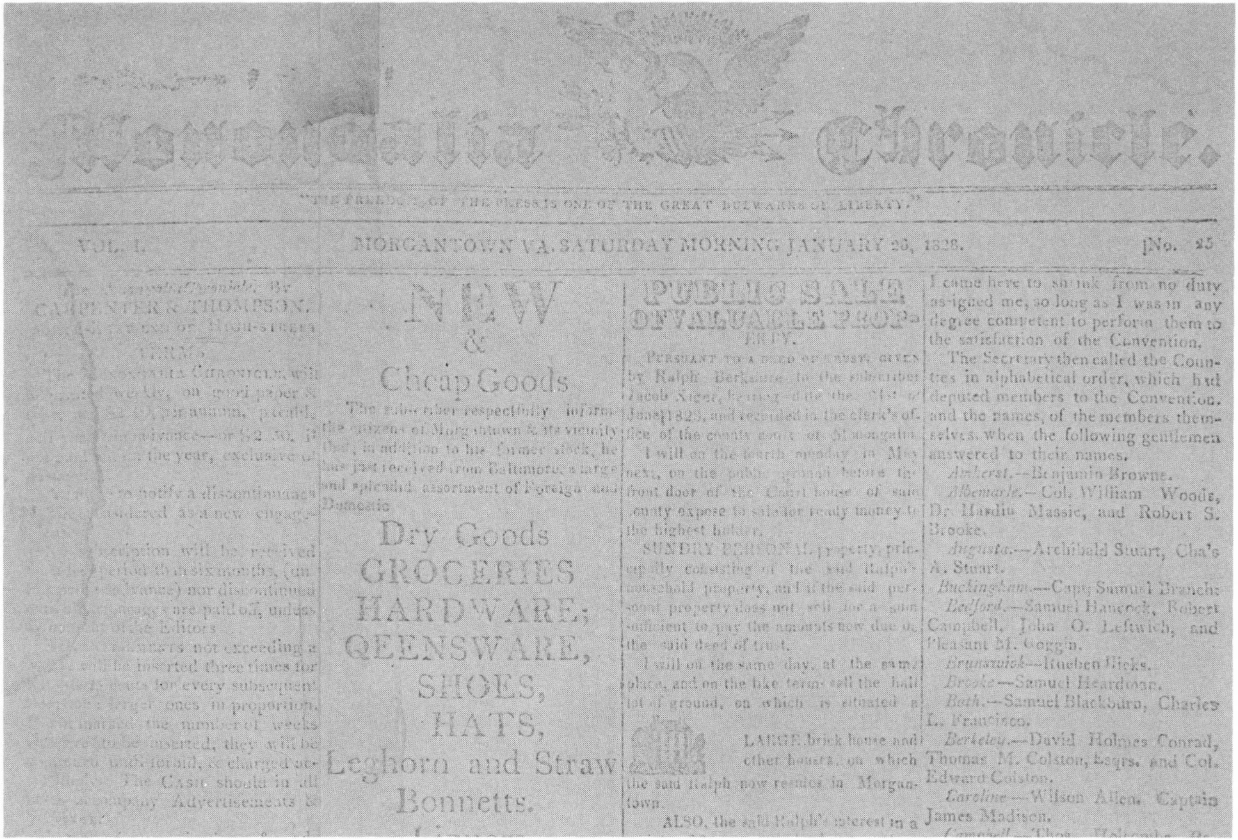
Monongalia Chronicle.

"THE FREEDOM OF THE PRESS IS ONE OF THE GREAT BULWARKS OF LIBERTY."

VOL. I. MORGANTOWN VA. SATURDAY MORNING JANUARY 26, 1828. No. 25

CARPENTER & THOMPSON.

TERMS.

NEW

&

Cheap Goods

The subscriber respectfully informs the citizens of Morgantown & its vicinity that, in addition to his former stock, he has just received from Baltimore, a large and splendid assortment of Foreign and Domestic

Dry Goods

GROCERIES

HARDWARE,

QEENSWARE,

SHOES,

HATS,

Leghorn and Straw

Bonnetts.

PUBLIC SALE

OF VALUABLE PROPERTY.

SUNDRY PERSONAL property, principally consisting of the said Ralph's household property,

LARGE brick house and other houses, on which the said Ralph now resides in Morgantown.

ALSO, the said Ralph's interest in a

I came here to shrink from no duty assigned me, so long as I was in any degree competent to perform them to the satisfaction of the Convention.

The Secretary then called the Counties in alphabetical order, which had deputed members to the Convention, and the names, of the members themselves, when the following gentlemen answered to their names.

*Amherst.*—Benjamin Browne.

*Albemarle.*—Col. William Woods, Dr. Hardin Massie, and Robert S. Brooke.

*Augusta.*—Archibald Stuart, Cha's A. Stuart.

*Buckingham.*—Capt. Samuel Branch.

*Bedford.*—Samuel Hancock, Robert Campbell, John O. Leftwich, and Pleasant M. Goggin.

*Brunswick.*—Rueben Hicks.

*Brooke.*—Samuel Heardoan.

*Bath.*—Samuel Blackburn, Charles L. Francisco.

*Berkeley.*—David Holmes Conrad, Thomas M. Colston, Esqrs. and Col. Edward Colston.

*Caroline.*—Wilson Allen. Captain James Madison.

Fig. 1. The *Monongalia Chronicle*. (Courtesy West Virginia University Library.)

"It is well known to the public & the subscriber's friends, that serious and continued indispositions had, several weeks ago compelled him to discontinue the publication, of the 'Monongalia Chronicle'. In taking that step, he was aware that some disappointment would naturally be felt by his late patrons; by those, more especially, who were anxious for the continuance of a newspaper in this county, as a vehicle of useful and interesting intelligence."[9]

He, therefore, made an arrangement with "Mr. William Thompson; who has undertaken to edit the paper, on impartial and independent principles, such as, it is hoped, will secure for it an extensive and liberal patronage."

Most of the issues carried very little local news; everyone knew it already. Foreign items were months late; even news of meetings of Congress was one to two weeks late.

David Carpenter died late in the year and Thompson continued alone. Under date of November 24 appeared a notice of a sale "at the house of D. S. Carpenter, dec'd.," of one mahogany printing house, type, cases, furniture, etc.

A new subscribers' route was proposed in the fall, provided sixty subscribers could be signed up. The route, starting at Morgantown, would go by way of "Boyers' Mill, Basnett's blacksmith shop, Brown's Mill on Dunkard, Statler Town, Miner Mill, Worley Tavern, Squire Thomas' Mill, Brookover Tanyard, Big Papaw Station, Shiveley's Mill, Price's Mill, Hess's shop on Indian Creek," thence returning to Morgantown. The paper was published on Saturday and subscribers were promised to have their papers on Sunday.

The paper was now being published at the "North-east End of High Street." The editor did not always find it easy: "Owing to the confinement of the Editor of this paper, at Waynesburg by high waters, and indisposition, our editorial summary will not appear this week."[10]

**The Hanging of Joshua.** On August 17, 1827, along Falling Run, just outside the town limits of Morgantown, there occurred the execution by hanging of Joshua, a Negro slave belonging to James Collins. He had been arrested for the rape of a white

9. *Monongalia Chronicle*, August 11, 1827.
10. *Monongalia Chronicle*, December 15, 1827.

woman and had been tried on July 13 by a county court called for the purpose, composed of Justices Dudley Evans, Richard Watts, David P. Morgan, Owen John, and Jacob Kiger. The court assigned Charles S. Morgan and Edgar C. Wilson to defend him and ordered that Collins pay each a fee of $7.50. Joshua was found guilty and sentenced to death by hanging. He was eighteen years of age and was valued at $250 by the court, which amount the state had to pay to his master.[11]

The case against Joshua brought out the unpleasant fact that he had been aided in his assault by the husband of the victim.

Only one other slave in the eighty-five-year history of slavery in Monongalia County was brought to court charged with attempted assault on a white woman. Moses, in 1825, was arrested on such a charge and the court record of his trial includes evidence presented by Bill, another slave, who reported that, two or three weeks before the assault, he and the prisoner had been going by the woman's house, "and the prisoner asked him who lived in that house, he replied he did not know, but that it was a woman who had been moved there—prisoner said 'there is a dam fine chance here' I replied yes for a white man—prisoner replied Yes for a black man either—I said your colour would submit here—prisoner replied Submit or not submit by God I'll make it submit—I said how will you make it submit—he said if I can't get it any other way I would choak her—I told him to drop it & not let any other person know it."[12]

For many years after the hanging of Joshua, residents of the area could see fearful ghosts gliding through the night shadows along Falling Run.

It should be pointed out that crime among black people in the county at this time was at a very low rate of incidence, and that slaves, especially, were often not given a fair show in the courts.

**John C. Evans Dies.** John Coleman Evans, second son of John ("Captain Jack") Evans, Jr., and grandson of distinguished pioneer settler Col. John Evans, died in New Orleans on

11. Samuel T. Wiley, *History of Monongalia County* (1883), p. 320. See Edward M. Steel, Jr., "Black Monongalians: A Judicial View of Slavery and the Negro in Monongalia County 1776-1865," *West Virginia History* 34 (1973):331-59.
12. Steel, *West Virginia History* 34:344, 345.

September 17, 1827. He was born in 1803, was educated for the profession of law, and studied law with his uncle, George F. Strother, in Missouri. He became interested in steamboating, however, and while in command of a boat running from Louisville to New Orleans contracted yellow fever, the cause of his death.[13]

**William Jolliffe Dies.** A prominent citizen of the Paw Paw Creek section, William Jolliffe,[14] died there May 1, 1827. He was a son of James and Hannah Springer Jolliffe, and was born near Uniontown, Pennsylvania, May 30, 1761. He married Catharine Collins and after her death in 1804, he married Charity Prickett.[15] Their home was near the mouth of Paw Paw Creek. William was a soldier in the War of 1812, and was wounded, which disabled him to some extent the remainder of his life, for which disability he received a pension.

To William and Catharine were born twelve children: James, William, John, Thomas, Hannah, Aaron, Amos, Levi, Elizabeth, Joseph, Job, and Nathan.[16]

**Benjamin Wilson.** Col. Benjamin Wilson, whose name figured prominently in the pioneer history of Monongalia County (see *Monongalia Story*, vol. 2, numerous entries), died December 2, 1827, near Clarksburg. He was born November 30, 1747, in Shenandoah County, the son of William and Elizabeth (Blackburn) Wilson. At the time of his death he was described as "the most prominent man in the Monongahela Valley."[17] Through his marriage to Anne Ruddle and then to Phoebe Davidson he was the father of thirty children. At the time of his death he was survived by twenty-four children, seventy-three grandchildren, and thirty-two great-grandchildren.

Another Benjamin Wilson (no known relationship) was living in Monongalia County at the same time and their names are frequently confused (as in *Monongalia Story*, vol. 1, p. 299). The other Benjamin (born about 1750, died by 1834) located

13. Wiley, p. 525.
14. See various references in *The Monongalia Story*, vol. 2; see also Glenn D. Lough, *Now and Long Ago* (1969), pp. 388, 389.
15. Core, vol. 1, p. 341.
16. *Cyclopedia of Monongalia County*, p. 130.
17. Dorothy Davis, *History of Harrison County* (1970), pp. 49, 50.

on Dents Run and he and his wife Ellenor are mentioned as giving an acre of land to the Mount Tabor Baptist Church in 1803. Their children were Eleanor, George P., William, Mary, James, Lydia, Elizabeth, Leven, Millie, and Benjamin (who died in 1825 in an accident while helping build a church).[18]

**A. G. Fairchild Resigns.** The Reverend Ashbel Green Fairchild,[19] popular minister of the Presbyterian Church in Morgantown, resigned his pastorate and moved to Fayette County, Pennsylvania, where he was installed as pastor of the Georges Creek and Hunt churches. His farewell sermon was given on April 15. But he would make frequent return visits to Morgantown.

**Paw Paw Methodist Church.** Near the headwaters of Paw Paw Creek a small, eighteen-foot square log house, built in 1815-16 on a two-acre plot of ground, was serving both as a schoolhouse and as the home of a Methodist congregation. Henry Boggess taught the school and held Sunday Bible classes. Circuit riders paid occasional visits.

In 1823 a church was organized with a membership of twelve; the Reverend Thomas Jamison was pastor.[20]

**Pitcher Chapel.** According to one account, the Pitcher church, on the west side of the Monongahela River just north of Barnesville, was built in 1826. (Another account says 1822.) Jonathan J. Pitcher, along with Benjamin Satterfield, gave the land on which the church was built.

Residents of the area are said to have worshipped in a schoolhouse there as early as 1787. Pioneer leaders were John Beall, Abraham Sisco, James Taylor, John Hoult, and others. Around 1800 Methodist circuit riders Thomas Daughady and John Kewly preached there. A letter written in 1803 by Ann Prickett Dragoo tells how, as a little girl, she and others waded across the

18. Ralph Shearer Rowland and Star Wilson Rowland, *Wilsons and Burchells and Related Families* (1976), pp. 9-14.
19. Core, *The Monongalia Story*, vol. 2, pp. 447, 500.
20. William Wilcox, *How Our Marion County Churches Began* (1976), p. 63. The church is now known as the Saint John Methodist Church, at Bassinettville.

river to attend services. The building was of hand-hewn logs fastened together with wooden pins.[21]

**Retailers and Artisans.** Among tradesmen operating in the county in 1827, as indicated by advertisements appearing in the *Monongalia Chronicle*, were J. H. McGee, who sold dry goods, groceries, queensware, hardware, shad, mackerel, herrings; Nathan Goff, who had dry goods, queensware, hardware, groceries, hats, shoes, leghorn and straw bonnets, spun yarn, and stationery; and William Griffey, who advertised cloths, cassinets, calicoes, muslins, cottons, cotton yarn, glass, china ware, tin-ware, dye-stuffs, sole-leather, shoes, molasses, confectionary, and Conemaugh salt. Griffey had a harrowing experience on November 5, shortly after dark, when he was attacked by two ruffians near Belleville, Washington County, robbed of twenty-five dollars, and beaten.

S. Trinkle advertised that he would do horse-shoeing at fifty cents all around if the customer found the iron, or seventy-five cents if he found it.

James Kidd, formerly of Edinburgh, Scotland, now of Waynesburg, Pennsylvania, solicited business as a stonecutter, supplying hearthstones, printing press stones, window sills, and tombstones, neatly lettered.

Lazier and Bayard were recommencing retail business in the brick house two doors south of Mrs. Dering's tavern, nearly opposite the courthouse.

**Land Grants Made in 1827.** Attention has been called in numerous earlier pages of *The Monongalia Story*[22] to various methods used by the commonwealth of Virginia to grant land to settlers in the western country. By the end of the Revolution most of the really good land had been claimed, although the establishment of ownership often involved long and bitter litigation.[23]

But in 1827, and for a long time thereafter, many thousands

21. Wilcox, *How Our Marion County Churches Began*, pp. 74, 75. Although moved to a new location when the railroad was built, and extensively renovated recently, the old historical building is still used for services. For John Kewly, see Charles H. Ambler, *The Wesley Methodist Church, Morgantown* (in *Waitman Thomas Willey*), p. 221.
22. E.g., Core, vol. 1, pp. 148-332; vol. 2, pp. 48-50, 100-102.
23. Core, vol. 2, pp. 489-92.

of acres of "waste" (unclaimed) land was still owned by the commonwealth and was deeded to purchasers (owners of adjoining tracts or newcomers) for very small considerations.

Records of these land grants are found in the land books of the various counties and we are indebted to Edgar B. Sims,[24] former West Virginia auditor, for a most "exhaustive and careful page-by-page examination of the copies of land grants filed" in his office. These records are of tremendous value in relation to the settlement pattern of the second quarter of the nineteenth century. Unlike holders of "tomahawk grants," many of whom went on West as the Indian danger lessened, most of these settlers were permanent, and their descendants still live here today.

The Monongalia County grants appear year-by-year on succeeding pages, becoming fewer each year, as might be expected. By the beginning of the Civil War very little "waste land" remained.

Spellings of geographical names (and of grantees) appear in many variations and in general are listed here as they are recorded in the original grants.

Grants made by the Commonwealth of Virginia in 1827 included:

| | | |
|---|---|---|
| Anderson, Charles G. | 100 a. | Dunkard Creek |
| Clagg, Alexander | 200 | Indian Camp |
| Conaway, Charles | 150 | Davids Run |
| Fleming, Benoni | 500 | Miracle Run |
| Goff, Byram | 38 | Adj. Thomas Clare |
| Haines, John and William | 175 | Piles Fork |
| Haught, Isaiah | 75 | Reubens Run |
| Hickman, Joshua | 28 | Glady Creek |
| Jarrett, William N. | 20 | Adj. Isaac Harrow |
| Jones, John and Samuel | 160 | Three Forks Creek |
| Linn, William | 60 | Glady Creek |
| Martin, Leonard | 112 | Pricketts Creek |
| Morgan, Charles S. | 150 | Davids Run |

24. Edgar B. Sims, *Index to Land Grants in West Virginia* (Charleston, 1952), 866 pp. For records of other early settlers see *General Index to Surveyors' Books of Monongalia County*, prepared by Bertha L. Pixler under the direction of Thomas Ray Dille, Morgantown, 1912.

| Murphey, Harrison | 112 | Pricketts Creek |
| Price, Caleb P. | 250 | Papaw Creek |
| Scott, Jacob | 5 | Adj. Isaac Lemaster |
| Sole, Jacob, Jr. | 100 | Dunkard Creek |
| Sole, John | 100 | Adj. J. Davis |
| Stafford, Seth | 85 | Waters Cheat R. |

**County Government:** Jesse Busey was sworn in as sheriff on March 26. Thomas Meredith and Matthew Fleming were sworn in as justices of the peace on July 23; Rawley Martin resigned on July 23 and John Wagner on August 28.

**Miscellany.** In 1827: Francis Billingsly acquired the tavern property on Lots 11 and 12, corner of Walnut Street and Middle Alley, formerly owned by Fauquir McRa (Callahan, p. 311). . . . W. L. Jackson, George J. Williams, and Daniel H. Polsley were admitted to the Monongalia County bar (Wiley, p. 317). . . . Sandford Pickenpaugh went into the tailoring business in Morgantown (Wiley, pp. 602, 604). . . . A party of five Indians passed through the county and spent a few days at Uffington. During their stay they got in a fight among themselves and one was critically injured (Wiley, p. 620). . . . The ice on "Buffaloe Creek" broke up and came down in a heavy body on January 29, carrying off part of the middle pier of the bridge near Middletown, so that the bridge was rendered impassable. Ice in the creek was fourteen to sixteen inches thick (*Monongalia Chronicle*, February 3, 1827). . . . Joseph Weaver, of Ice's Ferry Road, died; his wife was Rebecca Foster (Owens, p. 100).

CHAPTER FIFTY-TWO

# 1828

By 1828 the new town of Middletown, halfway between the county seat towns of Morgantown and Clarksburg, was growing steadily and the residents were beginning to speculate that it, too, might become the seat of government for a new county.

**The Growth of Middletown.** Middletown had been laid by Boaz Fleming in 1819 and it was legally established as a town by the Virginia General Assembly in 1820.[1] Fleming had begun in 1817 the work of clearing a portion of his farm for the town site and Glenn D. Lough,[2] quotes from a letter written by William Haymond, Jr., the surveyor, concerning the first day's activities: "Boaz and his boys chopped down 13 large trees, lamed an ox, killed two copperheads, and uncovered a human skeleton, thought to be that of an Indian killed by Jonathan Bozarth, who first owned the land Fleming owns now."

Eighty-five lots were included in the original plat of the town (see map, *Monongalia Story*, vol. 2, p. 450). The first twelve were numbered from the Monongahela River along Jefferson Street to Jackson Street. Josiah Wolcott bought Lot 1 on September 9, 1820, and Lot 2 on April 15, 1822. According to Lough, he established a ferry here and sold the lots and the ferry on May 21, 1825, to Thomas Fleming.[3]

Lots 3 and 33 (on the opposite side of Jefferson Street) were bought by William Nuzum on December 6, 1822. James F. Davies bought Lots 4 and 35 on April 19, 1822, and Lots 5 and 6 were purchased by Samuel Jackson August 6, 1819. Lots 7

1. Core, *The Monongalia Story*, vol. 2, pp. 450, 455, 456.
2. Lough, *Now and Long Ago*, p. 416.
3. Lough, *Now and Long Ago*, pp. 420-27.

and 8 were sold to Andrew McCray on April 10, 1824. Matthew Fleming bought Lot 9 on May 13, 1826, and Joseph E. Gray bought Lot 10 on the same day.

Lots 11 and 58 were sold to Frederick Ice on April 15, 1822. Cornelius Van Zant, says Lough, was Middletown's first merchant; he bought Lots 13, 25, and 26 on December 22, 1829.

Lots 13 to 20 were along Monroe Street, starting at Jackson Street. Some of these lots were not sold until after Boaz Fleming's death, on March 20, 1830. Lot 17 was bought by William Cochran on December 4, 1822. Elisha Barrett bought Lot 18 the same day. Later he built a house on it, sold it to Solomon Holland and he in turn to Frederick Chisler on April 13, 1829. Lough says Chisler operated a blacksmith shop here. Lots 19 and 20 were bought by Samuel Billings on March 8, 1823.

Lot 21, at the corner of Monroe Street and Hull Alley, was sold to the school trustees for one dollar on April 12, 1828. Later that year a one-room log schoolhouse, called the Middletown Academy, was built on the lot, the town's first school.

Lots 21 to 26 were along Monroe Street. Lot 22 was purchased by Hazo Parsons on December 18, 1822. Simon Shore bought Lots 23 and 28 on April 10, 1824, and Archibald Fleming's heirs bought Lot 24 on March 20, 1830.

Lots 27 to 30 were along Barney Street. Horasha Morgan bought Lots 29 and 46 on Christmas Day, 1822. Lot 30 was purchased by Daniel Polsley on April 15, 1820.

Lots 31 to 42 were along Jefferson Street, starting at the river. Ebenezer Newcomb bought Lots 31 and 32 on June 6, 1822.

Boaz Fleming's original log cabin was on Lot 36. He built a new house on Lot 47 and sold his first house and lot to Isaac White on August 13, 1825. Glenn Lough says White opened a coal bank on it, one of the earliest mentions of mining activity in the area. John Conaway bought Lot 37, William Fleming bought Lot 38, and Alexander Fleming bought Lot 39.

Lot 40, at the corner of Jefferson Street and Porter Alley, was sold by Boaz Fleming for one dollar to the Presbyterian Association. A church was built on the lot in 1828 and a cemetery was maintained there. Boaz Fleming was buried there, in 1830.

Lots 43 to 53 were along Madison Street, starting at Jackson

Street and running to the river. Nuzum Leonard bought Lot 43, and Lots 44 and 45 were purchased by John Park.

Lot 48 appears to have been the first lot sold in Middletown. It was bought by Jehu Lash on August 6, 1819, for twenty-seven dollars. Lots 52 and 53 were bought by William Fleming in 1825. He built and operated a tanyard on the property, which he transferred to James Burns in 1827.

Lots 54 to 64 were along the opposite side of Madison Street, numbered from the river. John H. Polsley bought Lot 54. The Polsley family was operating a gristmill across the river and a post office, Polsley's Mills, was established there, the first in the area. Lots 59 to 70 were purchased by William Fleming as acreage. John W. Kelly bought Lots 73, 74, and 75 in 1819, selling Lots 73 and 74 to Thomas and John S. Barns and Lot 75 to Robert McGee. Lots 76 to 85 were sold by Boaz Fleming to his son William, who held them in open acreage for several years; this land bordered on Quincy Street.

So gradually the Middletown community was growing. By 1828 there was a school, a church, a store, across the river a mill and a post office.

But Boaz Fleming was interested in more than just the establishment of a town. He wanted to see a new county established, too, for which Middletown would be the county seat. His first petition called for the new county to be called Madison, in honor of President James Madison. Fleming's friend, John G. Jackson, was married to Mary Payne, who was a sister to the president's wife, Dolly Madison, famous for her beauty and charm as a hostess; she was an occasional visitor at Middletown.

Fleming died, however, without realizing his dream of a new county and another dozen years were to elapse before the new county was formed. Then both the county and the town would have new names.

**County Newspapers.** The *Monongalia Chronicle* continued to be published each Saturday, by "Carpenter & Thompson," at the "North-East End of High Street." But on February 16, 1828, several changes were made; that issue was Volume 1, Number 1, of a new series. The paper was printed on a super-royal sheet, the publication date eventually changed to Friday, and the publisher was given as "William Thompson."[4] Agents for the paper were listed as Ebenezer Newcomb, Middletown; Jacob Boyer, Fairplay Mills; John Brookover, Brookover's Tanyard; William Thomas, Miracle Run; C. A. Swearingen, Clarksburg; Levi Morris, Mount Morris, Pennsylvania; George Morris, Jr., Newtown, Pennsylvania; B. F. Black, "Greensburg" (Greensboro), Pennsylvania; Thomas Fletcher, Jefferson, Pennsylvania; and Israel Baldwin, Kingwood.

The new paper's motto was "Internal Improvements—Domestic Manufactures—'Open to all Parties—Influenced by None.' "

The publication was not without its problems: "Owing to an accident which occurred in this office, on Thursday last, the publication of the paper has been delayed beyond the usual time. While making up the first side of our paper, a *galley*, on which was deposited for *imposition*, Governor Giles' inflammatory address to the Virginia Assembly, gave way, and precipitated the Governor and a column and a half of his message, with an awful crash, on the floor, and instantly changed this public document to *pie.*"[5]

In Volume 1, Number 11, the editor apologized "for the non-publication of this paper for the last two w'ks" and announced that, being "now supplied with printing ink (which had unexpectedly failed) we resume the publication."[6]

The paper advertised for a "News Rider," "a young man or boy about sixteen years of age, to carry the newspapers to distant parts of the county." The editor would find a horse and pay expenses. But often he had to apologize for not "performing our route regularly."[7]

Collections were slow in coming, and, after several issues had been missed, Volume 1, Number 22 was printed on a "medium sheet," with an explanation for "our late embarassments and irregularities." Several "of our subscribers (respectable gentlemen of both political parties) have called upon us and in a most

4. David S. Carpenter had died the previous autumn (see p. 6).
5. *Monongalia Chronicle*, March 8, 1828.
6. *Monongalia Chronicle*, May 9, 1828.
7. E.g., *Monongalia Chronicle*, June 13, 1828.

handsome way, paid up their subscriptions."[8] But this was the last issue known to have been published.

A new paper was started the same year, known as the *Monongalia Farmer*. It was published by Francis Madera and Enos D. Morgan and was a sheet twenty by thirty inches in size. No issues for 1828 are known to be extant.

**"Down on the Farm."** Life on the farms was simple, full of hard work, but food was mostly plentiful, even though limited in variety. In the Middletown section it is recorded that John O. Manley every other year took a packtrain load of furs and pelts to Winchester or some other eastern market, returning with rice, sugar, tea, coffee, and other articles of luxury. With the establishment of stores, these articles became more easily available locally.

During harvesttime breakfast was served early and dinner at noon. Often, about five o'clock, apple pie was served in the field and the laborers then worked on until dark before coming to the house for supper.

Housewives made "apple leather" by spreading sliced pieces of apples out on a board to dry. During the winter the "leather" was cooked a little at a time, as needed.

Sausage making was a laborious process. An 1828 account tells of a gathering of neighbors for the purpose. The men of the party laid the meat on a wooden bench and chopped it into small pieces with cleavers. After it had been seasoned with sage, salt, and pepper, it was smoked and hung in bags on rafters to be used in the winter months.[9]

**Retailers and Other Businesses.** Henry S. Morgan, in March, opened in "Mr. Thompson's store house, next door to Mr. M'Gee's store in Morgantown," a "New and Cheap Store," selling "dry goods, groceries, hardware, queensware, tin-ware, powder, spun-yarn, steel, shoes, hats, bonnetts, dyestuffs, lead, shot, sugar, fish, glass, &c."[10]

Frequent notices were inserted in newspapers of the times and places that stallions would "stand" for service. Familiar

8. *Monongalia Chronicle,* September 26, 1828.
9. Dora Lee Newman, ed., *Marion County in the Making* (1917), pp. 142-46.
10. *Monongalia Chronicle,* March 29, 1828.

names of horses were Western Spy, Sir Solomon, and Young Snapdragon.[11]

Miss Rachel Hurry advertised her services, "in the art of Millinery and Dress Making, to the Ladies of Morgantown and vicinity." She had studied under the well-known Misses Dickson, in Pittsburgh.[12]

Lazier Bayard and Company announced that: "We have again commenced making IRON at the Cheat Iron works, of the very best quality, and of every variety and kind, which we can confidently recommend to our customers and friends generally; and will at all times keep at our store, a large and general assortment of iron nails, and castings, which will be sold low for cash, or in exchange for country produce of every description."[13]

William Veatch advertised a "House of Private Entertainment," at the "Sign of the Horse," on "Water-street nearly opposite the Post Office." Travelers and others would be well accommodated and charged moderately. "A constant supply of oats and other horse feed will be kept on hand."[14]

**Progress on the Railroad.** "No public work has been commenced with more energy, or prosecuted with greater spirit and zeal than the Baltimore and Ohio Rail Road. The company appear to have completed all the preparations preliminary to a commencement. They have obtained a charter, explored and located the route and raised funds for its prosecution. The next anniversary of our National Independence is the day fixed upon for a formal commencement of this important work; and to the venerable patriot, *Charles Carroll*, has been tendered the honor of laying the corner stone."[15]

Everyone knows how Charles Carroll (1737-1828), the last survivor of the signers of the Declaration of Independence, did indeed turn over the first spadeful of earth in the important project, on July 4, 1828, and how he commented: "I consider this among the most important acts of my life, second only to signing of the Declaration of Independence, if even it be second to that."

11. *Monongalia Chronicle*, April 11, 1828.
12. *Monongalia Chronicle*, March 15, 1828.
13. *Monongalia Chronicle*, March 22, 1828.
14. *Monongalia Chronicle*, June 20, 1828.
15. *Monongalia Chronicle*, April 18, 1828.

**Slave Auction at Williamsport.**[16] A group of seventy-seven slaves were driven, in the early summer of 1828, from Winchester via the old State Road to Morgantown, thence to Bulltown,[17] in southern Monongalia County, to the home of Jefferson Keener. Here they were locked for the night in a log pound and next day the owners, Frederick Burdett and Mortimer Johnson, took them across the Tygart Valley River to Williamsport and auctioned them off. Prices ranged from $276 to $1,695 each, a total of $41,788 for the "buckes, wenches, and gals," as the auctioneer termed them.

Fig. 2. A slave auction. (From an old engraving.)

Not all were sold immediately, however, and Absalom Knotts, pioneer settler of the area, told of slaves, in pairs shackled to poles, who were rented or hired out to farmers of the community by the day, week, or month. Actually very few farmers of the section could afford to own slaves.[18]

16. Now known as Pruntytown.
17. Now known as Knottsville.
18. (Anonymous) *Historical Anecdotes of Early Taylor County*, p. 19.

**Slavery in Monongalia.** The black population of Monongalia County was never very high during slavery days. Dr. Steel[19] presents a graph indicating that the highest percentage of black inhabitants was shown by the 1820 census, when the 3.39 percent slave and 1.06 percent free totaled 4.45 percent of the county's population. From that time there was a steady decline in percentage until by the outbreak of the Civil War they constituted only about 1 percent of all residents.

Slavery, according to Dr. Steel, was a declining institution in Monongalia County after 1820. Numerous silent decisions adverse to slavery were made in the county, slaveholders imported few slaves, and many negroes who were freed left the county.

The problems involved in ownership of slaves were often troublesome. For one thing, they were convenient forms of property for law officers to seize to satisfy a judgment against an owner. Courthouse records relate that John Stealey and his endorser, Ralph Berkshire, in 1817, failed to meet an obligation, whereupon the sheriff seized a quantity of iron and four slaves belonging to Stealey and ten barrels of whiskey and a negro woman named Rachel from Berkshire. These were all advertised at a sheriff's sale.

But a sheriff could create problems for himself by such an auction, as Sheriff John Goff discovered in 1801. He levied on Elisha Griffith's property to satisfy a judgment and seized an eight-year-old slave named Jenny, valued at three hundred dollars. Jenny was sold at a sheriff's sale to Philip Doddridge, who paid forty dollars for her. But it turned out that Jenny had already been sold by Griffith to Thomas Chipps, now deceased, and Joanna, his widow and administratrix, sued both Doddridge and the sheriff.

Problems also arose when slaves were part of an estate that was in process of settlement. The administrators of the estate of Augustus Werninger, in 1825, sought permission via the county court of his heirs, who were minor children, to sell his slaves, not only to pay his debts, but also "because the said negroes are now confined in jail to keep them from running away."

Slave owners were responsible for their property and were not permitted to allow their slaves to look after themselves

19. See footnote 11, p. 7.

without going through the legal procedure of freeing them. George Dorsey was brought into court in 1823 to show cause why he should not support Christina, "a black woman going at large in this county." Rebecca Dering, in 1824, was charged with "permitting her negro man slave named Sawney to trade as a free man," a practice condemned as an "evil and pernicious example" to the community. Sawney, it was said, had rented a house and was buying and selling whiskey.

Forcible seizure of slaves was difficult to resist. Margaret Jenkins, she said, paid four hundred dollars for a Negro named Samuel. But he was seized in 1801, by Thomas Wilson for another man who claimed to own him and she had to sue to recover him. Thomas John and Elihu Horton seized Littleton, the slave of William Martin, on a public road and refused to surrender him until brought in court by Martin. Some such seizures were perhaps carried out by would-be slave stealers.

All in all, it might be said that mildness characterized the institution of slavery as it existed in Monongalia County, and that as a group the black residents of the county were generally law abiding.

**Bethel Methodist Episcopal Church.** A new church building was constructed in 1828 about two miles from the mouth of Scotts Run, on top of a hill between that stream and Robinsons Run. The congregation apparently was organized in 1824 (or earlier), with fifty-three members, two pastors, and five trustees. The two pastors ("circuit riders") were Rev. P. H. Hudson and Rev. Asbury Poole, followed in 1826 by Rev. D. Breckingham and Rev. Richard Armstrong. The class leader in 1824 was George Courtney.

The original church building was destroyed by fire about 1827 and the new structure was built across the road, on a lot purchased from Michael and Nancy Ann Courtney. The land was deeded to the trustees, John Courtney, William Courtney, Marcus Moore, Alexander Ware, and Michael White.[20]

**Salt Wells.** Salt was an item necessary to the diet and one of the few things which the pioneers brought across the mountains on packtrains. The settlers noted numerous "salt licks" (see

20. Gideon S. Dodds and Mrs. Gideon S. Dodds, *Churches of Monongalia County*, pp. 114, 115. The building was still in use in 1978.

Fig. 3. The Bethel Methodist Church. (Photo Dr. and Mrs. Gideon S. Dodds.)

*Monongalia Story*, vol. 1, pp. 11, 12; vol. 2, pp. 214, 215), and made efforts to drill wells to obtain sufficient quantities to supply needs.

In a well drilled at the mouth of Quarry Run a very rich stream of salt water was struck. Jonah Bayles and others boiled down some of the water and obtained a fine grade of salt.[21]

Another well was drilled in 1828 near Hoult "just below the mouth of Hawkinberry Hollow; when they got the well done, it made three bushels of salt per day. Salt sold for $3.00 per bushel at that time. The well was making money, but the demand for a greater output led them to ream the hole in order to increase the flow. They struck a soft place and it caved in. This caused some oil to seep in and spoil the salt-making. After that they called the well 'the Devil's Stinkbag.' "[22]

21. Wiley, p. 690.
22. Lough, *Now and Long Ago*, p. 536.

**Nimrod Evans Dies.** One of the eight children of Colonel John Evans,[23] pioneer settler near Morgantown, was Nimrod Evans, who preceded his father in death, passing away February 27, 1828. He was born January 13, 1770. Nimrod succeeded his father as clerk of the county court January 1, 1807, and held the office until his death. In 1807 he purchased the old "National," a tavern built in 1798 by Isaac Hite Williams, on High Street opposite the courthouse, and lived there the remainder of his life. He became clerk of the Superior Court of Law on September 2, 1811, and held this position, too, until his death.

He married Elizabeth Strother and they had no children, but adopted French Evans, son of his brother John ("Captain Jack").[24]

Nimrod Evans was one of the organizers of the Monongalia Farmers Company of Virginia in 1814 and one of the trustees who supervised erection of the Presbyterian Church in Morgantown in 1819.

**Joseph Bunner.** A member of an early pioneer family of the Prickett's Fort section, Joseph Bunner, died in November 1828. Joseph and his brothers, Casper and John (Reuben may also have been a brother), of Irish extraction, settled near White Day Creek shortly after the Revolution (see various references in *Monongalia Story*, vols. 1 and 2). Joseph was born in 1752 in Pennsylvania and served in a Pennsylvania regiment during the war. His will listed children as Marcy, Catherine, Elizabeth, Joseph, Ruth, John, Casper, Margaret, and Henry. Bunners Ridge memorializes the family name.[25]

**Election Results.** The vote for president in Monongalia County was:

| | |
|---|---|
| Andrew Jackson, Democratic | 490 |
| John Q. Adams, National Republican | 181 |

The vote for state senator and delegates to the general assembly follows:

23. Core, *The Monongalia Story*, vol. 2, p. 253.
24. Wiley, p. 524.
25. *The 175th Anniversary* . . ., pp. 394, 395. See also Jack W. Bunner, in Balderson, *Prickett's Fort*, pp. 180-88.

|                    | Courthouse | Pawpaw | Swamps | Total |
|--------------------|-----------|--------|--------|-------|
| Senate             |           |        |        |       |
| C. S. Morgan       | 421       | 158    | 82     | 661   |
| House of Delegates |           |        |        |       |
| Richard Watts      | 401       | 143    | 76     | 620   |
| E. C. Wilson       | 301       | 70     | 56     | 427   |
| Capt. Z. Morgan    | 186       | 44     | 23     | 253   |
| Aaron Baker        | 52        | 52     | . .    | 104   |
| T. S. Barnes       | 50        | 18     | 5      | 73    |
| P. Holland         | 32        | 2      | 14     | 48    |

**Land Grants Made in 1828.**[26] Grants of land in Monongalia County in 1828 included:

| | | |
|---|---|---|
| Anderson, John | 100 a. | Days Run |
| Bare, Michael | 50 | Miracle Run |
| Bartley, James | 91 | Dunkard Creek |
| Bland, Elenor | 58 | Kellums Run |
| Collins, Isaac | 62 | Kellums Fork |
| Cox, Thomas | 4 | Adj. S. Grubb |
| Cunningham, George | 100 | Waters Cheat R. |
| Eddy, Isaac | 147 | Pappa Creek |
| Highly, Peter | 77 | Miracles Run |
| Jennings, William | 100 | Dunkard Creek |
| Lewis, Benjamin | 100 | Days Run |
| McDaniel, Uriah and Nancy | 232 | Flat Run |
| Nolan, Joshua | 90 | Elk Lick Fork |
| Patterson, Philip | 240 | Pricketts Creek |
| Sine, Moses | 19½ | Stradlers Run |
| Tarlton, Elijah | 100 | White Day Creek |
| Wiley, John W. | 54 | Middle Run |

**County and Town Government.** Jesse Busey was sworn in for his second term as sheriff on March 24, 1828. Levi Anderson resigned as justice of the peace on May 20, 1828. Sworn in as justices on August 25 were Hillary Boggess, Benjamin B. Thorn, and, on August 26, Nimrod Dent. Trustees for the town of Morgantown in 1828 were J. H. McGee, Mathew Gay, E. M. Wilson, J. A. Shackelford, and N. B. Madera.

26. See p. 11.

**Miscellany.** In 1828: Dr. Robert Travis was practicing medicine in Smithtown (Wiley, p. 467). . . . So far as known, the second steamboat to reach Morgantown was the "Monongahela," on April 22 (Wiley, p. 542). . . . The Cheat Iron Works were leased to Lazier, Bayard and Company on May 22 (Wiley, p. 682). . . . Nimrod and Marmaduke Dent took over from their father, Captain John Dent, the operation of the milling, merchandising, and distilling business at Laurel Point (Wiley, p. 722). . . . The executors of Nimrod Evans conveyed his property, Morgantown Lot 9, to Edgar Wilson, who immediately conveyed it to E. M. Wilson (Callahan, p. 310). . . . Twelve families were living in Middletown (Lough, p. 547). . . . Jacob Pindall died February 23, aged seventy-two years.

# CHAPTER FIFTY-THREE

# 1829

A new chapter in the educational history of Monongalia County began in 1829, with the completion of "a large edifice" to house the town's academy, a growing institution with a great future.

**The Monongalia Academy.** Morgantown had been an educational center almost from its very beginnings. In 1788, only three years after the establishment of the town, the trustees of the Randolph Academy, set up by the Virginia General Assembly, met in Morgantown to organize the institution. The decision to locate the academy in Clarksburg, as nearer the center of population of northwestern Virginia, must have been a disappointment to Monongalians.[1]

But they lost no time in undertaking the development of a school of their own. In 1803 a brick building at the corner of Spruce and North Boundary streets was placed into operation as a school. It should be remembered that there were no public free schools at that time, so the school was the result of the efforts of civic-minded individuals.

This interest on the part of local citizens was eventually the background of a request to the general assembly for a charter for the Monongalia Academy. The incorporating act, dated November 29, 1814, allocated to the new academy one-sixth of all surveyors' fees collected in Monongalia County, which since 1787 had been paid to Randolph Academy. The act also authorized the collection of tuition fees and vested the management and control of the new school in a board of ten trustees, namely, Thomas Wilson, Augustus Werninger, John Evans, Jr., Ralph

1. Core, *The Monongalia Story*, vol. 2, pp. 165-67.

Berkshire, Enos Daugherty, John Shisler, Rawley Evans, George Dorsey, James Scott, and Dudley Evans.[2]

Something of the activity of the school is indicated by an advertisement in the *Monongalia Spectator* for March 9, 1816: "The Tutor of said Academy shall attend to the instruction of about twenty-five scholars in the several branches usually taught in the schools and academies, for which the Trustees of said Academy will pay said Tutor four hundred dollars per annum, by quarterly installments." Most records of the academy for the next ten years have been lost but there is evidence that Ashbel G. Fairchild was the tutor in 1821.

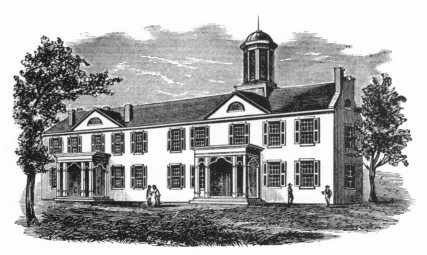

Fig. 4. Monongalia Academy. (From Wiley's *History of Monongalia County*.)

A lottery venture raised about eight thousand dollars and the academy took on new life in 1827. The trustees began looking for a new site and planning to erect a larger building. After some delay in which a number of sites were considered, the lots at the corner of Walnut and Spruce streets were purchased in 1828, from John Evans, Jr., and his wife, Gilly.

2. Core, *The Monongalia Story*, vol. 2, pp. 404, 405.

Work immediately began on the new building, a brick building, two stories high, seventy by forty feet in size. The building was completed in 1829 but not in time to allow its use to begin in that year.

**The Constitutional Convention of 1829.** The first constitution of Virginia was adopted on June 29, 1776, during the troublous early days of the Revolutionary War, under the stress of haste and preoccupation with many other pressing problems. Western Virginia, of course, had scarcely a voice in its formation, being represented only by delegates from Berkeley and Hampshire counties and from the District of West Augusta.

By the 1776 constitution there was established a general assembly, to meet annually, composed of two houses, the house of delegates with two representatives from each county, and the senate, of twenty-four members, one member from each of twenty-four districts. Suffrage was confined to freeholders who had been in possession of their property for at least one whole year before the issue of the writ for the election.

"With the election of the members of the general assembly" says James Morton Callahan[3] "the voice of the voting population ceased." The other major state officers were chosen by joint ballot of the two houses of the general assembly. These officers included the governor, treasurer, secretary, attorney general, and the judges of the superior courts.

Nor did the people have any more voice in government at the local level. The twelve-member county courts had general management of all local affairs and they were self-perpetuating bodies, with vacancies filled by the governor from nominations presented by the sheriff, who was himself drawn, ordinarily, from the court membership. "Clothed with executive, legislative, and judicial power," says Otis K. Rice,[4] "the court appointed civil officials of the county and all military officers below the rank of brigadier general, laid the county levies, and filled numerous honorary and remunerative positions."

By the end of the first half century of independence the defects in the hastily drawn constitution had become well

3. James Morton Callahan, *Semi-Centennial History of West Virginia* (1913), p. 127.
4. Otis K. Rice, *The Allegheny Frontier* (1970), p. 362.

known. But even many of the people who protested strongly against these defects were reluctant to propose a new constitution for fear it would turn out to be worse.

But at last, in 1828, the general assembly scheduled a referendum to determine the wishes of the people with respect to holding a constitutional convention. Tidewater Virginia voted strongly against it, but the valley and western counties were strongly in favor; supporters cast 21,896 votes, opponents numbered 16,646. The vote in Monongalia County was:

|            | For | Against |
|------------|-----|---------|
| Courthouse | 422 | 69      |
| Swamps     | 77  | 8       |
| Pawpaw     | 136 | 28      |
|            | 635 | 105     |

The general assembly acted slowly to carry out the mandate of the people but finally ordered an election for delegates to the convention, four from each senatorial district. The districts were still based on the census of 1810, so the western counties were at the very outset placed at a disadvantage, in view of the fact that their population had increased greatly since that time.

The convention was regarded in Monongalia and the other western counties as perhaps the most important issue since the Declaration of Independence and great interest was shown in the selection of delegates. The election, held on May 25, showed the following results:[5]

|                | Courthouse | Pawpaw | Swamps | Total |
|----------------|------------|--------|--------|-------|
| C. S. Morgan   | 369        | 60     | 53     | 482   |
| E. M. Wilson   | 337        | 85     | 42     | 414   |
| Phil. Doddridge| 236        | 27     | 55     | 318   |
| Alex. Campbell | 249        | 48     | 6      | 298   |
| Samuel Sprigg  | 155        | 14     | 40     | 209   |
| A. McClean     | 132        | 43     | 1      | 176   |
| Wm. G. Brown   | 80         | 34     | 35     | 149   |
| John Fairfax   | 6          |        |        | 6     |
| Israel Nicklin | 3          | 1      |        | 4     |
| Scattering     | 8          |        |        | 8     |

5. The *Republican*, May 30, 1829.

It was an August assemblage which met at Richmond on October 5, 1829, to open the convention. Representatives of the district to which Monongalia County belonged were Philip Doddridge, Alexander Campbell, Charles S. Morgan, and Eugenius M. Wilson. Among other members of the convention were two former presidents, James Madison and James Monroe, Chief Justice John Marshall, John Tyler, a future president, two United States Senators and eleven members of the House of Representatives. The convention drew national attention and numerous spectators attended. James Monroe was elected president.

Most of the debates were on two questions: representation and suffrage. The easterners in general favored a representation based on white population and taxation combined, while the westerners stood solidly for white population alone. Eastern members cited the importance of property rights and pointed out that three-fourths of the state's taxes were paid by citizens east of the mountains. The westerners, in rebuttal, asked who were the men who had fought the battles.[6]

When Abel P. Upshur, in a two-day long speech, endeavored to show that there was no natural source for the law of the majority, Doddridge asked, if the majority do not have the right to govern, "whence does the gentleman derive the power in question to the minority?" Campbell extolled "King Numbers" as the most dignified personage under the canopy of heaven.

As a partial compromise, a plan of apportionment was worked out, following no particular principle, but which seemed to favor the East more than the West. It was at last approved by the convention.

The convention then turned to the matter of suffrage. Reformers urged free white suffrage as a natural right, while conservatives insisted on property qualifications. Those in favor of extending the suffrage pointed out that twenty-two of the twenty-four states had already done so. Charles S. Morgan, of Monongalia County, maintained that universal manhood suffrage would unite the citizens in common interests. The conservatives, however, triumphed and the right to vote was extended to only small groups.

6. Callahan, *Semi-Centennial History of West Virginia*, pp. 130-36; Rice, *The Allegheny Frontier*, pp. 367-73.

Fig. 5. Virginia Constitutional Convention, 1829-30. Alexander Campbell is seventh from the right in the back row. (From a painting by George Catlin.)

31

The western delegates were full of bitterness; Campbell considered calling them together in a separate convention to discuss
secession, and westerners in general hoped it might fail of ratification when submitted to the vote of the people. Here again
they were disappointed; at the referendum, held in April 1830,
the constitution was ratified by a vote of 26,055 to 15,566.

The vote in Monongalia County was as follows:[7]

|              | *For* | *Against* |
|--------------|-------|-----------|
| Courthouse   | 282   | 219       |
| Swamps       | 7     | 59        |
| Pawpaw       | 112   | 126       |
| Dunkard      | 62    | 30        |
|              | 463   | 434       |

**Baltimore and Ohio Railroad.** Dispatches from Baltimore newspapers indicated rapid progress on the railroad construction
project:[8]

"The rapid progress of this great work is really astonishing
and the amount of excavation and embankment completed and
advanced towards completion in the last month appear almost
incredible."

"The foundation stone of the bridge or Viaduct to be constructed for the passage of the Baltimore and Ohio Rail Road
over Gwynn's Falls near the western boundry of this City, and
in the first section of the road, was laid on Saturday last. This
bridge will have a larger span than any other stone bridge in the
United States, with the exception of that on the National Road
where it crosses the Youghogeny river."

Reflecting the continued interest in the progress of the railroad, numerous other notices appeared in Morgantown newspapers through the year, including the following:

"The Board of Engineers have commenced laying the rails
upon the division of the road within the City of Baltimore, & it
is calculated that the entire line between Baltimore & Ellicotts
Mills may be finished during the ensuing spring."[9]

7. Wiley, p. 270.
8. The *Republican*, June 6, 1829.
9. The *Republican*, November 10, 1829.

**Weather in Morgantown, 1829.** The weather in Morgantown for 1829 was summarized by E. D. Morgan as follows:[10]

| Number of Days | Clear | Cloudy | Rain | Snow | Changeable |
|---|---|---|---|---|---|
| January | 5 | 5 | 9 | 10 | 2 |
| February | 7 | 1 | 5 | 9 | 6 |
| March | 10 | 3 | 5 | 11 | 2 |
| April | 1 | 1 | 14 | 4 | 10 |
| May | 11 | 1 | 11 | | 8 |
| June | 11 | | 10 | | 9 |
| July | 7 | 4 | 15 | | 5 |
| August | 15 | 2 | 8 | | 6 |
| September | 4 | 1 | 17 | | 8 |
| October | 8 | 3 | 15 | | 5 |
| November | 3 | 2 | 12 | 8 | 5 |
| December | 5 | 5 | 9 | 4 | 8 |

**The Republican.** A new county newspaper was started by Enos D. Morgan, with the assistance of Francis Madera, in 1829. Known as the *Republican*, it was a four-page sheet, nineteen by twenty-four inches in size, four columns to the page, published each Saturday, at $1.75 per annum in advance. On August 1 it was enlarged to nineteen by twenty-six, with five columns to a page.

The name "Republican," used for the paper, referred to a political party by that name, but it was not the Republican party of today. Rather, it was the party led by John Quincy Adams and Henry Clay and was more nearly the forerunner of the Democratic party of today.

Volume 1, Number 1, published on March 28, contained a long section giving debates on the proposed constitutional convention, with a speech by Edgar C. Wilson, of Monongalia County. The inaugural address of General Andrew Jackson also appeared, on page 1.

The issue of September 19 "completes the first six months of THE REPUBLICAN,—we have met with tolerable good support

10. The *Republican*, January 26, 1830.

since the commencement of this paper and our subscription list continues still to increase."

The name of the paper, beginning with the issue for October 10, 1829, was enlarged to the *Republican, and Monongalia and Preston Advertiser.* Thereafter, starting with the issue of October 21, the paper was published on Tuesday, "in order to suit the mails." Emphasizing the great local interest in the constitutional convention, the proceedings were published at full length, week after week.

**The Carding Business.** John H. and Joryar Hoult advertised "that they still intend carrying on the CARDING BUSINESS on the Monongahela River, about 2 miles below Middletown near the mouth of Buffalow Creek, and about one mile above the mouth of Pawpaw, in Pricket's settlement. They respectfully solicit a share of the public patronage.

"If they are accommodated with good wool, in good order for the machines, & one pound of grease to every eight or ten pounds, they give their assurance that good work shall be done. . . .

"The price of carding will be five cents per pound if paid in advance; 6 3/4 if paid on or before the 1st of Jan.

"Country produce will be taken; such as Wheat, Rye, Corn and Oats, if delivered at their Mill, at the Morgantown prices. . . .

"For the accommodation of those on the west side of the river, they will ferry them over at R. Holt's Ferry, on their own expense, when the wool is brought; also, when the rolls are taken away and paid for."

Prices allowed for produce were listed as "Flax-Seed (per bushel) 33 1/3 cents. Bees wax (per pound) 25. Tallow, 6¼. Wool, 25. Rolls, 6¼."[11]

**Internal Improvements.** Great interest was being shown in the development of better forms of transportation, as witness this editorial comment:

"Unless steam can be called in to the aid of canals, rail-roads (assisted as they are by stationary or self-moveing steam engines,) must, in many cases supersede the use of canals.—

11. The *Republican,* May 2, 1829; see also *Monongalia Story,* vol. 2, pp. 508, 509.

There seems to be no definable limit to the introduction of steam. Carriages are said to be on the eve of being introduced in England, that can run 15 miles in the hour and economise fuel to a very great extent. . . . Few states in the Union have a greater interest in such results than Virginia has."[12]

Some people, however, still felt canals were the answer to transportation problems:

"The Pittsburg Statesman of the 15th inst. says—The Chesapeake & Ohio Canal is progressing rapidly. It is under the superintendence of competent and active Engineers. Judge Roberts is now in this city and his surveys are said to be very favorable and satisfactory. We are told that he entertains no doubt of the practicability of an entire water communication from Washington City to Pittsburg."[13]

**Services Rendered.** Newspaper advertisements gave glimpses of business and industry of the day:

William Veatch "continues to keep a house of Private Entertainment at the sign of the Black Horse on Water Street, where travellers and others can at all times be accommodated with victuals, lodging & horse-feed. He has also opened a shop on Main street near the Courthouse and intends keeping a constant supply of cakes, beer, cider and confectionary. He also carries on at the latter place the Boot & Shoe Making Business, and has on hand, an assortment of coarse, kipskin, calfskin and morocco shoes."[14]

During the summer it was announced that the partnership of Thomas J. Massie and Josiah Boyers had been dissolved and Massie was carrying on the retail business alone.

John A. Derbins advertised for "a Journeyman Cabinetmaker and House-Joiner, to whom good wages will be given. Also, an Apprentice to learn the Cabinet Making business."[15]

**Morgantown Physicians.** Several physicians were practicing medicine in Morgantown, in the late 1820s, including Drs. B. R. C. O'Kelly, Charles McLane, Daniel Gettings, and a Dr. Evans.

12. The *Republican*, May 23, 1829.
13. The *Republican*, August 1, 1829.
14. The *Republican*, September 5, 1829.
15. The *Republican*, August 8, 1829.

Notices of some of these appear in advertisements in local newspapers:

"Dr. C. M'Lane having removed to the house lately occupied by Dr. M. Gettings, tenders his professional services to the public as heretofore. He intends to keep on hand a general assortment of medicines, which he will retail on as good terms as they can be purchased on, in the western country."[16]

"Dr. O'Kelly, having removed to Morgantown, respectfully tenders his professional services to the public. His Shop is nearly opposite the Post-Office on Water-street."[17]

Dr. Evans "Respectfully informs the citizens of Morgantown and the public generally, that his services are tendered to them at the different branches of his profession. His residence is in the white house opposite the Market."[18]

**Election Results.** Results of the election, Monday, April 27, appear below:[18]

|                      | Pawpaw | Swamps | Courthouse | Total |
|----------------------|--------|--------|------------|-------|
| Congress             |        |        |            |       |
| Philip Doddridge     | 87     | 80     | 385        | 552   |
| Joseph Johnson       | 90     | 21     | 149        | 260   |
| House of Delegates   |        |        |            |       |
| R. Watts             | 153    | 77     | 430        | 660   |
| F. Billingsley       | 147    | 51     | 268        | 466   |
| E. C. Wilson         | 53     | 64     | 332        | 449   |
| E. S. Pindall        | 14     | 10     | 65         | 89    |

**William N. Jarrett.** One of the distinguished pioneer residents, William N. Jarrett, died November 2, 1829. He was born June 15, 1776,[19] the son of John Jarrett, who came from New Jersey and settled near Ice's Ferry at an early date.[20] He married for his first wife Sarah Morris, daughter of Absalom Morris, for whom Morris Cross Roads, in nearby Fayette County, Pennsylvania, was named.

16. The *Republican*, November 3, 1829.
17. The *Republican*, June 13, 1829.
18. The *Republican*, May 2, 1829.
19. Wiley, p. 600.
20. Wiley, p. 481.

By 1805 Jarrett was operating a tavern on Lot 81 (corner of High Street and Maiden Alley) in Morgantown[21] and was a justice of the peace for Monongalia County about the same time.

The tavern had been started by Hugh McNeely[22] and upon his death Jarrett married his widow Mary ("Polly") and continued the business. He was a charter member and treasurer of Morgantown Lodge No. 93, A.F.&A.M., organized December 15, 1812. He was captain of a company of cavalry ordered (but too late) to the defense of Washington, D.C. The first bank in Monongalia County, the Monongalia Farmers Company of Virginia, was organized at his house December 1, 1814.[23]

A newspaper editor commented:

"His honorable conduct, social feelings and domestic habits, secure to him the respect and esteem of a large circle of acquaintances—in all his transactions as a neighbour, kind and benevolent; as a friend, stedfast and sincere; as a parent, affectionate to a fault; as a master, kind and humane. Such a loss claims from a friend, the expression of sincere sympathy in the bereavement which his afflicted and amiable widow and children has suffered by his death."[24]

**Jesse Hughes.** The famous old Monongalia County Indian fighter, Jesse Hughes (*Monongalia Story*, vol. 1, pp. 220-22, etc.; vol. 2, pp. 25, 26, 57, 77, 191, etc.), died in Jackson County in 1829. After leaving the Monongahela Valley he had lived for a short time in Vincennes (now Indiana) and then in eastern Kentucky.

"With eyes described as like those of a mountain panther or a rattlesnake, Jesse was reported to be able to see at night as well as a wild animal, to outrun any Indian prowling in the forest, and to enjoy the killing of any Indian, young or old. For each Indian scalped, he notched his gun barrel. Next to Indian killing, Jesse excelled in snake kills."[25]

21. Core, *The Monongalia Story*, vol. 2, p. 371.
22. Wiley, p. 339.
23. Core, *The Monongalia Story*, vol. 2, p. 407.
24. The *Republican*, November 3, 1829.
25. Phil Conley and William Thomas Doherty, *West Virginia History* (1974), p. 147.

Land Grants Made in 1829.[26] Monongalia County grantees in 1829 included:

| | | |
|---|---|---|
| Anderson, Levi | 18 a. | Dunkard Creek |
| Brown, Abraham | 25 | Dunkard Creek |
| Cooms, Philip | 33 | Waters Monongahela R. |
| Cunningham, George | 50 | Deckers Creek |
| Eddy, Gavin (The Third) | 100 | Papa Creek |
| Eddy, Michael | 100 | Furtneys Fork |
| Ewel, Thomas | 8 | Adj. Robert Ferrell |
| Gochenaur, John | 100 | Dunkard Creek |
| Hanway, John | 670 | Waters Tygerts Valley |
| Haught, Jacob | 148 | Statlers Run |
| Hewes, Vincent | 63 | Johnnycake Run |
| Minor, Samuel | 272 | Days Run |
| Nuzum, John | 170 | Waters Tygert Valley |
| Parrell, Joseph | 196 | Wickwares Creek |
| Patterson, Richard M. | 1 | Cole Run |
| Stafford, Seth | 5 | Adj. Lemuel John |
| Tennant, Nimrod | 110 | Upper Run |
| Tennant, Peter | 100 | Statlers Run |
| Tennant, Richard D. | 120 | Upper Run |

**County Government.** Anthony Smith was sworn in as sheriff on March 23, 1829. William Thomas resigned as justice of the peace September 28, 1829. Seth Stafford and Henry Boggess were sworn in as justices on August 24.

**Miscellany.** In 1829: A tavern kept by John Addison in a brick house at the southeast corner of High and Pleasant streets was sold to Asby Pool (Callahan, pp. 117, 118). . . . Nancy Miller died on June 20, aged ninety-two (Wiley, p. 633). . . . "We are authorized to state that the Rev. Alexander Campbell of Brook County, will preach in Morgantown on Friday the 25th inst; and in Kingwood on Sunday the 27th inst." (The *Republican*, September 12, 1829). . . . "The Monongalia Guards will meet in the Court-House yard in Morgantown, on the 4th of July, at 9 o'clock A. M. precisely; completely equipped for parade, for the purpose of celebration the anniversary of National Independence. By order of James Shay, O. S." (The *Republican*,

26. See p. 11.

June 27, 1829). . . . As an example of rapid transportation, it was noted that a letter from New York had reached Berlin, Prussia, in only twenty-seven days (The *Republican*, April 18, 1829). . . . The Frederick mail stage (Stockton and Stokes) was robbed "last Saturday night" (The *Republican*, April 18, 1829). . . . The stump of the famous Pringle sycamore tree (*Monongalia Story*, vol. 1, pp. 64, 171) could still be seen (Withers, p. 119). . . . Alexander Fleming sold Lot 39, in Middletown, to Solomon Holland (Lough, p. 423). . . . Henry Henthorn (1777-1842) furnished the stone for the Monongalia Academy (Owens, p. 85). . . . Jacob Miller (1800-1885) settled on West Run (Owens, p. 89). . . . Thomas L. Dunn was operating a store west of Cheat River (Owens, p. 145).

CHAPTER FIFTY-FOUR

# 1830

The Dunkard Creek valley was among the earliest sections of Monongalia County to be permanently settled. A temporary settlement at the mouth of the creek by the four Eckerlin brothers in 1751 gave the stream its name.[1] They, and others with them, practiced baptism by immersion and were referred to as Tunkers, from the German, tunken, to dip; this presently became Dunkers and finally Dunkards. The earliest records in the Monongalia County courthouse spell the name as Dunker Creek.

When the French and Indian War began, conditions on the frontier became dangerous because of hostile Indians and the Eckerlins relocated in what they regarded as a safer place, on Cheat River, clearing a tract on a floodplain which became known as Dunker's Bottom. But in 1757 this settlement was destroyed by the Indians, and the Dunkards disappear from our history, having left their name on two geographical features.

The French and Indian War was hardly over before other white settlers came cautiously into the Dunkard Creek valley. The treaty of 1763 had indicated the land west of the Alleghenies should belong to the Indians and this was confirmed by the Treaty of Fort Stanwix in 1768. But the settlers came, anyhow.

Later, after the Declaration of Independence, land grants were given to these early pioneers and dates were supplied for their settlements.[2] But since the earliest of the settlements had been made illegally, it is possible that some of these dates may

1. Core, *The Monongalia Story*, vol. 1, pp. 151-53.
2. *The Monongalia Story*, vol. 1, pp. 156-60.

have been advanced to make it look some better. It is, therefore, not possible, to say exactly when the first permanent settlers arrived in the Dunkard Valley.

Among the first must have been Bruce Worley and his brother Nathan who located, perhaps by 1765, near the site of the present village of Pentress.[3] Nearby, on a rich bottom land, John Statler and his wife located in 1770.[4] They had been survivors of the Decker massacre in 1759 at what later became Morgantown. John's two brothers, Jacob and Joseph, came along and settled not far away on a branch of Dunkard Creek which came to be known as Jacob Statler's Run, Jakes Run, or Statlers Run. When the Revolutionary War broke out, Statler's Fort was built on John Statler's land, for protection against the Indians. Adam Brown, for whose family Brownsville, in Fayette County, was named, was another early settler and married Christina, a sister of the Statlers.[5]

Downstream a short distance was the settlement of Frederick Husk, at the mouth of a stream called then Husk's Run but which soon after came to be called for another early settler, Rudolph Snider's Run, or, from his nickname, "Dol" Snider's Run, finally Dolls Run.[6]

Upstream from Statler's Fort, on another tributary, Thomas Day had settled by 1772. The branch was named for his family Days Run, as was the later community of Daybrook.[7]

Still further upstream another tributary was named Miracle Run. No known miracle suggested the name for this branch; instead, it was a variant spelling of the name of early settler John Merrical.[8]

**Blacksville is Laid Out.** At the site of the present town of Blacksville, on lands owned by John Baldwin, was built another bulwark against Indian raids, known as Baldwin's Blockhouse. It was here that the last encounter in Monongalia County between the Indians and the frontiersmen took place in June 1791, re-

3. Wiley, *History of Monongalia County*, p. 753, note; Core, *The Monongalia Story*, vol. 1, pp. 236, 356.
4. *The Monongalia Story*, vol. 1, pp. 154, 184, 279.
5. *The Monongalia Story*, vol. 1, p. 150.
6. *The Monongalia Story*, vol. 1, pp. 157, 159, 183, 250.
7. *The Monongalia Story*, vol. 1, pp. 163, 168, 208, 247.
8. *The Monongalia Story*, vol. 1, pp. 11, 238.

sulting in the deaths of three settlers and capture of two others.[9]

Around Baldwin's Blockhouse there soon began to grow up a cluster of houses, a kind of a community center for Dunkard Valley, known locally as New Hampshire or Hampshire Town. Some of the settlers had come across the mountains from Hampshire County. On August 14, 1797, a county court manuscript records, John Statler and Eve, his wife, sold two lots in "Hampshier Town," adjoining John Baldwin, to Peter Miers for four dollars.

On October 10, 1829, David Black laid out a proposed new town and placed an advertisement in the weekly newspaper, the *Republican*, as follows: "The subscribed has lately laid out a town on his farm on Dunkard Creek, Monongalia County, Virginia, called Blacksville, and which will be incorporated during the winter; it is situated on the State road from Morgantown to Wheeling, and on the road from Clarksburg to Pittsburgh and Waynesburg:—the distance from Morgantown 20 miles, 45 from Wheeling, 14 from Waynesburg, and 35 from Clarksburg—the town will be surrounded by a large population, and is a very healthy situation, etc., etc. David Black."

The General Assembly of Virginia, on February 3, 1830, passed an act to establish the town, naming it Blacksville, for the owner of the land. John Fordyce, surveyor, prepared a plat of the new town, "on Dunkard Creek in Monongalia County in the State of Virginia so far as said town lies within said state." (Some of the houses were across the Mason and Dixon line, in Pennsylvania.)

The streets, Fordyce said, "are North and South with a variation of two degrees West, the Lots are 110 feet by 58." A board composed of William Thomas, Samuel Minor, and John Lantz "caused the lands allotted for said town lying within said County to be laid off into lots, streets and alleys, as exhibited on the foregoing diagram." This was produced to Thomas P. Ray, clerk of the county court, on July 18, 1832, and admitted to record.

9. *The Monongalia Story*, vol. 1, pp. 350, 351; vol. 2, pp. 2, 51, 61, 105, 189, 344.

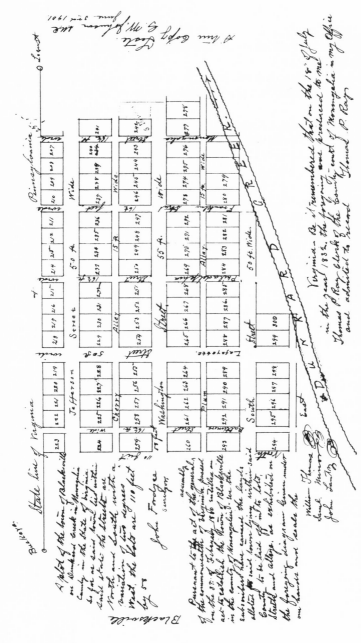

Fig. 6. Original plat of the town of Blacksville, produced to Monongalia County Clerk Thomas P. Ray in 1832.

43

**Jacksonville is Founded.** About 1827 Peter A. Layton built the third house on a site at the head of Scotts Run, eight miles west of Morgantown, and a village was on its way to becoming a kind of business center for the agricultural area on Scotts Run and adjacent areas.

The first house at this site was a schoolhouse, built about 1800 (possibly earlier), a building used not only for educational, but, says Wiley,[10] "for masonic and religious purposes" as well. Davis Shockley and William Slater were recorded as pioneer schoolmasters.

The first dwelling house was built not far away by Caleb Hurley, who owned much of the land in the vicinity.

Peter Layton and others soon began to provide services of value to local farmers. Layton started a tannery, which, through various owners, continued to operate for more than a half century. On the small expanse of flat land near the head of Scotts Run, along the old Morgantown and Fishing Creek state road, Layton, about 1830, proceeded to lay out a town which he called Jacksonville.[11] The town was mostly laid out on lands of Caleb Hurley and Leven Fleming.

A horse mill was built near the schoolhouse at an early date, some say by Davis Shockley, others by James Lemasters. Later it had a carding machine attached, to serve wool producers of the area.

From an early date a physician was located in the village. William Slater, pioneer schoolmaster, "doctored the people," at a time when an M.D. degree and a license were not necessary for the practice of medicine.[12]

**The New Academy Opens.** After the completion of the new building at the corner of Walnut and Spruce streets, in late 1829, classes of the Monongalia Academy were opened in the new location in 1830, under the principalship of Jonathan R. Haddock.

Opening of the academy in the new building was announced in a Prospectus, copies of which were "struck in the form of

10. Wiley, *History of Monongalia County*, p. 701.
11. Andrew Jackson had become president of the United States the previous year.
12. Earl L. Core, *Chronicles of Core*, 3d ed. (1975), pp. 33, 41.

hand bills, for circulation throughout the country." The school functioned, so the Prospectus said, under the management of a "principal teacher" with as many assistant teachers as the trustees deemed necessary. The students were divided into the following groups:

First Class: Reading, Arithmetic, English Grammar and Geography.

Second Class: Spelling, Reading, Writing and Arithmetic through division.

Third Class: Spelling and Reading.

Fourth Class: Greek, Latin, French, one class in each language.

Fifth Class: Moral and Intellectual Philosophy.

Sixth Class: Algebra, Rhetoric and History.

Seventh Class: Natural Philosophy and Geography.

Eighth Class: Mathematics and English Grammar.

Ninth Class: Surveying and Navigation.

Tenth Class: Algebra.

The "Regulations for the government" of the academy denied admission to persons who could not read and write. Noisy conduct and obscene language were forbidden in the building, and students were not permitted to accept challenges to fight duels or to act as seconds in duels. Gaming, habitual intoxication, use of profane language, and other gross offenses were forbidden under penalty of expulsion. Class records were reported regularly to the trustees. Teachers were expected to use corporal punishment.[13]

The academy in Virginia during the first half of the nineteenth century was somewhat the equivalent of the high school of today, although of course they were private subscription schools for the middle class element and did not serve the population as a whole. Although academies were chartered by the general assembly, the state actually exercised very little control over them, since only a small amount of financial support was provided by the state.

**Educational Summary.** The 1830 census reports for Monongalia County one academy, having fourteen scholars. In addition,

13. Charles H. Ambler, *History of Education in West Virginia* (1951), pp. 81, 82.

there were twenty-eight primary and common schools, having an enrollment of 629. A total of 169 poor children were being educated at public expense. There were in the county 2,132 persons over twenty years of age who were unable to read or write.[14]

**The Census of 1830.** The census of 1830 showed that Monongalia County was continuing to make a steady increase in population. There was not the dramatic increase characteristic of the early pioneer decades; many of the people who came to the Monongahela Valley were simply on their way farther west and did not tarry long. And most of these immigrants no longer came by way of Morgantown, following, instead, the new National Road to cross the Monongahela at Brownsville and reach the Ohio at Wheeling.

The abstract of the census is shown below:

|                  | Aggregate | Free   | Slave | Federal or Representative |
|------------------|-----------|--------|-------|---------------------------|
| East Monongalia  | 6,688     | 6,455  | 233   | 6,594                     |
| West Monongalia  | 7,368     | 7,239  | 129   | 7,316                     |
| Totals           | 14,056    | 13,694 | 362   | 13,910                    |

Twenty-three counties later to be part of West Virginia had been established by 1830. Of these only two, Ohio and Harrison, exceeded Monongalia at the time of the Fifth Census. Wheeling, in Ohio County, had come into prominence with the completion of the National Road to that point in 1818 and its subsequent extension through the state of Ohio. By 1830 Ohio County's population had grown to 15,584, from only 9,182 ten years earlier. Harrison County was also making substantial growth, having reached a population of 14,722 by 1830. The central location of its county seat town, Clarksburg, made it a suitable place to collect materials for shipment to the East.

Kanawha County, in 1830, still had only 9,326 people, Wood only 6,429, and Cabell only 5,884.

Monongalia County had grown from a population of 11,060 in 1820 to 14,056 in 1830, an increase of 3,996, or 36 percent. The area of the county was about seven hundred square miles,

14. Wiley, p. 381.

so that there were about twenty people to the square mile, still not a very dense population.

Agriculture, in 1830, remained the principal occupation of the people. Transportation of agricultural products was difficult and for most breadstuffs too expensive to show a profit. Therefore, the surplus grain was fed to horses, cattle, and hogs, which could be transported on the hoof to eastern markets. Great droves were conducted to Baltimore or Philadelphia every year. Cattle raising brought money into the county and stimulated new improvements, such as water mills, the introduction of frame and stone buildings to replace the original log cabins, the beginning of mercantile business in town and village stores.

The manufacture of iron was the second most important occupation. By 1830 the iron works along the Cheat River employed several hundred people and were continuing to expand. The manufactured products, beyond the needs of the territory centering in the Morgantown market, were sent down the river on flatboats to Pittsburgh.

Other county industries, in 1830, were the preparation of country millstones (from Pottsville Conglomerate rocks), the operation of carding and fulling mills, the manufacture of pottery, wagon making, boat building, and tanneries.

Transportation remained one of the greatest handicaps to the further economic growth of the county.

**The Election of 1830.** There were four voting places in the county in 1830, although elections were not very important in those days. Most public offices were appointive; members of the house of delegates and the senate were about the only state officers who were elected. Results of the 1830 election for house of delegates are shown below:[15]

| Candidates | Courthouse | Pawpaw | Swamps | Dunkard | Totals |
|---|---|---|---|---|---|
| E. C. Wilson | 386 | 80 | 82 | 57 | 605 |
| Richard Watts | 308 | 104 | 81 | 71 | 564 |
| F. Billingsley | 222 | 126 | 54 | 45 | 447 |
| S. H. Morgan | 67 | 33 | 16 | 3 | 119 |
| E. A. Barker | 57 | 29 | 1 | 8 | 95 |

15. Wiley, p. 302.

**Stagecoach Service Proposed.** A meeting was held at the courthouse on May 9 and a committee was selected to secure better
mail service for Morgantown through a line of stagecoaches connecting with Uniontown and Clarksburg.[16]

A few days later a newspaper editor commented:

"Our readers will find in another part of to-days paper the
proceedings of a public meeting held in this place to take into
consideration the propriety of petitioning the Post Master General to cause mail to be carried in stages from Uniontown, Pa.
by way of this place & Clarksburg to Parkersburg, Va.—The
growing population, wealth & commerce of the country demand the facilities sought for. In a pecuniary point of view the
Post office department would be almost immediately benefitted
by the transportation of the mail three times a week in stages
on this route. It would pass through the fine Vallies of the
Monongahela and Little Kenawha rivers being a distance of
about one hundred and thirty three miles. This country . . . has
struggled alone, from the times of Indian massacres and Indian
wars, and grown populus and rich through neglect of the governments . . . & now appeals with confidence of success to the
proper authorities for that which can be alone afforded by
them."[17]

Soon thereafter a letter to the editor, signed "Clinton" called
attention to some of the problems such service would face:

"As it is evident to all that our roads are barely sufficient for
the introduction of stages; and, that if there were now stages
running on the road in its present narrow and incomplete state,
it would be very much cut up, and without a great deal of
additional work would soon be almost impossible,—particularly
in the winter and spring seasons. And as there is reason to hope,
that we shall have a line of stages at some period not very
distant, running from Uniontown, Pa. to Parkersburg on the
Ohio river, the question presents itself forcibly to our minds, 'In
what way shall we effect a more valuable improvement. . . ?'

"All feeling a like interest in making a great road through the
county branching from the National Road, we should freely

16. Callahan, *Making of Morgantown*, p. 165.
17. The *Republican*, June 5, 1830.

compare opinions, and finally adopt that plan which promises to be the best."[18]

**The Republican Fails.** July 10, 1830, was the date of the last issue known of the weekly paper, the *Republican and Preston and Monongalia Advertiser.* The paper had been launched by Enos D. Morgan, a son of Captain Zackwell Morgan, on March 28, 1829. On April 20, 1830, the masthead was changed to "Morgan and Dunnington." Like all other newspapers of the day, collections were difficult. The issue of March 16, 1830, contains a typical appeal: "Next Monday being court day, we hope our subscribers, and those that are in arrears for advertisements and job work, will not forget that we are in great need of money at that time—and that we are bound to meet our engagements."

But after July 10 the county was once again without a newspaper.

**Steamboat Arrivals.** The arrival and departure of occasional steamboats were noted with interest by the newspapers:

"The steamboat MONONGAHELA arrived at this place from Pittsburg on Friday the 16 inst. and departed on the 17th. The same boat again arrived on Saturday the 24th, and started for Pittsburg same day.

"We notice these arrivals with pleasure, and we believe that in a few years the river trade of our country will be principally carried on by Steamboats. The Monongahela with little improvement will afford three feet water for nearly six months in the year, besides occasional freshets during the summer and fall months."[19]

"The Steam-boat ODD FELLOW arrived at this place on the 6th inst. from Pittsburg and departed the next day for Brownsville."[20]

**Boaz Fleming Dies.** Boaz Fleming, an early settler and an active civic leader in the Middletown area, died March 20, 1830. He was born in Delaware on January 3, 1758, and married Elizabeth Hutchinson (1764-1823) in 1784. Fleming led a party of

18. The *Republican,* June 26, 1830.
19. The *Republican,* March 30, 1830.
20. The *Republican,* June 12, 1830.

pioneers to Monongalia County in 1787 and was instrumental in laying out Middletown in 1819.

Children of Boaz and Elizabeth were: Clarissa (1786-1863), married James Hamilton (1783-1854); William (1789-1862), married Elizabeth Hudson, then Sarah Miller; Mary, born April 1, 1791; Elizabeth (1793-1843), married Benjamin Bartlett; David G. (1796-1883), married Sarah Fox (1801-1884); Sarah, born November 18, 1798; Lemuel (1802-1883), married Hulda Toncray (1810-1869); Jane (Jean) (1804-1879), married George M. Richardson; Joannah, born September 23, 1810; Margaret (1814-1882), married Andrew Cummins, then John Nelson.

After the death of his first wife, Fleming married Eliza Laidley and they had one child, Derexa (1827-1914), married George W. Hunsaker.[21]

**Fatal Accident.** "On the 27th ult. as Mr. John Foster was engaged in repairing a millstone at his mill on Decker Creek, about 5 miles from this place, [he] was most shockingly mangled by falling into one of the wheel pits, about 17 feet deep, on a solid rock; his skull was fractured so as to cause his death on the 5th inst. Mr. Foster was among the most worthy and respected citizens of this County."[22]

**John Cooper.** "Died, on Wednesday morning last, at his residence in this town, Capt. John Cooper, aged 73—after a protracted illness of three years during which time he was confined to his room—this gentleman entered the army of the Revolution at an early age and was at the memorable engagement of the storming of Stony Point—he was a man of strong and vigorous mind and had read much of ancient and modern history—he resided in this place more than thirty years, and maintained the character of a peaceable and honest mind."[23]

**The Railroad Starts Service.** Great interest continued to be manifested locally in the progress of the work on the Baltimore and Ohio Railroad. A Morgantown newspaper commented:

"A new car was put on the road on Friday, and another on Saturday, with two floors, the lower apartment was occupied

21. Lough, *Now and Long Ago*, p. 387.
22. The *Republican*, February 9, 1830.
23. The *Republican*, February 16, 1830.

by ladies, and the upper by gentlemen, amounting to forty persons, drawn by a fast moving horse with much ease. Its singular appearance afforded much interest and amusement to the crowds of spectators along the road as it passed."[24]

The first brigade of cars, each pulled by one horse, began making trips three times daily between Baltimore and Ellicott City on May 24, at a speed varying from seven to thirteen miles an hour. Soon after experiments were made with a lighter car rigged with a mast and square sails to take advantage of the wind. A horse motor car of the treadmill type was also tried. Finally, in August, Peter Cooper made the trial run of the first American steam locomotive. "Although on the return trip the crude locomotive lost in the historic race with the gray horse, it solved the problem of steam power for the railroad."[25]

"The iron horse breathing fire and smoke from its nostrils had begun its epic journey on American soil. The future destiny of this beast was so far beyond human conception that the greatest minds of the day failed to visualize the momentous gravity of this new departure in transportation. Some of the more radical 'prophets' even went so far as to predict that the day would come eventually when people would be whisked across the country side at the inconceivable rate of twenty-five to thirty miles per hour."[26]

Fire!—"On Tuesday night last the citizens of this place were alarmed by the cry of fire. It was however extinguished before any material damage was done. The building which took fire was that of Mr. John W. Thompson's, occupied as a Potter's shop."[27]

Later in the same year, according to Wiley,[28] the pottery did burn down, on August 29, and Thompson started, on September 30, construction of the steam pottery that was to serve the community for the next half century and more.

Frederick Cleaveland Webb, brother-in-law of Thompson, related the story of the fire in his diary.[29]

24. The *Republican*, January 26, 1830.
25. Callahan, *Semi-Centennial History of West Virginia*, p. 111.
26. S. T. DeJournett, "From Baltimore to Wheeling," *West Virginia History* 4 (1942):164-71.
27. The *Republican*, February 23, 1830.
28. Wiley, *History of Monongalia County*, p. 260.
29. Film 848625, L. D. S. Genealogy Society, Salt Lake City.

Fig. 7. Replicas of early B.&O. engine and passenger cars, displayed in Morgantown at the Monongalia County Sesquicentennial, October 21-23, 1926. (Courtesy West Virginia University Library.)

Fig. 8. John Wood Thompson. (Portrait courtesy Janet Crommett, Camp Hill, Pennsylvania.)

Fig. 9. Deborah Vance Thompson. (Portrait courtesy Janet Crommett, Camp Hill, Pennsylvania.)

"Arrived at Morgantown on Wednesday the 21st of July where I found my brother-in-law with his family in good health, excepting his wife who has poor health. Mr. Thompson is keeping his store and also carrying on his trade of crockery. John Wood Thompson, son of James and Dorcas, was born in the town of Belair, on the 14th of Sept. 1784. Married to my sister Mary,[30] daughter of Nathaniel and Charlotte Webb.

"August 29, 1830. About 3 o'clock in the morning Mr. J. W. Thompson's shop was consumed by fire, burned all his tools. Lost $400. The whole damage estimated $1600."

**Fourth of July Celebration.** "The 4th of July was celebrated at Granville . . . on Saturday the 3d inst. by a military parade of Capt. Hamilton and Capt. Boyers' Companies.—The rain interrupted much of the arrangement. Those who joined in the celebration late in the afternoon sat down to a good dinner prepared and well served up,"[31] at which voluntary toasts were offered by Capt. Josiah Boyers, John A. Fogg, Joseph E. Allen,

30. Actually he was married twice, the second time to Deborah Vance (see Fig. 9).
31. The *Republican*, July 10, 1830.

Noah Ridgway, Jr., James S. Hamilton, Col. C. S. Morgan, and others.

**Retailers and Tradesmen.** Newspaper advertisements give an idea of the types of commercial enterprises operating in the county:

"New Store! in Morgantown; John W. Thompson has just received and is now opening in his Store Room, lately occupied by Morgan & Henry, a general assortment of fall and winter goods."[32]

"J. W. Thompson still continues to carry on the Potting Business in all its various branches, and will sell that article on the most accommodating terms, either wholesale or retail."[33]

"Tailoring. Thos. S. Tricket respectfully informs his friends and the public generally that he has commenced the above business in Morgantown opposite Mr. F. Billingsley's Dwelling house, where he will execute all work in his line of business with neetness and dispatch; and upon the shortest notice."[34]

"The subscriber having purchased a *New Rope* and has got the Ferry at this time in complete repair. Every attention will be paid to travellers and others, who may call on him for the purpose of crossing.

"N. B. All who are in arrears for ferriage, for the first six months, will do me a very great favour to come forward and settle the same.

"Morgantown                                          John Core."[35]

**The Pulse of the County Seat.** The growth of Morgantown was by now proceeding at a slower rate, since heavy westbound traffic bypassed the town, following the new National Road to Brownsville and Wheeling. Previously many emigrants had reached Morgantown by wagon roads from Cumberland or Western Port and either located here, at least temporarily, or bought boats for the voyage down river to Ohio, Kentucky, and beyond. The flood of emigration into Morgantown virtually stopped, however, with the completion of the National Road, and the county seat became a quieter town.

32. The *Republican*, January 5, 1830, etc.
33. The *Republican*, January 26, 1830.
34. The *Republican*, May 8, 1830.
35. The *Republican*, July 10, 1830.

But one beneficial effect of the opening of the new road was in the greater ease in securing manufactured products from the East, for sale in the county's stores. This had the effect of increasing the diversity and abundance of material things in people's lives.

Efforts were now directed towards securing an improved road from Morgantown over the nearest and best route to the National Road. Not much improvement was made for a long time but there was increased traffic over the old road from Morgantown to Ice's Ferry, thence on to Uniontown at the base of Laurel Ridge, entering Uniontown on Morgantown Street. This route also served the growing community about Jackson's iron works and other industries east of Cheat River. Over this route Morgantown merchants brought from Philadelphia, Baltimore, and other eastern cities the goods which they sold to people from a large area of surrounding country who came to Morgantown to buy.

**The Williamsport Conference.**[36] The Methodist Episcopal denomination became established in Monongalia County at an early date (*Monongalia Story*, vol. 2, pp. 160-63, 218-20, etc.) but in 1820 dissension arose among members at the action of the general conference in denying local congregations the right to choose their own presiding elders. This resulted in the organization, at a conference in Williamsport[36] Harrison County, of the Equal Rights Society, who declared "we must protest, organize, and demand a square deal." This society eventually became a separate denomination known as the Methodist Protestant church and Pruntytown can claim the distinction of being the site of the foundation of this society or church group.[37] When, in 1830, Rev. Cornelius Springer came to Williamsport to organize a Methodist Protestant congregation, he found twenty-eight citizens of the village ready to assist in formation of the new church body.

**Monongalia Temperance Society.** The Monongalia Temperance Society was organized April 20, 1830, by the Reverend A. G. Fairchild and the Reverend Norval Wilson. On the first Monday

36. Williamsport was later renamed Pruntytown.
37. I. A. Barnes, *The Methodist Protestant Church in West Virginia* (1926), pp. 234, 235.

in May the following officers and directors were elected:
Mathew Gay, president; A. P. Wilson, vice-president; Thomas P.
Ray, secretary; and the Reverend J. A. Shackleford, William
Fleming, Nathan Goff, Henry Lazier, and Thomas P. Ray, di-
rectors.[38]

**Land Grant Made in 1830.**[39] The only Monongalia County
grantee in 1830 was:

Lazier, William                    105 a.                    Adj. Wm. Worth

**County Government.** Anthony Smith was sworn in for his second term as sheriff on March 22, 1830. William J. Willey was
sworn in as commissioner of the revenue for the Western District, succeeding Rawley Evans.

**Miscellany.** In 1830: Joseph W. Ray, son of Patrick and Mary
Day Ray, died (Callahan, p. 93). . . . Rev. Joel Stoneroad was
the Presbyterian minister in Morgantown (Callahan, p. 153). . . .
Dr. B. R. C. O'Kelley purchased Lot 19 in Morgantown, with the
brick house on it (Callahan, p. 189). . . . Lot 80 in Morgantown
was conveyed by T. P. Ray to Joseph Kern (Callahan, p. 319).
. . . Lot 98 was transferred by James Chadwick to Nicholas
Pickenpaugh (Callahan, p. 323). . . . William McCord was admitted to the Monongalia County bar (Wiley, p. 317). . . . Dr.
Marmaduke Dent sold his share of a business at Laurel Point to
his brother Nimrod and moved to Granville (Wiley, pp. 483,
722). . . . John Thomas was minister of the Forks of Cheat
Baptist Church; John McFarland and Daniel Medsear were
chosen deacons (Wiley, p. 686). . . . Nicholas Vandervort was
operating Ice's Ferry (Owens, p. 70). . . . Joseph Cummins, "A
shouting Methodist," moved to a farm one mile west of Cheat
River (Owens, p. 78). . . . Archibald Fleming's heirs bought Lot
24, in Middletown (Lough, p. 422). . . . William Fleming sold
Lot 38 to Benjamin B. Bartholow (Lough, p. 423). . . . Skin caps
were popular in Middletown, made from the pelts of muskrats
(Newman, p. 158).

38. Wiley, p. 451.
39. See p. 11.

# CHAPTER FIFTY-FIVE

# 1831

In colonial times educational opportunities for girls were very meager. O. P. Chitwood says: "They were taught reading, writing, sewing, embroidery, and good conduct."[1]

On the frontier, educational opportunities, such as then existed, were about equal for girls and boys. Both attended, if they were able, the short terms of the subscription schools. No free public schools existed, although by the end of pioneer times, some funds were available for the education of indigent children.

But the academies, which offered the only form of "higher education," were for boys only. The Monongalia Academy, the first in Monongalia County, was incorporated November 29, 1814, by the General Assembly of Virginia and by 1830 had outgrown its original quarters and moved into a new two-story brick building, "a large edifice," completed the year before.

**An Academy for Females.** A lottery venture floated by the trustees in 1827 had raised about eight thousand dollars, allowing for the construction of the new building on a better site, and the trustees decided to use the old building, at the corner of Spruce and North Boundary streets, for "the education of females." The proposed school would be operated, according to their proposal, as a department of the Monongalia Academy, but would be separate and distinct from it.

However, the trustees had some doubts as to their authority to make such use of their property, and by the time the boys had moved out of the old building, this plan was abandoned.

1. Oliver Perry Chitwood, *History of Colonial America*, 3d ed. (1961), p. 456.

But, says Wiley: "Those public spirited citizens who founded Monongalia Academy for the education of their sons, were not forgetful of the education of their daughters."[2] At a meeting on January 3, 1831, the trustees of the Monongalia Academy ordered "that Rev. Joseph A. Shackelford, John Rogers, Henry Lazier and Alpheus P. Wilson be appointed a committee to prepare a memorial to the Legislature for authority to convey the old academy lot and apply the proceeds of the sale to the erection of a female academy."

On March 23, 1831, the general assembly passed an act granting the authority to the trustees to establish a separate school for females and to sell the old property. Thomas P. Ray and A. P. Wilson, on September 5, 1831, selected Lot 113, at the northwest corner of Bumbo Lane and Middle Alley as the site for the new building. This property belonged to Elizabeth Morgan, wife of Zackquill Morgan II.

But on November 7 a proposition was made to a Morgantown Baptist congregation that if they would give $350, Lot 1 would be selected, a school building constructed on it, and the Baptists could use it on Sundays for church purposes. This proposition, however, did not work out and the trustees returned to their original proposal, to build on Lot 113.

**The Monongalia Academy.** Meanwhile, under the principalship of Jonathan R. Haddock, the Monongalia Academy was getting well under way in its new quarters. Newspaper advertisements called attention to its programs. Two courses were offered, the English Elementary and the Classical and Scientific.

The English Elementary included classes in Reading, Writing, Orthography, Arithmetic, Bookkeeping, English Grammar, and Geography.

The Classical and Scientific course embraced Ancient and Modern Languages, Mathematics, Natural, Intellectual, and Moral Philosophy, Belles Lettres, Chemistry, and the various branches of Natural History and Natural Sciences.

Tuition was $2.00 per quarter for the Elementary course and $7.50 per quarter for the Classical. Board cost $1.00 to $1.50 weekly. Classes were held throughout the year, except for the

2. Wiley, *History of Monongalia County*, p. 397.

first three weeks of July and from the second Monday of December to the first Monday of January.[3]

Occasional lecturers came to town and gave addresses to students and townspeople, sometimes selling books:

"Mr. H. Winchester delivered a 'lecture' (Tuesday evening last) on the progress, improvement and great advantages of 'Education', in which he in a very masterly, and forceable manner, proved the advantages of 'Education', particularly, to the 'Female mind.' "[4]

**The Growth of Learning.** Morgantown, following the opening of the National Road, was no longer on a main migration route to the west, and its citizens were living a quiet life, without many visitors from the outside. But they were interested in learning and perhaps freedom from the distraction of heavy traffic encouraged this. The town was already starting to gain a reputation as an educational center.

"A Visitor" described the town in 1831 in a long poem, "Sic Esto," a portion of which follows:

> "Beyond where Alleghany's cloud-capped brow,
> Admits the cultivation of the plough,
> *There* on a picturesque, romantic plain,
> The arts and sciences commence their reign.
>
> Where erst the war-whoop, to the heart so chill,
> Was echo'd by the Indian from the hill;
> Where bloody tomahawks were flourished, *there*
> The modes of civil life the traveller cheer.
>
> But what will soothe the mind, yet raise surprise,
> Here MORGANTOWN arrests his wand'ring eyes;
> Its people bland and hospitably kind,
> In customs and in morals much refin'd."
>
> "Lo, here we see the humble schoolhouse rise,
> And seminaries greet our joyful eyes."[5]

3. The *Monongalian,* December 24, 1831.
4. The *Monongalian,* March 12, 1831.
5. The *Monongalian,* August 13, 1831.

**"Chronicles of Border Warfare."** In May 1831, a very interesting book appeared from the press of Jacob Israel, in Clarksburg, and was advertised in the Morgantown newspaper.[6] It was written by Alexander Scott Withers and dealt with the border wars, chiefly of western Virginia. Since many of the participants in the warfare, or their descendants, were still living in the Monongahela Valley, the book, describing events so graphically, was well received and read with avidity around country firesides.

Fig. 10. Alexander Scott Withers. (From *Chronicles of Border Warfare.*)

Fig. 11. Simon Kenton. (From an old print.)

A. S. Withers was born in Fauquier County, October 12, 1792, and married Melinda Fisher in August 1815. They settled near Clarksburg about 1827, relocating later near Weston. After the death of his wife, in 1853, he moved to near Parkersburg, where he died January 23, 1865.

The reader will recall that we quoted at great length from this work in our accounts of the pioneer period in Monongalia County.[7]

6. The *Monongalian*, March 26, 1831, etc.
7. Core, *The Monongalia Story*, vol. 2, pp. 3, 10, 192, etc.

**New Constabulary Districts.** The county had been divided, on June 8, 1807, into nine constabulary districts, but with the establishment of Preston County, in 1818, the Third, Fourth, and Fifth Districts fell into that county. It was felt that a new organization was needed, so, on June 27, 1831, the county court subdivided the county into four districts and appointed constables for each, as follows:

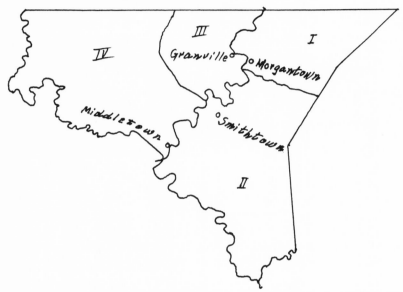

Fig. 12. Map showing approximate boundaries of the constabulary districts, 1831.

Constabulary District No. 1. All that part of the county east of the Monongahela River, and northeast of a line commencing at the mouth of Cobun Creek, and up the same to the head thereof at the Preston County line. Constables appointed were George W. Dorsey, John Watts, Jeremiah Stillwell, George Jenkins, Nelson Berkshire, and Madison McVicker.

Constabulary District No. 2. All that part of the county east of said river and southwest of the above described line. Constables named were William Meredith, William Swearingen, Amos Jolliffe, Amos Meeks, Horatio Morgan, and Benjamin Bradley.

Constabulary District No. 3. All that part of the county west of said river and northeast of a line running up Indian Creek to the head thereof; thence to Peter Tennant's mill; thence down Days Run to Dunkard Creek; thence with the creek to the Pennsylvania line. Constables were William M. Harrison, John D. Martin, Benjamin H. Barker, Hosea Wade, Andrew Brown, and Caleb Tanzey.

Constabulary District No. 4. All that part of the county west of said river and southwest of the last above described line. Constables, John Musgrave, Thomas Wade, Haze Parsons, George Dawson, Thomas L. Boggess, and William Lantz.

Thus there were two districts east of the Monongahela River and two west of the river.

**The Circuit Superior Court.** By the Virginia Constitution adopted in 1830, the old Superior Court of Law, which, under one name or another, had met in Morgantown twice a year since May 4, 1789, was designated the Circuit Superior Court of Law and Chancery. An act of the general assembly on April 16, 1831, placed Monongalia in the Twentieth Circuit, Tenth Judicial District. Judge Joseph L. Fry, of Wheeling, opened the first session of the new court in Morgantown on May 28, 1831.

This was a significant change in judicial procedure. It had been the policy of the state of Virginia ever since the Revolution to keep jurisdiction of common law and chancery separate. The Constitution of 1776 had authorized the general assembly to appoint "Judges in Chancery." From that time until 1831 the two jurisdictions were kept entirely separate and were exercised by separate courts, except that county and corporation courts had jurisdiction in both common law and chancery; even here separate "order books" were required.

In 1777 three chancellors were authorized by the assembly to hold the "High Court of Chancery," although only one, George Wythe, was appointed. He held this court until 1802, when two additional chancellors were appointed. Subsequently the state was divided into four districts and this system continued until the chancellors' courts were abolished by the Constitution of 1830 and chancery jurisdiction given to the judges of the Circuit Superior Court of Law and Chancery.

An act of the general assembly on December 22, 1788, had divided the state into five districts, with at least two sessions of court to be held every year in each district. These district courts were courts of general jurisdiction except that they had no chancery powers.

In 1809 the District Court was abolished and in its place the Circuit Superior Court of Law was substituted. The state was divided into circuits and courts were held in every county of the circuit. Monongalia County, in 1809, was in the Eleventh Judicial Circuit and the first session of this court in Morgantown was opened by Judge Hugh Nelson on Monday, May 15, 1809. Judge Nelson resigned and was succeeded, on January 22, 1812, by Daniel Smith, who was chosen by the general assembly and commissioned by the governor. Judge Smith, of Harrisonburg, who served until 1831, was about "six feet tall, with a round full face, black hair, and pleasant countenance . . . a man of fine presence."[8]

Prosecuting attorneys were appointed by the various courts; the first to serve the Circuit Superior Court of Law in Morgantown was Noah Linsly, an attorney who located in Morgantown in 1797, moving to Wheeling two years later. Linsly Military Institute was named in his honor.[9] Following Linsly's death in 1814, James McGee was appointed and then, on September 10, 1821, Eugenius M. Wilson. Guy R. C. Allen was the first prosecuting attorney of the new Circuit Superior Court of Law and Chancery, opening May 28, 1831.

Clerks of the District Court, from 1789 to 1809, were John Williams and William Tingle. For the Superior Court of Law, from 1809 to 1831, the clerks serving were William Tingle, Nimrod Evans, and Thomas P. Ray; Ray was also appointed the first clerk of the Circuit Superior Court of Law and Chancery, May 28, 1831.

Wiley says of the Monongalia County bar that "it was always a credit to the county and the State."[10] He points out some of the attainments. Its members have served, he says, "in both houses of the Virginia . . . Legislature. It has given judges to the judicial circuits . . . and to the State Supreme Court of Appeals. It has furnished members to represent Virginia . . . in the House of Representatives of the United States."

8. Wiley, pp. 308, 322.
9. Core, *The Monongalia Story*, vol. 2, pp. 413-15.
10. Wiley, *History of Monongalia County*, p. 316.

**Election of 1831.**[11] The vote for members of the House of Delegates in the August election was as follows:

|                    | C. House | Swamps | Thomas' | Pawpaw | Middle-town | Total |
|--------------------|----------|--------|---------|--------|-------------|-------|
| Richard Watts      | 289      | 34     | 60      | 21     | 21          | 425   |
| Francis Billingsly | 288      | 35     | 51      | 57     | 85          | 516   |
| William G. Henry   | 305      | 56     | 37      | 28     | 63          | 489   |
| Thomas S. Haymond  | 205      | 81     | 10      | 9      | 143         | 448   |
| Robert McGee       | 44       | 4      | 1       | 23     | 214         | 286   |
| Stephen H. Morgan  | 76       | 15     | 34      | 35     | 46          | 206   |

**E. M. Wilson Dies.** Eugenius M. Wilson, a son of Thomas and Mary Poage Wilson,[12] died on April 23. He was born in 1797 and admitted to the Monongalia County bar in 1819. The local newspaper reported:

"Died, On Monday evening the 23d inst about 8 o'clock (at the residence of his brother) Eugenius M. Wilson, of Wheeling, in the 34th year of his age. His death was not only inflicted on his family and friends a wound which nothing but christian resignation to the dispensation of Providence can cure; but has left a space in the different stations which he filled, that cannot be easily filled. His life has been amiable and exemplary—his death was that of a christian."[13]

**Prominent Pioneer Businessman Passes Away.** John Stealey, among the best known of Monongalia County's early businessmen, died on September 18, 1831. He was operating the Rock Forge Iron Works by 1815.[14] The local newspaper commented:

"Died, at Jeffersonville, Indiana, on the 18th ult., John Stealey, Esq. formerly a resident of this town. This gentleman removed from Alleghany county Maryland to this place at an early day, and without money education or friends acquired a large estate—he was distinguished for a strong vigorous mind, and uniform attention to business—his house was distinguished for hospitality, and no man ever resided in the county, gave more encouragement to young men setting out in life—the eve-

11. Wiley, p. 302; the *Monongalian*, September 3, 1831.
12. Core, *The Monongalia Story*, vol. 2, p. 515.
13. The *Monongalian*, May 28, 1831.
14. See Core, *The Monongalia Story*, vol. 2, p. 422.

ning of his life was clouded, to the regret of a large portion of the community."[15]

He was active in politics and was appointed a member of the county court. He was also active in church affairs and was a trustee of the Methodist Episcopal congregation, helping to build Morgantown's first church, in 1819, and was also a trustee of the Presbyterian church.

He married Prudence Cozad and of their children Elizabeth married Cornelius Berkshire, Sarah married Jacob Kiger, Christina married Rawley Scott, and Catharine married Col. Richard Watts, then William Hart."[16]

**The Monongalian.** A new weekly newspaper, the *Monongalian*, began publication on Saturday, January 22, 1831, succeeding the *Republican and Preston and Monongalia Advertiser*, which had ceased publication the previous summer. It was nineteen by twenty-six inches in size, with twenty columns on four pages. The price was two dollars per annum. The publisher was Elisha Moss, who also operated a store "late in the possession of John W. Thompson."

Like other papers of the day, it carried very little local news but had detailed reports of activity in the Congress and the legislature, usually one to two weeks late. There was also foreign news, stories, poetry, etc., and long discussions of political affairs. Also like most papers, it was well edited.

**The Business Scene.** Advertisements in the newspaper gave glimpses of the types of activity going on in 1831:

John Hurry announces "that he continues to carry on the Wheel-right business in the shop lately occupied by James Hurry decd., in Morgantown; where he intends keeping on hand, a variety of first rate spinning wheels. . . ."[17]

John Lawlis advertised that he intends to carry on weaving "at the house of Mr. Leving Fleming, at the head of Scotts run, near Peter Layton's Tan-yard," including "Double Coverlets, Single Coverlets, Table-linen, double and single Twill-flannel, Linen & Lindsey."[18]

15. The *Monongalian*, October 8, 1831.
16. Wiley, pp. 254, 262, 313, 589, 591.
17. The *Monongalian*, January 29, 1831.
18. The *Monongalian*, March 12, 1831.

Fulling and carding will be commenced at Middletown Mills the first of May by John S. Barns and Jonathan H. Haymond. Payments will be accepted in cash, grain, or other trade.[19]

Chadwick and Watts announce that they "have just received a first-rate spring selection of merchandize, including dry goods, groceries, hardware, queen's ware, medicine, etc."[20]

James and John Wilkins announce they will go into the copper and tin business, "in all its various branches, in a new shop prepared for the purpose, opposite the market house in Morgantown."[21]

Of course, farming was the principal occupation and farms were frequently offered for sale, their advantages listed:

Thomas Hamilton offers for sale a farm of eighty acres, four and one-half miles west of Morgantown, including "cleared land, a part of which is in meadow, a comfortable dwelling house, a convenient barn, good orchard, sugar camp, with extensive mines of stone coal."[22]

**Highway Improvements Urged.** Problems of transportation continued to plague the people. The local paper quoted a long section from the Richmond *Enquirer* which was applicable to most counties, including Monongalia:

"Our Roads are the Laughing-stock of strangers. Except a very few turnpikes, the high ways and the bye-ways are any thing else than what they ought to be. The system itself is radically defective. They are put under the superintendence of the Overseers of the Road in each county—who call out the laborers from the neighbouring farms, to work upon them, from time to time—and Heaven knows, in what a slovenly and perishable manner."[23]

Soon thereafter the paper published a long letter from C. S. Morgan, proposing that the state borrow $2 million for improvement of waterways and highways, including $48,000 "To

19. The *Monongalian*, April 9, 1831.
20. The *Monongalian*, April 23, 1831.
21. The *Monongalian*, September 3, 1831.
22. The *Monongalian*, January 22, 1831.
23. The *Monongalian*, February 12, 1831.

make a road from the mouth of Fishing Creek by Morgantown to the Pa. line near Smithfield."[24]

Later in the year, William G. Henry, in a long open letter to the people of Monongalia County, urged improvements in methods of transportation.

"What then does wisdom dictate to us? Is it not to push the opening of a road from the mouth of Fishing Creek to Smithfield in the direction of Cumberland, which would pass through more than 40 miles of this county; and to urge the opening of the navigation of our river?" It was "not yet known where the Baltimore rail road will terminate—when it will be finished," but it seemed safe to guess that transportation from Cumberland to the seaboard would soon be provided, either by railroad or canal.[25]

As a local improvement, the county court, through its commissioners, Alex Wade, Nimrod Dent, and John Fortney, called for bids "for making the new road from Cores Ferry to the mouth of Scotts Meadow Run"; also for building "a bridge across the mouth of said run."[26]

**The Northwestern Turnpike Is Located.** From the earliest pioneer times the construction of a good road across the Alleghenies had been a prime concern of the settlers on the western waters. The rugged terrain meant that a good road would be very costly and one suggestion was that charging tolls to travelers would help provide funds.

The general assembly in 1827 had passed an act incorporating the Northwestern Turnpike Company to construct a road from Winchester to some point on the Ohio River near the mouth of the Little Kanawha. The company was subject to all the general rules provided in the Turnpike Act of 1817. The provisions of this act were not put into operation, however, and the assembly of 1831 reorganized the project.

The chief engineer was Colonel Claudius Crozet (Fig. 24), a French officer of artillery under Napoleon Bonaparte in the Russian campaign and later professor of engineering in the United States Military Academy (1816-23).

24. The *Monongalian*, February 26, 1831. Near Smithfield (later called Somerfield), at the "Great Crossings" of the Youghiogheny, connection would be made to the National Road; George Swetnam and Helene Smith, p. 195.
25. The *Monongalian*, July 16, 1831.
26. The *Monongalian*, July 30, 1831; i.e., from Morgantown to Granville.

Crozet began the work of locating the road in the spring of 1831. He laid it out through Hampshire County, thence crossing the Potomac River to run through the state of Maryland for a distance of eight and three-quarter miles, then entering Preston County at the German Settlement (Aurora).

Continuing westward the route crossed the Cheat River and Laurel Ridge to pass through the southern extension of Monongalia County near Bulltown.[27] It then crossed the Tygart Valley River and passed by Williamsport[28] to Clarksburg. Crozet did not complete the location to the Ohio River, since he resigned at the end of the year and was succeeded by Charles B. Shaw, who had been assistant engineer for a number of years.

It was specified that the road would be sixteen feet wide, exclusive of ditches, and the types of materials to be used in construction were specified.

**John Thorn Dies.** "Died, on the 21st ult. after a short but painful attack of fever, John Thorn of this county, in the forty-first year of his age. In the death of Mr. Thorn the county has lost one of its best citizens—society a most amiable member—and his large and interesting family, a kind and provident husband and father."[29]

**Church History.** From 1825 until about 1831 the Methodist Episcopal Church in Morgantown was included in the Monongalia Circuit of the Pittsburgh Conference. Ministers serving the local church during this period were:[30]

    1825  Samuel R. Brockunier, Nathaniel Callender
    1826  William Hank, Richard Armstrong
    1827  Shadrach Chaney, George McKaskey
    1828  Shadrach Chaney, John Spencer
    1829  Robert Boyd, Edmund Sehon
    1830  Robert Boyd, Clarke Brown
    1831  John West, Andrew Coleman

Ministers serving the Presbyterian Church[31] after the resig-

27. Later Knottsville.
28. Later Pruntytown.
29. The *Monongalian*, September 3, 1831.
30. Wiley, p. 444; see also Grafton T. Reynolds, *Manual of the Pittsburgh Conference of the Methodist Episcopal Church* (1928).
31. Op. cit., p. 592.

nation of Rev. Ashbel Fairchild (p. 9) were Joel Stoneroad, 1830-31, and Rezin Brown, 1831.

"The Rev. Cyrus Beecher Bristol, a missionary under the (Presbyterian) Assembly's Board, commenced preaching on Stewart's run in December, 1831."[32]

**Middletown Presbyterian Church.** On November 4, 1830, the Reverend Cyrus Beecher Bristol, a member of the Bedford Presbytery, began a long pastorate at the Presbyterian church in Middletown. He had been sent as a missionary but continued as a regular pastor.

The church had been organized in the home of Asa Hall, near the mouth of Buffalo Creek, in 1815 (*Monongalia Story*, vol. 2, p. 423). Boaz Fleming, Jordan Hall, and Thomas Hall were ordained elders. Occasional visiting ministers in the next few years were the Reverends James Adams, J. Green, R. Condit, and A. G. Fairchild. About 1828-29 S. Reed, a licentiate, preached six months as a stated supply. Elisha D. Barrett was licensed as a candidate for the ministry about the same time.[33]

In 1831 a church was built on a lot on Jefferson Street donated by Boaz Fleming. The building, adjacent to a cemetery, was nearly square, one story high and unpainted. There were two entrance doors, one for men and the other for women, while inside there were two sections, for the same purpose. "The ministers were of the regular Presbyterian type of those days—stern and unsmiling—who thought the Sabbath Day a most holy institution which must be kept to the last letter of the law."[34]

**The "Old Salem" Church.** Among the earliest meetinghouses of the county was the Salem Methodist Church, near the site of Prickett's Fort, across the Monongahela River from the mouth of Paw Paw Creek. The congregation was organized in 1830 and the building was constructed in 1831. The deed for the lot was made by Jacob Swisher September 2, 1831, to Joseph Hartley, Methodist Protestant trustee, Raphael Hoult, Methodist Episcopal trustee, and Horatio Morgan, public trustee. Leaders in

32. Wiley, p. 729.
33. Newman, *Marion County in the Making*, pp. 325, 326.
34. Op. cit., p. 327.

the establishment of the church were the Reverend Daniel
Helmick and J. J. ("Jenk") Harris.

The building, against the hillside in a wooded area, faced
westward, and, like most other buildings of the period, was also
used as a school.[35]

**Land Grants Made in 1831.**[36] Monongalia County grantees in
1831 included:

| | | |
|---|---|---|
| Batson, John W. | 78 a. | Plum Run |
| Brookover, John | 100 | Paw Paw Creek |
| Brookover, John | 175 | Sugar Camp Run |
| Bush, Peter | 12 | G. Lick Run |
| Campbell, Robert | 245 | Laurel Run |
| Cleland, Patrick | 112 | Buffalo Creek |
| Core, Christopher | 20 | Rudolphs Run |
| Cox, Andrew | 100 | Dunkard Creek |
| Eddy, Margaret | 5 | Adj. James Barker |
| Fetty, John | 100 | Adj. F. Cole |
| Freeland, John | 150 | Piles Fork |
| Hambleton, Benjamin | 78 | Meadow Run |
| Haught, Peter | 225 | Scotts Run |
| Johnston, Thomas | 100 | Wickwares Creek |
| Lowe, Philip | 35 | Spring Run |
| Lowe, Philip | 20 | Wts. Monongahela R. |
| Metz, Peter | 194 | Piles Fork |
| Morris, Ezekiel | 50 | Dolls Run |
| Myers, John | 240 | Hazel Run |
| Price, Charles P. | 245 | Laurel Run |
| Remley (?),[37] Emanuel | 48 | Dunkard Creek |
| Shriver, John | 60 | Dunkard Creek |
| Smith, Jacob C. | 250 | Morris Run |
| Snodgrass, Elisha | 37 | Farrows Run |
| Sole, John | 100 | Dunkard Creek |
| Strasser, George | 240 | Hazle Run |
| Taylor, Abraham | 70 | Dunkard Creek |
| Thomas, George | 80 | Flat Run |

35. Wilcox, *How Our Marion County Churches Began*, pp. 83, 85. The
building, near the later Montana Mines, was dismantled in 1895; Barnes,
*M. P. Church*, pp. 80, 81; Balderson, *Prickett's Fort*, p. 68.

36. See p. 11.

37. Lemley.

| | | |
|---|---|---|
| Thomas, Isaac | 50 | Miracles Run |
| Toothman, Adam | 116 | Plum Run |
| Wade, Thomas | 46 | Dunkard Creek |
| Warman, Thomas | 10 | Corner J. Smith |
| Weaver, John | 60 | Days Run |
| West, David | 20 | Indian Creek |
| Williams, James | 1,250 | Wickwares Creek |
| Wilson, John, Jr. | 76 | Adj. Jemima Scott |
| Wilson, Stephen | 42½ | Papaw Creek |
| Youst, Peter | 100 | Pappaw Creek |

**County Government.** David P. Morgan was sworn in as sheriff on March 30, 1831. Ralph Berkshire was sworn in as commissioner of the revenue for the Eastern District of Monongalia County, succeeding Isaac Cooper. Dudley Evans resigned as justice of the peace on September 26, 1831. He had been appointed before 1796. Rawley Evans resigned the same day, having been sworn in May 14, 1810. The county levy was fifty cents.

**Miscellany.** In 1831: Joseph Jolliffe, who had bought the Jeffs property at Smithtown,[38] built a new gristmill and sawmill on it (Wiley, p. 614). . . . Casper Orth sold his tannery at Stewartstown to William Robison, son of James Robison (Wiley, p. 674). . . . Robert P. Hennen purchased Lot 9 on Front Street in Morgantown and there began the manufacture of high grade furniture, a business that was to grow in importance and endure for more than three-quarters of a century (Callahan, p. 136). . . . William Lazier acquired Lot 54 on Spruce Street and erected on it a large frame mansion (Callahan, pp. 189, 318). . . . Mrs. Eveline C. O'Kelly, wife of Dr. B. R. C. O'Kelly, died April 26, survived by her husband and a son and daughter (the *Monongalian*, April 30, 1831). . . . The steamboat "Tariff" arrived the port of Morgantown on March 6 (Wiley, p. 542). . . . Hugh Sidwell, of West Run, died (Owens, p. 96). . . . William Nuzum sold Lot 33, in Middletown, to James Burns (Lough, p. 420). . . . Andrew McCray sold Lots 7 and 8 to Benjamin Fleming (Lough, p. 421). . . . William Fleming sold a tract of land near Quincy Street to Francis Pierpont (Lough, p.

38. See Core, *The Monongalia Story*, vol. 2, pp. 339, 519.

426). . . . In January, snow fell to a depth of three feet, the deepest since 1780 (*Chronicles of Core*, p. 43). . . . Captain James Hurry, distinguished military commander of the War of 1812 (*Monongalia Story*, vol. 2, p. 408), died on January 1; he was born July 15, 1776.

# CHAPTER FIFTY-SIX

# 1832

Faced with tremendous problems related to transportation, and having a broad river flowing through the middle of the county, local residents still experienced great frustration in making proper use of it. Canoes, flatboats, and keelboats all suffered from fluctuations in the water level. Now, when steamboats seemed about to take much of the labor out of the process of moving people and goods, the same difficulties remained.

Typical of efforts to solve some of the problems involved in river transportation was an act passed by the general assembly on February 25, 1832, providing for the opening and improving of navigation on the Monongahela River in Monongalia County. A committee was appointed to raise twenty thousand dollars. But any substantial improvement was still far in the future.

Keelboats and barges continued to carry most river freight. Business increased and boats were built larger and larger. "The keelboatmen, moreover, anchored by self-interest to the old ways, were frankly contemptuous of the steamboat. In their eyes it was a scheme to destroy their business and expose people's lives."[1]

A tragic accident on a riverboat took the life of a young and talented citizen of Monongalia County early in 1832.

**Alpheus Poage Wilson.** The Wilson family had figured prominently in the annals of the county from the very beginning. Thomas and Mary Poage Wilson came to Morgantown before the end of the Revolutionary War and he was admitted to the county bar while Morgantown was still a frontier community.

---

1. Leland D. Baldwin, *The Keelboat Age on Western Waters* (1941), p. 191.

They had five sons and three daughters, "distinguished for talent and ability."[2]

Alpheus Poage Wilson was born at Morgantown on March 2, 1794. After reading law with his father he was admitted to the bar in 1821. In September of the same year he married Eliza Evans, daughter of Jesse Evans, of Springhill Township, in Fayette County, Pennsylvania.

In 1816 he was appointed by the county court to serve as coroner and as acting sheriff. The next year he was appointed sheriff and served until July 27, 1818, when Rawley Evans was appointed as his successor.

He was elected to the House of Delegates of the Virginia General Assembly in 1819 and to the state senate in 1821, where he served four years.

In 1826 A. P. Wilson was a delegate to a meeting in Washington, D.C., for discussion of a proposed canal to connect the waters of Chesapeake Bay with those of the Monongahela. Their proposal, the Chesapeake and Ohio Canal, got under way slowly, however, and soon came into competition with the Baltimore and Ohio Railroad.

In 1825 Wilson took over the operation of the Deckers Creek iron works at Rock Forge, a position which led indirectly to his accidental death seven years later.

The Rock Forge iron works had been started at least as early as 1798, by Samuel Hanway, pioneer county surveyor.[3] Later the works were operated by John Stealey, who in 1815 advertised for hands to work at the furnaces. Between that date and 1824 the plant was operated by Col. Richard Watts and Jacob Kiger, sons-in-law of Stealey. According to tradition, stoves were made at Rock Forge before 1824. Probably most of the production, however, was in the form of bar iron, which was purchased by local farmers and blacksmiths for making horseshoes and agricultural implements. Some of the iron may have gone to Hawthorne's nail works,[4] on Aaron Creek; nails were probably also made at Rock Forge. At one time, according to

2. Callahan, *Making of Morgantown*, p. 92.
3. Core, *The Monongalia Story*, vol. 2, pp. 266-69.
4. Core, *The Monongalia Story*, vol. 2, pp. 290-92.

Moreland's history of the iron works,[5] the Rock Forge establishment consisted of "the furnace—quarterstack—and a forge. The forge had three fires and one hammer run by water power."

Some of the iron was loaded on flatboats for shipment downstream. On February 10, 1832, A. P. Wilson fell from a load of iron near Brownsville, Pennsylvania, and was drowned. The issue of the local newspaper for that week is missing in the West Virginia University Library, but soon thereafter a newspaper notice offered for sale his "Law and Miscellaneous Library" of four hundred volumes.[6]

**The Road to Morgantown.** One of the earliest examples of Monongalia County folk literature is the famous "Road to Morgantown," the author of which is unknown but believed to be Joseph Park and the date likewise unknown but apparently about 1832.

The story concerns Robin Darrah, a resident of Miracle Run, in western Monongalia County, who is directing a stranger to the county seat. Along with illustrating the garrulous nature of some backwoodsmen, the account gives sidelights on living conditions of the day and the people mentioned were real men and women living in the area at the time.[7]

The text follows:

"STRANGER. My friend, can you tell me the road to Morgantown?

"ROBIN DARRAH.[8] (Throwing down an armful of chips

5. James R. Moreland, *The Early Cheat Iron Works* (1940), pp. 103, 104.

6. The *Monongalian*, March 17, 1832.

7. Many of the persons named in this story can be identified as landowners in western Monongalia County in the 1830s from deed records in the courthouse, and are also named as heads of households in the 1830 and 1840 census reports.

Most of the names also appear in a genealogical book, *Andrew Park our Ancestor*, by Harry and Ruth Park, Earl and Ruby Park, Elias and Kate Park, and Ethel Park Stemple (148 pp., privately printed, date not given but about 1970). Further footnote references to this book appear as Park, etc. See also "History of Bula" in Book Two (Battelle School District) of Lynn Hastings, *School and Local History* (1960).

8. Robert D. Darrah (1769-1848). He married first Anna Campbell, then Barbara Coon. Their children were Sarah (married James Park), Joseph (married Margaret Jones), Robert, Jr. (married Barbara Jones), Henry (married Ann Tennant), Mary (married, possibly, Joseph Park), Ruth (married Benjamin Shuman), Elizabeth (married James Park), and William (married Delia Ann Park). Pers. comm., W. L. Darrah, Route 1, Box 1, Eddyville, Iowa 52553. See also Park, etc., pp. 16, 86, 94.

which he was carrying from the yard). By the grace of God I can tell you as well as any man in the county, for I've been there myself. You come past old Joe Tuttle's,[9] didn't you? With his lip stickin' out like your foot, and the amber running off his lip sufficient to swim ducks. He chaws tobaccy, sir!

"STRANGER. I care nothing for him. I've come past there. I wish to get to Morgantown.

"ROBIN DARRAH. Well, you'll take up the hill past old Blink-eyed Baldwin's,[10] all the blacksmiths we have in the county; the cussedest iron roaster you ever saw in the born days of your life. He will burn up forty plowshares a year, if you'll take 'em to him. A few days ago, Jake (dang his name) and Bets (dang her, too! For I can't think of either of their names), was running off to get married over in Pennsylvania, and stopped at Blink-eyed Baldwin's to get their hosses shod. He blowed and blowed and the devil a shoe he made and whether they got married or not I'm unable to tell. He's got a little stewed up old woman for a wife about as big as your fist, about so high! and she keeps the whole country in an uproar with her lies, running from house to house, and tattling. And she's got her name up, so that it's Mattie Baldwin here and Mattie Baldwin there and Mattie Baldwin in everybody's mouth. And there's not a lawsuit in the county in which she is not summoned as a witness for somebody, and whether she swears or not I'm unable to tell you, but I believe she swears lies.

"You'll take down the hill from there to old Dave Chew's[11] that married old Aaron Foster's widder.[12] You'll turn around his farm to the right—that road will lead you down to Dan Cokes,[13] the dog shooter; he has killed all the dogs in this county, so if you're afraid of dogs you needn't be alarmed, for there's not a dog left to bark at you, and it's Dan Cokes here and Dan Cokes there and Dan Cokes in everybody's mouth. He ought to be made pay for the dogs, and I think he will before he gets through with it. The other day me and my son, Joe, was going through a field and up jumps a fox and the dog took after

9. Joseph Tuttle lived on Miracle Run.
10. Perhaps intended for John Baldwin. Park, etc., p. 93. John Baldwin was a road surveyor in 1821.
11. The Chew family was among the earliest settlers (see *The Monongalia Story*, vol. 2).
12. Aaron Foster lived near Miracle Run.
13. The Coke family was living on Days Run in 1836. Park, etc., p. 95.

it, and we've never heard of the dog or fox since till this day, and then the fox was about 350 yards ahead of the dog till he hasn't got back yet, and I expect Dan Cokes killed him.

"You just keep down the run from there and you'll come in among the fattest, lustiest set of Negroes you ever seen in all the days of your life. Their name is Dowd[14] and its Dowd here and Dowd there and its Dowd in everybody's mouth. I've one of the cussedest lawsuits with them you ever heard of in your life, and it's all about slander and there's Tom P. Ray,[15] Clerk of the county court at Morgantown and Edgar C. Wilson[16] the best lawyer in the Virginny, both say I'll beat 'em as slick as a bone and it's all about slander, though I never slandered anybody myself.

"You'll cross over a pint there and fall over to another run. By turnin' to the right you'll come down to old Bill Messers.[17] He married a Metz and her name is Peg, and she's the cussedest woman to swear you ever heard in all your life, sir. Her hair sticks out like a scrub broom. She don't comb it from one week's end to another and it's Peg Messer here and Peg Messer there and Peg Messer in everybody's mouth and she can out-swear Mattie Baldwin!

"You'll turn there to the left and that will take you to a pint and you will fall over into Jake's Run, named after old Jake Straddlers in Indian times,[18] and it's settled with Tennants[19] from head to mouth! And they are the cussedest set of men to fight you ever saw in all your born days. Whenever they have a log-rollin' or any comin' together of the people, their jackets are off, and the blood a flyin' and all hollerin' fair play. The father will fight the son and the son will fight the father. The brothers will fight one another. There's old Enock Tennant,[20] a steppin' around with his head a stickin' to one side; I believe he is the foulest Tennant among 'em. But there's Black Ben, Pete Tennant's[21] slave, I'd like to forget him. He's the only white man among the Tennants.

14. The Dowd family lived on Days Run.
15. See p. 215.
16. See p. 492.
17. On Paw Paw Creek.
18. Core, *The Monongalia Story*, vol. 1, p. 184.
19. Core, *The Monongalia Story*, vol. 1, pp. 305, 306; vol. 2, p. 464.
20. Son of Joseph and grandson of Richard.
21. Peter Tennant, son of Richard.

"You'll turn up that run by turnin to the right, no road to turn you off, till you fall on the head of the Little Paw Paw, to my son-in-law's Ben Shuman's,[22] one of the ugliest men you ever saw in your lifetime and it's Ben Shuman here, and it's Ben Shuman there and it's Ben Shuman in everybody's mouth; he keeps the whole neighborhood in an uproar with his lies. But I must say that Ben Shuman has the best breed of dogs in the county, and he's going to have a lot of pups soon. My Joe spoke a pup and I 'low to go over day after tomorrow myself and buy the mother and sell her to my brother-in-law, Joe Koon, for a gallon of whiskey, or a bushel of corn.

"John Hood's[23] got the best store in Blacksville. There's going to be a famine on the creek for Shep Lemaster[24] and Joe Park[25] are selling their corn out at 25¢ a bushel and they'll have to give 50¢ for the same corn back again between this and harvest. And Bill Lantz[26] and Bill Thomas[27] have got a barrell of whiskey apiece and are retailing it out at a bushel of wheat to the gallon and they'll get all the wheat in this neighborhood and that wheat will go from there to Pittsburgh and I'm drawin' a pension at this time, and devil a bit more right have I to it than they have, but there was old Andy Cobley[28] and Jake Brookover[29] got me before the squire and didn't care what I swore so they got part of the money. All the exploit I ever done in my life was to kill my mother and then the gun went off by accident.[30]

22. Benjamin Shuman is listed in the 1830 census as a householder in Monongalia County.

23. John Hood; see p. 247.

24. Perhaps Septimus Lemasters (1800-1873); Park, etc., p. 2.

25. There were several Joseph Parks living on or near Miracle Run, including Joseph (born 1795), son of pioneer settler Andrew Park (1760-1848) and his wife Mary; also Joseph (1818-1911), son of Andrew Park, Jr. (1792-1863) and his wife Sarah Humes. Park, etc., pp. 1, 2.

26. William Lantz was a landowner on Miracle Run. Park, etc., p. 94.

27. William Thomas owned land on a branch of Miracle Run called Thomas Run. Park, etc., p. 94.

28. Andrew Cobley was disallowed a road order by the county court in 1822.

29. Jacob Brookover in 1824 received a grant of one hundred acres on Days Run. Sims, *Index*, p. 450. He is listed as a householder in the 1830 census.

30. While cleaning his gun he accidentally shot and killed his mother, who was lying in bed (Hastings, "History of Bula").

"STRANGER. Goodday, sir!

"MRS. DARRAH. Robin, the gentleman don't know no more about the road now than if you hadn't said a word.

"ROBIN DARRAH. Hold your tongue, old woman. By the grace of God, he can't miss the way, and I know he recollects it, for he said good morning and we parted."

**The Monongalia Academy.** In 1829 an act of the general assembly (see p. 26) enabled the trustees of the Monongalia Academy to raise, by lottery, as much as twenty thousand dollars for the endowment fund of the academy. Thomas P. Ray was appointed to secure lottery drawings under this act, and, on January 26, 1832, a contract was signed with Yates and McIntyre, of New York.[31]

Meanwhile, William Griffey, Fielding Kiger, and Mathew Gay placed the following notice in a local newspaper:

"The subscribers will on the 28th inst. in front of the Court House, in Morgantown, offer for contract to the lowest and best bidder, the building of a two story Brick House in said town for the purpose of a Female Academy. The lower story only to be furnished, and that in a plane substantial manner."[32]

The contract was awarded to John Rogers, who proceeded to construct the building, on the east end of Lot 113.

**Primary Schools.** The report of the school commissioners for the year ending September 30, 1832, lists eighty schools in operation in the county. A total of 776 names of poor children appeared on the treasurer's list, but only 637 were actually taught. A majority of the schools remained open for only three, four, or six months; only two or three in the entire county were open for the entire year. This difficulty is attributed to a lack of good teachers, "the cause is that people here is two careless about educating their children." "The primary system of teaching adopted by the Legislature . . . in its operation is very defective and inopperative."

31. Wiley, p. 395; Ambler, *History of Education in West Virginia*, p. 81. Ambler says that "for sometime thereafter the trustees seem to have been more interested in augmenting their funds from the sale of lottery tickets than from effective teaching and curriculums. Success in lottery ventures led to abuses. . . ."

32. The *Monongalian*, January 21, 1832.

Names of the teachers were listed and the names of the commissioners, by school districts, were: 1. Hillery Boggess; 2. Robert McGee; 3. David Musgrave; 4. Aaron Barker; 5. Andrew Brown; 6. Thomas Lazzell; 7. William John; 8. Thomas S. Haymond; and 9. Fielding Kiger.

**Revolutionary War Veterans.** Wiley[33] gives two lists of soldiers of Monongalia County in 1832 who had seen service in the Revolutionary War. The first list includes those who had been pensioned under an act of Congress of March 18, 1818:

| | |
|---|---|
| Stephen Archer | Richard Johnson |
| Richard T. Atkinson | Daniel Lee |
| Joseph Bunner | Christian Madera |
| Ezekiel Burrows | Zadoc Morris |
| Benjamin Chesney | Thomas Malone |
| Asaph Colegate | Joseph Sapp |
| Henry F. Floyd | Gabriel Williams |
| Jesse Jaskins | Stephen Watkins |
| Youst Heck | Ebenezer Blackshire |
| Edward Raymond | |

The supplemental list includes names of men, some (or all) of whom had been pensioned by 1832:

| | | |
|---|---|---|
| Peter Bartrugg | Jacob Holland | John Stone |
| John Burdin | Peter Hammer | Charles Simpkins |
| Solomon Chaffin | Peter Haught | Henry Stone |
| Elisha Clayton | Purnell Houston | Philip Snell |
| James Collins | William Hall | George Tucker |
| Lieut. John Dent | George Keller | James Tryon |
| Henry Dorton | Peter Miller | James Troy |
| Samuel Dudley | Zackwell Morgan | Richard Thralls |
| James Devers | Amos Morris | Henry Williams |
| Simeon Everly | Evan Morgan | George Wade |
| Col. John Evans | Richard Price | John Wills |
| William Ford | Zachariah Piles | William Wilson |
| Caleb Furbee | Isaac Reed | William Wilson II |
| Stephen Gapen | James Scott | Henry Yoho |

33. Wiley, *History of Monongalia County*, pp. 487, 488. Some of the men on these lists had died before 1832.

**New Building for Forks of Cheat Church.** The historic old Forks of Cheat Baptist Church[34] received a new home in 1832. The congregation was established in 1775 and met in the homes of members until a log building was constructed at the old Baptist burying ground at Sunnyside in 1784. Robert Stewart and Catherine, his wife, sold the land to the church for five dollars on September 10, 1806, William John, John McFarland, and Samuel Bowen being agents for the church. Tradition says this structure was destroyed by fire.

The second church building was constructed in 1803, when Samuel Bowen, William John, Richard Cain, and John McFarland agreed to hew the logs for the structure that was twelve rounds high and twenty-six by twenty-two feet in size. The building stood about two hundred feet south of the old church. Both these buildings were also used for school purposes.

"The furnishings for the first churches were crude. It was necessary to depend on the craftsmanship of the congregation who was very often too busy to construct elaborate furniture. The furniture was constructed simply from wood. The windows were covered with paper greased with lard to let in the light while candles were used for evening services.

"According to the records of Miss Millie Hunter, who had researched the old records, the church always met on the first Saturday of each month, for business. These meetings were either in the meeting house or in a member's home. The meeting always opened with prayer, and business in many cases questioned disputes, slander, profane swearing, drunkenness, and disorderly walk. . . ."[35]

The third structure, built in 1832, was of brick, forty by thirty feet, and was built on a new site, deeded by Jacob Conn and his wife Elinor and by John McFarland and his wife Elenor. Furnishings, as in previous buildings, were constructed by the members, seats, pulpits, etc., but glass was used in the windows. A bell in the steeple, donated by Lancelot John, called the

34. See Core, *The Monongalia Story*, vol. 1, pp. 175, 309-12, 352, 407; vol. 2, pp. 90, 137, 152, 153, 154, 161, 175, 229, 320, 373, 420, 423, 428.

35. Joseph C. Gluck (and others), *Forks of Cheat Baptist Church* (1975), pp. 29, 30.

people to worship, and they sang hymns to the accompaniment of an organ. The cost of the building was $2,200.[36]

**The Monongalian Ceases Publication.** In the issue of January 14, 1832, Elisha Moss, editor of the *Monongalian*, commented:

"This week concludes the first volume of the Monongalian—we are thankful for the liberal support we have received, and on commencing the second, we hope it will increase, as nothing on our part as to care and attention shall be omitted to make the paper interesting to our patrons."

Fig. 13. Franklin Hotel, on Walnut Street, built about 1796. (West Virginia University Library.)

Nevertheless, only a few months later, without further notice, the paper ceased publication. The last number seen by the writer was for June 9, 1832. Once again the county was without a newspaper.

**Elections of 1832.** Results of the April election in Monongalia County for members of the general assembly follow:[37]

36. Op. cit., pp. 30, 31.
37. The *Monongalian*, April 28, 1832.

Senate

| | Richard Watts | Guy R. C. Allen | William B. Zinn |
|---|---|---|---|
| Morgantown | 460 | 102 | 38 |
| Swamps | 62 | 27 | 29 |
| Middletown | 76 | 47 | 175 |
| Pawpaw | 76 | 25 | 6 |
| Dunkard | 108 | 9 | 8 |
| | 782 | 210 | 256 |

House of Delegates

| | William G. Henry | William J. Willey | Thomas S. Haymond | Isaac Cooper |
|---|---|---|---|---|
| Morgantown | 427 | 248 | 242 | 305 |
| Middletown | 92 | 222 | 245 | 25 |
| Pawpaw | 80 | 91 | 25 | 14 |
| Dunkard | 72 | 112 | 25 | 14 |
| Swamps | 44 | 27 | 77 | 87 |
| | 715 | 700 | 614 | 445 |

In the vote for president, later in the year, the following totals were recorded for the county:[38]

Andrew Jackson, Democratic . . . . . . . . . . . . . . . . . . . . . .860
Henry Clay, National Republican . . . . . . . . . . . . . . . . . .230

**John Hennen Is Killed.** John Nelson Hennen, a farmer in the western part of Monongalia County, was accidentally killed by a falling tree on January 3, 1832. He was the son of Thomas and Anne Hennen and was born in Greene County, Pennsylvania, December 9, 1800. He married Sarah Pitsenberger, and they had three children, George Nelson, Asbury, and Sarah Anne, the latter born after the death of her father.[39]

**John Evans, of Crooked Run, Dies.** Two Monongalia County pioneers were named John Evans, one settling on each side of the Monongahela River. The John Evans of Crooked Run, on the west side of the river, died June 26, 1832, aged seventy-six years. He had settled in the area before the Revolutionary War. "He was a thorough-going and industrious man, and accumu-

38. Wiley, p. 269.
39. Dorothy T. Hennen, *Hennen's Choice*, vol. 1, pp. 39, 75, 76, 77.

lated extensive landed interests, giving each of his sons a farm."[40]

He was twice married, the first time to Sarah Williams; they had three children, Enoch, Lewis, and a daughter.

By his second marriage, with Elizabeth Raber, he had ten children, David, Samuel, Otha, Eli, Hugh, Alfred, Isaac, Nancy, Sarah, and Aramiah.

**Other Deaths.** John A. Berkshire, pioneer settler, died in 1832. In April 1806 he bought from George Barns a tract of sixty-three acres on Scotts Meadow Run and located there. He was married about 1772 and the couple had three sons, William, Ralph, and Cornelius.[41]

Daniel Strother Evans, son of John ("Captain Jack") Evans, Jr., and grandson of pioneer settler John Evans, was born in 1806 and was lured at an early age to the newly developing steamboat business on the Ohio and Mississippi rivers. It was while he was commanding a boat running from Louisville to New Orleans that he fell a victim to yellow fever, dying in 1832. An older brother had already met death in a similar manner (see p. 7).[42]

Philip Doddridge, celebrated lawyer and statesman, who was representing this district in Congress, died in Washington on November 19, 1832. His term had begun in 1829. His home was in Wellsburg, but he had been admitted to the Monongalia County bar on May 4, 1795, and served as prosecuting attorney of the Superior Court in Morgantown from May 1803 to May 1804. Born May 17, 1773, he was a son of John and Mary Wells Doddridge, and a nephew of the Philip Doddridge who was a pioneer settler in Monongalia County.[43] He was a brother of Joseph Doddridge, author of *Notes on the Settlement and Indian Wars.*[44] He had gone to Washington to meet his colleagues

40. *Cyclopedia of Monongalia County*, pp. 186, 187; Gordon C. Baker, "John Evans of the Border," *Monongalia Chronicle* (April, 1975), pp. 16-21.

41. Callahan, *Making of Morgantown*, p. 104.

42. Wiley, p. 525.

43. Core, *The Monongalia Story*, vol. 1, pp. 190, 238. For biography, see Waitman T. Willey, *A Sketch of the Life of Philip Doddridge* (1875), 96 pp.

44. Core, *The Monongalia Story*, vol. 2, p. 494.

on a special committee which was to make a report to the session of Congress convening December 3, 1832.

James Henderson, a native of Ireland, died November 8, 1832, at his home on Dunkard (or Henderson) Ridge, at the age of ninety years and was buried in the family cemetery. His children were Matthew, who moved to the head of Little Indian Creek; James, who "went west"; Jesse, who married Amanda Fox and moved to Tyler County; Rachel, unmarried; David, who married Elizabeth Morris and remained on the homeplace; Sarah, who married Abraham Horner; Alexander, who married Catherine Lemley; and a daughter who was killed when a child by a limb of a tree falling on her.[45]

**Road Construction Continues.** The building of wagon roads throughout the county continued year after year and county court records include dozens of reports each year. The following actions for 1832 are typical.

The county court received a report on a review of a petition for "a road from Jacob Metz's on Piles Fork of Buffaloe Creek to the Tyler County line near Nehemiah Glover's," with the recommendation of the reviewers for construction of the road, suggested workers and supervisors, and consent from landowners.

Commissioners were appointed to "view and mark out a road from the Poor House to the widow [Mary] Miller's residence"; "from the forks of Falling Run to [Robert] Tobin's coal bank"; "from Jackson's Forge to the Pennsylvania line"; "from a small drain by Michael Courtney's meadow to intersect the Waynesburgh and Morgantown road"; etc.

**Land Grants Made in 1832.**[46] Monongalia County grantees in 1832 included:

| | | |
|---|---|---|
| Batson, Charles W. | 70 a. | Plum Run |
| Batson, John W. | 138 | Plum Run |
| Camp, John | 26 | Indian Creek |
| Campbell, Joseph | 100 | Plum Run |

45. Core, *Chronicles of Core*, pp. 43, 44; a distinguished descendant was Joseph Lindsey Henderson (June 27, 1869-December 8, 1965), grandson of Alexander, professor at the University of Texas and author of *Educational Memoirs* (Austin, 1940), 335 pp.

46. See p. 11.

| | | |
|---|---|---|
| Carter, Lloyd | 78 | Waters Monongahela R. |
| Demoss, James | 260 | Three Forks Creek |
| Gallahue, Henry | 78 | Pricketts Creek |
| Hanway, John | 67 | Swamp Run |
| Hanway, John | 150 | Sandy Creek |
| Hanway, Samuel | 100 | Glade Run |
| Henry, Otho | 13½ | Meadow Run |
| Hirons, Thomas | 100 | Grassy Run |
| Lazzell, Thomas | 24 | Robinson Run |
| Minor, Alexander | 92 | Dunkard Creek |
| Murphy, Marshall | 110 | Adj. Wireman's Survey |
| Norris, George | 115 | Tygerts Valley R. |
| Poe, Francis | 90 | Wickwares Creek |
| Poe, William | 65 | Wickwires Creek |
| Ray, Thomas P. | 3,000 | Laurel Run |
| Rogers, William | 150 | Grassy Run |
| Sharp, Aaron | 150 | Mill Run |
| Sole, John | 100 | Dunkard Creek |
| Tennant, Adam | 110 | Statlers Run |
| Tennant, Richard D. | 68 | Doss (Days) Run |
| Wade, George R. | 4 | Adj. Joseph Wade |
| Wilson, Thomas S. | 50 | Booths Creek |

**County Government.** David P. Morgan was sworn in for his second term as sheriff on March 26, 1832. Sworn in as justices of the peace (members of the county court) were John Wagner, January 23; Joseph Gray, February 27; William Thomas, February 27; Isaac Cooper, February 27; and William Lazier, March 28. The county levy was set at $0.50.

**Miscellany.** In 1832: Rev. Thomas Martin was supply minister at the Morgantown Presbyterian Church and Samuel Brand was ruling elder (Wiley, p. 592). The Reverend Mr. Martin, a licentiate, "labored as a missionary amidst many discouragements for six months" (Callahan, p. 153). . . . Michael Kerns, Jr., was keeping a tavern on Front Street (Callahan, p. 117). . . . N. B. Madera in March conveyed Lot 8 to Nicholas Shisler (Callahan, p. 310). . . . At about the same time Shisler conveyed Lot 17 to Reuben B. Taylor (Callahan, p. 311). . . . John W. Thompson in April sold Lot 121 to George Hill (Callahan, p. 329). . . . John

Everly (1802-1879), a cooper by trade, was making nail kegs at the mouth of Maple Run, along Cheat River (Owens, p. 81). . . . "The Rev. Asa Shinn is expected to preach in the Court House in Morgantown, on Friday next at early candle-lighting" (The *Monongalian*, April 28, 1832).

## CHAPTER FIFTY-SEVEN

# 1833

The construction of the National Road from Cumberland via Uniontown to Wheeling was both bad and good for the economic health of Morgantown. County residents had been accustomed to being on a main route for westward migration, the immigrants reaching Morgantown by wagon through the Sandy Creek area, then taking boats for the trip downstream. Now the main route missed the county and the community lapsed into a period of quietude and tranquillity. Growth was nearly at a standstill.

But it was also good, because Morgantown was less than thirty miles away from one of the best roads in America. The completion of the National Road through Uniontown had made possible "rapid transit" lines for hauling goods and passengers across the mountains to and from Baltimore and Washington and this made it easier for local people, too.

Stagecoach Days. James Kinkead, Jacob Sides, and Abraham Russell established the first line of passenger coaches west of Cumberland, says T. B. Searight[1] and as early as 1818 John and Andrew Shaffer, Garrett Clark, Aaron Wyatt, Morris Mauler, John Farrell, Quill and Nathan Smith, and Peter Null were drivers on this line. The line was subsequently purchased by and merged in the National Road Stage Company, the principal and most active stockholder of which was the colorful Lucius W. Stockton. Born in Flemington, New Jersey, September 1, 1799, he appeared in Uniontown as a stage proprietor some time before 1824, and soon became widely known in his field. One

---

1. Thomas B. Searight, *The Old Pike* (1894), new edition by Joseph E. Morse and R. Duff Green (1971). Citations are to the 1971 edition.

incident in his early career, it is said, was a race between his horse and buggy and a locomotive from the Relay House to Baltimore, in which he came out ahead.

"He had a pair of 'Winflower' mares," Searight recalled, "which he drove frequently from Uniontown to Wheeling between breakfast and teatime, tarrying two or three hours at midday in Washington. At the watering places he ordered a little whiskey to be added to the water given these spirited and fleet animals, and they became so accustomed to it that, it is said, they refused to drink unless the water contained the stimulating element. He would also drive from Uniontown to Cumberland in a day, stopping at the stations to transact business, and from Cumberland to Hagerstown, sixty-six miles, was an ordinary day's drive for him."[2]

James Reeside was a competitor of Stockton and put on a line of stages which Stockton nicknamed the "June Bug," predicting that it would not survive the coming of the June bugs. Stockton later bought out the line and merged it with his own.

But another competitor came to stay. This was the Good Intent line and "was equal in vim, vigor and general equipment to the Stockton line...."[3] In Uniontown the headquarters of the Good Intent line was the McClelland House, where the passengers took their meals, the horses being stabled nearby. The headquarters of Stockton's "old line" was at the National House, on Morgantown Street. A lively spirit of competition flourished between the drivers of the two lines and a popular ditty all along the road was:

> "If you take a seat in Stockton's line,
> You are sure to be passed by Pete Burdine."[4]

**Stagecoach to Morgantown.** The first regularly scheduled stagecoach service through Monongalia County was started early in 1833. It was subsidized as a carrier of the United States mail, in addition to the transportation of passengers. It was a line of four-horse stages from Uniontown to Morgantown by way of Ice's Ferry, operated by Colonel Richard M. Johnson.[5] At

2. Op. cit., p. 102.
3. Op. cit., p. 103.
4. Op. cit., p. 103; Peter Burdine was an employe of the Good Intent line.
5. A year later a tri-weekly mail in two-horse stages was established between Uniontown and Clarksburg by way of Morgantown.

Uniontown connection was made with through lines operating east and west on the National Road.

One of the most eccentric of the old Stockton drivers, Henry Wise, carried mail and passengers for many years between Uniontown and Morgantown. He claimed descent from aristocracy and said that he drove the stage only for amusement. He customarily wore a silk hat and held the reins so slack that his horses frequently strayed from the narrow road.[6]

"The stage coach of those days had a large body supported by leather bands instead of metallic springs. It was painted with vermillion without and was plush-lined within. There were boots in front and rear as receptacles for trunks. The huge vehicle always had 'room for one more,' and was drawn by either four horses or six. The king of the freight wagons . . . was the huge conestoga, costing $250. It had a bed eighteen feet long and so deep as almost to hide a man standing within. The bed was painted a deep blue. Above was the white canvas cover and below were the broad tired wheels."[7] These coaches, of course, operated on the main lines; the coaches to Morgantown were smaller.

Fig. 14. A stagecoach and inn on a western Virginia turnpike. (Sketch by J. H. Diss Debar, courtesy West Virginia Department of Archives and History.)

6. Callahan, *Making of Morgantown*, p. 165.
7. Oren F. Morton, *History of Preston County* (1914), p. 206.

**Early Mail Service.** The development of improved communication through the establishment of a stagecoach line connecting Morgantown with the National Road at Uniontown, in the early 1830s, made it possible to provide better postal service. There had been a post office at Morgantown since 1794; now small post offices were established at various points throughout the county, mostly supplied by horseback riders once a week.

United States Post Office records for this early period are rather fragmentary, but the following list, supplied by the National Archives, probably includes all the Monongalia County post offices established up until 1833. An office might be set up under one name with a postmaster named, then on the postmaster's death, removal, or resignation, the office would be discontinued but perhaps a new office, with a new name and a new postmaster, would be set up to serve the same general neighborhood.

*Barnes' Mills.* Thomas Barnes, Jr., was likely the first postmaster, with R. Martin named on July 13, 1824. This was at the mouth of Buffalo Creek. The office was discontinued March 2, 1833.

*Blacksville.* This post office, at the newly established town of Blacksville, served the Dunkard Creek settlements. Fletcher Brock was the first postmaster, succeeded by S. Wilson and W. Brock on July 5, 1832.[8]

*Dunkard.* This was probably the first post office on Dunkard Creek, a mile or two west of Blacksville, with Thomas Reynolds as postmaster.[9]

*Granville.* Melford P. Massie is listed as the first postmaster of this office, which was established in 1830. Marmaduke Dent became postmaster March 2, 1833.

*King's Ferry.* This office, along the Tygart Valley River, had as its first postmaster Job Springer, succeeded by M. Jeffries May 24, 1826.

*Knottsville.* Near Threeforks Creek, this office had Absalom Knotts as its first postmaster.[10]

8. Anthony Conrad became postmaster May 30, 1835.
9. Dunkard Post Office was discontinued June 11, 1834.
10. Rawley Gandy became postmaster July 14, 1834, and the place was popularly known as Gandeeville.

*Lakeville.* George Lake was the postmaster at this office, near Tygart Valley River, which was discontinued January 19, 1833.

*Morgantown.* Nicholas B. Madera became postmaster at Morgantown in 1822 and was still serving in 1833.

*Mount Linus.* This post office, on the western side of the Monongahela River between Morgantown and Middletown, was established January 4, 1831. Gouldin Arnett was the first postmaster; a county court record dated 1828 mentions Goulding Arnett as the "infant" son of Daniel Arnett, with W. J. Willey as his guardian. L. Shaidly and Clement Morgan were appointed February 29, 1833.

*Palatine Hill.* William Haymond was the postmaster at this office, across the river from Middletown. No date is given for the establishment.

*Park.* This post office was established December 30, 1833, with Thomas Johnson as the first postmaster.[11]

*Polsley's.* The first post office at Middletown was known as Polsley's, (or Polsley's Mills), from pioneer settler Jacob Polsley, the first postmaster. The post office was established December 11, 1820. John H. Polsley became postmaster in 1822 and Ebenezer Newcomb in 1827.

*White Day.* Joseph Jolliffe was postmaster at this office near Smithtown, on White Day Creek. No date is given.

Mail mostly came into the county from Uniontown by way of the "mail hack," or stagecoach, which usually had seats for three or four passengers. When the mail pouches reached Morgantown, the pouches were unlocked and the mail was sorted. The items which had local addresses were placed in boxes to await the coming of the person to whom they were addressed. Since mail did not arrive every day, and most residents did not receive letters or parcels in every arrival anyway, some of the pieces might be held by the postmaster for a long time. Some of them were never called for. Unclaimed mail might be advertised in Morgantown newspapers, or even in newspapers in other towns, as Clarksburg, Uniontown, or Wheeling.

Mail addressed to other Monongalia County post offices was put into the bag of a particular carrier, who might have several offices on his route. When the day came for his trip over that

11. He was succeeded by Thomas Steel and Peter Johnston February 6, 1834. The office was dicontinued October 11, 1839.

route, the bag was locked and the carrier departed, with the bag on his horse. When he arrived at a particular post office, he descended from his horse, took the bag into the post office, and handed it to the postmaster, who unlocked it with his key. The postmaster sorted through the items within, removed those which bore the address of his office, then replaced the others, together with any he might have on hand for dispatch from his office. He then locked the bag and handed it to the carrier, who departed towards the next office.

Longer horseback routes led to Clarksburg by way of Middletown (later replaced by the stagecoach), to Washington, Pennsylvania, by way of Waynesburg, and to Kingwood.

**Louisa Ann Lowrie.** "The first missionary from Monongalia to heathen lands was Mrs. Louisa Ann Lowrie. She was the daughter of the Hon. Thomas Wilson, of Morgantown, and was born November 2, 1809. In 1833, she married the Rev. John C. Lowrie, eldest son of the Hon. Walter Lowrie, Secretary of the Senate of the United States. Mr. and Mrs. Lowrie embarked in May, 1833, at Philadelphia, as missionaries to India. Mrs. Lowrie but reached the chosen land of her labor to find a grave. Threatening symptoms of consumption at the time of her sailing developed rapidly during the voyage into that fatal disease, that ended her life in Calcutta on the evening of the 21st of November, 1833. She was laid to rest in the Scotch burial-ground at Calcutta. Thus ended the short but brilliant life of an eminent Christian and devoted missionary. Her memory is well preserved in the memoir of her life by the Rev. A. G. Fairchild, D. D."[12]

**Churches.** A Presbyterian church was built at Smithtown about 1833, by Presbyterians and Episcopalians, jointly. William Morris, "a liberal Welshman," was a prime mover. The Reverend Cyrus Beecher Bristol preached there. The building was used by several denominations.[13]

A Methodist Protestant church was organized in 1833 in Jacob Smith's dwelling house, near the Jackson iron works, by

12. Wiley, *History of Monongalia County*, p. 449. Mrs. Lowrie's obituary appeared in the *Monongalia Farmer*, April 12, 1834.
13. Wiley, p. 625. The last services in the church were held about 1878.

the Reverends John Lucas, William Dunlavy, Asby Pool, and Joseph Shackelford. The class organization included William Donaldson, class leader, and Lewranah his wife, William Norris and Rheuhama his wife, John N. Baker and Nancy his wife, Aaron Hamilton and Mary his wife, Mr. and Mrs. Thomas Burch, Mr. and Mrs. Jacob Breakiron, Mrs. Amelia Norris, Mrs. Hannah Smith, William and Matthew McConnel, William Lewellin, Jacob Smith, Elizabeth, Eleanor, Mary, Eliza, and Sarah Norris, and Elizabeth Baker. William Donaldson attended the first quarterly meeting in Fairmont on November 16, 1833.[14]

Residents of the Baptist faith in the Glady Creek community, near the Tygart Valley River, organized a congregation on December 28, 1833, known as the Hebron Baptist Church. The first building was a log cabin which also served as a schoolhouse.[15]

**Building Roads.** For more than a third of a century Monongalia County residents had been engaged in the construction of a system of wagon roads and this continued unabated throughout 1833.

Petitions were presented to the county court for new or relocated roads "from Jackson's works to the Pennsylvania line in the direction to Evanes Furnace"; "from Morgan Town to Beverly, sending it by way of Henry Hambleton and others by taking the road on the present Clarksburg road, up the Monongalia river to the poor hous lands, then leaving the same taking a south easterly direction"; "from the mouth of Little Creek going by or near a new sawmill now building by Jacob Swisher and from thence to Pricketts Creek near Isaac Hills saw mill from thence to intersect the road (known in the neighbourhood by the name of the Paw Paw road)"; "from McDaniels Ferry on the Valley River to Isaac Marquiss' Mill on Sandy Creek"; "from the Bridge near Bakers Mill to intersect the road near John Hayman's leading to Morgantown"; "Beginning at the

14. Wiley, p. 688; Dodds and Dodds, *Churches of Monongalia County,* p. 153.
15. Wilcox, *How Our Marion County Churches Began,* pp. 98, 99. The present church building was constructed in 1869; Balderson, *Prickett's Fort,* pp. 76-78. For history of Glady Creek, see Balderson, ibid., pp. 164, 165.

State Road leading from King Wood to Clarksburg at Philips saw mill . . . hence to John Jones intersecting the Road leading from Clarksburg to Morgantown"; "from the road near Joseph Tennants thence up Henrys Run and down Pedlars Run and to intersect the State Road near George Wilyards at the mouth of Pedler Run"; "leading from the State road at William A. Hurleys to Nathan Johnsons, state road"; "from William Thomas' Mill to Peter Tennants' Mill"; "a way for us to travel to Boyles Mill on Piles fork of Buffaloe from the mouth of Mods run"; "from Holts Mill[16] to Barns Mill"; "from holts ferry up the River by the way of T. Halls mills and thence to Goosmans forde"; "commencing at the road [leading from the widow Wades to Collins Mill] at Daniel Deusenberrys . . . to intersect the road leading from Morgantown to Waynesburg"; etc.

"Whereas the road leading from Glady creek . . . to Bulltown or Knotsville in the swamps has been much complained of by those who frequently travel the same by reason of the said Road being located through a very hilly part of that Region inasmuch that tis almost inaccessible for a loaded waggon and team," the petitioners asked for a new road.

When a signed petition was presented to the county court, a committee was appointed to review the route as to public need, ease of construction, and willingness of landowners to donate land for the road. If the review was favorable, a foreman was appointed to employ "hands" (local men) to grade out the road, mostly by pick and shovel.

An important feature of the wagon roads was the watering trough, the "service station" of the nineteenth century. The early troughs were hewed out of a log of a tree and were placed by the side of the road every few miles, where a spring flowed out. They were a necessity for horses. Later troughs were made of heavy wood planks about twelve feet long and two feet wide, bound together with iron bands and bolts.[17]

Problems in construction frequently arose, as the following:

16. For history of the Hoult community, see Balderson, ibid., pp. 173, 174.
17. See Alvah J. W. Headlee, "Greene County in 1865," in reproduction of J. L. McConnell's *Map of Greene County, Pennsylvania* (Waynesburg, Pa., 1977), 39 pp.

"a new road that is laid out near Willyards that you have ordered Barton Morris and his hands to make wee find it too hard for us to accomplish—pleas to order Michael Coar and his hands to help us make the road."

A new major highway, conceived as a competitor of the National Road, was the Northwestern Turnpike, incorporated in 1827 and effectively organized in 1831. It was designed to connect the Monongahela and Ohio settlements with communities east of the mountains. Governor John Floyd, in his address to the legislature on December 2, outlined progress:

"The Northwestern Turnpike road, which was authorized to be constructed, is in progress, and promises to be extensively useful, as its friends expected. The entire location of it has been finished, and seventy four miles of the distance has been put under contract for its construction, twenty four miles of which has been completed in a style highly gratifying to its friends and the public generally."[18]

**The Railroad.** Meanwhile the Baltimore and Ohio Railroad was very slowly creeping towards the Monongahela Valley. Callahan relates the progress made and the numerous frustrating delays encountered:

"The completion of the track to Point of Rocks on the Potomac, on April 1, 1832, was followed by a steadily increasing traffic and travel from the river above which assured the future success of the road and indicated that it had outgrown the earlier conception of a mere improved form of toll road. At this point the enterprise was halted by a decision of the Court of Appeals in favor of the Chesapeake and Ohio canal, which contested the right to occupy the narrow valley of the Potomac and generously invited the railroad company to abandon its work and devote its resources to the completion of the canal. By interference of the legislature which compelled a compromise, the railroad company subscribed for 2500 shares of the canal stock and submitted to obnoxious regulations to prevent fright of the tow-path horses—including a demand to haul its trains by horses through the passes along side the canal.

"After securing the repeal of these petty regulations, the directors of the road, after May, 1833, pushed their tracks for-

18. *Monongalia Farmer,* December 28, 1833.

ward to Wager's Bridge opposite Harpers Ferry . . . , producing an immediate stimulus to the business of the road, coincident with the introduction of better cars and additional engines and the invention of various devices such as switches and turn tables."[19]

Governor Floyd, in his December 2 message, commented:

"Roads and canals, or rail roads, which now seem to be a valuable substitute for rivers, carry the products of distant countries to market, with a velocity which annihilates space, and bringing distant countries almost together, are only wanting to enable us to reach the highest state of improvement and prosperity, which any people ought to desire."[20]

**Michael Kerns.** One of the earliest settlers of Monongalia County, Michael Kerns, Sr., died July 10, 1833. He was born in Holland about 1740 and was married in Lehigh County, Pennsylvania, to Mrs. Susannah Weatherholt, about 1766. They came to Monongalia County by 1770 (*Monongalia Story*, vol. 1, p. 177, etc.; vol. 2, pp. 148, 331).

Michael and Susannah had at least four children, Michael, Jr., (ca. 1768-1833), Christiana (born ca. 1770, married Fleming Jones), John J. (born ca. 1778, married Elizabeth Toothman), and Susan (married Jacob Stealy?).

Following the death of Susannah, Michael married Mrs. Barbara Riffle, of Fayette County, Pennsylvania.

Michael Kerns, Jr., also, apparently, died in 1833, a few months after his father. He married Catherine Criss and they had seven children, namely, Elizabeth (married John G. Cooper), Susannah (married Reuben Chalfant, then William Culan), John (married Maria, daughter of Moses Cox), Michael, III (married Eliza, daughter of William O'Neal), George (married Polly C., daughter of Jesse Payne), James (born March 4, 1796, died January 8, 1870, married Mary, daughter of Godfrey and Margaret Guseman), and Jacob (married Sarah, daughter of James McVicker).[21]

19. Callahan, *Semi-Centennial History of West Virginia*, pp. 111, 112.
20. *Monongalia Farmer*, December 28, 1833.
21. From data in Morgantown Public Library, researched by Mrs. Hilda Moore Anderson and Mrs. Patsy Moore Laird. See also Callahan, *Making of Morgantown*, pp. 33, 34, 108, 144; and numerous references in *The Monongalia Story*, vol. 2.

**Fire!** On the night of December 21, 1833, "between the hours of 6 and 7 o'clock, the barn of Dr. Caleb Dorsey of this county was totally destroyed by fire, together with seven head of horses, farming utensils, and a considerable quantity of grain and hay, with which the barn was principally filled. It is not known as yet, we believe, how the fire originated; but there cannot be a doubt, but that it was the work of some unknown incendiary.

"The loss is estimated to be about 1200 dollars."[22]

**The Monongalia Farmer.** After the county had been without a newspaper since the *Monongalian* ceased publication June 9, 1832, about a year and a half went by before a new paper was founded.[23]

The *Monongalia Farmer* began publication December 21, 1833, next door to William Griffey's store and exactly opposite the courthouse. It was printed on a super-royal sheet and the subscription price was two dollars, in advance. Francis Madera and Company was the publisher; the motto was "Our Country— and our Country's Friends."

The following announcements appeared in the first issue:

"Notwithstanding the many fruitless and faithless attempts that have been made for the successful establishment of a public Journal in Morgantown, and the many gross impositions which have been practiced upon the citizens of Monongalia County heretofore, we come before you fully determined to give the matter a full and fair test, and to ascertain if possible by a course which we will presently state, where the fault lies, whether in the liberality and patriotism of the citizens of Monongalia, or in the honesty, industry, and economy of those by whom the business has been conducted heretofore. . . .

"The publication of 'The Monongalian' having ceased, and the present proprietors of the press being sensible of the necessity of a medium thro' which the news of the day may be disseminated, propose the publication as above."

**Monongalia Academy.** "The semi-annual examination of the students of this institution took place on Thursday and Fri-

22. *Monongalia Farmer,* January 4, 1834.
23. Wiley, p. 433, says the *Monongalia Farmer* "was started about 1828" and adds: "No copies of it can be found." But vol. 1, no. 1, in the West Virginia University Library, is dated Saturday, December 21, 1833.

day . . . and their various recitations . . . was witnessed by a large number of persons, with great and increased attention and pleasure; and a general opinion of Mr. Horner's indefatigable exertions and skill, were attested by the progress made by all his students, beyond the expectations of the most sanguine. This examination was closed by a short, pertinent, and eloquent address, from the Rev. Mr. Drummond, in which he pourtrayed to this rising generation, the general effects of a good education. . . .

"This institution deserves to be patronized, and under such teachers, it will flourish—situated in one of the most healthful spots on the banks of the Monongahela; in a village noted for its morality and intelligence—parents and guardians cannot select an institution more advantageous."

On Friday evening, the principal, Thomas Martin, "delivered an address in his usual eloquent, forcible and impressive manner, upon Education, to a large number of persons; the effect was better felt, than can be described."[24]

**Land Grants Made in 1833.**[25] Monongalia County grantees in 1833 included:

| | | |
|---|---|---|
| Batton, Henry | 50 a. | Indian Camp Run |
| Copenhaver, Isaac | 100 | M. Morgans Run |
| Frederick, John | 95 | Booths Creek |
| Holt, Elijah | 22 | Adj. John Holt |
| Holt, Raphiel | 8 | Waters Monongahela R. |
| Jennings, William | 100 | Coxs Run |
| McElfresh, Joshua | 18 | Waters Monongahela R. |
| Metz, Leonard, Jr. | 50 | Buffalo Creek |
| Reed, Stephen | 20 | Toms Run |
| Smith, Anthony | 200 | Maple Run |
| Smith, Anthony | 140 | Wolf Pen Ridge |
| Stafford, James H. | 12 | Waters Cheat R. |
| Watson, James | 100 | M. Morgans Run |
| Wiley, John W. | 100 | Coxs Run |
| Youst, William | 200 | Piles Fork |

24. *Monongalia Farmer*, December 21, 1833. John S. Horner was an assistant teacher (Wiley, p. 395).
25. See p. 11.

County Government. Thomas S. Haymond was sworn in as sheriff on March 25, 1833. Thomas Watson was appointed commissioner of revenue for the Western District. Andrew Brown, Moses Cox, Leonard Lamb, Thomas Watson, Fielding Kiger, and John Clayton were sworn in as justices of the peace on September 23, 1833. The county levy was $0.87.

In a reapportionment of United States Congressional Districts, Monongalia, along with Preston, Tyler, Ohio, and Brooke counties, constituted the Twenty-first District. Previous to 1833, Monongalia had been in the Eighteenth District, along with Brooke, Ohio, Harrison, Tyler, and Preston.

Miscellany. In 1833: Waitman T. Willey located in Morgantown in June and was admitted to the Monongalia County bar on September 9 (Wiley, p. 316). . . . William Werninger was admitted to the bar on April 16 (Wiley, p. 318). . . . Thomas Martin became principal of the Monongalia Academy (Wiley, p. 395). . . . The steamboat *Yancey* arrived at the Port of Morgantown on February 4 (Wiley, p. 542). . . . Caleb Dorsey began the practice of medicine in Morgantown (Wiley, p. 584). . . . George M. Reay, son of John Otho and Elizabeth Reay, located in Morgantown (Wiley, p. 598). . . . A gristmill with two sets of stones (one set buhrs) was built near Flickersville[26] by Caleb P. Price (Wiley, p. 724). . . . Thomas P. Ray bought Lot 1 in Morgantown from John W. Thompson (Callahan, p. 308). . . . Fielding Kiger bought the west end of Lot 103 from Thomas P. Ray, trustee (Callahan, p. 325). . . . Lot 10, in Middletown, was sold by Joseph E. Gray to Matthew Fleming (Lough, p. 421). . . . James Burbridge bought Lot 72 from John S. Smith (Lough, p. 425). . . . John D. Jester bought sixty acres on Dunkard Creek from Christian Goodnight on April 22 (*Chronicles of Core*, p. 44). . . . Jacob Statler conveyed a tract of land on a ridge between Pedlar Run and Statler Run to Shadrach Huggans and his wife Jane (*Chronicles of Core*, p. 44). . . . The home of Enoch Ross (1799-1870), just west of Cheat River, was made a community voting place (Owens, p. 94). . . . On November 13,

---

26. Flickersville is said to have been named for the abundance of flickers (*Colaptes auratus*) along Flaggy Meadow Run. Pers. comm. Alice (Low) Conley.

from 2 a.m. until daylight, occurred the famous phenomenon of shooting stars,[27] causing many to believe the world was coming to an end (Owens, p. 36). . . . John Ray, brother of Thomas Patrick Ray, died in 1833; he was born in 1798 (Callahan, p. 93).

27. See Denison Olmsted, "On the Cause of the Meteors of November 13th, 1833," *Amer. Jour. Sci.* 29 (1836):376-83.

# CHAPTER FIFTY-EIGHT

# 1834

Before the end of the pioneer period, differences between eastern and western Virginia on policies relating to banking, credit, and money supply were subjects of bitter sectional and political controversy which continued into the 1830s and beyond and were among the major causes of the separation into two states during the Civil War.

In pioneer Monongalia County what little surplus money existed was generally deposited in some eastern city, or at Pittsburgh. It was usually sent by special carrier, a method considered safer than transportation by mail.

An early bank within more convenient distance from Morgantown was a branch of the Bank of Philadelphia, which opened for business in Washington, Pennsylvania, in July 1809. Captain W. N. Jarrett's day book, under date of January 23, 1810, has this notation: "Ralph Berkshire, Dr. to ¼ of $3.75 which was G. McNeely's expense to Washington, Penna., to put our bonds and notes in the Bank of Washington—$0.94."

Soon afterwards, in May 1812, there appeared the first bank in Uniontown, the Union Bank of Pennsylvania, still more convenient for residents of Monongalia County.

The industrial development of western Virginia was handicapped, of course, by inadequate transportation methods but also through the shortage of investment capital and a lack of credit facilities. The state of Virginia was much slower in the development of banking than the neighboring states of Maryland and Pennsylvania, or even in the new state of Ohio. By the close of the War of 1812 there was not one incorporated bank in all of western Virginia and there were only two in the entire state, both of them in Richmond. Residents of Wheeling, in a petition to the general assembly in 1815, stated that, although there was not a single incorporated bank in the county, there were four banks in Ohio within twenty-two miles and six in Pennsylvania within sixty miles. A petition from Clarksburg in 1816 said no person in that area had ever had a note discounted by any bank of Virginia.

A group of Wheeling people formed an unincorporated private facility known as the Ohio Company, which began operation in July 1814 with a capital of $60,000. In the same year the Charleston Manufacturing Company opened for business in Charleston with a capital of $200,000 to be used "principally for Banking purposes." A group of Harrison County residents, in August 1814, formed a joint stock company which they called the Farmers Bank of Virginia, but failed to secure a charter from the general assembly. The group then formed a company which they called the Virginia Saline Bank, with a capital of $150,000, in operation by December 1815, to promote the manufacture of salt, iron, wool, cotton, and other products, the encouragement of agriculture, and the improvement of the Monongahela River as an artery of transportation. Morgantown's first bank was the Monongalia Farmers Company of Virginia, dating from December 1, 1814 (*Monongalia Story*, vol. 2, p. 407) but it had limited facilities.

**The Merchants' and Mechanics' Bank.** An act of the general assembly, passed March 7, 1834, established the Merchants' and Mechanics' Bank of Wheeling, with provisions for a branch at Morgantown. The county newspaper announced this great news as follows:

"By Tuesday night's mail, a letter was received from Richmond, directed to a gentleman in this place, communicating the passage of a bill, chartering a Bank at Wheeling, to be styled the Merchant's and Mechanic's Bank, with a branch at Morgantown.

"We are certain that the large majority of the people of this and the neighbouring counties, will receive this intelligence with much pleasure, and acknowledge that no act has ever passed the Legislature that will confer greater benefits upon this portion of the community."[1]

---

1. *Monongalia Farmer*, March 15, 1834. The full text of the act, quite lengthy, appeared in the issue for April 12 and copies were distributed to all persons interested.

Fig. 15. The Merchants' and Mechanics' Bank building, constructed about 1836. (Morgantown Public Library.)

According to the act, superintendence of the organization of the Morgantown branch devolved upon George McNeely, Mathew Gay, Reuben B. Taylor, Richard Watts, Nicholas B. Madera, William Lazier, John Rogers, James Chadwick, John H. McGee, and Thomas P. Ray.

The actual organization proceeded slowly, but by August arrangements were about completed and it was hoped the sale of stock would soon get under way.[2] About the middle of September the books were opened for taking stock, but only ten thousand dollars was subscribed the first week.[3]

Sale of the stock proceeded slowly and Francis Madera became concerned:

"Having the National road North, and the North Western turnpike South of us, we may look to be deprived of all trade unless this bank is established. Therefore, no lukewarmness should be felt in so important a matter."[4]

2. *Monongalia Farmer*, August 30, 1834.
3. *Monongalia Farmer*, September 20, 1834.
4. *Monongalia Farmer*, October 11, 1834.

But at last the goal was reached:

"It gives us pleasure to inform our readers, that more than 50,000 dollars has been subscribed on the books opened in this place to the stock of the Merchants' and Mechanics' Bank, and that it may be expected to commence business about the first of January."[5]

The banking enterprise was formally organized on November 6, with Thomas P. Ray as the first president and James Robb the first cashier. Its first location was in a building at the southwest corner of High Street and Maiden Alley.[6] The new bank did not, however, start discounting until after Christmas, because the engravers were unable to complete the notes as early as had been expected.[7]

Banking problems, however, continued to be subjects of controversy between eastern and western Virginia throughout the 1830s. The 1834-35 session of the general assembly increased the stock of the Bank of Virginia in Richmond, and added new branches in eastern cities, but blocked efforts to set up banks in western towns.

**The Methodist Protestant Church.** On March 1-4, 1834, the quarterly conference of the Middletown Circuit of the Methodist Protestant Church was held in Morgantown, the first quarterly conference of the new Methodist reform movement to be held here.

Numerous Methodist circuit-riders or "itinerants" had visited Monongalia County since early pioneer days, including Bishop Francis Asbury (*Monongalia Story*, vol. 2, pp. 160-63, etc.) and the Reverend Henry Smith (*Monongalia Story*, vol. 2, pp. 190, 218-20, etc.). The first Methodist church in the county was at Fort Martin (*Monongalia Story*, vol. 2, p. 423), an old log building dating from 1784. The first Methodist church in Morgantown was constructed on Pleasant Street in 1819 (*Monongalia Story*, vol. 2, pp. 447, 448).

The early organization was known as the Methodist Episcopal Church, but on the American frontier a branch movement de-

5. *Monongalia Farmer*, November 1, 1834.
6. Wiley, p. 462. The bank moved into a large new brick building at the corner of High and Pleasant streets about 1836 (Callahan, p. 189).
7. *Monongalia Farmer*, December 13, 1834.

veloped, based on the principle that laymen have a right to a part in church councils. This eventually developed into the Methodist Protestant Church (see following).

The Reverend I. A. Barnes says that the Methodist Protestant Church was "a potent factor in the progressive development of the civilization of the American people. . . . General and President U. S. Grant is reported to have remarked on occasion 'that the Methodist Protestant Church is the only really democratic organization in America.' "[8]

The reform movement in the Methodist Episcopal Church resulted in the formation of the Methodist Protestant Church in the 1820s and a conference of "Reformers" was held at Cincinnati in October 1829. At this conference the Reverend Asa Shinn, a well-known minister of the Monongahela Valley, was elected president, two deacons and twelve elders were ordained and twenty-two regular ministers were stationed. The new conference was named the Ohio Conference and included all the country west of the Alleghenies.

Reverend Cornelius Springer was one of the ministers assigned to a "territory" within the conference. He was a native of Wilmington, Delaware, but for fourteen years had been a successful minister of the Methodist Episcopal Church in the area about Zanesville, Ohio. Now he cast his lot with the reformers and aided in the organization of the new conference.

The "territory" to which the Reverend Mr. Springer was assigned was the entire Monongahela Valley. In 1829-30 he organized a great circuit including church bodies at Waynesburg, Morgantown, Middletown, Williamsport, and Bald Hill. General headquarters were established at Middletown, where the Reverend Asa Shinn had already formed a society in the home of Thomas Barnes (p. 140).

Barnes vividly describes the organization of the Morgantown society:

"In February, 1830 Dr. George Brown, who had been a presiding elder in the M. E. Church, and Rev. Cornelius Springer came to Morgantown, which was then a village of only 150 houses. These ministers were entertained in the home of Joseph

8. Barnes, *The Methodist Protestant Church in West Virginia*, p. 6. For history of the formation of the Methodist Protestant Church, see Smeltzer, *Methodism*, pp. 140-50.

Shackelford, a local preacher of the M. E. Church. For this act of Christian hospitality, Mr. Shackelford was expelled from the M. E. Church. The charges against him were: 'Entertaining in his home reform preachers, and praying for their success'. Mr. Shackelford was a man of unquestioned piety and business integrity, and many of his friends were indignant at the arbitrary manner in which he had been expelled from the church. A number of these friends met at the home of Mr. Shackelford on the 11th day of February, and Dr. Brown preached to them, and he and Mr. Springer later organized a Methodist Protestant society. Among the charter members of this first society were: Mr. Shackelford and wife and two daughters, Levi Hennan and wife, Peter Davis and wife, Daniel Stewart and wife, Mrs. Amhurst Miller and a few others. Soon after the society was formed a revival was held and a large number of converts joined the new church.

"Mr. Shackelford in the old stone house on what is now called Chestnut street, where services were held regularly until a suitable building could be secured. This stone house might properly be called the first Methodist Protestant Church of Monongalia County, and I should like to see the Methodist Protestants of Monongalia County buy this old building and preserve it as a memorial to the men and women who planted the banner of Mutual Rights and American Methodism in this great county."[9]

Other early members of the Methodist Protestant society in Morgantown were the Reverend Asby Pool and the Reverend John Clark, who had formerly been Methodist Episcopal ministers. In 1833 Dr. Peter T. Laishley and his wife joined the society. Dr. Laishley was born in Southampton, England, January 1, 1798, and came to America at the age of eighteen. In 1833 he was practicing medicine in Fayette County, Pennsylvania, but soon after he purchased a farm near Easton, in Monongalia County, where he lived the remainder of his life. In Fayette County he was a preacher in the Republican Methodist Church (the "O'Kelleyites") and at the conference in Morgantown in March 1834, was received as a minister in the Methodist Protestant Church. The Reverend Mr. Barnes, after naming these distinguished new members, concludes: "Thus it will be

9. Op. cit., pp. 115, 116; for biography of George Brown, see Smeltzer, ibid., p. 126; see also Brown's *Recollections of Itinerant Life* (1868). For the old stone house see Fig. 77, p. 452.

seen, the membership of the Methodist Protestant Church, at its beginning in Morgantown, was of a very high character, intellectually and socially, as well as religiously."[10]

In 1834 the Methodist Protestant Church in the upper Monongahela Valley (then part of the Pittsburgh Conference) was organized into the Hackers Creek, Pruntytown, and Middletown circuits.

**Middletown Methodist Protestant Church.** A church building was erected on Quincy Street in Middletown in 1834 for use of the Methodist Protestant congregation. Members of this denomination first organized here in 1829, when they gathered to hold their services in the "Old Horse Mill" in Barnesville. Thomas Barnes was a leader in this church, aided by his brother-in-law, the Reverend Asa Shinn, who began as an itinerant preacher among the hills of northern West Virginia while he was still a teen-ager. The congregation in Middletown was organized in 1830 by the Reverend Cornelius Springer.[11]

**Brown's Chapel.** In July 1834, a separate Presbyterian Church was established at Stewartstown. Minutes of the session meeting on July 5 were recorded as follows:

"Session convened at Stewartstown constituted with prayer, Rev. Mr. J. Stoneroad, Moderator. Elders present were James Robison, Gasper Orth, George D. Hill, Samuel Brand, and Moses Cox. Received on Examination Miss Sarah Sergeant. Dismissed with a view to be organized into a separate church, the following members of the church of Morgantown, according to the act of Presbytery April 2nd, 1834:

"Gasper Orth, Margaret Orth, Isabella Bowen, Sarah Sadler, Mary Ann Burchinal, Martin Bear, Mary Bear, John Frankleberry, Susan Trough, Sarah Sergeant, Margaret Sergeant, Sarah E. Hamilton, Robert Blaney, George Rogers, Sophia Porter, Margaret Sadler, Catherine Burgess, Samuel Bixler, Ezechiel Sergeant, Nancy Haney, Catherine Sadler, Mary Robinson, Harriett Henderson, and David Trough."

The first known meeting of the group at Stewartstown was on October 24, 1818, at the home of Elder Gasper Orth. In

10. Op. cit., p. 116.
11. Newman, *Marion County in the Making*, pp. 331, 332; Barnes, *M. P. Church*, pp. 68-70.

1830 he gathered together a few of his neighbors of the Presbyterian faith and organized what was known as Brown's Chapel, named for the Reverend Rezin Brown, pastor of the Morgantown church. In 1832 Orth conveyed to John Henderson, Jonathan Gordon, Gasper Orth, and David Tropf, trustees of the Presbyterian Church at Stewartstown, a lot of seventy-two poles whereon the church then stood "as surveyed and set apart by the Rev. Rezean Brown."[12]

Callahan adds a footnote concerning the Reverend Rezin Brown, saying that he "evidently did not suit the blue stocking members of the congregation, according to the early church historian. By making 'common cause with the Methodists, by mingling with them in all their meetings, he sunk Presbyterianism to the level of Methodism—an evil which required years to correct.' "[13]

**Fire Again, and Again.** Two other fires (see p. 98) occurred in Morgantown during the winter:

"On the night of the 28th ult. our citizens were aroused by the sudden cry of fire, which proved to be the stable of Captain Lazier, of this place, containing then ten head of horses, and which were fortunately rescued from the flames, by the unremitting exertions of our citizens. The origin of the fire is not yet ascertained, and it is feared never will be, as circumstances almost conclusively prove, that it was the work of an incendiary."[14]

A reward of $250 was offered for information leading to the conviction of the guilty person.

The third fire in about as many months came in March:

"Our citizens were aroused on the morning of the 27th inst., about 2 o'clock by the alarming cry of fire. It was first discovered in the loft of a stable situated on the premises of Nathan Goff, Esq., and now in the occupancy of Mr. Larkin H. Dorsey. There were three horses in the stable which were rescued by the exertions of Mr. William Griffey, who has a

12. James R. Moreland, *The First Presbyterian Church of Morgantown*, pp. 112, 113. See also Wiley, pp. 446, 687, 688; Fred Hamilton Weltner and Harry Leroy Jeffries, Sr., *The Stewartstown Story* (1971), p. 39. The church apparently had a rather short span of existence.
13. Callahan, *Making of Morgantown*, p. 153.
14. *Monongalia Farmer*, February 1, 1834.

second time risked his safety to save this noble animal from the fiery element. Fortunately for the surrounding buildings the night was calm, and by great exertions the fire communicated to no other buildings. The stable was entirely consumed."[15]

Again, it was assumed that arson was the cause.

**Colonel John Evans Dies.** One of the best known and most highly respected of the early pioneer settlers died on Sunday evening, May 18, 1834; "as a public servant his integrity was never questioned, as a private citizen his character was always above suspicion."[16]

John Evans was born December 9, 1737, near Alexandria, Virginia, where he attended school and married Ann Martin. He is said to have crossed the mountains first about 1763, returning in 1765 to build a cabin. In 1769 he brought his family to the Monongahela Valley, settling on a plantation he called Walnut Hill, about two miles north of the mouth of Deckers Creek (*Monongalia Story*, vol. 1, p. 166).

In Dunmore's War of 1774 he was a lieutenant and in the Revolution he attained the rank of lieutenant colonel. From 1782 until 1807 he was clerk of the county court (*Monongalia Story*, vol. 2, pp. 83, 253-55, etc.), and was active in public affairs. He encouraged education and aided in the establishment of the Monongalia Academy (*Monongalia Story*, vol. 2, pp. 404, 405).

John and Ann Evans had eight children, namely: Margaret (1764-1851), married Captain John Dent; Dudley (1766-1844), married Annarah Williams; John ("Captain Jack," 1768-1849), married Gilly Coleman Strother; Nimrod (1770-1828), married Elizabeth Strother; Rawley (1772-1859), married Marie Dering; Enoch, married Amelia Jenkins; James (1782-1870), married —— Buckner; and Marmaduke (1784-1816), not married.[17]

"Col. Evans led an active and enterprizing life, and probably done as much in furthering the settlement of this part of the country, as any man who ever emigrated to it; he was the steadfast and uniform friend of all the early settlers; & by his ex-

15. *Monongalia Farmer*, March 29, 1834.
16. Wiley, p. 527.
17. Wiley, pp. 521-527; Callahan, *Making of Morgantown*, pp. 78-81; pers. comm., Marion Tapp.

ample, was of great advantage in the settlement of a new country."[18]

**"Another Revolutionary Soldier Gone."** Thus the local newspaper announced the passing of Colonel Samuel Hanway,[19] who had entertained General George Washington on his visit to Monongalia County in 1784 (*Monongalia Story*, vol. 2, pp. 112-19). The newspaper account follows:

"Died, at his residence, yesterday morning, in this place, Col. Samuel Hanway, aged ninety years. In the year 1775 Col. Hanway raised a volunteer company in Amelia County, Va., to march against Lord Dunmore, at Williamsburgh, and whilst engaged in that service, the Legislature organized the 'Minute Men', in which corps he was commissioned a Lieutenant, and some time afterwards was commissioned as a Captain of Marines."[20]

He was later captured by the British and held in custody until exchanged, upon condition of not again entering the service.

He was appointed county surveyor in 1783 and continued to hold the office until 1831. He was never married, and when his work became burdensome to him he sent for his nephew, John Hanway, to come to assist him.

"He lived a temperate and active life, & maintained an unsullied reputation. Few men have lived in this county more respected, for all the moral worth pertaining to man, and the strictest regard to honorable conduct."

**James G. Watson.** On March 8 died "James G. Watson, aged 78 years. Mr. Watson removed from Charles County, Maryland, about thirty years ago, and has resided in this county since that time. Respected by all who knew him, he has left an aged widow, and a numerous family connexion to mourn their loss."[21]

He had settled at first near the mouth of Cheat River about 1800 and lived there three years, when he purchased a farm on White Day Creek, formerly the property of Robert Ferrell.[22]

18. *Monongalia Farmer*, May 24, 1834.
19. Wiley, p. 601.
20. *Monongalia Farmer*, May 3, 1834.
21. *Monongalia Farmer*, March 15, 1834.
22. Wiley, p. 635.

James G., the son of Scottish emigrant James Watson, was born February 23, 1756, and married Ann Swan Dyson on July 13, 1776; after her death he married Ann Reeder. He had five children, Thomas, Henry, James D., Margaret, and Mary G.

"Mr. Watson was a rather large and corpulent man, of social, jovial, disposition, loved the society of friends, and, delighting in the chase, kept a kennel of dogs, and mounted on his favorite horse, 'Steamboat', followed the music of his moisy pack o'er hills and valleys, far and near."[23]

**George Tucker.** George Tucker, one of the early settlers of the Jacksonville section, died February 1, 1834, as the result of a fall from the steps of a hotel near Steubenville, Ohio, on the return trip from a visit to his children near Columbus. He was seventy-two years old. He was probably born in Kent County, Maryland, the son of Morgan Tucker, and came to Monongalia County in early pioneer times, where his strong personality and indefatigable efforts made him a leader in the community and a bulwark against Indian incursions. He served in the Revolution, having enlisted in Delaware, under Captain David Crane.[24]

George Tucker is said to have been married three times. His first wife was Mary Hutchinson, whom he had rescued from the Indians (*Monongalia Story*, vol. 2, p. 187). His second wife was Elizabeth Hudson, but the name of the third is unknown. His children included William (married Eunice Payne), Nancy (married Andrew Thompson), James, Richard, Andrew, Jesse, Levi (married Mary Glisson) (*Monongalia Story*, vol. 2, p. 370), Morgan (married Christena Moore), Rachel (married Ahab Keller?), Phebe (married Philip Boor?), Mary, Sarah, Thomas, and Aaron.[25]

**John Caruthers Dies at Smithtown.** John Caruthers, whose ancestors were said to have lived in Dumfrieshire, Scotland, near the fort Caer-rhy-thyr, died August 18, 1834.

John was born in 1759 in Ulster, Ireland, and married Cath-

23. *Cyclopedia of Monongalia County,* p. 171; see *The Monongalia Story,* vol. 2, pp. 328, 339.
24. Core, *Chronicles of Core,* p. 45; *Cyclopedia of Monongalia County,* pp. 94, 95.
25. Wiley, p. 703; pers. comm., Dr. Eldon Tucker, Jr., 1599 Monaco Circle, Salt Lake City, Utah 84121.

arine McCauley in 1785. He was in the English navy in 1782 under Vice Admiral George Brydges Rodney, who went in pursuit of Count de Grasse, the French commander planning to sail to the aid of the Americans.

Caruthers came to America in 1789, locating for a short time at Wilmington, Delaware, then coming to Crooked Run, just across the line in Greene County, Pennsylvania. About 1800 he moved to the White Day Creek section, where he lived the remainder of his life. John and Catharine had nine children, including Mary, who married David W. Jones.[26]

**The Brand Settlement.** John Brand, pioneer settler of Monongalia County, on Dents Run, died January 12, 1834, at the age of eighty-two. Of Scotch ancestry, he bought 190 acres of land from Thomas Dawson on February 11, 1793, and settled on it, the region thereafter being known locally as the "Brand Settlement." He was a farmer and blacksmith.

He married Jane McCray (or McRa), sister of William McCray, also an early settler, and they had eight children, namely, Mary, George, Margaret, Jean, John, James, William, and Agness (Nancy).[27]

**County Election.** The election held on Monday, April 28, for members of the legislature produced the following results.[28]

|  | Waitman T. Willey | Stephen H. Morgan | Francis Billingsley | William Lazier | Joseph F. Harrison | Isaac Cooper |
|---|---|---|---|---|---|---|
| Courthouse | 205 | 187 | 298 | 225 | 178 | 153 |
| Pawpaw | 114 | 96 | 27 | 1 | 1 | 9 |
| Jarrett's | 8 | 16 | 9 | 20 | 20 | 15 |
| Dunkard | 128 | 123 | 13 | 3 | 3 | 13 |
| Swamps | 67 | 35 | 44 | 27 | 8 | 59 |
| Ross' | 49 | 80 | 16 | 12 | 18 | 15 |
| Middletown | 257 | 248 | 44 | 33 | 12 | 15 |

26. *Cyclopedia of Monongalia County*, pp. 146, 147.
27. See Franklin Marion Brand, *The Brand Family* (Morgantown, 1922), 426 pp.
28. *Monongalia Farmer*, May 3, 1834.

**The Monongalia Academy.** Examinations commenced on Friday, June 13, and citizens were cordially invited to attend.

Tuition fees for the term beginning July 7 were announced as: Reading, writing, and arithmetic, eight dollars; English grammar, geography, history, algebra, etc., ten dollars; Latin, Greek, French, etc., fifteen dollars.[29]

At the Female Academy, which had been finished in 1833, Miss Sarah Green announced that her first session at the Female Academy would begin on April 1. Terms of tuition, per quarter, were announced as three dollars for English Education, and five dollars for Drawing, Painting, etc.[30]

**The Militia.** Monongalia, Preston, Brooke, and Ohio counties, in 1834, comprised the Tenth Brigade of the Third Division; in all, the Third Division was made up of the Seventh, Tenth, Sixteenth, and Twentieth brigades.

At that time each county was divided into regimental districts of not less than three hundred men. Each regimental district was divided into two battalion districts, which were in turn subdivided into four company districts, each company numbering from fifty to one hundred men. Colonel, lieutenant colonel, and major were elected by the officers of the several companies. A captain and four lieutenants were elected by each company. Each captain appointed five sergeants and six corporals. Every able-bodied man between the ages of eighteen and forty-five was enrolled.

If called into service, camp equipment allowed for the Third Division included one kettle for every six men, one axe and spade for every twenty, and one wagon for every eighty.

About the first Monday of each May a well-trained officer came to each county, drilled all the county officers for three days, and then on each succeeding day helped to drill one regiment, until all the regiments had been drilled. About the first of October, each battalion drilled for one day. On the first Saturday in April and in October each company drilled in its own area.

After all these drills, about the last of October, the officers of each regiment met and held a court martial; every man who had

29. *Monongalia Farmer*, May 31, 1834.
30. *Monongalia Farmer*, March 29, 1834.

Fig. 16. A general muster of the militia at a western Virginia county seat, about 1840. The captain, a veteran of the War of 1812, is giving the new colonel and his staff information on military tactics. (West Virginia Department of Archives and History.)

been absent at one of the drills had to present a lawful excuse or he was fined.[31]

**At the Racetrack.** Horse racing began on the frontier at an early date (*Monongalia Story*, vol. 2, p. 434), and betting went along with it. A small racetrack was in operation in Monongalia County in 1834: "The races for the ensuing Fall will commence on Wednesday, the 22nd of October next, at the farm of Mr. Costelo, on Decker's Creek 2 miles from Morgantown and continued 4 days. A handsome purse may be expected to be run for, and therefore good horses may also be expected."[32]

**The End of the Monongalia Farmer.** The *Monongalia Farmer* continued to publish throughout 1834, with considerably more emphasis on local affairs than most of the earlier newspapers. The editor lapsed into poetry to describe the paper's beginning and its goals:

"Last year amid the various scenes of Earth
MONONGALIA FARMER had auspicious birth . . .
We tell the doctrines of our country clear,
And golden rules by which men ought to steer;
The news we give, from North, South, East and West,
Of all we think, read, hear, we give the best."[33]

But its progress was not easy. There were shortages of various materials, but especially of income. And on occasion news was short, too:

"Owing to the failure of the mails arriving on Sunday last, in consequence of high waters, which were far above an ordinary height, we were obliged to occupy our columns this week, to a considerable extent, with miscellaneous matter. . . ."[34]

With the issue for December 13 (vol. 1, no. 52) the *Monongalia Farmer* came to an end. The following notice had appeared earlier:

"We are thankful for the patronage we have received, though limited, and falling far short of our expectations. The Farmer will be conducted, at the expiration of the present volume, by Enos D. Morgan. It will be enlarged to an imperial size. The plan

31. Wiley, pp. 516, 517. Evan Shelby Pindall was later a brigadier-general for the Tenth Brigade.
32. *Monongalia Farmer*, October 4, 1834.
33. *Monongalia Farmer*, January 4, 1834.
34. *Monongalia Farmer*, January 18, 1834.

taken by him should certainly be encouraged by all who feel an interest in the perpetuation of knowledge, and the welfare of his country's prosperity."[35]

**John Wolverton Blue.** John W. Blue, of Hampshire County, was in charge of the construction of the Northwestern Turnpike from Aurora to the Tygart Valley River. Brinkman tells of his arrival in 1833 in southern Monongalia County, near the mouth of Threefork Creek:

"Stopping overnight with the hospitable family of James Current, a settler of land now occupied by the present suburb of Grafton,[36] Blue, upon awakening the next morning, heard the wife of Current sobbing bitterly.

"Asking the cause of her grief, Blue was informed that she was saddened because the right-of-way, as surveyed by the engineers, would destroy their cabin home, cause the destruction of her vegetable and flower garden, and would cause them to rebuild and reseed elsewhere.

"Mr. Blue, a Virginian of the old school, was greatly moved by the woman's grief and made the Currents an offer of $300 for the 900 acres of land and their ruined home. His offer was quickly accepted and this one-day beautiful suburb of Grafton was transferred to Mr. Blue. . . .

"In the following year, 1834, the Northwestern Turnpike was completed to the banks of the Tygart Valley River, and Mr. Blue superintended the construction of the historic old covered wooden bridge placed across the stream."[37]

**Land Grants Made in 1834.**[38] Monongalia County grantees in 1834 included:

| | | |
|---|---|---|
| Cannon, James | 60 a. | Slaters Run |
| Carter, Lloyd | 14 | Waters Monongahela R. |
| Demoss, Charles | 50 | Three Forks Creek |
| Fleming, Elizabeth | 140 | Adj. Wilson's Forge |
| Fluharty, John | 30 | Flees (Flat?) Run |

35. *Monongalia Farmer*, November 1, 1834.
36. Blueville.
37. Charles Brinkman, *History of Taylor County*, chapter 13, May 2, 1939 (published in installments in the Grafton *Sentinel;* see also Paul C. Bartlett, ed., *Historical Anecdotes of Early Taylor County*, p. 103.
38. See p. 11.

| | | |
|---|---|---|
| Glover, Samuel | 100 | Buffalo Creek |
| Hall, John | 50 | Buffalo Creek |
| Hanway, John, et al. | 1,200 | Morgans Run |
| Jackson, Josiah, et al. | 1,200 | Morgans Run |
| Leeson, Thomas | 48 | Pricketts Creek |
| Lemley, George | 115 | Elk Lick Fork |
| McMasters, John | 50 | Indian Creek |
| Morgan, David | 30 | Mud Lick |
| Morgan, David, Jr. | 30 | Pricketts Creek |
| Morgan, Jacob | 68 | Waters Monongahela R. |
| Myers, Jacob | 250 | Laurel Run |
| Park, William | 150 | Miracles Run |
| Rose, Thomas | 100 | Joys Run |
| Ross, Henry | 23 | Pricketts Creek |
| Shriver, Abraham | 100 | Dunkard Creek |
| Straight, John M. | 27½ | Straight Run |
| Talkington, Isaac | 120 | Mods Run |
| Tanzey, Caleb | 23½ | Adj. Philip Lewis |
| Troy, James | 100 | Days Run |
| Underwood, David F. | 90 | Flat Run |

**County Government.** Thomas S. Haymond was sworn in for his second term as sheriff on March 24, 1834. For commissioners of the revenue Isaac Cooper was appointed for the Eastern District and Nimrod Dent for the Western District. On July 28 Josiah Boyers and Reuben B. Taylor were sworn in as justices of the peace; William Lazier resigned on May 26. The county levy was $0.31¼, the lowest it had been since 1822.

**Miscellany.** In 1834: On the fifteenth of May the snow was four inches deep in places, and ice one-third of an inch in thickness formed (Wiley, p. 246). . . . The winter of 1833-34 had been very mild; old-timers recalled that the deepest snow totaled only four inches and ice was only ¼ inch thick (Owens, p. 36). . . . Guy R. C. Allen, on April 8, was sworn in as prosecuting attorney for the circuit superior court of law and chancery (Wiley, p. 311). . . . Samuel Arnold was admitted to the county bar on April 11 (Wiley, p. 318). . . . Lot 45 in Morgantown was conveyed to Robert Hawthorn by Horatio Morgan (Callahan, p. 66). . . . The first parsonage for the Morgantown Methodist Episcopal Church was provided in May by purchase of the southeast corner

of Lot 16 from Rebecca Dering (Callahan, pp. 149, 311). . . .
Morgantown secured tri-weekly mail deliveries by two-horse
stagecoaches running from Uniontown to Clarksburg (Callahan,
p. 165). . . . William Lazier conveyed Lot 10 in Morgantown to
James D. Wright (Callahan, p. 310). . . . John H. McGee conveyed
a portion of Lot 43 to Joanna Lowman (Callahan, p. 317). . . .
Jesse Jarvis and his wife, Sarah Werninger Jarvis, conveyed a
portion of Lot 80 to James Chadwick and William Alexander
(Callahan, p. 319). . . . Nicholas Pickenpaugh acquired Lots 105
and 109 (Callahan, p. 327). . . . A new type of bellows was invented and patented by James Robe, vended by William Griffey
(various notices in the *Monongalia Farmer*, October,
1834). . . . "The body of Mr. Archie Wilson, of this county, was
yesterday found in the river about one mile above town, nearly
opposite the poor house. He had apparently fallen in the river
and drowned. His horse was hitched to a tree nearby (*Monongalia Farmer*, April 19). . . . Zadock S. Morgan, formerly of
Morgantown, died at Louisville, Kentucky, on July 31 (*Monongalia Farmer*, August 16, 1834). . . . "The Rev. C. F. Frey, the
converted Jew," preached at the Forks of Cheat at 11 a.m. and
at Morgantown at 4 p.m. on July 9 (*Monongalia Farmer*,
June 28, 1834, announcing the coming services). . . . H. D.
Murphey was carrying on the business of wool carding at
Thorn's Mill, one half mile below Morgantown (*Monongalia
Farmer*, April 12, 1834). . . . A new firm, George McNeely and
Henry Dering, Jr., went into business in Morgantown (*Monongalia Farmer*, June 7, 1834). . . . A second structure was erected
for the Fort Martin Methodist Episcopal Church, replacing the
old log building said to have been dedicated by Bishop Asbury
in 1784; George Waters gave one hundred dollars to the building
fund (Dodds and Dodds, p. 116). . . . David McGee sold Lot 39,
in Middletown, to John Brome (Lough, p. 423). . . . William
Fleming sold Lot 42 to Hugh Creighton (Lough, p. 424). . . .
Elizabeth Haught Piles, wife of John Piles, of Dunkard Creek,
died March 18, 1834, aged forty-nine years (*Chronicles of Core*,
45). . . . Jesse Henderson bought a forty-four-acre farm on
Pedlar Run (*Chronicles of Core*, p. 45). . . . John Pixler (1801-
1839) purchased a farm from Nicholas Vandervort, west of
Cheat River (Owens, p. 92).

# CHAPTER FIFTY-NINE

# 1835

Joseph Martin in 1835 published his famous "New and Comprehensive Gazeteer of Virginia,"[1] containing a description, county by county, of the entire state of Virginia. It might be of interest to quote from Martin's account of Monongalia County, for the picture presented of conditions at the end of the first third of the nineteenth century.

**Monongalia According to Martin.** "The face of the country," Martin says, "is generally mountainous and hilly; one-third of the territory of the county, lying upon what is called in this country the 'Laurel Hill', it being the last western regular ridge of the Alleghanies; the other two-thirds, or western part of the county, being intersected by hills and valleys.

"Notwithstanding the mountainousness of the country, the soil is very fertile; producing good crops of all kinds of grain and vegetables common to this latitude. And it is remarkably well timbered, both as to variety and size."[2]

The county was bordered on the north by Greene and Fayette counties, in Pennsylvania, on the east by Preston, on the southeast by Randolph, on the south by Harrison, and on the west by Tyler. The rivers watering the county were the Monongahela, Cheat, West Fork, and Tygart Valley.

1. *A New and Comprehensive Gazetteer of Virginia and the District of Columbia: containing a copious Collection of Geographical, Statistical, Political, Commercial, Religious, Moral and Miscellaneous Information, Collected and Compiled from the most Respectable, and chiefly from Original Sources* (Charlottesville). The work may actually have been published in 1836; some copies say 1835, others 1836 or "1835," while some bear no date. The quotations are from the 1968 reprint in vol. 2 of *West Virginia Heritage* (Richwood).
2. Op. cit., p. 45.

"The Monongahela . . . is navigable from its head (the junction of the West Fork and Tygart Valley), in time of freshets, for flat-boats of the largest size. And steam-boats have frequently ascended from Pittsburg to Morgantown, ten miles above the mouth of Cheat. From Pittsburgh to Morgantown, the navigation of this river is very easy for steam and flatboats, and unobstructed, except by low water, and is becoming very considerable. From Morgantown upwards the navigation is more difficult, and can only be effected in times of freshets. . . . The Tygart's Valley although a considerable stream is only navigable about ten miles; it being obstructed by very high falls . . . Cheat River . . . empties into the Monongahela, two miles below the Pennsylvania line. Although it is a considerable stream, affording nearly as much water as the Monongahela, it is only navigable as high as Jackson's Iron Works, a distance of eight or ten miles. . . .

"The principal exports of this county are stock (horses, cattle, hogs and sheep), iron, lumber and some flour. There are three forges and three furnaces (and another being erected) in this county; which manufacture large quantities of iron annually. There is also one nail factory, and several good merchant flour mills. Jackson's Iron Works, on Cheat River, are considered the most valuable in Western Virginia, or perhaps in the western country. There has lately been a salt-well sunk in this county, which promises well."[3]

In 1834 there were 184 slaves, 5,417 horses, thirty-six studs, three coaches, five carryalls, and three gigs. In 1832 $887.15 was spent in educating poor children, and in 1833 $870.92.

Eleven post offices were named, including Barnes' Mill, Blacksville, Dunkard Creek, Granville, King's Ferry, Mount Linus, Middletown (or Polsley's Mills), Morgantown, Palatine Hill, Smithfield (Smithtown), and White Day.

Blacksville and its environs were described as follows: "It contains 11 dwelling houses, 2 mercantile stores, 1 common school, 1 temperance society, 1 tan yard, 1 saddler, and 2 blacksmith shops. Dunkard Creek is navigable to this place, and boat building is carried on to some extent. The face of the surround-

3. Op. cit., p. 46.

ing country is uneven, but very fertile, producing wheat, rye, corn, oats and buckwheat in abundance. . . . Population 52, including 1 physician."[4]

Granville, two miles below Morgantown, "contains 21 dwelling houses, 1 house of public worship free for all denominations, 1 common school, 3 mercantile stores, 2 taverns, 2 warehouses, 1 saddler, 1 smith shop, 2 cabinet makers, 2 boot and shoe factories, 1 cooper and 1 chair maker. Population, white males 44, females 56, colored 10—total 110—and 1 resident physician."[5]

Middletown, eighteen miles of Morgantown, "contains 30 dwelling houses, 2 houses of public worship (1 Methodist and 1 Presbyterian), 1 colonization society, 1 tract, 1 temperance, and 1 humane mission society, and 1 common school, 4 mercantile stores, 1 distillery, 2 taverns, 1 pottery, 3 cabinet makers, 1 chair maker, 1 wheelwright, 1 wagon maker, 1 smith shop, 1 gun smith, 2 boot and shoe factories, 1 saddler and harness maker, 1 brick maker, 2 hatters shops, 2 saw and grist mills. . . . Population 200 persons, of whom 2 are physicians."[6]

In the immediate vicinity of Middletown "are 2 carding and fulling mills, 4 saw mills, and 2 manufacturing flour mills. The face of the country is somewhat hilly, in parts very much broken. The soil is generally of a rich loamy clay, producing all the staples common in the middle and southern states—well adapted to grazing and raising of cattle, horses, hogs, &c., large numbers of which are raised for the eastern markets. This section of country holds out innumerable advantages for the establishment of manufactories. The forests abound with the finest timber, and the earth is stored with iron ore, and the best stone coal. Large quantities of the latter are shipped from this place for the Pittsburg and Cincinnati market, and frequently to New Orleans."[7]

Morgantown, Martin says, "is a flourishing and wealthy village, holding out incalculable advantages to the manufacturer and mechanic. Its healthy situation on the bank of the Monongahela River,—the various productions of the country by which

4. Op. cit., p. 47.
5. Op. cit., p. 47.
6. Op. cit., p. 47.
7. Op. cit., pp. 47, 48.

it is surrounded,—the inexhaustible coal mines which abound in almost every hill, and the rich and innumerable iron banks which are everywhere to be found in this vicinity are perhaps not to be surpassed in Western Virginia.

"Besides the ordinary county buildings it contains 120 dwelling houses, 2 houses of public worship (1 Methodist and 1 Presbyterian), and 1 . . . academy called the 'Monongalia Academy', comprising 2 departments—Classical and Preparatory. Its standing fund at interest is $10,000, and it averages 40 pupils,—size of building 70 feet front, 40 feet deep, 2½ stories high, a handsome and spacious brick building, pleasantly situated; . . . 2 temperance societies . . . , 1 Sunday School, 1 Bible and 1 colonization society, 1 poor asylum, 7 mercantile stores, 1 apothecary shop, 2 houses of entertainment, 1 fulling and dying establishment, 1 windmill manufactory, and 1 printing office from which is issued a weekly paper, 2 tan yards, 2 saddlers, 4 boot and shoe factories, 1 wheelwright, and chair makers, 5 cabinet makers, 1 copper and tin plate worker, 1 red and stone ware manufactory, 4 tailor shops, 3 hat manufactories, 2 gun smiths, 1 wagon maker, 3 smith shops, and 1 plough manufactory.

"The United States Mail passes thru' this village 3 times a week. Population 650 persons, of whom four are resident attorneys, and three regular physicians. . . . This town and county will at no distant day rank among the most flourishing and prosperous in Virginia."[8]

**Colonization Societies.** Martin's *Gazetteer* says that in 1835 there was one "colonization society" in Middletown and one in Morgantown. The object of colonization societies was to resettle, preferably in Africa, freed American Negro slaves. The National Colonization Society of America, organized in 1816, formed the colony of Liberia in 1820 but withdrew its help from the settlers in 1827 and thereafter the societies were not very successful.

**The Dolls Run Christian Church.** On March 28, 1835, a group of neighbors living in and near the valley of Dolls Run, along the state road leading from Morgantown to the mouth of Fishing Creek, came together and adopted the following significant articles of agreement:

8. Op. cit., p. 48.

"We the members of the Christian Church on the waters of Dunkard and Naborhood of John Myers do jointly agree to imbody our selves in a church capasity to watch over Each other in Love taking the New Testament for our Rule of faith and prattices in Agreement whear of wee have hear unto set our Names March 28th, 1835."

Fig. 17. The Dolls Run Christian Church, built about 1846. (Sketch by Elizabeth C. Davis.)

The following thirty-three names were affixed: "Father Sines, Pegy Sines, Jaccob Sines, John Myers, Mary Myers, Magnes Henderson, Rachel Henderson, Mother Sines, Mary Mathews, Sary Sines, Rebecky Sines, Pegy Right, Mary Right, Sary Right, Robert Butcher,[9] Permelly Kelly, Wm. Mer-

9. The Robert Butcher mentioned was a schoolmaster who lived for about twenty years in the neighborhood. He was a son of Robert, Sr., and Lydia (Stevenson) Butcher and was born about 1796. He married Rachel, daughter of George and Mahala Hennen, and they had eight children, Frances Ann, James Harrison, William Jackson, Matthew Hennen, Elizabeth Jane, George Washington, Thomas, and Lydia Ann (see Dorothy T. Hennen, *Hennen's Choice*, vol. 1, pp. 29, 30; vol. 2, pp. 564-67).

renner,[10] Sarah Merrener, Stevenson Merrener, Mymy Piles, Lyda Butcher, Rachel Butcher, Nancy Merriner, Rebecca Shriver, Rebeccah More, Catherine Piles, James Main, Nimrod Merriner, Matthew H. Merriner, Robert H. Merriner, Margaret Hanes, Catherine Right, and Frances Ann Merriner."[11]

The "Naborhood" of John Myers was on Pedlar Run, the site of the old "Pedlar's Camp," where, tradition says, two pre-Revolutionary War pedlars or Indian traders had been found frozen to death.[12] "Father Sines" was Jacob Sines, Sr., and "Mother Sines" was his wife Rebecca; they appeared to be leaders of the group and some of their children, including Jacob, Jr., were among the members named.

**The Restoration Movement.** The group thus established was the result of the preaching of various itinerant ministers representing the so-called Restoration Movement, persons who called themselves simply Disciples of Christ, or Christians, after the New Testament custom. Early meetings of these ministers and their adherents were held in the log cabin home of John and Mary Myers. One early minister was a man named Garrison. The movement was new and coldly received by some. On one occasion, while a meeting was in progress, a man repeatedly called the Reverend Mr. Garrison a liar. The minister finally ended these interruptions by picking up the fellow and tossing him out the window, an act of defenestration similar to the one that set off the Thirty Years War, in 1618.[13]

This Restoration Movement included numerous church bodies calling themselves Disciples of Christ, Churches of Christ, Christian Churches, etc. In the early years of the nineteenth century the various bodies, while not at all or only loosely organized with respect to each other, were at least fairly close

10. William Leonard Merrenner (Mariner), son of Dr. Stephenson (Stevenson) and Sarah (Butcher) Mariner, was married to Frances Ann, daughter of Robert and Rachel (Hennen) Butcher. About 1838 they left Dolls Run and migrated to Tyler County, near the site of Hundred. *Hennen's Choice*, vol. 1, pp. 60, 61; vol. 2, pp. 564-67.

11. Core, *Chronicles of Core*, p. 63; *Morgantown Disciples*, pp. 9-15. The document was preserved among papers of "Father Sines" and discovered by his great-granddaughter, Catherine Myers, in 1936.

12. Core, *The Monongalia Story*, vol. 1, pp. 129, 176.

13. Core, *Morgantown Disciples*, p. 12.

so far as their interpretation of religious principles were concerned.

Tucker and McAllister point out, in the most recent comprehensive history of the movement,[14] that the Christian Church (Disciples of Christ) is one of the largest religious bodies to have originated on American soil and that it, along with other somewhat related groups, developed as a result of peculiar conditions existing on the American frontier in the opening years of the nineteenth century.

"Those hearty and adventurous persons," say Tucker and McAllister, "who had come to America's shores in the colonial period had discovered that large areas of land, sparsely inhabited, made possible religious diversity and experimentation scarcely imagined before. They could dream of a new beginning, free from the traditions, prejudices, and persecutions of the Europe they had left behind. In church, as well as in public affairs, they planned so that the laity increasingly could demand and get a greater share in decision-making and authority. . . .

"The American religious experience prior to 1800 had led the people to believe that in this land mankind truly had the opportunity for a new beginning. Life here could attain the potential which God had intended it to have. . . . In this new land men and women could escape the poverty, wars, social stratification, and lack of opportunity which they believed were the fate of Europeans."[15]

The Disciples are indebted to a few key leaders whose witness gave birth to the movement. Among them were Thomas Campbell and his more distinguished son, Alexander. At first there was no agreement on the matter of choosing a name. Tucker and McAllister continue: "Peter Cartwright, a volatile and outspoken Methodist circuit rider on the American frontier, was one of many detractors to refer to Disciples as Campbellites. This nickname was used as a means of poking fun at the upstart Disciples and they resented it. Although Alexander Campbell

14. William E. Tucker and Lester G. McAllister, *Journey in Faith. A History of the Christian Church (Disciples of Christ)* (1975), 505 pp. Dr. McAllister is a one-time interim minister of the First Christian Church of Morgantown; see also Perry Epler Gresham, "Proud Heritage," *West Virginia History* 15 (1954):99-117.

15. Tucker and McAllister, *Journey in Faith*, pp. 38, 39.

never won a medal for his humility, he certainly had no intention of seeing the movement saddled with his name."[16]

**Religion in the 1830s.** Americans had thrown off European traditions of aristocracy and adopted equal rights, but "looked to free religion, free schools, and free land to guarantee their privileges.

"Religion was the first of the guarantees they invoked, not only because its concerns were central to their lives, but also because they were heirs to a long tradition of evangelical effort. At the same time, the fact that they shared a complex religious heritage meant that they were compelled to work out a fresh conception of their faith in its relationships with society. Had they persevered literal-mindedly in their traditions, they might well have had to choose between democracy and religion. By conceding free religion, however (taking that term in its volunteristic rather than its anticlerical sense), they converted it into the first bulwark of their liberties."[17]

"The church was a strong influence for the improvement of society. The generous and hardy people appreciated religious services. The sermons might have been on the divinely approved old-time Methodist single-breasted coat and the plain bonnet, or on the unusual temperature of the bottomless pit, but the preacher's words were the Word of the Lord. Congregations gathered in the welcome of the pioneer homes or the groves and sang . . . ,

> 'When I can read my titles clear
> To mansions in the skies,
> I'll bid farewell to every fear
> And wipe my weeping eyes.'

Sometimes the worship would overflow with emotion."[18]

**Stewarts Run Presbyterian Church.** "The Rev. Cyrus Beecher Bristol, a missionary under the Assembly's Board, commenced preaching on Stewart's run in December, 1831. From time to

16. Tucker and McAllister, *Journey in Faith*, p. 26.
17. Rush Welter, *The Mind of America, 1820-1860* (1975), p. 253.
18. Manford Grover Flowers, *The Western Virginia Conference of the Methodist Episcopal Church, 1850-1939* (Master's thesis, West Virginia University, 1947), pp. 25, 26.

time a few members were added to the church of Middletowh. In 1835, a church was organized, as may be seen from the sessional records."[19]

The Stewarts Run Presbyterian Church was organized August 1, 1835, with the following charter members: William Stewart and Elizabeth his wife, Evan Stewart and Jane his wife, John Stewart and Elizabeth his wife, John Lough, Isaac Cordray, John Pratt and Hannah his wife, Isaac Cox, Mary Kelley, Areli Stewart, Malinda Cordray, Elizabeth Lough, Nancy Barrackman, and Asa Hall and Elizabeth his wife.

The Reverend C. B. Bristol was the first pastor and William Stewart, John Lough, and John Stewart were the first ruling elders. The congregation worshipped alternately at William Stewart's and John Lough's. Communion services were generally held in the grove on Stewarts Run or in John Lough's barn.

**The Pierpont Methodist Episcopal Church.** On the historic old Pierpont farm, on the Brandonville Pike where the Pleasant Hill road crosses, a log cabin was constructed in early times which served as both church and school.

In 1835, Zackquill, son of John Pierpont, and Dorcas his wife deeded to the trustees of a Methodist Episcopal congregation (William Vandervort, Henry Henthorn, Eli Moore, Zackquill Pierpont, and John M. Cobun) one-half acre of land for a cost of ten dollars, on which to build a church. The conditions were that "a church must be erected for the members of the M. E. Church of Monongalia County." The new church was small in size, of frame construction. It was set fifty feet farther north and thirty feet farther east than the first location, since Francis Tibbs owned the land along the road.[20]

**Educating Poor Children.** The abstract of the schoolmasters' accounts for the tuition of poor children, in county court records, listed seventy-eight teachers, 646 children on the treasurer's account, and 496 actually taught. Textbooks supplied included the United States spelling book, Webster's spelling

19. From the session book; see Wiley, p. 729.
20. Ivan C. Owens, *Easton-Avery Community History*, pp. 102, 170; Dodds and Dodds, *Churches of Monongalia County*, pp. 151, 152.

book, American grammar, English readers, Pike's arithmetic and the Bible.

**The Democratic Republican.** Enos D. Morgan bought the press of the *Monongalia Farmer* late in 1834 and early in 1835 started a new weekly paper, the *Democratic Republican*. It was twenty by thirty inches in size, four pages, twenty-four columns. Its motto was "Our Country and Our Country's Friends." Subscriptions were two dollars per annum.[21]

**The Northwestern Turnpike Crosses Preston County.** By 1835 the new turnpike was complete across Preston County. It entered the county at the German Settlement (Aurora), crossed the nearly level plateau, and then descended the steep escarpment by a three-mile grade to the Cheat River. For about four miles the road followed the river, crossing the stream about midway in this distance on a covered wooden bridge costing eighteen thousand dollars, completed in 1835.[22] With many short curves the road climbed to the top of Laurel Hill, then pursued a gentler incline to the banks of Sandy Creek. In general it was built as a dirt road, but was broad, smooth, and well constructed, the maximum grades never being more than five degrees. The average construction cost was about one thousand dollars a mile and the road was kept in repair by a regular work crew.

**Tygart Valley Bridge Is Completed.** During the same year the road was completed across the narrow southern extension of Monongalia County and the bridge carrying the Northwestern Turnpike across the Tygart Valley River was constructed in 1834 and opened for traffic in 1835. John Blue, who had been the foreman for construction of the road from the Maryland line to Clarksburg, moved into bachelor quarters near the bridge and became bridge tender to collect the tolls.[23]

21. Unfortunately, no issues of this paper for 1835 or 1836 are known. See pp. 137, 151, etc.

22. Oren F. Morton, *History of Preston County*, p. 205. The covered bridge over Cheat River was destroyed by fire in 1964.

23. Brinkman, *History of Taylor County*, chap. 13; *Historical Anecdotes of Early Taylor County*, p. 103. Blue later married a Miss Means, of The Swamps. About 1838 he moved east a few miles and set up a ten-room house as the Blue Tavern, a stagecoach and mail stop and a relay point for horses.

Fig. 18. Northwestern Turnpike Bridge across Cheat River, built in 1835.
(Photo W. R. Lenhart.)

**New Wagon Roads.** Meanwhile, the routine construction of new
wagon roads, and improvement of existing ones, continued
throughout the area, as 1835 county court records indicate.
These include:

A petition for a new road "from Jackson's forge by the
mouth of Quarry Run and Lamb's furnace to the Crab Orchard
road"; "from the old state road near Richard B. Tennant's up
the Long Drain to intersect the road between Shadrach Hugens
and John Mires on the head of Pedlar Run"; "from Maracles
Run to the three forks of Dunkard Creek"; "from . . . Nicholas
B. Madera's meadow to the Sandy Hollow near Joel Ridgeway's," in the Falling Run section; and a petition for improvement of the old Line Ferry road.

**Kramer's Potash Factory.** Probably in 1835 Theophilus Kramer
located at Middletown to establish a potash factory. This was an
important industry at the time and Kramer paid twelve and
one-half cents a bushel for wood ashes delivered at the plant.
The requisite was that they must not have been exposed to rain,
since they were valueless if not kept dry. Ashes in fireplaces in

homes could be left in place as long as there was room for them, then stored in barrels. Ashes where log-heaps were burned in clearings had to be gathered promptly.

The ashes, in the factory, were placed in slacking or bleaching bins (hoppers). Water was then poured on them, producing lye; the water, boiled down, precipitated potash. This was packed in barrels or bags and shipped down the river to Greensboro and New Geneva, where it was used in the manufacture of glass.[24]

**Land Grants Made in 1835.** Monongalia County grantees in 1835 included:

| | | |
|---|---|---|
| Alton, Benjamin | 520 a. | Miracle Run |
| Alton, Samuel | 50 | Dunkard Creek |
| Carder, Joseph | 215 | Short Creek |
| Carter, Lloyd | 250 | Coburns Creek |
| Cartwright, Isaac | 75 | Waters Monongahela R. |
| Davis, Belah | 100 | Deckers Creek |
| Davis, Elijah | 75 | Wickwares Creek |
| Evans, Enoch | 7 | West Run |
| Fast, Adam, Jr. | 100 | Long Drain |
| Freeland, John | 65 | Piles Fork |
| Freeland, John | 100 | Piles Fork |
| Gallahue, Henry | 50 | Pricketts Creek |
| Glover, William | 80 | Dunkard Creek |
| Hanway, John | 9 | Pricketts Creek |
| Hanway, John | 230 | Days Run |
| Harney, Dorthy | 100 | Adj. J. Jacobs |
| Hawkins, Isaiah | 50 | Reubens Run |
| Henderson, Jesse | 44 | Pedlars Run |
| Leyming, John | 54 | Pricketts Creek |
| Malone, Thomas | 220 | Pricketts Creek |
| McGill, Joseph | 100 | Plum Run |
| Morgan, Zebulon | 100 | Pricketts Creek |
| Morris, Richard | 35 | Piles Fork |
| Musgrave, Zebulon | 100 | Pricketts Creek |
| Remley (Lemley) (?), Henry | 75 | Dunkard Creek |
| Satterfield, John | 6 | Pricketts Creek |
| Shahan, William | 125 | Horse Run |

24. Lough, *Now and Long Ago*, pp. 441, 442. For pioneer glassmaking, see *The Monongalia Story*, vol. 2, pp. 232, 233.

| | | |
|---|---|---|
| Straight, William | 73 | Adj. Peter Straight |
| Strosnider, Abraham | 100 | Dunkard Creek |
| Tennant, Peter | 100 | Miracle Run |
| Underwood, Thomas | 42 | Plum Run |
| Walton, Thomas | 250 | Coburns Creek |
| Winter, Samuel | 100 | Piles Fork |

**County Government.** David Musgrave was sworn in as sheriff on March 23, 1835. Hillary Boggess was appointed commissioner of the revenue for the Eastern District. Sworn in as justices of the peace were John Rude (January 26), John S. Shisler (May 25), and George Dawson (May 25). The county levy was $0.37½.

**Miscellany.** In 1835: James Travilla McClaskey, son of William and Rebecca McClaskey, moved from Randolph to Monongalia County (Wiley, p. 289, Owen, p. 89). . . . G. D. Camden was admitted to the Monongalia County bar (Wiley, p. 317). . . . Augustus Haymond, son of William Haymond, Jr., moved from Palatine Hill to Morgantown, where he engaged in mercantile business (Wiley, p. 353). . . . John Mills succeeded John S. Horner as assistant teacher in the Monongalia Academy (Wiley, p. 396). . . . Thomas P. Ray built "a magnificent brick residence" at "Beech Hill," overlooking the river at Falling Run (Wiley, p. 403). . . . Addison S. Vance, born in Frederick County in 1812, moved to Morgantown (Wiley, p. 602). . . . John Robinson moved from Valley Furnace, Preston County, to Monongalia County (Wiley, p. 659). . . . Elizabeth (John) Weltner, of Stewartstown, died (Wiley, p. 675). . . . Tassey, Morrison and Sample became operators of the Cheat Iron Works on November 16 (Wiley, p. 682). . . . Alexander Hayes bought a lot along the Monongahela River opposite Morgantown, including the rope ferry which he operated (Callahan, pp. 100, 114). . . . John Watts, wheelwright and constable, acquired the south half of Lot 42 in Morgantown (Callahan, p. 317). . . . Charles S. Morgan conveyed Lot 120 to Thomas F. Brooke (Callahan, p. 329). . . . Thomas Fleming sold Lots 1 and 2, in Middletown, and a ferry across the Monongahela River, to Octavius Haymond (Lough, p. 420). . . . Frederick Ice sold Lots 11 and 58, with a tavern operated by Benjamin B. Bartholow, to Benjamin B. Burns (Lough, p. 421). . . . Unlike the previous winter, this one was very cold; the temperature was twenty-four degrees below zero on February 9 (Owens, p. 36).

CHAPTER SIXTY

# 1836

In the *American Journal of Science* (New Haven, Connecticut), issue for January 1836, there appears an article by Dr. S. P. Hildreth, of Marietta, Ohio, entitled "Observations on the Bituminous Coal Deposits of the valley of the Ohio . . . ," that includes one of the earliest detailed accounts of the geology of the Monongahela Valley. In view of the fact that in the years ahead coal was to be basic to the industry of Monongalia County, some special attention should be devoted to this article.[1]

**Geological Survey of the Monongahela Valley.** The Monongahela Valley, Dr. Hildreth says, "occupies a space of about one hundred and eighty miles in length, by sixty or eighty in breadth, and lies between the Alleghany mountains and their collateral ranges on the east, and the Ohio river on the west. Its general direction is north and south, with a rapid declination from its southern borders to its northern extremity. The waters of the Monongahela pursue a course directly opposite to that of the Ohio . . . and although the descent in the beds of the streams is very great, yet it occupies about three days for the rains which fall on the head branches, and occasion rapid rises in its waters, to arrive in the Ohio, at Marietta; whereas, could they pursue a direct course like many of the streams below, they would reach the point in one third of that time."[2]

Tygart Valley, in Randolph County, was a most interesting

1. "Observations on the Bituminous Coal Deposits of the valley of the Ohio, and the accompanying rock strata; with notices of the fossil organic remains, and the relics of vegetable and animal bodies." Illus. *Am. Journ. Sci.* 29:1-154.
2. Op. cit., pp. 51, 52.

region to Dr. Hildreth. "The river," he says, "meanders through its whole length with a calm and placid surface. Environed by ridges of lofty mountains, and shut off from the strife and tumult of the surrounding world, this valley affords, at certain seasons of the year, all the natural and picturesque beauties of the fabled valley of Johnson. Here may be found nearly all the rare and curious shrubs, and flowering trees, indigenous to the western country. Enticed by the depth and warmth of the valley, protected from the cold winds by the lofty ridges which surround it, flora here commences her earliest labors."[3]

The Cheat River, he says, near its headwaters on the Shavers Fork, runs "in a narrow glade, on the top of one of the mountain ranges, . . . through a mountainous region of wilderness . . . , one of the most gloomy and desolate tracts to be found in all the ranges of the Alleghany. The water from this elevated district has a descent of at least two thousand feet to the settlements of 'Dunkard's Bottom'. . . . The waters of the Cheat river are noted for their dark, sombre color, supposed to arise from the hemlock roots and leaves over which the water passes. It takes its name from the numerous accidents that have happened to travellers in fording it."[4]

But in all the vast region under consideration, it is the coal that most impressed Dr. Hildreth: "Down the valley of the Monongahela, we find one of the richest and most abundant deposits of coal, in all the valley of the Ohio." He includes a sketch and descriptions "furnished by the Rev. C. Elliott, who has traversed the coal measures, and examined them minutely, for several years."

In the illustration the coal deposits "are numbered in the order of their superposition. The figures above the curved lines denote the height of the several beds above the river at different places, while those below denote the depth of the two deposits underneath the river at Pittsburgh. . . . At Morgantown where the illustration commences, the hills near the river are from three hundred and fifty to four hundred and fifty feet in height. No less than four distinct deposits of coal are found from the tops of the hills to the bed of the river. No. 1 lies at an elevation

3. Op. cit., pp. 54, 55.
4. Op. cit., p. 57.

of three hundred feet, is six feet in thickness, and affords coal of a moderately good quality. No. 2 is one hundred and fifty feet above the river, is seven feet in thickness, and the coal of a very excellent quality. No. 3 lies near the base of the hills, and only thirty feet above the water in the river. The coal is of rather an inferior quality, and only three feet in thickness. No. 4 is a few feet beneath the surface at this spot, but four miles above, it appears in the bed of the river, and continues so to do for fifteen or twenty miles. It is six feet in thickness. This coal is of a very superior quality, highly bituminous and free from sulphur, or sulphuret of iron, and in repute for smith-work. There are in all the beds twenty two feet of coal. At the bottom of the best coal beds, is found a deposit of about eighteen or twenty inches of coal of great purity, and which for the manufacture of iron is fully equal to charcoal; burning without leaving any cinders, and very little ashes."[5]

The No. 3 bed dips upstream. "A person sailing up the river can easily perceive as he ascends, that the coal banks are becoming nearer the water's edge at every hill he passes, until at Greensboro' and Morgantown, they are within a short distance of the water: as you retire from the river and follow out the creeks, you find this stratum on their shelving banks, and sometimes forming the beds of the runs; and when you reach their heads it has sunk beneath the surface too far to be reached at all, except by shafts."[6]

Deposit No. 1, Hildreth says, Elliott has "been unable to find at any other place except near Morgantown and Somerset, Pa. There is no bed west of the mountains corresponding to this; for it is No. 3 alone that makes its appearance at so many points on the Monongahela and Youghiogheny rivers, except near Morgantown and Greensboro'. But it must be recollected that the hills in these neighborhoods are prolongations, or spurs of the mountain ranges, which may account for its appearances in these places only."

These "immense beds of bituminous coal . . . fill the mind with wonder and surprise" as one reflects on the vast forests required in their formation and the uncounted ages during

5. Op. cit., pp. 63-65.
6. Op. cit., p. 66.

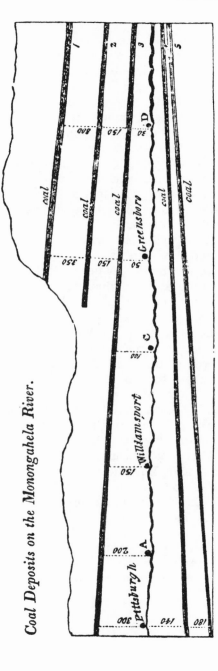

Explanation—A, Elizabethtown,—C, Brownsville,—D, Morgantown.

Fig. 19. Coal deposits on the Monongahela River. (*Amer. Jour. Sci.*, 1836.) According to Carl J. Smith, West Virginia Geological Survey, the numbered seams are as follows: 1. Waynesburg; 2. Sewickley; 3. Pittsburgh; 4. Upper Freeport; 5. Upper Kittanning.

which they were being compressed. The "Almighty and liberal hand" has provided man with a bountiful resource, which he will not be very slow in utilizing.[7]

**The Democratic Republican.** During 1836, it may be presumed, Enos D. Morgan continued to publish the weekly newspaper which he had started early the previous year. However, no copies for 1835 and 1836 can now be found.

The term Democratic Republican was in allusion to one of the major political parties of the day, favoring a strict interpretation of the constitution to restrict the powers of the federal government, and emphasizing states' rights. It was, therefore, opposed to the Federalist party (*Monongalia Story*, vol. 2, pp. 474-77) and was the party that had elected Andrew Jackson to the presidency in 1828 and again in 1832. It was the ancestor of the Democratic party of today. Earlier it had been called simply the Republican party.

Enos D. Morgan (1807-1857) was a son of Captain Zackwell Morgan and a grandson of Colonel Zackquill Morgan, the founder of Morgantown.

**Morgantown Merchants.** Among retail merchants in Morgantown in 1836, with dates their business began, were Martin Callendine (1832), Chadwick and Alexander (1832), L. H. Dorsey (1833), E. and U. Billingsley (1835), McNeely and Dering (1835), and Chadwick and Sons (1835).

**Ordinaries and Houses of Private Entertainment.** An ordinary, or tavern, was a center of social life in the community in early times. Here travelers stopped to eat or spend the night, and men of the neighborhood came to hear the news, drink, gamble, bowl, or discuss politics. A house of private entertainment was a place of meeting, where food and drink were sold, but on a smaller scale. Licenses were charged, and certain standards required.

County court records, year by year, preserve the names of persons licensed as "ordinary keepers," "keepers of houses of private entertainment," "Hawkers and Pedlars and Exhibitors of Public shows." Typical is the record for the year ending August 31, 1836:

7. Op. cit., p. 123.

Private entertainment: John Core, James Williams, John Johnson, Susannah Chalfant, William Frum, Doctor Thorn, Joseph Jolliffe, Fred A. Dering, Patsey Massie, Arthur Fitch, John Worley, John Cleland, Joseph Shuttleworth, William Haymond, Michael Kern, Isaac Riggs, and Joseph Perrell. License fees were about two dollars each.

Ordinary: John Jones, William F. Martin, William Meredith, James M'Vicker, James Fleming, Curtis Hayes, Alexander Hayes, Jacob Cartright, Daniel B. M'Vicker, Benj. B. Barthlow, Ishmael S. Massie, John Core, and Samuel Costolo. License fees were eighteen dollars.

Public Show: J. B. Green. Thirty dollars.

**Union Baptist Church.** Residents along Miracle Run, in the western part of the county, in 1836, organized at Cross Roads the Union Baptist Church. Alexander Eddy, Sarah Cross, Barbara Yost, and Jacob Haught were among early members of the church. A small frame building was constructed, and this served for a time, not only for church purposes, but also as a school.[8]

**The Last of the Indian Fighters.** Simon Kenton (Fig. 11), one of the last of the old Monongalia Indian fighters, died April 29, 1836, near Zanesville, Ohio. He was born April 3, 1755, probably in Fauquier County, Virginia. In 1771 he appeared at Ice's Ferry on Cheat River, introducing himself as Simon Butler; he had knocked a man unconscious in a fight and fled, thinking he had killed him. Here he stayed "for about six weeks, during which time he became acquainted for the first time with 'real borderers,' Indian fighters, long-hunters, traders, Indians, and a few renegades. For 'the ferry' knew them all, good and bad, Christians, sinners, ministers of the gospel, cutthroats, coming and going, and 'pausing for a while, at this early wilderness outpost, west of the Alleghenies.' "[9]

Later he lived for a while on Paw Paw Creek, spent the winter of 1773-74 on Big Sandy River, served in Lord Dunmore's war as a spy, worked with and once saved the life of Daniel Boone, and was at Prickett's Fort in 1778 when George Rogers Clark

8. Dodds and Dodds, *Churches of Monongalia County*, p. 131.
9. Lough, *Now and Long Ago*, pp. 524-26; see also Edna Kenton, *Simon Kenton, His Life and Period, 1755-1836* (copyrighted 1930).

was there recruiting men for the expedition against Kaskasia (*Monongalia Story*, vol. 2, pp. 35-37). He was captured by the Indians and taken to Detroit, where he escaped in 1779. Learning that the man he thought he had killed was still alive, he returned to Virginia in 1782, then went with his father's family to settle in Kentucky in 1784.

Like Boone, he moved farther west as the settlements began to destroy the wilderness, but in 1824 appeared in Frankfort, Kentucky, to petition the state to release lands claimed by him. His appearance at first excited ridicule, but, on being recognized by General Thomas Fletcher, he was hailed as "the second great adventurer of the west" (after Daniel Boone), his lands were restored, and Congress granted him a pension of $240 a year.

**Colonel Richard Watts.** Richard Watts died in 1836. Born in Maryland in 1788, he married Catharine, daughter of John Stealey, and with his father-in-law and brother-in-law, Jacob Kiger, operated the Rock Forge Iron Works from 1815 until 1824.

He was sworn in as a member of the county court August 28, 1820, and the same year became lieutenant colonel in the Seventy-sixth Regiment, Virginia Militia.

He was elected to the House of Delegates in 1828, 1830, and 1831, and to the state senate in 1832.

**Henry Dorton.** A free black man who had been among the earliest settlers in Monongalia County, Henry Dorton (or Dalton), died in 1836. He was born at Bladensburg, Maryland, in 1748 and enlisted in the Revolutionary army three different times.

His first enlistment was in 1777 at Redstone Old Fort in Capt. Joseph Foard's company, a unit eventually ordered to Fort Graves on the Ohio River. The company, composed largely by Virginians, found the fort burnt, and on their return trip, along the river toward Wheeling, they were attacked by about seventy Indians who killed nearly half of the detachment. Dorton was one of the survivors who accompanied the burial party sent out ten days later from Fort Pitt to the site of the engagement. He was discharged soon afterward.

He was called up again in 1778 at Redstone and went to Fort Pitt, thence down the Ohio and helped in building Fort

McIntosh and Fort Lawrence. After six months of service, he was discharged and returned to his old home at Bladensburg.

Once more he was drafted and served at Savannah, being discharged after Cornwallis's surrender at Yorktown.[10]

About 1790 he moved to Monongalia County, settling south of Morgantown (*Monongalia Story*, vol. 2, pp. 263, 307). He had three sons, Bethuel, Levi, and John, and father and sons at various times owned farms of as much as two hundred acres each. The sons were hunters of some prowess, filing numerous claims for bounties on wolf and fox scalps.

"In 1832 Henry Dorton, old and inform, applied for a pension based on his Revolutionary service. Thomas P. Ray, the commissioner who took evidence on such claims in Monongalia County, approved the claim with a note that 'He was the only applicant in this county that had preserved his discharge.' He received a pension in 1833 and yearly until his death in 1836. In an unmarked grave about a mile from Clinton Furnace lie the remains of one black Monongalian who fought for his country in the American Revolution."[11]

**Thomas Barnes.** Thomas Barnes, (or Barns), one of the earliest settlers at the site of Middletown, died October 19, 1836. He was born December 9, 1750, at Frederick, Maryland. He probably settled at the mouth of Buffalo Creek before 1775 and may have traded with the Indians.[12] On December 25, 1783, he patented the land where Middletown was later established, as an assignee of Jonathan Bozarth; in pioneer times this was referred to as the "Christmas Gift tract" and the land was considered lucky.[13]

Barnes was a sergeant in Abner Crump's Company, First Virginia Regiment, commanded by Colonel George Gibson, October 1777 and his name is on the list of those receiving certificates for balance of pay, July 15, 1783.

He was sworn in as a member of the Monongalia County court sometime before 1796, resigning on May 15 of that year.

10. Rachel Cox, *Revolutionary Soldiers who applied for Pensions in Monongalia County* (typescript), p. 11; Ross B. Johnston, *West Virginians in the American Revolution*, p. 92; Wiley, p. 610.
11. Edward M. Steel, Jr., *West Virginia History* 34(1973):333, 334.
12. Lough, *Now and Long Ago*, p. 92.
13. Op. cit., pp. 235, 236.

He was a religious leader of the area about the mouth of Buffalo Creek (see *Monongalia Story*, vol. 2, p. 219) and was a charter member of the Monongalia County Bible Society, organized in 1823.

He married Sarah Scott about 1776; she was born in Ireland May 20, 1752, and died in Monongalia County December 17, 1803. Their children were: (1) William, born January 28, 1779; (2) Sarah (1780-1830), married William Willey, Jr.; (3) John Scott (December 14, 1781-February 23, 1858), married Susannah, daughter of Samuel Swearingen; (4) Catherine, born February 12, 1783; (5) Phebe, born December 28, 1784, married Rev. Asa Shinn; (6) Thomas, Jr. (October 15, 1785-December 12, 1856), married Rachel Pindle (1792-1818), daughter of Jacob Pindle, then Elizabeth Pindle (1794-1894); (7) Mary Ann, born November 18, 1788, married James Tharp; and (8) James, born June 24, 1790, died March 20, 1843.[14]

**Election Results.** In the spring election, William S. Morgan was elected to Congress, without opposition. For House of Delegates, Thomas S. Haymond and Horatio Morgan were elected. The results appeared in the local newspaper, but the surviving copy of the issue is fragmentary.[15]

|  | Thomas S. Haymond | Horatio Morgan | Tansey | John Boggess |
|---|---|---|---|---|
| Morgantown | 247 | 213 | 221 | |
| Middletown | 234 | 146 | 44 | |
| Ross' | 62 | 67 | 5 | |
| Pawpaw | 14 | 66 | | |
| Snodgrass | 5 | 32 | | |
| Swamps | 69 | 21 | | |
| Blacksville | 45 | | | |
| Jacksonville | 11 | | | |
| Jarrett's | 8 | | | |
| Flat Run | 13 | | | |

**Jacob Boyers.** A well-known gristmill operator, Jacob Boyers, died January 22, 1836. A son of Leonard and Catherine Boyers, he was born December 7, 1782.

14. Lough, *Now and Long Ago*, p. 383.
15. The *Democratic Republican*, April 22, 1836.

He married Elizabeth Lock and they had twelve children, namely, Josiah, Catherine E., Harriet, William G., Morgan Lock, Hyrcanus J., Hezekiah, Julianna, Mary, Jacob, Simon L., and Henry G.

His business, known as the Fairplay Mills, was located on Scotts Run.[16]

**Land Grants Made in 1836.** Monongalia County grantees in 1836 included:

| | | |
|---|---|---|
| Bateman, Daniel | 12 a. | Waters Cheat R. |
| Brookover, John | 200 | Miracle Run |
| Caldwell, James | 150 | Laurel Run |
| Clark, Abisha | 230 | Dunkard Creek |
| Cox, Jefferson | 100 | Dunkard Creek |
| Cunningham, George | 7 | Wests Run |
| Farrell, William | 250 | Wickwares Creek |
| Farrell, William | 54 | Wickwares Creek |
| Feltimore, W. W. | 43 | Wickwares Creek |
| Ferrell, Wilsby | 40 | Pricketts Creek |
| Frew, Samuel | 43 | Wickwares Creek |
| Hanway, John | 40 | Adj. John Nuzum |
| Hanway, John | 35 | Waters Tygart Valley |
| Haynes, William | 75 | Miracles Run |
| Hindgarden, Samuel | 50 | Dunkard Creek |
| Hood, John | 17½ | Days Run |
| Jacobs, Benjamin | 18 | Laurel Run |
| Knox, Daniel | 1 | Scotts Run |
| Lantz, Lot | 1,700 | Dunkard Creek |
| Lemasters, Anthony | 80 | Deckers Creek |
| Lemasters, Lewis | 100 | Flat Run |
| Lemasters, Thomas | 38 | Buffalo Creek |
| Miller, Jesse | 6 | Pumpkin Run |
| Morgan, James, Sr. | 20 | Pricketts Creek |
| Morgan, James, Sr. | 58 | Pricketts Creek |
| Myers, James | 92 | Indian Creek |
| Myers, Solomon | 120 | Pedlar's Run |
| Nuzum, George | 100 | Pricketts Creek |
| Ochiltree, Isaac | 150 | Laurel Run |

16. *Upper Monongahela Valley*, p. 447.

| Philips, Elinton | 65 | Wickwares Creek |
|---|---|---|
| Powell, C. | 37 | Days Creek |
| Reed, William | 72 | Waters Cheat R. |
| Stafford, James H. | 20 | Waters Cheat R. |
| White, Stephen and John | 380 | Yeagers Fork |
| White, William | 850 | Dunkard Creek |
| Wiley, John W. | 1½ | Dunkard Creek |
| Williams, James, Jr. | 95 | Wickwares Creek |
| Woodyard, Samuel | 325 | Wickwares Creek |

**County Government.** David Musgrave, on March 28, 1836, was sworn in for his second term as sheriff. William John succeeded Hillary Boggess as commissioner of the revenue for the Eastern District. The county levy was $0.50.

**Miscellany.** In 1836: George H. Lee was admitted to the Monongalia County bar (Wiley, pp. 317, 318). . . . George Kramer came from Greensboro, Pennsylvania, and located in Morgantown (Wiley, p. 604); he bought Lot 20 (Callahan, p. 312) and Lot 44 (Callahan, p. 317). . . . Christianne, wife of James Watson, died December 5, aged 23 years (Wiley, p. 618). . . . John W. Sturgis was running a store at Stewartstown (Wiley, p. 673). . . . A portion of Lot 27 was conveyed to the Merchants' and Mechanics' Bank (Callahan, p. 314) which built a large brick building on it (Callahan, p. 189). . . . Portions of Lots 85 and 86 were conveyed to Fielding Kiger (Callahan, p. 321). . . . James Chadwick conveyed a portion of Lot 98 to Sanford Pickenpaugh (Callahan, p. 323). . . . John A. Durbins conveyed a portion of Lot 102 to Larkin H. Dorsey (Callahan, p. 325). . . . Lot 124, which had been the home of the Monongalia Academy in 1815, was sold at public auction to Guy R. C. Allen, for $1,405 (Callahan, p. 329). . . . The town of Newport[17] (later Catawba) was laid out on Jacob Swisher's land and the first lot (Lot 12) was sold by him and his wife Drusilla to Thomas Harden; Lot 27 was deeded to the school trustees for a schoolhouse (Lough, p. 544). . . . Lands were surveyed for James Shriver on Dunkard Creek, for Abraham Shriver on Dunkard Creek, and for Joseph Sutton on Rudolph Sniders Run (*Chronicles of Core*, p. 66).

17. For history of Newport, see Balderson, *Prickett's Fort*, pp. 175, 176.

# CHAPTER SIXTY-ONE

# 1837

The manufacture of iron in Monongalia County had begun in pioneer days (see *Monongalia Story*, vol. 2, pp. 265-69, 289-92, 294, 422, 458-60). By 1837 it might be said that the industry was approaching its zenith.

**The Cheat Iron Works.** Most of the industry centered in the area beyond Cheat River from Morgantown, where the iron ore beds outcropped. Moreland described the industrial community as it existed in the late 1830s:[1]

"The magnitude or extent of the iron industry on Cheat River and in Cheat Mountain is hard for those of the present generation to appreciate. That it was, at a very early date, of no inconsiderable magnitude can be easily established, but to conceive an industrial community on Cheat River which about 1840 was four times as large as the then town of Morgantown is difficult for those of us who now know the quiet rural community of Cheat Neck to comprehend or imagine. To visualize a thriving community of over 100 homes, housing several hundred people, in the immediate vicinity of the present old Henry Clay Furnace is too much for our imagination. Yet those are the well authenticated facts."

Moreland continues: "To consider the Cheat Mountains as an industrial section of such magnitude that the American nation was dependent on it in the War of 1812 taxes our credulity, yet

1. James R. Moreland, *The Early Cheat Mountain Iron Works. Some notes on the early history of Cheat Neck, and the territory embraced in the West Virginia Forest Reserve and Game Refuge, on the Cheat Mountains, and of the Iron Industry carried on at a very early date as well as in nearby parts of Monongalia and Preston Counties, West Virginia* (1940). Typescript, in various Morgantown libraries.

that some of the shot fired by the cannon of General Jackson at the Battle of New Orleans and some of the mills and iron work of Perry's squadron on Lake Erie came from Jackson's Iron works, and were made from iron smelted there in Cheat Mountains, appears to be well established.

"To imagine a town on Cheat River, more than 100 years ago, with macadamized streets and a system of water works over-taxes our imagination, yet such were the facts, as living witnesses have verified."[2]

**The Henry Clay Furnace.** The Henry Clay Furnace, four miles from Ice's Ferry by way of what was called the Bruceton Pike, was built by Leonard Lamb about 1834 to 1836, for Tassey and Bissell. Why it was named for Henry Clay is not known, although the Kentucky senator was largely instrumental in having the National Road built through Fayette County rather than through Pittsburgh, as was proposed by some promoters.

According to Moreland, William Smith, "who lived all his life on top of the Cheat Mountain," testified in 1912 in a court suit against the Ball Land and Lumber Company that he was then eighty-two years old and "that about 1840, when he was a boy of 10 or 12 he went to Henry Clay about every week to sell eggs and other products, and that there were then employed there at the Furnace, and in digging ore, making charcoal, etc., about 200 men, and that there were about 100 houses in its immediate vicinity, with a community of nearly 500 people living there. They also had a school and church where the Reverend Peter T. Laishley, a Methodist Protestant minister, taught during the week and preached on Sunday. Reverend Samuel Clawson also preached there."[3]

The furnace was a cold blast, run by steam, and had a capacity of about four tons of pig iron each twenty-four hours. In the early years all the iron made was boated down the river, but later much of it was used locally.

After the original operators, Tassey and Church ran it next, then Tassey, Morrison and Semple, and finally the Ellicotts. They built seven or eight miles of tramway. It was located on

2. Op. cit., p. 58.
3. Op. cit., pp. 81, 82.

Fig. 20. Henry Clay Furnace, as it appeared in 1890. (West Virginia University Library.)

the John Davis survey of two thousand acres, which Leonard Lamb bought in 1837 from Thomas S. Haymond.

Moreland describes the remains in 1940: "All that remains at this day is the square stone stack about thirty feet high with an opening near the ground on each face. To one side is a stone wall to hold the bank, along the top of which ran the road up which they hauled the ore, limestone and charcoal with which to charge the furnace. From that bank on top of the wall there was a bridge over to the top of the furnace, across which the ore, etc., were hauled in wheelbarrows and dumped into the top of the stack. Below and by the side of that wall is a pit of water into which the slag was drawn to cool. In the woods nearby are a few corner foundation stones and an occasional chimney butt for some of the log houses."[4]

Doubtless the conditions surrounding the furnace in the 1830s would have saddened the hearts of ecologists, had any existed at that time. (The word ecology had not yet been coined.) The great bare areas where strip mining had been carried on to uncover the ore-bearing rocks, the slashings where trees had been cut for charcoal, and the various waste products from the manufacturing process left scars on the beautiful mountain slopes.

Moreland adds: "We often read of the romance and attraction of searching ancient ruins for evidence of forgotten civilizations. So completely gone are the evidences of the forgotten industrial civilization once existing in that quiet sleepy section that any one inclined to search ruins for romance and excitement need not go farther away than to our neighboring Cheat River country to satisfy that desire."[5]

**Valley Falls.** On November 13, 1837, Washington W. Fetterman and his wife Sarah acquired the land around the falls of the Tygart Valley River. This land had been patented October 3, 1781, to David Gray and Samuel Hanway, described as a tract "on both sides of Tygers Valley River, including the Great Falls of the said river." Samuel Frew, who sold the land to the Fettermans, had cut a millrace through the massive Connoquenessing Sandstone over which the river pours and completed a sawmill which began operations July 15, 1837.

4. Op. cit., p. 81.
5. Op. cit., pp. 58, 59.

In 1837 the general assembly ordered a survey for a canal around the "Big and Little Falls" of the Tygart Valley River; such a canal was to have provided navigation from Pittsburgh to near Beverly.[6]

**Monongalia Baptists.** The Baptists had been the very first religious group to organize a congregation in Monongalia County. The first church in the county, as it now exists, had been the Forks of Cheat Baptist Church, organized by the Reverend John Corbly on November 5, 1775. Even before that, in 1774, the Reverend John Sutton had organized the Simpson Creek Baptist Church, at what is now Bridgeport, then in the District of West Augusta, later Monongalia County, and still later Harrison County. This may have been the first organized church in northwestern Virginia. By 1777 four Baptist churches had been formed in the Monongahela Valley, totaling 121 members, strong enough to form the Redstone Association. One of these churches was on Whiteley Creek (now Greene County, Pennsylvania), where the family of the Reverend John Corbly was killed by the Indians in 1782. Another early Baptist church was the Mount Tabor Church near Laurel Point.

**The Goshen Baptist Church.** The Goshen Baptist Church, about ten miles south of Morgantown, was organized August 2, 1837, by the Reverends J. W. B. Tisdale and John Curry.[7]

The first members of the Goshen Baptist Church were Mr. and Mrs. Rezin Holland, Sr., Mr. and Mrs. Leven Howell, Mr. and Mrs. John Huffman, Elizabeth Fleming, Nancy Howell, Joanna Holland, and Rebecca Jones. The congregation held its first meetings in the home of Rezin Holland. "Shortly after the church was founded, a building site was selected and named Goshen."

The following notice appeared in a Morgantown newspaper a short time later:

"A protracted meeting will commence on Tuesday the 26th,

6. Ross B. Johnston, "Valley Falls," *West Virginia History* 15 (1953):58-67; Balderson, *Prickett's Fort*, pp. 166-71.

7. Through the courtesy of the Reverend Stacy Groscup, pastor of the church in 1976, and Spencer McBee, a member of the congregation, an anonymous manuscript history of the church was presented to the Morgantown Public Library and is the source of much of the information used here. See also Dodds and Dodds, *Churches of Monongalia County*, p. 139.

instant, at 11 o'clock, with the Goshen Baptist Church, on the farm of Reson Holland, 5 miles from Morgantown, on Booth's creek, attended by Elders J. Curry, Wm. Davidson, Wm. Wood, and others; at which meeting the Lord's Supper will be administered. It is also expected that Leven Howell will be ordained to the gospel ministry. There will be preaching also in Morgantown, on Monday evening the 25th inst, by early candlelighting, by some one of the ministers mentioned above. J. W. B. Tisdall."[8]

Rezin Holland was a son of Capel Holland, who was among the early pioneer settlers. Rezin, born in 1776, died in 1851, is said to have built the first windmill in Monongalia County.

Other pioneer settlers in the Goshen Community were two bachelor brothers, James and Josiah Wilson (before 1777), Jacob Holland (1801), John Austin (about 1806), Robert and William Robe (1773), B. H. Griffith (about 1817), and Henry Dolton (or Dorton), a black man who had fought in the Revolutionary War.

Thomas Steele was an early settler and hunter, for whom Toms Run was named. It is said that he habitually wore a blue hunting shirt, with a red fringe, and on one occasion shot a bear on his own land, weighing over four hundred pounds after being dressed.

The Sayer family settled in the area about 1778 and the old Sayer Trail was a transportation artery in days when most people traveled horseback or on foot.

**Sunday Schools.** Considerable rivalry existed between local congregations of Morgantown churches. On May 17, 1837, the Methodist Episcopal Sunday school was organized, with W. R. Willey as superintendent.[9] Later in the same year, the Presbyterians, taking a definite stand against their earlier custom of attending the Methodist Church when their own church was not having a service, organized their own Sunday morning services, under the direction of Thomas Martin, principal of Monongalia Academy.[10]

Modern Sunday schools had been started by English publisher Robert Raikes in 1780, to aid children of poor families by

8. *Democratic Republican,* August 19, 1837.
9. Wiley, pp. 450, 591.
10. Wiley, p. 593; Callahan, *Making of Morgantown,* p. 154.

teaching them reading, writing, and the principles of religion. In America the Sunday school movement became widespread after the Revolutionary War and the American Sunday School Union was formed in 1824.

**Morgantown Central Temperance Society.** A temperance society was formed on July 4, 1837, with John Rogers president and E. C. Wilson secretary. For carrying on the work of the society the county was divided into four districts, one central and three auxiliary, as follows: First District, Morgantown Central Society; Second District, Pisgah Society, between Booths Creek and Pricketts Creek; Third District, Middletown Society; Fourth District, Gilboa Society, south of Indian Creek.[11]

**Andy Mundel and His Tall Tales.** On August 1, 1837, Andrew Mundel and Elizabeth, his wife, purchased from John Hanway a thirty-five-acre farm at the head of Pedlar Run. Andy Mundel had a fertile imagination and his neighbors enjoyed listening to his exaggerated tales; some of them are still told today.

"On one occasion, he said he was walking along the road when he heard a noise in the woods nearby. Investigating, he found the cause to be a detached limb, so crooked it could not lay still, and therefore flopping about from side to side. Before leaving the scene, his eye chanced to fall upon a bright looking pen knife. Picking it up, he found it to contain sixteen blades.

"Another time, out hunting, he came upon a deer. He had a gun but no balls for it. A peach tree grew nearby, so seizing a peach seed from the ground, he rammed it into his gun and fired. The seed struck the deer in the head but did not kill it. A year or so later he returned and found the same deer peacefully grazing, a young peach tree growing from its head. . . .

"Yet again he came upon twenty-four wild turkeys roosting on a single limb of a tree. He wished to secure as many as possible of them but had only one bullet. Standing at one end of the group, he took aim and fired. Every turkey fell from the limb. The ball had passed successively through the bodies of each of the birds."[12]

11. See p. 55; see also Wiley, pp. 451, 452.
12. Core, *Chronicles of Core*, pp. 66, 67.

**Abraham Shriver Dies.** Abraham Shriver, a son of Adam Shriver and one of the few survivors of the pioneer settlers on Dunkard Creek, died November 11, 1837, aged sixty-nine years. He and his wife, Mary Keckley Shriver, had a large family, including the following children: Adam, Benjamin, Ellis, Isaac, John, Joseph, Jacob (married Margaret Core), Elizabeth, Catherine, Christena (married Michael Core), and Abraham, Jr.[13]

**The Democratic Republican.** The county weekly newspaper, the *Democratic Republican*, which had been started by Enos D. Morgan early in 1835, continued to be published. Only fragments survive, however, of issues dated before June 3, 1837 (Vol. 3, No. 10, Whole No. 114).

Very little local news appeared in this paper, although there were large numbers of advertisements, which helped the paper to survive. The rates for these were announced as, for one square or less, three times or less, $1.00; extra insertions, per square, $0.25.

**Revolutionary Veteran Dies.** "With regret we announce the death of Joseph Sapp, a patriot of the Revolution, who departed this life on the 16th inst., at his residence in this county. Mr. Sapp was a brave soldier in the field of battle. He struggled without a murmur for the liberties he afterwards enjoyed in a free and independent country. As to his age we have no particulars, but is said to be one of the oldest pensioners in the State."[14]

**John Madera Dies.** "Died this morning, at 7 o'clock, after a long and painful illness, Mr. John Madera, in the 44th year of his age."[15]

John Madera was a brother of Nicholas B. Madera, Morgantown postmaster, and a son of Christian Madera, who had settled in Morgantown probably in the early 1790s (*Monongalia Story*, vol. 2, pp. 477, 478).

13. See *The Monongalia Story*, vol. 2, pp. 302, 332, 392, 418; Core, *Chronicles of Core*, p. 67. Mary, his wife, died December 8, 1838, aged sixty-eight years.
14. *Democratic Republican*, September 30, 1837. See *The Monongalia Story*, vol. 2, p. 538; see also Core, *Morgantown Disciples*, pp. 69, 70. Finley Sapp (1867-1952), a distinguished Disciples of Christ minister, was a grandson.
15. *Democratic Republican*, September 16, 1837.

John Madera had three children, Elizabeth, Sarah, and Christian.

**Other Deaths.** "Died, on Tuesday morning last, after a short illness, at his residence in this town, Mr. Harmon Watts. He has left a large family to mourn his untimely end.

"On Thursday evening last, at her residence in this place, after a long and severe illness, Mrs. Ann Britton, at an advanced age."[16]

"Departed this life, on Sunday morning last, after a lingering illness, which she bore with christian meekness, Mrs. Precilla Protzman, wife of Mr. John Protzman, of this place, in the 33d year of her age."[17]

"On Sunday the 17th inst., after a short illness, Mr. William McCanse, an aged and respectable citizen of this county. He has left a family, and a large circle of friends and relatives, to lament their irreparable loss."[18]

**Fire at Middletown.** "We are informed that a fire broke out in Middletown in this county, some two weeks ago in the storeroom of Mr. Vanzant, merchant of that place. As it regards the particulars in which the fire originated, we are not in possession of exactly. It appears, however, that his son was in the act of measuring oats, and returning from the store had neglected to take with him the candle, and from which it is supposed the fire originated. A number, however, collected to the scene immediately, and by great exertions, rescued the largest portion of the goods, but unfortunately the store-room was consumed, together with a Tailor shop belonging to Mr. Robberts, attached to the store-room, was also left in a [state] of ruin. We have not the estimate of the damage sustained, but is supposed to be considerable."[19]

**Chesapeake and Ohio Canal.** Even after many frustrating delays, hopes were still strong that a canal might some day connect the Monongahela Valley with the Atlantic seaboard, as evidenced by the following notice:

16. *Democratic Republican*, November 25, 1837.
17. *Democratic Republican*, December 2, 1837.
18. *Democratic Republican*, December 23, 1837.
19. *Democratic Republican*, October 28, 1837.

"The Cumberland Advocate states that the contractors on the line of canal, from Cumberland eastward, are preparing for active operations. The Advocate adds: 'It is one of the heaviest undertakings known in the country, and will require many thousand labourers in order to complete it. The number now employed is computed to be about six thousand, and when the whole line is under way it is thought the number will be increased to about 15,000. Average the wages & board of this number at one dollar & twenty-five cents each, per day, and the sum expended per week will be one hundred and twenty thousand five hundred dollars.' "[20]

**Stagecoach Travel.** These were the days of turnpikes and travel by stagecoach. A mail coach connected Morgantown with the National Road at Uniontown, where transfer could be made with through coaches east and west. That this form of transportation was not always safe is indicated by this dispatch appearing in a Morgantown newspaper:

"On Wednesday night the 8th inst. an accident had befallen the Mail Coach about five miles east of Handcock's, Md. The occurrence is dreadful to relate. It appears at this time of this causality, the passengers were nearly all asleep, but were aroused to their utmost astonishment, finding the coach on the brink of a precipice, not less than sixty feet perpendicular, which in a moment found themselves at its bottom. The number of passengers the coach contained at the time, we are not informed, but all we understand were more or less injured. And horrible to tell, the accident proved fatal to a white lady, and two female servants, who survived but a few moments. Two of the horses were killed on the spot, and the balance so much injured as rendered them useless for any service."[21]

"Stagecoach drivers were young men with tested driving skill, wearing big hats, leather gloves, and bright clothes. The stagecoaches were always brightly painted, the horses were the

20. *Democratic Republican*, November 11, 1837. The 184-mile long canal was finally completed to Cumberland thirteen years later and opened with a formal ceremony October 10, 1850. But the celebration came too late; the predicted packet service never materialized. By the time of its completion the canal was already outdated, the railroad having taken its place. See Harry I. Stegmaier, Jr. (and others), *Allegany County: A History* (1976), pp. 120-27.
21. *Democratic Republican*, August 19, 1837.

best money could buy, and the sleek harness adorned with bright ribbons and tinkling ornaments. Stagecoaches carried passengers and baggage to the extent of twenty pounds a person."[22]

**More Wagon Roads.** The building of an ever-enlarging network of wagon roads continued through 1837. Petitions presented to the county court for new projects include: "a road from the mouth of Pantherlick run and up the same to the forks thence up the right hand fork . . . crossing the ridge to . . . little paw-paw"; "from near Joseph Shuttlesworth by the way of Newport to the mouth of Pawpaw Creek"; "from the Days run road at the mouth of Long drain to the ridge at the head of said run"; "from the road near Dents mill at William Jones' old shop to Little Indian creek"; "from the Clarksburg Road at the Widow Santees on to Isaac Philips and to intersect the Buffalow Road at or near Jacob Metz's on piles fork of Buffalow"; "from Hayes ferry landing to Wm. Wilkins store"; "from the Jakes run Road to the Days run Road beginning at the old place where Richard Tenant lived"; "from Pawpaw creek to . . . Jakes run"; "from the mouth of sugar camp run to the low gap at the head of Flat run"; "from Thomas mill to intersect the road leading from Blacksville to pawpaw at or near Elias Hoskinson's"; "from the Coburns creek bridge to the Preston county line"; "from Snodgrass to the mouth of Little Pawpaw Creek"; "from the North western Turnpike at Mr. [Isaac] Blue's to Mr. John Abraham Guseman's mill as far as the sign post where it intersects the present road leading from Knottsville."

An unusual effort was made during the year to upgrade the much-used road leading from Morgantown to the Dunkard Creek settlements. W. T. Willey, Andrew Brown, and William Price were appointed to review the road between Blacksville and Courtney's, on Scotts Run. This committee presented a long report to the county court recommending numerous relocations and improvements, most of which were made during the next six or eight years.

The major change recommended was along Dolls Run, where the old road was mostly to the west of the stream, whereas the

22. Frank   Ball,   "Stagecoach   Days,"   *West   Virginia   History* 7(1946):332-34.

new road would be mostly east of the stream. Excerpts from the report give an idea of the changes suggested:

"Marked an alteration near the mouth of Dolls Run where we crossed leaving the present road to the left hand and continuing along the base of the hill (lying on the east and s.e. side) and running nearly parallel with the present road and following sd. direction and keeping on the s.e. side of the run through the land of A [braham] Brown till we leave his possession near Jacob Sines . . . running almost in a parallel direction with the present road up to Michael Core's, then leaving sd. Core's house on the right, then taking a curve and passing in front of his dwelling house and crossing the run and from thence through his meadow wherein his barn stands and crossing it to where a gum tree stands. . . . This alternative avoids four bad crossings of Dolls Run, is some shorter than the present road, on as good ground and with the exception of a few rods will not require much labor to make it."[23]

**James Miller Moves to Palatine.** James Miller was born near Hartford, Connecticut, in 1780, and married Sarah, a daughter of Abner Messenger. In 1802 he started with his wife and father-in-law for the Muskingum Valley, but, taking a fever at Marietta, he returned with his wife to Morgantown, where he opened a coopering establishment, employing four persons. In 1820 he went to Greensboro, Pennsylvania, which he left in 1837 to go to Middletown, where he ran a coopering establishment and ran the ferry between Middletown and the new town of Palatine, in which town he bought the first laid-out lots and to which he moved in 1839.[24]

**New Martinsville.** Presley Martin, "Mouth of Fishing Creek," had an advertisement in a Morgantown newspaper announcing that he "is laying out a portion of the farm in TOWN LOTS, situated in Tyler County, Virginia, at the Mouth of Fishing Creek, on the Ohio river, and to be named MARTINSVILLE." He said that "A State road is located from Smithfield on the

23. See Core, *Chronicles of Core*, pp. 54-57.
24. *Cyclopedia of Marion County*, p. 69; Newman, *History of Marion County*, p. 277; Balderson, *Prickett's Fort*, pp. 130-34. It is said that the name Palatine was suggested because many of the early settlers were from the section of Germany known as the Palatinate.

National Road to the Mouth of Fishing Creek, and is finished to Morgantown, Va."[25]

Presley Martin was a son of Charles Martin, builder of Fort Martin, in Monongalia County (see *Monongalia Story*, vol. 1, p. 353; vol. 2, pp. 43, 45, 51, 293, etc.).

**Rivesville.** On February 23, 1837, a post office was established at the mouth of Paw Paw Creek, called Rivesville. The first postmaster was Elisha Snodgrass, the proprietor of the town, who had laid out several lots.[26]

The town was perhaps named for some member of the Rives family. Lough[27] says it was named for Rives Hoult, father of John and Lawrence Hoult, but Hardesty[28] says it was named for Hon. Henry C. Rives and Kenny[29] says William Cabell Rives.

In early records the community was called Milford (*Monongalia Story*, vol. 2, p. 279) and it was just across Paw Paw Creek from the town of Pleasantville (*Monongalia Story*, vol. 2, pp. 97, 98, 278, 279).

**Land Grants Made in 1837.** Tracts of land in Monongalia County were granted in 1837 to:

| | | |
|---|---|---|
| Alton, Samuel | 440 a. | Dunkard Creek |
| Bruin, Elija | 39 | Pricketts Creek |
| Clark, Abisha | 70 | Middle Fork |
| Cotton, William | 110 | Adj. Peter Meirs |
| Cunningham, John | 80 | Drake Run |
| Fleming, Joab | 60 | Dunkard Run |
| Hains, William, Jr. | 640 | Miracle Run |
| Haught, Evan | 112 | Miracle Run |
| Haymond, John | 355 | Wickwares Creek |
| Hostatler, Nathaniel | 70 | Dunkard Creek |
| Hostatler, Nicholas | 50 | Dunkard Creek |
| Jennings, William | 100 | Dunkard Creek |
| Keck, John | 375 | Days Run |

25. *Democratic Republican*, December 23, 1837.
26. Early sales were to Arthur Cowen, Jonathan Musgrave, John Prichard, William Willey, Thomas Barns, Jr., Moses McCurdy, Eugenius Snodgrass, and Simeon S. West. Lough, *Now and Long Ago*, p. 527.
27. Ibid., pp. 265, 408.
28. *Historical and Geographical Encyclopedia, Marion County*, p. 306.
29. *West Virginia Place Names*, p. 533.

| | | |
|---|---|---|
| Knight, Joshua | 118 | White Day Creek |
| Knight, Joshua | 60 | White Day Creek |
| Laggit, Enoch B. | 75 | Adj. T. Williams |
| Lantz, Lot | 1,400 | Dunkard Creek |
| Matheny, Moses | 150 | Dunkard Creek |
| Mercer, William | 185 | Slaters Run |
| Molisee, Henry | 100 | Deckers Creek |
| Moore, William | 30 | Adj. Cannon's Survey |
| Murphey, Harrison | 212 | Pricketts Creek |
| Murphy, William | 170 | Dunkard Creek |
| Patterson, Philip | 4 | Island, Tygart Valley R. |
| Phillips, Isaac | 210 | Peters (?) Fork |
| Ray, Thomas P. | 3,000 | Waters Cheat River |
| Roby, Randolph | 65 | Adj. Henry Barnes |
| Shafer, David and Henry | 200 | Bee Run |
| Shriver, Abraham | 50 | Dunkard Creek |
| Shriver, John | 400 | Dunkard Creek |
| Sutton, Joseph | 12 | Snyders Run |
| Swisher, Jacob | 40 | Pricketts Creek |
| Thomas, William | 295 | Adj. J. Brookover |
| Toothman, Adam | 96 | Plum Run |
| Toothman, Adam | 250 | Plum Run |
| Tucker, Morgan | 126½ | Slaters Run |
| Wade, Thomas | 270 | Dunkard Creek |
| Wilson, John | 90 | Pricketts Creek |
| Wise, George | 50 | Dunkard Creek |
| Wise, James | 120 | Adj. Hixenbaugh, Nolan |
| Wise, Levi | 22½ | Dunkard Creek |
| Youst, George | 98 | Peppers Creek |

**County Government.** David Musgrave was sworn in on April 24, 1837, for his third consecutive term as sheriff. John Hanway was appointed county surveyor, succeeding his uncle, Samuel (see *Monongalia Story*, vol. 2, pp. 100-102); he was only the third person to have held this position since the county's formation. Henry Boggess was appointed commissioner of the revenue for the Western District. Sworn in as justices of the peace on April 24 were Francis Billingsley, John S. Smith, John Lemley, and John Bowlby; on May 22, Elijah Tarleton, William Swearingen, John Musgrave, William Price, and Joseph F.

Harrison; on June 25, George S. Renshaw and Rawley Holland.
The county levy was $0.62½.

**Miscellany.** In 1837: Monongalia County was feeling the effects
of the financial panic of 1837, but not so severely as other parts
of the country (Wiley, p. 461). . . . Mathew Gay was elected
president of the Merchants' and Mechanics' Bank, succeeding
Thomas P. Ray (Wiley, p. 462). . . . New stores opened in Morgantown (or new names for existing stores) were Chadwick and
Son, H. and F. A. Dering, Haymond and Perry, George Kramer,
I. and J. F. Cooper, and William Lazier (Wiley, p. 580). . . . J. B.
Tisdale was minister at the Forks of Cheat Baptist Church
(Wiley, p. 686). . . . John Hood and Company started a store at
Hamilton on December 5; Morgan L. Boyers was also running a
store there (Wiley, p. 703). . . . J. B. Price started a blacksmith
shop at Flickersville (Wiley, p. 725). . . . David Baldwin was manufacturing plows two miles north of Morgantown (Callahan, p.
134). . . . In August T. Jones and Company announced the
opening of an iron store on Water Street, one door south of the
post office (Callahan, p. 134). . . . Zackwell Morgan was running
a blacksmith shop in Morgantown (Callahan, p. 134). . . . The old
brick house on Lot 19 in Morgantown became the mansion
house of John Hanway (Callahan, p. 188). . . . Robert Boggess
acquired Lot 123 (Callahan, p. 329). . . . Thomas P. Ray bought
Lot 3 in Middletown (Lough, p. 420). . . . C. B. Bristol bought
Lot 22 (Lough, p. 422). . . . Peter Thomas Laishley (1798-1884)
purchased a farm on West Run (Owens, p. 87).

# CHAPTER SIXTY-TWO

# 1838

By 1838 the population of Morgantown had grown to about 650 inhabitants and it was felt that the community should have a new form of government to replace the close corporation which had ruled the town since pioneer days.

**The Borough of Morgantown.** The act of the general assembly creating the new charter reads, in part, as follows:

"An act to incorporate Morgantown in the County of Monongalia (Passed February 3, 1838).

"Be it enacted by the General Assembly, That the inhabitants of so much of the county of Monongalia as are within the bounds of Morgantown, or that may hereafter reside within the said bounds shall be, and they are hereby made a body politic and corporate, by the name and style of 'the Borough of Morgantown,' and as such, and by that name, may contract with, sue and be sued, plead and be impleaded, answer and be answered unto, and may purchase, take, receive, hold and use goods and chattels, lands and tenements, and choses in action for the proper use of the said town, and the same may grant, sell, convey, transfer and assign, let, pledge, mortgage, charge or incumber in any case, and in any manner, may have and use a common seal; and generally shall have all the rights, franchises, capacities and powers appertaining to municipal corporations."

The charter of 1838 for the borough of Morgantown provided for seven trustees, elected at large annually in April at the courthouse, by *viva voce* vote of all borough householders and owners of land. There was no provision for ward representation. The original act of the general assembly establishing the town, in 1785, (*Monongalia Story*, vol. 2, pp. 123-25), had provided for five trustees who were appointed to their positions by the assembly. Vacancies were filled by the assembly, upon nomination by the remaining members of the corporation. The first step toward self-government had been taken in 1810, when the assembly passed an act making the trustees elective by the freeholders.

The charter of 1838 also gave the trustees increased powers. They were to be assisted by two officers, the tax collector and the treasurer, both chosen by the board, but neither of whom were members of the board. George Kramer was the first treasurer and Charles Watts the first collector. One of the duties of the collector was to clear rubbish from the streets. A few years later the trustees appointed a gauger for inspection of weights and measures, particularly of coal and hay, and a wharf master for control of river traffic.

The trustees were vested with power to establish and regulate markets, to maintain streets and sidewalks, provide for market buildings, the supervision of public safety and sanitation, and the levying of taxes (not to exceed fifty cents on the one hundred dollars). Assessments at first were made by the trustees, later by an assessor appointed by the trustees. In 1851 the local county constable was given the power of police and required to enforce the borough ordinances.

Borough records are complete from 1838 and are now filed in the City Hall on Spruce Street. The records indicate that the tax levy in the early period was usually twenty to twenty-five cents. Often increases were made only to be reduced after the next election, quite a contrast to today's pattern of government. In 1838 the total tax collected was $250.08¾, which included the tax on twenty-two slaves, at an average valuation of $286. The first license tax was for peddling tin.

**The First Meeting of the New Trustees.** The first trustees of the new borough government under the charter of 1838 were Thomas P. Ray, Waitman T. Willey, Frederick A. Dering, Elias Stilwell, Jr., William Lazier, Robert P. Hennen, and John Evans.

The minutes of the very first meeting of the board follow:

"At a meeting of the trustees of 'the borough of Morgantown' on Thursday the 5th of April in the year 1838, assembled pursuant to an act of the Assembly passed on the 3d February 1838, entitled an act to incorporate Morgantown in the county of Monongalia.

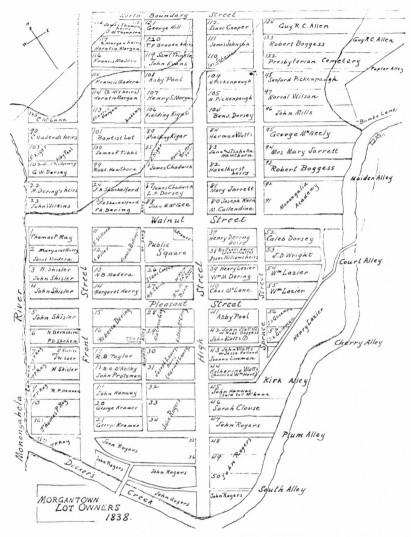

Fig. 21. Morgantown lot owners, 1838. (From Callahan's *Making of Morgantown.*)

"Present, William Lazier, Waitman T. Willey, Robert P. Hennon, Elias Stilwell junr., Frederick A. Dering and Thomas P. Ray.

"Resolved, That William Lazier be appointed President and Thomas P. Ray Clerk of the board.

"Resolved, That Waitman T. Willey and Elias Stilwell jr. be appointed a committee to settle with the collectors of the tax for the year 1836 and 1837 and make report thereof.

"Resolved, That Waitman T. Willey and Thomas P. Ray be appointed a committee to prepare a code of bye-laws and ordinances for the government of the borough and make report thereof.

"Thereupon the board adjourned."

**The Northwestern Turnpike.** The construction of the National Road across the Alleghenies to the Monongahela River north of Morgantown resulted in rival activities elsewhere to secure the advantage in transportation facilities for western trade. A road that was to have a considerable influence on the history of Monongalia County was the Northwestern Turnpike, conceived as an all-Virginia route to the Monongahela and the Ohio (see p. 67).

The act of its incorporation, in 1827, had authorized subscriptions at towns along the projected route, including Winchester, the point of beginning, Romney, Moorefield, Kingwood, Pruntytown, Clarksburg, and Parkersburg. But the stock languished on the market when engineering problems delayed the construction across the mountains.

At last, in 1831, the enterprise was revived by an act of the general asembly which organized a company, with the governor as president and a member of the board of directors, having the power to borrow money ($125,000) on the state's credit to construct a turnpike road of a minimum width of twelve feet "from Winchester to some point on the Ohio River to be situated by the principal engineer." The company was to have the right to erect bridges or to regulate ferries already in operation and to establish tollgates on each twenty-mile section.

The route as finally established was all in Virginia except for an 8¾-mile section through the corner of Garrett County, Maryland. In Hampshire County it was laid out through Capon Bridge, Hanging Rock, Pleasant Dale, and Augusta to Romney,

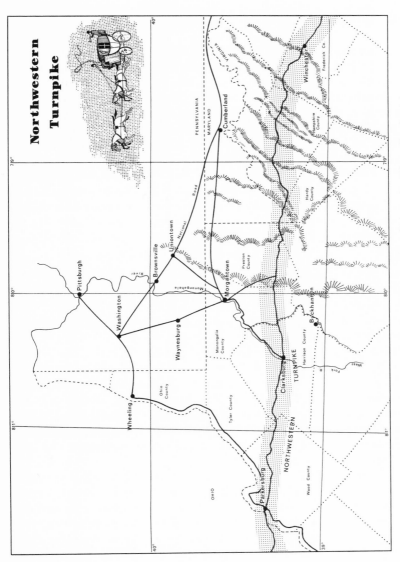

Fig. 22. Route of the Northwestern Turnpike. (Drawn by Diane Lenhart.)

163

crossing the South Branch just west of Romney. The road then passed westward to cross Patterson Creek at Burlington and New Creek at Rees' tannery, then climbed Allegheny Front Mountain and reached the North Branch of the Potomac at Gormania. Here it passed into Maryland and reached its highest point (over three thousand feet) before emerging into Preston County just east of the German Settlement (now Aurora). Then it crossed the rugged and picturesque Cheat River Valley considerably south of Kingwood, through which it was originally planned to go, by way of Evansville to the Tygart Valley River at Fetterman, thence to Pruntytown and Clarksburg. It then ran to Salem, at the head of Ten Mile Creek, crossed Middle Island Creek at West Union, and passed via Toll Gate to Parkersburg. Much of the route passed through a vast wilderness.

**The Road Is Completed.** At last, in 1838, the Northwestern Turnpike was completed to the Ohio River, and, while it crossed only a small portion of Monongalia County, it did, like the National Road to the north, make transportation easier for all the county's citizens.

Wiley describes the road and the traffic over it:

"It was wide and well built, in places being macadamized, with substantial bridges crossing all streams of any size. When finished, an amount of travel passed over it, which we can hardly credit today. Great numbers of travelers on foot passed and repassed over it, mail stages ran night and day, horsemen thronged it, two-horse wagons, four-horse wagons and six-horse wagons, singly and in streams, wound up and down its hills, and every night at some point along the road was a tide of travel claiming food, drink and shelter. The emigrant, with his little all, was daily pushing westward over it to the Ohio, to seek, or better, his fortune. Long lines of horses, flocks of sheep, and droves of hogs, intermingled with the cattle, and all together worked their way by the week slowly to the eastern markets. . . . The men in charge at night were hungry and tired, and to provide for their wants, taverns and stopping places sprang up as if by magic all along the road. Provision and forage had to be gathered in large quantities from the surrounding country. The immense business made the road a lively place, and forward and backward ran the farmer's wagon over a hundred country roads, transporting to these stands, flour and pork and beef and corn and potatoes and vegetables to feed the hungry traveling multitudes; while hay by the ton, oats and corn by the wagon load, came in to feed the animal masses.... In summer's heat or winter's cold, alike through storm or sunshine pressed on this great stream of travel. Two miles apart, and sometimes for every mile post on the road was a tavern, or stopping place for this great travel, with stabling, wagon-yards and fields fenced in for droves."[1]

Fig. 23. Tavern along the Northwestern Turnpike. (From *Aurora Community*, courtesy Lewis E. Stemple.)

**Retrospect.** An address delivered before the Newcomer Society in New York City by a Morgantown minister gives a retrospect of the Northwestern Turnpike from the twentieth century viewpoint:

"Today, if you would see beauty, it invites you to climb its easy grades to where you catch the sweep of mountain ridge on mountain ridge stretching away to where the blue shuts off the distance. Or to follow down some mountain side the track,

1. *History of Preston County* (1882), pp. 77, 78.

which it seems only a giant's finger could have traced, into some broad valley. . . . And perhaps as you go you will catch—if the ears of memory are keen . . . the rumble of Conestoga wagons, or the tinkle of pack-horse bells, or the soft thud of Indian moccasins taking the war-path again. Oh, it has seen history, this winding old road! It has helped to make history. Along it events travelled that gave birth to a State, a great state—and greater yet to be."[2]

**Steam Cars A Comin'!** The age of turnpikes, only just arriving, was already threatened by the approach of another method of transportation. James Hall, writing in 1838, told how Robert Fulton, building his first steamboat at Pittsburgh, "traveled across the mountain in a stage in company with several young gentlemen from Kentucky. His mind was teeming with those projects, the successful accomplishment of which has since rendered his name so illustrious—and his conversation turned chiefly upon steam, steamboats and facilities for transportation. At length, in the course of some conversation on the almost impassable nature of the mountains, over which they were dragged with such great toil, upon roads scarcely practicable for wheels, Fulton remarked, 'the day will come, gentlemen—I may not live to see it, but some of you who are younger probably will—when carriages will be drawn over these mountains by steam engine at a rate more rapid than that of a stage on the smoothest turnpike.' The apparent absurdity of this prediction, together with the gravity with which it was uttered, excited the most obstreperous mirth in this laughter loving company, who roared, shouted, and clapped their hands in the excess of their merry excitement."[3]

**The Steamboat Shannon.** In the spring William Lazier advertised that he had just received, per the steamboat *Shannon*, a shipment of goods for sale, including, "5 Tons Rolled Iron (war-

2. William E. Brooks, "The Northwest Turnpike—and West Virginia," *West Virginia History* 4 (1942):151-63. Also separately printed by the Newcomer Society.

3. Callahan, *Making of Morgantown*, p. 168. This story, while interesting, is doubtless apocryphal. It makes reference to an account, also apparently without foundation in fact, of the construction of a steamboat (the *Robert Fulton*) by Samuel Frisbee for Mr. Fulton, in 1808. See Wiley, *The Monongahela*, pp. 127-29. See also Henry W. Dickinson, *Robert Fulton, Engineer and Artist. His Life and Works* (1913), 333 pp.

ranted) assorted sizes, 2 Tons Juniata Hammered Iron, amongst which is an extensive assortment of Plough Irons . . . , 40 Kegs of Nails assorted from 3 to 20, 10 do. Brads, 8 and 10, 4 doz. Patent Buckets, Cordage of every description, Mackerel, Tobacco, Timothy-seed, Clover-seed, Spades, Shovels, 4 doz. Tea Kettles, Wagon Boxes, Mould Boards, Salt, Orlean Sugar, Meal Sieves, Cockle Sieves, etc."[4]

**Independence Day Is Celebrated.** In the first half of the nineteenth century the social life of the county was still much circumscribed, and recreation was usually combined with business and work, such as logrolling and cornhusking. But the celebration of the Fourth of July was usually the occasion of special neighborhood gatherings.

In July 1838, it is recorded, the Independence Day procession formed in front of the courthouse, and, led by three veterans of the Revolution who carried the flag, marched a mile and a half to the residence of Augustine Wells, Jr., where a "repast was served" and thirteen regular toasts and twelve voluntary toasts were offered. The long procession of toasts began with a series to Washington, Lafayette, President Van Buren, and the Union, included a series to education, steam navigation, and internal improvements, and closed with an appropriate one to the ladies.[5]

**James Robb Resigns.** In 1838 James Robb, the first cashier of the Merchants' and Mechanics' Bank, resigned and left Morgantown to engage in banking in New Orleans. He was succeeded as cashier, on October 1, by William Wagner.[6]

Robb was born in Brownsville, Pennsylvania, and came to Morgantown in 1834. He married Louisa Werninger, daughter of Augustus Werninger, Morgantown merchant, and their residence was on the northeast corner of Spruce and North Boundary streets.[7]

4. The *Republican*, April 21, 1838.
5. Callahan, *Making of Morgantown*, pp. 125, 126; the *Republican*, July 7, 1838.
6. Wiley, pp. 462, 463.
7. Robb was afterwards very successful, and his famous daughter, Isabella, Marchioness of San Roman, revisited Morgantown, her birthplace, many years later (see p. 447).

**Morgantown's First Foundry.** Iron production, as has been frequently noted, was one of Monongalia County's first industries. The manufacture of iron was mostly done near the outcrops of ore, along the western slopes of Chestnut Ridge, near Cheat River, at Rock Forge, and elsewhere.

Foundries for manufacture of much needed iron products were developed in connection with the furnaces. Stoves, grates, wagon parts, plowshares and other items were made in these foundries. In 1838 (or soon thereafter) the first foundry in Morgantown was built by Joel Nuzum and Henry and Hugh Daugherty. It was at the corner of Long Alley at its intersection with Plum Alley, a thoroughfare which eventually came to be called Foundry Street.[8]

**Morgantown Female Academy.** From its first inception, Morgantown's school for girls was a struggling institution, as compared to the Monongalia Academy. From time to time funds were diverted to it from the treasury of the boys' school. In 1837 the Female Academy was allocated $250 from Monongalia County's share of the Literary Fund.

Finally, on December 22, 1838, the trustees of Monongalia Academy petitioned the general assembly to have the female branch separately incorporated, as the Morgantown Female Academy, allowing them to give towards its endowment the lot on Bumbo Lane at Long Alley, the school building, and two thousand dollars. It was felt that this would give greater efficiency to its operation.[9]

**James Davis New Presbyterian Pastor.** The Reverend James Davis was installed as the regular pastor of the Morgantown Presbyterian Church in the autumn of 1838, having filled the pulpit acceptably as a stated supply minister since the fall of 1837.

The son of Rev. Thomas and Hannah Gilley Davis, he was

8. Wiley, p. 262; Callahan, *Making of Morgantown,* p. 134.
9. Wiley, p. 398; Ambler, *History of Education in West Virginia,* pp. 82, 83. The request was granted by an act of the assembly dated January 30, 1839, establishing the Morgantown Female Collegiate Institute. Its government and control was vested in a board of trustees; the first members appointed were William Lazier (president), Guy R. C. Allen, W. T. Willey (secretary), George Hill, and Reuben B. Taylor, largely members of the local Methodist Episcopal Church.

born in Pittsburgh October 28, 1808. He graduated from Western Theological Seminary in 1837 and was licensed by the
Presbytery in April of that year. Morgantown was his first pastorate and during his long stay the church would increase
steadily in strength and numbers. During 1838-39 the old dilapidated church edifice was repaired.[10]

**Jacob Holland.** Jacob Holland, a farmer south of Morgantown,
died September 17, 1838, aged eighty years. He had served four
years as a noncommissioned officer in the Revolutionary
War.[11] He came to Monongalia from Berkeley County in 1801.
He raised a family of seven sons and one daughter. One son,
William, was chased by a bear when thirteen years old and told
many interesting stories of his hunting experiences.[12]

**Thomas Laidley.** Morgantown's first merchant, Thomas Laidley,
died March 17 in Cabell County, where he and his wife, Sarah,
had gone to live with their son, John Osborn Laidley, at Lamer-
tine.

Thomas Laidley was born in Scotland January 1, 1756, emigrated to New York in 1774, and served in the Revolutionary
War.[13] In 1783 he settled in Monongalia County, established a
store in Morgantown,[14] and acquired a large number of town
lots and many widely scattered tracts of land in western Virginia, becoming a man of wealth and influence. His land patents
aggregated twenty-five thousand acres. He represented Monongalia County in the general assembly for three separate terms.

He married Sarah Osborn (October 12, 1760-March 24,
1844) in Philadelphia in 1778 and they had nine children:
James Grant (1781-1821), married Harriet B. Quarrier; Sarah
(1787-1848); Eliza Stewart (1789-1828), married Boaz
Fleming, of Middletown; John Osborn (1791-1863), attorney of
Parkersburg and Barboursville, led movement for establishment
of Marshall College in 1838; Thomas H. (1793-1881), a physician of Morgantown and Greene County, Pennsylvania; Jane B.

10. Moreland, *The First Presbyterian Church*, pp. 50, 51; Callahan,
*Making of Morgantown*, p. 154.
11. *The Monongalia Story*, vol. 2, p. 533.
12. Wiley, p. 609.
13. *The Monongalia Story*, vol. 2, p. 534.
14. *The Monongalia Story*, vol. 2, pp. 98-100.

(1796-1879); Leander S. (1798-1868); Edmond (1800-1815); and Corrine (1803-1805).[15]

**Mrs. Dorsey Dies.** "Died, on Friday morning at 9 o'clock, Mrs. Lovina Dorsey, consort of Benjamin Dorsey, aged 42 years and 9 months.—She was a kind and affectionate wife, a tender and indulgent parent, a humane mistress and an obliging and friendly neighbor. She has left a husband and a large family of children, and a wide & extensive circle of relatives and friends to mourn their melancholy loss."[16]

**"Another Soldier of the Revolution Gone."** "Died, on the 21 ult., Mr. Peter Miller, an old and respectable citizen of Monongalia County, upwards of 80 years of age; being among the last of the remnant of the soldiers of the Revolution. His funeral was largely attended and military honors paid to his memory by the Middletown Blues."[17]

**Joshua Boyles Dies.** Joshua Boyles, of Indian Creek, died May 25, 1838. Of Irish lineage, he was born in Monongalia County in 1807. "In his religious faith he was a strict and consistent member of the Methodist Episcopal Church, whilst in his political adherence he was a democrat."

He married Sarah, daughter of Samuel Jones, and they had four children, Matilda, married Lawrence May; Charles W., married Anna L., daughter of John Batson; Elizabeth, married Samuel Chroyer; and Samuel.[18]

**"Public Sale of a Negro Man."** A newspaper notice, with the above heading, announced: "The subscriber will offer at public sale on Monday the 22d inst. (being court day) a young negro man, about 20 years of age—he is a good looking, strong, active young man. Any one desirous of purchasing such a negro would do well to attend the sale.

"Terms made known on the day of sale. Wm. Wroe."[19]

15. Callahan, *Making of Morgantown*, pp. 81-85; see also Roderick Koinig Eskew, *History of the Quarrier, Laidley, Bickers, Eskew, and Allied Families* (1971).
16. The *Republican*, Saturday, January 20, 1838.
17. The *Republican*, May 12, 1838.
18. *Cyclopedia of Marion County*, p. 120.
19. The *Republican*, January 13, 1838.

**Palatine Is Laid Out.** Across the river from Middletown, the new town of Palatine was laid out in 1838 by W. H. Haymond and Daniel and John Polsley, sons of pioneer settler Jacob Polsley.[20] The area was 197 acres.

The first known settlers in this area were Robert Lowther,[21] Andrew Davisson, Tegal and Arthur Trader,[22] Abraham Sisco,[23] and Nathaniel Springer,[24] who located here around 1770. Jacob Polsley married Margaret, daughter of William Haymond, Jr., and acquired part of the Trader tract after 1790.[25]

**The First Dentist.** The earliest notice seen of a dentist practicing in Morgantown is the following: "DENTISTRY. Dr. Gibbs will remain a short time in Morgantown, and offers his professional services to its inhabitants and to those of its vicinity. He will perform all the operations in the line of his profession, with *neatness and durability*, all of which will be warranted. An early application is requested. His residence is at Mrs. Jarrett's."[26]

Dentistry, during this period, was undergoing transformation from an unimportant, often despised, occupation, into an

Fig. 24. Claudius Crozet. (From an old print.)        print.)

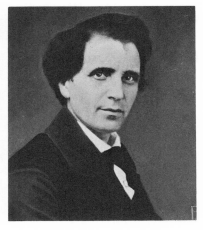

Fig. 25. Simon P. Hullihen. (Courtesy, School of Dentistry, West Virginia University.)

20. *The Monongalia Story*, vol. 2, pp. 133, 326, 450, 456, 485, 494.
21. *The Monongalia Story*, vol. 1, p. 181.
22. *The Monongalia Story*, vol. 1, p. 230.
23. Lough, *Now and Long Ago*, p. 121.
24. *The Monongalia Story*, vol. 1, pp. 130, 215.
25. Lough, op. cit., p. 433.
26. The *Republican*, September 1, 1838.

essential and honored portion of the health professions. It is interesting to note that a good part of the change was brought about by a dentist from the neighboring town of Wheeling, Dr. Simon P. Hullihen (1810-1857), regarded as the founder of modern oral surgery (Fig. 25).[27]

**The Willyard Hollow.** George and Elizabeth Willyard (Williard, Willard) in 1838 were living in a small ravine, a branch of Dolls Run near the residence of Michael Core. The family name was Vieillard originally, derived from the name of a French village called Vieillar. Nicholaus Vieillard joined the Huguenot migrations and moved to Otterberg, Germany, about 1655. One of his children, Jakob (born September 15, 1667) had a son Dewald (1711-1781), who married Anna Katherine Kirch; he and his wife came to Philadelphia in 1750. One of their children was George, who came to Monongalia County. He was born about 1765 and married a widow, Elizabeth (Hume) Ghanz.

George and Elizabeth Willyard (Williard) had seven children, namely, George, Jr. (married Sudna Lowther), Elias (his wife's name was Jane), Jakob (went to California in the gold rush), Dorothea, Isaac (married Catherine ———), Elizabeth (married William Shanks), and Charlotte (married Archibald Lowther).[28]

**Land Grants Made in 1838.** Monongalia County grantees in 1838 included:

| | | |
|---|---|---|
| Alton, Joseph | 190 a. | Paw Paw Creek |
| Ammons, Joshua | 90 | Days Run |
| Banack, Henry | 40 | Paw Paw Creek |
| Barnett, Solomon | 100 | Plum Run |
| Boggess, Henry | 180 | Indian Creek |
| Brookover, Abraham | 400 | Miracle Run |
| Brookover, John | 1¾ | Dunkard Creek |
| Corbley, Andrew | 25 | Dunkard Creek |
| Corbley, Andrew | 100 | Dunkard Creek |
| Cox, Moses | 1½ | Adj. Geo. Gallaspie |
| Dunlapp, Andrew | 120 | Waters Cheat R. |

27. A Simon P. Hullihen Memorial Award and Lecture is sponsored annually by West Virginia University. For biography of Dr. Hullihen, see Robert L. Murphy, "Father of Oral Surgery," *West Virginia University* magazine, Spring, 1977; editorial by D. M. Laskin in *Jour. Oral Surg.*, July 1973; see also *Wheeling Hospital News Bulletin*, November, 1976.

28. Core, *Chronicles of Core*, pp. 68, 69; pers. comm., McKinley Willard.

| | | |
|---|---|---|
| Dunn, Thomas | 75 | Waters Cheat R. |
| Dunn, Thomas | 162 | Lick Run |
| Eddy, Michael, Jr. | 60 | Lit. Paw Paw Creek |
| Evans, James | 130 | Plum Run |
| Fetty, John | 200 | Paw Paw Creek |
| Fluharty, William | 200 | Indian Fork |
| Fogle, Henry | 150 | Papaw Creek |
| Freeland, Elija | 100 | Piles Fork |
| Freeland, John | 160 | Piles Fork |
| Freeland, Stephen | 156 | Buffalo Creek |
| Furbee, Caleb | 94 | Piles Fork |
| Furbee, Caleb, Jr. | 185 | Piles Fork |
| Glover, William | 127 | Dunkard Creek |
| Haines, Abraham | 50 | Dudleys Fork |
| Hanway, John | 450 | Adj. John Ogden |
| Hanway, John | 300 | Adj. David Piles |
| Hanway, John | 60 | Dunkard Creek |
| Hanway, John | 600 | Three Forks Creek |
| Hanway, John | 400 | Three Forks Creek |
| Hanway, John | 90 | Drakes Run |
| Haught, Joseph | 200 | Miracle Run |
| Haynes, Abraham | 97 | Flat Run |
| Haynes, John | 150 | Piles Fork |
| Hixenbaugh, George, Sr. | 50 | Adj. A. Hixenbaugh |
| Holland, William | 6½ | Toms Run |
| Hughs, William | 150 | Johnnycake Run |
| Johnson, Henry | 100 | Adj. Levi Kelly |
| Johnson, Henry H. | 60 | Plum Run |
| Joliffe, Amos | 100 | Booths Creek |
| Jones, James | 18 | Pawpaw Creek |
| Jones, William | 150 | Papaw Creek |
| Kelley, Levi | 100 | Mods Run |
| Lantz, Lot | 1,000 | Miracles Run |
| Lantz, Lot | 115 | Dunkard Creek |
| Layton, Peter | 90 | Drakes Run |
| Leggit, Isaac | 45 | Indian Creek |
| Lemasters, Shelton | 140 | Mahons Run |
| Lemley, George | 110 | Dunkard Creek |
| Lemley, George | 66 | Adj. Wm. Cotton |
| Marple, Ezekiel K. | 100 | Coburns Creek |

| Martin, Thomas | 46 | Flat Run |
|---|---|---|
| McDaniel, Nancy | 8½ | Flat Run |
| Meredith, William | 5 | Little Creek |
| Minor, Samuel | 33 | Dunkard Creek |
| Moore, Jacob | 134½ | Statelers Run |
| Moore, Philip | 48 | Statelers Run |
| Murphey, Marshall | 100 | Adj. Wm. Poe |
| Parks, Joseph | 100 | Days Run |
| Poe, James A. | 190 | Wickwires Creek |
| Poe, Jonathan | 90 | Wickwires Creek |
| Poe, Stephen | 90 | Wickwires Creek |
| Poe, William G. | 75 | Wickwires Creek |
| Price, John | 13 | Paw Paw Creek |
| Price, John | 20 | Adj. Thomas Pindell |
| Price, William | 150 | Statlers Run |
| Price, William | 37 | Statlers Run |
| Ray, Thomas P. | 600 | Three Forks Creek |
| Ray, Thomas P. | 400 | Three Forks Creek |
| Rose, Thomas | 100 | Dunkard Creek |
| Santee, Samuel | 178 | Adj. Moses Matheny |
| Shriver, James | 129 | Dunkard Creek |
| Smith, George | 33 | Adj. Amos Smith |
| Talkington, Alexander | 250 | Mohones Run |
| Tennant, Richard B. | 44 | Statlers Run |
| Thomas, Isaac | 25 | Flat Run |
| Trippett, Topliff | 200 | Dunkard Creek |
| Wade, Alexander | 200 | Dunkard Creek |
| Wade, Hosea | 6 | Scotts Run |
| Watson, James O. | 250 | Dunkard Creek |
| Watson, John P. | 5½ | Corner to Cunningham |
| Whetsel, John | 450 | Sugar Camp Run |
| White, James G. | 200 | Joys Run |
| White, William | 125 | Dunkard Creek |
| Williams, James, Jr. | 170 | Three Forks Creek |
| Wilson, Levin | 60 | Adj. Henry Fogle |
| Wilson, William | 124 | Robinsons Run |
| Wise, Levi | 175 | Dunkard Creek |
| Yost, Aaron | 300 | Mud Run |
| Youst, John | 52 | Lick Run |
| Youst, Jehu D. | 136 | Corner S. Canby |
| Youst, Nicholas | 239 | Papaw Creek |

**County Government.** John Nuzum was sworn in as sheriff on March 26, 1838. As commissioners of the revenue Seth Stafford was sworn in for the Eastern District and George Dawson for the Western District. The county levy was $0.85.

**Miscellany.** In 1838: The Redstone Presbytery met in Morgantown on October 2 (Wiley, p. 447). . . . The Steamboat *Shannon* arrived at the port of Morgantown in March (Wiley, p. 542). . . . Camilla, wife of Evan Morgan, died on June 2, aged seventy-one years (Wiley, p. 633). . . . Elisha, son of John Snider, died (Wiley, p. 697). . . . Horatio Morgan conveyed a portion of Lot 114 in Morgantown to Zackquill Morgan III; Lot 116 was conveyed by Nicholas and Susannah Madera to Francis Madera (Callahan, pp. 66, 328). . . . Anna Madera, widow of Christian Madera, died (Callahan, pp. 88, 236). . . . James Kern, wishing to move west, offered his hat store for sale (Callahan, p. 129). . . . Patrick D. Shehen in May conveyed the southern part of Lot 6 in Morgantown to William Snider (Callahan, p. 309). . . . For the widening of Plum Alley (Foundry Street) John Rogers in October conveyed to the borough a strip of Lot 35, and of the unnumbered lot west of it, in return for which the borough later conveyed to him all of Long Alley south of Plum Alley (Callahan, p. 315). . . . The northern half of Lot 88 was conveyed, for $1,075, by James Johnson to George D. Evans and John F. Dering (Callahan, p. 321). . . . Lot 96 was conveyed by Norval Wilson to John Mills (Callahan, p. 323). . . . Stephen Morgan bought four lots in the newly laid out town of Newport[29] (Lough, p. 544). . . . Solomon Holland sold Lot 38 in Middletown on June 20 to Hiram Haymond and James O. Watson for $400 (Lough, p. 423). . . . On March 5 an act was passed by the general assembly declaring Dunkard Creek a public highway and directing the owners of dams to construct slopes and draw gates, the specifications of which were included in the act (*Chronicles of Core*, p. 70). . . . The summer was very dry and the Monongahela River at Morgantown could be crossed dry-shod (Owens, p. 36).

29. Later Catawba.

CHAPTER SIXTY-THREE

# 1839

The basic occupation of residents of Monongalia County during the 1830s continued to be agriculture. The county was nearly self-sufficient, so far as the production of food was concerned. But by the end of the fourth decade of the nineteenth century, industry was producing in the Monongahela Valley many of the articles needed by the residents, saving the long haul by wagons across the mountains.

**Early Industries.** Even before the end of the pioneer period, primitive industries were established to serve the population and several of these were dealt with in early volumes of this series. Among these were boatyards (*Monongalia Story*, vol. 1, p. 213; vol. 2, pp. 180-82), gristmills (*Monongalia Story*, vol. 2, pp. 147-50), potteries (*Monongalia Story*, vol. 2, pp. 127-30), distilleries (*Monongalia Story*, vol. 2, pp. 177-79), tanneries (*Monongalia Story*, vol. 2, pp. 193-95), iron furnaces (*Monongalia Story*, vol. 2, pp. 265-69, 289-92), nail works (*Monongalia Story*, vol. 2, pp. 290-92), wagon works (*Monongalia Story*, vol. 2, pp. 302-5), cooper shops (*Monongalia Story*, vol. 2, pp. 314-16), print shops (*Monongalia Story*, vol. 2, p. 317), gunsmiths (*Monongalia Story*, vol. 2, pp. 360, 361), saddlers (*Monongalia Story*, vol. 2, pp. 432-34), carding mills (*Monongalia Story*, vol. 2, pp. 507-9), and so on.

**Industries of the 1830s.** Most of these industries continued into the 1830s and beyond, and new industries were being developed. Callahan notes that several hatters were in business in Morgantown in the thirties. "In September, 1837, A. S. Vance, the hatter, advertised a runaway indented apprentice. . . . In June, 1838 Joseph Kern, wishing to move to the west, advertised a hat store for sale. In May 1839 Berkshire and Baker were engaged in tailoring, in an up-stairs shop, 'three doors west of William Lazier's new building'. In March 1839, J. W. Saer was making part of the boots and shoes which he sold."[1]

John W. Thompson had been in the pottery business since at least 1814 on Lot 88 in Morgantown and about 1830 installed steam machinery to replace his old shop, which had been destroyed by fire (see p. 51). He also operated a pottery on Lot 7. Several tanneries were being operated in Morgantown and at various other places in the county, including Stewartstown, Middletown, and in the Dunkard Creek neighborhood.

The first foundry in Morgantown, so far as known, was built about 1838 by Joel Nuzum and Henry and Hugh Daugherty (see p. 168). It was located on the east side of Long Alley (now Chestnut Street) at the corner with Plum Alley (now Foundry Street). Stoves, grates, and various other household and farm articles were manufactured by the early foundries.

David Baldwin, as early as April 1837, was manufacturing plows two miles north of Morgantown, and in April 1839 L. G. Robinson was advertising an "iron store" in the High Street house formerly occupied by James Chadwick's store, at the corner of Maiden Alley (now Wall Street). T. Jones and Company announced the opening of an iron store in August 1837.

Blacksmithing was an important trade in every section of the county. Zackwell Morgan, grandson of the founder of the town, was operating a shop in Morgantown in the thirties. Shops were conveniently located and prices were reasonable. An old invoice records that there was charged for "the removing of one pare of old shews, 12 cents; making and driving one pare of shews, 25 cents."

Robert P. Hennen was one of the first cabinetmakers in Morgantown, beginning the manufacture of high grade furniture on Lot 9 on Front Street in 1831. The business had a steadily growing reputation and remained under the management of the family for three-quarters of a century.

Wagon making for local needs had been started in Morgantown as early as 1802 by John Shisler, who later associated his son Michael with him in the business, located on the river bank

1. Callahan, *Making of Morgantown*, p. 129 note.

Fig. 26. A blacksmith shop. (Sketch by Diane Lenhart.)

at the end of Pleasant Street. In 1832 he secured as an apprentice James Kern, who built the first buggy in the county in 1841.

**John Rogers.** One of the leading businessmen of Morgantown in the thirties was John Rogers. He bought the property of Michael Kern along Deckers Creek in 1816 and after 1823 he and three nephews, Thomas, Jacob, and James Rogers, operated not only a water-powered gristmill but also a paper mill (at the Hogback) and a sawmill (at the foot of High Street). In June 1837 he leased a new sawmill at the mouth of Deckers Creek to Samuel R. Dillner. He also operated a carding mill, which he leased, in May 1838 to Charles Wolverton. At that time wool carding was also being done at Guseman's mill, four miles up Deckers Creek, and at Thorn's mill, one mile below Morgantown, on the river.

In 1839 Rogers built, at a cost of six thousand dollars, a large four-story stone building along Deckers Creek for papermaking. Known as the Live Oak Paper Mill, it was leased to Tillton and Crowl, who began paper manufacture on September 2 of that year.

Meanwhile Rogers acquired town lots in Morgantown, in addition to the Kern tract across Deckers Creek. He secured the property along the Creek west of High Street and south of Plum Alley to the covered bridge across Deckers Creek, near Front Street. He also bought Lots 32, 33, and 34, north of Plum Alley between High Street and Long Alley, later conveyed to the trustees of the Morgantown Female Academy.

**The Cheat Iron Works.** The iron industry continued to be the county's most important manufacturing enterprise. Most of this activity was to the east of Cheat River, in the Cheat Neck Community and on the slopes of Chestnut Ridge. The Jackson family, which had been the principal developer of the industry, sold its interests to Evan T. Ellicott and Brothers on April 22, 1839, and they continued the operations for about a decade, adding a rolling mill, a puddling and boiling furnace, a nail factory (Joshua Swindler was the first nail maker), a foundry, machine, wagon and blacksmith shops, and a large number of dwelling houses. By 1840 Morgantown was beginning to feel the prosperity of the Cheat industry, said to have supported a village of about seven hundred people at Cheat Neck at that time.

**Prices of farm products.** Although agriculture was the principal occupation of the people, prices were low and very few products were shipped out of the county. The table on page 181 gives prices of farm products on January 1 of each year (except 1828), from 1827 to 1839.[2]

**Turnpike Days.** Stimulated by the brilliant success of the National Road, completed to the Monongahela River in 1818, and to a smaller degree by the less dramatic Northwestern Turnpike, completed to the Tygart Valley River by 1835, the people of the Monongahela Valley during the thirties and forties engaged in a tremendous flurry of "turnpike" building. Strictly speaking, a turnpike road is one that has turnpikes, or tollgates, established by law at regular points to collect tolls from the users to defray the cost of construction, maintenance, etc. Actually, these turnpikes (usually shortened to "pikes"), seldom collected enough revenue to provide for operation and repair, to say nothing of the original cost. But carrying out of the conception, haphazard and faltering though it was, did contribute measurably to the improvement of transportation facilities in the Monongahela Valley, including Monongalia County.

The sale of lottery tickets seemed the easiest way to raise money for the construction of roads. Unfortunately, although many lotteries were authorized by the general assembly, few were very successful.

The two decades following 1830 might be referred to in Monongalia County annals as the "Age of Turnpikes."

**The Morgantown and Beverly Turnpike.** On February 29, 1832, an act of the general assembly was passed authorizing commissioners "to raise by way of lottery or lotteries, any sum of money not exceeding forty thousand dollars, which shall be applied to the purposes of opening and constructing a road from Beverly, in the county of Randolph, to Morgantown, in the county of Monongalia." This road connecting the county seats of Randolph and Monongalia counties, passed through the

2. Wiley, p. 249.

| Year | Eggs per doz. | Butter per lb. | Beef per lb. | Bacon per lb. | Potatoes per bu. | Buckwheat per bu. | Rye per bu. | Oats per bu. | Corn per bu. | Wheat per bu. |
|---|---|---|---|---|---|---|---|---|---|---|
| 1827 | $0.06 | $0.08 | $0.02 | $0.02 | | $0.25 | $0.33 | $0.16 | $0.25 | $0.40 |
| 1828 | | | | | | | | | | |
| 1829 | | .08 | .02 1/2 | .02 1/2 | | | .37 | .20 | .31 | .75 |
| 1830 | | .08 1/3 | .02 1/2 | .03 | | | .33 | .25 | .25 | .50 |
| 1831 | | .08 1/3 | .02 | .02 1/2 | | | .33 | .18 | .31 | .44 |
| 1832 | | .08 | .02 1/2 | .03 | | | .37 | .20 | .31 | .62 |
| 1833 | | .08 | .02 1/2 | .02 3/4 | | | .33 | .20 | .25 | .62 |
| 1834 | | .08 | .02 1/2 | .03 | | | .40 | .20 | .37 | .62 |
| 1835 | | .10 | .03 | .03 1/2 | | | .33 | .16 | .31 | .62 |
| 1836 | | .10 | .03 | .04 1/2 | .25 | | .50 | .25 | .37 | .87 |
| 1837 | | .12 1/2 | .04 | .05 1/2 | .75 | | .50 | .25 | .40 | 1.10 |
| 1838 | | .12 1/2 | | .04 | | | | .25 | .50 | 1.00 |
| 1839 | | .15 | | | | | .75 | .50 | .75 | 1.00 |

Fig. 27. Toll station on a turnpike road. (Sketch by Diane Lenhart.)

town of Evansville, on the Northwestern Turnpike, and was known locally as the Evansville Pike.

Specifications of the Beverly Road were set forth as follows: "The road is to be graded according to the location—clear, uniform and smooth, sixteen feet wide . . .—the side banks must be at an angle of 45 degrees except when solid rock is to be removed—the timber is to be cut at least ten feet on each side of the road—culverts and brakes are to be made where specified on each contract. . . ."[3]

**The Brandonville and Fishing Creek Turnpike.** On March 15, 1836, the general assembly authorized "Presly Martin of the county of Tyler, Thomas P. Ray and Richard Watts of the county of Monongalia, and Harrison Hagan, of the county of Preston . . . to superintend and direct the construction of a road from the Ohio river at the mouth of Fishing Creek in the county of Tyler, by way of Morgantown in the county of Monongalia, and Brandonville in the county of Preston, to the state line in the direction of Smithfield on the National Road. . . . The said road shall be cleared at least thirty feet wide, and shall be improved and made suitable for the passage of wagons and other wheeled carriages, for a space of not less than fifteen feet wide throughout the whole extent." The directors were authorized, when a twenty-mile section of the road was completed, "to erect a toll gate or gates on some suitable point or points of such section, and to demand and receive thereat a tariff of tolls not exceeding the rate of tolls now authorized by law on an equal section of the North-western Turnpike." This road was designed to carry traffic from the National Road near Smithfield (later called Somerfield), Pennsylvania, through Brandonville and Morgantown to the mouth of Fishing Creek at the site of New Martinsville (established 1838 and named for Presley Martin, son of Charles Martin, the builder of Fort Martin).

The road ran from the Pennsylvania line past Brandonville to Ice's Ferry, thence to Morgantown, crossing the river there and thence via Laurel Point to Middletown, thence up Buffalo Creek and down Fishing Creek to the Ohio River. It was mostly built between 1836 and 1839.

3. The *Republican*, June 16, 1838.

**The Brandonville, Kingwood, and Evansville Turnpike.** A similar road, entirely in Preston County, was authorized March 13, 1837, "from some point on the Pennsylvania line, in Preston County, by Brandonville and Kingwood, to some point of the North-western turnpike at or near Evansville." This road, the "Brandonville, Kingwood and Evansville turnpike," when finally completed, connected the National Road with the Northwestern Turnpike by way of Kingwood.

In the same year, on March 30, an act had provided for the construction of a road, the Morgantown and Clarksburg Turnpike, from the Pennsylvania line, in Monongalia County, via Ice's Ferry, past Smithtown to Clarksburg.

And, also in the same year, the assembly incorporated the Pennsylvania, Morgantown, and Beverly Turnpike to run from the Pennsylvania line near Fort Martin, crossing the Monongahela River at Collins Ferry, thence via Morgantown to Evansville and Beverly.

**A Turnpike to Wheeling.** To connect the Northwestern Turnpike with Wheeling, a road was authorized April 6, 1838, "from the North-western turnpike at the Tygart's Valley bridge, by way of Middletown, to Wheeling." Commissioners named to secure subscriptions were Thomas Barnes, John S. Smith, Job Springer, C. C. Vanzant, John S. Barnes, and Matthew Fleming. The road would not have to be paved or covered with stone or gravel, but it was to "be cleared thirty feet wide, and be improved for a width of eighteen feet, except at difficult places, but shall no where be less than twelve feet wide, and shall not exceed a grade of four degrees."

**The Dunkard Creek Turnpike.** The road to Fishing Creek not having fully materialized, the general assembly, on February 1, 1839, authorized the "Dunkard Creek turnpike company" to construct "a turnpike road from the mouth of Scott's run, in Monongalia County, by way of the valley of Dunkard Creek, to intersect the Middletown and Wheeling turnpike, at some suitable point." Books for receiving subscriptions were authorized up to fifteen thousand dollars, in shares of twenty dollars each. The books were to be opened at Blacksville, under the direction of Andrew Brown, Samuel Minor, John Hood, William Thomas, and Thomas P. Ray. It was provided, further, that the turnpike company "shall not be required to make a summer road or side road to their said turnpike, nor to cover it with stone or gravel; and that said turnpike shall be made sixteen feet wide, and at a grade no where exceeding four degrees."

The Morgantown and Clarksburg Turnpike Company, incorporated in 1839, was formed to build a road by way of Morgantown and Ice's Ferry to the Pennsylvania line. Nothing was done beyond locating the road.

It could not be said that any of these projects, from the viewpoint of what had been envisioned, were actually completed. The lotteries did not raise enough money and people who were invited to buy stock in a company whose future was dubious were not inclined to invest. On many of the projects, however, some improvement of the roads was made, with the result that by 1840 wagon traffic throughout Monongalia County and to the main roads on the north and south moved satisfactorily, at least in good weather.

Bridge contracts for highways, awarded in 1838 and paid by the county court in 1839, included one over Flaggy Meadow Run, for $199.93; Scotts Mill Run, $550; and Buffaloe Creek, $2,550.

Commissioners William Thomas, William Price, and S. Lemley met at Statler Town on January 26 to award a contract for a bridge over Dunkard Creek at that point.[4]

**Arrivals and Departures of the Mails.** A schedule of mail service for Morgantown in 1839 appeared as follows:

"Eastern Mail will arrive on Saturday evening—departs for Clarksburg on Sunday morning.

"Clarksburg mail arrives on Sunday evening—departs for Uniontown on Monday morning.

"Eastern mail arrives on Tuesday evening—departs for Clarksburg on Wednesday morning.

"Clarksburg mail arrives on Thursday evening—departs for Uniontown on Friday morning.

"Wheeling Mail leaves on Monday morning—arrives on Thursday evening."[5]

**The Female Academy.** The new Morgantown Female Collegiate Institute, incorporated January 30, 1839, was proceeding to

4. The *Republican*, January 26, 1839.
5. The *Republican*, February 16, 1839.

develop with greater vigor the property set aside by the Monongalia Academy for the use of females, at the corner of Bumbo Lane and Long Alley.[6]

Lot 113, the east one-third, on which the school building was constructed, was conveyed by Elizabeth Morgan to the academy in December 1832, and her heirs later conveyed the remainder of the lot. The portion of Lot 114 adjoining the academy was sold by Horatio Morgan to the academy in April 1839 and eventually all of Lot 114 also became property of the academy.[7]

Miss E. Doggett was appointed principal in 1839.[8]

**Morgantown Churches in the 1830s.** Three churches stood within the borough limits of Morgantown during the 1830s.

The Methodist Episcopal Church was built in 1819, on Pleasant Street at the corner of Long Alley (*Monongalia Story*, vol. 2, pp. 446, 447). From 1825, the church was served by ministers of the Monongalia Circuit, Pittsburgh Conference (see p. 68).

In 1833 Morgantown became a station, with its own ministers; those who served, for the next few years, were:[9]

1833. James Drummond.[10]

1834. J. Mills.

1835-36. G. S. Holmes.

1837. H. Gilmore.

1838. T. Stinchcomb.

1839. J. Spencer.

Members of the Presbyterian church, in connection with members of the Protestant Episcopal Church, also began the construction of a building in 1819 (*Monongalia Story*, vol. 2, pp. 447-49) and got the walls up and the roof on, but then ran out of money and the project lapsed for a year or two. Then the women took up the enterprise, worked up wool and flax into

6. Wiley, p. 398.
7. Callahan, *Making of Morgantown*, pp. 327, 328.
8. Wiley, p. 399.
9. Wiley, p. 590.
10. James Drummond was born in Manchester, England, May 19, 1804, and died at Cadiz, Ohio, May 7, 1888. He was a brother of Thomas Drummond (p. 336). "He was truly a great man; a mighty preacher of the gospel, and a walking cyclopedia of poetry, history and Scripture." George Cleaton Wilding, *Promoted Pioneer Preachers* (1927), p. 118.

cloth, and from its sale realized one thousand dollars, which, with a gift of one hundred dollars, was sufficient to finish the church. This building was on High Street at the corner of Kirk Alley.[11]

The Reverend Ashbel Green Fairchild served as minister from 1817 until 1827, when he resigned to go to Fairchance, Pennsylvania. He had a broad education, spoke eight languages, and wrote several books. His religious fervor and pleasant manner made him much loved. He did not lose contact with Morgantown, for his son and daughter continued to live here; his son, Ashbel, was a wagon manufacturer, and his daughter, Anna, married attorney Lycurgus S. Hough.[12]

From the departure of the Rev. Mr. Fairchild, in 1827, until the coming of Rev. James McDougal, in 1834, the church was without a regular pastor. Several persons served for short periods as supply ministers or "missionaries."

Rev. Richard Armstrong was one of these. The son of James Armstrong, he was born in Pennsylvania April 13, 1805, graduated from Dickinson College and Princeton Theological Seminary, and married Clarissa Chapman. He was in Morgantown from 1827 until 1831, during which time he established the first Sunday school in the county, a union school. In 1831 he sailed as a missionary to the Marquesas and Hawaiian Islands, eventually serving as Minister of Public Instruction for the Hawaiian government until his death on September 23, 1860.[13]

The Reverend Joel Stoneroad, son of Lewis and Sarah Gardner Stoneroad, was born in Mifflin County, Pennsylvania, January 2, 1806. He graduated from Princeton Theological Seminary and served the Morgantown church as a missionary in 1830 and 1831.[14]

The Reverend Rezin Brown preached here in 1831 (see p. 109), and made a deep impression on the community in his brief stay, as is indicated by the fact that the Presbyterian church at Stewartstown was called "Brown's Chapel."[15]

11. Wiley, p. 591.
12. For biography, see James R. Moreland, *The First Presbyterian Church* . . ., pp. 45-48.
13. See biography in Moreland, pp. 48, 49.
14. For biography, see Moreland, p. 49.
15. Moreland, op. cit., pp. 49, 50.

Rev. Thomas Martin was born in County Down, Ireland, on December 16, 1804. He graduated from Belfast College and Princeton Theological Seminary and became principal of Monongalia Academy in 1833. For the next three years, even after leaving Morgantown, he served as stated supply.[16]

James McDougal was the next pastor, serving from 1834 to 1836. He was born in Newark, New Jersey, March 16, 1805, and graduated from Princeton. He preached half time at Morgantown, the other half at Stewartstown and Sandy. He resigned in 1836, "convinced that Presbyterianism could never flourish in such uncongenial soil." He was married to Julia Kitchell.[17]

James Davis filled the pulpit for about a year, beginning in 1837, and then became the regular pastor. He was the son of Rev. Thomas and Hannah Gilley Davis and was born in Pittsburgh October 28, 1808. He graduated from Western Theological Seminary in 1837. His pastorate lasted eighteen years, during which time the church steadily increased in strength and numbers.[18]

The Methodist Protestant congregation was organized in Morgantown in 1830 and for over ten years met in various places, including the old stone house on Long Alley (see p. 107).

Ministers serving the congregation for its first decade were:[19]

1830. John Lucas, William Dunlavy

1831. William Collins

1832. Israel Throp, Daniel Kinney

1833. James Piper, William Menhall

1834. James Hopwood

1835. Zachariah Regan

1836. James Palfreyman, William Dunlap

**Zion Methodist Church is Built.** To serve the population of the town along Cheat River at Ellicott's Iron Works, a new church building was constructed in 1839, by members of the Methodist Protestant and Methodist Episcopal churches jointly. The building stood on a low hill overlooking the town and the river.

16. For biography, see Moreland, op. cit., p. 50.
17. For biography, see Moreland, op. cit., p. 50.
18. For biography, see Moreland, op. cit., pp. 50, 51.
19. Wiley, pp. 593, 594.

Fig. 28. The Zion Methodist Church. (Photo Dr. and Mrs. Gideon S. Dodds.)

A Methodist Protestant congregation had been organized here in 1833 by Rev. Valentine Lucas in the home of Jacob Smith; Asby Poole and Joseph Shackelford were ministers assisting. The first steward of the class, William Donaldson, attended the first quarterly meeting in Fairmont on November 16, 1833.[20]

**The Democratic Republican Passes Away.** One more local weekly newspaper came to an end during 1839. The *Democratic Republican* had been started in 1835 by Enos D. Morgan. In April 1839 the paper moved to "the room directly over Mr. Willey's Law Office, on the public square."[21] The issue for April 13 was skipped on account of the move. Scattered issues (some titled only, *The Republican*) are found in the West Virginia University Library, but the last paper seen was dated May 18, 1839 (see p. 129).

20. Dodds and Dodds, *Churches of Monongalia County*, p. 153; Barnes, *M. P. Church*, pp. 123, 124; "An old lady still living in the community told the writer she had seen Samuel Clawson jump over the pulpit during a great meeting there. Dr. George Westfall had a notable meeting here in 1858, at which Uncle Jack Baker is said to have reached the high water mark in Methodist shouting."
21. The *Republican*, April 20, 1839.

**Elijah Hartley Settles on the Head of Dunkard.** Elijah Hartley, a graduate of Shelbyville Academy, Shelbyville, Indiana, located in western Monongalia County in 1839 to pursue the career of teaching.

He was a son of Rodger and Judah (Cross) Hartley and was born at Newtown, Greene County, Pennsylvania, January 18, 1815. He was of English-Quaker descent, his grandfather, Mahlon, a native of Philadelphia, having migrated to Greene County in 1797.

At Shelbyville Elijah was a classmate of Thomas Andrews Hendricks, who was elected vice-president of the United States in 1884. Elijah's first teaching position was in Muskingum County, Ohio, where he taught three terms, then two terms in Allegheny County, Pennsylvania, before coming to the head of Dunkard Creek to spend the remainder of his life.[22]

**Alexander Smith.** A remarkable frontiersman who indirectly played a prominent role in the history of Morgantown, Alexander Smith, died in March 1839. Born in Scotland, he emigrated to America, settling first at Georgetown, Maryland, where he married Volinder Suter. In 1794 he moved to the upper Potomac crossing of the old Winchester-to-Morgantown wagon road, where he entertained many people traveling to and from Monongalia County.

His family, of one son and nine daughters, was well educated, some of them talented musicians. It is said that he brought the first piano over the Alleghenies to his farm mansion. Six of his daughters later resided in Morgantown, namely, Janette (married Thomas P. Ray), Margaret (married Mathew Gay), Delia (married Hannibal Pugh), Ann Amelia (married Dr. Adam F. Hornback), Isabella (married James Caldwell), and Eleanor (married Thomas Brown).[23]

**The Old Market House is Sold.** On May 15, 1839, the old market house was ordered sold by the trustees. From pioneer days this had been the site to which farmers brought produce to sell to townspeople (*Monongalia Story*, vol. 2, p. 377). Certain days were specified as market days and the hours were specified,

22. *Cyclopedia of Monongalia County*, pp. 219, 220.
23. Callahan, p. 91.

usually from daylight to 10:00 a.m. The long frame building stood along High Street, on the public square.[24]

**Bank Directors Picked.** Directors of the Morgantown branch of the Merchants' and Mechanics' Bank of Wheeling for 1839 were announced as Thomas P. Ray, William Lazier, Edgar C. Wilson, William M. Dering, Mathew Gay, John Hanway, and Fielding Kiger.[25]

**John McFarland Dies.** John McFarland, a pioneer settler of the Stewartstown section, died October 11, 1839, aged ninety years. He was living along Cheat River as early as 1771 (see *Monongalia Story*, vol. 1, p. 188) and was a charter member of the Forks of Cheat Baptist Church (*Monongalia Story*, vol. 1, p. 311).

Traveling over an old packhorse road that crossed the mountains near Wimps Gap, came down Rubles Run and crossed Cheat River at Pack Horse Riffle, McFarland "operated a pack horse train of twelve horses himself and each horse had around its neck a bell which was stopped up with leaves or moss through the day but left open when he camped at night, so that the horses could be easily found or when he was nearing his home so that the home folks might know that he was coming. On these pack horses was loaded salt, sugar, coffee and other articles not raised by the early settlers."[26]

In 1823 McFarland, along with William John, Samuel Bowen, and Richard Cain, hewed logs for a new church building twenty-two by twenty-six feet and twelve rounds high, built near the old church.[27]

**Land Grants Made in 1839.**[28] Monongalia County grantees in 1839 included:

| | | |
|---|---|---|
| Tower, Edwin W. | 200 a. | Buffalo Creek |
| Yager, Peter | 8 | Dunkard Creek |

24. Wiley, p. 604; Callahan, *Making of Morgantown*, p. 137.
25. The *Republican*, January 19, 1839.
26. Weltner and Jeffries, (Colebank), *The Stewartstown Story*, p. 13.
27. Op. cit., p. 11.
28. See p. 11.

**County Government.** John Nuzum was sworn in for his second term as sheriff on March 25, 1839. The county levy was $0.75. The county was authorized by the general assembly to borrow $10,000 to build bridges and to aid internal improvements.

**Miscellany.** In 1839: On January 17, Thomas P. Ray was elected president of the Merchants' and Mechanics' Bank (Wiley, p. 462). . . . Johns and Evans were proprietors of a store at Stewartstown (Wiley, p. 673). . . . John Hood, with William Launtz, was operating a store at Blacksville (Wiley, p. 723). . . . Lot 117 in Morgantown was conveyed by Horatio Morgan to Thomas Meredith (Callahan, p. 66). . . . Volunteer firemen were provided with ladders and hooks by borough trustees in an effort to control fires in the town (Callahan, p. 127). . . . The Presbyterians repaired their dilapidated old church building, at a cost of $700 (Callahan, p. 154). . . . Lot 45 was conveyed to Charles McLane (Callahan, p. 317). . . . Part of Lot 53, west of Rogers' mill road, was conveyed to George D. Evans (Callahan, p. 318). . . . Part of Lot 86 was sold by Frederick A. Werninger, son of A. F. Werninger, to James Chadwick, for $500 (Callahan, p. 321). . . . Lot 100 was conveyed by James F. Tibbs to Joel Nuzum (Callahan, p. 324). . . . A portion of the former public square was sold by Thomas P. Ray in February to William Lazier for $4,600 (Callahan, p. 330). . . . John S. Barns bought Lot 43 in Middletown from Michael Carney for $350 and James Kerns bought Lot 50 and part of Lot 49 from Cornelius C. Vanzant for $50; these lots were on Madison Street, near the bridge (Lough, p. 424).

# CHAPTER SIXTY-FOUR

# 1840

Hu Maxwell estimated the population of Monongalia County as 5,580 at the time of its establishment in 1776 (*Monongalia Story*, vol. 2, p. 62). The area at the time of its greatest extent, in 1780, was about 8,485 square miles, which was reduced to 1,325 square miles by the creation of Harrison County in 1784.

The first census, in 1790, gave Monongalia County 4,768 people, and the second census, in 1800, reported 8,540 inhabitants, an increase of 79 percent. Another sizable increase, of 50 percent, was registered by the third census, in 1810, when the count was 12,793.

A decrease was noted in the fourth census, in 1820, but this was occasioned by the formation of Preston County in 1818, whereby the area of Monongalia County was reduced from 1,325 square miles to only 700 square miles. Actually, when Monongalia's 1820 population of 11,060 is added to Preston's 3,422, we get a total of 14,482 people for the area in which 12,793 lived in 1810, a gain of 1,689.

The fifth census, in 1830, gave Monongalia County a population of 14,056, an increase of 36 percent. Thus we might conclude that by 1840, the county, now sixty-four years old, had shown a steady increase in population throughout its entire history, although at a gradually reduced rate.

In 1810 Monongalia County was the most populous of the sixteen counties then in existence in the area later to become West Virginia. By 1820 this rating had been transferred to Jefferson County, although, had Monongalia and Preston been counted together, as in 1810, the largest population was still recorded here.

By 1830, however, the effects of the construction of the National Road were showing, and Ohio County, with 15,584 inhabitants, was the leading county in western Virginia, with Harrison County (14,722 people) second and Monongalia County a close third.

**The Sixth Census.** The sixth census, in 1840, gave Monongalia County a population of 17,368, a 24 percent increase over the 14,056 reported ten years earlier. Although the frontier had by now moved on much farther to the west, and the great wave of population growth had subsided, there was still much unused land here and new settlers continued to arrive.

The 1840 census showed Monongalia County still third in rank in western Virginia, but Berkeley County, with 19,972 people, was now in first place. Harrison had grown to 17,669, a growth due at least in part to the construction of the Northwestern Turnpike. Monongalia (17,368) was still a close third, Jefferson, with 14,082 inhabitants, was fourth, and Kanawha, now growing rapidly following the completion of the James River and Kanawha Turnpike, about 1835, was in fifth place, with 13,567 people. Ohio County, in first place in 1830, had fallen to sixth place by 1840, but this was only an apparent decline in population. Marshall County, formed from Ohio in 1835, had 6,937 people in 1840 and this, added to Ohio County's population of 13,357 in that year, would have still made that area the most populous in western Virginia.

**The Agricultural Census.** Statistics relative to agricultural production, mostly lacking in earlier census reports, are as follows:

| | | | |
|---|---|---|---|
| Wheat, bushels | 166,496 | Hay, tons | 6,938 |
| Rye, bushels | 6,259 | Wool, pounds | 51,316 |
| Corn, bushels | 381,316 | Honey, pounds | 930 |
| Buckwheat, bushels | 8,936 | Orchard products, value | $9,582 |
| Oats, bushels | 320,092 | Horses, number | 5,560 |
| Tobacco, pounds | 14,915 | Sheep, number | 28,817 |
| Hops, pounds | 636 | Swine, number | 19,885 |

The four principal population centers in 1840 were Morgantown, Middletown, Blacksville, and Cheat Neck. Martin's *Gazetteer*, in 1835, had given the population of Morgantown as 650, of Middletown (later Fairmont), 200, and of Blacksville 52. Cheat Neck was a growing center of iron manufacture and the area probably included a population of several hundred people. Most Monongalia County residents, of course, were farmers.

**Coal Banks.** Despite the abundant deposits of coal recognized as available in the county (see p. 134), only a limited and very local use was made of it. At places where the seams outcropped against the hillsides, farmers dug against the bank (or face) of the coal, and continued to follow it in tunnels extending short distances into the hillsides. The coal was carried out in baskets or in small cars pushed or pulled on crude tramways, and piled in bins, from which the farmer transported it to his house, or sold it to his neighbors.

The 1840 census reported that 73 men were engaged in coal mining in Monongalia County (certainly part time only), producing 167,200 bushels that year.[1]

**Rev. William Hanna Visits Morgantown.** The Reverend William Hanna was a distinguished Presbyterian minister and author of southwestern Pennsylvania in mid-century days and his narrative of a trip to Morgantown in 1840 gives a vivid picture of the life of the times.[2]

William Hanna was born in Trumbull County, Ohio, May 6, 1820, the son of Isaac and Martha Davis Hanna and a descendant of Robert Hanna, the founder of Hannatown, Westmoreland County. He preached at various churches in Fayette, Greene, and Allegheny counties, and wrote a history of Greene County (1882).

In April 1840, "extremely despondent, being in debt for books, tuition, boarding, and clothes," he heard of a job opening in Morgantown—"Messrs. H. & H. Daugherty . . . wished to employ some one to make the wood work of four hundred plows, for which they would pay four hundred dollars. This was to my mind then almost a fabulous sum, and a desire to get the job soon dissipated my despondency, as I thought I saw, in the good providence of God, the means of extinguishing all my indebtedness."

1. See James T. Laing, "The Early Development of the Coal Industry in the Western Counties of Virginia," *West Virginia History* 27 (1965):144-55.
2. See his book, *Biography and Recollections of Rev. William Hanna from the year 1826 to the year 1880* (Pittsburgh, 1881).

Two weeks later, "I left the Town of Smithfield in the stage for Morgantown. While waiting in New Geneva for dinner, Rev. James Davis . . . came into the room and engaged passage in the same coach. He was at that time pastor of the Presbyterian Church of Morgantown—a gentleman whose presence brightened our journey and seemed to shorten the way. I always regarded my meeting with him on that occasion as providential, as he forthwith interested himself in my welfare, bidding me welcome to his house and to his church, introducing me to some of the best citizens of the place, etc. During my entire stay he was the same kind hearted, whole souled man. I was let down from the stage at the house of Mr. George Hill, with whom I was to board."

Mr. Hill "was one of the most intelligent, humble, upright, and pious men I ever knew." He had been married to the former Miss Julia Henderson of "Forks of Cheat" a year or so earlier. "Their first child was then a few months old. This boy was named Robert Fairchild Hill, partly for the maternal grandfather and partly for Rev. A. G. Fairchild, the former pastor."

"My friend Rev. Davis introduced me to Thomas P. Ray, a man of untiring energy in all things connected with the best interests of the town, the church, and schools. I also formed the acquaintance of Mr. John Rodgers (not the man who was burnt in Queen Mary's reign), who was just then building a large brick house (see Fig. 203) where the two ways met at the end of the Decker's Creek bridge. This man was a devout Episcopalian, one of the first men I ever heard reading out the 'responses' in the church. He was considered one of the 'pillars.' I was also introduced to old Dr. McLane, a bland, mild, and exceedingly polite Scotchman, whose pills and vermifuge have given him almost a world-wide reputation."

"The year of my sojourn in Morgantown was one of intense political excitement. 'Tippecanoe and Tyler too!' could be heard in all directions. I spent several of my autumn evenings in listening to political speeches, in which I noticed this marked difference in men: Some always dogmatically denounced all who differed with them, while others condescended to reason with their political opponents. One of each of these two kinds of speakers is as distinctly remembered by me as though it were but yesterday. The dogmatizer I will not name, but I mention with feelings of high regard the man who spoke so pleasantly and reasoned so well. It was Hon. Edgar C. Wilson, a member of the Monongalia County bar, and an elder in Rev. Mr. Davis's church. He had also represented his congressional district in the National Legislature. His first wife was Miss Mary Ann Oliphant, a daughter of Andrew Oliphant, of Fayette County, Pennsylvania. His second wife was Miss Eliza Oliphant, sister of my benefactor, F. H. Oliphant, of Fayette County.

"One evening, while sitting in Mr. Hill's dining room, Rev. Thomas Martin, a native of the 'Emerald Isle,' but then principal of the Morgantown Academy, unexpectedly stepped in. Among his other peculiarities, promptness and brevity were very prominent, as I can well testify, and as the following will illustrate: Mr. Martin had an appointment for preaching at Evans School House (see p. 336) at six o'clock in summer time. Asa Hall, Charles Hall, Henry Smith and myself started in good time, but did not walk fast enough, for just as we arrived at the enclosure in which the house stood, the twenty minutes sermon was over and the audience dismissed."

"On the lot adjoining the one on which Mr. Hill resided, immediately below, there lived in 1840 Mr. Richard Forest, who had been married the year before to Miss Nancy Henderson, who had been a missionary, sent out by the 'Western Foreign Missionary Society,' among the Indians in Iowa. She was a sister of Mrs. Hill, and, as they lived within fifty feet of each other, I was frequently in their house while I boarded with Mr. Hill. These two ladies were born in the extreme southwestern corner of Fayette County, Pennsylvania, in the 'Forks of Cheat.' This name was given the peninsula of land between the Monongahela and Cheat Rivers—more particularly that 'smoothing iron' shaped piece of land formed by the two rivers and the 'Mason and Dixon' state line, which crosses Cheat River at what is yet called the 'Line Ford.' "

Why the stream was called "Cheat" "I never was informed, but the first time I ever saw it it cheated me." He was ten years old and was sent to take Miss Sarah Henderson, his schoolteacher, home. At "McFarland's old mill the water was perfectly clear, as it usually was as it came rushing down the mountains." Miss Henderson thought they could ride it, but it was deeper than they thought. His horse stepped on a rock and fell down and the boy was soaked.

Another house, three hundred feet from Mr. Hill's house, was the old "Wilson mansion," the birthplace of Mrs. Louisa A. Lowrie, a missionary to India. "This lady I saw several times at Esquire Oliphant's and Rev. A. G. Fairchild's, her former pastor."

**The Presidential Campaign.** The presidential campaign of 1840, as noted previously (p. 196), was carried on in Monongalia County in a most enthusiastic manner.

The county seat was feeling the influence of the Cheat iron industry, which was about at the peak of its prosperity, and supported a village of about seven hundred inhabitants. As a feature of the political campaign, a Whig procession in Morgantown included wagons loaded with iron workers, about twelve hundred in all, who threw sample nails on the streets as signs of prosperity.[3]

Ballots were cast at ten voting places, viz., Courthouse, Ross, Swamps, Jacksonville, Snodgrass, Middletown, Jarrett's, Paw Paw, Flat Run, and Blacksville.

Although of course the Whig candidate was successful, the vote in Monongalia County was strongly Democratic:

Martin Van Buren . . . . . . . . . . . . . . . . . . . . . . . . . . . . . . .1236

William Henry Harrison . . . . . . . . . . . . . . . . . . . . . . . 681

**Revolutionary War Veterans.** Surviving veterans of the Revolutionary War living in Monongalia County June 1, 1840, were: Evan Morgan, aged eighty-eight; James Devars, eighty-six; William Wilson, eighty-four; Isaac Reed, eighty-two; George Keller, eighty-one; John Dent, eighty-five; James Collins, eighty-five; Elisha Clayton, eighty-three; Charles Simpkins, eighty-two; Benjamin Chesney, eighty; Zadoc Morris, seventy-nine; Asaph M. Colgate, seventy-seven; Samuel Dudley, seventy-seven; Amos Morris, seventy-seven; James Scott, seventy-five; and Robert Darrah, seventy-one.[4]

**End of "The Monongalia Farmer's Company."** Morgantown's first bank, an unchartered bank of exchange, discount, and

3. Callahan, *Making of Morgantown*, pp. 12, 133.
4. Wiley, p. 488.

deposit, called "The Monongalia Farmer's Company of Virginia," came to an end in January 1840. Organized December 1, 1814,[5] Thomas Wilson was its first president and C. Berkshire the first clerk.

But the incorporated Merchants' and Mechanics' Bank of Wheeling, through its Morgantown branch, since 1834 had been adequately handling the county's financial affairs, so in 1840 the Farmer's Company wound up its business and directed Mathew Gay to distribute equitably all money on hands among the stockholders. He proceeded to collect the assets, and, after paying the liabilities, distributed the residue.[6]

**New Retail Merchants.** Retail merchants opening for business in Morgantown in 1840 included James Chadwick and Company, Chadwick and Pickenpaugh, Perry and Billingsley, and Isaac Cooper, who kept a tavern on Chancery Row. John Addison was also a tavern-keeper in Morgantown. Alexander Hayes was engaged in the hotel and stagecoach business. Josiah W. Saer was keeping a tavern on Lot 23.

**Waitman T. Willey.** A relatively new citizen of Morgantown, Waitman Thomas Willey, in 1840 was rapidly building up a lucrative law practice. He distinguished himself as an advocate of a superior quality and became well liked through his genial manners and very accommodating disposition.

Waitman T. Willey was the grandson of William Willey, who was born in 1767 in Sussex County, Delaware, and moved to Monongalia County in 1782-83, locating near Collins Ferry, on the Burris farm. A few years later he purchased a farm near the site of Cassville, where he later died.

In 1802 William Willey, Jr., son of the pioneer William, bought and settled on a tract of land on Buffalo Creek, near the site of the later town of Farmington. As his second wife he married Sarah Barnes, daughter of Thomas Barnes, who had settled at the mouth of Buffalo Creek.

Waitman Thomas Willey, the son of William and Sarah Willey, was born on October 18, 1811, in his parents' little log cabin not twenty feet square. Wiley says of the community in which

5. *The Monongalia Story*, vol. 2, p. 407.
6. Wiley, pp. 339, 461, 462.

he was born: "Then it was an exceptionally isolated community. The few scattered settlers along the stream from thence
to its head were thirty miles or more from the county seat.
They were situated on no great thoroughfare which marked the
tide of emigration to the great West. A few log cabins with the
curling blue smoke, in the midst of a small 'deadening' were all
that denoted that the restless spirit of the Anglo-American
courage had attacked the vast primeval solitudes of the upper
waters tributary to the Monongahela."[7]

In the wilderness there were few opportunities for schooling.
By the time he was twelve years old he had received a total of
only about nine months in school. In 1823 his father purchased
a farm at the mouth of Paw Paw Creek and moved his family
there, across the creek from the village of Pleasantville (later
Rivesville).

Wiley says this move made a great change in Waitman T.'s
life. "He soon felt the impulse of achievement, which seems to
pervade the minds and hearts of all dwellers by the side of deep
flowing streams. He never wearied of sitting on the banks of the
river and listening to the monotone of its steadily moving currents."[8]

This, however, did not keep him from long hours of hard
labor on the farm, interrupted only by two months of grammar
school during the next five years. Five books, the *Iliad*, the
*Essay on Man*, *Pilgram's Progress*, Pike's Arithmetic, and the
Bible constituted the family library and these he read and
reread. "The more he read the more his wonder grew . . . new
thoughts rose to stir within him new desires. He longed to join
in the scenes of the great world around him . . . and to partici-
pate in the grand conflict where each for himself hews out the
pathway to honor."[9]   Finally he asked his father to provide him
the means for obtaining an education.

On Christmas Day, 1827, he left home for Madison College,
in Uniontown, Pennsylvania. Wiley describes him as he was at
the time, seventeen years of age: "He was over six feet high and
weighed two hundred pounds; he wore the native home-spun

7. *History of Monongalia County*, p. 165.
8. Wiley, p. 166.
9. Wiley, p. 167.

jeans of the butternut hue; his entire earthly effects were carefully wrapped up in a bandanna handkerchief which he carried
in his hand, as, with a light heart and an unconquerable courage,
he walked the whole of the distance, forty miles, in one day—a
feat he performed at each vacation during his college course."[10]

He graduated in June 1831, from Allegheny College, Madison
having in the meantime been consolidated with that school. For
the next year he remained at home, working on the farm, reading at every leisure hour. Then in May 1832 he entered the law
office of Philip Doddridge, at Wellsburg, reading law under his
direction until Mr. Doddridge died in Washington in November
of that year. He completed his law studies under John C. Campbell, of Wellsburg.

On the twenty-fourth of June 1833 he located at Morgantown and was admitted to the bar in September, at first in
partnership with E. C. Wilson, then in an office of his own. In
his journal, noting his location in Morgantown, he added
"where I now live and where I expect to die," indicating his
location was intended to be a permanent one. On October 9,
1834, he was married to Elizabeth E. Ray, daughter of Patrick
Ray, and sister of Thomas Patrick Ray.

Gradually he purchased from John Rogers a large tract south
of Deckers Creek, an area which became known later as
Chancery Hill. His first purchase entitled him to the use of
"Dutch George's spring," on later Spring Street.

In 1839-40 he constructed his residence (Fig. 34), here, equip-
ping it with running water half a century before that utility was
in general use in Morgantown. Ambler describes the home:[11]

"The residence fronted east of north, and entrance was by a
five-columned roofed veranda. A path led thence to a patio
which then formed a part of present Prairie Avenue to the brink
of the terrace below. Thence descent was over stone steps to the
'road leading to Clarksburg,' otherwise called 'the Palatine
road.' A westward entrance over an open veranda commanded
a beautiful view of the Monongahela River, as did also the main
entrance."[12] A covered bridge across Deckers Creek was built
in 1840 (replacing one built in 1830), serving the Clarksburg
road.

10. Wiley, pp. 167, 168.
11. In *Waitman Thomas Willey* (1954), 282 pp.
12. Op. cit., p. 16.

In the erection of his pretentious residence, Willey was doubtless motivated by confidence in the future of Morgantown. But he was doubtless unaware of the glorious future that lay ahead for him.

Willey's powers as an orator soon became widely known and in 1840 the Whig Convention in Richmond placed him on the Harrison-Tyler electoral ticket.

"Into that exciting canvass he entered with all the enthusiasm of the impassioned orator impelled by profound convictions of duty. He made over forty speeches in North-western Virginia and Western Pennsylvania. His peculiar oratory made him a favorite with the masses. He not only pleased them with the smoothness of his speech and convinced them with the soundness of his logic, but he swayed them with the indefinable subtility and the nameless spirit of eloquence. Out of that campaign he came with a most definitely established reputation as an orator; it was reserved for other times and issues to demonstrate his ability as a statesman."[13]

He was, of course, greatly gratified at General Harrison's election to the presidency.

**Captain John Dent Dies.** "In the history of Monongalia the Dent family has played a prominent part, and bears an honorable record in the county's annals. The first of the name upon the soil of the county was Captain John Dent, who came from Loudon County, Virginia, to Monongalia in the early spring of the historic year of 1776. He served in the Broadhead and McIntosh campaigns on the western frontier. . . . He was a captain in the frontier militia under Colonel John Evans, whose only daughter, Margaret, he married. Captain Dent became possessed of a large landed estate upon the waters of Dent's Run (which was named for him), and was a member of the Virginia Assembly, a justice of the peace, and served a . . . term as sheriff. He died September 20, 1840, aged eighty-five years."[14]

John and Margaret Dent had twelve children, namely: Elizabeth (married Rawley Martin); John Evans (married Rebecca Hamilton, moved to Illinois); George (died at New Orleans in

13. Wiley, pp. 170, 171.
14. Wiley, p. 482; see also Callahan, *Making of Morgantown*, p. 81. His wife survived him, dying November 23, 1851, aged nearly eighty-eight years.

1805); Dudley Evans (married Mahala Berkshire, drowned in the Kanawha River); Nancy (married Captain Felix Scott); Nimrod (married Susan Graham); Margaret ("Peggy," married John Rochester); Enoch (married Julia Gapin); James (married Dorcas Berkshire); Marmaduke (married Sarah Price); Ann Arah (married Peter Fogle); and Rawley Evans (married Maria Miller).

**New Morgantown Homes.** John Rogers, one of Morgantown's best known businessmen, in 1840 built a new brick home on Plum Alley (see p. 196). Previously he had lived in an old stone-walled house occupied earlier by Michael Kern near Deckers Creek at the foot of High Street. It is related that while the building was under construction a tar barrel was burned on the top of one of the chimneys to celebrate the election of William Henry Harrison.[15]

Fig. 29. The St. Clair Hotel, corner Front and Walnut streets. (Courtesy West Virginia University Library.)

Another home built in or about 1840 was the brick house of Dr. Charles McLane at the southwest corner of High Street and Kirk Alley (Fig. 70, p. 394).

15. Callahan, *Making of Morgantown*, p. 96.

**Zechariah Piles Dies.** According to his widow's application for a pension, Zechariah (Zachariah) Piles died on November 15, 1840, in the Dunkard Creek settlement. Dates of his birth and death vary considerably in published accounts but the pension application gives his birth date as July 15, 1758, in Frederick County, Maryland. He was the son of James and Lydia Owens Piles.

James Piles was killed in an Indian attack in 1778 near Fort Statler (see *Monongalia Story*, vol. 2, pp. 28, 29), in which twenty-year-old Zechariah was himself wounded in the heel.

Zechariah was an active citizen in the pioneer community, assisting in such public enterprises as road improvement and bridge construction.

He was married twice. His first wife was Rachel Wright (1760-1812) and they had at least ten children, namely: Elisha (1794-1876, married Rosanna Knight); John (1795-1874); Nancy (married a Parks); Hannah (1802-1887, married Jacob Sines); Joshua (married Margaret Henderson); Zechariah, Jr.; Rebecca (married a Cordray); Lydia (married George Petty); Sarah (married an Eddy); and Elijah ("Eli" born ca. 1810). On July 7, 1813, he was married to his second wife, Susannah Lezar (1781-1873), and they had one son, Uriah ("Riley," born 1817).[16]

**Middletown in 1840.** The village of Middletown by 1840 was becoming a vigorous rival to Morgantown and its citizens were actively promoting the notion of a new county, of which the village would be the county seat.

Lough presents some interesting slants on what life was like in Middletown in 1840. He quotes Eusebius Satterfield of Rivesville, who was certainly not completely serious:

"In Middletown in 1840 there were 5 coal banks, 7 sawmills, 2 tanneries, 27 stills, 2 brickyards, 1 house of ill fame, Aunt Sukey's, 5 saloons, 1 fortune-telling parlor, 1 hot bath hall, a brass drum for sale, a lost calf, a runaway slave, who was later found drunk on hard cider, a hitching post with Benedict

16. The early history of the Piles family of Monongalia County is not very well known but the principal facts are given in the recent excellent treatment by Ralph Shearer Rowland and Star Wilson Rowland, *Wilsons and Burchells and Related Families, 1608-1976* (Fairfax, Va.: 1976, 359 pp.), pp. 166-88.

Arnold's picture on it, a fiddle-player for all occasions. My father told me so."[17]

A more serious view of life in Middletown may be gained from a letter written by "Nancy and Mirtle" on April 4, 1840:

"Dear Cousin Josie: We are all well and pray you are the same way. It is raining today. I bet it is not raining in Indiana is it? There are 71 houses hereabouts being lived in now but when you was living here there was only 10 or was there more? We have fixed our place up some and Sam dug us a well. It is not very deep but the water is very good. Talk talk talk is all we hear of getting a county and a courthouse for Middletown. Doctor Kidwell[18] is going to live in the old Bartholow[19] house. They say he is very good in the medicine he peddles. Young Watson[20] sold him the property and told he paid cash. On the first Friday of last month a steam boat tried to get up from Morgantown but got stuck on the bottom at Joliffs. There's been a lot of rain and the river was very high.

"The name of the steam boat was little napoleon (see p. 210). I hear the other little napoleon met his water loo too ha ha. Catherine Billings died last week on Monday of a fever. She was keeping company with George you know who and people said they would get married. George got on his horse and rode out of town right after the funeral and nobody knows where he went or if he will ever come back. He left here sobbing like his heart was broke.

"We heard a wolf last night that was over the river. When you lived here we heard them every night but not any more so much. Bill Sandy took his dogs and gun and went after it but did not get it.

"There are two stores here now Magees and Vanzants, and out around town there are five others, at Barnses and up the river. Everybody in town has their gardens plowed and most are already planting them. It will soon be time to pick greens and then the garden truck will come on and we won't have to skimp so much.

"Maude Ashcraft was here for two weeks and visited around.

17. Lough, *Now and Long Ago*, p. 444.
18. Zedekiah Kidwell.
19. Benjamin B. Bartholow.
20. James O. Watson.

She walked in from their place but went home with Dan and Etta in their wagon. Pet Moore has a new boy born last Wednesday this makes her eight. My goodness Frank and Mirtle and me are going to Morgantown come this next Saturday. We need so much stuff and the new stuff is in at the stores. The roads all around are just mud and every day and night dozens of wagons and rigs go by on their way to Clarksburg loaded down heavy. The mud is still up to the horses knees and bellies and it is still pouring the rain down."[21]

**First Sewing Machine.** Miss Ferris, it is said, put into use Middletown's first sewing machine. She was one of the best dressmakers of the period, having learned her trade in London. Her shop was on the corner of Quincy and Jackson streets. The sewing machine was about a foot long and six inches wide. It was screwed to the top of a table, was hand propelled, and sewed with a lock stitch. The machine cost eighty dollars.[22]

The "pin back" dress was of this general period. Its peculiarity was that, instead of buttons or other fastenings from the neck to the waist, there were many pins, placed as close together as possible. Thorns were often used instead of the bright "store-bought" pins, which were considered highly ornamental.

Men of the wealthier class were beginning to wear ruffled shirts with stiff pleated fronts and, at the neck, a stock collar with a bow, commonly called a "stand-up dickey."[23]

**Cabinetmakers and Undertakers.** William Clyde Hennen, Jr., was a son of William and Rebecca Hennen and was born in Greene County, Pennsylvania, March 15, 1817. He married Louisa May Dye and they moved to the Dolls Run section of Monongalia County, where they resided only a short time. By 1840 they had removed to the Wadestown area, where William followed the trade of carpenter and cabinetmaker. He was also an under-

21. Lough, *Now and Long Ago,* pp. 443, 444.
22. Newman, *Marion County in the Making,* p. 163. The date, 1840, given by Newman, is certainly an error. Elias Howe is said to have made and patented his first sewing machine in 1846 and Isaac Merritt Singer's first machine dated from 1850. See Ruth Brandon, *A Capitalist Romance. Singer and the Sewing Machine* (1977), 244 pp.
23. Newman, pp. 163, 164.

taker, making his caskets of black walnut with a highly polished finish.[24]

A first cousin of his, Robert Painter Hennen, also born in Greene County (December 22, 1802), located in Morgantown about 1831. He married Elizabeth Wilkins and by 1840 he began the manufacture of furniture at his shop on Lot 9. He is remembered as one of the first expert cabinetmakers in Morgantown.[25]

**Monongalia Baptist Church.** On March 12, 1840, James Griffin and Abram Hanes met with Jesse Price at his home on Mods Run for the purpose of organizing a Baptist church in the McClelland Community. The church was established and named the Monongalia Baptist Church. A building was constructed on Plum Run.[26]

**Newport Methodist Protestant Church.** When Jacob Swisher laid out the village of Newport at the mouth of Little Creek, he also organized a Methodist congregation there, which served the thriving logging community of about 120 persons. Early meetings of the congregation were held in Swisher's home and the Reverend John Clark served as pastor. In warm weather he preached out of doors, standing on a large rock near the riverbank.[27]

**Building Mill Roads.** The system of wagon roads was by 1840 nearing completion, but short links of new roads, or improvements and relocations of existing roads, were subjects of petitions to the county court, to make it easier to get to mill or to market. A few excerpts indicate the nature of these projects: "from John Shively's old mill to David Scott's farm"; "from Asa Sutton house to point on the road leading from Jacksonville to Mount Morris"; "from the Pricketts Creek bridge down

24. Dorothy T. Hennen, *Hennen's Choice*, vol. 1, p. 53. W. C. Hennen died at Wadestown September 29, 1884.

25. *Hennen's Choice*, pp. 54, 115, 116. In 1865 he was joined in this business by his son, Matthew, and after Robert's death, October 30, 1873, Matthew and his brother Frederick continued the business as Hennen Brothers, adding the manufacture of caskets and coffins to items previously made. See also Wiley, pp. 262, 263.

26. *Bicentennial Church Histories of Marion County*, p. 44.

27. Wilcox, *How Our Marion County Churches Began*, pp. 86, 87; Barnes, *M. P. Church*, p. 92. A building was erected in 1854.

said creek to Pricketts sawmill to where it will intersect the new
port road"; "from Grandville to Jacob Scotts from thence by
way of Thos. Boices to intersect the state road near Robert
Finnels"; road under construction "from Jesse Mercers ferry to
Henry Barbs, it Being a part of the Middletown road a road of
very Considerable Consequence"; "Mill Road from my house to
the mouth of indian Creak to intersect the River Road leading
to the Morgantown Road"; "a Road Commencing at the road
leading from Middletown to Knotsville near Robert Hendersons
through by Marshall Murpeys to intersect the road that leads
from James Morgans to William Rogers Mill near francis Poes
for a mill road"; "from the town of New Port to the Steam
Boat yard at Morgans Eddy"; "from McVickers Mill to an old
Sawmill on West Run"; "George Lake, William Lynn and William Reese view and mark out a road near Francis Poe's";
"Grant us a Mill Road Leading from Shadrach Hogens to intersect the road at James Eddys, leading from indian creek down
statlers run"; "alteration in the road leading from the state road
near James Arnetts to the fishing creek pike in the direction of
Dents Mills"; "from Clark Morris on the Dunkard Mill run to
Boaz Flemings farm on Plum Run"; "A Good Road Leading
from the Bridge across the Valley River to Nuzums Mill, Down
the River."

Improvement of the road from Morgantown to Uniontown in
1840, by way of Ice's Ferry, made the stagecoach ride easier.
The establishment of Ellicott's rolling mill on Cheat the same
year furnished new impetus to secure still better roads for that
section.[28]

**Indian Warfare Victims Re-interred.** At the battle of Dolls Run,
in 1778 (*Monongalia Story*, vol. 2, pp. 28, 29), eighteen settlers
had been killed and their bodies were buried along the stream,
on the site of the battle. After the passage of a half century,
some of the skeletons were exposed as the stream cut into the
burial ground, and, says Wiley: "On Washington's Birthday,
some time between 1830 and 1840, two volunteer military
companies—one from Greene County, Pa., and the other from
Monongalia County—took up the bones of the murdered men

28. Callahan, *Making of Morgantown*, p. 165 note.

where they were buried on the run, and re-interred them in Core's graveyard with the honors of war."[29]

An eyewitness of the ceremony, Andrew Anderson, tells of his memories: "I was at the resurrection and burial of the bones. My father, Col. Levi Anderson, had charge and burried the bones of Jacob Statler, Piles, Brookover, and others at Cores meeting house.[30]

"Zachariah Piles and Schumaker made their escape. Zach Piles was shot in the head in his flight on horseback. I knew the old man when I was a kid."[31]

**Land Grants Made in 1840.**[32] Monongalia County grantees in 1840 included:

| | | |
|---|---|---|
| Austin, James | 30 a. | Booths Creek |
| Downes, Robert | 23½ | Buffalo Creek |
| Haynes, John | 65 | Piles Fork |
| Macabee, Zadock T. | 27 | Booths Creek |
| Martin, James | 30 | Booths Creek |
| Rice, Isaac | 17 | Pappaw Creek |

**Joseph Carraco.** Joseph Carraco died in Morgantown April 19, 1840. He was a son of William Carraco, a native and lifelong resident of the eastern shore of Maryland, where Joseph was born in 1780. Joseph located along the Tygart Valley River near Three Forks Creek in 1800, but ten years later moved to Morgantown. His occupation was farming. At first he was a member of the Roman Catholic church, but after coming to Morgantown associated himself with the Methodist Episcopal Church.

He married Catharine Beauregard and they had seven children, four daughters and three sons, of whom one, John William, was reared from the age of seven by Dr. Charles McLane.[33]

29. *History of Monongalia County*, p. 67.
30. *The Monongalia Story*, vol. 2, p. 486.
31. From an undated letter, copy in West Virginia University Library. Pers. comm., Mr. and Mrs. Leslie Wheeler, Tiskilwa, Illinois, and Mr. and Mrs. Orville Smith, Villa Park, Illinois. Levi Anderson (see Core, *Chronicles of Core*, pp. 39, 40, 54) married Mary Brown, daughter of Adam Brown. Andrew was born about 1824. Core's Meeting House (see *The Monongalia Story*, vol. 2, p. 486) was built near the mouth of Statler Run before 1815, by Michael Core, whose father, John, had been killed in the battle.
32. See p. 11.
33. *Cyclopedia of Monongalia County*, p. 109.

**Charles Glasscock.** Born in Fauquier County, Virginia, July 20, 1775, Charles Glasscock died on Indian Creek February 16, 1840, where he had settled as a young man. He followed farming and milling. He married Mary Arnett, a granddaughter of James Arnett, a Revolutionary War soldier. Daniel Glasscock was a son.[34]

**County Government.** John Evans was sworn in as sheriff on March 23, 1840. Commissioners of the revenue appointed by the county court were Thomas Watson, for the Eastern District, and John Musgrave, for the Western District. Sworn in as justices of the peace were John Stewart, July 27, 1840, John Hood and William Bradley, on August 24, 1840, and Leander S. Laidley, September 28, 1840. The county levy was $1.37½.

**Miscellany.** In 1840: P. S. Ruter was appointed principal of the Morgantown Female Academy, succeeding Miss E. Doggett (Wiley, p. 399). . . . Dr. Hugh McNemera was a practicing physician at Blacksville. Physicians at Morgantown included Drs. Charles McLane, Thomas Brooke, Daniel Gettings, Colastian Billingsley, and B. R. C. O'Kelly[35] (Wiley, p. 467). . . . James Evans was elected colonel of the seventy-sixth regiment of the county militia (Wiley, p. 515). . . . The steamboat *Little Napoleon* arrived at the Port of Morgantown April 27 (Wiley, p. 542). . . . John H. Bowers came from New Geneva, Pennsylvania, and settled near Cheat River; he married Levarah G. Baker (Wiley, p. 672). . . . Burrs were placed in Jacob Ruble's gristmill near Cheat River (Wiley, p. 677). . . . James Hare moved from New Geneva and settled between Morgantown and Cheat River; he married Mary Vandervort (Wiley, p. 691). . . . Andrew Brown refitted the well-known Brown's Mill, on Dunkard Creek (Wiley, p. 746). . . . Lot 117 in Morgantown was conveyed by Thomas Meredith to Francis Madera for $125 (Callahan, pp. 66, 328). . . . Lot 80 was sold by Joseph Kern in March to Charles McLane for $1,275 (Callahan, p. 319). . . . Lot 97 was sold in February by Norval Wilson to George Lemmon for $160 (Calla-

34. *Cyclopedia of Monongalia County*, p. 113; see also *James Arnett and his descendants. . .*, in papers of L. D. Arnett, WVU Library, called to my attention by Dr. William S. Arnett.

35. George Brown, an M. P. minister, traveling in 1843 with his wife and two children, tells of visiting with Dr. O'Kelly. One of his children, playing in the yard with the doctor's children, fell and broke his arm, "but the bone was immediately set by the doctor." *Recollections of Itinerant Life*, p. 295.

han, p. 323). . . . Guy R. C. Allen acquired Lot 123, including Deep Hollow (Callahan, p. 329). . . . Lot 32 in Middletown was sold by Simon Shore to Albert Shore (Lough, p. 422). . . . Cornelius McShane was operating Ice's Ferry (Owens, p. 70). . . . John Hare (1787-1881) bought a farm just west of Cheat River (Owens, p. 83). . . . Fredrick Moore, a teamster, located on West Run (Owens, p. 90). . . . Zackquill Pierpont, son of John, died; he was born in 1782 and married Dorcas Ridgeway (Owens, p. 92).

CHAPTER SIXTY-FIVE

# 1841

Disease and accident were common among the citizens of Monongalia County during the first half of the nineteenth century and physicians were few. The remote communities, far removed from the seaboard cities, were not inviting fields for the practice of medicine. Many of the physicians who did come were poorly equipped for the conquest of disease.

The most common remedies used were secured from native or introduced plants. Some of the medical plant lore was brought from Europe, where similar plants might have been used; some of it was learned from the Indians.[1]

Among the diseases then prevalent here was intermittent fever (malaria), although not as common along the Monongahela as along the Ohio. When present in Monongalia County it was of distant origin, say accounts of the time. It was treated by bark of dogwood (*Cornus florida*), cherry (*Prunus* sp.), or poplar (*Populus* sp.) digested in whiskey, or by a similar concoction of boneset (*Eupatorium perfoliatum*).

Dysentery took a heavy toll. "Oak ooze" was administered internally by some in treatment of this common ailment, while others advised a "decoction" made from mayapple (*Podophyllum peltatum*) root, walnut (*Juglans nigra*) bark, and slippery elm (*Ulmus rubra*) tea, plus hot fomentations to the abdomen.

The diagnosis of "lung fever" was applied to most chest ail-

1. An excellent treatment of the subject is Charles F. Millspaugh's *American Medicinal Plants. An Illustrated and Descriptive Guide to Plants Indigenous to and Naturalized in the United States Which are Used in Medicine* (1892), 806 pp. Dr. Millspaugh was botanist at West Virginia University, in Morgantown, from 1889 to 1892.

ments and was usually treated by steaming the patient with vapors of whiskey. Virginia snakeroot (*Aristolochia serpentaria*) was used for all coughs.

Measles and scarlet fever broke out in epidemics on an average of every five years. Typhoid was endemic in all communities. Diphtheria was known as putrid sore throat. Many adults were ready every spring to have their blood purified by one or more bleedings. A common practice was to purge by the use of large doses of senna and manna or a decoction of rhubarb and molasses. These drugs were also used to stimulate the kidneys and to keep the bile flowing freely.

Accidents were frequent, as travel over mountain paths and rough, narrow wagon roads, often across swollen rivers and creeks, was extremely hazardous.

**"Old" Dr. McLane.** In 1841, and for many years before and after, the best known physician in Monongalia County was Dr. McLane. There were three McLane doctors in Morgantown—father, son, and grandson—who practiced medicine here for almost one hundred years. The one in 1841 was the father, hence, "Old" Dr. McLane.[2]

The ancestral home of the McLane (or MacLean) family was the Isle of Mull, Scotland. Alan McLane emigrated to America about 1760, returned to locate in Ireland, then came back to America in 1804, with his wife and two sons, William and Charles. Charles was born in Tyrone County, Ireland, in 1790.

The family settled near Lancaster, Pennsylvania, where Charles read medicine. Later, Charles attended lectures at the University of Pennsylvania, where he received a degree. After a short practice in Greensburg and Connellsville, Pennsylvania, he moved to Morgantown in 1823. He was thirty-three years old, married to Eliza, daughter of John Kern, of Greensburg, and had two children.

Questions of diagnosis were often quite baffling, as indicated by this letter Dr. McLane received in 1826 from the well-known Dr. Philip Syng Physick of Philadelphia:

2. See Simon B. Chandler, "The Three McLane Doctors of Morgantown," *Bull. Hist. Medicine* 25 (1951):269-76. Dr. Chandler was professor of medicine at the School of Medicine, West Virginia University. See also biography of Dr. McLane by A. L. Wade, *Morgantown Post*, March 5, 1887.

Philad. 24th April, 1826

Dear Sir:
   Your letter, without date, describing the state of Wm. Evans eyes came to my hands this day—I am sorry to inform you that without an opportunity of examining them I cannot form a satisfactory opinion of the nature of the blindness—If the pain in the forehead continues, I would advise a low diet—frequent purging—the application of leeches over the painful part—blisters to the back of the neck and issues on the forehead or on the temples near the margin of the orbit—I am gratified by your polite letter and I remain very respectfully

Your faithful pro P. S. Physick.

   Dr. McLane's son, Joseph Alan (born in 1820) "read" medicine with his father and at the age of seventeen enrolled in Jefferson Medical School in Philadelphia. In December he wrote his parents:

Philadelphia Dec. 6th 1837

Dear Parents:
   . . . You inform me in your letter that the small pox is near Morgantown. On this account (as soon as I read the letter) I ran up to Dr. McClintock's on 5th St. to get the vaccine matter. He had none on hands but had a few days before been vaccinating. So of course I had to wait until last evening, when he divided a scab with me. I sent you this matter under the transparent wafers on the 1st page. . . . If Emily is not too busily employed this winter, I wish that she would take the trouble of noting down the temperature of the atmosphere (out from the house) at about 9 o'clock each morning and about 4 o'clock in the afternoon each day from this till the last of February. I will do the same here & see whether there is much difference of the two places. . . . . I met Thos. Benton as I passed through Cumberland and at a tavern on this side of the mountain I had the honor of conversing alone with Henry Clay. He is a polished gentleman but not at all proud.

Yours truly etc
Jos. A.

   Dr. McLane replied:

Morgantown, Jan. 3rd, 1838

Dear Joseph,
   . . . Since I wrote last, I purchased Mr. Robb's[3] fine traveler at $100 . . . I am in hopes that he will be quite a good horse by spring. Within a few days, I have been in Pittsg. and since my return, I attended a case above the Horse-Shoe, 60 miles up Cheat. I got back on Monday the 1st—on the 2nd I attended a case in Greene County (Pennsylvania) and to-day I attended one beyond Cheat. . . .

3.  James Robb. See p. 167.

Mrs. McLane added a note: "We vaccinated Virginia on the same evening we received the letter 4 days from Philadelphia. It took very well. . . . The thermometer stands at 66 between 3 and 4 p.m."

In 1840 Dr. McLane erected a brick house at Kirk and High streets, which was to be the family home for many years. He invented "the liver pills known by his name and which have a great sale in America, and are known in almost every civilized country on the globe."[4]

In addition to practicing medicine, he was a local preacher in the Methodist Episcopal Church.

He was about five feet eight inches in height, and had a round face, auburn hair, and blue eyes.

Joseph A. McLane (born 1820), Charles's son, after reading medicine with his father, graduated from the Pennsylvania Medical College at Philadelphia in 1841 and returned to Morgantown to practice with his father.

**Thomas Patrick Ray.** Thomas P. Ray (Fig. 30), one of the best known citizens of Monongalia County, died in Baltimore, Maryland, on the fourteenth of October 1841, only forty-six years of age. Wiley says of him that, "for many of the latter years of his life, his history would be, essentially, the history of the county, so far as material development, and public improvements are related to it."[5]

Mr. Ray was born May 14, 1796, on the Isle of Wight, the son of Patrick and Mary Ray. When he was six weeks old his parents sailed with him from England, arriving, after a long and tedious voyage, in Philadelphia. They at first located near Wellsburg, Brooke County, removing, nine years later, to Wheeling, Ohio County. At the age of fifteen Thomas came to Morgantown to "write" in the office of Nimrod Evans, clerk of the county court. He gained not only the confidence of his employer, but also the esteem of the bar, the bench, the citizenry. Through his diligence, industry, and ability, he became known as one of the most expert of the young clerks in the state.[6]

4. Wiley, p. 472.
5. Op. cit., p. 349.
6. See biography in Wiley, pp. 348-52.

When Mr. Evans died, Mr. Ray was appointed to his position (in 1828) and after the adoption of the amended state constitution, erecting Circuit Superior Courts of Law and Chancery in each county, he was appointed clerk of that court also (May 28, 1831). He continued to hold both offices until the time of his death.

He was married, on June 22, 1819, to Miss Jennett Smith and they had three children, George S., Volender, and Delia, who married Col. James Evans. Their home in Morgantown, says Wiley, "soon became the very seat of hospitality—a hospitality most cordial and generous. His house was always open to his friends, and persons from abroad ever received from him those courtesies and kind offices which are so grateful to the stranger."[7]

But, Wiley continues, "his distinguishing trait of character was his public spirit; and the distinguishing feature of his history was his assiduous, persistent and unselfish efforts to promote the public welfare by all available and proper instrumentalities."

It was principally through his exertions that funding was provided for the Monongalia Academy after the construction of the new school building in 1829 and he was a member (and treasurer) of the new board of directors. It was also through his instrumentality that a branch of the Merchants' and Mechanics' Bank of Wheeling was opened in Morgantown. He was president of the bank for many years.

A less successful effort, to which he devoted a great deal of time, was in trying to secure the improvement of the Monongahela River for slack-water navigation from the Pennsylvania line to the junction of the West Fork and Tygart Valley rivers. He was able to have a survey made, but nothing further was accomplished.

He was more successful in securing the improvement of wagon roads through the county. Through his personal and persistent efforts, state charters were secured and legislative aid was obtained to construct what was known as the Brandonville and Fishing Creek Turnpike and the Beverly and Pennsylvania Turnpike. Not satisfied, says Wiley, "with obtaining the means to

7. Op. cit., p. 350.

Fig. 30. Thomas P. Ray. (From Wiley's *History of Monongalia County*.)

Fig. 31. James Vance Boughner. (From Wiley's *History of Monongalia County*.)

Fig. 32. George Frederick Charles Conn. (From Wiley's *History of Monongalia County.*)

Fig. 33. Alexander Luark Wade. (From Wiley's *History of Monongalia County.*)

prosecute these works," he also "gave much of his time and attention to surveying and locating them, and still further super-intending their construction."[8] Although these highways were by no means built to the standards of the National Road, and could scarcely be said to operate as "turnpikes" at all, yet they were greatly improved for the movement of local traffic. "There were no improvements of general interest to the county, during the mature years of his life, of which he was not the principal factor; and to no other citizen, during these years, was the County of Monongalia so largely indebted for its material pros-perity and development."[9]

Indeed, it is possible that overwork may have caused, or at least accentuated the illness which caused his death in Balti-more, where he had gone for treatment.

A Morgantown newspaper thus commented on his life and death:

"Mr. Ray has been long and favorably known as a citizen of our town. He was a man of strong mind—of great business habits, and of unquestioned integrity. As clerk of our County and Superior Court, it is believed that there was no officer of the kind in the State his superior, and few that were his equals. He attended to more business of a public nature, and without compensation, than we have ever known attended to by one of our citizens. As the active and managing head of several road companies and incorporations—as Trustee of the Borough—as Treasurer and Trustee of the Monongalia Academy—as President of the Bank in Morgantown; and in the various offices and appointments with which he was entrusted, he displayed the most untiring industry, judgment, and ability. Mr. Ray was truly the friend and assistant of the poor; his heart and purse were ever open to their wants. He contributed liberally to the support of the Gospel, to all charitable and benevolent associa-tions, and to the internal improvement of the county. Few men have departed this life more generally and more sincerely la-mented within the circle of his acquaintance."[10]

His large brick house, constructed about 1835, was on what

8. Op. cit., p. 351.
9. Op. cit., p. 351.
10. *Democratic Republican*, October 16, 1841.

he called Beech Hill, on the site later occupied by the first
buildings on the campus of West Virginia University.

Fig. 34. Home of Waitman T. Willey, on Chancery Hill, built in 1840.

**Willey Succeeds His Brother-in-Law.** In November 1841, W. T.
Willey was elected clerk of the county court, succeeding to the
place made vacant by his brother-in-law; and, in the same
month, was appointed by Judge Joseph L. Fry clerk of the
Circuit Superior Court of Law and Chancery, being sworn in on
November 22. Both of these offices he was to serve with perseverance and the utmost devotion to duty. Amidst these
labors, however, he did much literary work and began the collection of a library which developed into a large, well-chosen
stock of books. At this time, too, he united with the Methodist
Episcopal church, an act, he recognized as "more important
than any or all acts of my life."[11]

He had been deeply affected by the untimely death of President Harrison earlier in the year and wrote in his journal: "In-
scrutable Providence! I loved him—his country loved him."[12]

11. Wiley, p. 172.
12. Ambler, *Waitman Thomas Willey*, p. 23.

By popular request he delivered a memorial address on the president's life and character in the Presbyterian church.

Willey's health was not very good (he suffered from hepatic trouble) and his journal contains numerous somber reflections. On March 17, 1841, he wrote: "Spring with its birds and blossoms will soon be here. Dreary nature will soon shake off her torpor, and infuse joy into both man and beast by her re-animated appearance. Old and young look to the approaching season with feelings of delight. But to me, alas! this pleasant season of the year will have few charms; for as the warm weather approaches my disease is aggravated. I feel despondent and hopeless. . . . My life bids fair to be short."[13]

**William Wroe.** William Wroe, of Morgantown, died about 1841. The son of William (1729-1781) and Grace Chancellor (?-1804) Wroe, he was born in Westmoreland County, Virginia, in 1762. He married his double cousin, Sarah Chancellor (born 1774), who survived him, and they had six children, Benjamin L. (born 1810), Matilda, William Chancellor, Grace M., Sarah Jane, and Elizabeth B.[14]

**Another Loss of Territory.** For the fifth time, in 1841, Monongalia County lost territory,[15] when all that portion of the county east of Chestnut Ridge (or Laurel Hill) was added to Preston County by the passage of a bill introduced into the general assembly by William G. Brown, a member from Preston.

The act, passed on the fifteenth of March, provided: "That so much of the County of Monongalia as lies east of the range of mountains called Laurel Hill, and north of Cheat River, next to and adjoining the County of Preston, and is contained in the following boundary lines, to wit: beginning on the line dividing said counties at the point where it crosses Cheat River, and running thence a straight line to the England Ore bank, on top of the mountain; thence a straight line to the Osburn farm, so run as to include the dwelling-house of said farm in the County of Preston; thence a due north course to the Pennsylvania line,

13. Wiley, p. 171.
14. From data in Morgantown Public Library, supplied by Mrs. Riley Brown, 729 South Margrave, Fort Scott, Kansas 66701.
15. See *The Monongalia Story*, vol. 2, pp. 95, 104, 284, 441.

shall be annexed to, and henceforth be a part of the County of Preston."

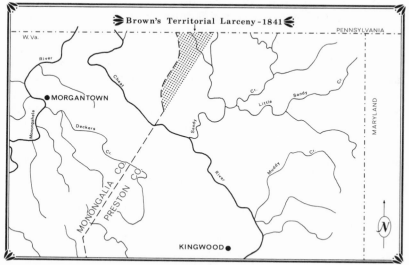

Fig. 35. Map showing "Brown's Territorial Larceny," 1841. (Drawn by Diane Lenhart.)

"Referring to this act," Wiley relates, "Mr. John J. Brown, in his Centennial address, says: 'In 1841, by an act of Assembly which Monongalians mildly designate as "Brown's Territorial Larceny'" the grand summits of Laurel Hill, away to the east where the King of day first heralds his glory, were rudely wrested from her [Monongalia's] unwilling grasp and added to Preston County.' "[16]

The territory involved included approximately twenty-five square miles.[17]

**Report of School Commissioners.** The annual meeting of school commissioners was held on October 25, 1841, and a report was submitted to the county court in relation to moneys provided from the Literary Fund for the education of indigent children. The report stated that eighty-five common schools and two academies were in operation the past year.

16. *History of Monongalia County*, p. 100 note.
17. Wiley, p. 561.

There were nine school districts in the county, with a commissioner for each district. The following list names the commissioners, with the schoolmasters in each district:

No. 1. Nathan Hall, commissioner; James W. Bowman, James Thomas, Francis C. Whiting, Lemuel Poe, Nathan Hall, Jr., Lewis Jefferies, Isaac Hall, Richard Howell.

No. 2. John Johns, commissioner; J. J. B. Tisdal, J. P. Wansley, Auburn McDoogle, John W. Batson, James Snodgrass, William Prichard, Harriet Henderson, G. T. Stub, Ingaber Shafer, John Anderson, Elizabeth Legitt, Davis M. Bruno, Thomas G. Stub, Amelia Pritchard.

No. 3. Henry Boggess, commissioner; James A. Hogue, Levy Straight, Absalom Prichard, Stephen Wilson, G. R. Stub, John Price, John Anderson, William T. Ash, Isaac O. Rittenhouse.

No. 4. Aaron Barker, commissioner; Moses Cox, Joseph C. Price, James P. Blair, Lary Holland, James A. Hoge, Susan Phillips, Mary Berkshire, Horatio Martain, John Polston, Isaac Cordery, Revlin Fennel, Bushrod Fennel, Jacob Basnett, Rachel Ann Combs, Eliza Tibbs, Wesley Wiseman.

No. 5. William Price, commissioner; Joshua M. Huggins, Joseph H. Piles, Oliver Galliher, B. Caldwell, Charles O. Dowd, Elig Hartley, Richard D. Tennant, Rawley Snider, James Cross, James W. Bowman.

No. 6. Joseph F. Harrison, commissioner; Joab Hoh, Joseph C. Price, William T. Ash, Asbury Stephens.

No. 7. Thomas Lewellan, commissioner; Alpheus Summers, Catherine Taylor, Asby Stephans, A. G. Brandon, Thomas Gibson, Catherine Taylor, James P. Blair, John N. Jaritt, Elizabeth Magill, Anne Kolyer.

No. 8. Thomas Wattson, commissioner; Fielding A. Knight, R. P. Nixon, Eliza Morgan, C. B. Ross, Isaac Nuce, Nancy Linn, William H. Wilson, John H. Biggs, Thomas Watson, Horace Brown, Lanyan Deavault, John H. Holt, James Wattson, John M. Armstrong, William Rae, Grace M. Rae, Harrison R. Ferrell.

No. 9. Fielding Kiger, commissioner; Joseph C. Price, John Vandivert, Asby Stephens, An Kolyer, David M. Zarley, Richard Howell, Alpheus Summers, Katherine Taylor, Thomas Clare, George W. Brown, John N. Jaritt, William Holland, Lewis Turner, Nancy Farrut, C. Nicholson.

**The Hopewell Methodist Church.** The Pisgah Methodist Episcopal Church, near Smithtown, was built in 1813.[18] When the reform movement in the Methodist church developed, resulting in the formation of the Methodist Protestant group, a society of reformers was organized, as early as 1833. Allen Holland attended the first quarterly conference, held at Middletown, November 16, 1833, as steward from that body.

The society worshipped in the Holland schoolhouse until 1841, when a frame church was built a short distance from the Pisgah church. Because they hoped to succeed as a new denomination, they named the new church Hopewell. Among the charter members were Allen, Richard, and William Holland, Zadoc McBee, Joseph Shuttlesworth, Isaac Powell, Stephen Stansberry, and their families.[19]

**James Fork Methodist Church.** On the first Sunday in April 1815 a Sunday school was organized on James Fork, a branch of Buffalo Creek, by Mrs. Thomas Laidley, who became its first superintendent. The first church building was a log house, in which the classes met and in which a circuit rider preached a few times each year.

In 1841 this building was torn down and a frame church was built. The deed for the new lot, recorded June 8, 1841, was made by John Toothman and wife Sarah to Joseph Martin, Arthur Watson, John McDougal, John Prichard, and Randolph Robey, as trustees.[20]

**Road Amendments.** The system of wagon roads for the county by now was nearly complete, needing only "amendment" (relocation to improve grades, etc.) or the construction of short connecting roads.

County court records for 1841 include petitions for amendment of roads "from the top of Walkers hill to Indian Creek"; "from the bethel meating house or near Hynson Smiths and through by the way of Michael Whites to intersect at or near Waitman Davis saw mill 'commencing at Capt. James Morgans running down Piney run to Pricketts creek' "; "from John M.

18. *The Monongalia Story*, vol. 2, p. 402.
19. Barnes, *The Methodist Protestant Church*, pp. 145, 146; cf. Wiley, p. 627.
20. *Bicentennial Church Histories of Marion County*, p. 50.

Ralphsniders to the county road near the widdow Mary Combs"; "from Frederick Swisher bridge on the little pappaw by way of John Toothmans and Benjamin Shumans to the crossing of Indian creek below Roarks old mill."

A "Mill Road" was requested "beginning at Jacob Metzes leading up the left hand fork to the low gap on the dividing Ridge between Monongalia, Harrison and Tyler Counties." A new road was requested "beginning at or near the mouth of Parish dreen at the Beverly pike and go up that dreen in a winding direction . . . to the Beverly pike at or near where Reason Everly now lives." A petition was presented for a road "from the Stateline at Blacksville by way of Kings Run to Tenants mill on Daies Run thence crosing pawpaw to the head of Dunkard Mill run." Another road was asked for "from the road leading from Morgantown to Clarksburg near the house of John Jones down Toms run to the little falls in the Monongahela river." Another petition said a new road was needed "from the old State road at Josiah T. Wilson to the North Western turnpike at or near the farm of Isaac Blew. the blacksmith shop at which the neighbourhood gets their work don is situated about half way between these points."

Viewers were appointed to look over the projects proposed and any further action depended upon the report submitted by the viewers.

**New Bridges.** One substantial improvement in the highway system was in the increasing number of streams that were being bridged, making it easier for wagons to cross in all kinds of weather. Typical of county court actions of the time is this decision to build a "bridge across Dunkard Creek near the Tanyard, about three miles below Blacksville." The report stated that the creek was nearly impassable at this point for several months of the year.

**Land Grants Made in 1841.**[21] Monongalia County grantees in 1841 included:

| | | |
|---|---|---|
| Billingsley, John | 125 a. | Buffalo Creek |
| Billingsley, John | 50 | Piles Fork |
| Blackshire, Elias | 55 | Drakes Run |

21. See p. 11.

| Byrne, John P. | 233 | Three Forks Creek |
|---|---|---|
| Clear, Edwin | 100 | Dunkard Creek |
| Davis, Belah | 100 | Dripping Springs |
| Dowd, Charles O. | 250 | Days Run |
| Eddy, Alexander, Jr. | 2¼ | Adj. John Downer |
| Eddy, Alexander, Jr. | 62 | Paw Paw Creek |
| Eddy, David | 72 | Paw Paw Creek |
| Eddy, Michael | 20 | Paw Paw Creek |
| Eddy, Michael | 49 | Paw Paw Creek |
| Hanway, John | 500 | Paw Paw Creek |
| Heck, Adam | 6 | Parkers Run |
| Jacobs, Benjamin | 98 | Coburns Creek |
| Jacobs, Benjamin | 41 | Coburns Creek |
| Lemley, George | 300 | Dunkard Creek |
| Lemley, Jacob | 100 | Dunkard Creek |
| Metz, Leonard, Jr. | 300 | Piles Fork |
| Nuzum, Richard B.[22] | 12 | Tygerts Valley R. |
| Ramsey, John | 3½ | Scotts Run |
| Roby, Randolph | 50 | Plum Run |
| Showalter, Daniel | 200 | Dunkard Creek |
| Thomas, George | 120 | Flat Run |
| Thomas, Isaac | 150 | Miracles Run |
| Thomas, Israel | 160 | Flat Run |
| Thomas, Joseph, Jr. | 300 | Flat Run |
| Thomas, William, Sr. | 5½ | Miracle Run |
| Tower, Edwin W. | 62 | Wickwires Creek |
| Tower, Edwin W. | 500 | Paw Paw Creek |
| Varner, William | 37 | Paw Paw Creek |
| Wilson, Edgar C. | 233 | Three Forks Creek |

**Wick Johnson Dies.** Wick Johnson, merchant and farmer, of
Scotch-Irish extraction, died along the Tygart Valley River in
the Knottsville section in 1841.

In his early life he kept a hotel in Kingwood, "where he was
well and kindly remembered as an excellent landlord a few
years ago, by the then surviving old people of that beautiful and
prosperous town." From Kingwood he went to Evansville,
where he engaged for sometime in the general mercantile busi-

22. The early Nuzum pioneers on Goose Creek were Quakers and organized the Gilboa Church, later turned over to the Dunkards. Balderson,
*Prickett's Fort*, pp. 159, 160.

ness. From there he went to the Tygart Valley, where he followed farming until his death. "As landlord, merchant, and farmer, Mr. Johnson was popular, and had the good will of all who knew him."[23]

He married Clarissa B. Zinn and they had nine children, one of whom was Harrison W. Johnson, a merchant of Mannington.

**County Government.** John Evans was sworn in for his second term as sheriff on March 22, 1841. The county levy was set at $0.75.

**Miscellany.** In 1841: Ralph L. Berkshire was admitted to the county bar on April 8 (Wiley, p. 316). . . . P. S. Ruter was named principal of Monongalia Academy (Wiley, p. 395). . . . Mathew Gay was elected president of the Merchants' and Mechanics' Bank on January 21, succeeding Thomas P. Ray (Wiley, p. 462). . . . Steamboats arriving at the Port of Morgantown included the *Wellsville* on April 19, the *Isaac Walton* on May 1, and the *Effort* on May 3 (Wiley, p. 542). . . . New Morgantown merchants included I. and J. F. Cooper; Postlewaite, Cragan and Company; and Madera and Watts (Wiley, p. 580). . . . Alexander Hayes bought the old tavern opposite the courthouse built by Fauquier McRa in 1797 and named it the Franklin House (Wiley, pp. 567, 604). . . . Samuel C. Bowlby, seventeen-year-old son of John H. Bowlby, died of typhoid fever, said to be the first case in the county (Wiley, pp. 711, 712). . . . Moses Strosnider located in Blacksville (Wiley, p. 745). . . . Harriet Sophia, infant daughter of Frederick Augustus Dering, died (Callahan, p. 86). . . . William Snider conveyed part of Lot 6 in Morgantown to John H. Snider (Callahan, p. 309). . . . John Rogers sold the west end of Lots 33 and 34 to Hugh and Henry Daugherty (Callahan, p. 315). . . . Christian Madera's executors, N. B. Madera and Fielding Kiger, conveyed a portion of Lot 90 to Charles Watts (Callahan, p. 322). . . . Samuel Trinkle sold Lot 119 to Thomas and James Evans (Callahan, p. 329). . . . Margaret McDougal Dudley, wife of Samuel Dudley, died (Lough, p. 387). . . . John Abel moved to a farm just west of Cheat River (Owens, p. 71). . . . Henry Shaffer, Jr., died (Owens, p. 95).

23. *Cyclopedia of Marion County*, pp. 195-97.

## CHAPTER SIXTY-SIX

# 1842

Once more, in 1842, the size of Monongalia County was changed, with the establishment of the new county of Marion. This was the eighth change in the size of the county since its formation in 1776. Increases had been made in the size in 1779 and 1780. Decreases were made in 1782, when the territory north of the Mason and Dixon line was yielded to Pennsylvania and in 1784, when Harrison County was formed. A small section was yielded to Harrison County in 1800 and in 1818 Preston County was taken off. In 1841 a small slice east of Chestnut Ridge was added to Preston.

**Marion County Is Formed.** Marion County was created by an act of the general assembly passed January 14, 1842. The new county had an area of a little over three hundred square miles, most of it coming from the southern part of Monongalia County, but with a portion from Harrison County.

The act of establishment, so far as it concerns Monongalia County, reads as follows:

"So much of the southern end of the county of Monongalia. . . . Beginning at Laurel Point (a corner of the line of Preston County), from thence to the mouth of Maple Run on White Day Creek; thence down White Day Creek to Barnabas Johnson's meadow; thence a straight line to a low gap on the top of a ridge on the lands of the Rev. John Smith, at or near where the road leading from Middletown to Morgantown crosses said ridge, and following said ridge to where the old State Road crosses said ridge, and thence a due west line to the line of Harrison County."

The new county was named for Revolutionary War hero Gen. Francis Marion.

Middletown became the first county seat of Marion County. Established on January 19, 1820, the name Middletown signified that it was halfway between the two county seat towns of Morgantown and Clarksburg.

But now Middletown was itself a county seat and to the residents, according to the *Marion Pioneer*, the county's first newspaper, it seemed "that a more appropriate title should be procured for the young metropolis than mere Middletown." Presently the paper reported: "We are glad to perceive . . . that a bill has passed the house of delegates changing the name of this place from Middletown to Fairmont. Thus it appears that Middletown is no more. This venerable town is numbered with the things that were. The days of Middletown have passed away forever and will be consigned to eternal oblivion, and Fairmont has made its appearance in our village, the bright harbinger of her future greatness and glory."[1] It is said that William Haymond, Jr., suggested the name Fairmont because the location of the town on high hills, with a beautiful outlook, "caused it to be in fact, as well as in name, a fair mount."[2]

The first court for the new county met on April 4, 1842, at the home of William Kerr, in Middletown. Justices present were John S. Barns, Thomas S. Haymond, Thomas Watson, and William Swearingen. The court adjourned to meet in the Methodist church, on Washington Street, where meetings were held until 1844, when the first courthouse was completed.

Zebulon Musgrove was the first crier of the court, Thomas S. Boggess was elected clerk, William C. Haymond was appointed commonwealth attorney, and Austin Merrill surveyor.

At the April term of court, recommendations for sheriff were made to the governor for Isaac Means, William J. Willey, and Matthew Fleming. A controversy apparently developed between those recommended and it seems that for a while all three served. At the May term nominations were again considered and the name of Benjamin J. Brice was substituted for Matthew Fleming. But the court stated that Isaac Means, a justice of the peace for twenty-two years in Monongalia County, was Brice's

1. The *Marion Pioneer*, February 11, 1843.
2. Lough, *Now and Long Ago*, p. 428.

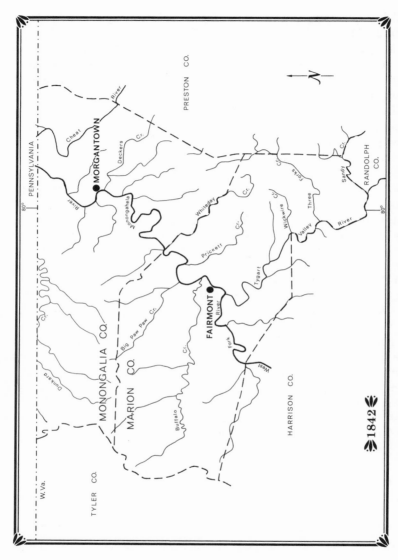

Fig. 36. Map showing formation of Marion County, 1842. (Drawn by Diane Lenhart.)

senior "as to sheriffalty," and the recommendation was passed to the governor. At the June term of court, however, Benjamin Brice was commissioned sheriff.

Elias Dudley was commissioned as the first coroner at the May term and William Swearingen was elected commissioner of revenue at the October term of court.

The county was divided into two poor districts, with Thomas S. Haymond, Jacob Means, and Henry Martin overseers for the Southern District, and John Clayton, Jesse Sturm, and John H. Martin overseers for the Northern District.

At the November term of court the county was divided into nine school districts, with Nathan Hall, John Linn, William Swearingen, Thomas S. Haymond, John Clayton, John S. Smith, Elias Blackshere, Jesse Sturm, and Thomas A. Little named as school commissioners.[3]

**The Circus Comes to Town.** " 'Well, here we are again!' sunshine and cloud; arbutus sprays and drooping lilies; robins and rabbits; cross-buns and buck-beer; dainty bonnets and pretty dresses; prima donnas skipping away and traveling-vans harnessing up; in short, spring has come, and 'the greatest Show on Earth' is on its way once more."

Thus Isaac J. Greenwood opens his little book on the circus, a theme, he says, that is humble and yet divine, tracing its beginning "when in dim time past Phaeton cried:

"O radiant Sire, grant me without delay,
To guide the Sun's bright orbit for a day."[4]

Public amusements date back to ancient times, when the Greeks gathered in the stadium to watch wrestling matches or the Romans assembled in the circus to see chariot races or gladiatorial combats.

On the frontier in America people gathered on the public square or on vacant lots to watch wrestling or bowling matches and cock fights. Gambling was often an accompanying form of entertainment. These "spectator sports" were "improvements"

3. Lough, *Now and Long Ago*, pp. 447, 448.
4. Isaac J. Greenwood, *The Circus, Its Origin and Growth Prior to 1835* (New York, 1898), 117 pp. See also Earl Chapin May, *The Circus, From Rome to Ringling* (1932), 332 pp.; Arthur C. Prichard, "A Circus is Coming," *Goldenseal* 4(1978):41-49.

over the usual recreational activities of the pioneers, such as husking bees, log-rollings, barn-raisings, and quilting bees, which were merely ways of turning hard work into play.

The circus came to America from Europe before 1793; President George Washington attended John Bill Ricketts' Circus in Philadelphia on April 22 in that year, the day he issued his famous proclamation of neutrality.

The larger cities on the seaboard had their places of entertainment but early in the nineteenth century traveling circuses began to make their way through the countryside. One of the best known of these "rolling-shows" was that of Aaron Turner, an Englishman who came to America in 1817 with his two sons, Tim and Napoleon, both good horseback riders and vaulters. Greenwood, in his history, estimates that by 1820 there were over thirty such shows on the road, moving throughout the New England and Atlantic states.

"At first," Greenwood says, "they were but small affairs consisting of a couple of wagons, four horses and some half dozen performers, mostly tumblers and vaulters, with perhaps a trick man and that indispensable—a clown. There was no band, save a fiddle or two; no lady in gauze and spangles, no ringmaster and no tent; but they carried some six-foot poles, around which, planted in a circle, was stretched, at each performance, a canvas to keep them from the gaze of outsiders, while a few boards served to build an inside platform, raised just above the ground, for acrobatic performances, jig-dancing and the like; the rest of their loads was baggage, cooking utensils and provisions. The place of exhibition was open to the sun and rain, though in time a covering suspended from a center-pole was introduced. There were no seats, except such as could be borrowed for the ladies, but sometimes the wagons were drawn in, so that the back crowd could mount upon them, and two hundred and fifty spectators, at an entry price of twenty-five cents, was a big house. Usually a man went ahead who placarded all conspicuous places, procured the five-dollar license and hired the ground; then presently a bugler on horseback announced the approach of the show, and on the village-green the clown would soon be proclaiming the time of performance."[5]

5. Greenwood, pp. 113, 114.

Greenwood says that "before 1847 none of the traveling circuses ventured farther west than Buffalo," but this is not quite correct, since licenses had been granted by the Monongalia County Court to about a dozen shows before that time.

So far as the records indicate, the first license "to exhibit a show" was granted September 24, 1825, to Messrs. Baldwin Smith, Kelly and Company. The fee was twenty-five dollars.

The next year, on June 30, a license was issued to Vanwyck Field and Company for twenty-five dollars "to exhibit a public show."

On September 9, 1829, a license was issued to Alexander McKinley and Chauncey Griswold, "exhibitors of public show."

Again, on October 14, 1829, for the same fee, a license was issued to Jonah Ogden and Company, and on August 7, 1832, to William and J. R. Howe, "exhibitors of public show."

By 1833 the cost of a license had risen to thirty dollars. On September 24 of that year a license was issued to Messrs. Miller, Mead, and Olmstead, "exhibitors of a show."

Typical of the records kept by the court is the following: "Recd. July 12th, 1834 of French Holby & Co. Thirty dollars the amount prescribed by Law to be paid for the privilege of Exhibiting animals and Circus and paintings, for one year from this date. Charles Madera, deputy, for Thos. S. Haymond, S. M. C."

Other licenses to exhibit shows in Monongalia County were as follows:

August 31, 1839. License fee thirty dollars, issued to James Husted, "exhibitor of public show."

July 15, 1840. License to Messrs. Fogg and Stickney for thirty dollars "to exhibit public show."

August 12, 1840. License to J. L. Humphrey "to exhibit show in Monongalia County."

September 8, 1841. "Receipt for $40 license fee issued to Titus Augustine & Co. to exhibit show."

Most of these shows probably did not exhibit animals but at least some of them did and local tradition tells how elephants, trudging slowly along, were required to wade through the streams for fear of breaking the bridges down.

Brinkman includes among travelers on the early Northwestern Turnpike "the gaudily painted wagons of the old John

Robinson circus and the lone elephant shuffling along in the rear, Robinson on his way to Williamsport to visit his boyhood friend, Abraham Smith."[6]

**The Regular Baptist Church of Morgantown.** Although the first church organized in the county was a Baptist congregation,[7] the denomination was late in forming a body in the county seat. About 1831 or 1832 they discussed plans to erect a house of worship in Morgantown and had the opportunity to secure joint use of the proposed Female Academy building by contributing to its construction. In 1833 they sought, acting through trustees of the "Baptist Church of the Forks of Cheat and Morgantown," to obtain a clear title to Lot 101, known in early town plats as the "grave yard lot." Affidavits were secured from Mrs. Rachel Chipps, a daughter of John McFarland, and from Colonel John Evans, a former county clerk; the latter stated that he "recollects that a deed was made by Z. Morgan to John McFarland, William John, Owen Davis, and Thos. Mills, as trustees of the Baptist church, to a lot of ground in Morgantown fronting on Front Street and numbered in plot of town No. 101, that said deed was recorded in the Clerk's office of the County Court previous to the burning of said office in 1796."[8]

On February 1, 1842, several members of the Regular Baptist Church residing in the community, with the assistance of four Regular Baptist ministers, organized a congregation in Morgantown, consisting of twenty-two members, each of whom signed the church covenant and the declaration of faith, agreeing among other things to be subject to the civil powers.

The Regular Baptists were the original English Baptists, before their division into the Particular and General Baptists. They were moderately Calvinistic in doctrine, practicing close communion and foot washing. Like later Baptists, they believed immersion to be the true form of baptism.

The twenty-three charter members were Jacob H. Shafer,

6. *History of Taylor County*, chap. 13; see also Balderson, *Prickett's Fort*, p. 160.
7. The Forks of Cheat Baptist Church; see *The Monongalia Story*, vol. 1, pp. 309-12.
8. Callahan, *Making of Morgantown*, p. 158. For background, see Jesse L. Boyd, *A History of Baptists in America* (1957); also Robert G. Torbet, *A History of the Baptists* (1950).

Ann Shafer, Jane Chadwick, Gideon Way, Jane Way, John Murphy, John Joseph, Sarah Joseph, Mary H. Shuff, Mary Evans, Elizabeth John, Malinda St. Clair, Abigail Houston, William Haney, Mathias Tilton, Elizabeth Tilton, Martin Callendine, Anna Callendine, Mary Ann Way, Wilson Crowl, Anna Crowl, Emily Kern, and Martha Evans.

Mathias Tilton was elected clerk, and Rev. A. J. Garrett was chosen as the first minister, with the Reverend John Thomas to preach once each month. Among the most prominent of the early members were Gideon Way and Martin Callendine; the latter, in August 1842, was elected collector and treasurer. Among early additions were James Evans, Elizabeth A. Eagle, and Perry Jones, a black man, all of whom were baptized in the river.

The first problem was to find a suitable meeting place. At first, services were held in the courthouse, and also sometimes in the Methodist church. On February 2, 1842, the Rev. Mr. Garrett suggested that the congregation consider raising money to build a meetinghouse on Lot 101. A fund raising campaign began and on August 20 the congregation chose as trustees, to secure a title to the graveyard lot, Edgar C. Wilson, Martin Callendine, and James H. Shafer. On September 7, these trustees appeared before the Circuit Superior Court of Law and Chancery, claiming that Lot 101 (although never occupied by the Baptists) had always been known as the Baptist graveyard lot. They presented the earlier affidavits of Rachel Chipps and John Evans and extracts from the records of the old Forks of Cheat Church as evidence of their right to hold the lot in trust for the Baptist church. The court gave its approval.

**"The Buffalo Creek Meeting House."** Meanwhile, a group of Baptists met in the home of Patrick Clelland, on the site of Barrackville, in 1841 to organize a new congregation. The Reverend A. J. Garrett provided leadership and in 1842 a church building was erected on a hill above Buffalo Creek. Since it was the only church in the neighborhood, it was commonly known simply as "The Meeting House." The Reverend Mr. Garrett served as pastor of the congregation for the next thirty-eight years.[9]

9. *Bicentennial Church Histories of Marion County*, p. 55.

**The B.&O. Reaches Cumberland.** After many long and frustrating delays, the track of the Baltimore and Ohio Railroad was finally completed to Cumberland on November 5, 1842. The end of track had reached a point opposite Harpers Ferry in 1833 and on December 1, 1834, connection had been made with the Winchester and Potomac Railroad at that point. Better cars and better engines were being built and various helpful devices had been invented, such as switches and turntables.

For the next several years westward extension was abandoned, as the general assembly continued to deny requests to construct the line through the counties of Northwestern Virginia.

Reconnaissances of engineers who had looked over proposed routes from Harpers Ferry to Wheeling[10] and from Cumberland to Pittsburgh were reported to the directors in 1837 and the directors then recommended extension of the line to Cumberland at a cost of $4.6 million. Maryland and Baltimore each agreed to subscribe $3 million but funds were not immediately available to finance the new construction or to rebuild the crude and experimental road already built so as to meet the needs of growing traffic. It was still necessary to overcome objections to extension of the railway line alongside the Chesapeake and Ohio Canal.

Finally, in 1838, the general assembly granted a five-year extension of the earlier charter, allowing for construction through Virginia territory from Harpers Ferry west to a point near Cumberland, with the provision that Wheeling would eventually be one of the termini on the Ohio. The assembly added a new subscription of $1,058,420 to the $302,100 subscribed to the stock of the company in 1836.

The directors, faced with overwhelming difficulties of obtaining ready cash, adopted the expedient of paying bills by certificates redeemable in Baltimore City 6 percent stock at par. Construction was then resumed in 1840 and the line completed to Cumberland two years later.[11]

10. One route considered would have passed through Morgantown (see p. 292).

11. Callahan, *Semi-Centennial History of West Virginia*, pp. 112, 113; see also Edward Hungerford, *The Story of the Baltimore and Ohio Railroad* (1928), 2 vols.

The completion of the railroad to Cumberland made it much easier to reach points beyond the mountains, including Uniontown, Morgantown, and other places. Traffic on the National Road across the Alleghenies, already heavy, increased greatly and it is said that there were so many competing stagecoach lines that often there were fifteen or twenty coaches entering and leaving Cumberland twice each day. There was a corresponding increase of traffic by wagons; forty often entered Wheeling in a day. Considerable obstruction to stagecoaches and wagons resulted from the numerous droves of cattle, sheep, and hogs, headed for the Eastern markets.[12]

**County Newspapers.** According to Wiley,[13] the weekly newspaper, *Democratic Republican,* ceased publication in 1842. Wiley says that in 1840 the editor, Enos D. Morgan, changed politics and became a Whig, and that the paper was Whig until it ended.

Another paper, the *Democratic Watchtower,* was projected about 1842 by Joseph H. Powell and a man by the name of Treadwell. But it was said that Treadwell got on a drunken spree about the time the first number was to go to press, and it was never issued.[14]

**New Roads Requested.** A few petitions for new roads or alteration of existing roads continued to be made in 1842. A new road was asked for, "commencing at or near some large rocks on the new road leading from Mercers ferry to Middletown. The rocks named is just below Moses Coxes house and from that point on the old county road and with it some distance then leaving it and going past the house of John Wagoner passing the barn that is on the sd. farm so as to strike the turnpike at or near a fill that George Lemons made then down a drain to the Grandville road."

Construction, maintenance, and repair of the roads were done by farmers of the neighborhood who were "impressed" by county court warrants to do the work, and to furnish wagons and horses when necessary. Protests against these warrants were sometimes filed, especially when it was felt the road in question

12. Callahan, *Semi-Centennial History of West Virginia,* p. 92.
13. *History of Monongalia County,* p. 434.
14. Wiley, p. 434.

was not important or work did not need to be done. "Surveyors" were appointed to supervise the work.

After the work was completed, allowances were granted by the court in payment. Typical amounts in 1842 were $1.75 a day for a "span of oxen cart and driver"; $1.00 per day for a man and "plough team"; and $1.75 for a sled, two horses, and a driver.

**Michael Courtney, Sr.** An Irish immigrant, Michael Courtney, died April 16, 1842, in Trumbull County, Ohio. He was baptized in Ireland October 1, 1758, the son of Thomas Courtney, and came to Monongalia County about 1786. He married Nancy Ann George and their children were Robert, Nancy Ann, Matthew George, John Wesley, Thomas R., Susan, Elizabeth, Sarah, Hester Ann, and Cassandra. Another son, Michael, Jr., according to tradition, was born out of wedlock.[15]

**Henry Michael.** Henry Michael, a farmer of Stewarts Run, died June 4, 1842. He was born in 1766, a son of Daniel Michael, a pioneer settler there, who "was industrious, soon succeeded in establishing a comfortable home, and eventually became one of the most thrifty and successful farmers of the county, owning at the time of his demise a large amount of real estate."

Henry Michael lived on a portion of his father's homestead and engaged in agricultural pursuits. "Energetic, industrious, and well trained and schooled under the direction of his father, . . . he was successful from the very start." He was married twice, first to a Fetty, with whom he had nine children, then to Anna Bayne, who bore him five children, including A. N. Michael.[16]

**Benjamin Reeder.** An early settler whose name appears on many pages of Monongalia County's pioneer history, Benjamin Reeder, died in Harrison County in 1842.[17] He was born in

15. Pers. comm., Eldon B. Tucker, Jr., Salt Lake City, Utah.
16. *Cyclopedia of Monongalia County*, p. 206.
17. Wiley (footnote, p. 403), referring to the later West Virginia University, says that the grounds "once belonged to Squire Benjamin Reeder, who lived on them in a large white frame house, and who lies buried not far from the present buildings." This must be an error, however, since he was apparently buried in a family cemetery near the later village of Enterprise.

1762, the son of Simon and Sarah (Greene) Reeder, who moved to Monongalia County about 1783. Benjamin Reeder married Eleanor Slaughton, of Alexandria, Virginia, in 1786; one of their children, Thomas Reeder (1800-1873), married Eliza, daughter of Asa Shinn.

Benjamin Reeder was a land speculator, dealing in Revolutionary War land warrants and patenting thousands of acres of land. Among other properties he owned was that on which Woodburn Female Seminary was later built (see pp. 464, 465). He moved to Harrison County in 1828.[18]

**Land Grants Made in 1842.**[19] Monongalia County grantees in 1842 included:

| | | |
|---|---|---|
| Baker, Nathan | 100 a. | Piles Fork |
| Clemens, John | 420 | Piles Fork |
| Davis, William B. | 120 | Piles Fork |
| Fetterman, Sarah B. | 2¼ | Three Forks Creek |
| Fleming, John S. | 100 | Buffalo Creek |
| Freeland, John | 31 | Adj. E. Blackshire |
| Hanway, John | 4½ | Adj. Wm. Stewart |
| Hanway, John | 44 | Kellums Fork |
| Hanway, John | 235 | Buffalo Creek |
| Hawkins, Elijah | 9 | Adj. J. Vandergrift |
| Hixenbaugh, Abraham, and George, Jr. | 150 | Briar Run |
| Jones, John | 1¾ | Adj. Josiah Wilson |
| Jones, Stanton | 23 | Three Forks Creek |
| Keefover, George | 174 | Piles Fork |
| Lockard, George | 190 | Piles Fork |
| Martin, Samuel G. | 18 | Wickwires Creek |
| Martin, Spencer | 115 | Piles Fork |
| Martin, Thornton F. | 365 | Johnnys Run |
| McDiffit, John | 100 | Piles Fork |
| Moore, John | 45 | Days Run |
| Scott, David | 4¼ | Adj. Jacob Shively |
| Wade, Alexander, Jr. | 210 | Dunkard Creek |
| Wade, Alexander, Jr. | 950 | Piles Fork |

18. Data from the *Book of Reeder* (typescript, 187 pp., without date), prepared by Benjamin Garnet Reeder, a great-grandson, and made available to the author by him.

19. See p. 11.

| Watson, James O. | 235 | Buffalo Creek |
| Wilson, Edgar C. | 100 | Laurel Run |
| Youst, John D. | 175 | Paw Paw Creek |
| Youst, Peter | 100 | Piles Fork |

**County Government.** Samuel Minor was sworn in as sheriff on March 28, 1842. W. W. John was appointed commissioner of the revenue for the Eastern District. New justices of the peace sworn in May 23 were John Watts, Martin Callendine, William Launtz, Morgan S. Bayles, Hugh Daugherty; Henry Watson, and James Evans. Augustus Haymond was appointed coroner. The county levy was $1.25.

**Miscellany.** In 1842: Waitman T. Willey was sworn in on April 8 as clerk of the Circuit Superior Court of Law and Chancery (Wiley, p. 312). . . . Eusebius P. Lowman was admitted to the county bar on April 26 (Wiley, p. 316). . . . Other attorneys admitted to the bar this year included E. M. Davisson and Charles A. Harper (Wiley, p. 318). . . . Lycurgus Stephen Hough moved to Morgantown from Loudoun County (Wiley, p. 356). . . . Miss ———— Faris was appointed principal of the Morgantown Female Academy (Wiley, p. 399). . . . "Furnace script," issued by the Cheat River Iron Works, was used as currency at the furnace stores (Wiley, p. 461). . . . Steamboats arriving at the Port of Morgantown included the *Traveller*, on January 12, and the *Alpine*, on December 10 (Wiley, p. 542). . . . New merchants in Morgantown were Haymond and Madera, Richard Serpell, George Kramer and Son, D. C. and J. C. Chadwick, N. Pickenpaugh, and W. and E. C. Lazier (Wiley, p. 580). . . . Susan Chalfant was running a tavern (Callahan, p. 117) and a grocery store on Front Street (Wiley, pp. 583, 587). . . . James House moved from Fayette County, Pennsylvania to West Run; he married Dianna Ross (Wiley, p. 676). . . . Rev. William Wood was pastor of the Forks of Cheat Baptist Church (Wiley, p. 686). . . . Alpheus Garrison came from Guernsey County, Ohio, and settled on Pedlar Run (Wiley, p. 754). . . . Mary Ann, widow of Alpheus Poage Wilson, died (Callahan, p. 93). . . . Dr. Joseph Alan McLane began the practice of medicine in Morgantown; his wife was Mary Lazier (Callahan, p. 97). . . . Joel Ridgway conveyed a portion of Lot 102 in Morgantown to James T. Davis (Callahan, p. 325). . . . Nancy Blue, sister of John W. Blue, drowned October 13 in the Tygart Valley River just below the Valley Bridge on the Northwestern Turnpike (Bartlett, p. 64).

# CHAPTER SIXTY-SEVEN

# 1843

The decade of the 1840s was the most prosperous period for the Cheat iron industry, which had begun operation as early as 1798, perhaps earlier.[1]

Monongalia County had been very fortunately endowed by nature for the production of iron. The ore was available in at least three seams outcropping along the slopes of Chestnut Ridge; limestone used in the processing was also in abundance; and charcoal, for fuel, was readily produced from wood of beech trees (or other trees), common in the forests.

**The Ellicott Industries.** Ellicott's rolling mill began operation on Monday, September 14, 1840.

Samuel Jackson, one of the earliest of the operators, had started "Jackson's Old Iron Works" about 1809, along Cheat River near Ice's Ferry. About 1822 Josiah Jackson, son of Samuel, built the Woodgrove Furnace, about three miles from Ice's Ferry, on Morgan Run at Darnell Hollow. It stood on the Samuel Canby one-thousand-acre tract, which Jackson had purchased in 1818 from the heirs of Amos Hough. This tract, along with seventeen other tracts, totaling over five thousand acres, was conveyed by Jackson on April 1, 1836, to John Tassey, Samuel Church, John Bissell, William Morrison, and Leonard Lamb, in consideration of the sum of $25,000, a very large amount at the time.

On April 23, 1839, Tassey, Morrison and their partners conveyed thirty tracts of land to Evans T. Ellicott and Andrew Ellicott for $92,000. These tracts included about 15,000 acres,

1. See *The Monongalia Story*, vol. 2, pp. 265-69, 289-92, 458-60.

with all the mills and improvements, as well as the Pleasant, Woodgrove, and Henry Clay furnaces. In 1842 the Ellicotts organized the Monongalia Iron Works and during the next few years the industry reached its zenith.

In addition to the furnaces thus acquired, the Ellicotts built the Anna Furnace about 1845-48 near Ice's Ferry. It was named for the wife of Evans T. Ellicott and at first used charcoal but later coke. Its capacity was eight to ten tons daily.

The rolling mill was built to roll out iron bars and plates of various sizes. They also built a puddling mill, for conversion of pig iron into wrought iron by subjecting it to heat and "puddling" (stirring) in the presence of oxidizing substances. They enlarged the nail factory and stove factory, already in operation, and built machine, wagon, and blacksmith shops, and a large number of dwelling houses. To transport the ore, charcoal, pig iron, etc., they built nearly fifteen miles of tramways, connecting all their furnaces. James R. Moreland, who has been the principal historian of the Cheat iron works,[2] estimates that these various industries, at their greatest extent, employed over 1,700 men and that 3,000 people, scattered through the mountainous area, depended on the iron company for their living.

Moreland describes the transportation system: "Those tramways, while used in connection with the iron industry, at first contained no metal in their construction at all. One witness in a suit at a much later date described the tramways in a very interesting way. He said they first graded the road bed, some of the cuts were five to six feet deep, it was well located according to the lay of the land, then they cut down tall straight young trees hewed square with as much length as the size would justify. They next cut the cross ties, which they notched at each end in such a manner that the notch would hold the wooden rail when a wedge was driven into the notch along the outside of the rail. Those notches were spaced just right to make the tram's guage suitable for the cars which they used and the wedges took the place of spikes to hold the rails in place. The

2. *The Early Cheat Mountain Iron Works*, pp. 77, 78. It is likely that there has been considerable exaggeration in these figures over the years. The 1840 census lists 65 men as employed in iron mining. The number engaged in all types of manufacturing in the county is given as 185 by the 1850 census.

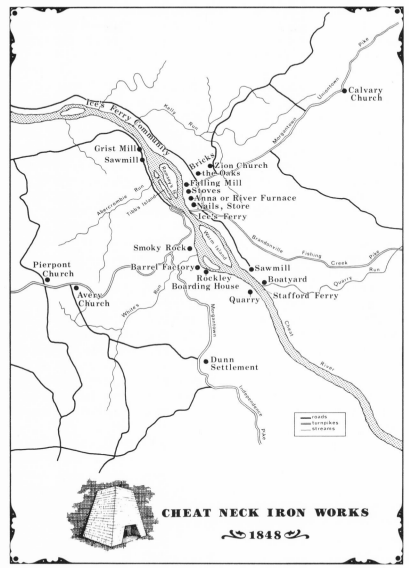

Fig. 37. a. Map of Ice's Ferry and vicinity in 1848, at the zenith of the
iron works. (Drawn by Diane Lenhart, from information furnished by Dr.
Kenneth L. Carvell.)

only iron used was in the wheels of the cars, as we gather that even the axles of the cars were wood. Wood was cheap and plentiful, labor was inexpensive, the men knew how to chop and hew, but iron cost $100.00 per ton in pigs so it had to be conserved."[3]

John L. Johnston, a professor of civil engineering at West Virginia University, talked with persons who had been familiar with the old iron works and brought some of the recollections together in historical notes (about 1909-12), which are quoted by Moreland. The tramways started, he said, at the Anna or River Furnace, and the Jackson or Laurel Iron Works, on Cheat River "and went up the mountain through the Andrew Ice 400 acre survey, through the Thomas Evans 220 acre survey, thence one branch through the Thomas Evans 460 acre survey, onto the John Davis 2,000 acre survey to the Henry Clay Furnace. The other branch started on the Evans 220 acre survey, through the Thomas Evans 460 survey, and the Stephens 140 acre survey, across John Davis' 700 acre survey to the ore beds on the Ross or Hope tract of 910 acres on the very top of the mountain. Some of the cuts, he said, were five or six feet and most of them were (in 1912) still well preserved. He said that the fills had been well graded and carefully built." Professor Johnston said that in later years a piece of strap iron was placed along the wood rail.[4]

No mention is made of any tramway used in connection with the Woodgrove Furnace. The ore came from the Johnson Hollow and was hauled down by wagons. Only pig iron was made here.

The Ellicotts were quite progressive. They introduced steam at the Woodgrove Furnace, although the hot blast process came later. Around the furnace were stores, stables, and other buildings with houses for from 150 to 200 men. In those days men had to live close to their work. The men lived in fifty or sixty hewed log houses near the furnace.

**Morgantown Female Academy.** The two Morgantown academies were making steady gains and in 1843 the girls' school had progressed to the point where more space was needed and an

3. Op. cit., p. 74.
4. Ibid.

Fig. 37. b. Cheat Iron Works, tramways, etc. (Photo courtesy Fred H. Weltner.)

addition to the building on Bumbo Lane was authorized. No school was held, then, for a year, while the improvements were being made.

Technically, the school was known as the Morgantown Female Collegiate Institute, from the term used in the act of incorporation by the general assembly.[5]

**Huggans' Chapel.** Shadrach and Jane Huggans, on December 28, 1833, bought from Jacob Statler a tract of land lying on the ridge between Pedlar Run and Long Drain, a branch of Jakes Run. They added to this farm by purchasing an additional tract from Jonathan Wright on June 3, 1843.

The Hugganses were members of the Methodist Episcopal Church and settlers in the area with leanings towards that faith met, in the 1830s at their home on the ridge. Finally a log church was built nearby, known as Huggans' Chapel.[6]

**Mooresville.** About 1840 to 1843 Rawley Moore (1817-1907) had William Price lay out a town on Jakes Run to be known as Mooresville. Rawley was a son of Michael Moore, Sr. (died 1812), and a brother of Michael, Jr. Michael, Sr., had moved to Monongalia County about 1785 from Hardy County, where his father, Philip More,[7] had settled prior to 1748. The town of Moorefield was established in 1777 on lands owned by Conrad More, another son of Philip.

The first lots in the village of Mooresville were bought by William Price, Jacob Moore, R. B. Tennant, John Piles, and William Sine; John Piles, it is said, built the first house. A tavern or two were opened, and it became a place notorious for liquor-drinking.[8]

**Edward Parrish and the Oregon Trail.** Edward Evans Parrish, Sr., arrived from Philadelphia about 1781 and settled in the

5. Wiley, p. 398. In later years it was known popularly as the Whitehall Female Seminary, on account of a white coat of paint having been applied to the building.

6. Core, *Chronicles of Core*, pp. 44, 65.

7. The family named was originally spelled More, and seems to have been changed to Moore, after settlement in Virginia.

8. R. B. Tennant, whose land adjoined the village, later became tired of the continual drinking and carousing, and bought up the town, lot by lot, and tore down all the houses but one. Wiley, p. 747; Core, *Chronicles of Core*, p. 71.

Crooked Run community in Monongalia County west of the Monongahela River (*Monongalia Story*, vol. 2, p. 537).

His son, Edward Evans Parrish, Jr., born here in 1800, was married in 1827 to Rebecca Maple, daughter of Rev. Thomas Maple. Edward, Jr., also became a minister and moved to Ohio with his family.

In 1843 the Parrish family joined a covered wagon train for Oregon, where they settled. On the long journey of fifteen months along the Oregon Trail he kept a detailed diary of events and conditions.[9]

**Samuel Baker.** Samuel Baker, a son of John Baker, of the Cheat section, died in 1843. John was a native of Germany, emigrating to this country at an early age, locating for a short time in Philadelphia, then removing to Monongalia County, where he spent the remainder of his life as a farmer.

Samuel Baker married Mary Dugan and they had nine children, namely, Thornton; Malinda, married Rev. Asby Stevens, of Palatine; John; Alcinda, married Eugene Bright; James; Elizabeth, married James P. St. Clair; Sarah, married Thomas Wilkinson; Henry C., married Eliza J. Everly; and Thomas M.

**John Hood.** John Hood, a well-known merchant of the Monongahela Valley, died in Monongalia County, March 21, 1843, when only forty-five years of age. He was a son of Archibald Hood, who was born in Scotland and migrated to Waynesburg, Pennsylvania. John was born in 1799 in Washington County, Pennsylvania. He was "one of the most remarkable and successful business men that southwestern Pennsylvania has ever produced."

John Hood operated two or three large farms, ran several lines of huckster and peddling wagons, and in 1836 started the large wholesale grocery and provision house of Hailman, Hood and Company, of Pittsburgh. He also ran a line of trading boats on the Monongahela and Ohio rivers, and operated several large saddlery and harness shops, whose products were widely sold.

9. Callahan, *Making of Morgantown*, pp. 13, 128. From this diary years later Emerson Hough obtained material used in writing *The Covered Wagon*, which in turn was the basis for the popular moving picture production of the same name. For further information on the Parrish family, see *Cyclopedia of Marion County*, pp. 74, 75.

In connection with these enterprises he also engaged in numerous other lines of business, one of which was the buying and selling of whiskey. The last dozen years of his life were spent principally in Monongalia County.

"At the time of his death he was entering upon a wider career of business that promised abundant prosperity to himself and usefulness to the commercial interests of western Virginia and western Pennsylvania. Prudent but energetic in his enterprises and enthusiastically hopeful in whatever he engaged, his untimely death was severely felt in the Monongahela valley from Pittsburg to Fairmont."

He married Letitia, daughter of John Smith, of Waynesburg, and they had ten children, namely, John S., farmer and mill owner of Lowesville; William, farmer of Shinnston; Alfred, first postmaster of Hoodsville, for whom the office was named; James, postmaster at Lowesville; Joseph A., merchant of Lowesville; Maria, married Philip Lowe; Letitia, married Jacob Huffman; Margaret; Caroline; and Mary Ellen.[10]

**William Jones.** A famous Indian encounter of pioneer Monongalia County involved the capture of two children of Jacob Jones on Dunkard Creek in 1777 (*Monongalia Story*, vol. 2, pp. 9, 10). After the capture of the children, the family withdrew to a safer situation, finally settling near Knottsville, in southern Monongalia County, in 1794. Jacob and his wife Dinah died about 1828, aged ninety-six and ninety-three years, respectively.

William was one of their eight children and continued to live in the Knottsville section. He was born in Monongalia County May 4, 1774, and followed the calling of a farmer. He married Sarah Anderson and they had ten children, namely, Jacob (1797-1879), Jane (married Jacob Means), Delight (1801-1856), Anderson, Fleming, Samuel (married Frances Limber), Uriah, Rebecca (married Melker Shroyer), Nathan, Eliza (married Andrew Miller).

William Jones died near Knottsville, May 17, 1843.[11]

**New County Papers.** The historian of Monongalia County of the early 1840s is not aided very much by newspapers of the times

10. *Cyclopedia of Marion County*, pp. 171-73.
11. *Upper Monongahela Valley*, pp. 874-79.

that have been preserved until the present. This is in spite of the fact that several papers are said to have been published in those years.

The *Democratic Republican*, which had been started by Enos D. Morgan in 1835,[12] came to an end in 1842, but Morgan started a new paper late in 1843, using a press he had purchased from the *Silk Culturist*, of Brandonville, Preston County.[13] The new paper, called the *Northwestern Journal*, was a four-page sheet, about twenty-two by thirty-two, with twenty-four columns. Although it is said to have survived until 1845, no copies have been seen.[14]

Another paper, the *Virginia Shield*, is said to have been issued about 1843, but no copies have been found. It was about twenty by thirty in size, edited by Joseph H. Powell, and was Democratic in politics.[15]

**Joseph H. Powell.** Although very little is known of the paper, the *Virginia Shield*, its editor was a very known journalist. Joseph H. Powell was the son of a Monongalia County farmer, Chalfant Powell. Joseph served an apprenticeship in a printing office before starting the *Shield*, which apparently did not last very long.

Powell then left Monongalia County with the idea of pushing to the West on the Northwestern Turnpike, but arriving at Clarksburg he gave up the idea and went into the printing and publishing business there. "He was a clear and interesting writer, and some of his articles on Indian border warfare and other subjects were read with attention and have been frequently quoted."

He married Sarah A. Pugh and their son, Larmer C., born

12. See p. 129.
13. *The Silk Culturist* was published, starting in June 1839, by Jacob Alter and Joseph Miller in a log house on "Mount Pleasant Farm" near Brandonville. It was a monthly magazine six by nine inches in size, consisting of sixteen to twenty-four double column pages. The full title was *Mount Pleasant Silk Culturist and Farmers' Manual: Devoted to the Growth and Manufacture of Silk and Belt Sugar, and the Improvement of Agriculture, Horticulture, and Rural and Domestic Economy.* It lasted about one year. Wiley, *History of Preston County*, pp. 87-89; Morton, *History of Preston County*, pp. 190-92. A few issues are preserved in the West Virginia University Library.
14. Wiley, p. 434.
15. Wiley, p. 434.

May 4, 1846, became a partner in 1874 with A. H. Fleming in the publication of the *Fairmont West Virginian.*[16]

**Land Grants Made in 1843.**[17] Monongalia County grantees in 1843 included:

| | | |
|---|---|---|
| Austin, William | 60 a. | Booths Creek |
| Clark, Samuel | 65 | Flat Run |
| Dunn, Thomas | 320 | Adj. C. Gallagher |
| Fleming, Elizabeth | 20 | Adj. T. Robinson |
| Fleming, Matthew | 72 | Miracle Run |
| Fluharty, Hannah | 50 | Glade Run |
| Jenkins, Wilson | 5 | Cheat River |
| Keener, George, heirs | 100 | Iron Ore Ridge |
| Poe, William | 8½ | Flat Run |
| Rice, Joseph | 27 | Scotts Run |
| Stafford, James H. | 15 | Waters Cheat R. |
| Thomas, William | 110 | Miracle Run |
| Tower, Edwin W. | 4 | Adj. Benj. Hamilton |

**County Government.** Samuel Minor was sworn in for his second term as sheriff on March 27, 1843. Anthony Smith was appointed commissioner of the revenue for the Eastern District and John Stewart, then William Hood, for the Western District. The county levy was set at $1.25.

**Miscellany.** In 1843: Waitman T. Willey addressed the literary society of Allegheny College on "The Influence of Virtue upon the Character, and its Effects upon the Higher Attributes of the Mind" (Wiley, pp. 172, 173). . . . Steamboats arriving at the Port of Morgantown included the *Aetna*, on April 6, the *Rambler*, on April 18, and the *Oella*, on December 25 (Wiley, p. 542). . . . George M. Reay, son of John Otho and Elizabeth Reay, built a house on the south side of Deckers Creek near its mouth (Wiley, p. 598). . . . Joshua Crowther and Rev. Edward Price came from England and inspected the iron ore seams along Deckers Creek at Rock Forge with the idea of developing them (Wiley, p. 654). . . . Mary Jane and "Menerva Harvy" young children of "Robbert and Ruth Harvy" (Harvey) died on October 25 and November 1 and were among the first to be buried

16. *Cyclopedia of Marion County*, pp. 42, 43.
17. See p. 11.

in a new cemetery on Dolls Run at the mouth of Smoky Drain (*Chronicles of Core*, p. 72). . . . Nimrod Madera in October conveyed Lot 90 in Morgantown to James Protzman (Callahan, p. 322). . . . Joshua Low died June 22, aged ninety years (see *Monongalia Story*, vol. 2, p. 144).

CHAPTER SIXTY-EIGHT

# 1844

One of the most persistent and nagging problems of Monongalia County from the very beginning of its history was that of transportation. A rugged mountainous territory separated the Monongahela Valley from eastern communities; road construction was difficult and traffic moved slowly at best.

It was particularly frustrating to know that a broad river flowed through the middle of the county, promising a solution to transportation difficulties, and then to realize that this promise was seldom fulfilled. Much of the time the water in the river was too low for dependable movement of large boats, or too high and swift for safety.

**Towards Slack Water.**[1] As early as April 15, 1782, the commonwealth of Pennsylvania made the Monongahela River in her territory a public highway and later appointed a commission to survey the river from Pittsburgh to the Virginia line and to estimate the cost of "locks, works or devices necessary to be made to render said river navigable." But nothing came from this survey.

Similarly, the Monongahela Navigation Company, a Virginia corporation chartered in 1817, accomplished nothing.

The first steamboat reached Morgantown in 1826 and thereafter one or two steamboats arrived most years, but they were of comparatively little value in transportation because of their uncertainty.

In 1837 a second Monongahela Navigation Company, a Pennsylvania corporation, was organized, and progress at last began

1. We are indebted to Richard T. Wiley, *Monongahela: The River and its Region,* pp. 153-75, for much of the material in this section.

to be made. It was determined that the river was 90½ miles long from Pittsburgh to the Virginia line and that the ascent in that distance was 74½ feet. It was obvious that, to provide for regular, dependable transportation, a system of locks and dams would have to be constructed, similar to those that had been used in canals in Europe since the fifteenth century and which had been used in the Erie Canal, completed across New York State in 1825. These structures, in rivers, of course, had to be much more sturdily built than in canals, because of damage likely to be sustained by frequent heavy floods that swept downstream. The dammed up water, more uniform in depth, and with a much reduced current, is known as *slack water*.

Various engineering surveys were made of the river between Pittsburgh and the state line and it was finally decided to construct four locks between Pittsburgh and Brownsville, where connection would be made with the National Road.

The next problem was to secure the money necessary for the construction. Efforts were made to sell stock in the company and the state of Pennsylvania encouraged the project by subscribing $125,000. But there were repeated delays because of lack of funds.

At last the company advertised for bids on the first two locks and placed notices in various newspapers. The Morgantown newspaper, for example, carried a "Notice to Contractors" from the Monongahela Navigation Company, for "constructing two Steamboat Locks, and two crab dams," the locks to be of cut stone 180 by 40 feet, the dams 900 and 1,200 feet long.[2]

Contracts were let late in 1838 and work began in the spring as soon as weather conditions would permit. More than once the work had to be suspended for lack of funds, but the autumn of 1841 saw the completion of work on Lock No. 1, in the Pittsburgh area, and Lock No. 2, a short distance above the mouth of Turtle Creek.

In the meantime contracts were let for No. 3, just below the mouth of Watsons Run, two miles above the boat landing at Elizabeth, and No. 4, about two miles below Belle Vernon. Their construction was also attended with much difficulty by reason of the financial stringency.

2. The *Republican*, November 3, 1838.

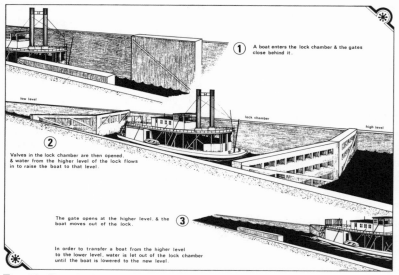

Fig. 38. Sketch showing how river locks work. (Drawn by Diane Lenhart.)

Various financial disasters threatened the project and 1843 was a dark period, when it looked as though the investors would lose everything. But persistence paid off and Nos. 3 and 4 were completed and put into operation in the autumn of 1844. Slack-water navigation between Pittsburgh and Brownsville became a reality.

The new locks and dams were described in an early engineer's report as follows:

"The locks are massive structures of cut stone masonry set in hydraulic cement, with chambers measuring 190 feet in length and 50 feet in width. The points of the heavy miter gates are suspended from the tops of the walls and swing clear of the floor. The gates are opened and closed by means of capstans placed on top of the walls.

"The dams vary in length from 605 to 1000 feet, with a base of 65 feet in width, and a height of from 13 to 16 feet, according to the depth of water where they are located. They are constructed of timbers, laid in alternate courses, forming open cribs, 7 and 9 feet each, spiked at all crossings and filled with stone. . . .

"The huge and apparently unwieldy gates, which are necessarily required to confine and discharge immense volumes of water contained in a lock of such unusual capacity as these of the Monongahela navigation, are worked by a mechanical contrivance of the simplest description, with an ease and celerity which enables the largest steamboats to pass through them in the incredibly short space of five minutes."[3]

Traffic was considerable from the beginning and grew rapidly. Connections were made with the National Road at Brownsville and with Ohio River packets at Pittsburgh. But the growing communities along the river also contributed their share of business for the conveyance of passengers and freight. The Pittsburgh and Brownsville Packet Company entered at once upon the career which long made it famous.

These developments were watched with interest by the people of Monongalia County. But almost a half century would go by before slack water finally reached Morgantown.

**Rock Forge.** The old Deckers Creek iron works, known as Rock Forge, were in operation at least as early as 1798.[4] In 1800 they were being run by Samuel Hanway, in 1815 by John Stealey and his sons-in-law, Richard Watts and Jacob Kiger. In 1824 Watts was succeeded by Jesse Evans, who put A. P. Wilson in charge of the works and the furnace, known as "Valley." About 1831 Alexander Clear and William Alexander were operating the works.[5]

In 1843 Joshua Crowther and the Reverend Edward Price came from England and inspected the Deckers Creek ores. Finding them promising, Joshua and his brothers, Joseph and Benjamin, sons of an iron producer in Wolverhampton, Staffordshire, England, formed Crowther and Company in 1844 and bought the works.

The outcome was not very successful. They ran the works for awhile, but presently ceased for want of transportation to market. The company then closed down and the owners left,

3. Wiley, op. cit., p. 166.
4. *The Monongalia Story*, vol. 2, p. 268.
5. Wiley, p. 255.

pronouncing the ores and coals abundant and sufficient for operation, when transportation to market could be provided.[6]

**The Strosnider Hotel.** The Strosnider Hotel was built at Blacksville by Moses Strosnider in 1844, and for the next half century was a popular resort for the traveling public in that section of the county.

Moses Strosnider was born January 12, 1806, on Whiteley Creek, Greene County, Pennsylvania, the son of Gasper Strosnider, a native of Germany, and Sarah Syphers Strosnider, of Virginia.

Fig. 39. The Strosnider Hotel, Blacksville, about 1865. (Courtesy Ruth Strosnider.)

"Moses Strosnider did not have the advantages for obtaining an education as are afforded the youth of today, but gained such knowledge as could be obtained in the subscription schools. He early evinced a mechanical turn of mind, and learned the trade of wheelwright, building the old and superannuated spring-wheel much in use in those days. He was a man

6. Wiley, p. 654. Wiley adds that Joshua Crowther located the ironworks at South Pueblo, Colorado, for Jay Gould and Company and managed them for several years.

of enterprise, and seeing a good opportunity for a woolen mill on Dunkard Creek, built and operated a woolen and grist-mill combined near Blacksville for many years, and afterwards moved the woolen mill to Blacksville. . . .

"He was a valuable addition to the town of Blacksville, entering with spirit and enthusiasm into every move which had for its object the good of the town, and the welfare and prosperity of the people at large. His kindness of heart, his benevolence of spirit, and his extreme humanity will be remembered among his most striking traits. He was strictly moral and was instrumental in the building of the Baptist church of Blacksville giving largely of his time and money to the consummation of the project."

He continued for many years operation of both the mill and the hotel.

He married Mary Thompson and they had ten children, namely, Thompson, a physician of Blacksville, married Sarah Thompson; Josephus, cabinetmaker and undertaker of Blacksville, married Elizabeth Thomas; Sarah, married William Morgan; Mary Ann, married Corbley Orndorff; Mahala Arlene, married Albert Gallatin Chaplin; Gasper F., who ran a gristmill near the mouth of Days Run, married Susan Virginia Marsh; Caroline Frances; Margaret Marie, never married, but succeeded her father as proprietor of the hotel, operating it for over forty years; Michael Leslie, a carpenter and woolen mill owner, married Carolyn Wallace; and James Neason.[7]

**The Avery Methodist Protestant Chapel.** The Avery Methodist Church, on the Brandonville Pike between Morgantown and Cheat River, was dedicated in September 1843. It was likely the result of a society organized in the settlement by Rev. George G. Westfall, a circuit rider. Jonah Vandervort, Leonard Selby, and P. J. Laishley, trustees, had met in 1842 in the old Pierpoint school to plan the new building.

The minutes indicate that Paul Bayles built the splitstone foundation, "Mr. Campbell of Fayette County, Pa." put up the frame, David Durr constructed the roof, Robert Holyfield and John Houston put on the weatherboarding, and John Bowers installed the windows, made the doors and laid the floor, with

7. *Cyclopedia of Monongalia County,* pp. 178, 179; pers. comm., Ruth Strosnider, Blacksville.

"nails at Ellicotts prices." Four other trustees were elected on December 26, 1843, namely, "Zack Pierpoint Joseph Cummons Ed Compton & John Weaver."

Motions were passed on April 19, 1844, considering the Methodist Episcopal church, Reformed Baptists, Presbyterians, and Lutherans included in the orthodox denominations that may use the new building, provided they hold themselves accountable for any damage it may sustain during the time of using. In all cases they must leave it swept or forfeit the right of using. It must not be used as a house for singing school.

Rev. Peter Laishley wrote to Charles Avery of Pittsburgh, telling him of the need for money to finish the church and suggesting that if he would contribute one hundred dollars, they would name the church for him. He sent the money and the church was named Avery Chapel.[8]

**Tales of the Town.** Morgantown during the second quarter of the nineteenth century grew slowly, contrasting with its fairly rapid growth during its pioneer period. In a way, the world had passed it by, with the construction of main highways just north and just south of the county.

The village was a closely-knit community where life went on quietly day after day, hardly anything escaping the attention of all the residents. Many interesting events took place, some of them being embellished in the telling, and it might be worthwhile to pause a moment in our narration of more serious affairs to consider some of the tales of everyday life.

Fortunately many anecdotes have been preserved that add flavor to the history of the times. One of the most valuable of the early collections of such stories was by Joseph Moreland, an attorney of the late nineteenth century.[9]

Moreland muses: "May we not hope that in the preparation

8. Owens, *Easton-Avery Community*, pp. 102, 190-97; Dodds and Dodds, *Churches of Monongalia County*, pp. 148, 149. The church was completed and put in use in 1846; Barnes, *M. P. Church*, pp. 127-33. For biography of Charles Avery, see Smeltzer, *Methodism*, pp. 125, 126.

9. His little 52-page book was entitled *Morgantown. Its Practical Jokes and Jokers; Its Thrice Told Tales; Legends, Ghost Stories, Exaggerations, Doings and Sayings, Marvelous and Incredible; Its Fun, Wit, Humor, Etc.* It was prepared as one of a number that were contributed to the centennial history of Morgantown for the occasion of the centennial celebration, October 29, 1885, and was published in 1885 by the New Dominion Steam Printing House.

of these sketches we are contributing at least to the future historian of Morgantown when she shall be of sufficient importance to take rank among the cities of the world. As the future historian of Morgantown passes over his field of observation and notes in detail the events that go to make up the history, its thrice told tales will be of the very *res gestae*. Its legends, ghost stories, exaggerations; doings and sayings, marvelous and incredible, will furnish beauty and adornment, and its jokes, its fun, its wit and its humor will give pith and point to the whole."[10]

Since Joseph Moreland was an attorney, it is not surprising that affairs at the courthouse were the objects of many of his jokes.

On one occasion, Moreland says, "Squire W——, a worthy and prominent citizen of Morgantown," was presiding at a meeting of the court. The clerk, as usual, had furnished the court with a docket, in the first and second columns bearing the names of plaintiffs and defendants, and in the third column a memorandum of the last order entered in each case. In numerous cases the last order was one directing another summons to issue against the defendants. Opposite each of these "was the clerk's memorandum in these words, *alias summons*, which, of course, meant that another summons was ordered. The President of the court, with his accustomed gravity, took his seat and commenced exercising his legal talents on the docket. Scanning the column in which appeared on almost every line *alias summons*, he turned to the clerk and said, 'Mr. Clerk, who is this *Elias Simmons*, he seems to have a great many cases in this court?' The Clerk explained and members of the bar smiled."[11]

Moreland also related numerous anecdotes of practical jokes played on physicians. One concerns Dr. Charles McLane, the most conspicuous traits of whose disposition, Moreland says, "were his kindness and his child-like simplicity. It is related that on one occasion as he was making a professional trip along a road that ran by a creek or deep stream, he came upon a robust looking individual sitting by the edge of the stream, apparently in great misery, for he was moaning at a great rate. The doctor,

10. Moreland, p. 1.
11. Moreland, p. 30.

in his kind way, stopped and inquired the cause of his apparent suffering and was told it was toothache. By request the doctor alighted and was proceeding to examine the tooth when the mischievous rascal, who was only feigning his suffering, closed his huge jaws upon the doctor's fingers and held on like a bull-dog. He thought it a smart joke to thus punish the doctor for his kindness, but he mistook his man. The 'Adam' was roused in the old doctor, and he leveled a left-handed blow at the butt of his ear that relaxed the jaws of the 'smart Alex' in a hurry, and sent him end over end into the creek. This anecdote furnishes a sample of the sort of people the early practitioner came in contact with."[12]

Fig. 40. Dr. McLane treats a mischievous patient. (Sketch by Diane Lenhart.)

**Rev. John Parker.** The Reverend John Parker was stricken by paralysis while preaching and never recovered, dying in 1844. He was born in Western Port, Maryland, but settled on Paw Paw Creek, Monongalia County, in 1795. "He was a blacksmith by trade; but resided on a farm and followed agricultural pursuits in connection with his trade. He was an exhorter and local minister of the Methodist Episcopal church; a pioneer of Methodism. His was the home of the ministers, and he lent the best efforts of his life to the furtherance and establishment of the Christian faith."

He was married twice and had six children, including John D. Parker, who also became a local minister in the Methodist Episcopal church.[13]

**Col. Dudley Evans.** Colonel Dudley Evans, a son of early pioneers John and Ann Evans, died in 1844. He was born in 1766, in Loudoun County, at the time his parents were planning to move to the Monongahela Valley.

Colonel Evans commanded a regiment in the War of 1812 under General W. H. Harrison and also was a member of the county militia. He served more than a dozen terms in the general assembly, between 1802 and 1820, with marked ability, besides serving as a member of the Monongalia County court from before 1796 until his resignation in 1831. He married Anarah Williams and they had four sons and four daughters.

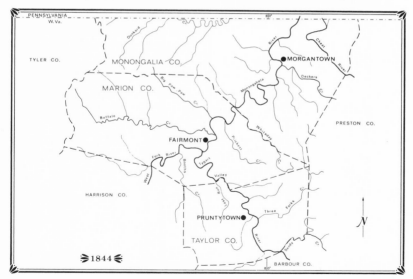

Fig. 41. Map showing formation of Taylor County, 1844. (Drawn by Diane Lenhart.)

13. *Cyclopedia of Monongalia County*, p. 110. Captain Eli L. Parker, who served in the Civil War, was a son of John D.

**Taylor County Is Formed.** The general assembly, on January 19, 1844, passed an act for the establishment of the new county of Taylor, named for Senator John Taylor (1750-1824), distinguished soldier and statesman of Caroline County.

Even before Marion County was organized, a movement had been started for the formation of a new county from the southern part of Monongalia and portions of adjoining counties. Petitioners cited the long distances they had to travel to reach the county seat. Edward J. Armstrong, of Williamsport, one of Harrison County's members of the general assembly, introduced the legislation that was finally adopted.

Parts of Barbour, Harrison, and Marion counties were included in the new county, the boundaries of which were described as beginning at Laurel Point, the corner of Monongalia, Marion, and Preston; thence direct to the upper end of the falls of Tygart Valley River, and down the river to the mouth of Lost Run; thence direct to the mouth of Booth Creek, at Poland's thence up the right fork of Booth Creek to Anderson Corbin's; thence southward to James McDaniel's on the Northwestern Turnpike; thence due south to Simpson Creek; thence up said creek to Joseph Bailey's; thence southeast to the Barbour line, at Samuel Bartlett's; thence direct to John H. Woodford's on Pleasant Creek; thence direct to the ford of Pleasant Creek, below Jedediah Sayer's; thence northeast to Tygart Valley River, crossing at the mouth of Big Sandy Creek; thence with the line of Barbour and Marion, and Preston and Marion to the point of beginning.

Williamsport was selected as the county seat, it being by far the largest town within the new county, and advantageously situated on the Northwestern Turnpike.[14]

**Land Grants Made in 1844.**[15] Monongalia County grantees in 1844 included:

| | | |
|---|---|---|
| Bell, Samuel | 160 a. | Booths Creek |
| Gallaher, James | 1 | West Run |
| Hanway, John | 500 | Statlers Run |

14. Williamsport was renamed Pruntytown on January 23, 1845, to appease, it is said, John Prunty, who had opposed formation of the new county on the grounds that "It's so damn small, I can stand on one edge and spit across it" (Brinkman, *History of Taylor County*, chap. 12).

15. See p. 11.

| Lawless, James | 40 | Gustins Run |
| Matheny, Moses | 164 | Dudleys Fork |
| Philips, Isaac | 220 | Piles Fork |
| Shafer, Henry | 50 | Lick Run |
| Tennant, Richard D. | 100 | Slaters Fork |
| Tower, Edwin W. | 500 | Statlers Run |

**County Government.** Owen John was sworn in as sheriff on March 25, 1844. William Lantz was appointed commissioner of the revenue for the Western District. The county levy was set at one dollar.

**Miscellany.** In 1844: Hugh Daugherty built the molding and engine room of Reay's steam foundry, across Deckers Creek from Morgantown (Wiley, p. 262). . . . Admitted to the county bar were I. J. T. Fox Alden, Lycurgus S. Hough (March 29), Andrew McDonald (April 8), John W. Harner (April 8), and Philip H. Keck (October 28) (Wiley, pp. 316, 318). . . . George D. Evans and Company opened a retail store in Morgantown (Wiley, p. 580). . . . Jesse Holland took over the operation of the "Old Dominion" tavern in Morgantown (Wiley, p. 586). . . . James Odbert, saddler, came to Morgantown from Washington County, Pennsylvania (Wiley, p. 604). . . . The Selby School, on the Pleasant Hill road near the Pierpoint School, became the second in that community (Owens, p. 103). . . . Sanford Pickenpaugh purchased Lot 17 in Morgantown from Henry Lazier (Callahan, p. 311). . . . Francis Demain acquired the south half of Lot 25 in October for four hundred dollars (Callahan, p. 313). . . . The southern half of Lot 38 was purchased by Augustus Haymond and Francis Madera for one thousand dollars (Callahan, p. 316). . . . Lot 112, the vacant "brick kiln" lot, was conveyed by Isaac Cooper to W. T. Willey in trust to secure a debt (Callahan, p. 327).

# CHAPTER SIXTY-NINE

# 1845

Despite the early interest in education in the commonwealth of Virginia, a survey in 1839-40 showed that illiteracy was on the increase. This was largely the product of the rather haphazard system by which schools were administered. The earlier schools were largely operated by churches and the struggle for separation of church and state often left the state with very little interest in the schools. The common schools, supported by subscription, and free district schools, supported by the churches, were largely creations of the provident middle classes. Only very slowly was a system put into operation for educating the indigent poor.

**Tract Societies.** An important assault on illiteracy in the western counties of Virginia, including Monongalia, was made by various "tract societies," especially the American Tract Society, organized in New York in 1825 for nonsectarian distribution of Christian literature. Charles H. Ambler describes the work of their agents, called colporteurs: "Combining the enthusiasm and unselfishness of the ideal schoolmasters with the piety and crusading spirit of the missionary, their agents conducted an aggressive campaign against ignorance. By use of horses and buggies colporteurs distributed thousands of religious tracts in the rural sections . . . and organized a number of societies to aid them. Sometimes they were showered with indignities, but they were persisent and, when they could not sell their wares, they gave them away."[1]

One colporteur, who began his work in Fairmont on April 1,

1. *History of Education in West Virginia*, p. 12.

1845, first visited Francis H. Pierpont, a young lawyer, who volunteered to accompany him to "every house in town." With his help three days were sufficient to place his "buggy load of books."

The same colporteur then replenished his stock and commenced work "in the country among the mountains." He related:

"It was like a translation from sunlight into darkness—from a high civilization into one of ignorance and superstition, with here and there a family of wealth and refinement.

"The very broken, rugged state of the country, with a sparse population, rendered it impossible for the people to support either schools or churches."[2]

**Mid-Century Agriculture.** By the year 1845, as the midpoint of the nineteenth century approached, agriculture was still the basic occupation of the people of Monongalia County, but it was gradually becoming a little less laborious.

Farms of considerable size had succeeded the pioneer clearings. With an abundance of land to be had for the clearing, farmers gave no thought to preservation of the fertility of the soil. A field was counted good for so many crops, and when "worn out" was turned over to hay production or allowed to grow up in thicket, while another field was cleared to take its place.

Corn was the principal crop. After two or three crops had been grown on "new" ground, winter wheat would be sown early in October, between the rows of corn shocks, and covered by harrowing. By 1845 grass seed was becoming available and was often sown broadcast in the wheat field in February or March. Timothy, orchard grass, and Kentucky bluegrass were favorites. Red clover was seeded with the grass. The seedlings would be well established by the time the wheat was ready to harvest, early in July. A good start was thus made for a crop of hay the next year.

Cutting the wheat in pioneer days was done with a grain sickle, a long, curved knife with a serrated edge. Its use was quite a gymnastic feat. The harvester "hunkered down," swinging the sickle with his right hand to cut a swath about four or

2. Op. cit., p. 11.

five feet wide, at the same time catching the cut stalks in his left hand, laying them in a row a handful at a time.

Using a wooden rake, the swaths were raked into sheaves, which were bound with a band made from wheat stems, tied with a twist knot. The sheaves were then bunched, twelve to a shock; ten sheaves were stood on end and the other two broken over just above the band and laid crosswise over the shock as cap sheaves. These cap sheaves not only shed rain, but protected the heads of the upright sheaves from bird depredation.

A substantial improvement in wheat harvest came early in the century with the development of the grain cradle. This was basically a scythe, such as was used to mow grass for hay, but was provided with four parallel wooden fingers on which the cut stalks fell. Instead of stooping, a cradler stood at his work and could cut four to six acres of grain in a twelve-hour day.

Then in 1831 Cyrus H. McCormick invented the reaping machine. It has been said that probably no other invention has contributed so much towards increasing the food supply of the human race. Of course the first reaper was a crude machine but its principle was carried out in later, greatly improved models. The apparatus, pulled by a team of horses, was supported on two wheels, gearing being attached to one wheel. The cutting was done by a cutter bar about six feet long, composed of triangular knives attached to a steel bar which slid back and forth in a groove in a system of guards. A reel bent the grain back against the knives and picked up bent stalks, so that all the grain was cut. The cut stalks were laid on a platform from which they were raked into piles by a man following the machine.

After drying, the cut stalks were threshed to beat the grains of wheat from the stalks. This was usually done by a flail, the Irishman's "two sticks of pleasure." The flail was an instrument consisting of a long handle joined to a heavier but shorter piece of wood by a stout leather thong. The stalks were spread on a tight floor and the grain was literally beaten out. Several men could work together but they had to keep the same rhythm or someone's head would get thumped. The chaff and grain would then be gathered from the floor and by pouring from one measure to another, on a windy day, the chaff would be blown away, while the heavier grain would fall straight down, thus "separating the wheat from the chaff," an expression which has persisted to our own day.

An improvement in this process came about with the development of the windmill, a contrivance with a large, hand-powered fan, a feed hopper, and various screens, an instrument which eventually supplanted the erratic natural breeze. Rezin Holland is said to have built the first windmill in the county about 1810, near the site of the Goshen Baptist Church.

The next improvement in the threshing process was the threshing machine. Wiley says that in 1840 John Durr, of Greene County, Pennsylvania, brought in a ground or chaffpiler threshing machine and set it up on the farm of Major W. W. John. "It was an object of wonder to all, and was feared by some, who could not be induced to go near it for fear 'it would bust.' "[3]

About the same time, or shortly after, William E. Watson and E. J. Evans purchased mowing machines, constructed somewhat like reapers, except that they did not have reels or platforms for catching cut stalks. They largely replaced scythes and eliminated much of the hard work from haymaking.

Gristmills, to which farmers took their grain for grinding, continued to be important community centers, strategically located so as to be within easy access to the population. One of the best in the county was the Morgantown mill, built by John Rogers in 1826. Guseman's mill, along Deckers Creek, was built by Abram Guseman about 1807. Ruble's mill, one of the first in the county, was still in operation along Cheat River. Other mills were at Jacksonville, Laurel Point, and along Dunkard Creek and Miracle Run.

**Eden Methodist Church.** About 1840 services began to be held in a log schoolhouse in the residence of "Doctor Frank John" and a Methodist Protestant society was organized. The first members were Isaac Conn, Elza Conn, Margaret Hoard, James Hoard, John Hoard, Ann Evans, Mary Hoard, Sarah Gray, Vincent Gray, William John, Oliver John, Robert Ross, Louisa

3. *History of Monongalia County,* p. 245. Andrew Ralston, near West Middletown, Washington County, Pennsylvania, in 1842 invented a type of threshing machine, of which five hundred were produced in Robert B. McClure's shop there before the business went bankrupt in 1859, the year of a disastrous frost. George Swetnam and Helene Smith, *Guidebook to Historic Western Pennsylvania* (Pittsburgh, 1976), p. 231.

Stewart, George Bowers, Alpheus Stewart, Tabitha Ross, Elizabeth Hoard, and Tabitha Rich.[4]

In 1844, William Stewart deeded a lot to the trustees of the
church, John Hoard, Simeon H. Laishley, and Edward Burgess
"for the purpose of building a meeting house." In 1845 Isaac
Zearley built the church, a small frame structure surrounded by
trees, and adjacent to a cemetery.[5]

**The Burnt Meeting House.** A log school and meetinghouse was
constructed about 1818 by Presbyterians living in the Brand
Settlement, south of Morgantown and west of the Monongahela
River. These people were members of the Morgantown church
but in 1835 the two church bodies were separated, so that quite
a loss of membership occurred in the Morgantown congregation.
The Barrackmans, Brands, Loughs, Coxes, Mercers, Robinsons,
Cordrays, and other residents of the Brand Settlement were in
the group.

In 1835 John Brand conveyed one-half acre of land to James
Robinson, Sr., Frances Marvel Brand, William T. Brand, Henry
G. Brand, Ulysses Camp, and Charles I. Brand as trustees "in
trust for a public burying ground and for use of an Old School
Presbyterian Church or house of public worship."

In (or about) 1845 the church burned down and was never
rebuilt. The cemetery continued to be used, however, and was
referred to as the Burnt Meeting House Graveyard.[6]

**James Vance Boughner.** On May 8, 1845, Dr. J. V. Boughner
(Fig. 31) married Louisa J., daughter of Andrew Brown, and
soon thereafter located at Brown's Mills, on Dunkard Creek, for
the practice of medicine.

He was born at Clarksburg April 9, 1812, the son of Daniel
and Mary Vance Boughner. When only sixteen years of age he
became postmaster at Greensboro, Pennsylvania, and it was said
of him that, "possessed of an active and ambitious mind, he
made up for want of early opportunities by extensive and gen-

---

4. *The Stewartstown Story*, pp. 11, 33, 34.
5. Dodds and Dodds, *Churches of Monongalia County*, "The Rev.
George G. Westfall is accredited with having conducted the greatest revival
ever known at Eden Church. This meeting was held in 1862," pp. 150,
151; Barnes, *M. P. Church*, pp. 125-27. The building was still standing in
1978. See Fig. 60, p. 364.
6. Moreland, *First Presbyterian Church*, p. 113.

eral reading and study, and acquired a very thorough knowledge of the standard English classics and of general history."

He read medicine with Dr. ——— Stephenson and attended lectures at Cincinnati Medical College. He first located at Mount Morris, Pennsylvania, practicing medicine on both sides of the Mason-Dixon Line. He represented Greene County in the Pennsylvania legislature before moving to Virginia.[7]

**New Roads.** The building and improvement of the county's system of wagon roads continued through 1845. Among projects worked on were: a road "leading from Laurel run bridge by Capel Howels Sawmill to the County road near John Pierponts"; "from the farm of Davis Weaver running through Lands of James McLasky, William Vandevort, Jonah Vandevort, intersecting Pike between the two Churches about Five Miles from Morgantown"; "from Peden Mercers on the old State road through . . . (Nancy) Linchs land"; "from Granville to William Tingle's "Colebank"; "from the low gap of Jakes Run to Jacob Formans on the right hand fork of pawpaw"; "from Jas. Parks hollow on land of David Haines Heirs . . . then on land of Richard Lewis . . . then on land of Wm. Thomas . . . then on the line between Adam B. Tennant & Septemus Lemasters" to Miracle Run; "from the town of Blacksville by way of Enos Tennants mill to the Marion County line at or near Jeremiah Conways farm"; "the Powells ferry road from White day Creek to Pisgah meeting house"; etc.

**The Mountaineer.** County newspapers were having problems during the 1840s. The *Democratic Republican* suspended publication in 1842. The *Northwestern Journal* ran from 1843 to 1845, the *Democratic Watchtower* was projected in 1842 but never published, and the *Virginia Shield*, a Democratic paper edited by Joseph H. Powell, had a brief life about 1843.

Another short-lived paper, the *Mountaineer* was published in 1845, renting the press of the *Northwestern Journal*. Democratic in politics, it was run by Andrew McDonald and Boaz B. Tibbs. It is said to have been a four-page sheet but no copies of it have been seen.[8]

7. Wiley, pp. 479, 480.
8. Wiley, p. 434.

**Edward Price, Furniture.** The manufacture of high grade furniture, as has been noted earlier (p. 177), was an industry which appeared in Monongalia County in the 1830s and 1840s.

In 1845 Edward Price, a skillful furniture maker, arrived in Morgantown from England, and in a small shop began the manufacture of chairs by hand, turning out most of the parts with a foot lathe he brought with him from England.[9]

He became a member of the Morgantown Baptist Church and was later ordained as a minister.[10]

**Ice's Ferry Post Office.** To serve the populous area beyond Cheat River, about Ellicott's iron works, a post office called Ice's Ferry was established June 9, 1841, with Evan T. Ellicott as postmaster. On August 22, 1845, John Bowers was named to succeed him.

By the middle of this decade it might be said that the Cheat iron industry was about at its zenith, with a small town nestling along the river just below the ferry.

**Land Grants Made in 1845.**[11] Monongalia County grantees in 1845 included:

| | | |
|---|---|---|
| Glover, Isaac | 100 a. | Piles Fork |
| Haught, Samuel | 72 | Adj. Isaac Thomas |
| Hennon, Jeremiah | 57 | Adj. Jacob Lemley |
| Lewellen, John | 40 | Morgans Run |
| Lewis, Benjamin | 80 | Days Run |
| Metz, John | 270 | Papaw Creek |
| Price, Caleb P. | 4 | Robinson Run |
| Ridgeway, Joel | 1½ | Falling Run |
| Tuttle, Andrew | 13½ | Miracles Run |
| Tuttle, Andrew | 270 | Miracles Run |
| Varner, William | 160 | Papaw Creek |
| Wade, Alexander, Jr. | 130 | Dunkard Creek |

**Henry Youst Dies.** Henry Youst (or Yost) died in 1845. He was a son of John Youst, who was born in Germany but migrated to America before the Revolutionary War. John first located in

9. Callahan, *Making of Morgantown*, p. 136; Wiley, p. 263.
10. Wiley, p. 595.
11. See p. 11.

western Pennsylvania but soon settled along Indian Creek, Monongalia County.

Henry was born in western Pennsylvania in 1787 and came with his father to Indian Creek. Like his father, he was a farmer and they together suffered the hardships of pioneer life, as they developed their farm. The country was sparsely populated and the settlers formed themselves into militia for mutual protection. "Henry Youst was a brave and courageous youth, and was found not unfrequently with the citizen guards."

He married Sarah, daughter of John Watson, of Buffalo Creek, and they had five children.[12]

**Thomas Lemasters Dies.** Thomas Lemasters, one of the pioneer settlers of the Monongahela Valley, died in Tyler County in 1845. Thomas and his brother Isaac were apparently in Monongalia County before 1780; one of the earliest deeds recorded for the site of Morgantown was in Isaac's name.[13] He left, and went on west, but it is not known where he located.

Thomas lived at various places in Monongalia County, chiefly in the western part, before settling finally in Tyler County. He was the father of about twelve children, most of whom settled in Tyler County.[14]

**County Government.** Owen John was sworn in for his second term as sheriff on March 24, 1845. W. W. John was appointed commissioner of the revenue for the Eastern District. The county levy was set at $1.25.

**Miscellany.** In 1845: The Anna Furnace, or River Furnace, was being built by the Ellicotts at Ice's Ferry. It was designed to burn charcoal but was later converted into a coke furnace. Its capacity was eight to ten tons in twenty-four hours (Wiley, p. 257). . . . David G. Thompson was admitted to the Monongalia County bar on April 7 and George S. Ray on September 8 (Wiley, p. 316). . . . Classes were resumed at the Morgantown Female Academy, after remodeling of the building, and E. J. Meany was appointed Principal (Wiley, p. 399). . . . Steamboats

---

12. *Cyclopedia of Monongalia County*, pp. 166, 167.
13. *The Monongalia Story*, vol. 2, p. 98; see also vol. 1, p. 215.
14. *Cyclopedia of Monongalia County*, p. 203. One son, Septimus, born in 1800, was a farmer on the head of Dunkard Creek before moving to Tyler County in 1857 (p. 78).

arriving at the Port of Morgantown included the *Harlem*, on March 7, the *Massachusetts*, on June 23, and the *Miner*, on November 11 (Wiley, p. 542). . . . George M. Hagans and Company opened a store in Morgantown (Wiley, p. 580). . . . James Caldwell and James McGlaughlin were ruling elders in the Presbyterian Church (Wiley, p. 592). . . . Charles Parker was minister of the Forks of Cheat Baptist Church (Wiley, p. 686). . . . John Lemley built a gristmill on Scotts Run below Jacksonville (Wiley, p. 706). . . . William P. Harshe succeeded C. B. Bristol as minister of the Stewarts Run Presbyterian Church (Wiley, p. 729). . . . George Kramer conveyed a portion of Lot 20 in Morgantown to Ralph L. Berkshire (Callahan, p. 312). . . . Henry Lazier sold the northern part of Lot 39 to William Lazier for two thousand dollars (Callahan, p. 316). . . . The several heirs of Michael Clouse conveyed their interests in Lot 46 to Dr. Charles McLane (Callahan, p. 317). . . . Edgar C. Wilson purchased Lot 82 (Callahan, p. 320). . . . Philip Low died November 2; he was born July 24, 1788.

# CHAPTER SEVENTY

# 1846

In the first half of the nineteenth century it was the custom for members of the general assembly to meet their constituents on court days, particularly on the first day of the quarterly terms of the county court and the first day of the circuit court, to tell them what had been done in the legislature and to justify their own acts therein. The newspapers of the day were not widely distributed and people had not been well informed, from that source, of what was doing in legislative sessions, nor of the acts of their representatives.

General political meetings and discussions of current issues of the day were also held on court days. These meetings, and also the elections, were well attended, and political campaigns were hotly contested.

**Political Campaigning, 1846 Style.** There was an early law, in the Code of 1819, that any person who had served seven years in the general assembly should not be "compellable to serve therein again," but a seat in the body was considered as great an honor then as now and there were usually numerous candidates.

For example, a local newspaper published announcements of seven candidates for the house of delegates, and gave a vivid account of the campaign:

"The greater part" of the first day of the quarterly term of the county court, Monday, March 23, 1846, "was occupied with the speeches of the several candidates for the Legislature. First upon the rostrum came Wm. W. John, Esq., who commenced by saying that he was a farmer, and ploughed with a true American, and that he aspired to direct the plough of state, and thought he could handle it correctly and plough a straight

273

furrow. . . . He advocated railroads generally, showing by a few simple but conclusive arguments and illustrations, their benefits and importance."

William John, a Democratic candidate, was followed by John F. Cooper, another Democratic candidate, who gave his views upon the railroad question, opposing the right of way (for the Baltimore and Ohio Railroad), and also the Wheeling terminus, unless the road would pass north instead of south of Morgantown. He sharply critcized the conduct of Monongalia's two members of the house of delegates.

"Next in order came Alexander Wade, who occupied most of his time" in answering the criticisms of Mr. Cooper, and gave "some account of the doings of the last Legislature." He urged the importance of a convention to amend the constitution and predicted "that a convention could never be obtained on the white basis," recommending "the acceptance of a convention on the mixed basis, as the best of a hard bargain, and the only means by which Western Virginia could ever hope to obtain redress. He also took his usual stand against the county court system."

Elias Stillwell, Jr., then made "a very mild and gentlemanly speech. He boldly declared himself a Whig; said that he was a mechanic, and that mechanics, farmers and laboring men were as much entitled to the respect and support of the people, as wealthy and professional men." Mr. Stillwell announced his opposition to "railroads and all monopolies."

Daniel Miller "informed the people that he was no longer a candidate for the Legislature at the coming election."

John H. Bowlby made a long speech and "declared himself a Jeffersonian Democrat, and laid down the principles that would govern him, if elected."

Alexander B. McCans advocated biennial sessions of the legislature.

"Last but not least," continued the account, "came the 'Old Wheel Horse of Democracy,' Abner Scipio Davis. We did not hear the beginning of Mr. Davis' speech, but learn that he commenced by saying that he regretted that he had not heard his brother candidates speak, having been engaged all day in ferrying his constituents across the river, he had just snatched a few moments from his occupation to come to the courthouse to let the people know he was still a candidate for the legislature, and the 'Old Wheel Horse' was not going to back out. He said that he sometimes felt discouraged and disposed to retire from the contest, when persons crossing the river would speak lightly of the qualifications of the candidates before the people. He acknowledged that they were all a set of fools, but he was now determined to run through, fodder or no fodder. Mr. Davis promised the people that on the day of election, he would be more fully prepared to give them his views, and informed the candidates that on that occasion, they might expect a complete currying; he would commence with the oldest and end with the youngest, raking from stem to stern. Mr. Davis concluded by assuring the people that there was no doubt of his triumphant election, but that they might do as they pleased about electing him, afterwards he would do as he pleased. He informed them moreover that if they did not choose to vote for him, they might go to —— and he would stay at home and attend to the ferry, which was a darn'd sight more profitable than going to the Legislature any how."[1]

**The Western Virginia Standard.** A new weekly paper, the *Western Virginia Standard*, succeeded the *Mountaineer*, the first issue appearing on Saturday, February 14, 1846. It was Whig in politics, edited by George S. Ray. It was a four-page paper, twenty-two by thirty-two inches, with twenty-four columns, and sold for $1.50 per year. The motto was, "A people to be truly free must first be wise and good." It was printed on the old press of the *Northwestern Journal*.[2]

**The Election of 1846.** The election was on Thursday, April 23, and resulted in the election of Andrew Brown, a Whig from the Dunkard Creek area. The *Standard*[3] reported the returns as follows:

1. *Western Virginia Standard*, March 28, 1846.
2. Only a few copies of the paper have survived, although it is said to have run until 1849 (Wiley, pp. 434, 435).
3. April 25, 1846.

|              | *Brown* | *Cooper* | *Bowlby* | *John* | *Stillwell* |
|--------------|---------|----------|----------|--------|-------------|
| Court House  | 132     | 103      | 85       | 76     | 89          |
| Jarrett's    | 38      | 3        | 1        | 20     | 1           |
| Smithfield   | 6       | 0        | 3        | 16     | 5           |
| Pawpaw       | 3       | 23       | 3        | 2      | 2           |
| Jacksonville | 22      | 28       | 34       | 9      | 1           |
| Blacksville  | 49      | 33       | 7        | 0      | 0           |
| Warren       | 12      | 5        | 47       | 2      | 0           |
| Totals       | 262     | 195      | 180      | 125    | 98          |

**The Primary School System.** It was with the intent of remedying the educational situation somewhat (see p. 79) that the general assembly, in an act of March 5, 1846, amended "the primary school system."

"This act authorized school commissioners in each county to appoint county superintendents who were required to give bond for the faithful performance of his duties. These duties included the functions formerly performed by school treasurers, such as keeping accounts, collecting and reporting data pertaining to schools and teachers, and making required reports to the superintendent of the Literary Fund. Among other duties were the allocation of county quotas among school districts, gathering data from teachers regarding courses of study and methods of presenting them, and determining the per diem compensation of teachers."[4]

Each teacher instructing indigent children made out his report of the same, had it certified by the commissioner who employed him, and delivered it to the superintendent, in order to receive his pay. Indigent children usually attended the same schools that subscription pupils attended and were looked down upon as being "poor kids."

So far as is known, John Watts was the first county superintendent of schools in Monongalia. The county court, on October 25, 1846, divided the county into twenty-seven districts, and appointed a commissioner for each, as follows:

4. Ambler, *History of Education in West Virginia*, p. 26.

Eastern District (east side of the Monongahela)—No. 1, Seth Stafford; No. 2, Reuben Sensabaugh; No. 3, William John; No. 4, James Evans; No. 5, Rev. Peter T. Laishley; No. 6, E. C. Wilson; No. 7, John Hanway; No. 8, Asby Pool; No. 9, Rawley Holland; No. 10, Leven Howell; No. 11, no record; No. 12, Elijah Tarleton; No. 13, Thomas Meredith; No. 14, Thomas Tarleton.

Western District (west side of the Monongahela)—No. 1, John H. Bowlby; No. 2, M. L. Boyers; No. 3, Gideon Barb; No. 4, Caleb S. Price; No. 5, John Stewart; No. 6, Michael Core; No. 7, William Price; No. 8, William Lantz; No. 9, Alexander Wade; No. 10, James White; No. 11, William Cotton, Jr.; No. 12, Enos Haught; No. 13, George Wilson.

In this "poor system" we see an advance by Virginia towards a free public school system, which was never, however, quite realized before the Civil War.

Another provision of the 1846 act provided that an optional system of free schools might be adopted by the "council of any city or town having a corporation court, or by the voters of any county at a special election held for the purpose."[5]

**Contract for a New Courthouse.** Construction on a new courthouse for Monongalia County was started late in 1846.

This was the fourth seat of government in the seventy-year history of Monongalia County. The first was merely a farm building on "Phillips' Choice," the plantation of Theophilus Phillips, in present Springhill Township, Fayette County, Pennsylvania, but in territory claimed by Virginia in 1776. Zackquill Morgan was the first sheriff and tradition says Joseph Coombs was the first clerk of the county court (*Monongalia Story*, vol. 2, pp. xii, 7).

After the running of the line and final agreement on the

5. Monongalia County never held an election for the purpose, but as early as 1850 a free school system was agitated locally. In that year the Reverend Peter T. Laishley, on his card as a candidate for a seat in the convention to revise the constitution, said: "I am in favor of having an item embraced in the Constitution, establishing a general system of education, so that in our primary schools the children of the rich and the poor may meet on an equality, extending to all the opportunity of acquiring knowledge." Such a system, though, still had to wait a few years longer.

permanent boundary between Virginia and Pennsylvania, a small frame building to be used as a courthouse was constructed in 1784 on the public square of a newly laid out town on property of Zackquill Morgan, established the next year by the general assembly under the name of Morgan's-town (*Monongalia Story*, vol. 2, pp. 107, 108).

In 1800 the county court approved a plan for construction of a new two-story brick courthouse and awarded the contract for its construction to Henry Dering and George Hite, at a cost not to exceed $4,500. The building was up and the roof on by the fall of 1801, but work continued slowly on the interior and apparently the new building was not placed into use until the spring of 1803. Both the county court and the district superior court met in the building (*Monongalia Story*, vol. 2, pp. 299, 300, 307, 308, 351).

This building, after forty years, began to be inadequate for the increased use and plans were drawn for construction of a new building. Various plans were advertised in the *Virginia Standard* and numerous bids were received during the summer of 1846. William Boyle and John Bradbury bid $12,900 for Plan No. 1, $10,500 for Plan No. 2, and $8,000 for Plan No. 3. Gabriel Getzendanner and W. S. Wintermute submitted a bid for $7,550. F. Madera, Waitman Davis, George Hawthorn, Christian Madera, and George Dorsey bid $7,000. James Davis also bid $7,000, Zedekiah Kidwell bid $5,700, and Elijah Morgan $5,975.

Joshua H. Zinn, of Fairmont, submitted the lowest bid, stating that he "proposes building a Courthouse according to the plan that the commissioners have laid out and according to the directions given by them and to finish the same in a good workman-like manner for the sum of $5,695 or finish the same building with a portico the whole width of the building and put up brick columns with Ionic Bases and capitals cut of stone with two tiers of steps, portico 15 feet wide if required for $6,490."

As finally decided upon, the new courthouse was to be a two-story brick building with two clerks' offices and a court room on the first floor, and a broad flight of stairs leading to the second floor, occupied by another court room and two jury rooms.

The contract to build the new structure was let to Mr. Zinn on August 24, 1846, for $5,695, with $300 extra for a pediment to be constructed by Martin Callendine, Wilson Crowl, and W. T. Willey.

**The Morgantown Baptist Church.**[6] James Morton Callahan devotes several pages to the early history of the Morgantown Baptist Church. "On December 16, 1843, the congregation appointed [Martin] Callendine to write a short history of the church, and also decide upon the expediency of selling 87½ feet of Lot 101 fronting on Front Street and 87½ feet fronting on Bumbo Lane in order to secure funds for the erection of the meeting house on the remainder of the lot."[7]

Fig. 42. The Regular Baptist Church of Morgantown, erected in 1846 at the corner of Long Alley and Bumbo Lane. (Courtesy First Baptist Church.)

Construction of the meetinghouse got under way soon but progressed slowly, because of the shortage of funds. Callahan continues:

"On June 14, 1845, the question of finishing the meeting house was mentioned by Callendine; but consideration was postponed, possibly because of a drive to pay the preacher for

6. See pp. 234-35.
7. *Making of Morgantown*, pp. 157-61.

the ensuing year. On July 19, 1845, a report on the question was requested; but Mr. Callendine was not ready to report, and the question was deferred. On October 18, 1846, the congregation convened in the new meeting house to hear the dedication sermon by William Penney."

**Snider's Temple.** According to tradition, a log church building stood on the Snider estate on the old state road between Morgantown and Middletown, a road after 1836 designated as the Brandonville and Fishing Creek Turnpike.

About 1846, a second log church was built there; David Snider and his wife, Elizabeth Cotton Snider, deeded a lot to the church trustees on March 5, 1846. Eugenus Wilson Snider and Asbury Snider built the church. The building was described as standing near the turnpike on the Snider plantation, by an old oak tree. Tradition says that John Snider slept under the tree as a boy when returning home after having been captured by the Indians.

In the deed the building was said to be "for the Episcopal Methodists to preach in and for the proper use and benefit of the people."[8]

**The Miracle Run Methodist Church.** A Methodist congregation was organized in 1846, meeting in the Tennant schoolhouse on Miracle Run. The Reverend G. H. Williams was the first pastor. A class consisting of eleven members was formed by the Reverend Asbury Stephens and he established the church as a preaching station.[9]

**George Frederick Charles Conn.** The Reverend G. F. C. Conn (Fig. 32) was ordained as a minister of the Baptist Church in September 1846, by the Reverend Cleon Keyes, the Reverend Leven Howell, and the Reverend Charles Parker. The ceremony took place in the Forks of Cheat Baptist Church.

Mr. Conn was born in Fayette County, Pennsylvania, July 25, 1809. His grandfather, George Conn, of Scotch ancestry, was a ship carpenter at West Point, married Lydia Flintham, and settled on Georges Creek, in Fayette County. His father, Jacob

8. Dodds and Dodds, *Churches of Monongalia County*, p. 107.
9. Dodds and Dodds, *Churches of Monongalia County*, p. 133.

Conn, married Ellen, daughter of Captain George F. Hartman, and they moved to the Stewartstown area about 1820.

In 1832 George Conn married Susannah, daughter of Lloyd Robey. In 1837 he was baptized by the Reverend James W. B. Tisdale and joined the Forks of Cheat Church.

His life in the ministry was destined to be a career of great distinction (see p. 301).[10]

**Huston Stewart Settles in Blacksville.** Said to have been a descendant of the beautiful Mary, Queen of Scots, Rev. Huston Stewart settled in Blacksville in 1846. He was born July 17, 1825, in Greene County, Pennsylvania, the son of James and Mary (Blair) Stewart. He was educated in the common schools and learned the trade of stone-cutter. He was licensed to preach in the Baptist church.

On December 11, 1845, he married Rachel E. Ross, daughter of Francis Ross, who was in the battle of Lake Erie and later settled in Cheat Neck. The Reverend Mr. and Mrs. Stewart had four children, Frank R., James L., Mary J., who married New-ton Straight, and Lucinda G.[11]

**The Statlerstown Bridge.** The first bridge across Dunkard Creek at Statlerstown was constructed in 1846, to eliminate a very dangerous fording place for traffic on the road referred to as the Dunkard Creek Turnpike.

According to a county court record dated July 24, the two abutments for the bridge were to be ten feet thick at the bottom and the wing walls nineteen feet long. Elijah Morgan contracted for the stone work for $682. The superstructure, built of wood, of the arched or curved ribbed type, weatherboarded and covered was contracted by W. W. Sayers for $6.94 per foot in length.

**Rebecca Dering Dies.** A familiar figure on High Street, in Morgantown, for more than half a century, Rebecca Dering, passed away January 26, 1846. She had been a tavern keeper since about 1787.

Born in 1766, Rebecca was the daughter of George and Christina Musser, of Lancaster County, Pennsylvania. She married

10. Wiley, pp. 457-59.
11. *Cyclopedia of Marion County*, pp. 138, 139.

Henry Dering (see *Monongalia Story*, vol. 2, pp. 350, 351) and they moved to Morgantown about 1787, when the town was hardly more than two years old.

Soon after their arrival they opened what was perhaps the first tavern in the town, on the corner of High and Walnut streets. Henry died in 1807 but Rebecca continued to keep the tavern until her death. They had eight children.

By her will of August 1844 (proved February 1846), Rebecca gave to her grandchildren (children of F. A. Dering), the lots on Water Street which she had bought from E. M. Wilson, and made provision for the freedom of her Negro slave Henry after two years and of her slave boy Tim when he reached twenty-one.[12]

**Obituaries.** Several deaths were reported in newspapers during the year, including the following:

"Departed this life on yesterday, about 4 o'clock P.M. Mrs. Kisiah Davis, consort of Mr. Peter Davis, of this vicinity.[13]

"Died, On Friday the 30th January last, Mrs. Lavina Madera, consort of Mr. Nimrod Madera of this place, aged 35 years and 4 days.

"Died, On Friday the 13th inst., Mrs. Mary Cox, consort of Mr. Lev. Cox of this vicinity, aged about 45 years.[14]

"Died, On the 13th inst. Maj. David Scott, a citizen of this county, in the 78th year of his age.

"He was a major in the last war, and served in the army of the North West, under Major General Harrison."[15]

**A Melancholy Accident.** "A melancholy accident befell Wm. Shaver, of this county, while in the act of sawing boat-gunnels. . . . The scaffold upon which the log rested, fell suddenly, and he being in the pit, was crushed to the ground by the gunnel. On examination it was found that both of his thigh-bones were broken."[16]

12. Callahan, *Making of Morgantown*, p. 85. "She came to reside here some 59 years ago; and lived to see herself, perhaps the sole survivor of the then existing generation." *Western Virginia Standard*, February 21, 1846.
13. *Western Virginia Standard*, February 21, 1846.
14. *Western Virginia Standard*, March 14, 1846.
15. *Western Virginia Standard*, March 28, 1846.
16. *Western Virginia Standard*, February 28, 1846.

**Fire Alarm.** "An alarm of fire was given on Thursday night about seven o'clock. It proved to be in the upper part of the old Jail. While the family was engaged down stairs, a bed standing near the fire, caught the blaze and burned considerably before it was discovered. It was happily extinguished by the exertions of some of the citizens, before much damage was done. We understand that Mr. John Beck lost a bed and beding and his lady the greater part of her wearing apparel."[17]

**Snow Blocks Mountain Roads.** "A gentleman who came from Kingwood yesterday, informs us that the road from there, is almost impassable; the snow on Laurel Hill being from two to three feet deep."[18]

**George Wade Dies.** George Wade III, son of George Wade II, and grandson of early settler George Wade I (see *Monongalia Story*, vol. 1, p. 290), died in Monongalia County in 1846. He was born here March 3, 1791. He married Clarissa Kendall, who died without children a few years later. George then went to Rush County, Indiana, where he married Anna Luark, daughter of John Luark. They then moved to Madison County, Indiana, and after about ten years back to Monongalia County, to the neighborhood where he was born, where he lived the remainder of his life.

The children of George and Anna Wade were Alexander Luark, Sarah, Elijah Luark, George McKinnon, Wilson Britton, and Julia Ann.

The first named, Alexander Luark Wade, born near Rushville, Indiana, February 1, 1832, was destined to play a prominent role in the history of Monongalia County.[19]

**Benjamin Thorn.** A prominent citizen of Indian Creek, Benjamin Thorn (see various references in *Monongalia Story*, vol. 2), died early in 1846. He had married Eleanor, daughter of Thomas and Pricilla Magruder, and they had at least ten children, including Justinion, Linda Ann, Mary, Eleanor, Anna,

17. *Western Virginia Standard*, March 28, 1846.
18. *Western Virginia Standard*, March 7, 1846.
19. Franklin Marion Brand, *The Wade Family* (1927), p. 398.

Dennis Magruder, Joanna, Eliza Jane, Benjamin B., and Margaret.[20]

**John Stevens.** A farmer, teacher, and shoemaker of the head of Booths Creek, John Stevens died in 1846. He was born in New England about 1762. He married Nancy Agnes Whitford and they located in Monongalia County before 1808. His feet were frozen on a hunting trip and had to be partially amputated. Names of the children include Eleanor, William, Elizabeth, Silas, Simeon, Sarah, Mahlon, Israel, and Blachlet.[21]

**Land Grants Made in 1846.** Monongalia County grantees in 1846 included:

| | | |
|---|---|---|
| Artis, Samuel | 100 a. | Waters of Cheat R. |
| Campbell, Nimrod | 140 | Buffalo Creek |
| Davis, Bela | 200 | Deckers Creek |
| Ellicott, Evan T. and Andrew | 41 | Waters Cheat R. |
| England, Samuel | 100 | Waters Cheat R. |
| Freeland, Elijah | 125 | Johnnys Run |
| Glover, Samuel | 250 | Piles Fork |
| Hanway, John | 10 | Days Run |
| Hanway, John | 260 | Buffalo Creek |
| Hanway, John | 80 | Piles Fork |
| Reed, John | 132 | Deckers Creek |
| Reed, Robert R. | 20 | Dunkard Creek |
| Shafer, David | 81 | Adj. Dolly Horner |
| Tennant, Adam, Sr. | 18 | Days Run |
| Tower, E. W. | 350 | Piles Fork |
| Tower, E. W. | 100 | Buffalo Creek |
| Wade, Alexander, Jr. | 29 | Dunkard Creek |
| Wade, Alexander, Jr. | 80 | Piles Fork |
| Wade, Alexander, Jr. | 260 | Buffalo Creek |
| White, Joseph S. | 8 | Dunkard Creek |

**County Government.** Aaron Barker was sworn in as sheriff on March 25, 1846. Rawley Holland became commissioner of the

    20. Gordon C. Baker, "The Benjamin Thorn Family of Monongalia County . . .," *Monongalia Chronicle*, April, 1974, pp. 1-5.
    21. B. F. Tatterson, "The John Stevens Family," *Monongalia Chronicle*, January, 1975.

revenue for the Eastern District and W. W. Lazzelle for the Western District. Gideon Barb was sworn in as justice of the peace August 24, 1846.

**Miscellany.** In 1846: William McKinley was admitted to the Monongalia County bar (Wiley, p. 318). . . . Rev. Silas Billings succeeded P. S. Ruter as principal of the Monongalia Academy (Wiley, p. 395). . . . Rev. Thomas McCune became principal of the Morgantown Female Academy (Wiley, p. 399). . . . Steamboats arriving at the Port of Morgantown included the *Motive*, on March 9, and the *Medium*, on May 10 (Wiley, p. 542). . . . The Morgantown Masonic Lodge (see *Monongalia Story*, vol. 2, pp. 399-401), after having been dormant since 1819, was granted a new charter by the Grand Lodge of Virginia on December 16 (Wiley, p. 548). . . . Lazier, McLane and Company opened a retail store in Morgantown (Wiley, p. 580). . . . Adam Myers was manager of the "Old Dominion" tavern (Wiley, p. 586). . . . Mary John died, aged ninety-four years, and was buried at Stewartstown (Wiley, p. 675). . . . The Reverend James Davis became pastor of the Stewarts Run Presbyterian Church, succeeding the Reverend William P. Harshe, who had succeeded the Reverend C. B. Bristol (p. 272) only a short time earlier (Wiley, p. 729). . . . Henry Young Dering, son of Henry and Rebecca Dering, died at the age of fifty-five (Callahan, p. 85). . . . George M. Hagans bought Lot 31 in Morgantown from Harriet Lowry and erected a brick home on it (Callahan, pp. 189, 314). . . . George Kramer conveyed the southeast corner of Lot 21 to Michael Chalfant (Callahan, p. 312). . . . John Abraham Guseman sold Lot 26 to George D. Evans, who constructed a brick store on it (Callahan, p. 313). . . . Frederick A. Dering conveyed Lot 93 to Monongalia Academy (Callahan, p. 322). . . . The Avery church building was completed and used for the first time; Rev. Peter Laishley was present, along with Rev. M. Stewart, the pastor (Dodds and Dodds, p. 149).

# CHAPTER SEVENTY-ONE

# 1847

From 1846 until 1848 the United States was involved in a war with Mexico, and Monongalia County men volunteered for service, as they had in all previous wars in which the country was involved.

The immediate cause of the war was a series of developments in Texas, which had been a part of Mexico under Spain's New World empire and later under the Republic of Mexico. In 1821 Moses Austin had secured permission to settle three hundred families from the United States in Texas. Other families followed, under Austin's son, Stephen, so many that the Mexican government became to be alarmed. In 1829 further settlement of Americans in Texas was prohibited by Mexico.

Following a series of incidents in 1835 and 1836, the Texans first established a provisional state government, and then proclaimed their independence. General Antonio Lopez de Santa Anna countered by taking the field against them but was defeated in a battle along the Rio San Jacinto on April 21, 1836. Britain, France, and the United States recognized the independence of Texas, which over the next nine years maintained its sovereignty with little difficulty despite loud Mexican threats.

It was during the war for Texan independence that there occurred, on March 6, 1836, the capture of the Alamo, a fortress in San Antonio, with the death of all the defenders. One of them, tradition says (although his name is not on the official list), was a man named Boultinghouse, a descendant of the Joseph Boultinghouse who was a charter member of the Forks of Cheat Baptist Church.

From the start Texans manifested an interest in annexation

to the United States, but politically the issue was too explosive for any administration in Washington to raise. Finally, however, Congress passed a bill for its annexation and it was signed by President John Tyler on March 1, 1845.

Among the reasons advanced in opposition to the annexation was the attitude of Mexico and the certainty that this would draw the United States into war with that republic. Aware of the feelings in Mexico, President James K. Polk, only a few weeks after his inauguration, ordered General Zachary Taylor to proceed with a body of troops to Texas and post himself near the Mexican border.

**The Mexican War.** Support for a war with Mexico came from most parts of the United States. In Monongalia County the Seventy-sixth Regiment of Virginia militia, under Colonel James Evans, met on May 25, 1846, to ascertain how many men would volunteer to go to Mexico as soldiers of the United States. The 104th Regiment, under Lieutenant Colonel B. F. Tibbs met in July for the same purpose.

In all, about two hundred men volunteered to go for one year, in Kramer's Monongalia Blues, with Captain Fowler's Cheat Invincibles and Captain Edison's Cavalry. However, the government refused to accept any one-year men and this did not materialize.

War with Mexico was declared on May 13, 1846, and events proceeded rapidly. General Taylor advanced into northern Mexico and General Winfield Scott landed near Veracruz on March 9, 1847, preparing to advance toward Mexico City. Meanwhile, in an entirely different operation, John C. Fremont, at the head of a small band in California, repeatedly defeated the Mexican forces and on July 4, 1846, declared the independence of California.

Early in 1847 Lieutenant (afterwards captain) George W. Clutter recruited a body of men in Monongalia County for Captain John Tyler, Jr.'s, company at Old Point Comfort, Virginia.[1] Their names follow:

| | |
|---|---|
| Charles Ball | Jesse J. Carraco |
| William Black | William Christy (died) |
| Levi L. Bryte | Henry Dean |

1. Wiley, p. 496.

William Dean
Wilson Dean
George Exline
Jac. Farr
Oliver Guthrie
Richard Hall
Aaron Hamilton (died)
George Hayes
John W. Hayes
Levi Hayes
N. N. Hoffman
Oakley Hopkins[2]
Alex Jenkins
Levi Jenkins

John Keefover
—— Koontz
John McFadden
—— McFarland
Amos Martin (died)
William Miller
Ellis Mitchell
William Pixler
Lewis Powelson
Benj. Scott (died)
Felix Scott
Jeff Scott
Davis Toothman

The men left Morgantown on May 21, 1847, and proceeded by Cumberland and Baltimore to Fortress Monroe, whence they sailed for Mexico on June 9 and arrived at Brazos Santiago on July 6.

The company then marched to Mier, July 14, with the thermometer at 110 degrees in the shade, and drilled there for three months, after which it was sent to Veracruz and served under General Scott. Their regiment, the Thirteenth, was in two guerrilla battles, one at the Robber's Bridge, with 650 Mexicans, the other at the National Bridge, where Major Lally, with about 2,000 Americans, charged two forts and drove out about 2,500 Mexicans. The Thirteenth Regiment lost thirty men, of whom two belonged to the company to which the Monongalia squad belonged. This company suffered at different times for food, from sickness, and sometimes greatly for water.[3]

The war proceeded rapidly, as is well known, with one American victory after another, and in September 1847, Mexico City itself was captured.[4]

2. Oakley Hopkins, son of William R. (1773-1871) and Nancy (Oakley) Hopkins, was born November 25, 1820, and was killed by a bushwhacker in the Civil War October 14, 1861. He was a great-grandfather of Morgantown attorney Oakley J. Hopkins.

3. Wiley, pp. 520, 521. The company shipped for home on June 12, 1848.

4. On February 2, 1848, terms of peace were agreed upon by American commissioners and the Mexican government, later ratified by congresses of both governments. President Polk proclaimed peace on July 4, 1848.

"If ever America fought an unavoidable war," says K. Jack Bauer,[5] "it was the conflict with Mexico over the delineation of the common boundary. The whole thrust of America's physical and cultural growth carried her inexorably westward toward the setting sun and the Great Ocean. Thrust in the way of this movement were three sparsely settled and inadequately protected Mexican provinces: Alta California, New Mexico, and Texas. If the inexorable demands of destiny drove the United States into Mexican lands, similar demands of nationalism and self-respect prevented Mexico from parting with those areas except to overwhelming force."[6]

Bauer concludes: "There are many similarities between the war with Mexico and the more recent one in Vietnam. In both instances the United States found itself at war because of miscalculations about the enemy which destroyed the effectiveness of a campaign of gradual escalation. Despite victories in the field, which by conventional standards were staggering, America could not force the opposition to negotiate seriously. When peace in Mexico did come, it resulted from a temporary combination of circumstances which made a weak interim administration willing to settle lest American demands increase exponentially."[7]

**Another Loss of Territory.** The ninth change in the boundaries of Monongalia County since its formation in 1776 occurred March 15, 1847, when the general assembly ruled that a small slice at the southwestern end of the county was to be added to Marion County. The act provided "that the line run between the counties of Monongalia and Marion shall hereafter run so as to include within the county of Marion all territory on the waters of Buffalo Creek."

This action resulted in a curve of the hitherto straight boundary between the two counties and had the effect of reuniting the Glovers Gap community with its neighboring communities farther down Buffalo Creek.

5. K. Jack Bauer, *The Mexican War, 1846-1848* (1974).
6. Op. cit., p. xix.
7. Op. cit., pp. 396, 397.

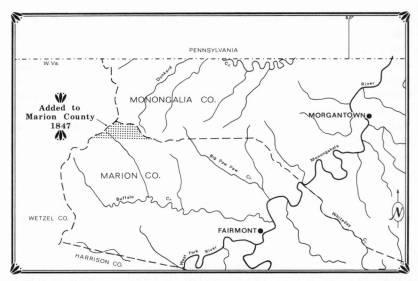

Fig. 43. Map showing minor boundary adjustment, 1847. (Drawn by Diane Lenhart.)

This adjustment in boundary brought the area of the county down to 368.82 square miles.[8]

**The Monongahela Navigation Company.** Encouraged by the progress made by the Pennsylvania group known as the Monongahela Navigation Company (see p. 252), citizens of Monongalia County renewed their efforts to secure slack water and sent a petition to the legislature praying for action.

In response to the petition, the general assembly, on March 10, 1847, passed an act incorporating the Monongahela Navigation Company, of Virginia, the object of which was to slack the Monongahela River from the state line to Fairmont. On March 19 another act was passed, empowering the company to increase its capital and to improve Cheat River to serve the iron works along that stream.

But, as had happened so many times in the past, nothing resulted from this action.[9]

8. This, as it happened, turned out to be the final change in the boundaries, although several unsuccessful proposals would be made from time to time.

9. Wiley, pp. 107, 127.

**Planning a Route for the Railroad.** Meanwhile, the Baltimore and Ohio Railroad Company, having completed its line to Cumberland in 1842 (p. 236), was preparing the extension that would finally bring it to the Ohio River.

The railroad had become a political issue in Monongalia County, as in all counties of western Virginia. Although at first western Virginians had been enthusiastic about the prospects of rail transportation and had pointed out its prospective advantages (see pp. 2, 18), many objections now began to be made.

Excitement was intense and all-absorbing. Citizens throughout the area (and in counties of southwestern Pennsylvania) gathered at schoolhouses, where the subject was warmly discussed. Among other things, it was suggested that the railroad would take the place of horses in transportation. Oats, which in 1846 sold for twenty-five cents a bushel, would drop to ten cents.

Rev. William Hanna relates some of the objections brought out in Greene County, Pennsylvania: "I listened to the sophistical arguments of some of the demagogues of that day, in which they asserted that the iron horse could not eat oats or corn. 'Let us just compel them to stop at Cumberland, and then all the goods will be wagoned through our country, all the hogs will be fed with our corn and the horses with our oats. Go away with your railroad! We don't want our wives and children frightened to death by the screaming of the locomotive. We don't want our hogs and cows run over and killed by the cars of a soulless corporation.' "[10]

On March 6, 1847, the general assembly, after a long delay caused in part by a conflict of possible routes, passed an act authorizing the Baltimore and Ohio Railroad Company to construct the extension of their road through Virginia to the Ohio River at Wheeling.

"Among the men of that day having the foresight to see the value of a railroad was Thomas Haymond, then the representative from Marion County. It is said by those acquainted with the circumstances, that Haymond never mentioned his county as desiring the road; but being well acquainted with the

10. Wiley, p. 107 note.

geography of north-western Virginia, he quietly got the following clause attached to the bill: 'That the said railroad to be constructed through the territory of Virginia, shall reach or cross the Tygart's Valley River at or within three miles of the mouth of Three Fork Creek in the county of Taylor.' Previous to this, surveys had been made down Muddy Creek, Preston County, to get on to Decker's Creek and reach Morgantown. Haymond's clause compelled the road to make near the mouth of Three Fork a point. When this was done there was no route left to get from there to Wheeling but through Marion; and Grafton became the junction. Morgantown most likely would have been, as the engineers pronounced the route by Morgantown the most desirable."[11]

The act required all parts of the road between the Monongahela Valley and Wheeling to be opened simultaneously for transportation of freight and passengers. It also annulled the stock subscriptions made by Virginia in 1837 and 1838 and made provisions for connections, depots, taxation, and other regulations. Wheeling was given authority to subscribe $1 million.[12]

**County School Report.** In 1847, it was reported to the county court, there were eighty-four schools in the county. The number of poor children eligible for state aid was 800; of these, 534 were sent to school for a total of 42,189 days, at a cost of $0.02½ per day. At the going rate, there was due the county from the Literary Fund $1,013.76.

**The Grandville Methodist Circuit.** Much of the territory of Constabulary District No. 3 (see pp. 61-62) was included in the new Grandville Methodist Episcopal circuit, formed August 21, 1847. Richard Jordan was minister in charge, and Morgan L. Boyers was a local preacher. Henry James and James Arnett were exhorters. Class leaders were John B. Lough at Cold Spring, Morgan Tucker at Huggans', Joseph W. Snider at Snider's, Elijah Snider at Laurel Point, and Sanford S. Scott at Grandville. Besides these charges there were four others, Union,

11. Wiley, p. 123 note.
12. Callahan, *Semi-Centennial History of West Virginia*, p. 115.

at Flickersville, Bend of the River, Arnett's, at Arnettsville, and Bethel.[13]

**The Goshen Church.** The Baptist congregation which had been organized in 1837 (see p. 148), began in 1847 the construction of a new church building. Bricks, and lime for mortar and plaster, were burned in kilns directly across the road. Massive beams and girders were hewn by hand.[14]

Fig. 44. The Goshen Baptist Church, constructed in 1847. (Photo by Wilbur Howell.)

**Dr. Robert Travis Dies.** One of the best known physicians of the county, Dr. Robert Travis, died in 1847. His father, Joseph Travis, had settled in Virginia about 1780, and Robert came to Monongalia County in 1803. He married Mary Trickett and settled at Smithtown for the practice of medicine about 1828, spending the remainder of his life at this location. Dr. Travis also kept a store in Smithtown.[15]

**Cassville (Jacksonville).** About 1840 residents of the growing community of Jacksonville (p. 44) began to agitate for the

13. Wiley, p. 727.
14. Dodds and Dodds, *Churches of Monongalia County*, p. 139.
15. Wiley, pp. 467, 614, 644.

establishment of a post office. However, it was not until several years later, September 20, 1847, that the proposal was finally approved. It was found that there was already a post office by the name of Jacksonville in Virginia, so Nicholas B. Madera, who was postmaster at Morgantown, suggested the name Cassville, in honor of American statesman Lewis Cass (1782-1866). This name was adopted for the post office and residents of the town changed its name from Jacksonville to conform to the name of the post office. Peter A. Layton was the first postmaster.

**New Brownsville (Pentress).** A village along Dunkard Creek, at first known as Statlerstown (see p. 6), was laid out as a town by Emanuel Brown[16] about 1847, and for years thereafter was called New Brownsville.

A post office, however, established August 23, 1847, was given the name of Pentress, and this name has persisted until the present time, gradually replacing the earlier names. It is said that William Price suggested the name Pentress because it was a familiar name in Wales, where his family originated. Cyrenius Cox was the first postmaster.

**Wadestown (West Warren).** By mid-century a village was developing at the junction of the three forks of Dunkard Creek, in the western end of the county, serving as the social and business center of District No. 7. The village came to be known as West Warren, but in 1847 a post office was established called Wadestown. William Kinney, on October 11, 1847, became the first postmaster.

One of the first settlers near the site of Wadestown was Phineas Kellum (or Kellam), who received a land grant by virtue of his settlement before the year 1778 on "Kellam's Fork of Dunkers Creek"; the name Kellam's Fork no longer appears on the map but it is probably one of the three forks of Dunkard Creek which join at Wadestown. A tract surveyed for Kellam in

16. Emanuel Brown was a son of Adam and Christina Brown, prominent pioneer settlers of the Dunkard Creek section, whose children, in addition to Emanuel, were John, Abraham, Andrew, Torissa Sarah, Catherine, Eve, Elizabeth, Mary, and Margaret. Adam Brown died in 1825; see numerous references in *The Monongalia Story*, vol. 2.

1784 was said to be "on the Head of a Run that Indeon John was killed on, it being a branch of Dunker Creek."

Lynn Hastings says Indians attacked the Kellam settlement in 1786, killing and capturing some of the settlers, burning their cabins.[17]

The Wade family, for which the community was later to be named, was there just as early as the Kellams. Records show that "Thomas Wade is intitled to four hundred acres of land in Monongalia County on the left hand fork of Duncar Creek about half a mile above the three forks of said Creek to include his settlement made thereon in the year 1775."

The Wadestown post office was served by a carrier who traveled at first once a week from Morgantown to Burton. Other post offices on this route were Scotts Run (established 1843, later Cassville), Jakes Run (established 1844, later Mooresville), and Blacksville (established 1832).

**Peter Henkenius Dies.** Peter Henkins, a farmer of the Dunkard Creek Valley, died in 1847. He was of German origin and the name was formerly written Henkenius. He was born in Chester County, Pennsylvania, February 19, 1769, and went to Frederick County, Virginia, in 1788, where he married Catherine Shriver on March 3, 1789. They moved to Shenandoah County in 1790 and to Monongalia County in 1798. He was a soldier in the War of 1812.

They were parents of Margaret (born June 11, 1789); Elijah (born May 22, 1791); Susanna (born in 1792); Christina (born March 15, 1794); Elizabeth (born March 11, 1795); Mary (born October 19, 1796); Rebecca (born March 24, 1798); Christiana (born November 9, 1799); George (born September 15, 1801); Alice (born September 18, 1803); Sarah (born July 18, 1805); Abraham (born February 16, 1807); and Carrie (born April 11, 1809).[18]

**Land Grants Made in 1847.** Monongalia County grantees in 1847 included:

| | | |
|---|---|---|
| Flum, Henry | 145 a. | Deckers Creek |
| Lewis, Richard | 240 | Amos Camp Run |

17. *School and Local History, Battelle,* p. 106.
18. *Cyclopedia of Monongalia County,* pp. 141, 142.

| McCurdy, Benjamin | 60 | Papaw Creek |
| Meredith, Thomas | 400 | Booths Creek |
| Miller, Jacob | 1½ | West Run |
| Price, Isaac | 4 | Flaggy Run |
| Riggs, Malone | 8 | Indian Creek |
| Robinson, John C. | 120 | Deckers Creek |
| Shafer, Aaron | 80 | Adj. Thomas Dunn |
| Tower, Edwin W. | 125 | Piles Fork |
| Tower, Edwin W. | 150 | White Day Creek |
| Tower, Edwin W. | 400 | Booths Creek |
| Vandervort, Jonah | 950 | Tibbs Run |
| Walker, Alpheus D. | 100 | Tibbs Run |
| Woodrough, Erastus, Sr. | 30 | Dunkard Creek |

**County Government.** Aaron Barker was sworn in March 22, 1847, for his second term as sheriff. R. L. Berkshire was sworn in as prosecuting attorney of the county court on February 22, 1847, succeeding Mathew Gay, who had served since 1814. William Haines, Daniel Dusenberry, Henry Daugherty, Henry Dering, and George M. Reay were sworn in as justices of the peace on July 26, 1847.

**Miscellany.** In 1847: The Dunkard Creek Turnpike, which had been projected unsuccessfully in 1839, was revived (Wiley, p. 539). . . . The steamboat *Danube* arrived at the Port of Morgantown on November 26 (Wiley, p. 542). . . . Alexander Hayes bought, for $1,100, the old hotel property, Lot 38, on High Street (Callahan, pp. 100, 316). . . . The Morgantown Baptist Church on March 27 voted to "sell the portion of the Baptist lot authorized by law" (Callahan, pp. 159, 160). . . . Henry Dering purchased Lot 44 and shortly thereafter built a brick house on it (Callahan, pp. 188, 189). . . . Lot 125 was conveyed by Charles McLane to Addison Vance (Callahan, p. 330).

CHAPTER SEVENTY-TWO

# 1848

The original settlers of Monongalia County were mostly of English, Scotch-Irish, or German ancestry, and, as the mid-point of the nineteenth century approached, the character of the population had changed but little. The pioneers "were contented with a life of rural simplicity and hospitality whose economy was in many cases mere subsistence. Their descendants usually lived amiably with their neighbors, maintained their urbanity and self-possession in the presence of strangers, and, beyond the efforts necessary to secure the necessaries of life, were often disposed to leave improvement of things to time and chance."[1]

They did, however, combine their efforts to improve moral and religious conditions through the organization of church congregations and related societies, such as lodges and temperance societies.

The first lodge, Morgantown Union Lodge No. 93, A.F. & A.M., was chartered December 15, 1812.[2] From 1819 to 1825 the lodge was inactive and in 1826 the charter appears to have been returned. On December 16, 1846, a new charter was granted. Peter T. Laishley was master in 1846-47, H. Reed and A. B. McCans in 1848.[3]

**The Independent Order of Odd Fellows.** On Thursday, January 27, 1848, Monongalia Lodge No. 62, Independent Order of Odd Fellows, was instituted through a dispensation granted

1. Callahan, *Semi-Centennial History of West Virginia*, p. 223.
2. *The Monongalia Story*, vol. 2, pp. 399-401.
3. Wiley, pp. 547, 548.

through Edmond C. Robinson, most worthy grand master of the Grand Lodge of Virginia. The application had been filed through the friendly association of five men, namely, P. R. Mitchell, John Beck, Rev. L. B. Dunlap, and J. U. Beall, of Morgantown, and E. L. Stealey, of Clarksburg.

The Independent Order of Odd Fellows originated in England, but no one knows exactly when; it was presumably in the early 1700s. The members of the order founded a system of benefits and the chief purpose was (and still is) to give aid, assistance, and comfort to the members and their families. It became a secret society, with its own system of rites and passwords. The three links in the symbol represent friendship, love, and truth, while the single eye represents the all-knowingness of God.

Fig. 45. The Masonic Hall, birthplace of the IOOF in 1848. The building at first stood at the corner of High and Walnut streets before being moved down Walnut Street. (Courtesy Morgantown IOOF Lodge.)

"The records show that the meeting was opened on Thursday evening, January 27, 1848, with A. C. Levit as Noble Grand, E. L. Stealey as Vice Grand, T. L. Moore as Secretary, E. M. Davidson as Warden, A. A. Lewis as Inside Guardian, and Cyrus Vance as Outside Guardian, all of them being members of Adelphia Lodge No. 47 of Clarksburg. Mitchell Dunlap, Beck, and Beall, being Odd Fellows, were admitted as brothers. Mitchell then presented applications for membership on behalf of the following men: George L. Reay, Richard B. Carr, William E. Grove, William Haymond, John L. Evans, William L. Evans, Thomas Evans, and Watson Carr, who were balloted on, elected, and initiated the same evening. A second meeting was held at ten o'clock the next morning, when the above candidates were given further degree work. At two o'clock of the same day, Friday, another meeting was held and the following officers were then elected: P. R. Mitchell, Noble Grand; Thomas Evans, Vice Grand; John Beck, Recording Secretary; R. B. Carr, Corresponding Secretary; George L. Reay, Treasurer; and Rev. L. B. Dunlap, Chaplain. At seven P.M. that evening, the newly elected officers being in their chairs, the following named men were appointed as a committee to make application for a charter: Watson Carr, William Haymond, John Beck, George L. Reay, and R. B. Carr. The first constitution and by-laws of this lodge were those used by Adelphia Lodge No. 47, which were adopted at this meeting."[4]

No further meetings were held until March 20, 1848, by which time the charter and other documents had arrived. The first trustees were William Haymond, Watson Carr, P. R. Mitchell, William Durbin, George L. Reay, and G. B. Tucker. The first report of the secretary showed nineteen men initiated and three admitted by card. The second report, dated September 28, 1848, showed nine more initiated. George L. Reay was the second noble grand and Thomas Evans the third.

On November 15, 1848, the first fine of 6¼ cents was imposed, for non-attendance. Similar fines were numerous thereafter. On November 22, 1848, Brother "John Doe" was summoned to appear before the lodge to answer a charge of conduct unbecoming an Odd Fellow. On November the twenty-ninth he paid a fine of one dollar.

Entries in the records for the next year or so provide information as to the operation of the lodge, as well as vivid glimpses of life in Morgantown at the time.

William Haymond, Jr., had been chosen for the honors of noble grand on July 7, 1848, but he did not live to take office,

4. Quotations from various historical pamphlets published by the lodge, the most recent in 1978. Courtesy Edmund Smith.

his death occurring on July 13. This was the first death in the new order, and was the occasion for the principal chairs in the lodge hall to be clothed in mourning for thirty days. Badges of mourning were worn by members for the same period. Death benefits at that time were $5.00 and $16.94 was allowed for funeral expenses.

**Sons of Temperance.** Temperance organizations were common at mid-century and enthusiastically supported. We have noted earlier the formation of the Monongalia Temperance Society (p. 150).

On Thursday evening, January 6, 1848, the Monongalia Division, No. 84, Sons of Temperance, was organized in the Masonic Hall in Morgantown by Joshua Mathiot, GWP, of Ohio. Charter members were L. S. Hough, S. Billings (chaplain), W. T. Willey, E. P. Fitch (treasurer), G. S. Ray (conductor), W. Carr (WA), H. E. Smith (RS), Guy R. C. Allen (WP), H. Dering (FS), J. E. Tucker (AC), H. Daugherty (IS), S. Merrifield (OS), and others.

Soon after, Granville Division, No. 194, and Willey Section, No. 37, Cadets of Temperance, were formed.[5]

**Prices of Farm Products.** With the improvement in economic conditions following the panic of 1837, prices of agricultural products declined, increasing again somewhat during the Mexican War.

Wiley[6] gives the following prices as of January 1, for the decade of the 1840s:

|      | Wheat per bu. | Corn per bu. | Oats per bu. | Eggs per doz. | Butter per lb. | Bacon per lb. | Beef per lb. |
|------|------|------|------|------|------|------|------|
| 1840 | $0.62 | $0.37 | $0.25 |       | $0.15 | $0.05 | $0.04 |
| 1841 | .50  | .31  | .20  |       | .10  | .03½ | .03  |
| 1842 | .75  | .31  | .25  |       | .10  | .03  | .05  |
| 1843 | .50  | .25  | .16  | .03  | .08  | .02¼ | .02½ |
| 1844 | .62  | .25  | .16  |       | .08  | .02½ |      |
| 1845 | .75  | .25  | .16  |       | .08  | .02½ | .02  |
| 1846 | .75  | .37½ | .25  |       | .10  | .03  | .03  |
| 1848 | .87½ | .50  | .25  |       | .12½ | .03½ | .03½ |

5. Wiley, p. 452.
6. Wiley, p. 249.

**School Statistics.** In 1848 the Board of School Commissioners reported that there were seventy-six primary schools in the county. The number of poor children who were entitled to state support was 1,335, of whom 725 were sent to school for a total of 46,076 days, at a cost of 2½ cents per day. The amount of money due the county from the Literary Fund was $1,013.76.

**Alexander Wade.** A sixteen-year-old boy, Alexander L. Wade, began teaching in a one-room school on Pedlar Run in 1848. He was destined to make most significant contributions to the advancement of education in Monongalia County and in the new state of West Virginia.

Alexander Wade was born February 1, 1832, near Rushville, Indiana, the eldest son of George and Anna Wade (see p. 283). In 1839 the family moved back to Monongalia County, where his father had been born, and where, in 1846, he died, "leaving the family no fortune save the force of a Christian education." Alexander, fourteen years of age, undertook to help his mother support the four younger children. "He had early imbibed a love for learning and an earnest desire to be a scholar. But schools were inferior and books were scarce, and his time was divided between labor and study, while his earnings went to buy bread for the family and books for the library."[7]

**G. F. C. Conn, Missionary.** The Reverend George Frederick Charles Conn (see p. 280) in 1848 received a commission from the General Baptist Association of Virginia to labor as a missionary in Preston County and adjoining areas. Under this commission he worked at Monongalia Glades,[8] where a church was organized with six members and increased to forty; at Elliotts Ridge,[9] where he baptized many; at the site of Gladesville,[10] where a house of worship was built and the membership grew from seven to one hundred; at Blacksville, where he organized the Minorsville church, which built a house of worship and attained a membership of forty; and at Laurel Point, in the

7. Wiley, pp. 371-72; see also *Cyclopedia of Monongalia County*, pp. 228, 229.
8. *The Monongalia Story*, vol. 1, p. 59.
9. *The Monongalia Story*, vol. 2, p. 220.
10. *The Monongalia Story*, vol. 2, p. 341.

bounds of the old Anti-Mission Baptist Church known as Mount Tabor.[11]

"His labors under this commission were abundantly blessed of the Lord; and Mr. Conn attributes any success he may have had as a Gospel minister, largely to the divine blessing upon this aid extended by the General Association of Virginia."[12]

**The Western Virginia Conference.** In the Methodist Episcopal Church in Western Virginia a considerable amount of dissension was developing with respect to slavery and abolitionism, some churches even refusing to accept the preachers sent to them. Some church leaders suggested that a Western Virginia Conference be formed from the Pittsburgh Conference: "A preacher identified with the people will be viewed with less suspicion as to abolitionism, and can more freely reprove the abuses of slavery, than one coming from a free and distant State."

Provision was thereupon made for the creation of a Western Virginia Conference, to include all of Virginia west of the Shenandoah range. The first annual meeting of the conference (held jointly with the Pittsburgh Conference) was held July 5-12, 1848, at Wheeling, presided over by Bishop L. L. Hamline. In the new conference were three districts, Morgantown, Clarksburg, and Kanawha.[13]

**The Monongalia Circuit.** The Monongalia Methodist Episcopal Circuit was formed August 19, 1848, essentially a renaming of the Grandville Circuit (see p. 292). The charges were Mount Hermon (formerly Huggans' Chapel) (see p. 246); Bethel (p. 21); Fort Martin (*Monongalia Story*, vol. 1, p. 186); Hawkins; Grandville; Cassville; and Wade's School-house. J. W. Reger and W. Fribley were preachers in charge.[14]

**Laurel Point Methodist Church.** Evan Pindall and Drusilla, his wife, on August 7, 1848, deeded to the trustees of the Laurel Point Methodist Church, a lot on which a log building had stood

11. *The Monongalia Story*, vol. 2, pp. 373, 374.
12. Wiley, pp. 457-59.
13. Smeltzer, *Methodism*, pp. 158-62.
14. Wiley, pp. 727-28; for biography of John W. Reger, see George Cleaton Wilding, *Promoted Pioneer Preachers*, pp. 58-60. "He was a preacher of marked ability, clear, pointed, forcible, sometimes eloquent, and always finding attentive hearers."

since about 1835, used both as a church and a school. The trustees were named as William Berkshire, James Brewer, John Snider, Benjamin Thompson, William Finnell, and John Mercer.

Families of the community who had organized the church included J. S. Potter, H. A. Snider, J. I. Snider, D. P. Thorn, E. M. Potter, and G. W. Snider.

**William Haymond Dies.** William Haymond, Jr., who spent some of his boyhood days around Kerns' Fort (see *Monongalia Story*, vol. 2, pp. 27, 54), died at Palatine, Marion County, on July 8, 1848. He was a son of Major William and Cassandra Clelland Haymond, and was born near Rockville, Maryland, June 11, 1771. He was engaged in the latter part of the Indian warfare, on the Monongahela frontier, and one summer patrolled the Ohio River near Parkersburg and Marietta.

He married Cynthia Carroll, daughter of Mr. and Mrs. James Carroll, a relative of Charles Carroll, signer of the Declaration of Independence, and they had seven children, Thomas S., William Calder, Hiram, Jonathan, Octavius, Augustus, and Marcus.

His father moved his family from Morgantown to Clarksburg in 1784, and William, Jr., lived there until 1794, when he moved to the site of Palatine.

**James Chadwick Dies.** A prominent Morgantown businessman, James Chadwick, died October 3, 1848. He was born October 6, 1784, and came to Morgantown from Fayette County about 1812. He was in business as Goff and Chadwick in 1825, Chadwick and Watts in 1830, Chadwick and Alexander in 1832, and Chadwick and Sons after 1835.[15] His sons, James, David H., and Daniel C., were associated with him.

**Halleck School.** A log schoolhouse was built at the site of the village of Halleck in 1848 and Oliver P. McRa[16] became the first teacher. Five years earlier, in 1843, the first school in the community had been built, on land belonging to Hugh Austin.

15. Wiley, pp. 580, 581, 601.
16. Oliver Perry McRa, born December 14, 1819, was a son of Duncan and Rebecca McRa, and a grandson of distinguished pioneer Farquhar McRa (*The Monongalia Story*, vol. 2, pp. 126, 204, 263, 371, 501). Oliver married Jemima, daughter of Elijah and Mary Jacobs, and they settled near Halleck. Their children were Edgar, Waitman, Elijah, Susan, Thomas Ison (a Methodist minister), Sylvester, Mary, and Virginia. See *Cyclopedia of Monongalia County*, pp. 188-91.

This school, known as the Gallaher School, had as its teachers for the first five years, Charles Johnson, James Johnson, and Oliver P. Jolliffe.[17]

**Land Grants Made in 1848.** Monongalia County grantees in 1848 included:

| | | |
|---|---|---|
| Brock, George | 24 a. | Dunkard Creek |
| Fetty, George | 3 | Indian Creek |
| Glover, Peter | 85 | Piles Fork |
| Jolliff, Joseph and Nathan | 85 | Booths Creek |
| Jones, John | 5 | Toms Run |
| Keck, Philip H. | 24 | Dunkard Creek |
| Kerns, James | ¾ | Adj. John Jones |
| Lazier, William | 350 | Booth Creek |
| McCord, John | 10 | Days Run |
| Moore, Daniel | 49 | Adj. Jacob Brookover |
| Ray, George S. | 24 | Dunkard Creek |
| Thomas, William | 32 | Miracle Run |
| Tower, E. W. | 115 | Laurel Run |
| Wheelright, William Thomas | 32 | Miracle Run |

**County Government.** George McNeely was sworn in as sheriff March 27, 1848. Nelson Berkshire was appointed commissioner of the revenue for the Eastern District and Gideon Barb for the Western District. The county levy was $2.85, the highest in history up to that time, reflecting costs of constructing the new courthouse.

**Miscellany.** In 1848: William Lazier, who had taken over the operation of Hugh Daugherty's foundry, put in a steam engine for power and associated James Nimon with him in the business (Wiley, p. 262). . . . Henry E. Smith and Samuel Woods were admitted to the county bar on April 6 (Wiley, p. 316). . . . Waitman T. Willey was appointed to the board of school commissioners, filing his bond on November 27 (Wiley, p. 364). . . . Richard J. Laishley, son of Rev. Peter T. and Sabina Laishley, was killed on September 27 by the bursting of the cylinder of a threshing machine (Wiley, p. 456). . . . Steamboats arriving at the Port of Morgantown were the *Star*, on May 10, and the *Hope*, on May 13 (Wiley, p. 542). . . . Thomas Purinton was

17. Hastings, *Clinton District Schools*, p. 56.

keeping a bookstore in Morgantown (Wiley, p. 583). . . . William Wood succeeded A. J. Garrett as pastor of the Morgantown Baptist Church (Wiley, p. 595). . . . The Goshen Baptist Church (see p. 293) dedicated a new house of worship on June 24; construction had started the previous year (Wiley, p. 626). . . . Samuel Kendall became pastor of the Forks of Cheat Baptist Church (Wiley, p. 686). . . . Dr. James Way was the first physician to locate at Cassville (Wiley, p. 702). . . . A Morgantown borough ordinance, adopted October 18, prohibited the keeping of wildcats, panthers, and bears in town (Callahan, p. 127). . . . David H. Chadwick conveyed the west end of Lots 15 and 16, in Morgantown, as far as the Methodist Episcopal parsonage, to Aaron Baird (Callahan, p. 311). . . . Lot 107 was conveyed by Henry S. Morgan to Samuel Merrifield and Alexander B. McCants (Callahan, p. 326). . . . Guy R. C. Allen acquired Lot 112, "the vacant brick-kiln lot" (Callahan, p. 327).

## CHAPTER SEVENTY-THREE

# 1849

The seat of government for Monongalia County was moved into a new building in 1849. This was the fifth structure to house governmental officials since the establishment of the county in the autumn of 1776. The first was a remodeled toolshed at "Phillips' Choice" (*Monongalia Story*, vol. 2, pp. 7, 19, 20), the second, very briefly, the house of Zackquill Morgan (Fig. 13), north of the mouth of Deckers Creek (*Monongalia Story*, vol. 2, p. 95), the third a frame building on the public square in Morgan's-Town (*Monongalia Story*, vol. 2, pp. 107, 108), constructed in 1784, and the fourth a brick building on the same site, completed in 1803 (*Monongalia Story*, vol. 2, pp. 299, 300, 307, 308).

**The New Courthouse Is Completed.** The building was evidently completed late in 1848, when allowances were made for various items of furniture, including (on October 21) "one wrighting table for clerks office, $6" and (on October 24) "repairing old table, $1.50." A year later payment was allowed for $16 for "one large desk for clerks office."

The final settlement for the construction, in 1849, ran a great deal higher than the original estimate (see p. 278) and Mr. Zinn submitted his bill of expense as follows:

| | |
|---|---:|
| Masonry and stone cutting | $ 956.32 |
| Brick and brick work | 2,047.00 |
| Lumber, timber, iron, and nails | 1,427.00 |
| Carpenter's work | 1,500.00 |
| Copper and spouting | 225.00 |
| Plastering and materials | 419.00 |
| Material and painting | 179.00 |
| | $6,753.32 |

The amount of the original bid, $5,695, had been increased by $470 for the pediment (evidently not completed by the first contractors) and other allowed expenses, for a total of $6,165, still $588.32 less than the amount claimed.

The commissioners approved the final settlement as follows:

| | |
|---|---:|
| Amt. of Mr. J. Zinn's contract | $5,695.00 |
| Amt. Agreement for pediment front and cornice | 405.00 |
| Amt. Extra in height of upper story | 100.00 |
| | $6,200.00 |

The commissioners concluded: "Allow $6,500 and this to cover all extras whatsoever, whether contracted with commissioners or otherwise, and to be in full for the entire courthouse."

Theodore Clouse was allowed two hundred dollars the same year for putting glass in the courthouse.

Between 1848 and 1850 a new two-story brick jail was built on the corner of Walnut Street and Long Alley. This building was constructed by Fielding Kiger and George Kramer.

The new jail replaced the famous "Old Log Jail," constructed about 1820 to 1825 of wooden blocks sawed about two by four feet and put together by iron bolts (*Monongalia Story*, vol. 2, pp. 505, 506).

Two other jails had preceded it, the original frontier building erected about 1784 and its replacement, a stone building forty-four by twenty feet in size, thirteen feet high, constructed in 1793 (*Monongalia Story*, vol. 2, pp. 270, 271).

**The Whipping Post.** The old whipping post was abolished by law in 1849. It had stood on the public square near Court Alley, about eighty feet from Long Alley. "Shortly after 1840 a white man named Whitehead was whipped. Later he became a very successful minister—an achievement which many attributed to the efficiency of the old time punishment. In 1849 a stern old judge from eastern Virginia imposed upon a negro a sentence of thirty-six blows with rawhide. The sheriff, whose duty was to 'lay on the lash,' shirked the unpleasant task which was therefore performed by Constable Vance in the presence of a large number of spectators. The negro was brought from the jail stripped to the waist, and his hands were tied firmly near the top of the post. Under the first blows, which left white stripes

Fig. 46. Monongalia County Courthouse, completed in 1848. (The statue of Patrick Henry was added in 1851.)

on his back, he cringed. Heavier blows followed until the blood trickled down. Thereupon, the spectators who kept the score of the strokes, reduced the punishment by counting faster than the blows were applied."[1]

George Hall, who arrived in Morgantown in 1845, recalled seeing the whip in frequent use as an aid to justice for nearly every petty judicial offense.[2]

**Failure of the Ellicotts.** A distressing development in 1849 brought to an end the period of prosperity of the Cheat Neck iron works, which had begun operation almost exactly a half century earlier. This was the failure and bankruptcy of the large Ellicott enterprises, which for the past decade had employed hundreds of people in various activities.

The entire holdings were sold at public auction; included were 15,000 acres of land, a rolling mill, a forge, a foundry, a nail factory, a gristmill, a sawmill, and three blast furnaces. A new company, formed in an effort to save the declining industry, composed of Mathew Gay of Morgantown, Butterford and Hersey of New Haven, and Lassey of Pittsburgh, purchased the property for $27,750.

Carvell summarizes the high points of the industry's history in the county:[3]

"In 1800 Samuel Jackson established Jackson's Iron works and made nails by hand at a forge close to the present bridge crossing. As demand for iron products increased, a nail-cutting machine, foundry and rolling mill (for making iron sheet and bars) were added. Iron production reached its zenith in the 1840's under the ownership of the Ellicott family. Four furnaces were in operation at that time, all connected to the shops along the river by tramroads. In addition, Ice's Ferry community contained a brickyard, sawmill, grist mill, boatyard, barrel factory, and post office (first known as Ice's Ferry and later as Laurel Iron works). During the 1840s, more than 3,000 persons lived along the river and about 1,500 were employed in the various shops and furnaces.

"Transporting iron products to market was the major

1. Callahan, *Making of Morgantown*, p. 124.
2. Callahan, ibid., p. 124 note.
3. *Wonderful West Virginia*, November, 1975.

problem. Roads were few and poor. Barges constructed at the boatyard at the mouth of Quarry Run were used to carry iron down the Cheat and the Monongahela and often to points as distant as St. Louis or New Orleans. Usually 14 by 30 feet, the barges were designed to slide gently over rocks and shoals. With each high water perhaps a dozen would leave, heavily laden with barrels of nails, stoves and other ironware. In dangerous water these craft might sink instantly. The life of a Cheat boatman was hazardous. At some point along the river the flatboat, barrels, nails and other cargo would be sold. The boat crew then walked back for another load."

Food for iron workers and their families, was provided, Carvell continues, "by local farmers who bartered their produce for iron and commodities at the company store. Money was scarce but scrip (company issued money) was common. Little is known of the social life, but one interesting bit of information survives—that one of the three islands in the river across from the settlement had a race track and fair grounds and shows of the 'wild west' kind drew crowds from 'near and far.'

"All of the land occupied by Ice's Ferry community is now under water. In its heyday it was the largest community in Monongalia County, with a population ten times that of Morgantown. The streets were paved with slag from the furnaces, and the town boasted running water. Wooden pipes, probably hollow logs, connected a reservoir to one of the mountain streams along the river community."

Dr. Carvell also mentioned[4] that for years the entire area was fragrant with the odor of burning charcoal, and that good charcoal burners were among the most respected people in the community.

One building of the old community has survived. This is the Zion Methodist Church (p. 188). "The odd orientation of this building," Dr. Carvell notes, "with the front door at the back," i.e., away from the present road, "is readily explained. The congregation hiked up the steep slope from the river to the church—the building actually faces toward the former town.

4. Pers. comm.

Today this structure is the only remnant of the many buildings that comprised this bustling community."[5]

The rapid decline of the works after the zenith in the 1840s was because of poor transportation and competition from richer iron-producing areas located more favorably with respect to markets. "The population gradually drifted away and a period of relative quiet reigned at Ice's Ferry."

**The Odd Fellows Move.** The first meetings of the Independent Order of Odd Fellows were held in Morgantown's Masonic Hall. But presently the lodge moved into its own quarters in Chadwick Hall, on the northwest corner of High and Wall streets. The first meeting at this site was held on January 5, 1849. P. R. Mitchell was the first steward. He was required to keep up good fires on Mondays, Wednesdays, and Saturdays, in addition to various other duties. His pay was fifty cents a week, with a "reasonable deduction when fires are no longer needed in the hall." The rent paid was fifty dollars a year.

On January 27, 1848, a resolution was passed making it an offense to spit on the carpet or on the stove. The fine was the same as for non-attendance, 6¼ cents.

On September 1, 1849, the bylaws were amended to state: "On the death of any married brother in indigent circumstances in good standing in this lodge every Brother shall be taxed by the secretary $1.00, the whole amount to be given to the widow."

The first appearance of Odd Fellows in regalia on the streets of Morgantown was on September 6, 1849, called a day of "procession."

**Laurel Point.** In 1849 Laurel Point was a flourishing village on the Brandonville and Fishing Creek Turnpike between Morgantown and Fairmont. Establishment of a post office here the previous year must have led to expectations that a small town would develop about it. A point of dry open forest land clothed

5. Business in Monongalia County was hard hit by the failure of the Ellicotts. The new owners tried to revive the iron works, but the industry was operated successively by the Taunton Iron Works (1849), The Monongalia Iron Works (1851), the Pridevale Iron Works (1854), and the Laurel Iron Works (1858), steadily becoming less effective. At last it was realized that the Cheat Iron Works were dead.

with mountain laurel (*Kalmia latifolia*), very lovely in flower, doubtless suggested the name.

Laurel Point is located along Dents Run, named for Captain John Dent, who came from Loudoun County to settle here in the early spring of the historic year 1776. He was a captain in the frontier militia during the Revolutionary War, serving under Colonel John Evans, whose only daughter, Margaret, he married. Captain Dent was a distinguished citizen, serving as sheriff of Monongalia County, a member of the county court and a member of the General Assembly of Virginia (see p. 202).

Marmaduke, a son of Captain Dent, was born February 25, 1801, and attended the subscription school at Laurel Point. He was of delicate health, afflicted with asthma, and his parents did not feel he was able to perform the arduous physical duties connected with farm life. He decided to study medicine, which he pursued under the direction of Dr. Enos Daugherty, of Morgantown, remaining with him for three years. He then moved to Kingwood, in 1825, to begin the practice of medicine, the first resident physician in Preston County. Here, in 1827, he married Sarah, daughter of William Price, one of the founders of Kingwood (*Monongalia Story*, vol. 2, pp. 441, etc.).

In 1828 Dr. and Mrs. Dent moved to Laurel Point, where he went into partnership with his brother, Nimrod, in an extensive business enterprise which had been started by their father about 1790. The enterprise began as one of the numerous gristmills in Monongalia County and Mr. Dent added merchandising and a distillery. To this establishment Dr. Dent brought the practice of medicine, making professional calls over a wide area, so that Laurel Point was an important center. Dr. Dent sold out his interest in the business, in 1830, to his brother, and moved to Granville, but this was not far away and his medical practice continued to serve the community.

The original mill at Laurel Point was destroyed by fire in 1800 and was succeeded by a stone building. The mill was operated by water power, from Dents Run.[6] Nimrod Dent installed steam machinery about 1841-42.

The first road through the community, the old "State" road, hardly more than a horseback trail, was built soon after 1787. A

6. Traces of the old mill race can still be seen along U.S. Route 19.

relocation of this road was the Brandonville and Fishing Creek "Turnpike" authorized by the general assembly in 1836. This was designed to run from the National Road near the Youghiogheny River to reach the Ohio at a point more southerly than Wheeling, where the National Road crossed. The design was scarcely realized but the road did become an important wagon road between Morgantown and Fairmont and was locally known as the Morgantown and Fairmont "Pike."[7]

The Laurel Point Post Office was established July 20, 1848, with John Jamison as the first postmaster, succeeded on October 3, 1848, by Edward G. Brooke. The post office was served by a route from Morgantown to Fairmont and return. An earlier post office in the community, called Dents Mills, had been established October 4, 1839, with Nimrod Dent as postmaster; it was discontinued May 24, 1843.

**New County Papers.** A new weekly paper, the *Monongalian*,[8] was started February 3, 1849, by George S. Ray, possibly to take the place of his defunct *Western Virginia Standard*. It did not last very long, however, and no copies have been seen.[9]

Another paper, the *Jeffersonian*, was started in 1849 by John Beck, proprietor. Only one issue was printed.[10]

The *Monongalia Mirror*, started on August 11, 1849, by the Reverend Simeon Siegfried, was more successful. Independent in politics, it was at first a folio, twenty by thirty-two, with twenty-four columns. The price was "$1.50 in advance, $2.00 after six months, and $2.50 if never paid—without coercion." It was printed on the old press of the *Northwestern Journal*.

The Reverend Mr. Siegfried was a minister in the Baptist church and had followed printing for thirty-three years before coming to Morgantown. He was a great advocate of temperance.[11]

7. This name persists even in 1978, although the technical name of this section is U.S. Route 19.

8. Not to be confused with the *Monongalian* of Elisha Moss, in 1831-32 (p. 65).

9. Wiley, pp. 435, 770, 771. Wiley says the issue for February 3 contains a denial of "Reports in circulation throughout the county" that smallpox and cholera were prevalent in Morgantown. George S. Ray (born 1823) was a son of Thomas P. Ray.

10. Wiley, p. 435.

11. Wiley, p. 435. Siegfried was born in New Britain, Pennsylvania, September 23, 1797. He married Mercy Johnson and they had five sons who entered the ministry.

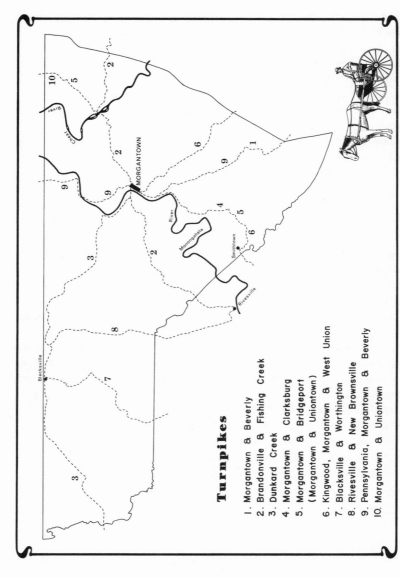

## Turnpikes

1. Morgantown & Beverly
2. Brandonville & Fishing Creek
3. Dunkard Creek
4. Morgantown & Clarksburg
5. Morgantown & Bridgeport (Morgantown & Uniontown)
6. Kingwood, Morgantown & West Union
7. Blacksville & Worthington
8. Rivesville & New Brownsville
9. Pennsylvania, Morgantown & Beverly
10. Morgantown & Uniontown

Fig. 47. Map of Monongalia County showing designated turnpike roads. (Drawn by Diane Lenhart.)

In October he announced the acquisition of new type and was aiming at one thousand subscribers.[12]

**John A. Dille.** A new law firm in Kingwood, Dille and Hagans, was formed in 1849, the partners being John A. Dille and M. B. Hagans. Dille was an enterprising young attorney, destined to play an important role in the formation of the new state of West Virginia and in the affairs of Monongalia County.

John A. was the son of Ezra Dille and was born on a farm in Washington County, Pennsylvania, July 19, 1821. After studying in the free schools of that county, at the age of sixteen he entered Greene Academy, where he spent a year which "opened new and broader fields for thought, and awakened and inspired a stronger desire for mental culture." In 1839 he entered Washington College, almost completing the full course of instruction before poor health caused him to withdraw. Hoping "that the purer air of the mountains would . . . restore his health," he moved to Kingwood in the spring of 1843, where he studied law under William G. Brown, who was later a member of Congress.

In March 1844 he was licensed to practice law in Virginia and opened an office in Kingwood, where his "diligence, energy, and fidelity to the interests of his clients soon won deserved success." In the spring of 1845 he joined Mr. Brown in the law partnership of Brown and Dille, a firm which continued until April 1849, when the partnership was dissolved and the new firm formed.

In the spring of 1849 he married Rachel Jane, daughter of Elisha M. Hagans, of Kingwood, a girl he had met when they were students in Washington College.[13]

**Stephen Morgan.** Stephen Morgan, son of David Morgan, died in 1849. He was born in 1761, near Pricketts Fort (*Monongalia Story*, vol. 2, pp. 39, 40). He was a farmer and mechanic and a member of the Episcopal church. He was justice of the peace for many years and served two terms as sheriff of Monongalia County.

He married Sarah Somerville and their children included

12. *Monongalia Mirror*, October 6, 1849.
13. Wiley, pp. 324-31; she died three years later, leaving one son, Oliver Hagans Dille.

Fig. 48. Rev. James Davis. (From the *New Dominion*, December 30, 1896.)

Fig. 49. Rev. Henry Weed Biggs. (From the *New Dominion*, December 30, 1896.)

Fig. 50. John J. Brown. (From Wiley's *History of Monongalia County*.)

Fig. 51. Mathew Gay. (From Wiley's *History of Monongalia County*.)

Charles S., Henry S., William S.,[14] Ann (married Horatio McLean), Elizabeth (married William J. Willey), Ruhanna (married Notly Carter), Albert, Sarah J. (married Austin Merrill), and George P.[15]

**William Jackson Butcher.** The Reverend William Jackson Butcher died at West Warren, November 2, 1849. He was the son of Robert and Rachel Butcher and was born April 8, 1821, in Monongalia County. He was a minister in the Christian church, serving congregations in Monongalia, Marion, and Wetzel counties; sadly his career was cut short by his untimely death. He was also a carriage-maker and wheelwright.

He married Marinda Ullom and they had two children, Nancy Jane and David.[16]

**Church History.** Morgantown's first church building, the Methodist Episcopal Church on Pleasant Street (*Monongalia Story*, vol. 2, p. 447), was destroyed by fire in 1849. Services were held in the Baptist church while a new building was being constructed. Ministers serving the church during the 1840s were: J. Spencer, 1841; W. D. Lemon, 1841-42; J. R. Coil, 1843-44; Edward Birkett, 1844-45; S. B. Dunlap, 1846-47; I. McClaskey,[17] 1847-48; J. D. Cramer, 1848-49; and J. S. Patterson, 1849-51.[18] W. T. Willey was superintendent of the Sunday school from 1837 until 1847, when he was succeeded by William Wagner. Presiding elders of the Morgantown District included H. Z. Adams (1848-55).[19]

The Presbyterian church continued to be served by the Reverend James Davis, who began his pastorate in 1837. The congregation steadily increased in numbers and strength. Ruling elders were Robert Robe, Jr., named in 1842 to succeed his

14. Served in the Virginia General Assembly and in the United States Congress. He was a distinguished naturalist, employed by the Smithsonian Institution.

15. *Cyclopedia of Marion County*, p. 153.

16. Dorothy T. Hennen, *Hennen's Choice*, vol. 1, pp. 61, 62.

17. Wiley, pp. 589-91; Callahan, *Making of Morgantown*, p. 159. For note on Isaac McClaskey, see Wilding, *Promoted Pioneer Preachers*, p. 113.

18. Jacob S. Patterson was born in Greene County, Pennsylvania, January 21, 1819, and died at Knightstown, Indiana, July 10, 1864. See biography, Wilding, *Promoted Pioneer Preachers*, pp. 15-17.

19. For biography see Wilding, *Promoted Pioneer Preachers*, pp. 115, 116.

father, Robert Robe, Sr., who had been an elder since 1822;[20] 1845, James Caldwell, James McGlaughlin; 1848, Edwin W. Tower, John McFarland, and Aaron Baird.[21]

Methodist Protestant ministers during the past decade were: 1840-42, Samuel Clawson,[22] John Bisher; 1844-46, Noble Gillespie; 1847, Samuel R. Porter; 1849, Peter T. Laishley. A church building had been erected on Long Alley, at the corner of Poplar Alley, in 1842. It was a brick structure thirty-four by forty-eight feet, built at a cost of $2,500. Many notable revivals were held in the building. The Sunday school superintendent in 1849 was Jesse Bell.[23]

The Reverend G. F. C. Conn became pastor of the Forks of Cheat Baptist Church in 1849.[24]

Thomas H. Monroe was preacher in charge of the Monongalia Circuit of the Methodist Episcopal Church in 1849.[25]

**The Regular Baptist Church of Minorsville.** On the Samuel Minor farm about two miles along Dunkard Creek east of Blacksville there was organized in 1849 a congregation known as the Regular Baptist Church of Minorsville. The first covenant was signed by Jacob Zearley, George Rogers, Joseph Guthrey, Huston Stewart, Barney Die, Marmelia Minor, Elizabeth Conn, Rachel Die, and Mary Rogers. The small church building was constructed and maintained by Samuel Minor.[26]

**The Liming Church of Christ.** Another church congregation in the western end of the county was organized the same year. This was the Liming Church of Christ on Liming Ridge, about four miles west of Wadestown. This congregation was a part of the so-called Restoration Movement of Alexander Campbell (see p. 125).

The first church building was constructed of logs, with

20. But his service was short, as he died May 3, 1845.
21. Wiley, ibid., pp. 592, 593; Moreland, *The First Presbyterian Church*, pp. 116, 120-23.
22. For biography, see Rev. James Robison, *Recollections of Rev. Samuel Clawson* (Pittsburgh, 1883), 246 pp.
23. Wiley, p. 594; Barnes, *The Methodist Protestant Church in West Virginia*, pp. 116, 120-23.
24. *Forks of Cheat Baptist Church* (Bicentennial), pp. 42-46.
25. Wiley, p. 728.
26. Dodds and Dodds, *Churches of Monongalia County*, p. 122.

greased paper windows and puncheon seats with peg legs. The building also served as a schoolhouse.[27]

**The Cold Spring M. E. Church.** The Cold Spring Methodist Episcopal Church, served by the Monongalia Circuit, was organized in 1849. The first leader was John B. Lough. Other members of the class were Charles and Sarah A. Bayles, Allen and Malinda Stevens, Aaron and Marion Barker, William N. Stewart, Thomas R., Leander B., Sarah A., James G., and Isabella Wilson, Dudley and Nancy Miller, Charlotte F., Christina, Isaac S., and Joseph N. Cox, David Herrington, John J. Kern, Hannah Wince, Stephen G., and Mary A. Snyder, Felix E. Bayles, Sarah Youst, Joseph and Adaline Lough. They at first met in the schoolhouse on Little Indian Creek.[28]

**The Baptist Church.** Ministers of the Morgantown Baptist Church during the 1840s were: A. J. Garrett, 1842-48; and William Wood, 1848-54. Gideon Way, Martin Callendine, and Jacob H. Shafer were deacons in 1842.[29] Lancelot John became clerk of the Forks of Cheat Baptist Church.[30]

**Sons of Temperance.** A great temperance reform was sweeping the country and Monongalia County members of the Sons of Temperance took an active part in establishing new divisions of the order. Waitman T. Willey traveled extensively through Virginia during 1849, producing favorable impressions as an orator and as a man.

"Mr. Willey's ability as a temperance orator at this period was of no meager character. He was deeply in love with his theme. To him it was as broad as humanity and as vital as eternity. His pictures of the desolation and ruin wrought by intemperance were as somber as the grave, and the magnetism of his glowing fervor pierced the shield of the stoutest opposer. Some of the greatest triumphs of his life were made during this eventful temperance campaign."[31]

27. Dodds and Dodds, *Churches of Monongalia County*, p. 132; Core, *Morgantown Disciples*, p. 18.
28. Wiley, p. 728.
29. Wiley, p. 595.
30. Wiley, p. 687.
31. Wiley, p. 173.

**Morgantown Female Academy.** In 1849 the board of directors of the Morgantown Female Academy was composed of William Lazier, president, W. T. Willey, secretary, William Wagner, treasurer, G. R. C. Allen, and Ralph L. Berkshire. The principal was Thomas McCune and his assistant teachers were Miss Luceba Brooks, Miss Isabel Armstrong, Mrs. M. E. McCune, and G. W. Fleming. There were 143 pupils enrolled, paying tuition ranging from four dollars to fifteen dollars for the five-month term. "Boarding (including lodging, fuel and lights)" might be had "in the family of the principal" for thirty-three dollars.[32]

A little excitement came in October: "The alarm of fire, on Thursday evening last, was occasioned by the burning of a curtain or blind in one of the windows of the Young Lady's Academy. One of the pupils was probably laboring so intensely to light up the cranium, that the external illumination was not immediately noticed. The fire was happily extinguished at once."[33]

**Francis Pierpont Dies.** Francis Pierpont, son of pioneer settler John Pierpont (*Monongalia Story*, vol. 2, pp. 242, 243), died at Fairmont March 3, 1849. He was born April 6, 1784, on the plantation of his father, a famous stopping place for travelers, visited by George Washington September 23-24, 1784. He married Catherine Weaver, daughter of Joseph and Rebecca (Foster) Weaver, on May 9, 1809. In 1814 they moved to Harrison County and in 1827 to Fairmont, where he built, owned, and operated a tannery.

Francis and Catherine Pierpont had seven children, namely, Joseph Weaver, Zackquill Morgan, Francis Harrison,[34] Larkin, Celinda Ann, Newton, and Rufus.[35]

**William Hall Dies.** "Died, On the 19th instant, at his residence near Rock Forge, in this County, Mr. William Hall, at an advanced age. He dropped down and died suddenly, without any known disease."[36]

32. *Monongalia Mirror*, September 1, 1849.
33. *Monongalia Mirror*, October 27, 1849.
34. Later recognized as the "Father of West Virginia." See p. 508 and Fig. 91.
35. *Cyclopedia of Marion County*, p. 23; Hedman, *The Pierpoint-Pierpont Family*, p. 445.
36. *Monongalia Mirror*, September 22, 1849.

**Morgantown and Bridgeport Turnpike.** The Morgantown and Bridgeport Turnpike Company was incorporated by the general assembly on March 25, 1849.

The Monongalia County portion of the road was built on the location of the Morgantown and Clarksburg road, from the Pennsylvania line beyond Ice's Ferry, through Morgantown and Smithtown, then through Marion County by way of Pleasant Valley, crossing the Tygart Valley River at Bentons Ferry.[37]

**Morgantown Prices.** Prices for ordinary commodities were low, as indicated by the local newspaper.[38]

| | | | |
|---|---|---|---|
| Dried Peaches, bu. | $1.25 | Wheat, bu. | $1.00 |
| Dried Apples, bu. | .37 | Corn, bu. | .50 |
| Flaxseed, bu. | .75 | Rye, bu. | .40 |
| Feathers, lb. | .31 | Oats, bu. | .25 |
| Nails | 4.00 | Buckwheat, bu. | .37 |
| Iron, lb. | .03½ | Flour, bbl. | 5.50 |
| Salt, bbl. | 2.25 | Bacon, lb. | .07 |
| Linen, yd. | .15-.20 | Butter, lb. | .08 |
| Linsey, yd. | .25-.31 | Eggs, doz. | .06 |
| Flannel, yd. | .35-.50 | Beans, lb. | .56 |
| Jeans, yd. | .40-.50 | Ginseng, lb. | .25 |

Construction work on the Baltimore and Ohio Railroad would soon cause marked increases in these prices.

**Daguerreotypes.** One of the earliest notices of photography in Morgantown is the following advertisement:

"E. Abercrombie, Daguerrian Artist, Second Story of Demain's Building, in the room formerly occupied by Prof. Russell, where he will remain but a few days. Ladies and gentlemen wishing a good Daguerrotype likeness, are respectfully invited to give him a call. Persons visiting the Gallery can have their miniatures or portraits taken in a style unsurpassed for beauty or elegance, and neatly set in morocco cases, gold lockets or breast pins, Copying from paintings, landscapes, views of residences, and likenesses taken from the deceased, without regard to weather.

"N. B. Ladies are recommended to dress in figured or dark material avoiding white or light blue. For gentlemen, a black or

37. Wiley, pp. 124, 538. For history of Pleasant Valley, see Balderson, *Prickett's Fort*, pp. 135-37.
38. *Monongalia Mirror*, September 1, 1849.

figured vest; also figured scarf or cravat, so that the bosom be not too much exposed.

"Instructions in the art will be given on liberal terms."[39]

The technique of making daguerreotypes was first described in 1839 by Louis Jacques Mandé Daguerre (1789-1851), in France. He made a polished silvered copper plate light-sensitive by subjecting it to iodine fumes. It was then exposed from three to thirty minutes in a camera. The image was developed by mercury vapor, and was "fixed" with sodium thiosulfate ("hypo"). Improvements made in 1840 increased the sensitivity of the plate by bromine fuming and enriched the image by gold chloride toning.[40]

**A New Water Pump.** Simeon Siegfried relates:

"While on a visit to Durbanna, the other day, we were shown a new Cast Iron Pump, the invention of Mr. John S. Gould. From the examination we were enabled to make of this Pump, we have no doubt that it is a great improvement on the iron pumps now in use. Having no complicated machinery, it is not liable to get out of order, and will not wear out in a lifetime. These Pumps can be made for $25 each, and considering their durability and efficiency, are cheaper by half than any article of the kind we have ever seen."[41]

The pump was made by the Durbannah Foundry, which also fabricated Anderson Coal Cooking Stoves, Brown and True American Ploughs, Grates, Wagon Boxes, and many other products.[42]

**"Workin' on the Railroad."** At last, in 1848, the Baltimore and Ohio Railroad Company began the extension of its line across the Alleghenies from Cumberland towards Wheeling. The route, as finally determined, crossed the Cheat River south of Kingwood, reached the Tygart Valley River at the mouth of Three Forks Creek, and crossed the Monongahela at Fairmont.

"At a meeting of the Board of Directors, held last week, contracts upon the second letting, embracing twenty-five miles west of Cumberland, were given out. The prices are in all cases

39. *Monongalia Mirror*, July 28, 1849.
40. See Beaumont Newhall, *The Daguerrotype in America* (1961).
41. *Monongalia Mirror*, September 8, 1849.
42. See their ad, *Monongalia Mirror*, September 16, 1849.

within the estimates of the Engineer, and there are now 45 miles in the hands of contractors, embracing the most difficult portion between Cumberland and the Ohio.—This fall 50 or 60 miles more will be let, which will bring the road to the Tygart's Valley River, whence a good turnpike of about 100 miles in length offers a connection with the Ohio at Parkersburg. The remaining portion of the contracts will be awarded in the spring. . . ."[43]

"Our Farmers and Merchants will be likely to get a share, though perhaps not a large one, of the funds to be diffused along and contiguous to the line of this improvement. There is a tunnel of nearly a mile in length, besides much other heavy work of excavation, embankments and bridging, to be achieved, which will employ several thousand hands, and call for large supplies of fuel, clothing and other necessaries."[44]

Although the line did not touch Monongalia County at any point, the construction work did make its economic influence felt in the county. The local newspaper carried an advertisement by Edward Lowe, superintendent, as early as the summer of 1849:

"Hands wanted to work on Section 87, B. & O. Railroad near Evansville, Preston County. Stone masons and laboring men will find steady employment at liberal wages. Horses and oxen wanted."[45]

Steamboat traffic on the Monongahela to Morgantown increased markedly, as construction equipment arrived from Pittsburgh, along with Irish laborers, food products, whiskey, articles of clothing, and other materials. The laborers walked across the country, inquiring their way to the "big toonel," to be built east of Evansville. The local newspaper estimated the railroad company would spend $5 million in the Morgantown area.[46]

The whiskey contributed measurably to the numerous riots and brawls between the opposing factions of "Corkonians" and "Fardowns," as, for example, on November 8, 1849, when

43. *Monongalia Mirror*, August 18, 1849.
44. *Monongalia Mirror*, August 25, 1849.
45. *Monongalia Mirror*, August 25, 1849.
46. *Monongalia Mirror*, December 22, 1849.

there was a riot of such magnitude that Kingwood and Evansville militia were called to quell the disturbance.[47]

"While the forty-niners were rushing to California, the railway was advancing towards Fairmont."[48]

**The Port of Morgantown.** The stimulation of work on the railroad resulted in increased river traffic at the Port of Morgantown. In October it was announced that the *John B. Gordon*, Alfred Yeager master, "will commence her regular trips on the first rise of water this fall, to points above Brownsville," leaving Brownsville every Tuesday, Thursday, and Saturday at 9 a.m., returning leaving New Geneva (or Morgantown, when water permits), Monday, Wednesday, and Friday at 9 a.m. The management expected to provide the service about two-thirds of the year.[49]

The steamboat made its first trip to the Morgantown area on November 1:

"The John B. Gordon was up within a mile of town on Thursday, laden with passengers and freight from Pittsburg. [A trifling improvement needs to be made.] Be that as it may, *that Boat must come up to town* on her future trips. A craft so trim and good looking, so well adapted to our trade, and so convenient for passengers, must not be compelled to hide herself away down behind the precipice."[50]

Fall rains resulted in a rise in the water in the river and soon the *John B. Gordon* was making regular trips to Morgantown, along with the *Robert Wightman*, the *Globe*, and the *Eclipse*, all heavily laden with passengers and freight.

Simeon Siegfried rode the boat and reported his experiences:

The editor had the pleasure of patronizing "our *line boat*, the *John B. Gordon*. . . . Some twenty-five passengers, including citizens, river-men and strangers, enlivened the trip, and united in favorable acknowledgements of the comfort of the boat, and the polite attention of her officers and crew." [They were] "conveyed right pleasantly to the port of Morgantown."[51]

47. *Monongalia Mirror,* November 10 and 17, 1849.
48. Callahan, *Making of Morgantown,* pp. 172, 176.
49. *Monongalia Mirror,* October 20, 1849.
50. *Monongalia Mirror,* November 3, 1849.
51. *Monongalia Mirror,* November 17, 1849.

"The daily arrival and departure of Steamboats, during the past week, may serve to show to the people, here and all along shore, what would be done all the time, if *Slackwater* was completed to this place."[52]

Earlier Siegfried had urged the resumption of efforts towards slack water:

"The citizens of Pittsburg, Morgantown, and all along shore, should wake up immediately, and *go to work* to slack the River from Brownsville—else the Rail Road will be completed to Cumberland before we are ready for it. We believe the *wind work* of this enterprize has been pretty well and handsomely done. The next thing in order is to subscribe the requisite amount of stock, raise the *dimes*, and then erect the dams."[53]

A long, two-column editorial, "Passenger and Freight Line to Pittsburg," later urged this even more fervently.[54]

A box, "Arrivals, Port of Morgantown," recorded the arrival of the *Globe* on December 18, with 150 bbls. flour; the *Gordon*, on December 19, with merchandise, flour and blue heads; the *Doddridge* on December 20, with salt and blue heads; and the *Gordon* on December 21, with flour, salt, cheese, merchandise and blue heads.[55]

**Land Grants Made in 1849.** Monongalia County grantees in 1849 included:

| | | |
|---|---|---|
| Garrison, John | 24 a. | Warrior Fork |
| Lemaster, Septimus | 48 | Building Run |
| Worley, David A. | 250 | Dunkard Creek |

**County Government.** George M. Hagans and Daniel Haldeman were sworn in as justices of the peace on September 24, 1849. Thomas Meredith succeeded Nelson Berkshire as commissioner of the revenue for the Eastern District. The county levy was two dollars.

**Miscellany.** In 1849: Masters of the Morgantown Masonic Lodge were J. E. Tucker and George S. Ray (Wiley, p. 548). . . . New retail firms started were William Lazier and Company, Fleming

52. Ibid.
53. *Monongalia Mirror*, August 25, 1849.
54. *Monongalia Mirror*, December 22, 1849.
55. Ibid.

and Guseman, and Lazier, McLane and Company (Wiley, p. 583). . . . Physicians locating in Morgantown were Watson Carr, Joseph Eidson, A. J. Bowman, and M. Y. Willey (Wiley, p. 584). . . . Mary Jarrett, widow of Captain William N. Jarrett, died (Wiley, p. 587). . . . Col. L. H. Jenkins was running a tailor shop at Stewartstown (Wiley, p. 674). . . . Julia Lowell Ray Dering, wife of Frederick Augustus Dering, died; she was born in 1815, the daughter of Patrick Ray (Callahan, p. 86). . . . Dr. Isaac Scott purchased from Rev. Asby Pool the brick house at the southeast corner of High and Pleasant streets, in Morgantown, formerly a tavern kept by John Addison (Callahan, pp. 117, 118). . . . Citizens of Morgantown in October discussed plans for a town hall, some proposing to locate it over the market place, others favoring construction of a new building with an adequate lecture room (Callahan, p. 182 note). . . . Lot 96 in Morgantown was conveyed by John Mills to Alpheus C. Dorsey (Callahan, p. 323). . . . Lot 100, south half, was conveyed to Zackwell Morgan III, and north half to Enos D. Morgan (Callahan, p. 324). . . . G. W. Fleming started a new drugstore in Morgantown (*Monongalia Mirror*, September 7, 1849). . . . Col. John Evans ("Capt. Jack") died on May 19; his children were Lucy Ann (married Nathan Goff), Louisa (married John H. Hoffman), Margaret (married Daniel C. Chadwick), Elizabeth, French Strother, John Coleman, George D., Daniel Strother, James and Thomas Clare (Callahan, pp. 79, 80).

# CHAPTER SEVENTY-FOUR

# 1850

By the middle of the nineteenth century at least nine changes had been made in the boundaries of Monongalia County since its first establishment, in 1776. The first two, in 1779 and 1780, were increases, bringing the total area to an estimated 8,485 square miles, its greatest extent. Running of the extension of the Mason-Dixon Line, in 1782, took away the portion north of that line, which had been claimed by Virginia. The formation of Harrison County, in 1784, brought Monongalia's area down to about 1,385 square miles. An area of about 60 square miles was added to Harrison in 1800, reducing the area to 1,325 square miles. The formation of Preston County, in 1818, reduced the area still further, to about 700 square miles.

In 1841 a small slice east of Chestnut Ridge, about 25 square miles, had been added to Preston County. In 1842 about 305 square miles was taken off in the formation of Marion County. Finally, in 1847, a small portion, about ten square miles, was taken from Monongalia to add to Marion County. This change brought the county down to its present size, 368.82 square miles.

**The Seventh Census.** By the census of 1850 the population of Monongalia County was recorded as 12,387, a decrease of 4,981 over the 17,368, recorded ten years earlier. But this decrease, of about 29 percent, was only an apparent decrease; in 1840 Monongalia County had an area of about seven hundred square miles, while in 1850 the area was only a little more than half as great. Wiley[1] estimated the population of the present area, in

1. *History of Monongalia County*, p. 561.

1840, as 8,820; the 1850 population, recorded as 12,387, therefore represented an increase of 3,567, or about 40 percent.

The 1850 census provided many details not noted in some of the earlier reports. For example, it was noted that the white population totaled 12,092, of which 5,987 were males and 6,105 females. The colored population included 119 free persons and 176 slaves. In the whole population there were 6,131 males and 6,256 females. Of these, 2,231 were born in the United States, but outside of Virginia, and 118 in foreign countries.

The census recorded that there were 2,124 dwellings in the county and 2,127 families.

A total of 109 pupils were enrolled in academies or private schools in the county, and these schools had an income of $3,334. In public schools 907 pupils were enrolled, with $2,139 paid for their education. A total of 2,317 white scholars were enrolled during the year in subscription schools, and it was recorded that there were 4,793 whites between the ages of five and twenty. Of whites over twenty, 1,204 could not read or write.

In 1850 there were 797 farms in Monongalia County, with 68,047 acres of improved land. The value of the farms, with improvements and machinery, was set at $1,620,331.

The census recorded 2,730 horses, asses, and mules; 8,516 neat cattle; 13,015 sheep; and 8,121 swine.

Farm products were listed as follows:

| | | | |
|---|---|---|---|
| Wheat, bu. | 52,370 | Butter & Cheese, lbs. | 155,962 |
| Rye & Oats, bu. | 114,173 | Hay, tons | 6,013 |
| Indian Corn, bu. | 184,379 | Hops, lbs. | 179 |
| Irish & Sweet Potatoes, bu. | 11,015 | Clover & other grass seeds, bu. | 536 |
| Peas & Beans, bu. | 392 | Flaxseed, bu. | 615 |
| Barley, bu. | 0 | Flax, lbs. | 12,293 |
| Buckwheat, bu. | 2,964 | Maple sugar, lbs. | 52,716 |
| Molasses, gal. | 2,403 | Wool, lbs. | 29,129 |
| Tobacco, lbs. | 3,750 | Beeswax & Honey, lbs. | 8,118 |

The value of animals slaughtered were given as $35,116, the value of produce of market gardens as $198, and the value of orchard produce as $301. The figures reflect the fact that most citizens raised their own food and there was very little local market.

The capital invested in manufacturing enterprises was put at

$231,730. There were 185 hands employed and the annual product was $358,634. In addition, a total of $17,946 of manufactured goods was produced in families.

By 1850 forty-two of the counties located in what is now West Virginia had been formed, and Monongalia stood fifth in rank, with respect to population. Ohio County, on the heavily traveled National Road, was first, with 18,006 people. Jefferson was second, with 15,357 people, while Kanawha County, on the James River and Kanawha Turnpike, was in third place, with a population of 15,353; Kanawha had been in fifth place in 1840. Hampshire County was fourth in rank in 1850, with 14,036 people.

Harrison County, in 1840, had been in second place, with 17,669 but in 1850 the population had dropped to only 11,728. The construction of the Northwestern Virginia Turnpike had resulted in a rapid increase in population in what is now central West Virginia, with the result that seven counties were formed between 1840 and 1850 from territory that had formerly been included in Harrison County. These included Marion (1842), Barbour (1843), Ritchie (1843), Taylor (1844), Doddridge (1845), Gilmer (1845), and Wirt (1848).

Marion County, which in 1840 had been included in Monongalia and Harrison counties, had a population of 10,552 in 1850.

The local newspaper reported the population of the borough as 827 free and 44 slave, for a total of 871. There were another 275 in the suburbs, so the town had a total population of 1,146.[2]

**Church Statistics.** The United States Census Report for 1850 indicated that there were thirty-one churches in the county, with a total value of $19,808 and a total of 12,310 "sittings." With 12,387 persons recorded as living in the county at the time, it is apparent that essentially all residents would have been able to attend church at a given time.

The report stated that there were nineteen Methodist edifices, with a value of $13,008 and 7,800 sittings; six Baptist buildings, having a value of $4,100 and 2,010 sittings; three Presbyterian churches, worth $1,700, with 1,200 sittings; and

2. *Monongalia Mirror*, August 31, September 21, 1850.

three Christian churches, with a value of $1,000 and 1,300 sittings.

**The Odd Fellows.** Early records of the Independent Order of Odd Fellows provide glimpses of life in Morgantown at mid-century.

On November 25, 1850, a committee was appointed to get straw to lay on the floor of the lodge hall, for better protection of the carpet.

By Odd Fellow rules, a local lodge can confer three degrees of membership. When a member has reached the highest of these three grades he is ready for membership in an encampment.

Orphan Friend Encampment No. 23 of Virginia was instituted in the lodge hall on February 2, 1850. The first officers were D. R. Hoxy, CP; Watson Carr, HP; F. I. Fleming, SW; P. R. Mitchell, scribe; James Nimon, treasurer; and Elijah Morgan, IW. Grand Patriarch William H. Hayden was present to institute the organization.

**General Educational System Proposed.** The "poor system," whereby the education of indigent scholars was paid for by money from the Literary Fund (*Monongalia Story*, vol. 2, pp. 368, 444, 451), was an early approach in Virginia towards a free school system.[3]

A further step forward was an act passed by the 1845-46 general assembly, providing for an optional system of free schools, which might be adopted by the "council of any city or town having a corporation court," or by the voters of any county at a special election held for the purpose.[4]

Although Kanawha, Jefferson, and Ohio counties had adopted this system by 1850, Monongalia never did bring it to a vote. The system was, however, agitated in this county. In 1850, the Reverend P. T. Laishley, in his card as a candidate for a seat in the constitutional convention, said: "I am in favor of having an item embraced in the Constitution, establishing a general system of education, so that in our primary schools the

3. See Ray C. Woods, "The Evolution of the Common School in (West) Virginia," *West Virginia History* 20 (1959):247-53.
4. Wiley, p. 364; Ambler, *History of Education in West Virginia*, pp. 53-64.

children of the rich and the poor may meet on an equality, extending to all the opportunity of acquiring knowledge."[5]

In Monongalia County in 1850 it was reported that there were eight "public" schools (accepting indigent children), employing eight teachers, having an attendance of 152 pupils and an income of $805. There were two academies, employing six teachers, with an enrollment of 109 pupils, and an income of $3,334. The number of pupils in attendance at all kinds of schools was reported as 2,319 white and 2 free black. There were 1,215 white persons (350 males, 865 females) in the county above the age of ten years who could not read or write. One school library was mentioned, with 150 volumes.[6]

An attempt was made in 1850 to merge the two academies into one, hoping to develop a college, but the project failed.

Numerous programs of a cultural nature were presented at the academies, e.g., a concert on June 22 by a "successful delineator of men and manners, and a much admired vocalist, violinist, and guitarist."[7]

**Joseph Campbell Dies.** "Died, at the house of Mr. Wamsley, in Marion County, Virginia, Joseph Campbell, Esq., sometime about the last of January. Mr. Campbell was formerly well known to the people of this county. It will be recollected by many that in 1804, he, in connection with Mr. Forbes Britton, established a newspaper in this town, which was entitled 'The Monongalia Gazette,' which they conducted for many years. That at the time it was first issued it was the only paper in the Northwestern part of Va., except one which was published at Wheeling. Mr. Campbell afterward acted as Sheriff and Coroner, in this county, for many years, much to the satisfaction of the Bar, and all others with whom he transacted business; and in all the relations of life he was considered an upright and honest gentleman. Mr. Campbell was an Irishman by birth, but came to Philadelphia as a lad, and was apprenticed to the Printing business. He was about 70 years old when he died."[8]

5. A long article by Laishley, with proposals for revision of the constitution, appeared in the *Monongalia Mirror*, June 22, 1850.
6. Wiley, p. 381.
7. *Monongalia Mirror*, June 22, 1850.
8. *Monongalia Mirror*, March 2, 1850.

**"Chunk" Morgan Dies.** Evan T. Morgan, a son of David Morgan, said to be the last Revolutionary War veteran in the county, died March 18, 1850, aged one hundred years and eighteen days. His wife, Camilla, had passed away June 2, 1838, aged seventy-one years. He was nicknamed "Chunk" Morgan, from being a short but heavy-set man. He was buried in the cemetery at the Fairview Methodist Episcopal Church.[9]

**John W. Williams Dies.** Born in Wales in 1800, John W. Williams died on Days Run May 25, 1850. He was reared in Wales but came to America in early life, locating first on Scotts Run, then on Days Run, adding to his property year by year until he came to own three hundred acres. He married Elizabeth Lallis.[10]

**Rev. Oliver Nay.** Rev. Oliver Nay died on Dents Run (Marion County) late in December 1850 and was buried on Christmas Day. He was a son of John Nay, an early Monongalia County settler and Revolutionary War veteran, and was born in 1807. He owned part of the land on which Mannington was later built and ran a gristmill there which was twice burned and rebuilt. He was a local minister of the Methodist Episcopal church and his home was a stopping place for ministers and missionaries traveling in the area. He married Triphena Teterick, daughter of Joseph Teterick, and they had thirteen children.[11]

**Sons of Temperance.** The Grand Division of Virginia, Sons of Temperance, held its third quarterly session, beginning May 24, 1850, in the Monongalia County courthouse. On the twenty-sixth there was a parade, with W. T. Willey chief marshal and Col. James Evans and Capt. Michael Shisler assistant marshals. It was reported that 461 persons marched in regalia. The music was furnished by the Morgantown and Waynesburg brass bands.[12]

A Total Abstinence Society was formed in Morgantown in 1850, with the Reverend Simeon Siegfried president, Daniel Haldeman vice-president, and William Durbin treasurer.[13]

9. Wiley, pp. 471, 488, 572, 633; *Monongalia Mirror*, March 23, 1850.
10. *Cyclopedia of Monongalia County*, p. 204.
11. *Cyclopedia of Marion County*, p. 130.
12. *Monongalia Mirror*, June 1, 1850. The paper called whiskey barrels "blue-heads" and said they were "blue ruin" to produce "red noses." The Sons of Temperance were nicknamed "Sonnies."
13. Wiley, p. 452.

**Mountain Music.** A very important part of the daily lives of people of Monongalia County, as elsewhere throughout the county in the nineteenth century, was folk music. This consisted largely of song, but also of music played on such instruments as the rebec, fiddle, banjo, guitar, parlor organ, harmonica, dulcimer, etc.

Folk songs were especially important. "They are called folk songs because they belong to the people and not to any one individual. One cannot compose a folk song. . . .

"Singing was part of the daily lives of the people, and they sang as they went about their work. Mother and grandmother sang as they worked at the spinning wheel or loom or as they went about the many chores of the household. Father and grandfather sang as they fed the stock, sharpened an axe, or as they sat before the fireplace. They sang not to entertain anyone but because it made them feel good to sing. Sometimes on the long winter evenings the children were entertained by songs and stories told by parents and grandparents."[14]

**A New Methodist Church.** A new church was constructed in Morgantown by the Methodist Episcopal congregation in 1850, to replace the building destroyed by fire the previous year. The new edifice, on the same lot at the corner of Pleasant Street and Long Alley, was a larger, brick building, forty-eight by seventy-two feet in dimension. The building cost $5,500, of which $2,500 was subscribed at its dedication, on October 1, 1850.

The stone work was done by Milton Rogers, the brick work by M'Cans and Rees, the carpentry by Elijah Morgan, the plastering by Uriah Rider, the painting by Ebenezer Mathers, and the dressing of sills and caps by B. P. Marsteller. The bell, weighing eight hundred pounds, was fabricated by Andrew Menelly, West Troy, New York.

"The dedicatory services in the new M. E. Church, in this town, on Tuesday last, were highly interesting and appropriate. After the reading of appropriate portions of Scripture by Rev.

14. *Mountain Heritage* (1975), part 6, "Music," by Patrick W. Gainer, p. 136; see also his *Folk Songs from the West Virginia Hills* (1975). Additional sources are Ruth Ann Musick, *Ballads, Folk Songs and Folk Tales from West Virginia* (1960); and *Singa Hipsy Doodle and Other Folk Songs of West Virginia* (1971), edited by Marie Boette, music notes by John Laflin, illustrated by Marcia Ogilvie.

Fig. 52. Mountain Music. (From Maurer, *Mountain Heritage*, Cedar Lakes, 1975.)

W. D. Lemon, the Presiding Elder, and the singing of a hymn adapted to the occasion by the Choir, to the unrivalled tune of Old Hundred, Bishop Janes, of New York, preached a most fitting and appropriate discourse. The sermon abounded with gems of thought, ably discussed the happily illustrated."[15]

**Drummond Chapel.**[16] The Drummond Chapel house of worship, in the section known as the Flatts, was constructed in 1850. The frame structure was built by James Sidwell, James Houston, and Robert Houston, while the solid sturdy furniture was fabricated by Joseph Weaver, of West Run, from "first class poplar lumber." Dedicatory services were held in October, with the Reverend James L. Clark in charge; a "tremendous crowd" attended.[17]

A church body had been organized around 1840, meeting for worship in a log school building known as the Captain James

Fig. 53. The     Morgantown     Methodist Episcopal Church, corner Pleasant Street and Long Alley, built 1850.

15. *Monongalia Mirror,* October 5, 1850.
16. Ira Baker, *History of Drummond Chapel,* MS, Morgantown Public Library; Dodds and Dodds, *Churches of Monongalia County,* pp. 81, 82.
17. The Reverend Mr. Clark's autobiography contains a brief account of Drummond Chapel (*Methodist Episcopal Times,* 1896.)

Fig. 54. Drummond Chapel Methodist Episcopal Church. (Courtesy Rev. Paul H. Smith and Ira M. Baker.)

Evans Schoolhouse, across the road from the church. James Evans was the Sunday school superintendent and a story is told that when he and Mrs. Evans heard that children were staying away from Sunday school because they had no shoes, they decreed that their own children would go to Sunday school barefoot.

The name Drummond was chosen for the new church to honor a young minister, Thomas Drummond, who had been stationed at Morgantown and who had been very popular and well liked. He was born in Manchester, England, January 27, 1806, but came to America with his parents when he was only five years old. He started preaching at the age of twenty-three and came to Morgantown in 1833, where he preached "with great acceptability and usefulness." He remained at Morgantown only one year and then, "filled with missionary zeal," volunteered to go west to Missouri. He was stationed at Saint Louis but died of cholera in less than a year, on June 15, 1835.

**Macadamized Roads.** By 1850 a rather feeble effort was being made to improve Monongalia County wagon roads so as to make them more easily passable in wet weather. A bill to appropriate money to macadamize the road from Morgantown to Ice's Ferry was introduced in the general assembly in 1850, but was defeated by a vote of fifty-four to forty-two.

The macadamizing process was developed by and named for John Loudon McAdam (1756-1836), a Scottish merchant and road engineer. The process consisted of raising the surface of the road slightly above the adjoining land, forming suitable drains alongside, and covering the surface with a series of thin layers of hard stone broken into angular fragments as nearly as possible the same size, no piece of a greater weight than about six ounces. Each layer of broken stone was gradually consolidated by allowing traffic to pass over it, and when the process was complete the covering of the road became a firm, solid surface, nearly impervious to water, and durable in proportion to the hardness of the stone from which it was made.

**"Our Roads."** Simeon Siegfried saw road improvement as one of the county's greatest needs:

"Much has been done, and is still doing, to prepare the leading roads through this County for the vast increase of business thrown upon them by their contiguity to the route of the B. & O. Railroad. An excellent Turnpike from this place to Palatine, opposite Fairmont, is in progress, and will probably be completed this Fall. It is well made (where finished), and already adds much to the comfort of travelling up the River. . . .

"The road towards Wheeling, by way of Jimtown, Cassville, Blacksville, &c., has been neglected much too long. It is true that our County has appropriated some Six Thousand Dollars to building Bridges on this route. But what has become of the state appropriation? And where are the Commissioners appointed to locate and make the road? We should like to know who they are, and have them stirred up to their duty. A vast amount of Produce and Stock is destined to pass over this road to the Railroad; and it is not at present in a fit condition for wagoning."[18]

**Railroad Construction Continues.** The excitement throughout the area caused by the construction of the Baltimore and Ohio Railroad from Cumberland to Fairmont continued throughout

18. *Monongalia Mirror*, August 10, 1850.

the year. Material for construction west of Tunnel Hill (Tunnelton) was being conveyed by temporary tracks over the top of the mountain to hasten the work, while awaiting completion of the big tunnel. During the spring of 1850 it was said that scarcely a day passed without witnessing the departure from Morgantown of a number of wagons heavily loaded with flour, bacon, and whiskey, and headed for construction camps. James Kerns filled an order for two hundred wheelbarrows for the railroad and expected to make one thousand more. The demand for Monongahela whiskey was constant; a brisk traffic resulted between the wharf and the brick building on Lot 25 where wagons were loaded for the camps. A runaway accident resulted in the loss of a wagonload of seven barrels of whiskey on the way to the railroad.[19]

**Port of Morgantown.** Stimulated by construction work on the railroad, the Port of Morgantown was busier than it had ever been in history. Steamboats from Pittsburgh and Brownsville arrived frequently when the water level permitted and the weekly newspaper carried a section on shipping news.

For example, on January 3 the steamer *Gordon* arrived from Brownsville with flour, whiskey, and sundries, but "navigation will now be suspended for a while, on account of floating ice."[20]

But on the ninth the *Philip Doddridge* arrived, with flour, salt, pork, brandy, and cheese, and on the twelfth the *Globe* tied up, with 567 barrels of flour and 312 packages of sundries, with thirty-seven deck and cabin passengers.[21]

On January 11 the *Doddridge* came in with flour, salt, molasses, groceries, and iron, and the *Globe* on the eighteenth with sundries.[22] The *Gordon*, arriving on the twenty-fourth, had 11,000 pounds of pork, besides sundries.[23] On the twenty-seventh the *Globe* arrived, with sundries and nineteen deck and cabin passengers, and the *Gordon* came in on the thirtieth.[24]

It was noted that the *Globe* left Pittsburgh at 10 p.m. on

19. Callahan, *Making of Morgantown*, pp. 172, 176.
20. *Monongalia Mirror*, January 5, 1850.
21. *Monongalia Mirror*, January 12, 1850.
22. *Monongalia Mirror*, January 19, 1850.
23. *Monongalia Mirror*, January 26, 1850.
24. *Monongalia Mirror*, February 2, 1850.

Fig. 55. Steamboat on the Monongahela. (Sketch by Diane Lenhart.)

January 31 and arrived at Morgantown at 6 p.m. on February 1, with sixty tons of cargo and fifteen deck and cabin passengers. The twenty-hour trip was regarded as remarkably rapid.[25]

To better serve the traffic, Walnut Street was macadamized from High to Front Street[26] and graded down to the wharf. A new wharf was constructed, with a log outline two hundred feet long, filled with rocks dragged from the river. The work was done by Captain M. Chisler.[27]

**First Steamboat to Fairmont.** The advance of the railroad from Cumberland toward Fairmont also stimulated efforts to develop steamboat navigation to the head of the Monongahela River at Fairmont. On February 11, 1850, at 5 p.m., the steamer *Globe* was successful in completing a trip from Morgantown to Fairmont with a load of flour. The *Globe* was 110 feet long and could carry forty-eight passengers.[28]

25. *Monongalia Mirror*, February 9, 1850.
26. *Monongalia Mirror*, September 28, 1850.
27. *Monongalia Mirror*, October 19, 1850.
28. Callahan, *Making of Morgantown*, p. 179. The *Globe* later made four other trips to Fairmont, and on the fifth trip, after unloading its cargo, it attempted to reach Clarksburg but failed. See a long story in the *Monongalia Mirror*, February 23, 1850, and notices in various other issues, including that of May 4, 1850.

It is said that D. S. Morris, editor of the Fairmont *Democratic Banner*, offered sixty dollars in gold to the captain of the first steamboat to tie up at Fairmont. A number of small steamers had tried for the reward and failed and Fairmonters had begun to despair of ever seeing a steamboat lying along their riverfront.

The previous fall was particularly rainy and the water in the river was higher than usual. Larkin Pierpont, a Fairmont tanner, brother of F. H. Pierpont, was in Morgantown early in February.[29] The steamboat *Globe* (Captain Hughes, of Rices Landing, Pennsylvania, skipper) was tied up at the wharf, with two hundred barrels of flour aboard. Being offered only $2.25 a barrel for it, he announced, "in language more emphatic than polite," that he was going to Fairmont with the flour, or sink his boat in the attempt.

Someone told the captain that Mr. Pierpont was familiar with the river and could pilot him to Fairmont; Mr. Pierpont being found, he agreed to show him the right channel over the falls (Little Falls) and they set out for Fairmont early the next morning.

The people of Fairmont were eating their supper when a steam whistle was heard down the river, and instantly a shout went up from a hundred throats, "A steamboat is coming! a steamboat is coming!"

"For a few minutes pandemonium seemed to reign, when all of a sudden everyone appeared to think it was his or her duty to be the first person at the river to meet the steamer. . . .

"They poured out of hotels, private dwellings, offices, and every place that contained a human being, like bees swarming or mad hornets coming out of their nests. Down the street they ran as if their lives depended—a hunk of meat or a piece of chicken in one hand and a piece of bread or some biscuits in the other."

Speeches were made, "felicitating Fairmont upon the auspicious event and lauding the captain, officers and crew of

29. A colorful account, giving the date as the first week of November, 1848, appeared in the *Fairmont Times,* November 6, 1907; see also Lough, *Now and Long Ago,* pp. 551-56. Other historians give the date February 11, 1850, which must be correct (see previous footnote); see also E. E. Meredith, *Fairmont Times,* December 9, 1940.

the Globe upon the fact of her being the first steamboat to land at Fairmont." The two hundred barrels of flour was sold at seven dollars per barrel and an entire week was spent there, carrying persons on short excursions.

The account relates that Morgantown citizens were jealous because the town had lost the title, "head of navigation," to Fairmont:

"To cap the incident some evil disposed or malicious persons let the rope of the ferry at Morgantown down so that it would sweep the pilot house, wheel, and smoke stack off the little boat as she went gliding down the river, which betrayed Morgantown's enmity toward Fairmont."

**Second Steamboat to Fairmont.** The second steamboat recorded as having traversed the Monongahela River above Morgantown to arrive at Fairmont is said to have been the *John B. Gordon*, perhaps in 1850. Captain Samuel S. Yeager (born at Greensboro, Pennsylvania, July 25, 1819), a pioneer in steamboat navigation on the Monongahela, operated the craft, which carried seventy tons of freight.

Samuel Ellis was a passenger on the boat. He had sailed from London, England, landed at New Orleans, there took a boat up the Mississippi and the Ohio to Pittsburgh. There he took passage on the *John B. Gordon*, and safely landed in Fairmont, perhaps the first (and only?) person to travel all the way by water. He made his home in Fairmont the remainder of his life.[30]

**"Durbannah Is Looking Up."** "That was the exclamation of an enterprizing citizen of the Village across the creek, the other day, as the steamer *Globe* lay cozily at the wharf on that side.— Well, it is a pretty spot, and no mistake, and deserves to be looking up. There is the Foundry, Tan-yard, Wheelbarrow Factory, and other industrial establishments; besides a number of new houses, and some splendid building lots yet to be improved."[31]

30. *Upper Monongahela Valley*, pp. 489, 490. This source gives the date 1847, obviously in error. Captain Yeager later went into. the mercantile business in Fairmont. He married Margaret Dent, daughter of Rawley Evans Dent, and died in Fairmont February 11, 1893.

31. *Monongalia Mirror*, May 5, 1850. The name Durbannah for the developing town was suggested by George Kramer for F. M. and William Durbin, who began building houses there around 1845; Wiley, p. 598; *Morgantown Post*, March 17, 1866. William Durbin died March 12, 1866.

**Uffington.** According to a family tradition, a man named Uffington, with his young daughter Martha and a small son came to the Booths Creek area in pioneer days and was killed by the Indians. The two children escaped by hiding in a clump of willows until dark, then making their way to a nearby fort. The boy died three years later, of scarlet fever, and Martha lived alone in a crude building near Raven Rocks.[32] She later married William D. Smith. They operated a store,[33] and a post office, named Uffington, was established in the store July 8, 1850, with Smith as the first postmaster.

**A Big Storm.** "Our town was visited, on the afternoon of Friday the 26th, by a very heavy thunderstorm. The rain poured down until the streets were flooded with water. We have seldom seen such a display of electricity as was then exhibited. Frequent and almost blinding flashes of lightning were followed in quick succession by crashing reports of thunder. A horse hitched to a post at the edge of town was killed. The lightning struck the post, and following the chain by which the horse was fastened, entered its neck, causing instant death. The horse was valued at ninety dollars, and belonged to a Mr. Hugus of this county, formerly a resident of Fayette County, Pennsylvania.

"The lightning struck the rod on the courthouse, and a tree in the locust grove back of the Male Academy. Several persons were severely stunned by the lightning, in town."[34]

**A Big Noise.** A loud report late in the afternoon of August 12 caused much speculation. A boatman at the mouth of Cheat said the water in the river was stirred and thought it was an earthquake. At Kingwood it was thought to be an explosion in the big tunnel under construction on the railroad and others suggested section superintendent Hoblitzel's powder magazine had exploded. Some thought a cannon had been set off. The Uniontown newspaper *Fayette Whig* said that a meteor had exploded and this seemed to be the general belief.[35]

32. See "A History of Uffington" (typescript in West Virginia University Library), by Belva Mae DeVault and Clara DeVault. Some sources spell the family name Uffing, but this name does not appear in any court records. On the other hand, an Anna Uffington figured in an 1856 action.
33. See advertisement, *Monongalia Mirror*, May 18, 1850.
34. *Monongalia Mirror*, August 3, 1850.
35. *Monongalia Mirror*, August 17, 24, 1850.

**Burns' Chapel.** One of the highest churches in the county, Burns' Chapel Methodist Church, on Chestnut Ridge, elevation 2,119 feet above sea level, was organized about 1850 by the Reverend Ephraim Cohen and the Reverend Marion Burns. Other members of the first class were Jeness Davis, Bela Davis, Harrison McKinney, and Solomon Robinson. Logs were cut by these men and a building erected, which served both as a church and school.[36]

**Sugar Grove Presbyterian Church.** A new Presbyterian church was built in 1850 near the head of Dents Run, about four miles from Laurel Point. Earlier services of the Presbyterian congregation had been held on Stewart Run and later in John Lough's barn on Dents Run. The new church, when first organized, was called the Dents Run Church. At the time of the dedication, however, it was renamed the Sugar Grove Presbyterian Church; it stood in a grove of sugar maple trees.

Fig. 56. Sugar Grove Presbyterian Church. (Photo Dr. and Mrs. Gideon S. Dodds.)

36. Dodds and Dodds, *Churches of Monongalia County*, p. 81.

The first pastor was C. B. Bristol, who began preaching on Stewart Run in 1831 (see p. 128).[37]

**Businesses of the 1850s.** Merchants and crafts-people advertising in the *Monongalia Mirror* during 1850 included J. B. Woodward, saddler and harness maker; James Cyphers, barber; Mrs. Jane T. Bear, milliner and mantua maker; George Hoskins and Richard Merryman, blacksmiths; John Beck, hats; E. Mathers, painting. G. W. Fleming's drugstore advertised a "Wonderful Curiosity, American Oil, or Great Medicine of Nature, from a well 185 feet deep." James Shay was at the "Hole in the Wall," M. Callendine at the "Two Big Doors," and W. A. Guseman and Company at the "Three Big Doors."

J. M. Abrams, of Brownsville, Pennsylvania, advertised that he visited Morgantown occasionally "to attend to all operations in Dentistry."

Lazier and McLane waxed poetic to advertise their business. A portion of one piece follows:
> "Messrs. Lazier & McLane
> Having 'cut to come again,'
> Have now on hand, at their Old Stand,
> The biggest pile, and latest style,
> And Lowest price, of something nice,
> In the shape of *Spring and Summer Goods*,
> That ever came to 'this neck of woods.' "[38]

**Slavery in 1850.** By 1850, slavery affected directly only a very few persons in Monongalia County. Slaves themselves, by the census report, amounted to less than 1½ percent of the population, and slave owners to .6 of 1 percent. The largest slave owner in the county was James D. Watson, who owned seventeen slaves, but even this would not have qualified him in the category of planter, as defined by most students of slavery. No other person owned as many as ten slaves; Evan Pindall and George W. Dorsey had nine each, and Jack Ridgway, seven. Sixteen persons were listed as owners of two slaves each and thirty-five as owners of one.[39]

37. Dodds and Dodds, *Churches of Monongalia County*, p. 110.
38. *Monongalia Mirror*, July 27, 1850.
39. Edward M. Steel, Jr., *West Virginia History* 34 (1973):339, 356, 357.

**William Hennen.** William Hennen, a farmer of Camp Run, near Wadestown, died early in 1850. A son of Matthew and Elizabeth Hennen, he was born in Washington (now Greene) County, Pennsylvania, about 1781. He married Rebecca Stafford and they had eight children, including Elizabeth, James, John O., Enoch, Thomas, William, Jr., and Alexander. They moved several times; about 1829 they located in the Dolls Run area and then, about 1846, to the western end of the county.[40]

**The James Cotton Family.** Ascha (Holloway) Cotton, widow of James Cotton, died September 15, 1850. She was born April 13, 1759, and married James Cotton (born December 25, 1749) in New Jersey. They settled before 1800 in western Monongalia County along Dunkard Creek, where James was killed February 20, 1806, by the fall of a tree. Children included Elizabeth, William, Mary, James, Richard, Robert H., Anny, and Jane.[41]

**Other Deaths.** "Died suddenly, on Tuesday night, in this county, Dr. Wesley J. Wisman, aged about 28 years.

"The deceased had been to his mother's and had returned in the evening, eaten his supper and retired to bed in usual health, and died during the night."[42]

"Died on Friday morning the 22d ult. at his residence in this county, Mr. Lemuel John, in the 66th year of his age."[43]

Mary McLane died on November 28, aged twenty-six years, eleven months, ten days.[44] She was the wife of Dr. Joseph A. McLane and a long tribute to her by Rev. W. D. Lemon appeared in the Pittsburgh *Christian Advocate.*[45]

**Land Grants Made in 1850.** Monongalia County grantees in 1850 included:

| | | |
|---|---|---|
| Fetty, John | 16 a. | Indian Creek |
| Hanway, John | 16 | Indian Creek |
| Minear, Philip | 200 | Booths Creek |

40. Dorothy T. Hennen, *Hennen's Choice,* vol. 1, pp. 24, 25.
41. Gordon C. Baker, "The James Cotton Family of Western Monongalia County," *Monongalia Chronicle,* April, 1975.
42. *Monongalia Mirror,* March 16, 1850.
43. *Monongalia Mirror,* March 2, 1850.
44. *Monongalia Mirror,* November 30, 1850.
45. Reprinted in the *Monongalia Mirror,* December 28, 1850.

**County Government.** William John was sworn in as sheriff on March 25, 1850. W. H. Stewart was appointed commissioner of the revenue for the Western District.

**Miscellany.** In 1850: There were recorded in Monongalia County 430 births, 168 marriages, and 153 deaths (Wiley, p. 470). . . . The Brandonville, Morgantown, and Fishing Creek Turnpike was let out in sections by William J. Willey, superintendent, for extensive repair from Maryland to Morgantown and thence nine miles towards Fairmont (Wiley, pp. 125, 538). . . . J. Beck and E. G. Brooke were elected masters of the Morgantown Masonic Lodge (Wiley, p. 548). . . . A. Haymond and Company was a new Morgantown mercantile establishment; other firms started were E. C. Lazier and W. A. Guseman and Company (Wiley, pp. 581, 583). . . . Dr. J. Sigsworth Guyer opened a medical office in Morgantown (Wiley, p. 584). . . . Matilda Gandy, wife of John Snider, died, leaving ten children (Wiley, p. 640). . . . The Reverend Samuel Clawson was pastor of Zion Methodist Protestant Church (Wiley, p. 688). . . . G. W. Sisler moved from Preston County to the Cheat River section of Monongalia County (Wiley, p. 693). . . . T. H. Monroe and S. King were preachers in charge of the Monongalia Methodist Episcopal Circuit (Wiley, p. 728); the Reverend Mr. Monroe organized six Sunday schools, including one at Cassville and one at Fort Martin (Wiley, p. 730). . . . The first town hall was constructed in Morgantown (Callahan, p. 182). . . . Mud holes on Front Street were filled and Walnut Street was improved to the wharf (Callahan, p. 184). . . . William W. and Susannah Price deeded land for the Laurel Flatts Methodist Church on Indian Creek (Dodds and Dodds, p. 105). . . . The Reverend F. C. Conn became pastor of the Minorsville Baptist Church (see p. 301) and preached his first sermon there on October 12, 1850 (Dodds and Dodds, p. 122).

# CHAPTER SEVENTY-FIVE

# 1851

The Virginia Constitution of 1830, although the problems dividing east and west had been hotly debated, did little to eliminate the hurts of sectionalism. James Morton Callahan summarizes the situation:

"The vast resources [of western Virginia]—forests of excellent timber, oil and natural gas, and 16,000 square miles of bituminous coal in workable seams—remained undeveloped because of the short sightedness of eastern leaders. The West, with no railroads and no canals, sorely needed improvements; but despite much public agitation and vigorous struggles in the general assembly, it had to remain content with paltry appropriations for turnpikes, obtained by log rolling, while vast sums were spent on badly managed improvements which were undertaken in the East."[1]

Equal representation in the legislature on the white basis was the demand of the westerners, while the easterners continued to favor the existing system, which tied suffrage to the property basis. Callahan says: "Several Easterners, arguing that much of the land in the West, fit only for a lair of wild beasts, was not worth a mill per acre and would never be of any value, were determined to draw the line of suffrage restriction even closer by fixing a minimum value for a freehold."[2]

The legislature had the power to reapportion the state after the census of 1840, but postponed it indefinitely, feeling that changes would be bound to be to the advantage of the western counties, which were rapidly increasing in population.

Sectional feeling became more pronounced. The west

1. *Semi-Centennial History of West Virginia*, p. 134.
2. Ibid., p. 132.

continued its fight for a greater share in the government. In 1842, at a meeting of delegates from ten counties held at Clarksburg, talk of dismemberment was current. A Charleston newspaper, the *Kanawha Republican*, proposed a new state to be called Appalachia.

The westerners finally settled into a determination to endure the evils of the constitution until after the census of 1850, satisfied that then the growth of the white population west of the mountains would be "so great that the East could no longer with any show of justice refuse them their proper share in the general assembly."

**The Constitutional Convention of 1850-51.** A constitutional convention bill before the legislature in 1850 was hotly debated. The east advocated election of delegates on the mixed basis; i.e., white population and taxes (every seventy cents of taxes would have a representation equal to one white person). The west, favoring white population only, was defeated, and in the August election for delegates to the convention, of the 135 members elected only 34 were from the counties that later became West Virginia.

The convention met October 14, 1850, adjourned November 4 to await census data, then reconvened on January 6, 1851. The committee on basis and apportionment found itself hopelessly divided in opinion and on February 6 presented two reports. One, favored by the western members of the committee and the convention, advocated white population as the basis for apportionment in both houses of the legislature. The other report, favored by the eastern members, advocated white population and taxes combined as a basis for both houses.

Every day, from February 17 to May 10, in committee of the whole, the convention discussed the reports of the committee, and various substitutes, without being able to agree on anything. Callahan says: "One session a day proved insufficient for the discussions. The reporter struck for higher wages, and the members, enamored with their own verbosity, agreed to his demands."[3]

The east had the votes to adopt its basis, but feared that the west would secede from the convention unless some compro-

3. Ibid., p. 136 note.

mise moderately satisfying to them could be reached. But each side clung to its views with bulldog-like tenacity. Feelings ran so high on May 10 that the convention was forced to adjourn until the next day. Finally a compromise committee was appointed in an attempt to prevent a split.

The leading citizens of Monongalia County had constantly participated in the western struggle for constitutional reforms. In the convention of 1850-51 they were ably represented by Waitman T. Willey. On the question of basis of representation "Willey made a speech which breathed the spirit of his native hills. He denied that wealth is properly the source of political power, and emphasized the idea that rights of persons are above those of property. He adhered to the rule that no men are entitled to exclusive or separate emoluments or privileges from the community but in consideration of public service."[4]

Ambler further describes Willey's great speech on the "Basis of Representation":

"He denied that property, even a 'peculiar' property, such as Negro slaves, needed power specifically conferred for its protection. In proof of this he reiterated a standing contention of the west to the effect that property had instrinsic powers more than sufficient for its protection in government."[5]

The constitution as finally adopted[6] was a compromise and, as with most compromises, not really satisfactory to either faction. But apportionment for the house of delegates was based on white population, and landed qualifications for voting were abolished.

An important provision was that hereafter all county officers were to be elected by the people. Heretofore, from the very beginning of Monongalia County, they had been appointed by the governor. A new spirit was about to enter county politics.

**The Rift Widens.** The president of the Virginia constitutional convention of 1850-51, at the close of many weeks of bitter debate, exhorted members of the convention on their return home to use all their influence to allay sectional strife between

4. The text of the speech appeared in the *Monongalia Mirror*, March 22, 1857.
5. *Waitman T. Willey*, pp. 25, 174-80.
6. The vote in Monongalia County was, for ratification of the constitution, 1,377; against ratification, 27.

East and West and to promote a cordial fraternal feeling. "Virginia united," he said, "has ever been one of the noblest states of the confederacy. I cannot contemplate what she should be if torn by intestine feuds of if frantically seeking her own dissolution. May you long live to see this ancient commonwealth united and happy at home, honored and respected abroad."

But despite this admonition, says Callahan, "the rift continued to widen in the decade of political agitation which followed. . . . Under the administration of Wise, the political hero of the West, efforts were made to conciliate the West and thereby to endeavor to bridge the chasm between sections. The West was exhorted to send her children to Virginian schools taught by Virginians, and various schemes for railroads and canals to connect the West and the East were proposed."[7]

But the interests of western Virginians were decidedly different from those of the easterners. Markets of the westerners were in Pittsburgh or along the Ohio and Mississippi valleys; rail connections to the East were with Baltimore rather than Richmond or Norfolk.

Daniel Webster, in his speech at the laying of the cornerstone for an addition to the Capitol in Washington, in 1851, forecast the future accurately:

"And ye men of Western Virginia who occupy the slope from the Alleghenies to the Ohio and Kentucky, what benefit do you propose to yourself by disunion? If you secede, what do you secede from and what do you secede to? Do you look for the current of the Ohio to change and bring you and your commerce to the waters of Eastern rivers? What man can suppose that you would remain a part and parcel of Virginia a month after Virginia had ceased to be part and parcel of the United States?"

Conley and Doherty[8] summarize the east-west differences: "Eastern Virginians and Western Virginians differed in economic, cultural, and political customs and ideals. In the east, there were large plantations on which one cash crop, such as tobacco, was grown. In the west, there were small farms producing many kinds of crops as well as pastures and grazing lands for varieties of livestock. It seemed possible that the west would

7. *Semi-Centennial History of West Virginia*, p. 139.
8. *West Virginia History*, p. 217.

develop industrially because of the valuable mineral resources which underlay the land.

"In the east many of the large estates were served by slaves, but in the west, a man's labor force consisted mainly of members of his own family. In the east, inexpensive transportation outlets were plentiful on the navigable rivers running from the Blue Ridge Mountains to the Altantic Ocean. In the west, because of the mountains, few rivers and roads had been made passable and only at great cost.

"The white people of eastern Virginia were mostly English, and the black population was African. The people of western Virginia were a mixture of many stocks, with very few of them coming from the eastern part of the state. On the eve of the Civil War, only 4 per cent of the total population in western Virginia was black, whereas in eastern Virginia at least a third of the people were Negro. Eastern Virginians were likely to conform to religious tradition; western Virginians were more often of dissenting faiths."

In politics, there were also sharp differences. Westerners, who had received help from national armies in quelling the Indians, and who sought funding from Washington for public improvements, were more likely to be Federalists, while easterners reflected the spirit of individualism and sectionalism associated with Thomas Jefferson.

The people of Monongalia County had long participated in the struggle of the westerners for state constitutional reforms to secure more nearly equal representation and more equitable taxation, as well as a larger share of appropriations for internal improvements. Their democratic views were ably expressed in the constitutional convention of 1829-30 by Philip Doddridge and in the convention of 1850-51 by Waitman T. Willey.

The constitution of 1850-51 quenched some of the fires of western discontent but it was not long until they were burning brightly again, as the westerners found out that they had lost in the new constitution. One blow was that all property was to be taxed at its true and actual value except for slaves, who were to be valued uniformly at three hundred dollars, even though some were sold for two thousand dollars or more. This shifted much of the tax burden to the west. Furthermore, the constitution prohibited the borrowing of money for construction of roads, canals, and other improvements needed in the west.

More and more, westerners came to believe that the only way for them to progress was to break away and form a new state.

**Making Carriages.** In 1841 James Kerns put together the first buggy made in Monongalia County, in a little shop on Maiden Alley, selling the vehicle to Harrison Postlewaite. By 1851 the manufacture of carriages, including various kinds of wagons, had become one of the leading industries in the county.

No one knows exactly when the buggy first appeared, or even the origin of the name. In England there was a two-wheeled vehicle by that name, with a folding top, but it was in America, in the nineteenth century, that it made its greatest development, as a four-wheeled carriage. The buggy came to be so universally used in the United States that, no matter what other conveyances a man might own, he usually had a buggy also. It was as important to a family a hundred years ago as an automobile is today.

By 1851 the road system of Monongalia County was fairly extensive and reached into every community. The roads were narrow, generally poorly engineered, rough and muddy or dusty, depending on the weather. There were, of course, no hard-surfaced roads; not even the so-called "turnpikes" were macadamized, except for short sections.

But the roads, poor by today's standards, were greatly improved over those of early pioneer days, which were scarcely more than bridle-paths. By mid-century they were good enough for vehicular traffic. Every farmer needed a wagon for transportation of materials; every family needed a buggy for transportation of people.

"Buggies were fairly comfortable; they were light and hence easy on horses; they were short-coupled so that they didn't need much space for turning, though (except for a later cut-under type) they could not turn sharp without cramping the front wheel against the body and upsetting. Buggies were strong, too; they are still made with perches. The first ones were entirely open; later they were more often made with folding tops, so often, in fact, that any folding top became a buggy top to an American. There was however a type with a fixed top, which later came to be known as a Jenny Lind buggy."[9]

Merchants used various forms of carts or light wagons to make their deliveries. Edwin Tunis takes note of some of these:

"There was no refrigeration in those days; nobody paid much attention to sanitation; flies were nothing more than a nuisance; so butchers delivered meat in open, shallow-bodied carts. Whether it was the need to get the meat to the customer quickly, before it spoiled, or only natural deviltry, butcher boys were proverbially wild drivers."[10]

Storekeepers also began using a light, open, spring wagon, with elliptical springs, a type of vehicle later called an express wagon.

Finally, there were the sturdy farm wagons, designed to carry heavy loads, lumbering and uncomfortable, but nevertheless essential to agricultural production.

All these kinds of carriages were manufactured in Monongalia County. John Shisler, in 1802, made the first wagons, in a shop on High Street, moving it in 1805 to the lower end of Pleasant Street, by the river, where he associated his son Michael with him. James Kerns, who later went into business by himself, became an apprentice to the Shislers in 1832. In 1849-50 Mr. Kerns built a steam buggy factory along the river, half a mile above the mouth of Deckers Creek.

The largest carriage factory ever operated in the county was that established in the year 1851 by Ashbel Fairchild and Ashbel Fairchild Lawhead. Samuel T. Wiley describes it as it was in his day (1883):

"The carriage manufactory of Fairchild, Lawhead & Co., . . . is one of the most extensive in the State. The buildings, if connected, would be 244 feet in length, and, with the lumber-yard, cover over an acre of ground. Two long two-story frame buildings (one 72 by 26, the other 102 by 32 to 40) are connected by a broad bridgeway above the first story. A one-story blacksmith shop, 50 by 30, and an office a story and a half, 20 by 14, comprise the establishment. The power is furnished by two engines, respectively, of 12- and 40-horsepower. The departments of the manufactory are, first, the machine shop . . . ,

9. Edwin Tunis, *Wheels* (1955), p. 58.
10. Ibid., p. 59.

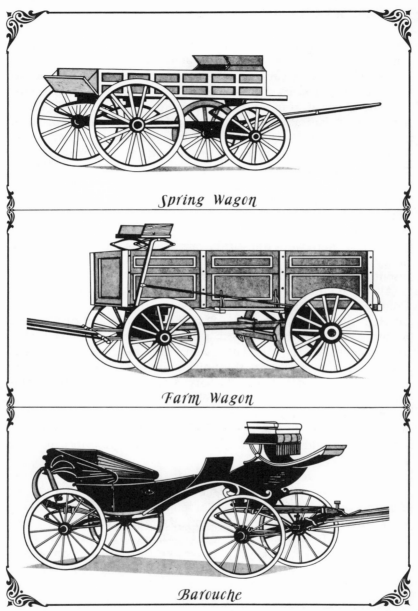

*Spring Wagon*

*Farm Wagon*

*Barouche*

Fig. 57. Types of carriages made in Morgantown. (Sketches by Diane Lenhart.)

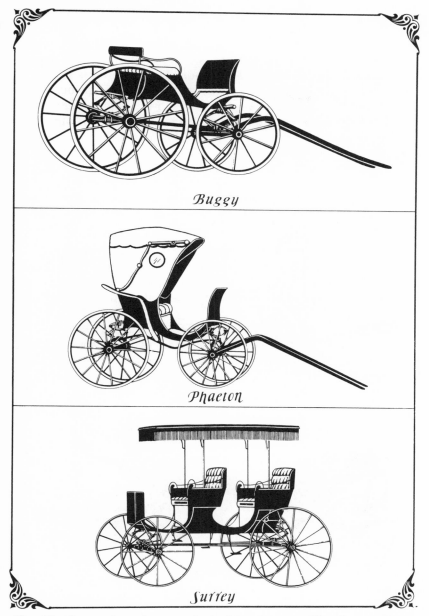

*Buggy*

*Phaeton*

*Surrey*

Fig. 58. Types of carriages made in Morgantown. (Sketches by Diane Lenhart.)

run by the forty-horse-power engine, where the necessary planing and spoke machinery dresses the rough material. Next is the wood-shop, . . . on the first floor. The material is next carried to the blacksmith shop, where five fires and all necessary machinery are run by a twelve-horse-power engine. The work from here goes up to the second story to the paint-rooms . . . , with varnish- and trimming-rooms attached. The work is now taken to the sales-room, 40 by 32 (on the first floor), where carriages, buggies, phaetons, barouches, spring-wagons, etc., are kept for the inspection of buyers. When running to its full capacity, the factory employs thirty hands. Vehicles from these works go all over this State, southwestern Pannsylvania, and in nine States, reaching as far west as Texas. All growing from a small beginning in 1851."[11]

**Street Improvement.** The maintenance and repair of streets in Morgantown was directly under the supervision of the entire board of seven borough trustees, who hired men to fill mud holes, repair sidewalks, and remove rubbish. In 1851 a plank walk replaced the flat rocks that served for sidewalks on High Street and on Front Street near the post office. Pleasant Street had been improved by gutters and permanent curbstones, and by macadamizing, with a layer of broken stone nine inches thick in the middle and six inches at the side.[12]

**The Kingwood Pike.** The Kingwood, Morgantown, and West Union Turnpike was incorporated in 1848.[13] In 1851 the maximum limit of the capital stock was increased, and on February 10 the Board of Public Works was authorized to borrow $2,800, with which to macadamize the pike between Morgantown and Cranberry Summit,[14] which was done. This was then, perhaps, the best road in this section of Virginia.[15]

Plank roads were being built in some places and promised to keep carriages out of the mud at all seasons. Commenting on the Kingwood Pike, the local editor said:

11. *History of Monongalia County*, p. 261.
12. Callahan, *Making of Morgantown*, p. 184.
13. At first called the Kingwood and West Union Turnpike Company; the name was changed in 1851.
14. Later named Terra Alta.
15. Wiley, pp. 124, 125, 539, 653.

"If *Plank Roads* can be made available in a hilly country—of which we entertain serious doubts—the road above mentioned will eventually become a Plank Road, and will accommodate the stock and other trade of a wide district of country."[16]

**Other Roads.** Monongalia County roads leading from the Port of Morgantown towards construction projects on the railroad were mostly in bad condition. The local newspaper reported on the Evansville Pike:

"A vast amount of heavy hauling to the Tunnel, during an open Winter and wet Spring, had cut up the bed of the road into mud-holes of every imaginable shape and size, so that a person on horseback, in broad daylight, must keep a sharp look-out to make his way in safety—but how wagons or carriages contrive to get along this deponent saith not."[17]

A "Solemn-choly" accident had occurred a littler earlier:

"A wagon load of Whiskey and Ale, destined for the Railroad, was upset the other day, a few miles from town, in consequence of the horses taking fright, and some three or four barrels of the *fire-water* were tetotally spilled! The only *real* loss, on the occasion, was that of a valuable horse, which came in contact with the tongue of the wagon as it fell over, and died of its wounds."[18]

**Stage Lines.** In 1851 six turnpikes radiated out from Morgantown[19] and on more and more of these stagecoach lines were being established for the transport of mail and passengers.

In the spring a new line was set up, as noted in the following announcement:

"Alexander Hays has commenced carrying the Mail weekly from this place to Brownsville, via Granville, Jimtown, Dornick, Maple's Mill, Carmichael, &c., going down on Friday, and returning on Saturday.

". . . Mr. James Protzman has the contract for carrying the mail on the new route hence to Evansville."[20]

"Alex. Hayes" was also "carrying the Daily Mail between this

16. *Monongalia Mirror*, May 31, 1851.
17. *Monongalia Mirror*, June 7, 1851.
18. *Monongalia Mirror*, March 29, 1851.
19. *Monongalia Mirror*, October 4, 1851.
20. *Monongalia Mirror*, March 1, 1851.

place and Fairmont." The stage for Fairmont left at 4 p.m. daily. The northbound stage left Fairmont at 3:30, arrived at Morgantown by 7:30 and left for Uniontown at 8.[21]

Other mail arrivals and departures were:

To Wheeling, via Waynesburg, every Tuesday by 3 p.m., returns Saturday by 6 p.m.

From Wheeling, via Blacksville, arrives Saturday by 10 a.m. departs Saturday by 11.

From Kingwood, arrives Saturday by 11 a.m., departs by noon.

To Evansville, departs Monday by 8 a.m., returns Tuesday by 4 p.m.

To Pruntytown, departs Wednesday by 8 a.m., returns Thursday by 5 p.m.

To Brownsville, leaves Wednesday by 8 a.m., returns Thursday 6 p.m.[22]

J. C. Rogers advertised a "New Mail Stage Line" daily between Morgantown and Clarksburg; "Seats may be taken at Hayes' Hotel."[23]

A four-horse coach to Brownsville, via New Geneva and Masontown, left Wallace's Hotel in Morgantown 7 a.m. Tuesday, Thursday, and Saturday, and returned leaving Brownsville Monday, Wednesday, and Friday at 7 a.m. The fare was two dollars.[24]

Accidents occasionally occurred, some of them fatal. A sixteen-year-old girl in Uniontown was run over by a stagecoach and killed instantly.[25]

A mishap near Cheat River was not so serious:

"We learn that the Mail Stage running between this place and Uniontown, was upset on Tuesday morning last, on Cheat Hill, and that the driver, Henry Wise, had a leg badly broken in two places. No passengers were injured that we hear of. It is said that the *top load*, that morning, was somewhat heavier than usual."[26]

21. *Monongalia Mirror*, July 12, 1851.
22. Ibid.
23. *Monongalia Mirror*, July 19, 1851.
24. *Monongalia Mirror*, September 13, 1851.
25. *Monongalia Mirror*, March 15, 1851.
26. *Monongalia Mirror*, November 15, 1851.

The stages did not always get through, on account of bad weather:

"Owing to the suspicion of ice in Cheat River, the Mail from Uniontown, failed to reach here on Thursday night."[27]

But in December the temperature dropped to eight degrees below zero and the Fairmont stage crossed the river on the ice at Morgantown.[28]

**Navigation Re-Opened.** "Such a stir as we had in town, on last Monday morning, when the steamers *Venture* and *Lindsey* made their appearance at the new wharf, and rolled out their ample freight to the view of beholders! It was the first arrival of a steamboat since early in the Summer, and every one was anxiously desiring a revival of trade, for every one felt in his pocket a sensation of emptiness consequent upon the stoppage of navigation."[29]

Meetings had been held during the year in an attempt to secure slack water up the Monongahela as far as Morgantown. The local paper commented:

"We are truly glad to see some signs of waking up to the importance of *slacking* our beautiful River, so as to render it navigable for Steamboats at all stages of water."[30]

**Jim Town.** A little village on the west side of the Monongahela River, at the mouth of Scotts (Mill) Run, grew up near the gristmill established by David Scott in the late 1770s. It was never very large, but has had two or three different names. During the nineteenth century it was mostly known as Hamilton, from James Hamilton, who built and operated a tavern known as the Hamilton House. A post office called Jim Town was started February 18, 1850, with William Pendleton Williams as the first postmaster, succeeded by Parnel Simpson February 26, 1851.

Morgan L. Boyers, with John Hood and Company, started a store December 5, 1837, succeeded as proprietors by John B. Arnett, Alf Yeager and Dunham, Fleming and Brooks, S. L.

27. *Monongalia Mirror,* February 1, 1851.
28. *Monongalia Mirror,* December 27, 1851.
29. *Monongalia Mirror,* November 22, 1851.
30. *Monongalia Mirror,* January 25, 1851.

Boyers, S. S. Yeager, and N. L. Furman. Another tavern, the Randall House, was started by John Dawson.[31]

Fig. 59. Statue of Patrick Henry, placed on the court-house dome in 1851. Since 1976 it has stood in the court-house annex; before that, for several years, it was in the Morgantown Public Library. (Photo by Mary Susan Dadisman.)

**Statue of Patrick Henry.** A statue of Virginia's "favorite son," Governor Patrick Henry, was placed on the dome of the court-house on August 20. The statue was proposed by L. S. Hough, who raised by subscription the necessary funds, and the work was done by E. Mathers.[32]

"The Statue is about nine feet in height . . . , admirably pro-portioned and well executed throughout. The left hand holds a scroll, and a mantle is gracefully hung over the right shoulder."[33]

The courthouse yard was improved, landscaped, and enclosed by an iron railing and gates.[34]

**The First Insurance Company.** On March 29, 1851, the Monon-galia County Mutual Insurance Company was incorporated by

31. Wiley, p. 703.
32. Wiley, p. 574.
33. *Monongalia Mirror*, August 30, 1851.
34. *Monongalia Mirror*, June 21, 1851.

the general assembly. The incorporators were Charles McLane, Edgar C. Wilson, George D. Evans, John E. Fleming, William Lazier, Addison S. Vance, Joseph A. McLane, and Elza C. Lazier; they were also named in the charter as the first board of directors. The company was to have its office at Morgantown and insure no property outside the county. The company, however, never did get organized to carry on business.[35]

Insurance for property did begin to be available in 1851, however, as H. P. Taylor opened an office as agent for the Pennsylvania State Mutual Insurance Company.[36]

**The Mountain Messenger.** The Reverend Simeon Siegfried, editor of the *Monongalia Mirror*, in 1850 started another paper, a religious periodical. It bore the name *Mountain Messenger*, or *Baptist Recorder*, and was distributed over the state in the interest of the Baptist denomination.[37]

The *Mirror*, meanwhile, moved to new quarters at the corner of Front Street and Court Alley, next door to the post office.[38]

**Riots on the Railroad.** Construction work continued on the B.&O. Railroad, interspersed with much consumption of Monongahela whiskey and numerous riots and brawls. On July 12, 1851, a big fight broke out at the tunnel, in which about one hundred Irish laborers were involved, armed with shillelaghs, stones, and pistols. The fight began at the east end of the tunnel and lasted from dusk to dawn, terminating at the west end. Four or five persons were fatally injured. The editor of the *Mirror* suggested that only Irish awkwardness in the use of firearms prevented a much larger number from being "kilt entirely."[39]

In August, following another riot in Marion County, one hundred Irishmen were arrested and, when Fairmont jails could not hold them all, two hack loads were transported to Morgantown, "where they were safely kept in the new jail across the

35. Wiley, p. 553.
36. *Monongalia Mirror*, September 27, 1851.
37. Wiley, p. 435. Random issues are on file in the West Virginia University Library.
38. *Monongalia Mirror*, April 12, 1851.
39. *Monongalia Mirror*, July 12, 1851.

street from the storage headquarters of the across-country whiskey trade which had stimulated all the trouble."[40]

A long account of a trip by a reporter to the "Mammoth Tunnel" gave an eyewitness report of the feverish activity at that site.[41]

**Mammoth Menagerie.** G. B. Quick and Company brought their circus and "mammoth menagerie" to Morgantown on September 25. A grand procession on the streets of the town preceded the show.[42] Simeon Siegfried did not give it a very high rating:

"If ever Beelzebub opened a *Recruiting Office* on earth, this is one. . . . There was more drunkenness and rowdyism in town . . . than we have witnessed here for years."[43]

**Monongalia Iron Works Sold.** On January 23 Rutherford, Hersey, Tassey and Gay took over the operation of the ailing Monongalia Iron Works, having purchased the property for $25,750.[44]

According to the sale notice, the property contained "15,000 acres of land, whereon are a Rolling Mill, Forge, Foundry, Nail Factory, Grist and Saw Mill, all driven by water power,— together with three Blast Furnaces. On this Land there is an abundance of Iron Ore, Stone Coal, Timber, and Limestone."[45]

**Fairview Methodist Episcopal Church.** Five miles south of Morgantown, on the Evansville Pike, a Methodist class had met in a school building, and then a congregation was formed which built a church. This, by 1851, was in such bad condition that Thomas Jeffrey, James Boyd, and Annie Grey started to raise money for its repair. They were so successful that the old building was removed and a new structure built on the same foundation.[46]

40. *Monongalia Mirror*, August 9, 1851; Callahan, *Making of Morgantown*, pp. 176, 177.
41. *Monongalia Mirror*, October 25, 1851.
42. See announcement in the *Monongalia Mirror*, September 20, 1851.
43. *Monongalia Mirror*, October 11, 1851.
44. *Monongalia Mirror*, June 28, 1851.
45. *Monongalia Mirror*, January 4, 1851.
46. Dodds and Dodds, *Churches of Monongalia County*, p. 141.

**Blacksville Methodist Church.** When Blacksville was laid out by David Black (p. 41), he offered to give a lot to the trustees of any Methodist congregation. There was no organization at the time, but some time later a log building was erected on the lot, used for both church and school purposes. A second church was built on the lot in 1851.[47] It was a building forty-six by thirty-six feet, with two doors and two aisles. Paul Vandervort was the first minister.[48]

**Pittsburgh Annual Conference.** The Pittsburgh Annual Conference of the Methodist Protestant Church was held in Morgantown in September 1851. George Brown, who attended the conference, gave an eyewitness account:[49]

"The church and citizens of that hospitable place entertained the Conference in their best style, and the impression made by the body on the public mind was, in all respects, favorable to our young Church. Rather contrary to my expectations, I was elected to the presidency again. During the Conference, the brethren took two perpetual scholarships, at five hundred dollars each, in Madison College; and shortly afterward the Board of Trustees took from our itinerant ranks Dr. P. T. Laishley, to act as agent for that institution. We all felt a deep interest in the prosperity of our newly-adopted college."

**Slavery in Decline.** For a quarter of a century and more, slavery in Monongalia County had steadily declined. The highest percentage was in 1820, when 3.39 percent of the total population were slaves. Slaveholders imported a few slaves and those who were imported were disposed of at a steady rate. There was no organized slave trade in the county, the nearest agency being at Clarksburg.

Black persons who were made free mostly left the county, so

47. Dodds and Dodds, *Churches of Monongalia County*, p. 125. Apparently the congregation only leased the lot; in 1896 the heirs of Thomas Brock conveyed it to the church trustees.

48. Paul Vandervort (*The Monongalia Story*, vol. 2, p. 167) was born in Monongalia County June 19, 1828, and died August 26, 1865, "in the prime of his life, and while he was attending to the duties of an effective preacher on the Blacksville Circuit." See biography Wilding, *Promoted Pioneer Preachers*, pp. 17, 18. Robert Laughlin traveled the Blacksville Circuit in 1864. Wilding, p. 24.

49. *Recollections of Itinerant Life*, p. 348.

that the percentage of black people in the total population also declined, from 4.45 percent in 1820 to less than 2.5 percent in 1850.

Most of the free blacks, in 1851, were listed as servants or farmers. Only Charles Dowd, of Long Drain, was listed as a laborer. Of thirty-three free blacks in 1851, twenty were farmers, ten were housekeepers, two were colliers, and one was a bloomer.[50]

Fig. 60. The Eden Methodist Church. (Photo Dr. and Mrs. Gideon S. Dodds.)

**New Brownsville Methodist Episcopal Church.** A Methodist Episcopal Church group was organized at Statlertown (New Brownsville, or Pentress) and a frame church was built in 1851. The first class was composed of Robert Chaffin and wife, Abram Brown and Elizabeth his wife, Andrew Brown and wife, Peter Henkins, and others.[51]

**Francis Taliaferro Brooke.** The first attorney to be enrolled on the Monongalia County bar, Francis T. Brooke, died March 3,

50. Edward M. Steel, Jr., *West Virginia History* 34 (1973):337-39.
51. Wiley, p. 750.

1851. He was born near Fredericksburg, Virginia, August 27, 1763. At the age of sixteen he was a lieutenant of artillery in the Revolutionary War. After the war he read law and in 1788 settled in Morgantown. He was admitted to the county bar May 4, 1789, and was appointed prosecuting attorney of the district court the same day. But the following year he resigned, being succeeded May 3, 1790, as prosecuting attorney by William T. McCleary, and returned to Fredericksburg. He was appointed a circuit judge, and, in 1815, was named as one of the judges of the Supreme Court of Virginia, a position he held until his death.[52]

**Captain Levi Tucker.** Levi Tucker died at Cassville August 10, 1851. The son of George Tucker, he followed agriculture to an extent but his main business was carpentry, building houses and boats. He built large flatboats on the Monongahela and transported the produce of the area to markets at Brownsville and Pittsburgh. He enlisted in June 1812 in the Twelfth United States Infantry, under Col. James P. Preston, and took part in the Second War of Independence. He married Mary A., daughter of Thomas Glisson (*Monongalia Story*, vol. 2, p. 369), and they had three sons, Thomas, John W., and James.[53]

**Adam Ice.** A member of one of the earliest pioneer families of Monongalia County, Adam Ice died July 5, 1851, near Fairmont. His father was Frederick Ice (see *Monongalia Story*, vol. 1, p. 172, etc.), who located at Ice's Ferry on Cheat River by 1758. Adam was born June 1, 1760, and a family tradition says he was the first white child born in Virginia west of the Alleghenies; this, however, has not been verified and is doubtful. He married Phoebe Bayles and their children were Sarah E., Margaret, Eleanor, William Bayles, Mary Magdaline, Rawley, David, Elizabeth, Jesse, Phoebe, and Abraham.[54]

**James Hoard.** James Hoard, the only male heir of Capt. John Hoard (see *Monongalia Story*, vol. 2, p. 37), died January 22,

52. See his biography in *Dictionary of American Biography*, vol. 2, p. 69; also Wiley, p. 333.
53. *Cyclopedia of Monongalia County*, p. 95; Core, *Chronicles of Core*, pp. 76, 77.
54. *Cyclopedia of Marion County*, p. 94; Lough, *Now and Long Ago*, p. 388.

Fig. 61. George M. Reay. (From *One Hundredth
Anniversary . . . , Methodist Protestant Church.*)

Fig. 62. Col. Joseph Snider. (From Wiley's
*History of Monongalia County.*)

1851. He was born on his father's farm in 1722 and devoted his life to agriculture, becoming well known as a prosperous and successful farmer and stock-raiser. He was a lieutenant in the Virginia militia.

He married Tabitha, a daughter of Levi Lewis, and they had ten children, Mary (married Charles Stewart), Sarah, John L., James, Elizabeth, William, Jemima (married David Keener), Tabitha (married Robert Ross), Margaret, and Aaron.[55]

**Thomas Watson.** Thomas Watson, a son of pioneer settler James G. Watson (p. 112), died September 20, 1851, at the age of sixty-three. He was born in Charles County, Maryland, and came to Monongalia County with his father, settling first near Stewartstown, then on White Day Creek.

Thomas married Rebecca, daughter of William and Cynthia (Carroll) Haymond, and they settled at "Cis-montaine," on Little Creek, where he died, leaving several children, including Henry and James D.[56]

**Daniel Clark Chadwick.** A grocer and general merchant of Morgantown, Daniel C. Chadwick died on September 27, 1851, at the early age of thirty-one. He was survived by his widow, Margaret Eliza (born 1821), daughter of John ("Captain Jack") and Gilley Strother Evans, and by four children (one other had died). His will, written only six days before his death, mentioned his mother, a sister, and a brother as members of his household.[57]

**Other Deaths.** Among other persons who died during 1851, was Margaret Evans Dent, widow of Capt. John Dent, who died November 23, aged nearly eighty-eight years.[58]

Rezin Holland, son of Capel Holland, died September 19, at the age of seventy-six, having been born in the year of American Independence.[59]

55. *Cyclopedia of Monongalia County*, p. 182; see also Clifford B. Hoard, *House of Capt. John Hoard* (1965).

56. *Monongalia Mirror*, October 4, 1851; *Cyclopedia of Monongalia County*, pp. 171, 172.

57. *Monongalia Mirror*, October 4, 1851. One of D. C. Chadwick's sons was French Ensor Chadwick, who was admitted to the U.S. Naval Academy September 28, 1861 (Paolo E. Coletta, pers. comm.).

58. *Monongalia Mirror*, November 29, 1851. A long account of her life is given, including numerous events of her girlhood in pioneer Monongalia County.

59. *Monongalia Mirror*, October 4, 1851.

Daniel Tucker died November 2, aged 21.[60] Twenty-seven-year-old Francis Warman died on August 11, and George Gould, for many years the mail carrier to Wheeling, via Waynesburg, died August 8, in Granville.[61]

Mrs. Mary Travis, widow of the late Doctor R. Travis, died May 16, near Smithtown; she was forty-six years old.[62]

"Died, on Saturday morning, the 8th of February, 1851, at his residence, near Smithtown, Monongalia county, Va., of Catarrhal Fever, Mr. Isaac Riggs, after an illness of some two weeks continuance. Had he lived two days longer he had arrived at the good old age of seventy years."[63]

**Land Grants Made in 1851.** Monongalia County grantees in 1851 included:

| | | |
|---|---|---|
| Cross, George | 34 a. | Dunkard Creek |
| Davis, Eugenious | 95 | Dripping Springs |
| Evans, James | 600 | Laurel Run |
| McKinney, Harrison | 150 | Deckers Creek |
| Meredith, John | 34 | Waters Monongahela R. |
| Tower, Edwin W. | 914 | Deckers Creek |
| Tower, Edwin W., et al. | 1,000 | Deckers Creek |
| Wheelright, Thomas William | 54 | Miracle Run |
| Wiley, Jacob | 2 | Dunkard Creek |
| Wilson, Edgar C., et al. | 1,000 | Deckers Creek |

**County and Borough Government.** William John was sworn in March 24, 1851, for his second term as sheriff. James F. John was appointed commissioner of the revenue for the Eastern District and John B. Lough for the Western District. Trustees of the borough of Morgantown were Elias Stillwell, J. E. Fleming, James Shay, H. Daugherty, J. R. Drabell, D. R. Lynch, and R. L. Berkshire. Borough real and personal property was taxed at the rate of twenty cents on the hundred dollars.

**Miscellany.** In 1851: Edward C. Bunker was admitted to the bar on April 5 (Wiley, p. 316). . . . Other attorneys admitted were E. B. Hall, Z. Kidwell, and U. M. Turner (Wiley, p. 318). . . . E. G. Brooke and J. E. Tucker were masters of the Masonic lodge

60. *Monongalia Mirror*, November 8, 1851.
61. *Monongalia Mirror*, August 16, 1851.
62. *Monongalia Mirror*, May 17, 1851.
63. *Monongalia Mirror*, February 22, 1851.

(Wiley, p. 548). . . . Haymond and Pickenpaugh opened a store in Morgantown (Wiley, p. 581). . . . G. L. Samuel opened a shop in Morgantown for making boots and shoes (Wiley, p. 602). . . . John Wallace purchased the National Hotel in Morgantown (Callahan, p. 114). . . . A borough ordinance required that "every sheep or goose found running at large within the borough limits shall be taken up and sold for the sum of $0.12½" (Callahan, p. 182). . . . Another ordinance required that no slaughterhouse be allowed within the limits of the borough from the first of April to the first of November, under penalty of a fine of five dollars for each and every offense; the deposit of dead animals or other nuisances on the streets was forbidden (Callahan, p. 183). . . . A new brick building on High Street, built by John Hanway, was occupied by the store of Carr, Smith and Company (*Monongalia Mirror*, March 29, 1851).

# CHAPTER SEVENTY-SIX

# 1852

Monongalia County, in 1807, for convenience of administration and law enforcement, had been divided into nine constabulary districts (*Monongalia Story*, vol. 2, pp. 347-50). Three of these were mostly taken into Preston County when it was formed in 1818. In 1831 the county was divided into four numbered districts (pp. 61, 62).

**Magisterial Districts.** On April 2, 1852, a commission was appointed by the general assembly to lay out the county into seven magisterial districts. The commissioners were William Lantz, N. Pickenpaugh, Gen. E. S. Tindall, Thomas Meredith, Alpheus Stuart, William Haines, and William Price. They reported as follows:

"District No. 1. Bounded and described as follows, to wit: Beginning at the mouth of Booth's Creek, on the Monongahela River, thence up said Booth's Creek to the mouth of Jacob's saw-mill run; thence up said run to where the road leading from said run by Benjamin Jacob's smith shop to the Beverly turnpike comes into said pike; thence a straight line to the ford where the Rock Forge road crosses Cobuns Creek; thence with said Rock Forge road to where it intersects the Morgantown and West Union turnpike road to the Preston line; thence with the said Preston County line to the chestnut corner of Monongalia, Marion, and Preston counties; thence with the Marion county line to the Monongahela River, and thence down said river to the beginning.

"District No. 2. Bounded and described as follows, to-wit: Beginning at the mouth of Booth's Creek, the beginning of District No. 1; thence down the Monongahela River to the mouth of West's Run; thence up said run, near by the house now occupied by Joseph Cummins, and with said road by Davis Weaver's to the Preston County line, and with said Preston County line to the West Union and Morgantown turnpike; thence with lines and boundaries of No. 1 to the place of beginning.

"District No. 3. Bounded and described as follows, to wit: Beginning at the mouth of West's Run, on the Monongahela River, thence down said river to the Pennsylvania line, and with the said Pennsylvania line, crossing Cheat River, to the Preston line; thence with the Preston County line, recrossing Cheat River, to District No. 2, and with the adjacent boundaries and lines of No. 2 back to the beginning at the mouth of West's Run.

"District No. 4. Bounded and described as follows, to wit: Beginning at the mouth of widow Brook's lane; thence with the road leading through said lane to the Morgantown and Evansville road; thence with said road to the Brandonville and Fishing Creek pike; thence with said pike to where the old State Road leaves said pike, near Scott's bridge; thence with the old State Road by the old Capt. Dent place on to where it comes to the new road leading by John Fetty's and with the said new road to the line of No. 6 hereinafter described; and with lines of No. 6 as hereinafter described to the Pennsylvania lines; thence with the Pennsylvania line to the Monongahela River, and up said river to the place of beginning.

"District No. 5. Bounded and described as follows, to wit: Beginning at the mouth of widow Brook's lane on the Monongahela River, the place of beginning for No. 4, and with the boundary lines of No. 4 to where said line strikes the boundary line of No. 6 as hereinafter described to the Marion County line; and thence with the Marion County line to the Monongahela River, and thence down the Monongahela River to the place of beginning.

"District No. 6. Bounded and described as follows, to wit: Beginning on the Pennsylvania line at David A. Worley's stable; thence crossing Dunkard Creek at the ford there and with the Day's Run road, commonly called the 'graded road', by the route of said road as surveyed and graded, to the Marion County line; thence with Marion County line to what is called

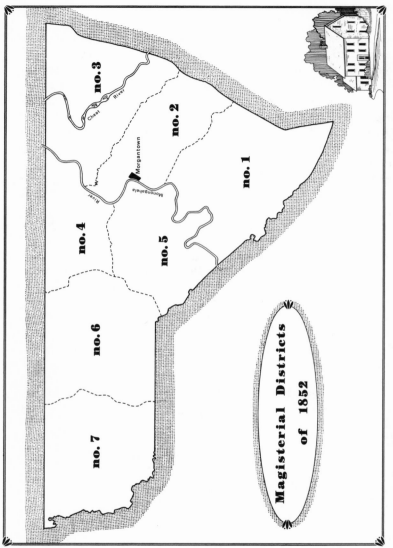

Fig. 63. Map of Monongalia County showing approximate boundaries of magisterial districts, 1852. (Drawn by Diane Lenhart.)

the Kennedy corner; thence a straight line to the mouth of the run on which Mrs. Dorcas Riggs lives; thence up said river to its head and the top of the ridge separating the waters of Stewart's Run, and the run on which John Hawkins lives; thence with the top of the ridge dividing the waters of Doll's Run, Stewart's Run and Little Indian Creek, keeping the highest ridge between Doll's Run waters and Dent's Run waters, and between Scott's Run waters and Doll's Run waters, until a knob not far from Smoky Drain of Doll's Run is reached; thence down a ridge in a north-east direction, including the Postlewait farm in No. 6, to the Jackson school-house on a run which puts into Dunkard Creek at Morristown; thence with the road leading therefrom to Morristown, to the Pennsylvania line, and with said Pennsylvania line to the place of beginning.

"District No. 7. Bounded and described as follows, to wit: Beginning at David A. Worley's stable on the Pennsylvania line, the place of beginning for No. 6, and with the line of No. 6 on the Day's Run road to the Marion County line; and thence with the Marion County line to the Wetzel County line; and thence with the Wetzel County line to the Pennsylvania line, and with the Pennsylvania line to the place of beginning."

**The County Court.** The county court for Monongalia County at the time of its first meeting, on December 8, 1776, was composed of several justices of the peace who had been appointed by Governor Patrick Henry. Future justices were to be appointed by the governor from names submitted by the court; hence it was a self-perpetuating body. Its members held office for life or during good behavior.

In addition to being the governing body for the county, it was also a judicial body, with both civil and criminal jurisdiction. The justices received no salaries, but candidates for the offices of sheriffs (and certain other county offices) were recommended from the body, to be appointed by the governor. For sheriff it was customary to recommend to the governor the name of the oldest commissioner of the court. The clerk of the court was selected from the body.

This method of selection of members of the court made it a prime target for popular attack. Otis K. Rice says: "Common complaints against the county courts centered around the undemocratic method by which members were chosen, the prevalence of nepotism, their inefficient administration, neglect of isolated areas of the counties, and lack of responsibility to the public which they were to serve."[1]

Petitions were repeatedly presented to the general assembly asking for extension of the franchise so as to make county officials elective. One such appeal reminded the legislature that it was the "declared right of taxing America, without representation, which produced the severance of these United States from their parent country."

The court system, a petition from Monongalia County charged, in 1818, "is nothing more than Mock Justice." One plea, with the usual catalog of hardships incident to traveling long distances to court and collecting witnesses, cited a case in which a plaintiff was awarded a judgment of $11.44 but won little more than a moral victory inasmuch as his ruinous bill of costs amounted to $11.28.[2]

Nevertheless, the Constitutional Convention of 1829-30 did nothing to change the system. Men of property urged successfully that suffrage was a conventional right (as contrasted to a natural right), and should be restricted to those most capable of exercising it judiciously.

But the Constitutional Convention of 1850-51 did extend the right of suffrage and reorganized the county court. Article VI, of the new constitution, specified:

"27. Each county shall be laid off into districts, as nearly equal as may be in territory and population. In each district there shall be elected, by the voters thereof, four Justices of the Peace, who shall be commissioned by the Governor, reside in their respective districts, and hold their offices for the term of four years. The Justices so elected shall choose one of their own body, who shall be the presiding Justice of the County Court; and whose duty it shall be to attend each term of said court. The other Justices shall be classified by law for the performance of their duties in court.

"28. The Justices shall receive for their services in court a *per diem* compensation, to be ascertained by law, and paid out of

1. *The Allegheny Frontier*, p. 363.
2. Ibid., p. 364.

the county treasury; and shall not receive any fee or emolument for other judicial services."

Other elective officers of the county named were the clerk of the county court, the surveyor, the attorney for the common-wealth, the sheriff, "and so many Commissioners of the Revenue as may be authorized by law."

Justices elected in the various districts, with dates they were commissioned, as recorded in county court papers, are as follows:

District No. 1. Capell Holland, Isaac Powell, Isaac Reed, July 13, 1852; and Joseph Shuttlesworth, November 15, 1852, in room of Thomas Meredith, who won the election.

District No. 2. Leroy Kramer, Henry Daugherty, Henry Kennedy, and Daniel Haldeman, July 13, 1852.

District No. 3. Charles H. Burgess, William Robinson, Seth Stafford, and John M. Cobun, July 13, 1852.

District No. 4. Purnell Simpson, James T. Davis, Daniel Du-senberry, and George Alexander, July 13, 1852.

District No. 5. John B. Yeager, James T. Hess, July 13, 1852; John N. Waters, April 12, 1853, in room of Philip Rogers, re-moved; and Gideon Barb, July 13, 1852.

District No. 6. Levi Haught, October 18, 1852, in room of John B. Lough, resigned; William Price, Enos Tennant, and Wil-liam Sine, July 13, 1852.

District No. 7. James Wise, Justus Gerard, John Anderson, and William S. Fletcher, July 13, 1852.

These twenty-eight commissioners were divided into groups of fours, each group being responsible for certain of the monthly meetings of the court.

The court chose its own president and selected, for the first four-year term, J. T. Davis.

**The B.&O. Reaches Wheeling.** The year 1852 was a high point in the history of transportation in northwestern Virginia. The Baltimore and Ohio Railroad, which had been organized in 1827, after many frustrating delays, at last reached the Ohio River, at Wheeling. After being stopped at Cumberland since 1842, the railroad finally, in 1848, had begun to feel its way across the Alleghenies.

The cost of the extension to Wheeling, two hundred miles in

Fig. 64. The B&O climbs out of the Cheat River canyon. (From Pangborn, *Picturesque, Historical and Descriptive B & O*, 1883.)

length, through the roughest region yet traversed by any railroad in America, was partly underwritten by sale of $1 million
of state bonds to Baring Brothers. Bonds were issued by the
company for rails to be bought in England. Chief Engineer B. H.
Latrobe and his assistants selected a route on which construction appeared practicable and estimated the total cost at
$6,278,000.

During the next four years (1849-52) the construction had
proceeded, through the mountains, over ravines and rivers,
through tunnels drilled in rocky mountain sides, up steep
ascents and around perilous curves. Operations in 1850 began
with thirty-five hundred laborers and seven hundred horses. The
completion of the section from Cumberland to Piedmont was
celebrated in 1851 with an excursion train from Baltimore, and
Latrobe promised that trains would run into Wheeling by January 1, 1853. Callahan paints a vivid picture:[3]

"Then followed a series of triumphs over the difficulties in
the mountains. The road was pushed from Piedmont westward
across Preston county through the haunts of roaming pack-
wolves, and parallel to the extensively travelled route whose
immense throng of people was soon to be diverted to newer
routes of more rapid travel. After passing over deep gorges on
high trestle work, and over turbulent streams by heavy masonry
work, at Tunnelton it passed through the longest railroad tunnel
which had yet been constructed in the world and continued
westward toward Fairmont creating new towns (Rowlesburg,
Newburg, etc.) in the region which was still sparsely settled, and
bringing the pioneer prospectors who prepared the way for the
later era of great industrial development based on coal and
timber. In order to hasten the work westward beyond the site
of the . . . tunnel which was not yet opened, and to get the road
to Wheeling on schedule time, a remarkable achievement was
performed by conveyance of materials over the top of the
mountain on a temporary track which had a grade of 530 feet
per mile. To this point cargoes of supplies, which for part of the
year reached Morgantown from Pittsburgh by steamboats, were
transported by wagons from the head of the Monongahela navigation. By the same route, or across the country from the

3. *Semi-Centennial History of West Virginia*, p. 117.

Fig. 65. The B&O crossing the Alleghenies. (*Illustrated London News*, May 18, 1861.)

Fig. 66. B&O Railroad bridge across the Monongahela River at Fairmont, built 1852.

National road, also came bands of Irish laborers inquiring their way to the 'big toonel.' "[4]

The railroad reached the Tygart Valley River at the mouth of Three Forks Creek.[5] From this point construction continued down the river to its mouth, thence following the Monongahela to Fairmont, to which the new road was opened early in 1852. The bridge across the Monongahela, at Fairmont, 650 feet long, was then the largest iron bridge in America (Fig. 66).

Westward from Fairmont the road followed Buffalo Creek and at the mouth of Pyles Fork stimulated the development of another town, named Mannington, for James Manning, a civil engineer of the new railroad.

"Northwestward from Mannington," says Callahan, "the route continued up Pyles Fork, thence across the divide between Glover Gap and Burton to the upper waters of Fish Creek (via Hundred and Littleton and Board Tree Tunnel) and finally across another divide to another stream which it followed from near Cameron to Moundsville." At the beginning of December, rails were being laid at the rate of two miles a day.[6] At Roseby's Rock the last rail was laid and the last spike driven on December 24, 1852.

It had not been easy. Newspaper reports through the year include reference to disasters, as well as triumphs. The blast that let daylight through the Big Tunnel killed one Irish laborer and injured two or three others.[7]

As the grading work neared completion, the Irish laborers were laid off and left rapidly, seeking employment elsewhere. By February, one hundred per day were arriving in Morgantown to secure transportation downstream by boat.[8]

Laying of track went forward steadily:

"They are expecting the Railroad Cars to reach Fairmont in two or three weeks, from this time. They passed through the Big Tunnel, and on to Fetterman, as we are informed, on

4. *Semi-Centennial History of West Virginia*, p. 117.
5. Here Grafton would be laid out in 1856.
6. *Semi-Centennial History of West Virginia*, p. 121; *Monongalia Mirror*, December 4, 1852.
7. *Monongalia Mirror*, January 31, 1852.
8. *Monongalia Mirror*, February 7, 1852.

Sunday last. The R. R. Co. and their Contractors evince a great deal of energy in urging forward this noble work."[9]

By July passenger cars were making regular trips, twice a day, as far west as Fetterman.[10]

A notice reprinted from the *National Intelligencer* said:

"It is with unfeighned pleasure that we have in our power to announce today the completion of the Baltimore and Ohio Railroad to the Monongalia river, a distance of one hundred and twenty-five miles from Cumberland. This great event took place on Saturday, the 5th instant. The progress of the track during the month of May, we are informed, has been most rapid, there having been *twenty miles* of road laid down during that month. . . .

"From Fairmont to Nile's Fork[11] the graduation is now ready for the rails. . . ."[12]

**Mail by Rail.** More rapid mail delivery was an important result of the end-o'-track reaching Fairmont:

"We are gratified to announce to our readers that instructions have been issued from the Post Office department, extending the mail route by railroad from Fetterman to this place. By this arrangement the Eastern mail will be delivered here in 17 hours from Baltimore, instead of two days as heretofore. . . . This arrangement is to go into effect on the first of October."[13]

Mail for Morgantown and Uniontown was also brought by rail to Fairmont and there transferred to stagecoach.

Stages left Morgantown for Fairmont daily at 7 a.m., "connecting with the cars on the Baltimore and Ohio Rail Road." Returning, the stages left Fairmont at 1 p.m. for Morgantown, there connecting with stages for Uniontown and Brownsville.[14]

**Steamer Thomas P. Ray.** "Our citizens were gratified by the appearance at our wharf, on Monday morning last, of the new and beautiful light draught steamer *Thomas P. Ray*. The craft was built at Brownsville expressly for the upper trade, and

9. *Monongalia Mirror*, May 15, 1852.
10. *Monongalia Mirror*, July 10, 1852.
11. Pyles Fork.
12. *Monongalia Mirror*, June 19, 1852.
13. *Fairmont Republican*, September 25, 1852.
14. *Monongalia Mirror*, October 9, 1852.

named in honor of one of the most enterprising citizens ever known in Morgantown. It is well adapted to the conveyance of passengers, having ample, neat and comfortable berths, and neatly furnished cabins. As a freight boat it is not surpassed in the trade, is of about one hundred tons burden, of ample power, the engines and machinery entirely new; and is neatly finished and furnished throughout.

"Capt. A. B. Gaskill has the command, with an efficient crew. . . .

"It is in contemplation by the company to give us a morning and evening boat to Brownsville, whenever there is sufficient water."[15]

A weekly box in the newspaper gave news of the Port of Morgantown, with arrivals and departures of steamers. An example:[16]

Arrivals

| February 23 | *"Thos. P. Ray"* |
| 24 | *"Thos. P. Ray"* |
| 26 | *"R. H. Lindsey"* |
| | *"Venture"* |

Departures

| February 23 | *"Thos. P. Ray,"* with 18 cabin and 87 deck passengers, mostly Irish railroad hands, freight. |
| 25 | *"Thos. P. Ray,"* 20 cabins, 60 deck passengers, freight. |
| 26 | *"R. H. Lindsey,"* railroad passengers, freight. |
| 27 | *"Venture,"* railroad passengers, freight. |
| | *"Thos. P. Ray,"* 18 cabin passengers, numerous deck passengers. |

The steamers occasionally tried the trip on to Fairmont. Simeon Siegfried, Jr., assistant editor of the *Mirror*, described his voyage on the *Thomas P. Ray*, on March 6. On the upstream trip, the steamer left Morgantown at 7 a.m. and made the trip in eight hours, including a few stops. Coming back, the running time was only two hours and twenty minutes.[17]

Steamer schedules, of course, were not very dependable, on

15. *Monongalia Mirror*, February 14, 1852.
16. *Monongalia Mirror*, February 28, 1852.
17. *Monongalia Mirror*, March 13, 1852.

account of fluctuations in depth of the water. The editor of the *Mirror*, Simeon Siegfried, gave a long account of his problems in securing newsprint paper.

He first sent to Pittsburgh with a friend but the trip was delayed by ice and he had to borrow paper from Uniontown. On January 2 he bought a ticket for a morning departure, but the steamer left an hour ahead of time and he missed it. He finally left at 11:30 a.m. on the *Venture*, Captain Wilkins, arriving in Pittsburgh early the next morning. He loaded the paper on the same boat which left at 5 p.m., the captain promising he would be in Morgantown in time for church the next morning. But the water was too low, so the passengers and freight were unloaded at Brownsville. On January 5 the *Globe* took them to New Geneva, but could go no further, so he borrowed a horse to ride to Morgantown and sent a wagon for the paper.[18]

**The Flood of '52.** The highest water on the Monongahela River in historic times, up to this time, occurred in April 1852. Old-timers told of the flood of 1832, which for a long time set the standard for high water in the valley, but no accurate record of its height was preserved, so exact comparisons could not be made.

April 6, 1852, was the date of the next high water which seemed to match (or exceed) that of 1832. Marks made then and long remaining showed the height reached above low water stage to be thirty-three feet and eleven inches.

Thirteen days later, on April 19, an even thirty-four feet was recorded, one inch higher than that reached earlier in the month.[19]

**The Age of Buggies.** With two carriage manufactories now operating in Morgantown, a new day was dawning for local transportation.

"We are glad to notice that our Farmers are throwing their old super-annuated and worn-out *pack-saddles* 'to the moles and bats'; and instead of packing their wives and sweethearts behind them on horseback to church and other gatherings, they are

18. *Monongalia Mirror*, January 10, 1852.
19. Wiley, *Monongahela: The River and its Regions*, pp. 160, 161. Floods of later years reached still higher levels, which some say is accounted for by the cutting of timber on the headwaters.

now supplying themselves with handsome buggies and carriages, and the luxury of a drive has become a *social* enjoyment. Thus one improvement is rapidly followed by another. The good graded roads that now pursue their winding way over almost every hill and valley, could not be properly appreciated without light vehicles to glide over them."[20]

Fig. 67. Buggy on a country road. (Sketch by Diane Lenhart.)

**The Democratic Republican.** Another newspaper called the *Democratic Republican* (see p. 249) was started in August 1852 by George M. Howard and B. F. Feall. The subscription price was $1.50 a year. It was a four-page sheet, twenty-four by thirty-seven inches, with twenty-eight columns. Its motto was "States' Rights—National Union," and it was Democratic in politics.

The paper was printed on the first iron press ever used in the county, earlier papers having used wooden presses.[21]

As might have been expected, a spirited rivalry developed between the town's two papers, the first time the community

20. *Monongalia Mirror*, August 7, 1852.
21. Wiley, pp. 435, 436.

had supported two papers. Mostly it was fortunate to have one. A sample of editorial exchange:

"The lads that put out the 'Republican' say that the MIRROR is not a *neutral paper.* Who ever said it was?"[22]

**Dornicktown.** Near the old Fort Martin Church was a blacksmith shop run by a man named Cartright, who also sold whiskey. It developed into a center of attraction for crowds of men, who threw stones ("dornicks") at a mark on a tree for the drinks. All the trees around the place were scarred and it became known far and wide as Dornicktown.[23]

A post office was established here, with this fancy name, on January 14, 1851, with William Hale the first postmaster, succeeded by David Rich January 27, 1851.

**James R. Moore.** On June 24, 1852, the Reverend James Robertson Moore became principal of the Monongalia Academy. It was under his able administration that the distinguished educational center, already having had a long career of usefulness, attained its greatest prosperity and the height of its honorable fame. Morgantown became an educational center to which students came from a wide surrounding area. In one year it had 176 students, from fourteen states.

The Reverend Mr. Moore was born August 20, 1823, in Columbiana County, Ohio, and graduated at Washington College. He became a minister in the Presbyterian church but had to resign because of a bronchial affliction. He was "a man of rather striking appearance and grave countenance—a man whose decision of character, great executive ability, and remarkable knowledge of human nature, won for him the respect and esteem of all who came in contact with him."[24]

The academy had experienced various ups and downs since moving into the new location in 1830. The trustees sponsored lotteries to raise funds for operation; success in lottery ventures led to abuses, as a result of which the trustees were indicted in 1840.[25]

22. *Monongalia Mirror,* May 14, 1853.
23. Callahan, *Making of Morgantown,* p. 167; Wiley, p. 705.
24. Wiley, p. 402.
25. Ambler, *History of Education in West Virginia,* pp. 81-84.

**New Building for the Female Academy.** The old home of the "Whitehall"[26] Seminary having deteriorated, the board of trustees in 1852 proposed to build a new structure and let the contract to Harrison Hagans for $3,500. Monongalia Academy contributed $1,750 towards the construction. The new building was located on the northwest corner of High and Foundry streets, on property conveyed by John Rogers.

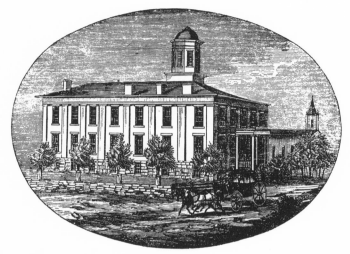

Fig. 68. Morgantown Female Seminary, corner of High and Foundry streets. (From the school's *Catalogue*, 1860-61.)

The Reverend and Mrs. Cephas Gregg had been employed in 1851 as teachers for the school. In announcing the appointment of Mr. Gregg as principal, the *Mirror* commented:

"The establishment of several seminaries, of the higher order, in any section of the country, contributes more than almost any thing else to raise the character and increase the prosperity of the citizens."[27]

A side benefit from the presence of two academies in town was the opening of a bookstore:

26. The name Whitehall was popularly used for the Morgantown Female Academy on account of a coat of white paint having been applied to the buildings. See Wiley, p. 398.

27. *Monongalia Mirror*, April 19, 1851.

"We take pleasure in informing the public, that through the enterprise of Mr. *Thomas Purinton*, one of the teachers in the Male Academy of this place, a good and extensive assortment of Books is now opened on High street, a few doors north of Walnut street. Such an establishment has long been needed in town, and ought to be well supported."[28]

Mr. Purinton was also, in his spare time, teaching girls' classes in the common branches.[29]

**Morgantown Circulating Library.** A public library was maintained at the Monongalia Academy for loan of books to citizens. Mathew Gay ran a notice in the newspaper, calling on persons who had borrowed books and failed to return them to deliver them to the Reverend Mr. Moore; "otherwise steps will be taken to recover them with cost."[30]

**Sudden Death.** "Died, very suddenly, on Saturday evening the 18th inst., supposed of *Apoplexy*, Thomas Meredith, Esq., of Smithtown, in this county, aged about 53 years. The deceased started to catch a horse, and not returning, was sought for, and found dead in the barn of Mr. Watson, near his own residence. He was a highly estimable and useful citizen."[31]

**The First Dentist, The First Photographer.** So far as can be determined, the first dentist to reside in Morgantown was Dr. James S. Aulabaugh, who opened an office in the Evans Hotel.[32] Wiley says one of the first was Dr. J. Lowry McGee, but gives no date.[33] Dentists from other towns had previously visited for short periods.

The first resident "Daguerrean Artist" may have been E. A. Mosier, who opened an office to take daguerreotypes over Dr. Carr's Drug Store.[34]

**Ice Cream Saloon.** "Mr. J. Cyphers, at the S. E. corner of High and Walnut streets, in this borough, has opened his Ice Cream

28. *Monongalia Mirror*, February 15, 1851.
29. *Monongalia Mirror*, April 26, 1851.
30. *Monongalia Mirror*, October 9, 1852.
31. *Monongalia Mirror*, September 25, 1852.
32. *Monongalia Mirror*, January 3, 1852. Numerous earlier dentists had visited here (see p. 171).
33. *History of Monongalia County*, p. 602.
34. *Monongalia Mirror*, May 15, 1852.

Saloon, in a manner to prove highly gratifying to his customers and the public. With spacious rooms and prompt attention, he will doubtless be able to give general satisfaction.—Try him!"[35]

**Zoar Baptist Church.** The Zoar Baptist Church, on Dents Run, was organized in 1852, with twelve members, by the Rev. G. F. C. Conn, who was to serve it as pastor for the next 28 years. The first members included Jarrett Lynch, Wilson Crowl and wife, Nancy Dent, Amelia Barker, Ann A. Barker, Ann Martin, James Arnett and wife, and Ann Arah Arnett.[36]

**The Calvary Methodist Protestant Church.** A group of families of the Cheat Neck area, about 1852, organized a Methodist congregation in a log schoolhouse that stood near where the Uniontown road crossed Darnell Hollow. Charter members included:[37]

| | |
|---|---|
| William Donaldson | Amy A. Costolo |
| Lewranah Donaldson | John Q. Saddler |
| William Lewellin | Sarah J. Saddler |
| Mary Lewellin | Thomas Irvin |
| James Donaldson | Catharine Irvin |
| Mary E. Donaldson | James McGee |
| Charles E. Donaldson | E. O. Hickle |
| Charity Donaldson | Mary J. Rankin |
| Ruth Cleaver | Joab R. Donaldson |

**Bishop Simpson.** Beginning on June 10, 1852, the fifth annual session of the Western Virginia Conference of the Methodist Episcopal Church was held in Morgantown. It was presided over by Bishop Matthew Simpson, who was ordained a bishop that year, so that this was the first conference at which the distinguished episcopant presided.[38]

35. *Monongalia Mirror,* May 15, 1852.
36. Wiley, pp. 458, 727.
37. Dodds and Dodds, *Churches of Monongalia County,* p. 150; Wiley, pp. 688, 689; Barnes, *M. P. Church,* pp. 124, 125; "A. G. Lewellan and wife and a goodly number of young people joined during a great revival held by Rev. Jeremiah L. Simpson in 1868. The most notable meeting ever held at Calvary was that of 1871 conducted by Rev. Peter T. Conaway.
38. For a record of the conference, see *Minutes of the Western Virginia Conference, 1848 to 1857.* Rowland Aspinall, Charles W. Evans, eds. (1939), pp. 129-64; Wiley, pp. 445, 446. Other sessions held in Morgantown were the thirteenth, March 14, 1860; Bishop Scott, and the nineteenth, March 21, 1866, Bishop Clark; Wiley, p. 445.

**The Hogs Lose Out.** Certain domestic animals, especially hogs, were hot issues in borough politics in the early 1850s. An ordinance of 1838 had prohibited a sow and her pigs from roaming at will on the streets. Many citizens desired to extend the ordinance to include the entire hog population. "Others were unwilling to curb the migratory and excavating instincts of hogs or pigs not longer requiring the personal attention of the mother hog."[39]

Simeon Siegfried evaluated the situation humorously: "The summary process of driving off, and selling under the hammer, every maternal swine with her progeny found running at large, has occasioned a bristling up at every corner, and the most eloquent grunts of disapprobation have been elicited."[40]

Callahan relates the final blow: "The hogs were several times victorious at the polls but finally lost in the borough election of 1852. Their final defeat, sentencing them to confinement in pens, was made more galling by an ordinance requiring their pens to be removed from positions abutting on streets and alleys."[41]

**Pierce Lynch (Linch) Dies.** Pierce Lynch, the son of John Lynch, a pioneer settler of Monongalia County, died in Greene County, Pennsylvania, in 1852. He was born on Indian Creek in 1797, but removed, in 1822, to the Georges Creek settlement in Fayette County, then to Greene County. He was a successful farmer and grazer and possessed considerable ability as a financier. He married Ellender Lough and they had fifteen children, including Jarrett Lynch, who returned to Monongalia County in 1847 to live near Laurel Point.[42]

**Samuel Billingsley Dies.** The owner and operator of Billingsley's gristmill, Samuel Billingsley, died in 1852 at the age of eighty. He was a native of Pennsylvania but settled along Paw Paw Creek, Monongalia County, in 1830, where he combined the occupation of milling and farming.

He married Elizabeth Snyder and they had twelve children,

39. Callahan, *Making of Morgantown*, pp. 182, 183.
40. *Monongalia Mirror*, May 10, 1851.
41. Ibid. After 1852 cows were the only domestic animals which had liberty to run at large in town, a privilege they retained until May 1878.
42. *Cyclopedia of Monongalia County*, p. 137.

including John, Samuel, Daniel, Thornton, Eugenus, Morgan, Dorcas, Maria, Malinda, and Mary.[43]

**Moses Holland Dies.** Moses Holland, a farmer of the old Holland section of Monongalia County, died in 1852 at the age of seventy-five.[44]

**Land Grants Made in 1852.** Monongalia County grantees in 1852 included:

| | | |
|---|---|---|
| Brady, John S. | 37 a. | Statlers Run |
| Lemley, Jacob | 6 | Adj. David Shockley |
| Plum, John S. | 22 | Waters Cheat R. |
| Tower, Edwin W. | 100 | Waters Cheat R. |
| Tower, Edwin W. | 19 | Cheat River |

**The Circuit Court.** By the Constitution of 1851 the Court of Law and Chancery (p. 62) was designated as the Circuit Court. Monongalia County was included in the Fifth Section, Tenth District, and Twentieth Judicial Circuit, composed, in addition to Monongalia, of Hancock, Brooke, Ohio, Marshall, Wetzel, and Tyler. George W. Thompson[45] was elected judge for eight years, and opened his first term of court at Morgantown on September 8, 1852.[46] R. L. Berkshire was elected prosecuting attorney.[47] George S. Ray was sworn in as clerk.[48]

**County Government.** The nature of the county government was drastically changed in 1852, as a result of the adoption of the new state constitution (see pp. 348-52). Thomas Meredith, on March 22, was sworn in as sheriff, the last such officer to be appointed by the governor. At the election, held in the spring, A. C. Dorsey was elected sheriff for a four-year term, beginning July 1, 1852. The terms of the appointed justices of the peace were terminated, and they were succeeded by elected officials (p. 374).

John R. Drabell was elected county surveyor, Michael R. Chalfant assessor for the Eastern District, and James A. Hogue

43. *Cyclopedia of Marion County*, p. 86.
44. *Cyclopedia of Marion County*, p. 191.
45. See biography, Wiley, pp. 322, 323.
46. Wiley, p. 308.
47. Wiley, p. 311.
48. Wiley, p. 312.

for the Western District. R. L. Berkshire was elected prosecuting attorney for the county court (and also for the circuit court). Marshall M. Dent was elected clerk.

**Miscellany.** In 1852: The stack of the old Woodgrove Furnace gave out, and the operator William (?) Claybaugh, replaced it with a new one (Wiley, p. 256). . . . Samuel McKelvey and Frederick D. Kay of Pittsburgh, on December 29, took over the operation of the Cheat Iron Works[49] (Wiley, pp. 257, 682). . . . R. E. Cowan was admitted to the county bar (Wiley, p. 318). . . . Dr. George W. John began the practice of medicine at Stewartstown (Wiley, p. 478). . . . J. E. Tucker and U. Griffith were masters of the Morgantown Masonic Lodge (Wiley, p. 548). . . . Moses D. Wells invented a seed sower, sold at five dollars each; about five thousand were manufactured and sold over many states. He also invented a rubber wagon lock (brake) and James Kern invented a sausage cutter (Wiley, p. 552). . . . The Commercial Building, on Lot 88, Morgantown, at the corner of High and Walnut streets, was constructed by George M. Hagans (Wiley, p. 581). . . . Frank Demain, John K. Shean, Shean and Rice, James Shay, and William Durbin were operating grocery stores in Morgantown (Wiley, p. 583). . . . Thomas Evans was running a tavern on the east side of High Street between Bumbo Lane and Maiden Alley (Callahan, p. 118). . . . H. W. Brock and Horatio N. Mackey began the practice of medicine in Morgantown (Wiley, pp. 584, 585). . . . John H. Smith was a tailor (Wiley, p. 602). . . . William Anderson, a native of County Tyrone, Ireland, settled in the West Run area (Wiley, p. 676). . . . William Sines was running a general store at Mooresville (Wiley, p. 747). . . . The temperature on January 20 was twelve degrees to eighteen degrees below zero, twenty-three degrees below zero at Jacob Miller's (*Monongalia Mirror*, January 24, 1852). . . . James O. Watson, with Francis H. Pierpont, organized (in Marion County) the American Coal Company, for the first commercial shipment of coal west of the Alleghenies. Watson has been called the "father of the bituminous coal industry" (Balderson, *Fort Prickett*, p. 109).

49. *Monongalia Mirror*, January 1, 1853.

# CHAPTER SEVENTY-SEVEN

# 1853

It is a fairly common belief that the men and women who laid the foundations of our modern society had robust health and unusual physical strength. It is true that men, women, and children worked hard, and this gave them a muscle tone that would be the envy of any jogging man of today. This undoubtedly pulled many of them through an attack of disease or injuries suffered from accidents.

But in general our ancestors were men and women whose physical vigor was sapped by privation, disease, exposure, and debilitating seasonal ailments. The years quickly took their toll and by the time the young people had become thirtyish fathers and mothers with children of their own, even the most healthy of them would probably have had a bout with fever or some contagious disease or begun to show the effects of too much raw whiskey, too much fried and greasy food, or too much childbearing or worry or anxiety.

**Health at Mid-Century.**[1] Monongalia County residents of the mid-nineteenth century were still mostly far from competent medical aid and, with frequent need for medical attention, the people largely became, of necessity, their own physicians. They had little knowledge of anatomy or of the causes and nature of diseases and made use of experimentation, superstition, or advice of persons who had suffered ailments like their own.

For drugs they sought roots, barks, herbs, some of which may have helped, by chance, some of which may have endangered their lives. Doddridge describes most of these remedies

1. Cf., pp. 212-13; see also Charles F. Millspaugh, *American Medicinal Plants* (1892).

as "harmless substances, which do wonders in all . . . cases in which there is nothing to be done."[2] In other words, the sick person's constitution would bring about his recovery without the aid of drugs.

Malaria was an affliction in western Virginia, although not as common in Monongalia County as it was in the Ohio Valley. It was known by various names, including intermittent fever, remittent fever, ague, dumb ague, shaking ague, or chill fever. Drinks made from bark of cherry, dogwood, or poplar were used in treatment, "digested in whiskey, or decoction of boneset." The herb boneset (*Eupatorium perfoliatum*) probably got its name because it would set the bones still, i.e., stop shivering with chills.

Fig. 69. Boneset, used in pioneer times for treatment of malaria. (From Millspaugh's *American Medicinal Plants.*)

A common complaint was rheumatism, especially among men who worked much of the time in cold, wet clothing. The most widely used treatment was bathing the aching joints with oil and baking it in before an open fire. Petroleum ("Seneca oil")

2. *Notes on the Settlement and Indian Wars,* p. 118.

discovered in western Virginia along the Hughes River in 1810, came into fairly general use for this purpose.

Winter weather brought pleurisy, colds, coughs, pulmonary disturbances. Cough syrups were made from spikenard (*Aralia racemosa*), elecampane (*Inula helenium*), Virginia snakeroot (*Aristolochia serpentaria*), Indian turnip (*Arisaema triphyllum*), or catnip (*Nepeta cataria*). Physicians recommended bleeding for pleurisy.

Asthma and consumption claimed many lives and the latter, especially, was held in somewhat the degree of fear that cancer is today. The people knew no real remedies and would try almost anything suggested. Dysentery was another dreaded affliction and took a considerable toll in human life. It was marked by distressing symptoms, acute inflammation of the intestines and a high fever.

Contagious diseases often virtually wiped out all the children of a family. "Black" diphtheria was one of the most dreaded of these. Monongalia County cemeteries bear many mute testimonies of the results of this scourge. For example, on Dolls Run in 1844, four children of Peter and Abigail Barrickman died within a few days; eight-year-old Mary on June 22, two others, eleven-year-old Peter T. and five-year-old John, on July 9, and sixteen-year-old Elma on September 3.

Typhoid fever was especially common, as the increased population brought about impure drinking water. Some years serious epidemics developed (see p. 402).

A disease especially prevalent in western Virginia was milk sickness or cow sickness, which led to chills, a high fever, vomiting, a swollen abdomen, delirium. Many cases ended in death. Not until the 1920s was its cause discovered. Cows that eat the herb white snakeroot (*Eupatorium rugosum*), very common in forest margins, have in their milk tremetol and this causes the disease in humans. It is thought that Abraham Lincoln's mother, Nancy Hanks Lincoln, had this disease.

Physicians were scarce, although they appeared about as soon as there were sufficient concentrations of population to warrant the practice of their profession. Training varied widely; there was no licensing and nothing to prevent a person from pursuing the practice of medicine, often "with an effrontery and presumption, directly proportioned to his own ignorance."

Fig. 70. Home of Dr. Charles McLane, corner of High Street and Kirk Alley, built about 1840.

Most early doctors gained their medical knowledge by apprenticeship and often combined it with other callings, particularly the ministry. At least five Monongalia County doctors received their preliminary training at the hands of Charles McLane. Another Morgantown practitioner, in 1832, entered into an agreement with the Reverend Peter Laishley by which he promised to instruct Laishley "in the Science of Medicine on the Old & reformed systems" and "to confer upon him Diplomas agreeable to the constitution of our Society, as soon as he is worthy to receive it." Dr. James Vance Boughner, on the other hand, studied at Cincinnati Medical College; he located, about 1850, at Browns Mills, on Dunkard Creek.

The medical profession of the day was not highly remunerative. After a doctor had ridden many miles in rain or snow to visit a patient, he often had to take payment in country produce, or perhaps go without payment. Doctors thus acquired a variety of objects, often useless to them, as large tubs, a plow beam, a gunstock, a cradle, a pair of shoes.

Drug preparations of the firm of I. Scott and C. McLane were having far-reaching sales. The most popular of these preparations were Dr. McLane's Improved Liver Pills and Vermifuge and Dr. Scott's White Circassian Liniment. The firm had a laboratory in the Evans building on High Street and employed more than a dozen hands.[3]

**The Railroad is Completed.** On January 1 the first train on the Baltimore and Ohio Railroad rolled into Wheeling.

Extensive preparations were made for a grand celebration in Wheeling. Nearly five hundred persons were aboard two trains that left Baltimore on January 10, including Governor Enoch L. Lowe of Maryland and Governor Joseph Johnson of Virginia. Editor Siegfried, of Morgantown, was aboard and published a vivid account of the trip behind snorting locomotives and an exciting ride on a frail and temporary switchback over the steep summit above awe-inspiring gorges at Board Tree Tunnel, which was not yet completed.[4]

About ten thousand persons (some said twenty thousand)

3. Callahan, *Making of Morgantown*, p. 174. See also numerous advertisements in the *Monongalia Mirror*.
4. *Monongalia Mirror*, January 22, 1853.

waited in Wheeling for their arrival late on Tuesday, January 11, but a locomotive suffered a broken axle near Mannington and the trains did not reach Wheeling until 2 a.m. on Wednesday, long after the citizens had gone to bed. The triumphal march, banquet and oratory was, therefore, postponed, but over nine hundred persons sat down for dinner at 6 p.m. in Washington Hall.

Soon after the completion of the railroad the following advertisement appeared in a Wheeling newspaper:

"The tunnels across the mountains are now completed. Connection with a fine line of steamers from Cincinnati at Wheeling. Leave Wheeling daily at 9 a.m. and arrive at Cumberland (201 miles) at 7 p.m., and allowing two hours there, arrive at Baltimore (380 miles) at 5 a.m. Passengers allowed ample time and opportunity at all points to get their meals. Tickets from Wheeling to Baltimore, $8.50."[5]

The new railroad brought about profound changes in Monongalia County. Passengers and goods which formerly came to Morgantown by stagecoach and wagon from Uniontown, where connections were made to the National Road, now came by railroad to Fairmont and thence traveled to Morgantown. And, since the railroad almost touched western Monongalia County at Burton, residents in the headwaters of Dunkard Creek had modern transportation facilities near at hand.

Stage to Fairmont. "We learn that Messrs. Alex. Hayes & C. Bright have become the proprietors of the Mail Stage line between this place and Fairmont. They have procured a neat and substantial new Coach from the factory of Mr. Kerns, which, with careful drivers and good stock, will enable them to convey passengers to their entire satisfaction. The line will leave Morgantown daily in time to connect with the Cars running east and west on the Railroad."[6]

Turnpikes. A considerable amount of effort was being devoted to improvement of turnpikes, to facilitate wagon, buggy, and stagecoach travel. The general assembly, in 1853, took several actions affecting roads in Monongalia County.

5. Callahan, *Semi-Centennial History of West Virginia*, p. 122.
6. *Monongalia Mirror*, July 30, 1853.

On March 12 the capital stock of the Morgantown and Bridgeport Turnpike Company was increased by twelve thousand dollars.

On February 10 the assembly appropriated twenty-two hundred dollars to complete the Maryland and Ohio Turnpike, and six thousand dollars to macadamize the section on Pharoahs Run.

The Blacksville and Worthington Turnpike Company was incorporated on March 26, with a capital of fifteen thousand dollars, the shares twenty-five dollars each. Books of subscription were to be opened at Blacksville by Egan B. Tygart, Thomas E. Hall, William Lantz, Enos Tennant, and John Shriver.

On March 1, the capital stock of the Pennsylvania, Beverly, and Morgantown Turnpike was increased by eight thousand dollars.

On March 29 the Smithtown Turnpike Company was incorporated, with a capital of ten thousand dollars.

An act was passed on February 15 providing for the extension of the Beverly and Fairmont Turnpike to Warren.

**The First Livery Stable.** James Protzman opened in 1853 what was perhaps the first livery stable in Morgantown.[7] Tavern and hotelkeepers from early times had provided quarters for stabling horses of visitors, but Protzman's establishment was independent of any hostelry. He kept horses and vehicles for hire and furnished stabling when required.

**Traffic Accidents.** The new type of transportation by light carriages was not without its hazards:

"Hon. E. C. Wilson had an escape—almost a miraculous one— on last Thursday evening. On returning from Court at Kingwood, in a buggy drawn by a young and spirited young horse, and descending the long hill this side of Mr. Way's farm, the animal, without any known cause, broke into a swift run, and demolished the carriage. We are happy to learn that Mr. W. escaped with a mere scratch."[8]

"A horse belonging to Dr. Dorsey, of this place, ran off with a carryall, on Tuesday afternoon last. No injury was done to the

7. Callahan, *Making of Morgantown*, p. 118.
8. *Monongalia Mirror*, May 14, 1853.

animal or vehicle, the horse having thrown himself against the fence, and upset the carryall, arresting his progress near Mr. Chisler's shop, where the animal was liberated from a complete state of entanglement by some persons who repaired promptly to the rescue."[9]

**Election Results.** The spring election for members of the House of Delegates gave the following results:[10]

|                | Lough | Combs | Stewart |
|----------------|-------|-------|---------|
| Court House    | 238   | 208   | 77      |
| Guseman's      | 32    | 27    | 7       |
| Jones's        | 64    | 21    | 50      |
| Osborne's      | 12    | 12    | 1       |
| Ross's         | 64    | 57    | 16      |
| Loftus's       | 55    | 70    | 7       |
| Cassville      | 108   | 93    | 6       |
| Cushman's      | 63    | 30    | 33      |
| Laurel Point   | 82    | 53    | 27      |
| Cox's          | 44    | 31    | 11      |
| Mooresville    | 47    | 46    | 15      |
| Tenant's       | 33    | 23    | 6       |
| Darrah's       | 25    | 24    | 13      |
| Warren         | 100   | 100   | 10      |
|                | 967   | 795   | 279     |

**Talking Slack Water.** The opening of the railroad to Fairmont stimulated efforts to bring slack water to the head of the Monongahela. The Monongahela Navigation Company had been chartered by the general assembly March 10, 1847, for that purpose, but no funds were available.

At a meeting held at the courthouse in Morgantown February 24, 1851, a committee of correspondence was appointed and subscriptions were ordered to be taken at eight different points in the county. Meetings were held in Pennsylvania to aid the project by arranging for subscriptions of stock to slack the river from Brownsville south to the state line. It was proposed that Monongalia and Marion counties raise $30,000, induce

9. *Monongalia Mirror*, May 21, 1853.
10. *Monongalia Mirror*, June 4, 1853.

Baltimore capitalists to invest $50,000 (to provide a connection with the railroad), and then try to get the state to subscribe $120,000. But, although a strong effort was made, the project failed.

Another meeting was held in 1852, to take steps to have the company's charter extended. This was done by the general assembly in March 1853, when it was enacted that work on the dams begin by 1855 and be finished by 1860. The board of public works would subscribe when Pennsylvania had completed its work to the state line. Later that month the Morgantown borough trustees were authorized to submit to a vote a proposition for the borough to subscribe up to $100,000 to the company.

A meeting was held in Morgantown on March 25, 1853, at which time a committee was appointed to go to Pittsburgh to solicit aid. The Pennsylvania navigation company was not proceeding with its work according to the terms of its charter and Morgantown citizens appointed another committee, in the spring of 1853, to bring suit against the company to compel it to go ahead or forfeit its charter. On November 26 the borough authorized by vote the levying of a tax to enable the committee to prosecute the suit. James Dunlap was employed as attorney. No suit was brought, however, as the Pennsylvania company got its charter extended.[11]

Practically every issue of the *Monongalia Mirror* throughout 1853 contained lengthy discussions of slack water.

**The Monongahela Belle.** The first, and only, steamboat to be built at the Deckers Creek boatyards was the *Monongahela Belle*, constructed by David B. Lynch and launched November 4, 1853. It ran from Morgantown for some time and then was sold to run on the "lower trade," farther downstream.[12]

One other steamboat was built in the county, at Ice's Ferry, about 1846. This was the *Lady Ellicott*, but it did not prove successful.[13]

Numerous flatboats had been built at Morgantown in pioneer times (*Monongalia Story*, vol. 2, pp. 180-82).

11. Wiley, pp. 127, 128; Callahan, *Making of Morgantown*, p. 180.
12. Wiley, p. 542.
13. Wiley, pp. 541, 542.

Lynch was also constructing barges for transportation of heavy materials. On April 20, 1853, he launched a barge "built for the coal trade below. The boat measured . . . 120 feet long by 20 wide, and its capacity twelve thousand bushels."[14]

**The Col. Morgan.** "On Friday morning last, the new and handsome steamer *Col. Morgan*, Capt. Wm. Kincaid, made her first appearance at this port. She was built at Brownsville, expressly for the up-river trade—is 125 feet keel, and 24 feet beam—draws 15 inches water.—The accommodations for passengers are ample and comfortable. . . . We learned, with peculiar pleasure, from the Captain, that this is, and will continue to be, a *Temperance boat—having no bar on board.* "[15]

**The Female Seminary.** By autumn the new girls' school building was nearing completion:

"The Female Seminary building, at the Southern extreme of High Street, is already under roof. When completed it will be decidedly an ornament to the town. It occupies a most beautiful and delightful situation, commanding a fine view of our Southern environs, which are not without their bright particular spots, to attract the eye and call up emotions of admiration.

"And, by the way, there is not within an hundred miles, a community so well adapted, in its pervading moral and religious sentiment, for the presence of an Institution for the education and training of 'the gentler sex' as that of Morgantown."[16]

The new school had bright prospects, which, however, were not to be fully realized:

"Had the Rev. Gordon Battelle,[17] an experienced educator and leader among the Methodists," says Ambler, "accepted the principalship of the Female Academy when it was offerred to him in 1853, he doubtless would, as desired by Trustee Waitman T. Willey, have developed it into a popular church sponsored institution. In the absence of effective leadership the

14. *Monongalia Mirror*, April 23, 1853.
15. *Monongalia Mirror*, April 9, 1853.
16. *Monongalia Mirror*, October 1, 1853.
17. See George J. Blazier, "The Pioneer Battelles and Their Contributions to the Building of Ohio and West Virginia," *West Virginia History* 15 (1954):258-68. Gordon Battelle was born November 14, 1814, and died August 7, 1862. See also Wilding, *Promoted Pioneer Preachers*, pp. 11-15.

school was however a struggling institution, sometimes referred to as the 'Methodist Seminary.' "[18]

**Harmony Grove Church.** When the old Presbyterian Church ("Burnt Meeting House"), about four miles south of Morgantown on the west side of the river, was destroyed by fire in 1845 (see p. 268), it was not rebuilt. Some of the Presbyterians united with the group on Dents Run to build the Sugar Grove church (see p. 343), and others joined with Baptists and Methodists of the Harmony Grove community to build a church in their own neighborhood. It was specifically stated in the deed for the church lot that it was to be for Episcopalians, Presbyterians, Methodist Episcopals, and Methodist Protestants.[19] A meeting was held October 8, 1853, "for the purpose of selecting a site and adopting laws and regulations by which said organization should be governed and maintained. . . . This house is to be used for the worship of God and to be a union meeting house." The meeting nominated Rawley Evans, president, and Ulysses Camp, secretary. Jesse Holland, Rawley Evans, and John Camp, Sr., were appointed trustees.[20]

**Zoar Church Dedicated.** "The meeting-house of the Zoar Baptist Church, situate 1½ miles north of Laurel Point, in this county, was dedicated to the worship of God on Sunday last, the 15th inst. The sermon was preached by Elder James Wood, of Ritchie County, who is assisting the pastor, Eld. Conn, in a protracted meeting."[21]

**Columbia Mouser.** Great excitement was caused in District No. 1 in April 1853 when a little girl named Columbia Mouser wandered away from her home and was lost in the woods. Friends hunted her for two days without success and then the entire neighborhood joined in the search. Jesse Sypolt was fortunate enough to find her at last, when she was nearly dead from hunger and fatigue. On the signal that she had been found, all the searchers gathered at her father's house. William Squires counted them and found they numbered 240 persons.[22]

18. *History of Education in West Virginia*, p. 83.
19. Deeded by Rufus Conn and wife.
20. Dodds and Dodds, *Churches of Monongalia County*, p. 103.
21. *Monongalia Mirror*, October 21, 1853.
22. Wiley, p. 633; *Monongalia Mirror*, April 23, 1853.

**Rev. George Amos.**[23] George Amos, a son of the Reverend
Henry Amos, early Monongalia County pioneer, died August 11, 1853. He was born on Indian Creek August 26, 1794,
and followed farming and cattle-raising most of his life; he
owned a farm of 240 acres of good land. He served at Norfolk,
Virginia, for a period of three months during the War of 1812.

Like his father, he was a licensed exhorter and local minister
in the Methodist Episcopal church. He had a good education for
the day and did considerable writing, some of which has been
preserved. He cleared off his farm, field by field, for a series of
grain crops and never plowed any of his land once it had come
into sod.

In 1818 he married Ida Hawkins, daughter of Rev. William
Hawkins, an herb doctor. Soon after the marriage they moved
to Paw Paw Creek, where they were among the pioneer settlers.
They had fourteen children, including Henry, Mary Ann (married Joshua Shuman), Asel, Rezin, Rhoda (married N. J. Snodgrass), John, Stephen, Elizabeth (married William Bell), Dorcas
(married George W. Smith), Zenia (married C. W. Satterfield),
Edgar W., George M., William T., and Bennett S.

**Jacob Zinn.** Jacob Zinn, of German lineage, died at what was
formerly called Monongalia Glades, in 1853, at the age of
eighty-four.[24] He was a pioneer Monongalia County settler,
having come from the vicinity of Hagerstown, Maryland. He
married Mrs. Sallie Bland, nee Byrne. Among their children
were William B. Zinn[25] and Parmelia, who married Samuel B.
Brown, of Preston County.

**Nicholas Pickenpaugh.**[26] Nicholas B. Pickenpaugh, prominent
Morgantown businessman of the second quarter of the nineteenth century, died November 5, 1853, during the great fever
epidemic of that year. He was born near Jimtown in Monongalia
County June 20, 1804.

He learned the trade of edge tool maker with James Chad-

23. *Cyclopedia of Marion County*, pp. 235, 238.
24. *Cyclopedia of Monongalia County*, p. 181.
25. He was a member of the convention that framed the constitution
for the new state of West Virginia.
26. *Cyclopedia of Monongalia County*, p. 39; *Monongalia Mirror*, November 12, 1853.

wick, who then supplied such tools over a wide area surrounding Morgantown. As this line of handmade tools came to be supplanted by machine-made tools, he learned the trade of blacksmith, which he followed for several years. He also spent some time in the mercantile business, and was a thoroughgoing businessman.

He was married twice, the first time to Abigail Chadwick (October 21, 1809-July 9, 1840), daughter of James Chadwick, by whom he had seven children, including Thornton and Abigail (married F. M. Durbin). After her death he married Eliza Jane Kauffman, by whom he had no children.

**Baltzer Kramer.** One of the early Monongahela Valley glassmakers, Baltzer Kramer (*Monongalia Story*, vol. 2, p. 233) died at Crawford's Landing, Pennsylvania, in 1853, at the age of seventy-seven. He was among the workers brought in by Albert Gallatin and worked at first in a plant on Georges Creek, making the first glass manufactured west of the Allegheny Mountains, much of it sold in Monongalia County. Later they built a larger plant on the banks of the Monongahela, one mile below Greensboro, at a place known for many years as the "Old Glass Works" (see map, *Monongalia Story*, vol. 2, p. 7). He married Jane, daughter of Theophilus Phillips and they had six children, including Theophilus Kramer.[27]

**Thomas Haymond.** Thomas Haymond, county surveyor of Harrison County, died August 31, 1853. He was a son of Major William and Cassandra Haymond and was born January 11, 1776, in Monongalia Glades, Monongalia (now Preston) County. Although but a boy he served a tour as a scout in the Indian wars, stationed at Salem.

He married Rebecca Bond January 6, 1803. He served in various county offices and succeeded his father as surveyor, serving from his father's death in 1821 (*Monongalia Story*, vol. 2, p. 472) until his own death in 1853.[28]

**Asa Shinn.** One of the most distinguished members of the pioneer Shinn family (*Monongalia Story*, vol. 2, pp. 32, 33, etc.),

27. *Cyclopedia of Monongalia County,* p. 169.
28. Henry Haymond, *History of Harrison County* (1910), p. 380; Davis, *History of Harrison County,* p. 422; *Monongalia Mirror,* September 17, 1853.

Asa Shinn, died at Brattleboro, Vermont, February 11, 1853. The son of Jonathan and Mary (Clark) Shinn, he was born May 3, 1781, in New Jersey, and moved with his family to the Monongahela Valley frontier at an early age. He was only sixteen when he began neighborhood preaching and at eighteen was appointed to the Monongahela Circuit by the Baltimore Methodist Episcopal Conference. In 1822 he was made presiding elder of the Pittsburgh District. In 1829, however, he, with numerous others, left the Methodist Episcopal Church and helped to found the Methodist Protestant Conference. In the next several years he was chosen for many important positions, including president of the Ohio Conference (1829), president of the Pittsburgh Conference (1833), president of the General Conference in Baltimore (1842), etc.

He was a prolific writer, his first book, *An Essay on the Plan of Salvation*, being published in 1813 (reprinted, 1831). His most important work, placing him "among the profound thinkers of the world," was *The Benevolence and Rectitude of the Supreme Being* (Philadelphia, 1840).

He was married to Phoebe, daughter of Thomas Barnes, and they had four children, William, James, Eliza, and Mary. His second wife was Mrs. Mary Bennington (Wrenshall) Gibson, daughter of John Wrenshall.[29]

**Land Grants Made in 1853.** Grants of Monongalia County lands were made in 1853 to:

| | | |
|---|---|---|
| Inskeep, John F. | 300 a. | Dunkard Creek |
| Tower, Edwin W. | 300 | Dunkard Creek |

**Borough Government.** Trustees of the borough of Morgantown sworn into office in 1853 were I. Scott, J. E. Fleming, J. R. Drabell, D. H. Chadwick, E. P. Fitch, D. B. Lynch, and M. Chalfant.

**The Post Office is Moved.** On April 6 James Shay was appointed Morgantown postmaster, succeeding Nicholas B. Madera, who had served in that capacity for more than thirty years. The post office was moved from Front Street, next door to the *Mirror*, to High Street, a few doors north of the bank.

Simeon Siegfried commented:

29. Josiah H. Shinn, *History of the Shinn Family in Europe and America* (1903), pp. 133, 134; Smeltzer, *Methodism*, pp. 130, 131.

"It is worthy of a passing remark that Mr. Madera (a uniform Democrat) was appointed by a Whig President and dismissed by a Democratic one."[30]

Editor Siegfried was not pleased by the change. In the first place, the site was by no means as convenient as it had been. And the new postmaster, perhaps because he was new to the job, did not give as satisfactory service. The public in general seems to have given him a hard time and there were threats of having him removed. Finally he wrote a long letter to Postmaster General Campbell setting forth his side of the matter; this letter was published in full in a local paper.[31]

**Miscellany.** In 1853: Capt. James Thompson equipped the old Morgantown pottery to operate by steam (Wiley, p. 260). . . . The first "Eclectic" physician to practice in the county was Dr. G. W. John, at Stewartstown (Wiley, pp. 467, 468). . . . U. Griffith and George S. Ray were masters of the Morgantown Masonic Lodge (Wiley, p. 548). . . . D. Haldeman invented a corn planter[32] (Wiley, p. 552). . . . D. H. Chadwick was a prominent Morgantown merchant (Wiley, p. 583). . . . A Sabbath school was organized in the Morgantown Baptist Church (Wiley, p. 595). . . . A Baptist church was built at Smithtown, one of its chief promoters being Daniel Harris (Wiley, p. 626). . . . George James was operating Ice's Ferry across Cheat River (Wiley, p. 680). . . . J. B. Price started a store at Flickersville (Wiley, p. 725). . . . Col. James Evans built a large frame mansion on his farm near Morgantown (Callahan, pp. 80, 81). . . . Jacob H. Shaffer, of the Morgantown Baptist Church, by vote of the congregation in February, was "set apart to improve his gifts in the gospel ministry" (Callahan, p. 159). . . . The meeting of the Northwestern Virginia Baptist Association was held at Morgantown on August 13, using the new Methodist Episcopal meeting house (Callahan, p. 160). . . . Public aid for the poor and unfortunate in Morgantown amounted to $155.37 in 1853, about one-fifth of the borough's total revenue (Callahan, p. 182). . . . Dr. L. K. Hummelshine had an office in Morgantown as "surgeon dentist" (*Monongalia Mirror*, February 5, 1853).

30. *Monongalia Mirror*, April 16, 1853.
31. *Monongalia Mirror*, November 5, 1853.
32. *Monongalia Mirror*, January 8, 1853; he also invented a burglar alarm; *Monongalia Mirror*, February 5, 1853.

# CHAPTER SEVENTY-EIGHT

# 1854

The Monongahela River from the earliest pioneer times gave promise of providing an excellent transportation artery for the county, but at the same time it constituted a very real obstacle to traffic moving in a different direction. The river flowed north approximately through the middle of the county, effectively dividing it into the East Side and the West Side.

Numerous ferries, as early as 1791, were established to get travelers across the river. One was operated across the river at the mouth of Scotts Mill Run; another from the lands of Dudley Evans to those of Reese Bullock; a third crossed the river from lands of George Hollinbaugh to those of Asa Hall; and a fourth from John Collins's at the mouth of Robinsons Run to lands of Jesse Martin. The general assembly, in approving these ferries, established the charge at three pence each for man or horse.

The next year (1792) a ferry was established at Thomas Evans's, near the mouth of Deckers Creek and the ferry at Morgantown soon became the busiest of the eight or ten in the county, some on the Monongahela, some on the Cheat.

But the ferries, at best, required considerable time in waiting. The equipment was often in poor condition and the operation closed for indefinite periods. High water forced a shutdown often lasting several days; ice might prevent crossing in winter. John Core, running a ferry in 1830, advertised in the county newspaper that he had secured some new rope and hoped to give better service in the future.

**The Suspension Bridge.**[1] It can well be imagined how residents of the county longed to see a bridge across the river, binding the two parts of the county closer together. It was proposed and agitated for many years but the magnitude of the project, and its great anticipated cost, caused a long delay before any work actually got under way.

The first important step towards the erection of a bridge was on March 11, 1850, when the general assembly by a special act created the Morgantown Bridge Company, with a capital stock of eighteen thousand dollars, having the authority to build a bridge and to levy reasonable tolls. Three-fifths of the capital was pledged by the state and the remainder was subscribed by May 1850.

By an act of the assembly on March 15, 1851, the capital was increased to twenty-eight thousand dollars. The stockholders, at a meeting held at the courthouse on July 5, 1851, elected Edgar C. Wilson, president, and Waitman T. Willey and James T. Davis directors, to act with three directors, John Rogers, Nicholas Pickenpaugh, and Guy R. C. Allen, chosen by the state.

The beginning of construction was delayed by negotiations with Jesse Mercer, who owned the land selected for the west-side approach. He also operated a ferry at that point and was faced with the loss of his business. The company offered him a price for his ground and stipulated that the ferry be moved to another site during construction. Mercer then presented claims for future damages and these required considerable time for adjustment.

Another cause of delay was likely the delinquency of sub-scribers, who were slow in paying for their stock until they could see evidence of substantial progress being made.

Dr. Isaac Scott was practicing medicine in Morgantown at the time and had patients on both sides of the river. In crossing to the west side he must use the ferry, or, at periods of low water, he would ford the stream, as did many others. One afternoon in February he was called to Fairmont and crossed at the Walnut Street ford without difficulty. On his return the next morning he found the river had risen quite high. In an attempt to ride across the swift stream, his horse was swept from under him,

1. See Wiley, pp. 133, 588.

and his life was endangered. Although encumbered by heavy boots, he held onto the bridle of his horse, which managed to swim ashore.

Following this experience Dr. Scott earnestly agitated the bridge proposal and used the county newspaper in an unusual way to keep the subject before the people. In a series of anonymous articles continued for several months, he would, in one piece, give an argument for building the bridge, the next week answering his own letter by giving possible objections to it. In turn he answered these objections conclusively in favor of the bridge. The articles continued so long that everybody was talking about the bridge and finally the subscriptions were paid up.[2]

In March 1853, the company authorized its president, E. W. Tower, to procure plans and specifications of the Fairmont suspension bridge, which had been completed in 1852. Soon thereafter bids were called for, resulting in contracts with Kelly and Kennett, of Fairmont, for the stone work for the towers and abutments; with J. H. Sandusky, of New Geneva, Pennsylvania, for the stone work for the anchorage; with Dewey and Company, of Wheeling, for the wire anchors; and with John Downey for the wire cables. Much of the material for the construction arrived on the steamers *Monongahela Belle* and *Forest City*.

In October 1853, permission was granted by the Morgantown borough trustees to occupy and use the lower end of Pleasant Street for the eastern abutment, cables, and anchors.

Financial difficulties threatened to slow the project, and finally, by an act of the general assembly in February 1854, the capital was increased to thirty-six thousand dollars.

Morgantown residents watched with great interest the progress of construction: "The suspending of the Bridge cables was completed on Saturday afternoon last."[3]

"The workmen are now planking the way leading up to the Eastern abutment, and filling and grading the street leading to the Bridge. The prospect of its being ready for winter crossing is quite fair at present."[4]

"The Suspenders and pendant joice are up two-thirds of the

2. Callahan, *Making of Morgantown*, p. 178 note.
3. *Monongalia Mirror*, October 14, 1854.
4. *Monongalia Mirror*, October 28, 1854.

Fig. 71. The Morgantown suspension bridge, built in 1854.

409

whole length, and in two or three days foot passengers may cross on the planks.—The toll-house is also up, and will be in readiness to receive the *spoils* by the time the Bridge is ready to take toll."[5]

At last, on the sixteenth of December 1854, the bridge was completed, having cost nearly thirty thousand dollars. Rates of toll were fixed, ranging from one cent per hog and three cents per pedestrian to fifteen cents for a one-horse vehicle and fifty cents for a four-horse vehicle. Some county residents still retain copies of annual passes for their family. A local newspaper told the story of the completion:

"It affords us pleasure to announce to the traveling public, that the Bridge over the River at this place was completed on Saturday last. It is a most substantial as well as a handsome structure, and is vastly convenient at this season of the year. Its solidity has already been pretty well tested, as several wagons from Oliphant's Works, each drawn by six horses and heavily laden with iron, have already crossed, producing scarcely a perceptible depression upon the cables."[6]

The completion of the bridge was one of the great landmarks in the history of the county. A safe and sure means was now provided for crossing the river at all seasons of the year.

**Clinton Furnace.**[7] Booths Creek enters the Monongahela River a few miles south of Morgantown, having cut for itself a deep channel through the hills, its headwaters far back on the slopes of Chestnut Ridge. Originally heavy forests of chestnut, oak, maple, hickory, walnut, and other trees covered the entire area. "The wolf howled here by day, and the panther screamed by night," said W. Scott Garner, an early historian. Wolves were still here in 1825, when the last bear is said to have been killed by Samuel Brown.

In the middle of the nineteenth century a fair-sized community was developing in the valley, with Clinton Furnace as the business and social center, promising to become a small town.

Early settlers in the Booths Creek area (some of whom

5. *Monongalia Mirror*, November 11, 1854.
6. *Monongalia Mirror*, December 23, 1854.
7. See Wiley, pp. 258, 262, 609, 610, 616, 617, 622, 630; pers. comm., W. H. Phillips, Troy, Michigan.

worked at the furnace) included John Frederick, Sr., Henry Banks, John Phillips, David Sayer, and Thomas Evans. James Jeffs settled here in 1810, buying land from William Buchannon. Benjamin Thorn had already, in 1803, started a gristmill and he sold his property to Jeffs. James Jeffs's son, John, a man of unusual business capacity, built a tannery about 1813. An improved gristmill, with a sawmill, was built about 1819, and a carding machine was added. The place was then called Jeffstown.

Hadley Johnson and his wife Rachel came from Washington County, Pennsylvania, in 1829, purchased the Jeffs property, and carried on the various business enterprises. About 1832 Abraham Pearl opened a small store, although it was not very successful and did not operate very long.

The community's busiest days began about 1846, when William Salyards came from Taylor County and purchased the property of John Frederick, Sr. Salyards had been connected with an iron furnace business in Taylor County and he commenced building a furnace along Booths Creek. This was the golden age of the Cheat iron works; the demand for iron was growing rapidly, and the industry gave great promise.

Salyards named his project Clinton Furnace, but its promise was scarcely borne out. About a year after it was commenced, the property passed into the hands of George D. Evans, Plummer Fitch, and Alfred Dorsey. They leased the furnace, about 1848, to Robert H. Bendle and John Burns, who did make the first iron, ran the furnace for a short time, and then failed. Dr. Watson Carr and George D. Evans were the next owners but they did not make any iron.

About 1853 the furnace was sold to George Hardman, who came from Courhessen, Germany. Alexander Campbell helped him financially at Wheeling, where he built the Cresson rolling mill. Hardman put the furnace, a quarter-stack, into production and operated it for several years. He made coke in ground ricks and put in a hot blast system.[8] Much of the manufactured iron was apparently shipped downstream by boat, as indicated by the following news item: "A boat containing 101 tons of pig

8. About 1858 Hardman made an assignment to Benjamin Ryan, who made the last iron. Hardman went on to Preston County, where he built Irondale Furnace in 1859 and Gladesville Furnace in 1870.

metal, from Clinton Furnace . . . , was sunk a few days since, at the 'Little Falls'. . . . It is said the loss is covered by insurance."[9]

In the growing community O. B. Johnson opened a general store in 1852 and continued the business for many years, even after the failure of the iron industry, selling to farmers over a wide area.[10] Clinton Furnace School (*School No. 6*) stood near the iron furnace.

Old-timers, a hundred years ago, emphasizing the fact that apples grow well in the area, told of three varieties, of great local popularity, which are said to have originated in Clinton District. One of these was the "Morgan Reds," from the Revolutionary War militiamen who fought the Indians; another was the "Granny Sweets," named for Polly Miller, wife of Thomas Miller, and the third was the "Grubb Cabin" apple, which originated at the log cabin of an early settler named Grubb.

Clinton Furnace was never served by a main traveled road. But the old road to Pettyjohn's Ferry and Clarksburg ran nearby and later the Evansville Pike was constructed from Morgantown to intersect the Northwestern Virginia Turnpike at Evansville; it, too, ran close to the community.[11]

**The Album.** A paper called the *Album* was issued about 1854 by Simeon Siegfried, Jr., and was said to have been a sixteen-page monthly. It was devoted to the interests of the Independent Order of Odd Fellows, but was published for only a short time.[12] No copies have been seen.

**Rock Forge Church.**[13] Sometime after the Reverend Ashby Poole came to Monongalia County in 1810, he organized a Sunday school in a log schoolhouse along the banks of Deckers Creek in the Rock Forge community. In 1854 a Methodist congregation was organized from this group and a church lot was

9. *Monongalia Mirror*, April 29, 1854.
10. About 1859 Johnson built a new sawmill and gristmill, but abandoned the tannery and carding business.
11. Today Clinton Furnace seems to have returned to the original forested condition, its furnace in ruins and forgotten, as are the nearby cave whose walls bear the names of many visitors, and the once well-known red sulphur springs.
12. Wiley, pp. 427, 436.
13. Dodds and Dodds, *Churches of Monongalia County*, p. 85.

purchased from William Horner and wife. The group began a building sixteen by twenty feet in size, which, however, they were unable to complete at that time (see p. 660).

Fig. 72. Wadestown, showing the covered bridge across a branch of Dunkard Creek, and the Baptist and Methodist churches, on the hill. (From a painting by Donley L. Stiles.)

**West Warren Baptist Church.** The Baptist congregation at Wadestown was organized in 1854 by William Haines, J. M. Haught, and J. DeGarmo. Members of the new church body had been previously affiliated with the Union Baptist Church of Cross Roads, Saint Paul's Baptist Church of Fairview, and Harmony Baptist Church of Burton. Twelve members constituted the original congregation. They adopted a church covenant, rules of decorum and articles of faith. The church was located on a hillside above the town and worshippers had to climb fifty-five steps to reach it.[14]

**The Western Virginia Conference.** The Western Virginia Conference of the Methodist Protestant Church was organized in 1854. The Methodist Protestant churches of this area had at

14. Dodds and Dodds, *Churches of Monongalia County*, p. 131. The first church building had loose siding that made a "squeaky" noise, so some years later it was taken down and rebuilt.

first been included in the Ohio Conference, organized at Cincinnati October 15, 1829. This conference included all the territory west of the Allegheny Mountains. In 1833 the Ohio Conference was divided, the Sandusky and Scioto rivers forming the dividing line. The western portion retained the name Ohio Conference, while the eastern portion, including the Monongalia County churches, was called the Pittsburgh Conference.

At a session of the Pittsburgh Conference in 1854, the southern churches were set off into the Western Virginia Conference.[15] All ministers appointed to pastorates within the territory of the new district automatically became members of the new conference, which extended from Pennsylvania on the north to the Great Kanawha River on the south, and from the top of the Allegheny Mountains west to the Ohio River. Twenty-four charges were included.

In Monongalia County there were reported 912 members, four local preachers, and eleven church buildings, valued at thirteen thousand dollars.[16]

**A County Fair?** On December 24, 1854, the Monongalia Agricultural and Mechanical Society was organized at a meeting in the courthouse. Col. James Evans was elected president, M. M. Dent secretary, and William Wagner treasurer. The society sought to buy grounds on the west side of the Monongahela River so as to start a county fair; the effort, however was not successful.[17]

**Stone-ware.** "The first kiln of Stone-ware ever manufactured in Morgantown, was burned this week at the Pottery of the Messrs. Thompson and from the specimens taken from the kiln, we are gratified to state the experiment has proven entirely successful. The enterprising proprietors of the well known establishment have put up the appliances necessary for the manufacture of every variety of Stone-ware, so that hereafter that article will be an article of export instead of import, as formerly, at our wharf."[18]

15. Renamed West Virginia Conference in 1863.
16. Wiley, p. 448; Barnes, *Methodist Protestant Church in West Virginia*, p. 471.
17. Wiley, *History of Monongalia County*, p. 248.
18. *Monongalia Mirror*, July 22, 1854.

**Building Barges.** Boat construction at the Morgantown yards continued through the year. A local paper commented: "The Boat Yard of Messrs. Lynch & Hagans (that *Bee-Hive* of the Monongahela in Virginia) presented a lively aspect on Monday last. A large cotton-barge built to order for a Southern firm, which had been finished for the water since August, was launched, and set afloat for its destination. Two very large coal barges were also in waiting for the freshet, and had been finished several weeks."[19]

**Thomas Smith, Shoemaker.** The son of Enos and Airy (Pitts) Smith, Thomas was born near Middlebourne, Tyler County, September 24, 1824, and learned the trade of cobbler from his uncle, Clayton Kearns, who lived nearby. In 1854 he came to Morgantown and on September 26 of that year was married to Barsheba B. Morgan, daughter of Clement Morgan.[20]

**New Post Offices.** A new post office, called Fort Martin, replaced the one previously known as Dornicktown. Joseph Snider, Jr., was the first postmaster, appointed May 16, 1854.

In the western part of the county, a post office called Miracle Run was established. Adam B. Tennant was the first postmaster, appointed June 6, 1854.

A post office called Pridevale (from the Pridevale Iron Works) succeeded the Ice's Ferry post office in 1854. Dr. Nathaniel Hoffman Triplett was appointed postmaster effective December 8, 1854.

**McCurdysville Or Center.** A small village was developing at the head of Little Paw Paw Creek, near the old state road (see *Monongalia Story*, vol. 2, p. 237), about fifteen miles west of the county seat. The community was locally known as McCurdysville, from the family of early settler Benjamin McCurdy, but in 1854 a post office was established, called Center. William Case was the first postmaster, his appointment effective July 3, 1854. The village consisted of a mill, a store, a church, the post office, and several dwelling houses.

19. *Monongalia Mirror*, December 2, 1854.
20. *Cyclopedia of Marion County*, p. 141. Smith did not remain long here, but moved, first to Farmington, then to Mannington, where he successfully operated his shop for many years and had an important role in the civic life of the community, including one term as mayor.

**Pridevale Iron Works.** In an effort to revive the ailing Monongalia County iron industry, the Pridevale Iron Company was chartered March 5, 1854, by Samuel McKelvey, John G. Holbrook, Ira Hersey, and others, to manufacture iron and other articles. The capital stock was set at one hundred thousand dollars to $1 million with shares at one hundred dollars each. The lands were limited to twenty thousand acres in Monongalia and Preston counties.[21]

**Kinsley Buys Valley Furnace.** The Valley Furnace at Rock Forge was purchased in 1854 by John Kinsley, who ran it for the next four years, the end of its history.

Kinsley was born in Ireland in 1827 and migrated to America with his father's family. He married Elizabeth J. Frum in 1858 and they had eight children, James A., John A., E. S., George H., Samuel A., Ida M., Margaret M., and Elizabeth. He was among the gold-seekers who went to California in 1849.[22]

**Deaths.** Among deaths during the year were Mrs. Margaret Prentis, wife of Jonathan Prentis, aged eighty;[23] Charles Madera, son of Nicholas;[24] and Henry Lazier, of Wheeling, formerly of Morgantown.[25]

**Isaiah Prickett Dies.** Isaiah Prickett, of the distinguished Prickett family that built Prickett's Fort, in pioneer Monongalia County, died November 7, 1854. He was born January 10, 1779, the son of Josiah Prickett and grandson of Jacob Prickett, one of the three brothers who built the fort (*Monongalia Story*, vol. 1, pp. 348-50; vol. 2, p. 100).

Isaiah married Sarah Ross and they had the following children: Levi, Henry, Nathan, Meredith, John, Eli, Maria, Ira, and Margaret. He was a farmer and ferryman near the fort.[26]

**James Hamilton Dies.** James Hamilton, a former resident of Monongalia County, died in Fairmont, Marion County, on October 10, 1854, at the age of seventy-four years. He was a son of Henry and Elizabeth (Fry) Hamilton, and came with his

21. Wiley, p. 682.
22. Wiley, p. 643.
23. *Monongalia Mirror*, March 4, 1854.
24. *Monongalia Mirror*, April 22, 1854.
25. *Monongalia Mirror*, May 13, 1854.
26. *Cyclopedia of Marion County*, p. 88.

parents to Monongalia County at an early age. In 1820 he purchased a farm on Plum Run and moved there; ten years later he moved to Middletown (later Fairmont).[27]

**Alexander Eddy Dies.** Alexander Eddy, a farmer of District No. 6, died January 1, 1854, at the age of ninety years. The family, of German origin, had located first in New Jersey but came to Monongalia County at an early date, one of "that host of pioneers who were clearing this region, and preparing it for the cultivation of the arts of husbandry." He married Margaret Kuhn and they had a large family of children, including Alexander, Jr., a farmer of Battelle Township, who was born November 17, 1802.[28]

**George W. Fleming Dies.** George W. Fleming, a former resident of Morgantown, died at Sandusky, Ohio, in April 1854. He was born at Mount Pleasant, Pennsylvania, and came to Morgantown about 1844, with his brother, John, and they opened the first drugstore in Morgantown. During his stay here he also organized and instructed what is said to have been Morgantown's first brass band.

He married Sarah J. Evans, daughter of Col. Rawley Evans, and they had two children, Julian E. and Elizabeth.[29]

**Dunkard Creek Pioneer Taken by Death.** Abraham Brown, an early pioneer settler of the Dunkard Creek section, died September 27, 1854. He was born in 1787, the son of Adam and Christina Brown. He married Elizabeth Core, daughter of Michael Core (*Monongalia Story*, vol. 2, p. 419) and they had the following children: Catherine, Michael C., Adam C., Jacob, Christina, John, William, George, and Norval, besides two children who died in a typhoid fever epidemic in 1851. He operated a farm and built a gristmill on Dunkard Creek at Core's ford.[30]

**Land Grants Made in 1854.** Monongalia County only grantee of state lands in 1854 was:

McGraw, Leonard                    20 a.   Lick Run

27. *Cyclopedia of Marion County*, p. 17.
28. *Cyclopedia of Monongalia County*, p. 197.
29. *Cyclopedia of Monongalia County*, p. 132.
30. *Cyclopedia of Monongalia County*, p. 123; *Chronicles of Core*, p. 78.

**County Government.** John T. Fleming[31] was elected sheriff. Michael R. Chalfant was elected assessor of the Eastern District.

**Miscellany.** In 1854: The summer was known for years afterwards as the "Dry Summer" (Wiley, p. 246). . . . The Woodgrove Furnace was being operated by Dr. Meredith Clymer, who put in a hot-blast (Wiley, pp. 256, 257). . . . The Fairchild Lawhead and Company carriage works were expanded (Wiley, p. 261 note). . . . James P. Smith was admitted to the county bar (Wiley, p. 318). . . . H. W. Emery was appointed principal of Morgantown Female Academy (Wiley, p. 399). . . . Homeopathic medicine was introduced to Morgantown by Dr. A. C. Miller (Wiley, pp. 468, 584). . . . Celia Wade died at the age of ninety-three (Wiley, p. 472). . . . The Rivesville and New Brownsville Turnpike was incorporated (Wiley, p. 539). . . . W. C. Wilson opened a store at Smithtown (Wiley, p. 615). . . . A. J. Stewart was keeping a store at Stewartstown (Wiley, p. 673). . . . Christian Jennewine migrated from Prussia and settled in the Cheat Neck area (Wiley, p. 691 note). . . . William Fear was running a store at Flickersville (Wiley, p. 725). . . . G. A. Burke opened a shop for making wagons at Blacksville (Wiley, p. 745). . . . Alexander Hayes bought from Sarah Hanway the old Hanway brick mansion house, on Lot 19 in Morgantown, known as the Washington Hotel (Callahan, pp. 100, 118, 188). . . . A new type of washing machine was invented by Elijah Morgan (Callahan, p. 175 note). . . . The Morgantown borough trustees were spending a considerable amount of money on general street repairs (Callahan, p. 184). . . . A brick office building was erected on Chancery Row by W. T. Willey (Callahan, p. 189).

31. For biography, see Wiley, p. 713.

# CHAPTER SEVENTY-NINE

# 1855

The wars with the Indians in northern Oregon between 1854 and 1857 involved, first of all, some former Monongalia County residents who had moved to Oregon, and, as the war continued, men from the county who volunteered for military service. As in all previous wars in which the country was engaged, Monongalia County men were there.

The coast of Oregon had been explored in 1543 by the Spanish under Sir Francis Drake. The Lewis and Clark expedition in 1804-1806 also established American claims to the territory.

A treaty between the United States and Spain, in 1819, fixed the southern boundary of Oregon, and the territory to the north was left to the United States and Great Britain. A threatening dispute arose between the two countries, as American settlers came into the Willamette valley in 1843 and organized a provisional government at Champoeg. This dispute gave rise to the rallying cry, "54-40 or fight," but was settled peacefully by a treaty in 1846.

**The Oregon War.** Wiley[1] tells the story of our participation in the Indian war: "It was the result of a general outbreak of the Indians along the Oregon and Washington frontiers. They had over 3,500 warriors engaged in the contest. Colonel Frank W. Thompson, of Monongalia, commanded Company A, 1st regiment Oregon mounted volunteers, which was afterwards reorganized as Company C, Battalion Oregon and Washington mounted rangers. Dallas Price and Oliver Price, two brothers who were descendants of the old Indian-fighting Morgans, and

1. *History of Monongalia County*, pp. 496, 497.

who were born and reared in Monongalia County, were in Thompson's company.

"Among the hottest contests of this war was a four-days fight on the Walla Walla River, at the point where Fort Bennett now stands—which fort, it is said, was named in honor of Captain Bennett, of Marion County, who was killed in that battle. The Indians were commanded by Peopeomoxmox, or Yellow Serpent, one of the most famous chiefs ever on the Pacific Coast. During the fight, Colonel Thompson saw this chief killed by a Missouri soldier named Sam Warfield, who knocked him in the head with his gun and afterwards scalped him, in retaliation for outrages committed by his warriors. After the chief had been scalped, Oliver Price cut a piece of skin from his back, had it tanned, and made a razor strop of it—another illustration of the savage hostility existing between the Morgan blood and the Indian race."

Fig. 73. John T. Fleming. (From Brand, *The William Fleming Family.*)

Fig. 74. Morris J. Garrison. (Photo courtesy Virginia Garrison Cole Ayers.)

Frank W. (actually Francis W.) Thompson was born in Morgantown on January 7, 1828. Wiley gives an account of his adventurous life: "He went West in 1850, and crossed the plains in 1852, when there was not a house between the Missouri River and the Cascade Mountains in Oregon. In the Yakima and other wars, he was captain of Company A, First Battalion of Oregon Mounted Volunteers. Col. Thompson learned several Indian languages while on the plains, and can yet speak some of them quite fluently."[2]

**Primary Schools.** State aid for county schools, financed through the Literary Fund, continued to be administered, but without

2. Wiley, pp. 529-31. Thompson's military life did not end with the Oregon War; see pp. 511, 512.

very much effect. Statistics for 1855 indicate that 750 poor children were sent to school, but that the average number attending was only 560 and they attended on the average only seventy-five days each. The average cost per pupil was $2.28 and the county had due from the Literary Fund and $1,080.48.[3]

Of course, many more children (and young people) attended the subscription schools and academies.

**Fertilizing Farms.** As the virgin soil of Monongalia County farms began to "play out," farmers began looking for ways to restore the fertility. James Kerns, of Pleasant Valley, began to use guano with good effect, as early as 1855. Lime was burnt and applied as quick-lime; Wiley[4] gives the nineteenth century view as to its activity, stating that "it imparts fertility partly by being dissolved in the surface waters, and so passing into the soil in such shape that the roots of plants can seize hold of it, but mainly by tending to decompose vegetable matter and so form a fertilizing humus."

"Soluble flour of bone" and "ammoniated super-phosphate" were the favorite fertilizers they purchased, but barnyard manure was the best of all and was available in great abundance.

**The Iron Works Decline.** By 1855 the Monongalia County iron works were fading out rapidly. Soon the old furnaces and other works would be ruins. John Kinsley had closed down his Rock Forge works, which had been in operation since the 1790s. The Davis or Pleasant Furnace had closed long ago. Dr. Meredith Clymer was operating the Woodgrove Furnace and the Anna Furnace, although without much success; he was also operating Cheat works for the Pridevale Iron Company. George Hardman continued to run Clinton Furnace on a small scale.[5]

**The Morgantown Telegraph and The American Union.** A new weekly paper, the *Morgantown Telegraph*, was started in 1855, by John W. Woody and John M. Coil; it was Democratic in politics. It is said to have been twenty-four by thirty-seven inches in size, four pages, and twenty-eight columns. Terms of

3. Wiley, p. 382.
4. *History of Monongalia County*, p. 246.
5. Wiley, pp. 254-58. For John Kinsley, see Wiley, p. 643.

subscription were $1.25 per year, in advance. The name was merely hopeful, since the first telegraph line did not reach Morgantown for many years (see p. 587). The motto was a quotation from Franklin Pierce: "To Preserve Sacred from all Touch of Usurpation, as the very Palladium of our Political Salvation, the Reserved Powers of the Several States and of the People." The paper carried very little local news, and was mainly political. The paper continued for only a few months.[6]

The last issue of the *Monongalia Mirror* appeared on June 23, 1855, and the paper was continued by Simeon Siegfried, Jr., as the *American Union*. The first number of this paper appeared June 30, 1855. It was twenty-four by thirty-six inches in size, four pages, and twenty-eight columns. In politics it was American ("Know Nothing"); its motto was "Liberty and Union, now and forever, one and inseparable."[7]

The paper was violently opposed to foreign immigration and Roman Catholicism. In many editorials it also opposed "Black Republicanism." Like its predecessors, it had financial problems and made frequent appeals to delinquent subscribers to pay up and offered to take various things, including squirrels and rabbits in payment of accounts. Besides financial problems, the paper had trouble with the post office, accusing it of not delivering his papers as promptly as those of the rival paper, the *Virginia Star.*

However, Siegfried, Sr., was perhaps the most scholarly of the early editors and the *Mirror* and *American Union* were excellent papers. The Reverend Mr. Siegfried urged his subscribers to file their papers for future use, and his care in preserving the papers himself provided one of the chief sources for studying the history of the county in his day.

The new name of the paper doubtless reflected editor Siegfried's enthusiasm for the American party:

"Believing the principles of the American party to be the principles of our country, in which are involved the safety and security of our glorious Union, and the perpetuity, beyond all

6. Wiley, pp. 427, 436, 771. The issue for May 31, 1855, has been preserved in the West Virginia University Library.

7. Wiley, pp. 427, 436. Simeon, Jr., was assisted by his father, who later took over the paper.

question, of our civil and religious institutions, we shall promulgate them with all energy and devotion."[8]

**New Inventions.** During 1855 numerous inventions were made by Monongalia County men, including the following: an automatic hand printing press feeder, by E. Mathers and W. D. Siegfried; a corn sheller, by James Nimon; a washing machine, by J. M. Kerns, and another by Daniel Haldeman; and a churn by J. Boyers.[9]

**Stagecoach Service.** Morgantown's system of public transporation was steadily improving and newspapers carried frequent notices of stagecoach (or "hack") service. In August 1855 Laughhead and Company started a new line from Uniontown to Fairmont, via Morgantown. The line operated every other day from Uniontown to Morgantown, and daily from Morgantown to Fairmont, where connections were made with B.&O. passenger trains. In July 1855 a tri-weekly stage line was established between Morgantown and Brownsville, connecting at the latter point with the evening boat to Pittsburgh. The noon stop for dinner was at Lantz's Willow Tree Tavern. Local newspapers carried notices reading: "Through Line! Daily and Tri-Weekly U. S. Mail Stage. Connection between the National Road and Baltimore & Ohio Rail Road."[10]

Steamboats continued to reach Morgantown but their schedules were uncertain because of fluctuations in water level.

**Traffic Accident.** The increasing use of carriages on streets and roads led to a rise in traffic mishaps, of which the following is an example:

"On Tuesday evening last, an old and heretofore well-behaved horse, belonging at Thompson's Pottery, attached to a light carryall, became restive from carelessness in hitching up and driving, ran down Front street and down the steep grade on Walnut street; and in attempting to 'make the turn' round the pottery, horse and wagon were precipitated over the embankment on to the wharf-paving below. Strange as it may seem, no person was hurt, the horse was not seriously injured."[11]

8. *American Union*, June 30, 1855.
9. Wiley, p. 552.
10. Callahan, *Making of Morgantown*, pp. 179, 180; *American Union*, July 21, 1855, August 4, 1855.
11. *American Union*, September 15, 1855.

**Street Improvements.** Streets of Morgantown and its suburbs were still mostly unimproved, except for High, Pleasant, and Walnut, which had been macadamized. Plank sidewalks were being built.

"We understand that the citizens over in Durbannah are about putting down a plank side-walk along their main st. This will add much to their convenience in getting about, and is a needed improvement.

"Our Borough Trustees, it is suggested to us, ought to fill up and repair the mud-hole and sideway at this end of the Creek Bridge, so that pedestrians may pass and repass without damage to the polish of their go-to-meeting boots, gaiters, and wardrobe generally."[12]

**H. W. Biggs New Presbyterian Pastor.** The Reverend Henry Weed Biggs was installed as pastor of the Morgantown Presbyterian Church on November 2. The services were conducted by the Reverend Dr. Ashbel Fairchild, the Reverend Joel Stoneroad, and the Reverend Robert M. Wallace.[13]

Biggs was born at Frankfort, Pennsylvania, May 15, 1828. He graduated from the University of Cincinnati in 1845 and from Princeton Theological Seminary in 1851. He was ordained April 10, 1852, and served as a missionary in Lebanon, Indiana, and stated supply at Princeton before coming to Morgantown.[14]

**Live Oak Paper Mill Destroyed by Fire.** John Rogers's paper mill came to an end in 1855, after a rather hectic existence. Designed to produce paper from rags, and of considerable significance to regional newspapers, it was built in 1839 and paper manufacture begun by Tillton and Crown, who were succeeded by Rogers and Tillton, later by Tillton alone. An unfortunate accident early in 1854 caused the death of the operator, Frederick Truedley, who had leased it only a short time earlier.[15] His lease was then taken over by Charles Arthur, of Beaver, Pennsylvania.

12. *American Union*, November 17, 1855.
13. *American Union*, October 27, 1855, advance notice.
14. Moreland, *First Presbyterian Church*, p. 51.
15. *Monongalia Mirror*, February 4, 1854.

**Fire at Blacksville.** One of the most destructive fires in the nineteenth century history of Monongalia County occurred at Blacksville on April 10, 1855. It started in the daytime in William Launtz's house and was said to have burned twenty-four houses.[16]

**Morgantown Businesses.** Among many business places advertised in local papers were Marble and Stone Cutting, by Burr P. Marsteller, Wool Carding, by Levin Gapen, Tailoring, by T. S. Ewan, and Gun-Smithing, by John K. Shean, who also repaired clocks.[17]

**Flood.** A series of destructive rains occurred early in July:

"Cheat River is reported to have been three feet higher than ever before known. Much damage has doubtless been done. We hear that the Rolling Mill at Pridevale Iron Works was inundated and partly destroyed; 500 pannels of fence, belonging to that company, washed away; and three large boats freighted with fire-brick (same locality), were sunk by the rapid rise of water and drifting trees, logs, &c."[18]

**Henry Runner.** Henry Runner, a Monongalia County farmer, died in 1855. He was born in Frederick County, Maryland, on March 17, 1777, and came to this county about 1810, locating south of Morgantown, where he remained until 1840, when he moved to The Flatts. He was twice married, the first marriage resulting in the birth of two children, who died in early childhood. His second marriage was to Elizabeth Thomas and they had eight children, namely, Michael, William, Daniel, Annie, James K., Henry, Elizabeth, and Lewis W.[19]

**Other Deaths.** Joseph Henderson died July 17, 1855: "he was stacking wheat and fell instantly dead." He was born in May 1777.[20]

Jeremiah Stillwell died July 30, 1855, aged about seventy years.[21]

16. Wiley, p. 744.
17. *American Union*, July 14, 1855.
18. *American Union*, July 14, 1855.
19. *Cyclopedia of Monongalia County*, p. 139.
20. Wiley, p. 633; *American Union*, July 21, 1855.
21. *American Union*, August 4, 1855.

**Land Grants Made in 1855.** Grants of Monongalia County lands were made in 1855 to:

| | | |
|---|---|---|
| Baird, Aaron | 4 a. | Deckers Creek |
| Liming, Reason | 3¾ | Scotts Run |
| Minor, Lancaster | 24¼ | Days Run |
| Moran, Robert | 170 | White Day Creek |

**Borough Government.** Trustees of the borough of Morgantown were Alexander Hayes, Michael Shisler, I. Scott, Daniel Fordyce, Jacob Kiger, James Odbert, and E. P. Fitch.[22]

**Miscellany.** In 1855: Alfred M. Barbour was admitted to the county bar on April 13 (Wiley, p. 316). . . . Lucy A. Lanham died at the age of ninety-three (Wiley, p. 472). . . . H. S. Reed was master of the Masonic lodge (Wiley, p. 548). . . . Drs. L. F. Campbell and M. L. Casselberry were physicians in Morgantown (Wiley, p. 584). . . . A. P. Stewart succeeded A. J. Stewart as storekeeper in Stewartstown (Wiley, p. 673). . . . Thomas M. Jarrett and Thomas Hawkins were operating Ice's Ferry (Wiley, p. 680). . . . A tannery was built at New Brownsville by Andrew Brown (Wiley, p. 746). . . . The brick Protzman House at the southwest corner of Front Street and Bumbo Lane was built (Callahan, p. 189). . . . A catfish weighing 63¾ pounds was caught in the river at Morgantown (Richmond *Dispatch*, June 2, 1855).

22. Wiley, p. 577.

CHAPTER EIGHTY

# 1856

The great almost overwhelming tasks to be accomplished in a developing country left, one would think, little time for recreational and cultural affairs. But, while it is true that the people of early Monongalia County worked hard, they played hard, too, and enjoyed some of the aesthetic things of life.

Some of Richard A. Bartlett's comments are applicable to nineteenth century Monongalia County:

"All sections had annual celebrations, most of them on the Fourth of July. Local talent competed in local tournaments or contests. . . . At other times there were corn-shucking contests . . . and the like. Women had their sewing bees, church dinners, and choir practices. Marriage, with the accompanying shivaree, could be a raucous occasion. Even funerals ended in big family dinners. . . . Halloween from earliest times included such high jinks as the buggy in the hayloft and the privy on the schoolteacher's front yard. An occasional circus, the county fair, and, in later years, a traveling Tom show could add to the interest of life."[1]

Before the end of the 1850s there were three academies operating in Morgantown and the town was already becoming widely known as an educational center, despite (or, probably, because of) its relative inaccessibility. No railroad reached the county and no important turnpike, while steamboat transportation was most unpredictable.

**Literary Societies.** In the serenity of this quiet community numerous literary societies developed, more or less associated with life at the academies.

1. *The New Country* (1974), pp. 397, 398.

The Thespian Literary Society flourished in the 1830s. It was dramatic in nature and the members performed Shakespeare's plays. Thomas P. Ray and Eli B. Swearingen were members.

The Young Men's Society for the Promotion of Literature, Science and Morality was organized at Morgantown in 1843. Wiley[2] said he could find no account of it, except that Waitman T. Willey, R. L. Berkshire, and other prominent men were members. Henry Clay, George McDuffie, and other United States senators were elected honorary members, and responded acknowledging their election. These letters have been preserved.

The Columbian Literary Society was started by students of Monongalia Academy after 1852. It was quite successful and came to have such a large membership that it was divided into two societies, a portion of the members organizing the Monongalian Literary Society. At the commencement exercises in 1856 the subject of a debate between the two societies was "Should Virginia adopt the Maine Liquor Law?"

Morgantown, in the 1850s, then, boasted of academies, printing establishments which produced newspapers, books, and periodicals, libraries both public and private, and flourishing literary societies. With such advantages, Morgantown and a few other little towns in western Virginia "stood as beacons—faint though their gleam may have been—whose rays reached into the recesses of the mountains and shed a glimmering of the light of knowledge upon culturally impoverished areas of the Alleghenies."[3]

**Slack Water Comes Closer.** Between 1854 and 1856 Locks and Dams Nos. five and six, in Pennsylvania, were completed, the slack water then reaching as far as New Geneva. Dam No. 5 was located at Denbo, about three miles above Brownsville, and No. 6 was at Rices Landing.[4]

Now that slack water was almost to the state line, the efforts of the Virginia Navigation Company was renewed but almost nothing was done for many years to extend navigation upstream. As Morgantown people feared, the effects of suspension of improvements gave New Geneva the advantage of being at

2. *History of Monongalia County*, p. 551.
3. Rice, *The Allegheny Frontier*, p. 235.
4. Wiley, *Monongahela: The River and its Region*, p. 167.

the head of navigation, thereby threatening the prosperity of upriver towns. Now that the excitement incidental to construction of the Baltimore and Ohio Railroad was over, relatively few steamboats came to Morgantown.

**The Virginia Weekly Star.** On August 9, 1856, the first issue appeared of a new weekly newspaper called the *Virginia Campaign Star*, with Marshall M. Dent editor and proprietor. A committee appointed by the Democratic party solicited subscriptions for it. Its motto was "Eternal Vigilance is the Price of Liberty." The sheet was twenty-four by thirty-three inches, four pages, twenty-four columns.

On November 15 the word *Campaign* was dropped from the title and it was thereafter issued at $1.50 a year, as a Democratic weekly paper.[5]

**New Inventions.** The ingenuity of Monongalia County citizens continued to come up with new devices to save labor. In 1856 there were notices of a dish saw and a grain sower, invented by James Kerns; a churn, by Dr. H. N. Mackey; and a shingle machine, by H. D. McGeorge. The latter was highly recommended by local newspapers.[6]

**Masontown and Independence Turnpike.** By 1856 turnpikes had been demonstrated not to be profitable, except for the main roads, but a few continued to be incorporated by the general assembly. In this year a road company called the Masontown and Independence Turnpike was organized, branching from the Brandonville and Fishing Creek Turnpike one mile west of Ice's Ferry, running to Masontown, Preston County, and thence to Tunnelton.[7]

**Lowesville.** A post office was established at Lowesville, with Levi Lowe as the first postmaster, his appointment effective February 13, 1856. Mail was delivered twice a week. Lowe was a miller and merchant in the thriving small river town at the mouth of Indian Creek (see pp. 248, 583).

**Union Methodist Church.** Methodists, Presbyterians, and Baptists, on Flaggy Meadow Run near Flickersville, built a log

5. Wiley, pp. 427, 436.
6. Wiley, p. 552; *American Union*, March 15, 1856.
7. Wiley, p. 539.

church on property given by Abraham Shafer to serve the religious needs of the community.[8]

**Mount Union Methodist Protestant Church.** Methodists of the Pierpont community in 1856 built a third church to serve the neighborhood (see pp. 128, 243). The new church was constructed near where the second one stood, and was designed according to the usual style of the times, with two doors and a dividing rail inside separating the men from the women.[9]

"Hurricane!" A severe electric and rain storm, with hurricane-like winds, struck the county on July 30. Trees and fences were blown over, windows blown in. The barn of G. V. Coombs, in the Pierpont area, was struck by lightning and destroyed by the resulting fire. A horse of William Addison, at the mouth of Booths Creek, was killed by a falling tree.

"The wire Suspension Bridge has more than ever proven its firmness and solidity. It was blown, so as to roll perhaps six feet in the flooring, and was lifted sideway once, so as to endanger a buggy crossing over at the time, but sank back to its place, sustaining no injury whatever. The side-cables, which secure the bridge on either side of the river, from being lifted by high winds, is a wise and salutary provision for the permanence of the structure."[10]

**Threshing Machine Accident.** The new threshing machines were still regarded with some well-deserved fear and accidents were reported every summer, similar to this one:

"Jonathan Hoffman, residing near Granville, . . . while engaged in feeding a Threshing Machine on Tuesday last, had his right arm so mutilated that amputation was rendered necessary. The hand was torn from the wrist, and passed through the machine; the arm was horribly torn to the elbow, above which it had to be taken off."[11]

The threshing machines went through the community, stopping at each farm where grain was to be threshed, mostly

8. Dodds and Dodds, *Churches of Monongalia County*, p. 108. During the Civil War there was a split in the church over the slavery question.
9. Dodds and Dodds, *Churches of Monongalia County*, p. 152. Repairs to the building were made in 1873. See *American Union*, June 14, 1856; Barnes, *M. P. Church*, p. 149.
10. *American Union*, August 2, 1856.
11. *American Union*, August 30, 1856.

Fig. 75. A threshing machine at work. (Sketch by Diane Lenhart.)

wheat, but some oats and a little rye. A crew of men followed the machines, mostly farmers exchanging labor with each other.

Christopher Core's ledger for 1854[12] contains a list of farmers for whom he did threshing and amounts he was paid for the work. Thirty-one names appear, including Adam Brown, wheat, $1.40; Jacob Sine, Jr., wheat, $1.10; Jacob Sine, Sr., wheat, $0.96; Isaac Willard, wheat, $0.50; James Berry, wheat, $0.68; Elizabeth Core, wheat, $2.80; Nimrod Barrickman, wheat, oats, $1.75; David Liming, wheat, oats, $1.87 1/2; Asa Suten, wheat, $2.10; and Ezekiel Morris, wheat, rye, $1.25.

**Railroad Schedules.** Mail stages from Morgantown made connections with Baltimore and Ohio Railroad trains at Fairmont and the time of arrival and departure of trains at Wheeling was announced as follows:

Mail Train, arrive 4.14 a.m., depart, 6.58 a.m., daily except Sunday.

Express, arrive 1.53 p.m., depart 4.23 p.m.

12. This old book was loaned by Norman Core, of Wadestown, a descendant of Christopher.

**The Old Stage Coach.** A poem in a local newspaper, lamenting the passing of stagecoach travel in the new railroad age, begins:

> "The good time when our fathers rode
>     In safety by the stage,
> Have passed before the onward march
>     Of this progressive age;
> And now no goodly coach-and-four
>     Draws up before the stage-house door.

> "How rang the laugh, the jest and joke,
>     As all together rode,
> Coach'd up in friendly jollity,
>     Like boys of one abode;
> The weary miles seem'd shorter then
>     As thus we rode o'er hill and glen."

The editor (apparently) added a postscript:

> "Our unknown poet, should he come
>     To Morgantown, he might
> Enjoy the ancient luxury
>     He praises well of right.
> A relic of the days 'lang syne',
>     The jolly stage and four,
> For Hayes & Bright's nice stage and stock
>     Pass daily by our door."[13]

**Beautiful New Coach.** "In addition to the travelling facilities heretofore placed at the disposal of the public by Messrs. Hayes & Bright, the proprietors of the Stage Line between Fairmont (via Morgantown) and Uniontown, they have had built a new commodious and beautiful coach. It was built at the Carriage Manufactory of Messrs. Fairchild, Laughead & Co., Durbanna, and like many other vehicles of their putting up, is a model of artistic workmanship."[14]

**Elcaney C. Bright.** "Uncle Caney" Bright, Morgantown's best known stagecoach driver, was born near Collins Ferry March 5, 1830. When only eleven years old he moved to Morgantown and started driving a wagon. At an early age he started driving a

13. *American Union*, January 19, 1856.
14. *American Union*, June 7, 1856.

stage, running at different times to Uniontown, Fairmont, and Clarksburg. He married Annie Isabell, daughter of Armous Miller, who operated a mill on Scotts Run. They had nine children, including Martha, George, Simeon, Minnie, and Jesse; the others died young.[15]

**Cold Winter.** "The weather, for three days past has been intensely cold, enabling us to sympathize with the crews in the Arctic regions, in search of Sir John Franklin! We don't experience colder weather in this latitude often than 9 deg. below zero, and such it was reported on Wednesday morning, at 7 o'clock; on Thursday morning 6 deg. and on Friday morning 8 deg. below zero. Whew! Rush up the bituminous!"[16]

"On Saturday morning last, the thermometer stood at 15 degrees below zero at daylight, and at 7 o'clock at 14 deg.—the coldest weather we have had for many years in this latitude."[17]

**Winter Activities.** On snow-covered streets and roads, sleighs often replaced carriages, often with melodious bells on the horses:

"We have had, in these parts, since Sunday last, first-rate sleighing, and a snow of 6 to 8 inches deep. There has been, also, on the part of our citizens, grave and gray, a pretty general disposition to enjoy it. A delightful opportunity has thus been afforded, and improved too by very many, of making family and social visits, reviving old friendships, creating new ones, &c., to say nothing of the facilities for love-making among the belles and beaux in the early dawn of Leap-year."[18]

Skating on frozen streams was a favorite sport:

"Deckers Creek has been frozen over tight and strong during the past week. Parties of skaters have been enjoying the sport much in the frosty moonlight for several evenings."[19]

15. *Cyclopedia of Marion County*, pp. 164, 165. "Uncle Caney" removed from Morgantown to Hampshire County in 1881 and continued to operate stages in that section for many years. "It is estimated that during his long experience as a stage-driver, he has traveled a distance that would encircle the globe and claims that he has owned in his lifetime not less than two hundred horses."
16. *American Union*, January 12, 1856.
17. *American Union*, February 2, 1856.
18. *American Union*, January 19, 1856.
19. *American Union*, December 11, 1856.

Fig. 76. Hayes and Bright's stagecoach proceeding down High Street. (Sketch by Diane Lenhart.)

**Carriage Repairing.** Wagons, buggies, and other forms of carriages, increasingly used on the county's roads, required constant repair. Many farmers and others were able to repair their own vehicles; others had neither the equipment, ability, nor time to do this and repair shops were opened:

"Messrs. John Fordyce and Alonzo Lynch have associated themselves in partnership, and have taken the shop lately occupied by Jas. M. Kern, near the Suspension Bridge, where they are prepared to repair carriages, buggies, carryalls, &c., at short notice and in good style. Mr. Fordyce is an excellent Blacksmith, and Mr. Lynch a first rate mechanic and coach maker, so that a patronizing public have every assurance of having work well done by the new firm."[20]

**G. R. C. Allen.** Guy Richard Champlain Allen, a prominent Morgantown attorney, died December 4, 1856. He was born in Wood County, August 18, 1803. He removed to Preston County, where he was appointed prosecuting attorney about 1832 serving until 1852. He was elected to the general assembly in 1828 and again in 1829.

Later he removed to Morgantown, "where he practiced law for many years, and was known as a lawyer of ability throughout the State, and was a very prominent man in Monongalia County during his life. . . . The Monongalia bar [following his death] adopted resolutions testifying to his worth and ability as a man and a lawyer."[21]

**James Miller.** James Miller, formerly a cooper of Morgantown, died near Fairmont on March 19, 1856. He was born near Hartford, Connecticut, in 1780 and migrated to Ohio in 1801. His stay there was not long and he settled in Morgantown, later moving to Greensboro, Pennsylvania, then to Fairmont in 1837. He was an old-line Whig and a member of the Methodist Church.

He married Sarah Messenger and one of their sons, William E. Miller, born in Morgantown July 29, 1822, was a captain in the Mexican War.[22]

20. *American Union*, June 14, 1856.
21. Wiley, p. 342; *American Union*, December 6, December 27, 1855.
22. *Cyclopedia of Marion County*, p. 155. Thomas Condit Miller, a son of William E., was named principal of the preparatory department, West Virginia University, in 1893.

**William Stewart.** William Stewart, of Sugar Grove, son of Stewartstown pioneer settler, John Stewart, died May 10, 1856, at the home of his son, Rev. W. Newton Stewart, having been stricken by paralysis while visiting his son. He was born at Stewartstown in 1783. "He followed the tranquil and peaceful pursuits of husbandry all his active life upon a portion of the tract of land originally settled and patented by his father. He was a valiant and brave soldier in the War of 1812, served under General Harrison, participated in the engagement at Fort Meigs, and many skirmishes with the Indian allies. He was a member and elder of the Presbyterian Church for many years, and was an active and liberal supporter."[23]

**G. S. Ray.** George S. Ray, son of Thomas and Jennett (Smith) Ray, died August 17, 1856, "cut down in the very prime of his life." He was born September 27, 1823. He graduated from Jefferson College, read law with Edgar C. Wilson, and was admitted to the bar September 8, 1845. He was editor of the *Western Virginia Standard* (see p. 275) in 1846 and of the *Monongalian* (see p. 313) in 1849. He was elected clerk of the circuit court in 1852 and served until the time of his death.[24]

**John Shisler.** Morgantown's first wagon maker (see *Monongalia Story*, vol. 2, pp. 304, 305), John Shisler, died December 28, 1856. He came to Morgantown in 1796. He married Elizabeth Criss and they had six children, Maria, Michael, Frederick, Catherine, John, and Edmund.[25]

The obituary in the local newspaper read:

"*Died*, In Morgantown, on Sunday morning, the 28th Dec., after a short illness, Mr. John Chisler, in the 86th year of his age. He was a peaceable and quiet citizen, a member of the Presbyterian Church, and, at the time of his death, the oldest inhabitant; having resided here during the last 60 years."[26]

**Benoni Fleming.** Early pioneer Middletown settler, Benoni Fleming, died February 6, 1856. The son of William and Jean (Jane) Frame Fleming, he was born February 17, 1768, in Kent

23. *Cyclopedia of Monongalia County*, p. 174; *American Union*, June 28, 1856.
24. Wiley, p. 352; *American Union*, August 23, 1856.
25. Wiley, *History of Monongalia County*, p. 600.
26. *American Union*, January 3, 1857.

County, Delaware. He served as a justice of the peace from 1820 to 1822, and operated a ferry from his land at the mouth of the West Fork River to the point of land between that river and the Tygart Valley River. He married Mary Stephenson and they had twelve children, George, Margaret, Boaz, John, Matthew, Rhoda, Alfred, Benjamin, Fielden, Nancy, Edward, and Stevenson.[27]

**Other Deaths.** Jonathan Prentis passed away in the seventy-ninth year of his life.[28]

Lloyd Roby, eighty-two years old, was drowned while crossing Cheat River in a skiff near Rude's Mill.[29]

Arthur Fitch died October 3, aged sixty-seven.[30]

David Crawford, of Cassville, died at the age of sixty-six.[31]

**Land Grants Made in 1856.** Monongalia County grantees in 1856 included:

| | | |
|---|---|---|
| Darling, James | 20 a. | Dunkard Creek |
| Lemley, Samuel | 151 | Dunkard Creek |
| Lemley, Samuel | 9½ | Dunkard Creek |
| Powell, Isaac | 12 | Jones Run |
| Roland, James | 60 | Waters Monongahela R. |
| Tower, Edwin W. | 4 | Booths Creek |
| Wilfong, George | 27¼ | Waters Monongahela R. |
| Wilson, Edgar C. | 83 | Waters Cheat River |

**Election Results.** The votes for sheriff and prosecuting attorney were reported as follows:[32]

| | Sheriff | | Pros. Atty. | |
|---|---|---|---|---|
| | Fleming, Democrat | Snyder, Indep. | Keck, Democrat | Blackshire, Independent |
| Jones' | 125 | 39 | 105 | 58 |
| Osborn's | 25 | 19 | 24 | 20 |
| Court-House | 156 | 153 | 75 | 246 |

27. *Cyclopedia of Marion County*, p. 249; Brand, *The Fleming Family*, pp. 559-63.
28. *American Union*, April 19, 1856.
29. *American Union*, August 16, 1856.
30. *American Union*, October 11, 1856.
31. *American Union*, April 19, 1856.
32. *American Union*, May 31, 1856.

| | | | |
|---|---|---|---|
| Guseman's | 25 | 7 | 16 | 14 |
| Ross' | 70 | 59 | 53 | 79 |
| Loftus' | 39 | 58 | 9 | 87 |
| Cushman's | 105 | 32 | 68 | 69 |
| Cassville | 149 | 3 | 120 | 30 |
| Laurel Point | 132 | 19 | 116 | 34 |
| Cox's | 86 | 9 | 72 | 15 |
| Mooresville | 186 | 6 | 133 | 51 |
| Tennant's | No poll taken | | | |
| Warren | 241 | 2 | 223 | 20 |
| Darrah's | 54 | 3 | 45 | 9 |
| | 1,393 | 409 | 1,059 | 732 |

**County and Borough Government.** John T. Fleming was elected to his second two-year term as sheriff. Thomas R. Miller was elected commissioner of the revenue for the Western District. P. H. Keck was elected prosecuting attorney for the circuit court and also for the county court. John B. Lough was president of the county court.

Justices (members of the county court) for the various districts, elected in 1856, were:

1. Jon. M. Heck, John Meredith, Isaac Reed, Moses Steele.

2. Manliff Hayes, Francis Madera, James Hawthorne, Lee Roy Kramer.

3. Charles H. Burgess, John Rude, William Donaldson, James T. McClaskey.

4. Joshua M. Davis, William W. Lazzelle, J. K. Barrickman, Purnel Simpson.

5. John B. Lough, Jesse Mercer, James Steele, Ulysses Camp.

6. John Wildman, Nimrod Tennant, E. B. Tygart, Noah Morris.

7. John Anderson, Justus Garrard, Josephus Eakin, Philemon Rice.

A new series of deed books was begun in the courthouse. Deeds recorded up to this date made up twenty-five volumes.

Trustees of the borough of Morgantown were I. Scott, E. P. Fitch, P. Rogers, R. P. Hennen, James Odbert, Daniel Fordyce, and Jacob Kiger.

**Miscellany.** In 1856: A. W. Lorentz was appointed assistant teacher at Monongalia Academy (Wiley, pp. 396, 419). . . . Peter Hayden was appointed principal of Morgantown Female Academy (Wiley, p. 399). . . . Sarah Newbrough died at the age of ninety-nine (Wiley, p. 472). . . . Dr. G. M. Dorsey was a Morgantown physician (Wiley, p. 584). . . . John H. Bowlby's large steam flouring mill was built near the head of Robinson Run; it was thirty by thirty feet, three stories high, with two runs of buhrs; he also had a sawmill, eighteen by forty-five feet (Wiley, pp. 707, 712). . . . Dr. James M. Price became the first physician at Arnettsville (Wiley, p. 723). . . . James P. Knox died (Wiley, p. 737). . . . The faculty of the Monongalia Academy discontinued the use of the cowhide as a means of discipline (Callahan, p. 142). . . . The old Morgantown Mills made extensive improvements which increased their grinding capacity to ten bushels per hour (Callahan, p. 174). . . . Pleasant Street was improved between High and Spruce by macadamizing (Callahan, p. 184).

CHAPTER EIGHTY-ONE

# 1857

Completion of the Baltimore and Ohio Railroad to Cumberland in 1842 and through Fairmont to Wheeling in 1852 stimulated efforts to secure a line to Morgantown. From the very beginning of the B.&O. Company, in 1827, there had been hopes that the main line would pass through Morgantown (see pp. 3, 4). There was some opposition, though, particularly on the part of wagoners, who thought the railroad would ruin their business, and for a couple of decades it was a hotly debated political issue (see p. 274).

But the success of the line already completed demonstrated the advantages of railroad transportation to Morgantown civic leaders and they sought ways and means to bring the steam cars into the county.

**Morgantown and Independence Railroad.** One of the first of these projects was in 1852, when, on November 30, the general assembly passed an act incorporating the Morgantown and Independence Railroad Company. This was to come up the Monongahela River from Pennsylvania to Morgantown, thence passing across the hills to intersect the Baltimore and Ohio line at Independence. The capital stock was to be two hundred thousand dollars, divided into shares of twenty-five dollars each. It was provided that books of subscription should be opened at Morgantown by John Hanway, William Lazier, Nicholas Pickenpaugh, and James Evans, and at Kingwood by William G. Brown, John P. Byrne, Elisha M. Hagans, and John A. Dille. When the sum of fifty thousand dollars was subscribed, the company was to be organized and construction was to begin by

1857. But the necessary amount of subscriptions could not be secured and work was never started.

**Monongahela and Ravenswood Railroad.** The next project was for a railroad to come up the Monongahela from Pennsylvania, through Morgantown, Fairmont, and Clarksburg, terminating at Ravenswood, Jackson County, on the Ohio River. An act incorporating the Monongahela and Ravenswood Railroad Company was passed by the assembly February 27, 1857. The act fixed the capital stock of the company at $4 million and the shares at one hundred dollars each. A meeting was held at Morgantown on April 24 and 140 delegates were selected to attend a convention at Fairmont on June 15. But the line never got beyond the talk stage.

**New Post Offices.** The Clinton Furnace Post Office, near the iron works by that name, was established July 9, 1857, with George Hardman as the first postmaster.

A post office was established at Cushman's "stone-pile," on Robinson Run, January 24, 1857, with Adonijah E. Cushman as first postmaster. It was called Maidsville.[1]

**Mathew Gay.** "Usefulness," says Samuel T. Wiley,[2] "is the largest factor in a successful life. The individual, measured by the highest standard, insofar as he lacks this essential element is comparatively a failure. A large majority of men who in many respects are distinguished and canonized as great, are distinctively so only in a limited and qualified sense; and the rightful measure of distinction to which they are entitled—whether national or local—is as justly their own, and should be as generously awarded to them by the historian, as it is to those by whom a larger field of action is occupied, and with whose illustrious deeds and useful lives mankind have been more strongly and deeply impressed. What a man makes of himself, and not what he is made by the aid and influence of friends and family, is the most potent and prominent thought that arrests the attention and deepens the conviction of his fellow men, and influences them—whether favorably or otherwise—in a just and impartial opinion. A calm and unbiased judgment of the life is more

1. *American Union*, March 21, 1857.
2. *History of Monongalia County*, pp. 336-42.

likely to be rendered when its labors are ended, and its ambitions and rivalries can no longer affect the award. There is a large class of useful men in every country who hold communities together, who are—to use the Yankee phrase,—'solid men,' and who, designated by the more generally popular and expressive, if not the more elegant term, are the backbone of society. These men, with pronounced individuality, patriotism, integrity, and usefulness, give tone to society, stability to its morals, ease and dignity to its manners, and progress and probity to its business affairs."

Of such a class of men, Wiley continues, was Mathew Gay (Fig. 51), who died on March 17, 1857, one of the most distinguished of Monongalia County's citizens of the first half of the nineteenth century.

Mathew, the oldest son of John and Margaret Gay, was born in County Tyrone, Ireland, about 1780. His mother's maiden name was McCleery and she was a sister of Colonel William McCleery, who located in Monongalia County in 1783, before Morgantown was founded (*Monongalia Story*, vol. 2, pp. 465-67). About 1799 Colonel McCleery lost his wife, and having no children, wrote to his nephew, Mathew, to come and live with him. The nineteen-year-old nephew sailed from Londonderry and after a long and stormy voyage, landed in Philadelphia and crossed the mountains to Morgantown.

Meanwhile, Wiley says, "Col. McCleery had fallen a victim to the charms of a young widow, who, before his nephew reached Morgantown, became his second wife. The nephew earnestly set about the work of learning the manners and business habits of the people of his new home, and, having determined to cast in his lot with them, commenced the study of law in his uncle's office; and, after a sufficiently lengthy residence in the country, on the 12th of June, 1805, renounced his allegiance to King George III, and became a naturalized citizen of the United States. In 1807, having obtained the legal certificate of residence and good character, Mr. Gay set out on his journey on horseback to Richmond, the Capital of the State, to be examined by three of the judges of the General Court of Virginia. On this journey he tarried over night at the house of Alexander Smith (see p. 190), on the north branch of the Potomac River, and saw, for the first time, the little blue-eyed girl, who, just fifteen years afterwards, became his wife. Having procured the signatures of Judges Archibald Stewart, Henry Hohms, and William Fleming, Mr. Gay returned to Morgantown and entered upon the successful practice of his profession, which he prosecuted until a few years before his death—a period of nearly half a century."

Mathew Gay held numerous offices during this period that illustrated the confidence bestowed on him by his fellow citizens. In June 1814, he was appointed the commonwealth's attorney in the Monongalia County Court, an office he held for thirty-three consecutive years, until 1847, when he resigned. He was a member of the board of directors of Morgantown's first bank, The Monongalia Farmer's Company of Virginia, during its entire existence (1814-1840), and was a director of the Merchants' and Mechanics' Bank of Wheeling at Morgantown from 1834 to 1841 and president from that time until his death. He was elected president of the Board of Trustees of Monongalia Academy in 1827 and reelected continuously until his death.

A Morgantown newspaper announced his death as follows:

"Died, on Tuesday morning, the 17th inst., after about a week's illness of pneumonia, Mathew Gay, Esq., President of the M & M Branch Bank of this place, aged seventy-eight years. The deceased was one of our oldest citizens, having resided here during the last fifty years. He enjoyed the esteem of his fellow-citizens. His remains were followed to the grave on Thursday afternoon last, by a large concourse of friends."[3]

The circuit court, on April 8, adopted a resolution honoring him, including the following: "That although Mr. Gay had, for many years, retired from the bar, yet his long professional career, his rigid integrity, and his character as a citizen in all the relations of life, had commanded the public respect and veneration in no ordinary degree. He died full of years, honored and respected by all who knew him."

Mathew and Margaret Gay had nine children, William M., Alexander S., John G. (married Martha Simonson June 27, 1865, both drowned July 30 on their way to Oregon), Mathew, Sarah A., Jane V. (married Andrew McDonald, Orlando, Florida), Jeanette J. (married Dr. N. W. Tate, Lexington,

3. *Virginia Star*, March 21, 1857; see also *American Union*, March 21, 1857, and a long tribute, *American Union*, April 11, 1857.

444　　　　THE MONONGALIA STORY

Missouri), Margaret P. (married William G. Brown, of King-wood), and Mary E. (married John J. Brown, of Morgantown).

**Another Cold Winter.** The winter of 1856-57, like that of the previous year, was unusually cold:

"The Monongahela is so firmly frozen over at this place, as to admit of the crossing of two-horse teams, &c., and many avail themselves of the opportunity to cross 'scott-free,' as there is no toll-gate at the natural bridge—for who shall collect toll for 'Old Boreas'?

"At Ice's Ferry, on Cheat River, the ice is said to be 20 inches thick! One day of last week, ELEVEN sleds, heavily freighted with grain, crossed there in close company."[4]

**Enos D. Morgan.** Enos D. Morgan, early Morgantown journalist, died January 27, 1857. He was a son of Capt. Zackwell and Elizabeth Madera Morgan and was born July 3, 1807. He was a printer by trade and edited and published several different newspapers between 1825 and 1845, including the *Monongalia Farmer*, the *Republican*, the *Republican and Preston and Monongalia Advertiser*, the *Democratic Republican*, and the *Northwestern Journal*. From 1845 until his death he was engaged as foreman and editor for other papers.

"Enos D. Morgan inaugurated a great improvement in the press of Monongalia County, and was largely copied by other editors. . . . Mr. Morgan was a man of talent and taste, and allowed his native modesty to keep him from public positions that he was especially qualified to fill with credit and honor. He was a natural musician, hardly having his equal as a violinist, and was the contemporary of the celebrated Capt. William S. Stoy, as a band instructor. He was a well-informed man for his day, and an earnest old-line Whig in political opinion. Modest and unassuming, he lived and died a gentleman in every respect."[5]

He married Martha B. Hanum and they had two children, Henry M., married Josephine A. Lazier, and Drusilla, married Dr. Joseph R. Mathers.

4. *American Union*, January 24, 1857.
5. *Cyclopedia of Monongalia County*, pp. 80, 81; Morgan, *Descendants of Col. Morgan Morgan*, pp. 241, 242; Wiley, pp. 433, 434.

**William Dering.** William Musser Dering died March 5, 1857. He was a son of Henry and Rebecca Musser Dering and was born in 1797. He married in 1822 Sarah Glisson, daughter of Thomas Glisson. Their daughter, Ann Musser, married David Hogue Chadwick.[6]

**Matthew Hennen, Jr.** A farmer and shoemaker of Granville, Matthew Hennen, Jr., died in 1857. The son of Matthew and Elizabeth Hennen, he was born in Washington (now Greene) County, Pennsylvania, about 1784. He married Nancy Stevenson, daughter of Robert and Lydia (Stevenson) Butcher, and they had several children, including Robert Painter, Elizabeth, Levi V., Harriet, George Washington, Rachel A., and Thomas Jackson Lazzell.

They moved to Monongalia County around 1810, living at various places, finally settling in Granville in 1849.[7]

**Thomas Jefferson John.** T. J. John died August 7, 1857. He was a son of Lemuel[8] and Susannah Fretwell John and was born in 1811, in the Stewartstown area and was an extensive and successful farmer, as well as a captain in the state militia.

He married Sarah Anne, daughter of David and Elizabeth Scott, and they had four children, David Scott, Lemuel Nimrod, James, and Elizabeth H.[9]

**Other Deaths.** John A. Hayes, twenty-seven-year-old son of Alexander and Phebe Hayes, died July 8.[10]

"Died near Clinton Furnace, in this county, on Monday, the 13th inst., Mr. Henry A. Ferrell, aged about 90 years; a soldier in the War of 1812, leaving an aged widow to mourn his loss."[11]

"Died, in this place, on the evening of the 19th inst., Mrs. Hester Ann Willey, wife of Dr. M. Y. Willey, and daughter of Mr. Alexander Hayes."[12] She was born December 27, 1831.

6. Callahan, *Making of Morgantown*, pp. 85, 86.
7. Dorothy T. Hennen, *Hennen's Choice*, vol. 1, pp. 26, 27.
8. See numerous references in *The Monongalia Story*, vol. 2.
9. *Cyclopedia of Monongalia County*, p. 200; *American Union*, August 28, 1857.
10. *American Union*, July 11, July 17, 1857.
11. *American Union*, July 17, 1857.
12. *American Union*, July 31, 1857.

Dr. Willey himself followed his wife in death only a few months later, dying of consumption on November 10, at the age of 35. A tribute of respect from the Hall of Monongalia Lodge No. 62, I.O.O.F., appeared in a local paper.[13]

"Died, at his residence, near this place, on the morning of the 25th instant, in the 47th year of his age, Mr. James S. Craig."[14] He was born in Westmoreland County, Pennsylvania, September 18, 1810.

**Woodland Methodist Church.** A deed was granted for the Woodland Methodist Church on February 14, 1857. The church was located next to the Woodland School, on the Cheat Road northeast of Morgantown. Thomas Warman was the first Sunday school superintendent.[15]

**Union Literary Society.** To provide a forum for discussion of live questions of the day, the Union Literary Society was organized January 1, 1857. The founders were E. H. Coombs, L. S. Layton, John Thorn, W. E. Wells, A. C. Pickenpaugh, F. M. Durbin, and Thornton Pickenpaugh. As time went by its membership was increased by the addition of John Marshall Hagans, Dr. H. W. Brock, E. C. Bunker, J. M. Heck, H. T. Martin, and many others. Meetings were held in one of the jury rooms in the courthouse.[16]

**Graduation Exercises.** Among the outstanding events on the calendar were the "Closing Exercises" of the Monongalia Academy, which by 1857 had grown into a "Commencement" lasting two days, with contests between the Columbian and Monongalian literary societies as added attractions.[17]

**Morgantown Female Seminary.** The Reverend A. S. Hank, A.M., became principal of the girls' school in 1857. He "was late principal of Cassville Seminary, Baltimore Conference. He has travelled extensively in Europe, and acquired the continental pronunciation of the French language."[18]

13. *American Union,* November 20, 1857.
14. *American Union,* July 31, 1857.
15. Dodds and Dodds, *Churches of Monongalia County,* pp. 90, 91.
16. Wiley, p. 552.
17. Callahan, *Making of Morgantown,* p. 186.
18. *American Union,* August 14, 1857; Wiley, p. 399.

**The Virginia Weekly Star.** With two newspapers in town, local citizens were amused by the jibes and criticisms they thrust at each other. For example:

"The Virginia Weekly Star made its appearance above the horizon on Wednesday evening last, considerably enlarged and improved in appearance. If it only had a *tail*, it might be mistaken for a comet; but then, altho' somewhat eccentric, it is more regular in its habits than a comet, hence it may be regarded, we presume, as a 'fixed star.' "[19]

**The Episcopal Church.** Although Episcopalians had joined with Presbyterians to erect a church building in Morgantown (*Monongalia Story*, vol. 2, pp. 447-49), Episcopal services were rarely held for many years. In 1852 and afterwards Rev. Robert Castleman, with Rev. James Page, who soon joined him, supplied Clarksburg, Weston, Fairmont, Morgantown, and Buckhannon, from centers in Clarksburg and Fairmont. An excellent church was built at Clarksburg and a building at Fairmont was purchased and repaired for church purposes.

But interest in Morgantown was apparently discouraging. Bishop William Mead, who visited Morgantown between 1853 and 1857, while Castleman was at Clarksburg, wrote: "Although our efforts thus far have failed at Morgantown I cannot pass it by without mention of the pleasant visits made to that place, and the hospitable reception given me by those worthy members of our church,—Mr. John Rogers and Mr. Guy Allen. Could the zeal and liberality of two individuals have sufficed for the establishment of the Episcopal Church at Morgantown, theirs would have done it."

One reason for Episcopal weakness in the area was that, although many of the settlers had migrated from eastern Virginia, they were usually either English who had deserted the church, often engaging in movements of violent hostility to it, or Scotch-Irish and Germans from the Shenandoah Valley, where the Episcopalian church did not exist in pioneer times.[20]

**The Marchioness de San Roman.** James Robb, it will be recalled (see p. 167), resigned his position in 1838 as cashier of the

19. *American Union*, August 28, 1857.
20. Callahan, *Making of Morgantown*, pp. 154, 155.

Merchants' and Mechanics' Bank, in Morgantown, and moved to New Orleans. Here he amassed a very large fortune in the banking business and was also involved in the railroad business. He was interested in politics and served a term in the Louisiana legislature.[21]

Becoming interested in investments in Cuba, he attracted the attention of Isabella II, Queen of Spain, and formed a partnership with her to purchase the Havana Gas-Works. This was a lucky venture which not only increased his wealth but brought him into high favor with the queen.

He had married in Morgantown Miss Louisa Werninger, daughter of Morgantown merchant, Augustus Werninger. While they were still living in Morgantown a daughter was born, named Isabella, from Isabella, wife of John Rogers, an intimate friend of Robb's. On a visit to Spain he was accompanied by his daughter, then a charming eighteen-year-old brunette. The daughter attracted the attention of a Spanish nobleman, the Marquis de San Roman, a cousin of the queen, who fell in love with her and eventually married her. The nuptials were celebrated at the Tuileries, in Paris, in 1857, the Empress Eugenia being present.[22]

**Morgantown Prices.** Prices prevailing in the local market in December were:[23]

| | | | |
|---|---|---|---|
| Flour, bbl. | $6.00 | Beef, lb. | .04 to .08 |
| Wheat, bu. | 1.00 | Dressed | |
| Corn, bu. | .50 | Turkeys, lb. | .05 |
| Oats, bu. | .37 | Live | |
| Butter, lb. | .15 | Turkeys, lb. | .04 |
| Eggs, doz. | .08 | | |

**New Luxuries.** The appearances of new luxuries and conveniences in Morgantown reflected a steady development of so-

21. The text of one of his speeches before the legislature appears in the *Monongalia Mirror*, January 3, 1852. For biography of James Robb, see *Dict. Amer. Biog.*, vol. 8, p. 644.

22. Callahan, *Making of Morgantown*, pp. 99, 100. A year or so later, the Marchioness, then at the height of her popularity, visited Morgantown and the scenes of her childhood as the guest of Mrs. Isabella Rogers. See also Moreland, *Anecdotes*, pp. 26, 27, reprinted as "The Four Isabellas," *Tableland Trails* 2 (3) (1958):133-36.

23. *American Union*, December 27, 1857.

ciety. An "Oyster Saloon" and restaurant, serving meals at any hour, and a livery stable which furnished "rigs" (horses and carriages) for driving, increased social opportunities. The local manufacture of Chalfants perfumeries and the opening of a jewelry store extended the list of local wants.[24]

PIC NIC. "One of the liveliest occasions of the season hereabout, was the Pic Nic excursion of our young folks, the beauty and chivalry of Morgantown, on Friday last. The company, some twenty-odd couples, cozily seated in carriages and hacks, headed by our excellent Brass Band, left town at an early hour in the morning for White-day, near Smithtown. The gay cavalcade made a most imposing appearance as it left town; and not less so as it returned in the evening. The Band discoursed most superb music, and we thought we never heard them do better. The company enjoyed the day finely, and the pleasure of the occasion was uninterrupted by the slightest untoward occurrence."[25]

**Railroad to Saint Louis.** The year 1857 was a great year in the railroad history of the United States and made travel to and from Morgantown easier, although the tracks were still no closer than Fairmont.

To secure a more direct line from Baltimore to the Ohio River, the Northwestern Virginia Railroad Company was projected and chartered in 1851, to construct a "branch" from the main line of the Baltimore and Ohio at Three Forks (later Grafton) to Parkersburg.

Stock was sold to interested people, especially those along the proposed route, and B. H. Latrobe was chosen chief engineer. Work got under way quickly and the line was one of the best constructed railroads in the country at the time, although passing through twenty-three tunnels. To relieve financial embarrassments, the company obtained a loan of $210,000 from the Baltimore and Ohio, and gave a mortgage on the line. Upon its completion, on May 1, 1857, the road passed to the management of the B.&O. Along the entire route opportunities for development and growth were provided and even in points not

24. Callahan, *Making of Morgantown,* p. 174.
25. *American Union,* August 21, 1857.

immediately touched efforts were stimulated to secure better transportation as a basis for new enterprise.

Simultaneous with the opening of the line to Parkersburg was the opening of the Marietta and Cincinnati Railroad (chartered 1847) and of the Ohio and Mississippi (chartered 1848 and first constructed on a six-foot gauge) from Cincinnati to Saint Louis. Completion of these three lines in one year, providing a through route from New York to Saint Louis was "enthusiastically observed by the 'great railway celebration' of 1857, beginning with a triumphal progress from Baltimore to St. Louis, punctuated by many stops and delays, and enlivened by the 'long-winded' speeches of aspiring orators bursting with burning rhetoric which nothing but the shrill shrieks of the locomotive could control."[26]

A local newspaperman rode the train across the mountains and reported favorably:

"The road is now thoroughly ballasted throughout its entire length, and the magnificent cars in which the passenger finds himself seated, pass over it at a good speed with a smoothness and ease we never found on any other road."[27]

Later he traveled on the Northwestern Virginia line:

"We made our first practical acquaintance with this great public improvement last week. Although so recently constructed, it is in admirable order.—The time tables are observed to a fraction. Conductors, engineers, and all others interested seem to understand their duties, & to discharge them with fidelity. The passenger trains make nearly 30 miles an hour—the Express train probably exceeding that rate of speed. . . . The number of tunnels is probably not exceeded any where, in the same length of road. It is said there are *twenty-seven* between Grafton and Parkersburg."[28]

**Stage to New Geneva.** The completion of Lock and Dam No. 6 (p. 428) extended slack water to New Geneva and boats from Pittsburgh reached this point thereafter on regular schedules. In the spring of 1857 Charles Wallace, proprietor of the Excelsior

26. Callahan, *Semi-Centennial History of West Virginia*, pp. 123, 124.
27. *American Union*, April 25, 1857.
28. *American Union*, August 28, 1857.

Livery Stable, announced a daily hack line between Morgan-town and New Geneva to connect with the Pittsburgh boats.[29]

**New Coaches.** "Mr. Alex. Hayes, the Proprietor of the Daily Line of Mail Stages between this place and Fairmont has recent-ly put upon the route two nice and handsome coaches. They are called 'Dr. Kane' and 'Kansas'—were built at the Excelsior Coach Manufactory of Messrs. Fairchild, Lawhead & Co.—and for beauty, comfort, and convenience, they surpass any vehicles heretofore employed on this line. Our main travel being over this route, connecting us with the Baltimore and Ohio Railroad, Mr. Hayes, we trust, will be handsomely remunerated in his efforts to accommodate the travelling public."[30]

An anonymous letter dated May 4, 1857, tells of a trip to Fairmont on the stage:

"Early in the morning . . . our indomitable Mail-Contractor A. Hayes could be seen on Main Street, drumming up passengers and packing them away in his *fine* coach until I, becoming completely demoralized, proposed to friend Hayes that he put me in the 'boot'. Here we were, three in a seat and one in the middle with band boxes in plenty occupying conspicuous places. The usual speed of this fast line was alarming on this occasion. Arrived in Fairmont in time to learn that the locomo-tive had passed an hour before, consequently ten hours had to be spent in the Mountain City. At eight o'clock the scream of the Iron Horse was heard with delight."[31]

**Steamboats.** The completion of Lock 6 also stimulated interest in completion of slack water to Morgantown:

"When shall we have the improvement extended to Morgan-town? What say you, men of capital and enterprise?—Will you suffer our goodly town to die a natural death—to be 'finished, fenced in and white-washed'—when a few thousand dollars would redeem it from otherwise inevitable decay? O! for slack-water to Morgantown!"[32]

29. Callahan, *Making of Morgantown,* p. 180; *American Union,* April 25, 1857.

30. *American Union,* July 4, 1857.

31. Quoted by Martha Brock in the *Woman's Edition of The New Dominion,* December 30, 1896.

32. *American Union,* January 17, 1857.

Fig. 77. Home of Joseph Shackelford, where the Morgantown Methodist Protestant congregation was organized. (Courtesy C. Roy Moyers and Spruce Street Methodist Church.)

Steamboats now rarely reached Morgantown, but occasionally one arrived, causing a great deal of excitement:

"We had a visit from a first steamboat on Monday evening last—the first in a period of nearly two years—and as might be expected it revived our town amazingly. It was the *Jefferson.* . . ."[33]

"On Tuesday last we had, at our wharf, a *live Steamboat.* The fine steamer, Luzerne, Capt. Bennet, came up laden with a cargo of seasonable merchandise, for our dealers."[34]

"The little Steamboat 'Gray Fox' has been making quite a splash in our waters of late. On her second trip here on Friday last she continued to try the channel between 'the head of navigation' and the 'Mountain city.' She left our wharf after 1 o'clock, and bid fair to make the quickest trip ever made to Fairmont, which no doubt she would have achieved but for the drowning of the engineer at Morgan's Eddy, at which point she abandoned the trip and returned to our port. She is a powerful

33. *American Union,* February 14, 1857.
34. *American Union,* November 13, 1857.

little craft, . . . and is more than a match for the strong current of the upper Monongahela."[35]

**Crime on the Streets.** A small lawless element in the town and vicinity was composed of persons who amused themselves by forming mobs to break up public meetings, by galloping their horses madly along the streets, or by using firearms in a careless manner. The newspaper editor reported:

"As a member of this establishment was passing over the suspension bridge in company with a friend, a rifle bullet fired by some one who was shooting at a mark on the river bank, came whistling past quite as near as was consistent with safety. Another ball entered the window of the office adjacent to the dwelling of Mr. Alexander Hayes. People are too careless about the way they use firearms in and about town."[36]

The town constable, the person responsible for enforcement of borough ordinances, was often helpless before gangs of boys. In March a mob broke up a lecture by Dr. Watson Carr on "The Future Influences of Females on Society."[37]

Later the constable, Uriah Rider, reporting that he was unable to break up gangs without assistance, was "authorized and empowered to summon sufficient assistance at any time to suppress all mobs and unlawful assemblages and to arrest all persons disturbing and annoying the citizens of this borough, and any person or persons refusing such assistance shall be subject to a fine of $5.00." Soon the jail was full and the newspaper reported:

"While a row was pending on Saturday night last, at the instigation of Captain Whiskey near the jail, one of the inmates of the 'jug' cried out, 'Be civil, be civil, boys, there's no more room in here,' a remark which contained more truth than it would have done at any time prior for five or six years."[38]

**Fire Protection.** As noted several times earlier, fires were frequent in nineteenth century Morgantown. After each fire, there was discussion of forming a bucket brigade and assembling fire

35. *American Union*, December 18, 1857; the engineer was a man named Nimon.
36. *American Union*, January 3, 1857.
37. *American Union*, March 7, 1857.
38. *American Union*, October 30, 1857.

fighting equipment, but then it was forgotten and nothing was done.

On November 2 a disastrous fire broke out, requiring nearly two columns in the *American Union* to describe it. The stable of Swan Tavern, of William N. Jarrett, opposite the newspaper office, was destroyed, although all the horses were led to safety by a heroic attendant. Efficient work of a bucket brigade saved the home of John W. Thompson. The stable of George R. Dering was also destroyed, but a horse, buggy, and other equipment saved. The stable of Michael Chisler was burned. Large quantities of hay in the stables were consumed. The total losses were estimated at over one thousand dollars.[39]

Later that month, stimulated by the fire, a meeting of the citizens of the borough was called to organize a fire company. The trustees also passed an order appointing Dr. Isaac Scott and John Wallace as a committee to procure two suitable ladders and four hooks and poles for use in fighting fires. "These measures," commented Callahan, "although they did not stop the fires, reduced the losses by fire."[40]

**Spalding and Rogers Circus.** A big "Three Circuses in One" outfit toured the area in September, advertising profusely in newspapers, showing in Uniontown on the eleventh, in Morgantown on the twelfth, in Waynesburg on the fourteenth, and in Wheeling on the fifteenth. Admission was fifty cents for adults, twenty-five cents for children. Editor Siegfried reported:

"The show came off on last Saturday, and such a crowd of persons as the occasion called together, we had not often if ever witnessed before in this place. Thirty-five hundred tickets were sold for the day performance; and over two thousand for the evening.—Our private opinion is that it is a grand shaving institution of the keenest Yankee construction. They are none of the whiskey bloats, but a set of wide-awake, unconscionable skinners. They are crack actors though."[41]

**Celebration of Christmas.** Christmas was rather a dry day in our burg; but little going on. The most interesting and profitable observance of the day that we are aware of was the anniversary

39. *American Union,* November 6, 1857.
40. Callahan, *Making of Morgantown,* p. 185.
41. *American Union,* September 18, 1857.

meeting of the Methodist E. Sabbath School, where religious services, addresses, the distributions of gifts to pupils, etc., afforded an agreeable pastime."[42]

**Borough Financial Statement.**[43] As an example of how Morgantown's borough government operated in mid-nineteenth century, the following financial statement for 1857 is given:

Receipts:

Cash received from taxes ..................... $654.91
Cash received from shows ..................... 12.50
Cash received from wharfage .................. 5.00
Cash borrowed from Henry Kiger .............. 300.00
Cash received from former collector ............ 5.00

Total amount of receipts .............. $977.41
Expenditures amounted to ..................... $899.01
Cash on hand ........................ $ 78.40

Outstanding debt:

Bond to Henry Kiger dated Oct. 11, 1857 ........ $300.00
Bond to C. Bell dated Oct. 1, 1857 ............. 375.00
Bond to H. Kiger dated Mar. 26, 1857 ........... 300.00
Due Dr. X for services to poor ................. 15.00

Total indebtedness ................... $990.00

**Land Grants Made in 1857.** Monongalia County grantees in 1857 included:

| | | |
|---|---|---|
| Carter, Notley T. | 54 a. | Waters Monongahela R. |
| Cole, Draper | 4 | Dents Run |
| Drabell, John R. | 45 | Deckers Creek |
| Drabell, John R. | 200 | Deckers Creek |
| Drabell, John R. | 118 | Deckers Creek |
| Drabell, John R. | 250 | Lick Run |
| Rose, Thomas | 6¾ | Browns Run |
| Smith, Benjamin F. | 15 | Days Run |
| Smith, Benjamin F. | 76 | Jakes Run |
| Tower, Edwin W. | 1661 | Deckers Creek |
| Tower, Edwin W. | 463 | Deckers Creek |

42. *American Union,* January 1, 1858.
43. Callahan, *Making of Morgantown,* p. 186.

**County and Borough Government.** James Hare became commissioner of the revenue for the Eastern District.

Borough trustees were I. Scott, D. Fordyce, D. H. Chadwick, H. Dering, E. P. Fitch, and John Wallace. Members of the new board of trustees, who assumed their duties on March 18, inaugurated a change in the manner of street improvement and maintenance. They selected a separate committee for each street, authorizing small sums for each: twenty-five dollars for High Street, thirty dollars for Bumbo Lane, twenty-five dollars for Spruce Street, fifteen dollars for Water Street and ten dollars for the High Street sidewalk. They requested citizens to keep the sidewalks adjoining their premises in good condition, safe at all times for night pedestrians, and warned them that any persons injured by an accident resulting from poor sidewalks could recover damages from the owner of the adjoining property. They enforced ordinances against feeding horses in the street and against placing obstructions on the sidewalks, but allowed "the owners of buggies and wagons the privilege of placing one buggy or one wagon close by the side of his own lot, but not in such a way as to obstruct the sidewalk."[44]

**Miscellany.** In 1857: A proposal was made to annex to Marion County that portion of Monongalia County south of White Day Creek and of Indian Creek, but nothing came of it (Wiley, p. 101). . . . Fairchild, Lawhead and Company, carriage makers, opened a branch in Clarksburg; they also had a branch in Uniontown (Wiley, p. 262). . . . Marshal M. Dent was named clerk of the circuit court (Wiley, p. 312). . . . Albert G. Davis, along with A. L. Wade, was making speeches advocating free schools in the county (Wiley, p. 364). . . . The financial panic severely affecting much of the country was not very severe in Monongalia County (Wiley, p. 461). . . . Francis Ross died at the age of ninety (Wiley, p. 472). . . . Elijah Morgan and H. Reed were masters of the Masonic lodge (Wiley, p. 548). . . . Callendine and Nye opened a store on Lot 81, Morgantown, in a building previously occupied by Carr, Hanway and Company (Wiley, p. 582). . . . Dr. W. H. Ravenscraft opened a medical office in Morgantown (Wiley, p. 584). . . . H. D. McGeorge invented a shingle machine patented March 3, 1857 (Wiley, p. 604). . . . S. G.

44. Callahan, *Making of Morgantown*, pp. 184, 185.

Snider was operating a tannery at New Brownsville (Wiley, p. 746). . . . Dr. A. W. Brown opened a store at Browns Mills (Wiley, p. 747). . . . The parsonage for the Methodist Episcopal Church was removed to Spruce Street on the west ends of Lots 56 and 57, purchased from John E. Fleming in December (Callahan, p. 149). . . . The suspension bridge was operated by Alexander Hayes under a thirteen hundred dollar lease (Callahan, p. 179). . . . A borough ordinance adopted in 1857 authorized the president of the board of trustees "to proceed at once against all women and girls who are moving themselves about in the borough of Morgantown corrupting the morals of the inhabitants of the said borough" (Callahan, p. 183). . . . A brickyard was being operated on the west side of the river below a point opposite the Walnut Street wharf, providing bricks for the many new buildings being constructed in town (Callahan, p. 189). . . . A Sunday school was organized at the Blacksville Methodist Church (Dodds and Dodds, p. 125). . . . Sarah, wife of D. H. Murphy, died March 2 (*American Union*, March 14, 1857). . . . John Clayton died, aged seventy years (*American Union*, March 21, 1857).

# CHAPTER EIGHTY-TWO

# 1858

Throughout the first half century of its history, Monongalia County's population was most unstable. Many adventurous persons came, stayed for a while, then moved on, looking for more adventure. Some even applied for land grants and perhaps received a grant, then conveyed it for little or nothing to an assignee, before moving on, looking for greener pastures.

This migration continued through the next half-century as well, although at a somewhat reduced rate. Families were large and, where there were several sons in a family, and opportunity seemed lacking, some of them were likely to go "out West," taking up land on the prairies or plains. The glowing reports they sent back beckoned still others to follow them.

Every year many persons studying their family history come to Morgantown, mostly from some state farther west, looking up traces of an ancestor who lived in Monongalia County a century or so ago. This is about the only way we here in the county can find out about the present generation, because in general we don't know where to look for them.

**Monongalia County, Minnesota.** One remarkable account of a band of Monongalians who "went West" is included in the brief history of Monongalia County, Minnesota.[1]

The Minnesota Territory was created in 1849 and Minnesota was admitted to the Union as a state on May 11, 1858. In the

1. This was brought to our attention by Dr. John J. Lawless, a former member of the West Virginia University Medical School faculty, who retired to live in Saint Paul, Minnesota. He verified his facts by consultation of the "Illustrated History and Descriptive and Biographic Review of Kandiyohi County," published by Victor E. Lawson and Martin Tew in 1905.

last Territorial Legislature, held early in 1858, in Chapter 124 of the General Laws enacted, the County of Monongalia was authorized, located about seventy-five miles almost due west from Minneapolis. The boundaries were described as follows:

"Commencing on a line between Meeker and Renville Counties at the SE corner of T118 and R33, west of the 5th principal meridian, west to SW corner of T118, R35; due North 30 miles, thence east to NE corner of T122, R33, thence south to place of beginning."

This was passed on March 8, 1858. The movement to have the county set up had been authorized by a group of Virginians who had settled in the spring and summer of 1857 in the area about Green Lake and nearby Carnelian Lake. The Virginians, several of whom were from the Morgantown section, included George C. Wilson, his father Eugenius M. Wilson, William Wheeler, and Newton Pierpoint and his wife.

On the shore of Green Lake they laid out a town, to be called Irving, in memory of a man who had spent the previous winter there, and then was apparently killed by the Indians, on his way to Saint Cloud, thirty miles to the northeast. Irving was to be the county seat of the new Monongalia County. At that time its total population consisted of Mr. and Mrs. Newton Pierpoint!

The first board of county commissioners, as designated by the act, was composed of George C. Wilson, Newton Pierpoint, and William Wheeler. The name of the county was said to be derived from Monongalia County, Virginia, "a Latinized form of the Delaware Indian name Monongahela."

The county commissioners were to designate certain officers (sheriff, etc.) and to arrange for selection and qualification of the officers. They named a sheriff, assessor, and clerk, none of whom qualified for their office; the next year new men were designated, but they also failed to meet the legal qualifications for office. The county was thus left without effective government.

Discussion and dissension followed, including the use of fire-arms (no casualties noted, however) concerning the location of the county seat, the rivals being Irving (population 2), Columbia (population not stated), and New London (population, a few). New London eventually won out.

Meanwhile, the people in the western and southern tiers of

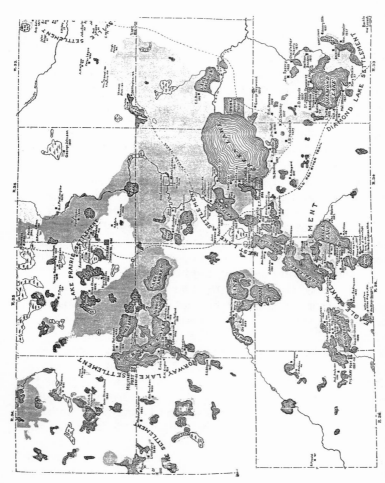

Fig. 78. Map of Monongalia County, Minnesota. (From Lawson and Tew, *Illustrated History . . . of Kandiyohi County.*)

townships were displeased, and succeeded in obtaining an amendment to the act, passed less than two weeks later, on March 20, 1858, dividing the total area, about forty miles north to south, and thirty miles east to west, into a northern half, Monongalia County, and a southern half, Kandiyohi County. Each consisted of twelve townships (432 square miles).

Apparently the majority of the population looked upon the Virginians as a group of promoters and land speculators who hoped to homestead desirable land, sell the best for a town, "and make a killing at the expense of those they possibly looked upon as a bunch of dumb Swedes."[2]

Dr. Lawless, writing March 11, 1973, describes the section as it is today:

"The area is beautiful country, with woods, good farm land, and many, many lakes. Green Lake is probably 3 x 4 miles, with wooded shores, and a popular resort now. This morning I had a fine brunch with a friend at Westwood Inn, which is on Green Lake and certainly close to, if not on, the site of Irving, of which there is no trace. New London persists as a town of 720, a quiet but busy country supply point, on the Crow River. . . . I looked in the phone books of New London, Spicer, Sunburg, Kandiyohi, and Willmar (the county seat), and find no mention of Pierpoints, Wilsons,[3] or Wheelers. They seem to have left no trace. There are plenty Andersons, Andersens, Larsons, Petersons (Swedish), and Pedersons (Norwegian), however."

The 1970 population of Kandiyohi County was 30,548.

**Capt. Felix Scott Disappears.** Felix Scott was a son of the distinguished pioneer, Captain David Scott, who was already living along the Monongahela River before Monongalia County was formed. Scotts (Mill) Run was named for David Scott and the stream now known as Dents Run was originally called Scotts Meadow Run.

Captain Scott and his wife had seven children, namely, Phebe and Fanny, killed by the Indians in 1779, Hannah (who married

2. However that may be, the project failed. Monongalia County, Minnesota, never did have an organized government, and in 1870 it was merged with Kandiyohi County. Thus ends its history.

3. But Eugenius M. Wilson was living in Minneapolis in 1873 and subscribing to the home-town paper (*Morgantown Weekly Post,* May 17, 1873).

Jesse, son of Colonel Charles Martin), James (married Amelia Daugherty), Robert (married a Cunningham), Felix (married Nancy, daughter of Captain John Dent), and Sally (married a Gapen).

Felix Scott read law in Clarksburg and was married about 1807, before being admitted to the Monongalia County bar on April 11, 1808. He served two terms in the House of Delegates of the General Assembly of Virginia, in 1812-13 and again in 1813-14. He was a captain in the county militia.

Captain Scott was the founder of the town of Grandville (now spelled Granville). The town was established by an act of the general assembly January 22, 1814, on "lots and streets as already laid off on the Monongahela River," the property of Captain Scott (*Monongalia Story*, vol. 2, pp. 412, 413). He was appointed as one of the first seven trustees. On June 6, 1814, the first lot sale was held, there being 43 lots in all. Captain Scott built the first house on the site, in 1812, and started a store there about the same time. A post office was established in 1830, with Melford P. Massie the first postmaster.

In 1819 Scott moved to Missouri, where he was elected a member of the legislature and later to the office of lieutenant governor. He was a candidate for governor of Missouri in 1832, but was defeated, owing to the opposition of Thomas H. Benton, who, it is said, feared him as a possible rival for a seat in the United States Senate.

About 1845 Captain Scott went to Oregon, where he soon amassed a fortune in trading. In 1858 he returned on a visit to his son, George, in Illinois. There he bought some blooded stock and started out to drive it across the continent to his home in Oregon. He never reached his home, however, and it was always thought that he was killed by the Indians while crossing the Rocky Mountains.

Wiley says of him: "Fearless, brave and generous, with a love for adventure, he had always pushed to the frontier."[4]

**Clinton Furnace Tragedy.** The wife of Joseph B. Sapp, Louise (Stewart) Sapp, of near Clinton Furnace, died very suddenly on October 18. She was buried, then when suspicions of foul play became general, the body was disinterred and a jury decided her

4. *History of Monongalia County*, p. 295.

death was by violence. Her husband confessed to her murder, was imprisoned, attempted suicide at least twice, and was finally successful.[5]

**Mason-Dixon Line Finally Established.** The extension of the Mason-Dixon Line to the southwestern corner of Pennsylvania was run in 1784 (*Monongalia Story*, vol. 2, pp. 109, 110), but west of the site of Blacksville two lines were marked, gradually diverging from each other until they were twenty-nine rods apart at the western end. By residents of the area, depending on where they lived, each of these lines was claimed to be the southern boundary of Pennsylvania. In the report of the Pennsylvania Commissioners of 1784, it appears that several temporary lines had been run and later corrected.

Finally, in 1858, in the case of *Michael White* v. *George Hennen*, in the circuit court of Monongalia County, with W. T. Willey as counsel for the defendant, the south marked line was proven to be the true state boundary line. The post at the end of this line was gone, but an old trapper, a man by the name of Roberts, testified that forty-nine years earlier, he had seen it standing there. White had unsuccessfully claimed land on which Pennsylvania school trustees had erected a school building. The notched white oak and black oak trees were gone and the vistas cut by the survey commissioners had been filled with a new growth of forest trees.[6]

**Simeon Siegfried, Jr., Leaves Morgantown.** The issue of the *American Union* for April 2, 1858, was the last for editor Simeon Siegfried, Jr. He had apparently started as junior editor of the paper, under his father, advanced to editor and then was succeeded as editor by his father.

"At the call of the Stillwater Baptist Church, in Belmont County, Ohio, the late editor of this paper, S. Siegfried, Jr., was ordained to the pastoral charge of the said church, on Thursday the 17th inst."[7]

5. *American Union*, October 29, 1858, January 7, 1859; Wiley, p. 633; Baker, *Daniel and Rebecca Stewart*, pp. 50, 57. Clark Sapp was the son of Joseph and Louise Sapp.
6. Wiley, p. 93; Callahan, *Making of Morgantown*, p. 51.
7. *American Union*, June 25, 1858.

Fig. 79. Woodburn Female Seminary. (Courtesy West Virginia
University Library.)

**Woodburn Female Seminary.** Morgantown was becoming widely
and favorably known as an educational center, under Methodist
influence, and "a company of gentlemen of considerable liberality" determined to locate a Presbyterian academy in the
community, to provide "North-Western Virginia with a permanent Female School of high order." Accordingly, they were
incorporated by an act of the general assembly of January 4,
1858, as the Woodburn Female Seminary Company. The incorporators were the Reverend J. R. Moore, W. A. Hanway, E.
W. Tower, and others. The company was authorized to hold not
over twenty-five acres of land, and to have a capital not exceeding fifty thousand dollars.

The company purchased the residence of Mrs. Thomas P. Ray
for use by the proposed seminary, and remodeled it into a
"large building." The site was a historic elevation of scenic
beauty overlooking the Monongahela River and the wooded
basin of Falling Run. The seminary was named Woodburn from
the nearby woods and a suggestion from Sir Walter Scott's *Guy
Mannering.* The trustees were authorized to grant diplomas and
degrees.

From its beginning the seminary was conducted by the Reverend James R. Moore, superintendent, with the aid of his wife, Mrs. Elizabeth I. Moore, principal, and four women teachers.[8]

"This institution went into operation on Wednesday morning the 5th inst. under the direction of Professor J. R. Moore, of Monongalia Academy, assisted by a corps of carefully selected, and, it is said, highly efficient teachers, one of whom is a daughter of Rev. S. Billings (formerly the Principal of our Academy), whose return will be cordially greeted by her friends of bygone days.

"This Seminary is located on one of the most beautiful knolls in all of the picturesque and lovely valley of the Monongahela. A spot long known as the attractive and elegant mansion of the late Thomas P. Ray, Esq., situate in the northern suburbs of our borough.

"The Trustees of this institution are constructing a substantial plank walk from the head of Main Street to the Seminary; an improvement greatly needed, as well for that specific object as for obviating the difficulty hitherto experienced in passing to and from the Methodist grave-yard when the streets are affected by rains and snows."[9]

"The influx of Pupils to our flourishing Seminaries has an enlivening tendency all around. The Boarding Houses are re-inforced, the congregations at Church doubly so, for the strangers go there, and the curious among our town's people go to get a look at the strangers."[10]

"M. C. D." told of the coming of the first students:

"Travellers who shall come in the twentieth century by electricity or some yet-undeveloped power to Morgantown will perhaps consider the stories of the adventurous stage riders from Fairmont thither as allegorical traditions. But as yet there are those who well remember their first trip on a day in May when the horses stalled in the mud on a hillside near Laurel Point, and the driver required his passengers—six inexperienced girls—to alight and walk to its summit in the falling rain, although each step seemed to be weighted with at least ten

8. Wiley, pp. 399, 400; Ambler, *History of Education in West Virginia,* pp. 101, 102; Callahan, *Making of Morgantown,* p. 143.
9. *American Union,* May 7, 1858.
10. *American Union,* May 21, 1858.

pounds of the heavy clay soil adhering to their shoes. It was a rather dismal preface to the new world upon which they were entering, but after the little stage rattled across the suspension bridge, through the quaint old town over which Patrick Henry's statue kept watch day and night, and out to the dignified country-seat which was to be their abode, and their eyes were delighted with the beautiful environment . . . , they forgot the vexations of the way."

"The scholars who resided at Woodburn that first year" lived and had their classes in the old Ray Mansion. "The school itself was held in the former drawing room . . . , whose spacious walls were hung with rare and costly paper, brought—it was said—from France unknown years before, on which were depicted classic carvings for frieze and dado, with rich draperies of lace and crimson velvet between. A chandelier with prism pendants was the only relic of the former furnishings, but there still remained most exquisite pictures in the views from its windows, which overlooked the quiet town half a mile away, the glittering river, the groves and hillsides beyond, and good eyes on a clear day could discern the stage as it came down the road toward Durbannah, or wound around the hill toward the bridge, bringing the latest tidings from the outside world."

"Of course study was the chief thing, and those who remember Mr. Moore know that he had the power of making his scholars feel that whatever branches they were pursuing were of the utmost importance."

But there was also time for recreation, "rambles in that bright summer . . . along the romantic Falling Run, gathering the wild flowers, from the meek blue Innocents to the lovely rose-pink Kalmias; in the long horse-back rides on Saturdays over the wild hill roads; in sitting in the white moonlight on the west porch, watching the river flowing like molten silver till it disappeared around the north bend; . . . and now and then listening to serenades in which the guitar and flute made night melodious."[11]

**McGuffey's Readers.** The most widely used textbooks in Monongalia County schools, as elsewhere throughout the country, in the second half of the nineteenth century were the

11. *Woman's Edition of the New Dominion*, December 30, 1896.

*Eclectic Readers* of William Holmes McGuffey (1800-1873). These were published for use in the first six grades of elementary schools. The simplest ones told stories, introducing new words, and were selected to win the pupils' interest. The more advanced readers contained works from the best English literature. The readers played a large part in forming the moral ideas and literary tastes of nineteenth century America.

McGuffey was born not far away, in Washington County, Pennsylvania, and graduated from Washington College. He taught at Miami University for ten years, during which time he published his readers, and was also president of Ohio University.

"Our America of McGuffey's day, like a young human being, was still forming its character. It needed the spiritual insight and moral stamina, the individual integrity and national unity so much emphasized by McGuffey. His selections represented the best thought for the guidance of a new nation whose individuals had the responsibility of an unheard-of freedom. . . . As some one has well said, George Washington was the Father of his Country, but it was McGuffey who reared the child."[12]

**Pleasant Valley Methodist Church.** A Methodist church, later called Pleasant Valley, was built along the Waynesburg road just south of the state line, in 1857, on property belonging to Coleman Wade. The property was deeded on January 14, 1858, to the trustees, named as Otho Wade, Presley Wade, Greenberry Wade, Denune Wade, Joseph Ingraham, Joseph Barrickman, Wenman Wade, and James Barrickman.[13]

**Revival Meetings.** "The series of meetings at the Methodist E. Church in this place, are still continued, and a large number have professed conversion. On Wednesday night the altar was crowded with penitents. The church at Pierpoint settlement is also enjoying a season of revival; and a meeting is also in progress at Granville; all under the auspices of the M. E. Church.

"At Harmony Grove, within about three miles of town, a meeting has been progressing under the auspices of the Baptist

12. Bruce Crawford, "McGuffey: Lessons in Goodness," *West Virginia History* 4 (1942):37-41.
13. Dodds and Dodds, *Churches of Monongalia County*, pp. 117, 118.

church; and on Monday last, three converts were baptized, and others await the ordinance."[14]

**Laurel Iron Works.** A charter was granted February 13, 1858, for the Laurel Iron and Coal Company, and permission was granted Meredith Clymer, John W. Seymour, R. C. Winterhoff, and others, to mine coal and minerals. The capital stock was set at one hundred thousand dollars to $1 million, with shares at fifty dollars each. Charles Carville and John A. Winterhoff were to receive subscriptions. The lands to be exploited were limited to fifteen thousand acres in Monongalia and Preston counties.[15]

**Stagecoach to Fairmont.** "Caney Bright runs a Hack to Fairmont, leaving Morgantown about 6 a.m., arriving in Fairmont in time to connect with the noon trains on the B. & O. Railroad. The Hack leaves Fairmont after the arrival of the trains. The service is provided on Tuesdays, Thursdays, and Saturdays."[16]

**Arrival and Departure of the Mails.** The following announcement was made by the Morgantown post office: Fairmont mail arrives at 12 to 1 p.m. and leaves at 1, daily except Sunday; Uniontown leaves at 7 a.m. and arrives at 2 p.m., every other day; Brownsville, via Fort Martin, Carmichaels, & c. arrives at 12 and leaves at 1 p.m., every Friday; Waynesburg, via Mount Morris, & c., leaves on Wednesday at 6 a.m. and arrives on Thursday evening; Burton Station, via Cassville, Blacksville, & c., leaves early on Monday morning and returns on Tuesday evening; Kingwood via Clinton and Gladesville, & c. leaves on Friday at 7 a.m. and returns on Saturday at 6 p.m.[17]

B.&O. trains arrived at Fairmont on the following schedule:[18]

|  | *West* | *East* |
|---|---|---|
| Mail train | 8:59 p.m. | 2:15 p.m. |
| Express train | 6:19 a.m. | 8:26 p.m. |
| Accommodation train | 1:23 p.m. | 2:41 p.m. |

14. *American Union*, January 22, 1858.
15. Wiley, p. 682.
16. *American Union*, September 24, 1858.
17. *American Union*, July 9, 1858.
18. *American Union*, June 4, 1858.

**Indians.** "There is to be a tall Indian Exhibition on Saturday, which may be worth looking at, as the tawny sons of the forest are fast passing aware [sic] before the rapid encroachments of the pale faces."[19]

**The Washington House.** "Mr. Alex. Hayes has fitted up and enlarged the before extensive buildings formerly owned and occupied by Mr. John Hanway, at the South end of Front street, in this Borough, and opened a Hotel, which he will keep in a style not easily surpassed for all that contributes to the comfort of the traveller or sojourner."[20]

**Picking Blackberries.** "The Blackberry business appears to be the order of the day just now. The mountaineers pack them in by horse loads; and the citizens go out after them in hacks, buggies, and on foot. This crop being abundant, and all other fruit a failure, our folks seem resolved to make the most of it."[21]

**Light! Light!** "Some enterprising genius has bro't to our town, within a few days, a lot of Lamps for burning Carbon Oil—an excellent idea. We have bought one, and having fired it up, found the light so brilliant that we had no occasion for spectacles. Call today on Fitch and Chalfant and examine them."[22]

"The light from this Lamp is as much superior to that from a candle, as the latter is to a farthing rushlight; and on the score of economy the contrast is still stronger."[23]

The "Carbon Oil" used in these lamps was petroleum, or a product refined from it (kerosine). Petroleum in eastern Ohio had been noted by S. P. Hildreth as early as 1826, in connection with salt wells, one of which, he said, "discharges such vast quantities of petroleum, or as it is vulgarly called, 'Snake Oil,' and besides is subject to such tremendous explosions of gas, as to force out all the water and offers nothing but gas for several days that they make but little or no salt."[24]

19. *American Union*, July 2, 1858.
20. *American Union*, July 16, 1858.
21. *American Union*, July 23, 1858.
22. *American Union*, June 25, 1858; Callahan, *Making of Morgantown*, p. 174.
23. *American Union*, July 2, 1858.
24. *Amer. Jour. Sci. and Arts* 10 (1826):7.

As early as 1825 George L. Lemon, in the Hughes River area, was collecting petroleum by digging pits in which the oil would accumulate and by 1858 the oil trade in that region had reached the amount of seventy-five barrels a year.[25]

**Steamboats, Again.** While carrying a considerable amount of freight to Morgantown, the arrival of steamboats, tied to the level of the water, was too uncertain to benefit the town fully.

"Local items are awfully scarce just now, partly owing to the dull times, no doubt. We have 'pretty much quit' having steamboats to visit us, and can't get up the usual interest in Slackwater discussion."[26]

Spring rains and melting snow in the mountains presently brought up the water level:

"The mouth of Deckers Creek presented quite a business aspect on Tuesday. Three barges, each from 125 to 130 feet in length, were being loaded with walnut boards and other lumber, for Pittsburg and a market. This shipment has been waiting a long time for water. Why can't this trouble be removed by slacking the river, a dozen miles or so, to this place.

"Wm Durbin loaded his barge with 125 tons of pig metal at our wharf on Wednesday morning."[27]

Several boats arrived while the water was up. "Another boat, the Telegraph, up on Thursday morning. Tall crowd at the wharf—boys cheering vociferously—men, especially monied ones, stand back and look on. A lady of our town says: 'they that are able, and will not help to dam the river, should blush every time they hear a steamboat whistle, and keep out of sight whenever one succeeds in getting up to our town.' "

"The Telegraph was up again last Tuesday night; and the Jefferson on Wednesday night. The latter brought a lot of Furniture for Woodburn Seminary, besides sundry merchandize."[28]

**George Kinney Dies at Wadestown.** George Kinney was born in Juniata County, Pennsylvania, in 1792. He was reared in that

25. Eugene D. Thoenen, *History of the Oil and Gas Industry in West Virginia*, p. 8.
26. *American Union*, February 5, 1858.
27. *American Union*, April 16, 1858.
28. *American Union*, April 23, 1858.

county and received an elementary education in subscription schools. He married Jane, daughter of John O'Neil, in that county, and shortly thereafter moved to Greene County, where he engaged in farming, stock-raising, and stock-dealing. In 1845 he removed to Wadestown, where he became a hotelkeeper, remaining in this business until his death in 1858.

They had nine children, namely, Alexander, Elizabeth, James W., Mary, Priscilla, William, Jane, Sarah, and George.[29]

**Benjamin Hayhurst.** Benjamin Hayhurst, a farmer of the Paw Paw Creek community, died April 2, 1858. He was born in Maryland in 1770, the son of David Hayhurst, who settled in Revolutionary War times near Ice's Ferry, later removing to Pharaohs Run.

Benjamin married Elizabeth, daughter of William Jolliffe, and they had eight children, namely, Nancy, Orlando, Charlotte, Catherine, Elizabeth, Sarah, John, and James.

Benjamin Hayhurst learned the trade of a blacksmith, but worked chiefly with farming and stock-dealing, owning a farm of 350 acres. He served in the War of 1812, in the Army of the West, under General W. H. Harrison.[30]

**Matthew Shanks.** Matthew Shanks, of German descent, died near Mannington, in Marion County, in 1858, aged seventy-five years. He was born in Fayette County, Pennsylvania, where he married Martha, daughter of Edward Jordan. They had seven children that grew to maturity, including John and William. In 1823 the family moved to Morgantown but soon removed to Dolls Run, remaining there until 1854.

He was a tanner by trade, but mostly followed farming. He was a Democrat and a member of the Church of Christ and served as a soldier in the War of 1812, being in the siege of Fort Meigs.[31]

**Alexander Rumble Settles in Monongalia.** Alexander Rumble was born at Smithfield, Fayette County, Pennsylvania, February 2, 1830, the son of Jacob and Susan (Gans) Rumble. Jacob Rumble was among the "old pike boys," who hauled on

29. *Cyclopedia of Monongalia County*, p. 201.
30. *Cyclopedia of Marion County*, p. 203.
31. *Cyclopedia of Marion County*, pp. 126, 127.

the National Road in its palmy days. Alexander moved to Morgantown in 1852. A year later he went to Greene County, where he remained until 1858, when he moved to a 108-acre farm near Clinton Furnace. He later added several hundred acres to this and became one of the well-known farmers of the area. He became a deacon in the Goshen Baptist Church.

He was married in 1853 to Rebecca Kinison and they had four children, namely, J. B., Susan, Jacob, and Grant.[32]

**Michael Courtney, Jr.** Michael Courtney was born in Ireland about 1786 (baptized January 2, 1786), the son of Michael, Sr., and came to Scotts (Mill) Run witb his two brothers, John and Robert, about 1816. In 1838 he moved to Preston County and in 1849 to the Clinton Furnace area, where he died August 12, 1858. He followed the trade of a weaver and a farmer.

He married Rebecca, daughter of Jesse Hanway, and they were the parents of six children, including Elizabeth, Ellen M. (married Harry Howell), John Hall, Samuel Hanway, Rachel (married William C. Fitzhugh), and Mary Jane.[33]

**Deaths.** Capt. John Lantz died September 1, 1858, at his home near Blacksville, aged eighty-three years.[34]

Dr. James F. Dorsey died, aged thirty-three years.[35]

Job Sims died October 11, at the age of sixty-three.[36]

Thomas Wells died October 29, aged sixty-six.[37]

Benjamin S. Wilson died at the age of fifty-five years, leaving a widow and ten children.[38]

Sarah, wife of John Joseph, died, aged sixty-three years, two months, seventeen days.[39]

Michael R. Shisler (or Chisler), son of pioneer carriage maker John Shisler (*Monongalia Story*, vol. 2, pp. 304, 305), died

32. *Cyclopedia of Monongalia County*, pp. 167, 168; Wiley, p. 640. Mrs. Rumble died in 1867 and he married Margaret E. Summers in 1868; they had two children, Clarence and Cora.

33. *Cyclopedia of Monongalia County*, pp. 137, 138; Wiley, pp. 432, 704; pers. comm., Dr. Eldon B. Tucker, Jr., Salt Lake City, Utah.

34. *American Union*, October 1, 1858.

35. *American Union*, October 8, 1858.

36. *American Union*, October 16, 1858.

37. *American Union*, November 12, 1858.

38. *American Union*, July 30, 1858.

39. *American Union*, August 13, 1858.

February 18, 1858. He was born in 1802 and associated with his father in the business, located at the bottom of Pleasant Street. He married Susan Hawthorne; Edmund was a son.[40]

**Philip Wisman.** A pioneer settler of the Laurel Point area, Philip Wisman, died November 26, 1858. The son of George Wisman, of German lineage, he was born near Woodstock, Virginia, in 1787. He married Christina, daughter of Abraham Hess, and the family moved to Monongalia County in 1816. He owned and operated a farm of several hundred acres and also ran a tannery. There were six children, including Silas and Abraham.[41]

**Land Grants Made in 1858.** Monongalia County grantees in 1858 included:

| | | |
|---|---|---|
| Bock, John | 23 a. | Waters Monongahela R. |
| Liming, Reason | 4 | Scotts Run |
| McLane, Joseph A. | ¾ | Deckers Creek |
| Weaver, William B. | 158 | Dry Run |

**County and Borough Government.** James Odbert was elected sheriff. James Hare was reappointed commissioner of the revenue for the Eastern District. Trustees of the borough of Morgantown were C. W. Finnell, L. S. Hough, Manliff Hayes, A. C. Dorsey, F. Madera, and R. L. Berkshire.

**Miscellany.** In 1858: The charter of the Virginia navigation company, sponsoring slack water, was revived and amended, on April 7, by the general assembly, and a capital stock of one hundred thousand dollars, in shares of twenty-five dollars, was authorized (Wiley, p. 128). . . . George Hardman, failing in his Clinton Furnace iron works, made an assignment to Benjamin Ryan, who continued the operation (Wiley, p. 258). . . . Lewis Layton was sworn in as clerk of the circuit court on July 1 (Wiley, p. 312). . . . Henry T. Martin was admitted to the bar on April 8 and Jonathan M. Heck on September 9 (Wiley, p. 316). . . . Others admitted to the bar in 1858, from outside the county, were W. P. Thompson, E. H. Fitzhugh, and Moses C. Good (Wiley, p. 318). . . . Jacob Bankard died at the age of

---

40. *American Union,* February 26, 1858. A tribute of respect was adopted by the Sons of Temperance, *American Union,* March 12, 1858.

41. Pers. comms. by Marietta Wisman Roby and by Robert S. Wisman; see also *Cyclopedia of Monongalia County,* pp. 149, 150.

ninety-four (Wiley, p. 472). . . . Steamboats arriving at the Port of Morgantown included the *Jefferson* and the *Arab* (Wiley, p. 542). . . . H. Griffith and I. Scott were masters of the Masonic lodge (Wiley, p. 548). . . . William Lazier was running a general store in Morgantown (Wiley, p. 583). . . . H. D. McGeorge patented a hemp brake, September 11, 1858 (Wiley, p. 604). . . . Isaac Powell was running a hotel at Smithtown (Wiley, p. 616). . . . A church was built at Clinton Furnace, by Methodist Protestants, but open to all denominations[42] (Wiley, p. 617). . . . The Andy Hole tannery, on White Day Creek, was constructed by Theophilus Devault (Wiley, p. 631). . . . A plat of the town of Arnettsville was made and lots were offered for sale (Wiley, p. 722). . . . "We hope our borough constable may convict and punish the depredators who amuse themselves at night by tearing up the board walk, etc., in town" (*American Union*, January 15, 1858). . . . In December the trustees gave constable A. C. Dorsey authority "to employ two competent persons to act as secret police to give information who the persons are that are committing depredations and improprieties almost every night upon the streets and alleys, so that they may be brought to punishment" (Callahan, p. 184). . . . Stones were laid for seven street crossings and the trustees encouraged the planting of more than one hundred shade trees along the streets (Callahan, p. 185). . . . Influenced by temperance movements the county court in May refused to grant liquor licenses for the coming year (Callahan, p. 188). . . . The Reverend George Westfall held great revivals in the Eden and Zion Methodist churches and many new members were added (Dodds and Dodds, pp. 151, 153). . . . "Kinsey Fife is out for Constable of our town. If you wish to sue and be sued *musically*, vote for him" (*American Union*, May 21, 1858). . . . "C. Wallace is running a daily Hack to New Geneva, to connect with the Line Boats to and from Pittsburgh" (*American Union*, May 21, 1858).

42. It was used for religious purposes until 1870 but after that ceased to be used, with the decline of the iron works.

## CHAPTER EIGHTY-THREE

# 1859

In the days just before the outbreak of the Civil War, Wadestown, or West Warren, after a slow start, was developing into the commercial and social center of District No. 7, in the extreme western end of the county, far away from the county seat.

**Wadestown.** The village that began to develop at the junction of the three forks of Dunkard Creek, serving the surrounding agricultural area came to be known as West Warren. It is thought that early settlers George, Elisha, and Thomas Wade migrated westward from Warren County, Virginia, hence the name. But when a post office was established in 1847, it was named Wadestown, from the Wade family of pioneer settlers.

Among other early settlers were Henry Church and his wife Hannah and Alfred Cotton. Dr. John McCarl was the first physician, Elijah Hartley an early schoolmaster, William Hennen a cabinetmaker and undertaker.

John H. Ewing, around Civil War times, owned large tracts of land nearby, pasturing herds of sheep and cattle in an area known as The Range or Range Run.

William Kinney was the first postmaster, appointed October 11, 1847; he was succeeded by John McCarl on December 29, 1854.

The Wadestown post office was served by a carrier who traveled at first once a week from Morgantown to Burton, a distance of forty-two miles.

Efforts were made early in the county's history to connect the communities in the western end of the county to the county seat by improved highways. In 1839 the general assembly enacted legislation providing for the Dunkard Creek

Turnpike Company. This failed because money could not be raised for construction and the act was revived in 1847 and again in 1848 and 1849, making it easier to raise funds.

But the completion of the Baltimore and Ohio Railroad to Burton and Wheeling in 1852 changed the picture immensely. Wadestown was now only six miles from the railroad, by a road leading up the North Fork of Dunkard, and was more favorably situated, in regard to transportation, than the county seat itself.

Efforts were redoubled, then, to complete the Dunkard Creek Turnpike. William Price, superintendent, reported on the condition of the western end for the year ending September 30, 1857:

"The road commences at the west end, at no public point, not reaching Burton (a station on the Baltimore and Ohio railroad) by something like three-fourths of a mile; and extending eastward across a ridge and down Dunkard Creek with the county road to a distance of six miles and 120 rods, passing but one village (and that of small importance) in its route—hence it may be seen that but a small amount of toll can be gathered. But should it be completed throughout its intended course, it will connect Burton with Morgantown, embracing in its route West Warren, Blacksville, Cassville, Hamilton and Granville, and connecting with several public ways before it reaches Morgantown."[1]

Two churches were established at Wadestown in the 1850s or earlier. The Wadestown Methodist Church is said to have resulted from a camp meeting held on an old Methodist Camp Meeting site on White Creek (or Camp Run), sometime before 1850; no dates are available. The West Warren Baptist Church was organized in 1854 by William Haines, J. M. Haught, and J. DeGarmo.

One of the first schools in western Monongalia County was located at Wadestown. It was a subscription school, entitled to receive indigent children whose tuition was paid for by money from the Literary Fund. It was likely in operation before 1830.

**The Big June Frost.** On June 5, 1859, occurred the "Big June Frost," an event which was recalled perhaps more frequently

1. For the year ending September 30, 1860, the amount of tolls and fines collected on the west end of the road was reported as only $128.50.

than any other in the nineteenth century annals of Monongalia County, with the possible exception of Jones's Raid during the Civil War.

"The growing season of 1859 had been a good one. An excellent crop of wheat on the verge of ripening was in prospect. Corn was belly-high to the horses used in plowing it. All vegetation was luxuriant, with the promise of fine yields from garden, orchard and meadow. During the afternoon and night of June 4 the weather turned suddenly cold. The air was still, the sky clear, and when the dawn came, all growing plants were white with frost crystals. The sun rose unclouded, and with its first rays, vegetation wilted and turned black. It was a beautiful Sunday morning, but it brought no joy to the people of this and other communities of the widely devastated region.

"Old timers recount that the first reaction of the people was panic and fear of financial ruin, even of starvation. Men gathered at their fences, in groups at the country stores and mills, and at the churches. They were stunned for the time, totally at a loss to see a way out in a country then very largely dependent on agriculture for wealth and comfort. They did recover from the shock, of course, and within a few days were working with a purpose.

"Wheat and blackened corn were plowed under. Some corn was replanted and grew to partial maturity before the killing frosts of the fall. Buckwheat was planted in the destroyed wheat fields, and quickly growing root crops of the hardier kind were substituted in the vegetable gardens. Men shared whatever they had for planting with their neighbors and every man lent aid wherever he could. A fine spirit of cooperation and neighborliness was born, and not for many years—never entirely—did it disappear. Out of the common misfortune came a real blessing. No one starved to death during the following winter. There was no real suffering. There was no financial crash. A diversification of crops was established."[2]

Wiley gives a brief summary: "When the light of day broke on Sunday, June 5, 1859, the trees and the earth were white as with a heavy snow. A great frost had fallen, and when the sun

2. The *New Dominion*, June 5, 1937. George Brown, living at the time in Fayette County, Pennsylvania, tells of the frost. *Recollections of Itinerant Life*, p. 401.

rose up in the eastern heavens, drooping leaf and wilting blade were cause of alarm to an excited people. Many supposed there would be a famine. Grain advanced with a bound to a high price. People turned from the wheat crop ruined, and, breaking up large fields, planted them in buckwheat, corn and potatoes. The remainder of the season proved favorable, and large crops were gathered from these late plantings"[3]

Henry Haymond also tells the story briefly:

"On June 5, 1859, occurred a heavy frost, which destroyed every living thing in the shape of crops, fruit and garden vegetables.

"Some few wheat fields that were above a certain line on the hills escaped damage.

"Corn was replanted and the wheat fields ploughed under and sowed in buckwheat and good crops were raised."[4]

The seriousness of this big frost is more fully appreciated when it is recalled that agriculture was the principal occupation in Monongalia County in 1859, that there were no railroads in the county to transport large quantities of foodstuffs from other parts of the United States, and that at that time the government had no programs for welfare or disaster relief. The people were on their own, and, except for a few indigent people who were cared for in the poor house, they expected no such aid from the public authorities.

Wiley, writing only a few years after 1859,[5] thought that Monongalia County, in soil and climate, was well adapted to agricultural purposes, especially for the raising of cattle, sheep, and horses. Shorthorn cattle (called Durham) were introduced as early as 1850, to improve the earlier stock. Merino sheep were brought in from nearby Pennsylvania.

Improved farm equipment, by 1850, was making possible increased production and elimination of some of the hard labor involved in farming. The first crude models of threshing machines, grain reapers, mowing machines, and horse-drawn hay rakes were already in use on a few farms in Monongalia County.

Intelligent farmers added one third to crop production through use of fertilizers, such as soluble flour of bone and

3. *History of Monongalia County*, p. 246 note.
4. *History of Harrison County*, pp. 186, 187.
5. *History of Monongalia County*, pp. 245-47.

ammoniated super-phosphate. Barnyard manure, however, was regarded as the cheapest and best article for county soils. Lime, burnt and applied as quick-lime, was beginning to be used.

**George Cookman Sturgiss.** George Cookman Sturgiss, destined to figure prominently in Monongalia County history, arrived in Morgantown November 11, 1859. He was born in Mahoning County, Ohio, August 16, 1842, the son of Alfred Gallatin Sturgiss, a minister of the Methodist Episcopal church. The name George Cookman was in honor of a distinguished clergyman by that name who went down with the ill-fated steamer *President* while crossing the Atlantic in 1841.

George's father died in 1845 and he had to make his own living from an early age. He learned the trade of a furniture varnisher, traveling in Ohio, New York, and Pennsylvania before coming to Morgantown to attend the Monongalia Academy.[6]

**The Morgantown Gymnasium.** An organization for development of physical culture was formed in 1859 and met in a room over T. Pickenpaugh's store. It had a membership of about thirty, including J. M. Hagans, Lowrie McGee, J. M. Heck, and A. C. Pickenpaugh. "It gave a couple of creditable public exhibitions."[7]

**United States Mail Stages.** In 1859 two stagecoach lines to Fairmont advertised service in Morgantown newspapers. Shanks' Line of United States Mail Stages left Morgantown Tuesday, Thursday, and Saturday at "6½ o'clock a.m.," returning, leaving Fairmont Monday, Wednesday, and Friday at 7 a.m. The advertisement stated that "persons travelling on this Line will always find comfortable Coaches, fast teams, and careful Drivers, ever attentive to the demands of Passengers."

But apparently a competitor, Bright's U.S. Mail Line, was more popular and operated over a much longer period. This line was run by E. C. Bright, known familiarly throughout the area as "Uncle Caney." His coaches left Morgantown at 6:30 a.m. every Monday, Wednesday, and Friday, traveling via Laurel Point, Arnettsville, Rivesville, and Barnesville, arriving at

6. *Cyclopedia of Monongalia County*, pp. 226, 227.
7. Wiley, p. 589. Apparently the organization was an early casualty of the Civil War.

Fairmont at 12:30 p.m. Returning, the coaches left Fairmont every Tuesday, Thursday, and Saturday at 7:00 a.m., traveling the same route and arriving at Morgantown at noon.

Bright said that "His teams are good, coaches comfortable, drivers agreeable, and he will spare no pains to give passengers a pleasant ride."

Half a century later a former stagecoach rider reminisced concerning stagecoach days and "Uncle Caney":

"No matter how deep the mud and slow the journey from Fairmont, when 'Uncle Caney' rounded the Bridge street corner and turned into Main Street the crack of his whip would be heard and the weary horses would make a last effort and dash up to the post office in a trot while two hundred lusty youths sang out, 'Here comes Uncle Caney!' "

The crowd of citizens and academy students would then wait for an hour or more while the postmaster sorted out the mail. When he was finished there would be a mad rush for the window to see if there was "Anything for us?"

" 'Uncle Caney' always generally lightened as much as was in his power the burdens of the weary traveler who journeyed with him on a cold, wintry day; when the one labor in life consisted of a vain endeavor to be cheerful with the thermometer ten below zero, a store box bumping every vertebra of his spinal column and two or three 'grip sacks', plow points, scythes and other sundries galavanting around his feet. Yes, the memory of the stage coach, the hot bath on reaching home, the home cough cure nostrums and the 'bad cold' that stayed with you for the balance of the winter, is pleasant when indulged in as a day dream while being whirled over the same route in a comfortable railway coach, or sitting in an easy chair waiting for the hustling letter carrier to deliver your mail."[8]

**Steamboats.** "There was a fine rise in the River last week, during which the steamers Jefferson and Telegraph made each a visit to our wharf, bringing a greatly needed supply of Sugar, Molasses, & c. and taking away a clever freight of our principal staples, *Pig Metal* and *Rags*. Say what you please about the bellowing of the steamboat horn, there is certainly music in it, as it echoes and re-echoes among our tall hills!"[9]

8. From Max Mathers Papers, in the West Virginia University Library.
9. *American Union*, February 25, 1859.

Steamboats mostly reached Morgantown during the winter and early spring, when the water was up. Almost every issue of local newspapers contained notices urging completion of slack water.

**End of the American Union.** A chapter in the journalistic history of Monongalia County came to an end March 29, 1859, when the last issue of the *American Union* appeared from the press. The editor, Simeon Siegfried, had offered his residence for sale in an issue a week or two earlier.

Simeon Siegfried came to Morgantown in 1849 and started the weekly *Monongalia Mirror* (p. 313). This paper continued until 1855, when it was succeeded by the *American Union*, with his son, Simeon Siegfried, Jr., as editor. The younger man, however, left Morgantown in 1858, and his father took over the paper.

Both papers were well edited and carefully preserved, so that essentially complete files are available, and are important sources of Monongalia County History.

The Reverend Mr. Siegfried moved to Grafton, where he established, later in 1859, a paper known as the *Grafton Guardian.* He had already, in 1855, founded the *Grafton Sentinel,* which lasted about six years.[10]

**Churches in the 1850s.** Ministers of the Morgantown Methodist Episcopal Church were: 1849-51, J. S. Patterson; 1851-53, S. G. Worthington; 1853-55, William Hunter; 1855-57, T. H. Monroe; 1857-59, James Drummond. Superintendents of the Sunday school were: 1847-51, William Wagner; 1851-54, William Lazier; 1854, George M. Hagans; 1855, William Wagner; 1856, William Lazier; 1857, Henry Dering; 1858, Ed. C. Bunker; 1859, William Lazier.[11] Presiding elders of the Morgantown District included H. Z. Adams (1848-55) and Gideon Martin.[12]

10. He located in New Richmond, Ohio, in 1860 as pastor of the Baptist church there. He died in Wilmington, Ohio, November 10, 1879, aged eighty-one years. See obituaries in Wilmington *Republican,* November 27, December 4, 1879; *Ohio Baptist Convention Annual,* 1880, pp. 35, 36; see also a journalism class paper on his biography, by Martha Meredith, January, 1957. This material was brought to my attention by Nancy M. Roman, reference librarian, American Baptist Historical Society, Rochester, N.Y.
11. Wiley, pp. 590, 591.
12. Gideon Martin was born in Lewis County, Virginia, April 30, 1815, and died June 9, 1902. He had a long and distinguished career. Wilding, *Promoted Pioneer Preachers,* pp. 80-82.

Ministers of the Morgantown Presbyterian Church were James Davis, from 1837 until 1855, succeeded by Henry W. Biggs. Among ruling elders were Leeroy Kramer and Joseph Sandusky.[13]

Ministers of the Morgantown Methodist Protestant Church were: 1851, Simeon Laishley; 1852, Henry Layton; 1854-56, Robert Sutton; 1857, P. T. Laishley; 1859, D. B. Dorsey.[14]

Ministers of the Morgantown Baptist Church were: 1848-54, William Wood; 1854-57, G. F. C. Conn; 1857, Simeon Siegfried; 1858-61, G. F. C. Conn. A Sunday school was organized July 1, 1853, and among Sunday school superintendents were: 1853, Rev. S. Siegfried; and 1857, M. Callendine.[15]

Ministers at the Forks of Cheat Baptist Churches included: 1849, G. F. C. Conn; 1854, S. L. Parcel; 1859-61, G. W. Hertzog.[16]

Ministers of the Zion Methodist Church were: 1850, Samuel Clawson; 1851, Isaac Francis; 1852, W. R. Wragg; 1853, P. T. Laishley; 1855, Jerry Simpson; 1856, W. R. Wragg; 1857-58, George Westfall; 1859-60, D. R. Helmick.[17]

Preachers in charge of the Monongalia Methodist Episcopal Circuit were: 1850, T. H. Monroe, S. King;[18] 1851, J. L. Clark;[19] 1852, J. L. Clark, Philip Green;[20] 1853, G. J. Nixon, A. Laughridge;[21] 1854, G. J. Nixon, Charles McLane; 1855, T.

13. Wiley, pp. 591-93.
14. Wiley, pp. 593-95.
15. Wiley, p. 595.
16. Wiley, p. 686.
17. Wiley, p. 688.
18. For biography of Spencer King (1825-1903), see Wilding, *Promoted Pioneer Preachers*, pp. 88, 89. He had an unbroken record of fifty-two years in the ministry.
19. For biography of James L. Clark, a charter member of the West Virginia Conference, see Wilding, *Promoted Pioneer Preachers*, pp. 86-88.
20. Philip Green was born in Rhode Island July 17, 1789, and died at Lumberport, Harrison County, January 24, 1870. "The ground he traveled over extended from the headwaters of the . . . Monongahela . . . to Lake Erie." See biography, Wilding, *Promoted Pioneer Preachers*, pp. 19, 20.
21. Abraham Laughridge was born October 31, 1821, in Allegany County, Maryland, and died in Granville October 22, 1854. He was licensed to preach in 1853. "But how mysterious the ways of divine Providence and how allusive are earthly prospects. Little more than half the Conference year had passed when it was discovered that that subtle disease consumption was fast preying upon his vitals." Wilding, *Promoted Pioneer Preachers*, pp. 6, 7.

H. Trainer, T. C. Hatfield; 1856, T. H. Trainer,[22] Nixon Potts; 1857, R. M. Wallace, T. R. Wilson; 1858, R. M. Wallace,[23] J. Sharp.[24]

**Westfall Chapel is Dedicated.** The Westfall Chapel at Maidsville was dedicated in June 1859, the dedicatory sermon being preached by Dr. Peter T. Laishley. The name honored Rev. G. G. Westfall, pastor of the church at the time of its construction.

The Methodist Protestant congregation at this place had its origin in the Cushman Class, founded in 1840 by the Reverend Laishley and Asby Poole at the residence of Adonijah E. Cushman, where the class had its meetings for the next eighteen years. Early members of the Cushman class were Mr. and Mrs. Joshua Davis, Mr. and Mrs. Isaac Dean, Mr. and Mrs. Lorenzo Davis, Mr. and Mrs. Thornton Conaway, Mr. and Mrs. John Hart, Mr. and Mrs. William Lazzell, and John Laird. This appointment, on the Methodist Protestant circuit, was known as the "Stonepile" (see also p. 441).

In 1858 a church was constructed on a plot of ground donated by James Sanders, a member of the Bethel Methodist Episcopal Church. Neighboring churches which gave assistance were Bald Hill, Taylortown, Morgantown, and others on the circuit.[25]

**Fletcher Methodist Church.** A Methodist congregation in the Cheat Neck area was organized in 1859 known as the Fletcher Church. Families concerned in the organization were the Holt, Jones, Warman, Costello, and Conn.[26]

**William L. Cordray.** Born in Monongalia County in 1818, William L. Cordray died in 1859. He had located at the head of

22. For biography of Thomas H. Trainer, see Wilding, *Promoted Pioneer Preachers*, pp. 54-56. He married Urana Loyd and then Elizabeth Tibbs, of Morgantown.

23. Richard M. Wallace was born in Butler County, Pennsylvania, August 29, 1817, and died at Clarksburg, October 2, 1893. See biography, Wilding, *Promoted Pioneer Preachers*, p. 63. He was a chaplain in Company H, Twelfth West Virginia Infantry.

24. Wiley, pp. 727, 728.

25. Dodds and Dodds, *Churches of Monongalia County*, p. 117; Barnes, *The M. P. Church in West Virginia*, pp. 133-42. Several persons who grew up in the church became ministers, including the Reverends Rufus Clark Dean, John Conaway, and William H. Hart.

26. Dodds and Dodds, *Churches of Monongalia County*, p. 151.

484 THE MONONGALIA STORY

Indian Creek in 1854. He was a farmer, a firm believer in the doctrines of the Presbyterian church, and a staunch Democrat.

He married Sarah Ann Lough and they were the parents of eleven children, including David E., John M., Eliza J. (married John N. Jones), M. L., Alles Ann (married Golden Michael, then Leven Varner), Mary E. (married Michael E. Fetty), Almira (married Alvin Michael), Calvin, Elizabeth, and Wilhelmina.[27]

**Joel Ridgeway.** Joel Ridgeway, a farmer of the Cheat section, died July 7, 1859. His father's name was also Joel. He had a three-hundred-acre farm and also supplied coal to residents of Morgantown, from custom mines. He married Jerusha, daughter of John Dawson, and they had twelve children, namely, Eliza (married Joseph Weaver), Sylvester, Dorcas (married Joseph L. Hill), George D., Susan (married Oliver McShane), Joel, William, Elihu H., Elizabeth (married David Beard), Mary (married Francis Costello), James, and Leroy.[28]

**Samuel Minor.** Samuel Minor, son of pioneer settler Capt. William Minor, died at his home on Dunkard Creek May 10, 1859, at the age of eighty years. He married Susan, daughter of Alexander Clegg, who with his two daughters, were captured by the Indians in 1791 (*Monongalia Story*, vol. 2, pp. 188, 189). Clegg and Susan, after some time, escaped from the Indians and were able to purchase the freedom of Susan's sister, Margaret. Both girls learned the Indian language and absorbed many of their manners and customs.

Samuel and Susan had eleven children. After Susan's death Samuel married Millie Lancaster and they had eleven children.

Samuel Minor located on a tract of six hundred acres near the mouth of Days Run, upon which he built and operated a gristmill.[29]

**Samuel B. Brown.** Samuel Brown, son of Thomas and Anna Ash Brown, was born in Prince William County, October 24, 1793, and came to Monongalia (now Preston) County, settling with his parents near Kingwood, in 1805. In 1833 he removed to District No. 1, Monongalia County, but returned in 1841 to

27. *Cyclopedia of Monongalia County*, p. 166.
28. *Cyclopedia of Monongalia County*, p. 88; pers. comm., Frankie Cline.
29. *Cyclopedia of Monongalia County*, p. 140.

Fig. 80. Rev. Asa Shinn. (From *History of the Shinn Family.*)

Fig. 81. Rev. John Clark. (From Barnes's *Methodist Protestant Church in West Virginia.*)

Fig. 82. Rev. Isaac Holland. (From Barnes's *Methodist Protestant Church in West Virginia.*)

Fig. 83. Rev. Samuel Clawson. (From Barnes's *Methodist Protestant Church in West Virginia.*)

Preston County, where he died March 18, 1859. He served in George I. Davinson's company in the War of 1812, the entire company walking to Norfolk.

He married Parmelia, daughter of Jacob Zinn, of the Zinn Settlement near Monongalia Glades. She was born May 4, 1804, and died April 7, 1886. Their children included Ashford, Lycurgus, Clarissa, William B., Granville, Amelia, Ruhama, Sarah A., Elizabeth, Loretta, and Marcellus J.[30]

**Alexander Faulkner.** Alexander Faulkner, the son of James and Elizabeth (Hawthorne) Faulkner, was born on the vessel bringing his parents across the Atlantic from northern Ireland, and died in Clinton Township February 27, 1859, aged sixty-eight years. His parents settled first at Dunkard Bottom and then moved to the vicinity of Morgantown. His father left on a trip to his homeland and was never heard of again; it was presumed that he had been murdered.

Alexander settled on a two-hundred-acre farm in 1837, spending the remainder of his life there. His trade was that of a scythe and sickle manufacturer; but his life was also devoted to farming, grazing, and stock-raising, being quite successful.

He married ——— and they had six children, Mary A., Thomas J., James A., John, William, and Eliza.[31]

**Fletcher Brock.**[32] Blacksville's first postmaster, Fletcher Brock, died June 2, 1859. The son of William Brock II and Margaret Dunn Brock, he was born May 5, 1807. He married Rachel, daughter of John Stephenson, and they had nine children, namely, Hugh Workman, Margaret E., Cynthia, Caroline, William, Martha, Luther Samson, Harriet, and Charley.

He was a licensed minister of the Methodist Episcopal church, but never had a regular charge. In addition to being postmaster, he ran a store in Blacksville for many years.

The Brock home was on the state line, part of the house in Virginia, part in Pennsylvania. He served several years in the Pennsylvania legislature and was elected to Congress from Pennsylvania.

30. *Cyclopedia of Monongalia County*, pp. 180, 181.
31. *Cyclopedia of Monongalia County*, pp. 198, 199.
32. Pers. comm., Lou (Brock) Reynolds, Bridgeville, Delaware.

**Births, Marriages, and Deaths.** Vital statistics for the 1850s were reported by Wiley as follows:

|      | Births | Marriages | Death |
|------|--------|-----------|-------|
| 1850 | 430    | 168       | 153   |
| 1854 | 204    | 65        | 129   |
| 1855 | 243    | 72        | 122   |
| 1856 | 244    | 59        | 111   |
| 1857 | 322    | 48        | 136   |
| 1858 | 385    | 57        | 122   |
| 1859 | 312    | 42        | 53    |

**Prices of Farm Products in the 1850s.** Wiley gives farm prices, carefully compiled from newspapers and private diaries, on January 1 each year, as follows on page 488.[33]

**Land Grants Made in 1859.** Monongalia County grantees in 1859 included:

| | | |
|---|---|---|
| Dunn, James       | 128 a. | Lick Run       |
| Liming, Reason    | 1      | Dunkard Creek  |
| Shafer, Dennis M. | 2      | Adj. John Camp |
| Shively, Michael  | 2      | Scotts Run     |
| Weaver, Jacob     | 32     | Wades Run      |

**County and Borough Government.** James Hare was reelected commissioner of the revenue for the Eastern District.

Trustees of the borough of Morgantown were M. Callendine, F. A. Dering, Alexander Hayes, D. H. Chadwick, W. A. Hanway, R. L. Berkshire, and M. M. Dent.

**Gas and Water Franchise.** Benjamin F. Smith and Jonathan M. Heck were given by the borough trustees the right to furnish water and gas for fifty years and to continue thereafter unless they failed to supply gas for a period of twelve months, whereupon the franchise would be revoked. They did drill a well and got some gas, but not sufficient for the purpose and the enterprise was abandoned.[34]

33. *History of Monongalia County,* p. 470.
34. City records, vol. 1, p. 251.

### Prices of Farm Products in the 1850s

|      | Wheat, per bu. | Corn, per bu. | Oats, per bu. | Rye, per bu. | Buck-wheat, per bu. | Butter, per lb. | Eggs, per doz. | Bacon, per lb. | Potatoes, per bu. |
|------|------|------|--------|------|------|--------|------|--------|------|
| 1850 | 1.00 | .45 | .31 | .44 | .37 | .12 | .08 | .07 | ... |
| 1851 | .75 | .37 | .31 | ... | ... | .12 | .08 | .10 | ... |
| 1852 | .60 | .40 | .31 | ... | ... | .15 | .10 | .10 | ... |
| 1853 | .65 | .37 1/2 | .25 | ... | ... | .16 3/4 | ... | .12 1/2 | .25 |
| 1854 | 1.00 | .40 | .33 1/3 | ... | ... | .15 | .09 | .12 | .50 |
| 1855 | 1.75 | .75 | .50 | ... | ... | .15 | ... | ... | 1.00 |
| 1856 | 1.50 | .37 | .22 | ... | ... | .15 | .12 | .12 | .37 |
| 1857 | 1.00 | .50 | .37 | ... | ... | .15 | .08 | .12 | .75 |
| 1858 | .60 | .37 | .25 | ... | ... | .12 | ... | .16 | .37 |
| 1859 | 1.00 | .75 | .40 | ... | ... | .12 | ... | .12 | .75 |

**Miscellany.** In 1859: John A. Dille, J. Marshall Hagans, and John G. Gay were admitted to the Monongalia County bar (Wiley, p. 316). . . . The rate of tuition in subscription schools was about 3¼ to 3½ cents per day (Wiley, p. 363). . . . George M. Hagans on January 13 succeeded Edgar C. Wilson as president of the Merchants' and Mechanics' Bank (Wiley, p. 462). . . . Dr. James V. Boughner, who had been practicing medicine at Browns Mills since 1845, retired and moved to Morgantown (Wiley, p. 480). . . . J. M. Mickle was master of the Masonic lodge (Wiley, p. 548). . . . Dr. Elisha H. Coombs and Dr. Samuel Kelley began the practice of medicine in Morgantown (Wiley, pp. 584, 585). . . . O. B. Johnson built a sawmill and gristmill at Clinton Furnace, but abandoned his carding and tanning business (Wiley, p. 617). . . . Charles Kerns was running a store and gristmill at Uffington (Wiley, p. 619). . . . Amelia, wife of Col. Amos Jolliffe, died on February 27, aged sixty-three (Wiley, p. 633). . . . The original property used by the Morgantown Female Academy, on Bumbo Lane, was conveyed to Harrison M. Hagans (Callahan, p. 143). . . . Bids were advertised for construction of a bridge across Deckers Creek near its mouth (Callahan, p. 166). . . . The leading business firms in Morgantown included William Lazier, R. L. and N. Berkshire, Chadwick and Neph., Callendine and Nye, and Rogers and Fogle (Callahan, p. 175). . . . The suspension bridge was leased to E. C. Bright for eleven hundred dollars (Callahan, p. 179). . . . Organization of an Anti-Tobacco Society was attempted but failed (Callahan, p. 188). . . . Nimrod Dent, son of distinguished pioneer Capt. John Dent, died.

# CHAPTER EIGHTY-FOUR

# 1860

Charles Henry Ambler, the distinguished West Virginia University historian, wrote his doctoral dissertation at the University of Wisconsin on sectionalism in Virginia, and presently published it, with considerable amplification, in book form.[1]

In the introduction to this work Dr. Ambler said: "The history of Virginia has been characterized by sectional antagonism. The natural features of her territory and the different elements in her population made such conflicts inevitable. In the early colonial days, even before population advanced into the Piedmont, the frontier settlers chafed under the rule of the older and more aristocratic planters. As population extended to the westward and became more diverse in nationality, the contrasts and conflicts between the older and newer societies became more pronounced."

In the first half of the nineteenth century, Ambler says, the sectional strife "was mainly a contest between a cismontane and a transmontane people. It was a contest between an older society with its peculiar institutions and a newer society fundamentally different from the older and inadequately represented in the law-making bodies. It was a contest between the owners of large estates and the owners of small farms; between a population largely English and one composed of various nationalities; and between a people whose economic interests and relations were with the South and a people whose interests and relations were mainly with the North. Unable to control the

1. *Sectionalism in Virginia from 1776 to 1861* (Chicago, 1910).

action of the state in 1861 . . . , most of the trans-Allegheny withdrew from the state and formed West Virginia."[2]

**Discord.** The citizens of Monongalia County were quite active in this sectional strife and we have called attention to this on numerous earlier pages of this work. Some concessions to the demands of the West were made in the Constitution of 1830, but they were insufficient and the agitation continued.

Still other gains were made in the Constitution of 1850. The principal matters of debate concerned representation and suffrage. A county newspaper editor commented, in 1850: "We ask for the right of representation for freemen, instead of being made 'hewers of wood and drawers of water' to those whose chattels are deemed of equal value with ourselves,"[3] a reference to the principle advocated by the Easterners that the amount of property owned should determine voting rights.

Monongalia people felt that the calling of a constitutional convention in 1850, on the eve of a new census, was taking advantage of the Westerners, since the western counties had been increasing in population more rapidly than the eastern counties.

But the convention was held[4] and some gains were made, but not all the objectives were attained. The landed qualification of voters was abolished and all property was to be taxed according to its value, but the basis of representation (denominated the "Mixed Basis") was based on the number of white inhabitants and the amount of state taxes paid, instead of the "White Basis," which demanded that each white man should have one vote, regardless of the amount of taxes paid.

The Constitution of 1850, then, was a step in advance; the West had extorted further concessions from the East but there were still many sources of strife left unhealed.

The profound excitement following the raid of John Brown at Harpers Ferry in the autumn of 1859 had not at all subsided

2. Ibid., p. 5. See also F. E. Chadwick, *Causes of the Civil War*, in A. B. Hart's *American Nation* series (1906). See also Richard Orr Curry, "The Virginia Background for the History of the Civil War and Reconstruction Era in West Virginia: An Analytical Commentary," *West Virginia History* 20 (1959):215-46.

3. *Monongalia Mirror*, quoted by Wiley, p. 154.

4. See pp. 348, 349.

by the opening of the presidential campaign in 1860. The campaign was bitter beyond precedent.

**The Presidential Election.** The vote in Monongalia County was as follows:

|               | Lincoln | McClellan |
|---------------|---------|-----------|
| Court House   | 283     | 75        |
| Ross's        | 140     | 42        |
| Burgess's     | 101     | 8         |
| Stumptown     | 126     | 124       |
| Laurel Point  | 147     | 59        |
| Arnettsville  | 58      | 79        |
| Mooresville   | 177     | 135       |
| Warren        | 100     | 142       |
| Clinton Furnace | 191   | 44        |
|               | 1,323   | 708       |

When it was determined that Abraham Lincoln was elected, the people of South Carolina at once passed an ordinance of secession from the Union. The governor of Virginia called an extra session of the general assembly to consider the crisis. No one understood that a terrible war was about to start, or that the problems between East and West in Virginia were coming to a head.

**Slavery in 1860.** Slavery was not a problem in Monongalia County. The number of slaves in Monongalia County had continued to decline during the past decade and Steel points out that if the statistical trends had continued, there would have been no slaves here, in another dozen years, even without the Emancipation Proclamation.

In 1860, only 101 slaves were recorded in the county. James D. Watson had 13, George W. Dorsey 10, William Talbott 6, Sarah Hanway 5; altogether, there were only 37 slave owners in the county.[5]

**E. C. Wilson.** Edgar Campbell Wilson, son of Thomas Wilson,[6] died in Morgantown April 24, 1860, escaping the agony of intrafraternal strife. He was born in Morgantown on October 18, 1800.

5. *West Virginia History* 34 (1973):337-39, 358.
6. See *The Monongalia Story*, vol. 2, p. 515.

Edgar C. read law in his father's office and was admitted to the county bar on June 24, 1822. Following in his father's footsteps, he was elected to the United States House of Representatives and served from 1833 until 1835. In September of 1833 he formed a partnership with a new lawyer in town, Waitman T. Willey, a union which lasted two years, when Willey opened an office of his own.

He was very active in civic and religious affairs. He was elected secretary of the Morgantown Central Temperance Society on July 4, 1837, and became a ruling elder in the Presbyterian church the same year. In 1842 he was appointed prosecuting attorney in the circuit court of the new county of Marion.

Several young men who later became distinguished lawyers studied in his office, including Lycurgus Stephen Hough, who came to Morgantown in 1842 and was admitted to the bar March 29, 1844, and George S. Ray, who was admitted to the bar September 8, 1845.

He was greatly interested in education and served as a trustee of the Monongalia Academy. On October 25, 1846, he was appointed school commissioner for District No. 6 (East Side), charged with supervision of schoolmasters in his district who received money from the State Literary Fund for instruction of indigent children; there were no "free schools" in that day.

On March 29, 1851, he was one of the incorporators of the Monongalia County Mutual Insurance Company, the county's first insurance company. Actually, however, the company never conducted any business.

As a development enterprise he laid out fifteen lots south of Deckers Creek as Wilson's Addition. Many years later this (with other areas) was incorporated under the name of Durbannah.

He was president of the Morgantown branch, Merchants' and Mechanics' Bank of Wheeling from March 26, 1857, to January 13, 1859.

The Monongalia County bar, following his death, passed the following resolution:

"That the character of Mr. Wilson as a lawyer, a gentleman, and a Christian, is eminently entitled to our respect, and we desire to enter upon the record of the court a permanent testimonial of our high regard for it."[7]

**Census of 1860.** The population of the county, by the census of 1860, was reported as totaling 13,048, classified as 101 slave, 46 free colored, and 12,901 white. By sexes, there were 6,453 males and 6,595 females. The free colored people, by sexes, were 26 males and 20 females; of slaves, there were 42 males and 59 females. The increase since 1850 had been only 661, about 5 percent. The number of persons per square mile averaged thirty-six.

The population of the town of Morgantown was given as 741, including 740 whites and 1 free colored; the number of slaves was not given. Neither was the population of the several districts into which the county was divided given separately.

Industrial statistics were reported as follows on page 495.

The total value of property in the county was given as: real estate, $3,535,232; personal property, $1,360,800; total, $4,896,032.

The census gave detailed agricultural information for the county:

| LANDS, STOCK, ETC. | | | |
|---|---|---|---|
| Acres in improved farms | 92,048 | Tobacco, lbs. | 1,380 |
| Acres in unimproved | | Wool, lbs. | 27,801 |
| farms | 86,310 | Peas and beans, bu. | 41 |
| Cash value of farms | $2,884,916 | Irish potatoes, bu. | 10,586 |
| Value farm implements | | Sweet potatoes, bu. | 565 |
| and machinery | $59,257 | Barley, bu. | 161 |
| Number horses | 3,904 | Buckwheat, bu. | 13,798 |
| Number mules and asses | 32 | Orchard products, value | $9,376 |
| Number milch cows | 3,881 | Wine, gal. | 45 |
| Number working oxen | 680 | Market garden | |
| Number other cattle | 7,090 | products, value | $ 103 |
| Number sheep | 10,945 | Butter, lbs. | 171,876 |
| Number swine | 8,028 | Cheese, lbs. | 6,116 |
| Value of live stock | $454,070 | Hay, tons | 6,353 |
| | | Clover and grass | |
| GRAIN AND PRODUCE | | seed, bu. | 376 |
| Wheat, bu. | 49,124 | Hops, lbs. | 32 |
| Rye, bu. | 4,999 | Flax, lbs. | 5,998 |
| Corn, bu. | 239,024 | Maple Sugar, lbs. | 32,608 |
| Oats, bu. | 126,198 | Maple Molasses, gal. | 1,812 |

7. Wiley, pp. 276, 277; Callahan, *Making of Morgantown*, p. 93.

## Industrial Statistics

| | Number of Establish-ments | Number Hands Employed | Annual Wages | Cost of Raw Material | Capital Invested | Annual Value of Products |
|---|---|---|---|---|---|---|
| Agricultural Implements | 2 | 5 | $1,152 | $ 1,100 | $ 5,200 | $ 3,100 |
| Carriages | 1 | 10 | 3,600 | 600 | 3,000 | 10,000 |
| Men's Clothing | 1 | 4 | 672 | 1,000 | 1,000 | 2,000 |
| Flour and Meal | 12 | 22 | 5,772 | 97,987 | 53,500 | 114,284 |
| Furniture, Cabinet | 1 | 2 | 480 | 247 | 1,000 | 887 |
| Leather | 4 | 9 | 840 | 4,815 | 8,300 | 6,700 |
| Lumber, Sawed | 7 | 8 | 2,088 | 3,910 | 6,800 | 7,475 |
| Pottery Ware | 1 | 2 | 600 | 497 | 1,500 | 2,000 |
| Wool, Carded | 3 | 3 | 180 | 7,200 | 5,000 | 8,000 |

| | | |
|---|---|---|
| Sorghum Molasses, gal. . | 7,722 | Animals slaughtered |
| Beeswax, lbs. . . . . . . . . | 111 | or sold for |
| Honey, lbs. . . . . . . . . . | 8,271 | slaughter value  . . . . . $46,994 |
| Home manufactures | | |
| value . . . . . . . . . . . . . $13,290 | | |

The number of farms in the county was reported as follows: between 10 and 20 acres, 11; between 20 and 50 acres, 159; between 50 and 100 acres, 453; between 100 and 500 acres, 335; between 500 and 1000 acres, 6.

Religious statistics gave the number of church edifices as forty-six (compared with thirty-one in 1850), having a total value of $39,350, with 15,350 sittings. These were classified as twenty-nine Methodist edifices, valued at $27,350, with 9,600 sittings; Baptist, ten, $7,000, 3,200; Presbyterian, four, $4,000, 1,650; and Christian, three, $1,000, 900.

**Navigation Company Charter Renewed.** The success of slack water below New Geneva renewed the interest of Morgantown people in efforts to secure money enough to bring it into Virginia. On March 8, 1860, the charter of the Monongahela Navigation Company was renewed by the Virginia General Assembly, and amended to authorize the company to extend slack water to Clarksburg.

At a meeting on April 24 Col. James Evans was elected president and Isaac Scott secretary. A committee composed of W. T. Willey, Col. James Evans, P. H. Keck, Prof. J. R. Moore, and Col. William A. Hanway was appointed to visit Pittsburgh to solicit aid.

In November Colonel Evans went to Pittsburgh and addressed the board of trade. Assurances of aid were received from the Pennsylvania navigation company. "Engineers employed to make a survey of the river, reported sixteen feet of fall from the Pennsylvania line to Morgantown, and that two locks and dams, costing $100,000, would be necessary to slack the river between these points. The borough trustees of Morgantown ordered a vote upon a subscription by the town of $5,000 to the enterprise. There is no record of such election having been held. The presidential election of 1860 and the beginning of the Rebellion called away the energies of the people to other subjects. . . ."[8]

8. Wiley, pp. 128, 129.

Fig. 84. Calvary Methodist Church. (Photo Dr. and Mrs. Gideon S. Dodds.)

**Calvary Church Dedicated.** The Calvary Methodist Episcopal Church, at Darnell Hollow, was dedicated by the Reverend Peter T. Laishley in 1860. Charter members were William Donaldson, Lewranah Donaldson, William Lewellin, Mary Lewellin, James Donaldson, Mary E. Donaldson, Charles E. Donaldson, Charity Donaldson, Ruth Cleaver, Amy A. Costolo, John Q. Saddler, Sarah J. Saddler, Thomas Irvin, Catherine Irvin, James McGee, E. O. Hickle, Mary J. Rankin, and Joab R. Donaldson.

The congregation had been organized about 1852, following a revival in a nearby log schoolhouse. The church was built in 1859.[9]

**"Hogeye" Church.** As early as 1860 a log church was built on the site of the later Mount Pleasant Methodist Protestant Church, on the Kingwood "Pike." Ephraim Cohen, Levi Dalton, William Clark, William Pool, and Daniel Brown and their families were leaders in the society. Hogs were allowed to run at

9. Wiley, pp. 688, 689; Dodds and Dodds, *Churches of Monongalia County*, p. 150.

large in the early days, and often crawled under the church to rest. Tradition says that, during a service one day, a boy looking down through a crack in the floor, saw a hog looking up at him, and cried out loud, "See the hog eye!" From that time on, Mount Pleasant was popularly referred to as "Hogeye" Church.[10]

**Episcopalians and Presbyterians Differ.** The Episcopalians at Morgantown began to exhibit signs of new activity in 1860. The Guy Allen Parish of the Diocese of Virginia, including Monongalia County within its limits, was organized by the Reverend H. S. Kepler at the house of E. B. Swearingen, on October 16, 1860.

By the autumn of 1860 a difference of opinion appeared between the Presbyterians and the Episcopalians concerning the rights of each in the Morgantown church property (see *Monongalia Story*, vol. 2, pp. 447-49, 499-501). The differences developed particularly in connection with the proposal of the Reverend D. J. Lee, of Fairmont, to preach for the Episcopalians.

On November 5, 1860, John Rogers, E. B. Swearingen, and J. R. Drabell signed a report to the Guy Allen Parish saying that they had conferred with a committee of the Presbyterians and had amically discussed the matters of difference and that the two parties had agreed upon a temporary plan of joint occupancy, as follows: "That said church should be set aside for Episcopal service on every Monday, and every fifth Sunday, commencing Monday the 12th inst., suiting our present necessities, and to continue until further arrangements are entered into by the parties; that the pending election of trustees for said church be deferred until the first Monday in January, 1861, that due notice may be given by the surviving trustees to all parties interested, that the interests of all may be consulted and met in said election; that both parties are at liberty to make arrangements for lights, fuel, and sexton as either party may deem proper."

The Episcopal vestry, to which this report was submitted on December 7, authorized Swearingen to notify the Reverend Mr.

10. Barnes, *The Methodist Protestant Church in West Virginia*, p. 149.

Lee of the arrangement for the place of worship. Mr. Lee, a man of pronounced pro-Southern views, had been expecting an invitation to preach and was promptly requested to come on the first Monday thereafter. In his letter to Lee, dated December 9, Swearingen explained that the negotiations with "our Presbyterian partners" had been "rather delicate and consequently tedious."

At a meeting of the Presbyterian congregation on December 19, called "to consider steps to build a new house of worship," Benjamin F. Smith introduced a resolution with the following preamble: "Whereas until very recently the larger part of this congregation was not aware of any right existing to this house of worship other than the one enjoyed by them and in pursuance of their right had inaugurated the policy of erecting a new building upon the same site; and whereas the P. E. congregation are now claiming a right of occupying this house a part of the time—inconsistent with our present arrangement and future plans, and also much to our discomfort—and yet we have temporarily granted with hope of some speedy arrangement whereby the distinctive rights of the two congregations could be ascertained and the property as a whole vested in one or the other."

At the same meeting a committee was appointed, composed of B. F. Smith, Rev. J. R. Moore, and Col. Lee Roy Kramer to meet with the Protestant Episcopal congregation to negotiate "for the sale or purchase of the respective rights of either in the church building."

But before the proposed meeting could be held, the Episcopalians were apparently embarrassed by tactless actions of the Reverend Mr. Lee, which occupied their attention to the exclusion of the matter of property title, and resulted in his dismissal by the vestry. At a meeting on December 29 the vestry requested Mr. Lee to furnish it with a copy of a "certain article or communication which appeared in the Southern Churchman about the 19th of October last, reflecting upon citizens of this place and vicinity and purporting to have been written by him."[11]

11. On January 4, 1861, the vestry resolved that "the spirit manifested on the part of the Rev. D. J. Lee be condemned as ill-becoming one of his position and highly disrespectful of the Vestry" and ordered that his services be dispensed with.

Meantime, steps had been taken to revive the old joint board of trustees which had been responsible for construction of the church building in 1819 (*Monongalia Story*, vol. 2, pp. 448, 449). Swearingen summarized the situation in a letter to Lee, dated November 9: ". . . We trust, Revd. and dear sir, that you will rejoice with us that we have accomplished so much in a peaceful and amicable manner, obtaining a comfortable house for our services altogether suited to our present necessities, with the right of the joint occupation hereafter when arrangements demanded. What is something remarkable in regards to this church property there has been no election of trustees since 1827. The articles of association provide, however, that the trustees elected remain in office until their successors should be elected. Being now about thirty years since the last election was held and our friend and brother churchman, John Rogers, Esq. is the only surviving trustee whose duty it will be to order an election which will be done on the first Monday in January next as agreed."[12]

**Amended Charter for Morgantown.** On March 20, 1860, an amended charter for the borough was granted by the general assembly. This charter provided for the election annually of a mayor, sergeant, recorder, and five councilmen. The boundaries given were those established in 1785 (see *Monongalia Story*, vol. 2, p. 125); the town had not increased in area in three-quarters of a century.

Philip Rogers was the first mayor, Manliff Hayes the first recorder, and A. C. Pickenpaugh the first sergeant. Councilmen elected were David H. Chadwick, William A. Hanway, Robert P. Hennen, Mathew Gay, Jr., and George Kiger.

The first action of the new town government was to order a revision of the ordinances which had been in force under the

12. The meeting was duly held, on January 7, 1861, and John Rogers, William A. Hanway, John P. Byrne, Lee Roy Kramer, and L. S. Hough were chosen as trustees. The title of the Presbyterian congregation to the property was quieted for the time being. Neither congregation had any deed to the Sepulchre lot (*The Monongalia Story*, vol. 2, p. 449); they had merely jointly built on it. The Episcopalians' claim was originally for only a half interest in the building, not in the lot. Wiley, p. 447; Callahan, *Making of Morgantown*, pp. 155-57; Moreland, *The First Presbyterian Church*, pp. 34-37.

old board of trustees. The mayor appointed William A. Hanway, D. H. Chadwick, and M. Hayes as the revision committee and they gave their report on July 4, 1860, which report was adopted.

The ordinances prohibited obstructions of sidewalks, discharge of firearms, drunkenness, gambling, etc., except under specified conditions. Disorderly conduct, such as indecent exposure, cursing, fighting, or rioting, was also forbidden. Dogs were taxed. Owners of hogs were fined if their hogs were found running at large. Racing of horses through the streets was prohibited. Buying, setting off, or shooting firecrackers, squibs, or other combustible material was prohibited.[13]

**George Waters.** A farmer of the Fort Martin community, George Waters, died December 11, 1860. He was born April 21, 1781, and was married (probably) three times. By his first wife, Mary (Hart), he had six children, Elijah, Mary, Eliza, Hannah, John Nelson, and Nancy. Tradition says he then married Mary Davis but no children are known. His next wife was Nancy, daughter of John, Jr., and Elizabeth Evans. Their children were George, Jr., Rawley, and Evans.[14]

**Land Grants Made in 1860.** Monongalia County grants in 1860 included:

| | | |
|---|---|---|
| Collins, Isaac | 1¾ a. | Dunkard Creek |
| Cumbridge, George F. | 15 | Dunkard Creek |
| Hanway, William A., et al. | 16 | Days Run |
| Smith, B. F., et al. | 16 | Days Run |

**County Government.** James Odbert was elected for his second consecutive term as sheriff.

Justices (members of the county court) elected, by districts, were:

1. Moses Steele, Alpheus Holland, Hamilton G. West, Thomas Tarleton.

2. Augustus Haymond, George M. Reay.

3. William W. John, John Bowers, William Donaldson, James T. McClaskey.

13. Wiley, pp. 576, 577; Callahan, *Making of Morgantown*, pp. 190-95.
14. Gordon C. Baker, "The Waters Family of ... Monongalia County ...," *Monongalia Chronicle*, April, 1975. The name is often spelled Watters in early records.

4. Daniel Duzenberry, J. K. Barrickman, Purnel Simpson.
5. John B. Lough, Jesse Mercer.
6. John Wildman, Nimrod Tennant, E. B. Tygart, Noah Morris.
7. S. H. Shriver, John A. Wiley, P. L. Rice, Justus Garrard.

The justices elected Augustus Haymond as president of the county court.

**Miscellany.** In 1860: Ashbel Fairchild added a two-story machine shop to his carriage works (Wiley, p. 262 note). . . . William A. Hanway was admitted to the Monongalia County bar on April 13 and Lowrie Wilson on September 4 (Wiley, p. 316). . . . William Berkshire died (Wiley, p. 323). . . . John Keck died (Wiley, p. 342). . . . The thirteenth session of the Western Virginia Conference of the Methodist Episcopal Church was held in Morgantown, beginning on March 14; Bishop Scott presided (Wiley, p. 445). . . . A charter was procured on February 20, for the Monongalia Bank of Morgantown (Wiley, p. 464). . . . Mary L. Henry died at the age of ninety-one (Wiley, p. 472). . . . Dr. George W. John opened a general store at Stewartstown (Wiley, p. 478). . . . William Britt was master of the Masonic lodge (Wiley, p. 548). . . . Charles Wallace was appointed postmaster of Morgantown (Wiley, p. 579). . . . A post office named Easton was established July 9, with Charles Lewellen the first postmaster; Dr. Charles McLane suggested the name Easton because it was east of Morgantown (Wiley, p. 676). . . . By a new arrangement, starting this year, collection of tolls on the suspension bridge was placed in charge of a toll taker employed by the directors. Already the bridge was stimulating the building of homes on the west side of the river (Callahan, p. 179). . . . Oil lamps were replacing candles in public buildings; the church minutes indicate Avery Chapel made the change this year (Dodds and Dodds, p. 149).

# CHAPTER EIGHTY-FIVE

# 1861

The American people at the beginning of the year 1861 awaited developments as men and women anxiously await the coming of a predicted tornado, not knowing if it will hit them or not, or what its intensity will be if it does hit.

"Men's motives . . . ," Bruce Catton says,[1] "are mixed and obscure, and none of the many separate decisions which brought war to America in 1861 is wholly explicable." Slavery was only one of many problems that were agitating the citizenry. Revolutionary changes were taking place at the middle of the nineteenth century, changes that were rocking society to its foundations.

Looking back, Catton adds, Americans "could see that something cherished and familiar was being lost," the early society governed by a common tradition. "That society, in retrospect, seemed to have been singularly uncomplicated and unworried—a loose amalgam of small cities, quiet towns, and peaceful farms, slow in movement, lacking railroads and telegraph lines and owning no factories of any consequence, simple and self-sustaining, owing the outside world no more than casual acknowledgment. . . ."

**The Coming Fury.** But now an Industrial Revolution was in progress, attracting immigrants by the thousands, "men of new tongues and new creeds and new folk ways, cut adrift from Europe by famine, by revolution, or by simple restless hope," adding to the complexity of the scene, when, on April 17,

1. Bruce Catton, *The Coming Fury* (1961), p. 79. For additional material on this period, see David M. Potter, *The Impending Crisis, 1848-1861* (1976), 638 pp.

1861, a special convention of the Commonwealth of Virginia voted for secession from the Union.

It was a fateful day. "With the rising of the sun," Wiley says,[2] "Virginia was united; with its setting, the East had pronounced for secession, and the West was assembling its first meeting in favor of revolution against any attempted disunion."

Excitement had been building in Monongalia County ever since Abraham Lincoln had been elected president, on November 6, 1860, and the movement for secession had gotten under way.

"The crisis has come," Marshall M. Dent commented, early in the new year adding: "We are in the midst of a Revolution. The country is becoming aroused in every direction. . . . Madness rules the hour. The North has commenced to arm, and soon we will be in the midst of a bloody internecine war. . . . We here warn you to beware of the insidious smiles of Secession. It commenced as a peaceable lamb, and has increased step by step until it has become a monster of strength and power. Again we call upon you to arouse to your interests—to choose for yourselves whether you shall be for or against your country."[3]

Excitement grew in the county. The Kramer Guards and Moore Cadets paraded in Morgantown on January 27; Waitman T. Willey made an impassioned speech to a large assemblage, which was received with applause. A Union pole and flag was raised in Morgantown, another in Granville. A Union meeting at Easton on January 30 had William J. Vandervort as chairman and was addressed by J. M. Holmes, Thomas A. Ryan, and W. S. Cobun. On the same day Daniel Miller presided over a similar meeting at Fort Martin.[4]

Pursuant to a previous notice—there was no telegraph line nearer than Fairmont and no way the citizens could learn what was then happening in Richmond—a large assemblage of people met in the Monongalia County courthouse on the evening of the very day on which the act of secession was passed. William Lazier was elected president, George M. Reay, William N. Jarrett, John Mikel, and Henry Dering, vice-presidents, and Drs. William M. Dent and Isaac Scott, secretaries. A committee on

2. Wiley, pp. 138, 139.
3. *Virginia Star*, January 5, 1861.
4. Wiley, p. 136.

resolutions, composed of Dr. J. V. Boughner, Francis Madera, Col. Leroy Kramer, R. L. Berkshire, and Dr. H. N. Mackey, reported a series of resolutions, including the following:

"Resolved, That in case an ordinance of secession is passed by our State Convention, that our delegates be requested to propose a division of the State, by some line that will sever us from all future connection with Eastern secessionists."[5]

The resolutions were unanimously approved and the meeting adjourned until Monday, April 22.

Marshall M. Dent commented:

"The whole West is on fire, and ere long the flames will reach the top of the Blue Ridge and proclaim to our oppressors and would-be masters, that our backs are not yet ready for their lash; that we have borne with their oppression and unjust taxation as long as we can, and that now, we must either be equals, or separate."[6]

Morgantown was bedecked with flags on the twenty-second, when the meeting reassembled. A delegation from "The Flats" numbered 300, one from Fort Martin 250; it was said over two thousand people were present. F. H. Pierpont and Fontaine Smith made speeches.

Waitman T. Willey[7] and Marshall M. Dent, Monongalia's delegates to the convention, arrived home in a few days, gave a report of the convention, and urged that western Virginia declare herself a separate and independent state.

The ordinance for secession provided for elections to be held in the various counties on May 23. Excitement was intense as Monongalia County people prepared for the vote. Over a thousand people assembled in a mass meeting on Adam Brown's farm at the mouth of Dolls Run, with great demonstrations, flags and banners flying, bands playing, and people cheering.

Other assemblies were held at the Evans schoolhouse, where over four hundred were present; at Clinton Furnace, at Easton, at Cheat Neck, at Captain Joseph Snider's, near Fort Martin.[8]

5. The full text of the several resolutions may be consulted in Wiley, *History of Monongalia County,* pp. 139-41.
6. *Virginia Star,* April 20, 1861.
7. Willey had delivered a powerful speech before the convention on March 2, in opposition to secession. See Wiley, pp. 184-88.
8. Wiley, p. 142.

Monongalia County's vote on the ordinance of secession was:

|  | For | Against |
|---|---|---|
| Court-house | 2 | 801 |
| Guseman's | 0 | 36 |
| Jones's | 9 | 146 |
| Osborn's | 0 | 84 |
| Ross's | 0 | 114 |
| Loftus's | 0 | 153 |
| Cushman's | 0 | 103 |
| Cassville | 1 | 133 |
| Laurel Point | 10 | 134 |
| Cox's | 62 | 63 |
| Mooresville | 0 | 201 |
| Tennant's | 7 | 35 |
| Darrah's | 2 | 66 |
| Warren | 22 | 190 |
|  | 115 | 2,259 |

While the people were voting, a rumor came that a Confederate force was gathering at Grafton. At Morgantown the borough council placed the town under the protection of Captain Jacob Hickman, of the Home Guards.

Excitement was intense on the following Monday, when a messenger reported an armed force only ten miles away, whose object was to capture the town. Runners were sent into the country districts and into Pennsylvania, asking for help.

All night long armed men poured into Morgantown in response to the call. The first was the Cheat Neck company of militia; next was a company from Smithfield, Pennsylvania. Then came Captain Hughes Oliphant's cavalry company from Fairchance Furnace, and a company from Morris Cross Roads, both in Pennsylvania, and Captain Joseph Snider's company. Word came that two thousand men were on their way from Wheeling to attack the Confederates at Grafton.[9]

All was confusion. No one knew what to expect next.

**Fearful Emergency.** For half a century differences between Virginians east of the Alleghenies and those to the west had been

9. Wiley, pp. 142, 143.

growing, the rift had been widening. "Now," by the Morgantown resolutions of April 17, "the measure of Eastern oppression is full and . . . the day is near at hand when Western Virginia will rise up in the majesty of her strength and repudiating her oppressors will dissolve all her civil and political connection with them, and remain firmly under the time honored Stars and Stripes."

Already, even before the vote on the ordinance of secession, the people of western Virginia were agitating again the idea of a new state west of the Alleghenies.

John S. Carlisle and others assembled over twelve hundred people in a mass meeting at Clarksburg at the same time, recommending that the people of each county of northwestern Virginia appoint at least five persons to represent them in a convention at Wheeling on May 13, 1861, "to consult and determine upon such action as the people of North-western Virginia should take in the present fearful emergency."

Monongalia County's meeting was held in the courthouse on May 4 and instead of five only, eighty-five delegates[10] were named to go to Wheeling. On the thirteenth over four hundred delegates had assembled in Wheeling, representing twenty-six western Virginia counties.

John W. Moss, of Wood County, was elected president; one of the secretaries was Marshall M. Dent, of Monongalia. The Reverend Peter T. Laishley, of Monongalia, offered a prayer:

10. The complete list of delegates: Joseph Jolliffe, Alex. L. Wade, Allen Fast, Joseph Shuttlesworth, Moses Steel, Thomas Tarleton, Abraham Devault, John W. Lanham, M. M. Dent, William Lazier, Henry Dering, Dr. H. N. Mackey, Dr. Isaac Scott, Dr. Charles McLane, Col. James Evans, W. T. Willey, W. A. Hanway, J. R. Moore, L. W. Runner, Leroy Kramer, Elisha Coombs, John Rogers, F. Madera, Samuel Howell, William Shaw, Philip Rogers, Charles Howell, A. C. Pickenpaugh, J. T. McClasky, John Bowers, N. C. Vandervort, William Anderson, Jacob Miller, Edgar St. Clair, John N. Baker, James Hare, C. H. Burgess, F. Furman, John Lemley, Joseph Snider, William Simpson, Amos S. Bowlby, Dr. W. M. Dent, A. S. Courtney, Col. Reuben Finnell, Joel Bowlby, Jesse Mercer, Dr. J. V. Boughner, J. N. Waters, S. G. Morgan, C. S. Price, William Fear, Benj. Thompson, Benj. Barker, James T. Hess, E. G. Tygart, Andrew Brown, Michael Core, John Wildman, Asa Tennant, William Price, Asa Lemley, A. Garrison, E. Morris, Dr. John McCarl, William Kinney, P. L. Rice, J. S. Lemley, Charles Edwards, Andrew Wiley, George Price, A. B. Pratt, E. C. Bunker, E. P. Fitch, A. G. Davis, Alex. Wade, Sr., Dr. D. B. Dorsey, James Lazzell, R. L. Berkshire, W. N. Jarrett, G. R. Dering, E. B. Swearingen, A. S. Vance, George McNeely, and George D. Evans. Wiley, p. 144 note.

"May the Almighty grant that the stars and stripes of the flag of our country ever wave all over this land, from the Atlantic to the Pacific, and from Maine to the Gulf of Mexico. O may those who would plunge us into the horrors of civil discord be over-reached by the omnipotent hand of Almighty God. O do Thou grant, we pray Thee, that this convention met here for the purpose of consulting upon the best interests of our beloved Virginia, may act promptly, decisively and harmoniously. May it act with reference to peace, principles and the universal happiness of our citizens and the country at large."[11]

As noted above, the ordinance of secession, when it came to a vote on May 23, passed by a strong majority in the state of Virginia, and the state seceded from the Union. But the majority against secession was even stronger in western Virginia. The die was cast.

At Wheeling, the convention, assembling on June 11, passed "an ordinance for the reorganization of the State Government," on the grounds that the Richmond government, having seceded, no longer was a member of the Union, and certainly did not represent western Virginians. Monongalia County's delegates to this convention were Leroy Kramer, Joseph Snider, Ralph L. Berkshire, William Price, James Evans, and D. B. Dorsey.

On the twentieth, as provided by the ordinance, the convention elected Francis H. Pierpont (Fig. 91) governor of the Reorganized Government of Virginia.[12] Governor Pierpont was a son of Francis and Catharine Weaver Pierpont and a grandson of John Pierpont (*Monongalia Story*, vol. 2, pp. 242, 243), pioneer settler of Monongalia County, with whom General George Washington spent a night in 1784.

The legislature of the Reorganized Government met on July 1, 1861, and elected Waitman T. Willey and John S. Carlisle United States Senators from Virginia; the acceptance of their credentials, along with those of the representatives elected, constituted official recognition in Washington of the Reorganized Government.[13]

The Wheeling Convention reconvened on August 6 and on

11. Wiley, p. 145 note.
12. See Charles H. Ambler, *Francis H. Pierpont, Union war governor of Virginia and father of West Virginia* (1937) 483 pp.
13. Excerpts from Willey's first speech in the Senate, on December 19, 1861, appear in Wiley, pp. 192-94.

August 20 passed an ordinance for the formation of a new state, to be called Kanawha, to be submitted to the people for vote in October; at the same election delegates were to be chosen for a constitutional convention, to convene if the ordinance was approved. Monongalia County's delegates to this convention were W. T. Willey and Henry Dering. The ordinance was ratified and the convention assembled November 26, 1861.

Monongalia County's vote on the proposition of the new state was:

|  | *For* | *Against* |
|---|---|---|
| Court-house | 452 | 2 |
| Guseman's | 35 | 0 |
| Jones's | 98 | 0 |
| Osborn's | 56 | 0 |
| Ross's | 70 | 0 |
| Loftus's | 98 | 0 |
| Cushman's | 76 | 0 |
| Cassville | 147 | 0 |
| Laurel Point | 92 | 1 |
| Cox's | 51 | 0 |
| Mooresville | 147 | 0 |
| Tennant's | 48 | 2 |
| Darrah's | 54 | 1 |
| Warren | 167 | 12 |
|  | 1,591 | 18 |

Meanwhile Fort Sumter had fallen on April 13 and the war was on. The Richmond government perhaps underestimated the character of the resistance manifested in the western counties and determined quickly to secure control of them. Another objective was to control the important Baltimore and Ohio Railroad, which would be of tremendous strategic value to the side that could use it.

General Lee, on May 4, ordered Colonel Porterfield, of Harpers Ferry, and Major Boykin, of Weston, to rendezvous at Grafton, call out volunteers, and prepare to move on Wheeling to secure the railroad.

But, in the face of the advance of General McClellan's troops from Wheeling and Parkersburg, and disappointed in his attempts to secure an adequate supply of arms, Porterfield did not advance; instead he retreated towards Philippi, and Colonel Kelley, from Wheeling, occupied Grafton without resistance.

Fig. 85. The battle of Philippi. (From a contemporary drawing in *Harper's Weekly*.)

On June 1 another body of Union forces, under General Thomas A. Morris, reached Grafton. Late the following day three thousand Union soldiers marched by two routes towards Philippi. They encountered heavy rains during the night but just before dawn of June 3 the two columns converged on the town and fired the opening guns of the first inland battle of the war.[14]

In the brief battle that followed no one was killed and the Confederates retreated precipitately, so rapidly that Northerners referred to the engagement as the "Philippi races." McClellan announced by military telegraph to the excited country the news of his victories and optimism was high. But the war would not be won so easily.

**Military Outfits.** The call of President Lincoln, on April 15, 1861, for 75,000 troops, met a prompt response, and Monongalia County did its part.

14. See Phil Conley, "The First Land Battle of the Civil War," *West Virginia History* 20 (1959):120-23.

*Company A, Sixth West Virginia Cavalry.* This company was recruited at Morgantown and mustered into the service of the United States at Clarksburg on June 25, 1861, originally as Company A, Third West Virginia Infantry. Frank W. Thompson was elected captain and acted as such until the organization was completed, when he became lieutenant colonel of the regiment. On August 13, 1864, the company was reorganized and became Company A, Sixth West Virginia Cavalry; many of the men were mustered out then, or soon thereafter.[15]

## Officers

James J. Thompson, captain, promoted from private, August 5, 1861.

A. C. Pickenpaugh, first lieutenant, prisoner of war captured Springfield, Virginia, June 26, 1864.

Nicholas B. Madera, second lieutenant, promoted from sergeant, May 20, 1862; prisoner, captured at Winchester, Virginia, April 4, 1864.

Oliver S. Jones, sergeant.

George W. Debolt, sergeant.

William F. Cullen, sergeant, prisoner, captured at Springfield, June 26, 1864.

Joseph J. Cline, sergeant.

Robert J. Fleming, corporal, prisoner captured at Springfield, June 26, 1864.

John M. Triplett, corporal.

Jacob T. Shroyer, bugler.

John Smith, bugler.

## Privates

Windsor Austin

Thomas L. Berry

Isaac W. Criss

Sanford Courtney, prisoner, captured at Springfield, June 26, 1864.

John A. Cox

Anthony Conard, prisoner, captured at Rocky Gap, Virginia, August 26, 1863.

Garrett T. Fogle

William Hennen, prisoner, captured at Greenbrier, Virginia, June 26, 1864.

15. Records of the West Virginia outfits are to be found in the *Annual Report of the Adjutant General of the State of West Virginia for the year ending December 31, 1864* (Wheeling, 1865). For Company A, Sixth West Virginia Cavalry, see pp. 626-28, 654-56.

George W. Harding, prisoner, captured at Winchester, April 8, 1864.

William Hess

John D. Jenkins

Thomas M. Johnson

Titus Lemley

Thomas H. McBee

Marshall Phillips

J. F. Ross

Charles A. Schiller, prisoner, captured at Jacksons River, December 19, 1863.

Solon Stone

John M. Solomon, prisoner, captured at Springfield, June 26, 1864.

George Wright

James Watkins

Charles E. Watts

### Recruits
#### (with dates mustered in)

Richard W. Blue, February 25, 1864.

George W. Collins, March 3, 1864.

John Dancer, October 24, 1863.

B. Jennewine, March 3, 1864.

James W. McKenny, October 24, 1863.

John E. Price, September 24, 1862.

Rezin L. Piles, February 28, 1864.

Theodore Stone, November 14, 1861.

Henry Shisler, October 24, 1861, prisoner, captured at Springfield, June 26, 1864.

William A. Schriver, September 24, 1861, prisoner, captured April 28, 1864.

William H. Tasker, March 3, 1864.

Wilford Watkins, October 24, 1863.

### Discharged

F. W. Thompson, captain, promoted to lieutenant colonel, August 5, 1861.

James F. Linn, sergeant, for disability, Little Rock, Pennsylvania, December 12, 1862.

John C. Davis, second lieutenant, May 20, 1862.

William A. Widney, sergeant, March 10, 1864.

David E. Holmes, corporal, March 10, 1864.

Elsey F. Haskins, corporal, for disability, Fort McHenry, Maryland, August 31, 1862.

George Garrison, corporal, March 16, 1863, from wounds received at Waterloo Bridge.

John Powell, corporal, for disability, Columbus, Ohio, September 17, 1862.

Henry C. Spitznagle, corporal, August 14, 1862, from wounds received at Bull Run.

### Transferred

Milton Berry, corporal            Sepheus Jenkins, corporal
James R. Matthews, corporal       William P. Goodwin, private

### Died

William D. Minker, killed in action at Bull Run, August 29, 1862.

Salathiel Burke, of smallpox in hospital at Cumberland, July 25, 1864.

William Cole, killed in action at Cross Keys, June 8, 1862.

John J. Frederick, killed in action at Cross Keys, June 8, 1862.

Charles M. V. Gould, of fever, July 17, 1862, at Woodville, Virginia.

William H. Guthrie, killed in action at Bull Run, August 29, 1862.

Thomas Herrington, August 15, 1862, from wounds received in action at Cross Keys.

Matthew Jenkins, in hospital at Richmond, Virginia, November 22, 1863.

James Kennedy, of fever, at home, Fayette County, Pennsylvania, April 30, 1862.

John H. McNemar, of fever, at Franklin, Virginia, date unknown.

Frederick G. Maze, killed in action at Catletts Station, Virginia, August 23, 1862.

William Piles, October 2, 1862, of wounds received in action at Bull Run.

James Scott, of fever, at Sutton, March 16, 1863.

James Woods, of fever, at New Geneva, Pennsylvania, April 2, 1864.

Martin Watkins, of fever, at Strasburg, Virginia, June 23, 1862.

### Deserted

James M. McVickers, at Cumberland, February 4, 1862.

### Veterans

(Re-enlisted February 1, 1864; after the war the company did duty on the western plains until May 22, 1866, when the members were mustered out.)

William W. Hickman, sergeant
William S. Cobun, sergeant
David L. Davis, sergeant
E. H. Baird, sergeant
William Collins, corporal
George Smith, corporal
Josiah Davis, corporal
John T. Baily, corporal
Marshall Scott, corporal
David G. Casey, corporal
George Adams, farrier
Charles Martin, blacksmith
William Doty, saddler
W. R. Batson, wagoner
James F. Ashley
John E. Blany
John E. Caruthers
John H. Cole
John H. Cortney
John A. Doty

W. W. Fleming
William Hawker
Stephen O. Lewellen
James McGraw
William McPeck
John N. Maze
Ephraim Provance
Joseph Provance
John Rogers
Henry Scott
Leonard Shank
Luther Sheats
Charles B. Shisler
Joseph Shisler
David Simpson
Jackson Steel
John L. Wardman
Jacob M. Widows
Oliver P. Widows
Solomon Wright

Aggregate, 114 men.

Fig. 86. Union Army volunteers along High Street, 1861. (Courtesy West Virginia University Library.)

*Company A, First West Virginia Cavalry.* This company, known locally as the "Kelley Lancers," was recruited in Monongalia County and mustered in at Morgantown July 18, 1861, for three years. The first captain was J. Lowrie McBee, who served until March 25, 1862, when he was succeeded by Lt. H. H. Hagans, who served until July 3, 1862, when he resigned and was succeeded by Charles H. Capehart. The company took part in engagements at Romney, Blue's Gap, Winchester, Port Republic, Orange C. H., Cedar Mountain, Kelley's Ford, Second Bull Run, Droop Mountain, Cloyd Mountain, etc., and was mustered out at Wheeling July 8, 1865.

Officers

J. Lowrie McBee, captain, promoted to major, Third West Virginia Cavalry, March 25, 1862, to lieutenant colonel, July 18, 1863, and to colonel, March 10, 1865.

N. N. Hoffman, first lieutenant; promoted from sergeant to second lieutenant, March 25, 1862, to first lieutenant, October 1, 1862.

H. H. Hagans, captain; enlisted as private, promoted to first lieutenant, December 15, 1861, to captain, March 25, 1862.

Thomas H. B. Lemley, first lieutenant.

Thomas D. Pugh, first sergeant.

John H. Conn, second lieutenant, promoted from sergeant, October 1, 1862.

William H. Jones, quartermaster sergeant.

William P. Merrill, company sergeant.

George W. Chandler, sergeant, promoted to second lieutenant, Company C, Third Cavalry, July 1, 1862.

| | |
|---|---|
| Thomas Dudley, sergeant | Michael P. Wells, corporal |
| Elias A. Dudley, sergeant | Samuel Goodwin, corporal |
| Abram Hess, sergeant | George R. Able, corporal |
| Shelby P. Barker, sergeant | L. W. Flanders, corporal |
| John Byre, corporal | George D. Ridgeway, corporal |
| John J. Jarrett, corporal | James Warman, wagoner |
| Edmund H. Selby, corporal | Bartholomew Jenkins, |
| Andrew J. Hibbs, corporal | blacksmith |
| John W. Phillips, corporal | Thomas H. Frost, saddler |
| Aaron Barker, corporal | James Kidwell, farrier |

Privates

William E. Abbott
William C. Anderson
Nimrod Austin
Jonathan Bausiman
Joseph F. Bausiman
Richard Berry
Francis M. Bird
Jacob Blosser
Peter J. Bower
William Brown
Daniel J. Carper
James P. Carroll
Moses W. Chesney
R. I. J. Claver
Thomas Collins
Caleb F. Conn
Daniel Cornell
William J. Deamer
John J. Dillworth
Jacob T. Eaglen
Thomas J. Edwards[16]
William H. Evans
William H. Fear
Alonzo Finnell
Simeon Furman
Clark Gidley
Samuel Goliday
John Goodwin
Thomas Griffith
William H. Guthrie
William H. Hagans
Jacob Hare
Arthur Hart
Edward Hart
Thomas D. Hawker
James Headland
John E. Hoffman[17]
Henry H. Hunter

John Izenhart
Virgil S. Jones
Herman Koster
Job Lawlis
John Lawlis
Leven C. Lawlis
William E. Lynch
Garrett L. McCauley
Festus H. McDougal
Reason S. Michael
Thomas Minear
Andrew J. Morris
James A. Neal
Nimrod Neely
James J. Page
John Papel
Isaac N. Phillips
John E. Phillips
Oliver P. Phillips
Hiram Piles
Conrad C. Potter
Daniel Rhodes
Daniel C. Riddle
William C. Riddle
Thomas Rose
Beckwith H. Saer
Jacob Sheets
Samuel Sheets
George W. Smith[18]
John H. Snyder
Charles Star
Lewis Sutton
Alexander J. Sweany
Sebastian Swink
Henry M. Tomlinson
John L. Tygart
Frank Vanswartown
Oliver P. Wade

16. Promoted to second lieutenant, Forty-fifth U.S.C.T., April 3, 1864.
17. Promoted to second lieutenant, Third Cavalry.
18. Taken prisoner; on Hunter's raid.

John Wells                              Edwin S. Wyatt
David Wiedman

### Discharged

George H. King, first lieutenant.

Jacob J. Jennewine, second lieutenant, promoted to first lieutenant, March 25, 1862.

Joel Donaldson, for disability, July 1, 1862.

Peter Hess, for disability, April 10, 1863.

Wilson Jones, for disability, September 13, 1863.

John W. Keller.

Samuel Merrifield, for disability, November 1, 1862.

John W. McCarty, for disability, November 1, 1862.

John W. McIntyre, for disability,. August 23, 1863.

William O'Reid, for disability, March 12, 1863.

Charles Snider, on account of wounds, November 13, 1863.

### Died

Richard Lee Henry, at Winchester, April 30, 1862.

Edmund W. Murphy, bugler.

Thomas Robinson, at Martinsburg, March 10, 1864.

Henry Rumble, killed at Lewisburg by a citizen, November 1863.

Calvin Sheets, shot by a sentinel at New Creek for forcing guard, October 10, 1861.

Joseph Smith, at Grafton, December 6, 1861.

William Sheridan, at Romney, December 2, 1861.

Aggregate, 125 men

*Company E, Seventh West Virginia Infantry.* This volunteer company was mustered into service at Grafton on July 31, 1861, and served until September 5, 1863, when it was consolidated into a battalion.[19]

### Officers

Henry B. Lazier, captain, resigned January 26, 1862.

Marcus Fetty, first sergeant, promoted to first lieutenant, May 26, 1863, to captain, June 26, 1863.

Isaac Hastings, first lieutenant, resigned May 26, 1863.

Anthony Jacquet, second lieutenant, resigned May 26, 1863.

Charles A. Calahan, sergeant, discharged September 7, 1863.

William J. Roger, sergeant.

19. *Ann. Rpt. Adj. Gen.*, pp. 202, 203, 226-29.

Cyrus B. Morgan, sergeant.
James P. Houston, sergeant.
Thomas E. Sullivan, corporal.
Calvin Bell, corporal.
William H. Cullison, corporal.
William E. Canthers, corporal.
Joseph W. Conway, corporal, died of wounds received at Antietam, September 17, 1862.
George T. Benthem, corporal.
Clark Kelly, corporal, discharged September 7, 1863.
Smith R. Irwin, corporal.
John A. Walters, musician, discharged August 10, 1864.
Jesse Poundstone, musician, discharged August 10, 1864.

Privates

William Adams
Aaron Austin, killed in action at Gettysburg, July 2, 1863.
Isaiah Adams
James C. Beatty
Thomas S. Beatty
Jonah Bayles
Thomas Bayles
William Bricker
John A. Butcher, died, date unknown.
John Blaney, killed December 31, 1862, at Fredericksburg.
Lawrence Blaney
Bartholomew Bishop, died, date unknown.
Levi Bricker, recruited September 6, 1862.
John Cunningham
Enos H. Cleavinger, missing in action, July 2, 1863, at Gettysburg.
Thomas P. Conwell
Mark Carney, died, date unknown.

Thomas Colebank
Samuel H. Cobin
Calvin Coburn
Thomas J. Cole
George A. Cummins
John Connelly, recruited October 6, 1861.
Alfred Dawson
Samuel Dornall
Jacob Eckhart, missing in action, December 13, 1862, at Fredericksburg.
Thomas V. Emerson
John P. Emerson
William R. Fowler
David S. Houston, died at Harrison's Landing, date unknown.
Ira M. Herrington, deserted, October 18, 1862.
Benjamin F. Herrington
Francis L. Hicks
Harvey Hoover
Isaac P. Hopkins, killed in action, September 17, 1862, at Antietam.

James C. Hostettler

Larkin Hall

Samuel Hall

John Holland

John J. Jenkins

William A. Jenkins

Aaron C. Jenkins, killed in action, May 3, 1863, at Chancellorsville.

Jacob Jarrett

John Knife

John W. Kennedy

Robert J. Linton, promoted to first lieutenant and adjutant.

Samuel C. Lewellen, died, date unknown.

A. G. Lewellen, recruited September 6, 1862.

Zadock Lanham

Eugenius Mayfield

Joshua Mayfield

Enoch Manning

Fred A. Merrifield, discharged, August 10, 1864.

Rufus J. Morgan

Samuel McCann, died, date unknown.

John H. Manning

W. M. V. Mayfield

Edward Moody

Oliver Miller, died at Harrison's Landing, date unknown.

Alph. S. McVicker, killed in action, July 2, 1863, at Gettysburg.

John Meckling

Samuel McKenney, recruited August 4, 1864.

Thomas K. Moore

G. R. Pickenpaugh

Oliver W. Powell

William Robe

John E. Roby, recruited September 6, 1862.

Philip M. Robinson

Martin E. Robinson

Edgar W. Ruble

Henry M. Ruble

Nelson Shaffer

Solomon Stafford, killed in action, September 17, 1862, at Antietam.

Joseph E. Stafford

Elza Stafford

John F. Sparks

James M. Sangston, deserted October 18, 1862, at Harpers Ferry.

Jacob H. Summers

George W. Shoemaker, died in hospital, date unknown.

John J. Swindler

Spencer Lucas, died June 1863, at Front Royal.

Lawrence Victor

George W. Widdows

David West

John Warman

William E. Wilkins

George W. Williamson

George R. Walker

Aggregate, 106 men

*Company C, Third West Virginia Cavalry.*[20] This company was organized at Brandonville October 1, 1861, and marched to Clarksburg, where it remained until January 15, 1862, when it proceeded to New Creek. It was in the engagements at Chancellorsville, Gettysburg, etc. Peter Tabler was captain. Men from Monongalia County on its roll included:[21]

Michael Ferrell, sergeant
Sylvester Ridgway, sergeant
Ulysses Davis, corporal
William Deets, corporal
Franklin C. Spencer, corporal
Alfred Porter, bugler
Eri Anderson
William Barthlow
Levi Bricker
James Deets
Jacob H. Hart
George Jenkins
Thomas Stoker
William G. Lazzel
George W. Rude, corporal
W. E. Kines, corporal
William Prossman, corporal
William C. Myers
Jacob Myers
Edgar C. Piles

H. R. Stansburry
John Smith
Lewis S. Stoneking
Samuel Tichnal
William Fleming
William B. Shaw[22]
Jonathan Stahl[23]
James S. Perry, first
  lieutenant
Andrew J. Statler
James P. St. Clair, sergeant
Middleton Roby, corporal
Balser Shaffer, farrier
Jacob Hart, blacksmith
Joshua Barthlow, bugler
David Shaffer
John E. Hoffman, first
  lieutenant[24]
Enos Myers
George W. Deen

**Philadelphia Baptist Church.** A Baptist congregation was organized on Miracle Run in 1861, called the Philadelphia Baptist Church.[25] The leaders were Alex Eddy, Ami Tennant, Martha Tennant, and George Keefover; there were thirteen charter members. The congregation met in a schoolhouse at first, then built a church structure at the forks of Miracle Run.[26]

20. *Ann. Rpt. Adj. Gen.*, pp. 546-49, 567-70.
21. According to Wiley, pp. 505, 506.
22. Captain, resigned May 24, 1862.
23. Captain, resigned, date unknown.
24. Killed in action, November 24, 1863.
25. Later called Bula Baptist Church.
26. Dodds and Dodds, *Churches of Monongalia County,* p. 130.

**Oil Excitement.** Col. Edwin L. Drake's discovery of oil near Titusville, Pennsylvania (his first well came in on August 27, 1859), stimulated the development of a tremendous industry in the Hughes River area, where petroleum production had begun as early as 1825 (see p. 470). Eugene D. Thoenen estimates that perhaps twenty thousand people were at Burning Springs in the spring of 1860.[27]

The excitement swept throughout western Virginia and J. Marshall Hagans, on February 27, 1861, wrote to his friend, W. T. Willey, at the convention in Richmond: "The oil 'fever' has settled into a regular epidemic here: capitalists can be seen congregating at all the public places discussing the 'slippery' subject. I understand that one company here made $1,200,000 without going to the oil region at all, this is rumor and may not be reliable."[28]

Thoenen comments: "When Hagans used the word 'rumor', he was using a term that would be as characteristic of the oil industry as the derricks themselves. Not only were rumors a part of the speculative side of the business but they were part and parcel of the active fields. Always there were the rumors of new wells, mystery wells, new leasing locations, the formation of new companies, and dry and flowing wells. The rumor, the antecedent of the truth, through the ever present grapevine, gave a spark to the oil-boom centers."[29]

H. Dering wrote to W. T. Willey on March 1, 1861: "I forgot to mention the fact of an epidemic prevailing among the male part of our citizens, that may prove fatal to some of our men. It is called the 'oil fever'. Several companies have been formed in this town who are sending agents to the Kanawha region to prospect and bore for oil. In our locality parties from Pittsburgh have been taking leases on the west side of the river along the Monongahela in our county."[30]

The quickening tempo of the local speculating companies is

27. *History of the Oil and Gas Industry in West Virginia*, pp. 13, 14. See also Howard B. Lee, *The Burning Springs, and Other Tales of the Little Kanawha* (Morgantown, 1968), 143 pp; and Gerald Forbes "The Civil War and the Beginning of the Oil Industry in West Virginia," *West Virginia History* 8 (1947):382-91.
28. Thoenen, ibid., p. 17.
29. Ibid.
30. Thoenen, pp. 17, 18.

gauged by another letter from J. Marshall Hagans to W. T. Willey, on March 19: "Our men here have a speculation in progress that may yield them about $5,000 to $10,000 a piece, there are 12 in the company."[31]

But the more intense excitement attendant upon the outbreak of war a few days later absorbed the oil excitement for the time.[32]

**Circuit Court Judge Resigns.** George W. Thompson, judge of the circuit court of the Twentieth Judicial Circuit, resigned his place on the bench, refusing to take certain oaths prescribed by the Wheeling convention of June 18, 1861. He turned to literary pursuits, and wrote a remarkable book, entitled the *Category of the Infinite.*

R. L. Berkshire was elected to succeed him and opened his first court on September 2. E. C. Bunker was elected prosecuting attorney.[33]

**Joseph Sutton.** Joseph Sutton, pioneer settler on Dunkard Ridge and Smoky Drain, died December 24, 1861. Born in 1771 in Manchester, England, his family came to America when he was only a boy, and tradition said he ran away from their home in Baltimore at the age of sixteen and located near Cassville.

He married Mary Snider, daughter of Rudolph Snider, and they had seven children, namely, Nancy (married Burton Pride), Asa (married Abigail Milburn), Amantha, John L. (married Teresa Trippett), Elizabeth (married George Wade), Margaret (married John Wise), and Hannah (married Henry Cunningham).[34]

**Benjamin Coogle.** Benjamin Coogle, a pioneer settler of Monongalia County, who located twelve miles west of Morgantown in 1807, died in January 1861. He was a son of Adam Coogle and was born near Baltimore in 1769. When he was eight years old the family moved to Hagerstown, where he learned the trade of weaver, which he followed until he located in Monongalia County, after which he was a farmer. He married Dorothea,

31. Thoenen, p. 18.
32. Wiley, p. 263.
33. Wiley, pp. 309, 311, 322, 323, 324.
34. *Chronicles of Core,* p. 95.

daughter of Christian Ridenour, and they had five children, Lyda, Sarah, Jonathan, Susanna, and John.[35]

**Moses Cox.** Moses Cox, a pioneer settler of Monongalia County, died at his home near Morgantown October 17, 1861. He was a son of Abraham Cox and was born near Hagerstown, Maryland, in 1780. He located on Indian Creek as a young man, working as a farmer, but he was interested in public affairs and served as a justice of the peace, "a position which his soundness of judgment and well-recognized probity of character made him eminently qualified to fill." He was twice married, the first time to Jane Musgrave, the second to Mrs. Charlotte (McDermott) Foster.[36]

**Isaac Wharton.** Isaac Wharton died on a farm near Cassville September 22, 1861. He was born in Greene County, Pennsylvania, in 1809, the son of Abner Wharton. He was reared and educated in Greene County and removed to Monongalia County in 1842, following agricultural pursuits the remainder of his life. He married Ruth Johnson.[37]

**Christopher Core.** Christopher Core, one of the last of the pioneer band which had wrested the county from the Indians, died May 20, 1861. He was born May 9, 1770, the son of John Core, who had been killed in the battle of Dolls Run (*Monongalia Story*, vol. 2, pp. 28, 29, 419). A family tradition says that Christopher saw one of the last Indian invaders on Dolls Run and caused him to flee by the old stratagem of appearing to call to a large body of friends. In the early days the rigorous requirements of pioneer days prevented him from obtaining an education and in 1815, when he was forty-five years of age, he was unable to write his name. Later he gradually learned this art, with many others which increasing leisure gave him opportunity to study. He lived near the head of Scotts Run.

He married Hannah, daughter of Rudolph Snider, and they had thirteen children, namely, Elizabeth (married Benjamin Liming), Margaret (married Jacob Shriver), Catherine (married William Piles), Christina, killed by a falling tree, Mary (married

35. *Cyclopedia of Marion County*, p. 107.
36. *Cyclopedia of Monongalia County*, p. 47.
37. *Cyclopedia of Monongalia County*, p. 162.

David Lough), Moses (married Elizabeth Piles), Michael (married Christina Shriver), Rebecca (married Benjamin Shriver), Abram, Asa, John (married Abigail Inghram), Sarah (married Wash Tennant), and Barton (married Nancy Fleming).[38]

**Fielding Kiger.** A well-known public figure of pioneer times in Morgantown, Fielding Kiger (see *Monongalia Story*, vol. 2, various entries), died September 7, 1861. He was born November 17, 1785, but names of his parents are not known. He was in Morgantown early in the nineteenth century and married Mary, daughter of Christian and Ann Madera, September 26, 1809. He was a member of the Monongalia County court and a trustee of Monongalia Academy.

He and his wife had nine children, namely, Fielding, Jr., George (married Mary Cooper), Jacob (married Elizabeth Wells), Leroy (married Mary Wells), Mary (married Edwin Billingsley), Amanda (married —— Laishley), Caroline (married James Demain), Eliza (married George Hoskins, then Edward G. Brooke), and Sarah (married Bernard R. C. O'Kelly).[39]

**Land Grants Made in 1861.** Monongalia County grantees in 1861 included:

| | | |
|---|---|---|
| Drabell, John R. | 330 a. | Dry Run |
| Dunn, James | 17 | Waters Cheat R. |

**Sidewalks.** Morgantown's main streets, still unpaved, were nevertheless becoming fairly well provided with walks for pedestrians. In January 1861 the borough board of trustees ordered stepping stones to be placed across High Street at Bumbo Lane, on condition that a boardwalk be placed on Bumbo Lane from High to Spruce and on the east side of Spruce from Bumbo Lane to the Presbyterian burial ground.[40]

**County and Borough Government.** In some counties of western Virginia, the maintenance of civil government practically broke down during the war, owing to bitter differences in sympathies between North and South. But in Monongalia, although there

38. *Chronicles of Core*, pp. 95, 96.
39. Pers. comm., Judge Marvin R. Kiger.
40. Callahan, *Making of Morgantown*, p. 196.

were some Southern sympathizers, these constituted a small minority, and civil authority continued without interruption.

Benjamin McCurdy was sworn in as commissioner of the revenue for the Western District. John E. Dent was chosen *pro tem* clerk of the county court.

Isaac Scott was elected mayor of Morgantown and John S. Dering sergeant; Manliff Hayes was reelected recorder. Councilmen were David H. Chadwick, William A. Hanway, Robert P. Hennen, Frederick A. Dering, and George Kiger.

**Miscellany.** In 1861: C. H. Hassler, Thomas H. Hanbury, and R. W. Blue were teachers in Monongalia Academy (Wiley, p. 396). . . . There were 313 births reported, 62 marriages, and 117 deaths (Wiley, p. 470). . . . Syefax Washington, a black man, died in Morgantown; he said he had been a slave of John Washington (Wiley, pp. 471, 472). . . . D. C. Pickenpaugh was master of the Masonic lodge (Wiley, p. 548). . . . The Union Literary Society was an early casualty of the Civil War (Wiley, p. 552). . . . Francis Madera was appointed as postmaster of Morgantown on May 13, succeeding Charles Wallace (Wiley, p. 579). . . . A. L. Nye and Company opened a store in Morgantown (Wiley, p. 582). . . . William Willey, father of Waitman T. Willey, died at Farmington, aged ninety-five years (Wiley, p. 699). . . . Eighty-five young ladies were attending Woodburn Female Seminary (Callahan, p. 143).

# CHAPTER EIGHTY-SIX

# 1862

The war was slowly but steadily getting out of control. It would not be the neat, short limited war both sides had predicted. At first, it is true, it was not much of a fight. Neither side was prepared; the generals were inexperienced, incompetent, cautious. There were shortages of good soldiers and supplies, excesses of both gloom and optimism.

But finally the conflict settled down to all-out war. Terrible swift swords caused rivers to run red, men and women to cry in distress.

**Terrible Swift Sword.**[1] In Monongalia County, as elsewhere throughout the nation, men and women were profoundly stirred. The first call of President Lincoln for troops, on April 15, 1861, met with a prompt response on the part of young men from the county. Nor did their promptness and zeal falter as they responded to the president's subsequent calls.

"They went from every township, from every neighborhood, and almost from every home. And many of them never came back any more. They wasted away with disease in the hospital, died of wounds on the field, or met sudden death in the terrible tide of bloody battle. The list of their names is a list of heroes. The record of their glorious acts is a history of which old Monongalia may well be perpetually proud."[2]

1. A woman, Julia Ward Howe, who had seen parading battalions from her hotel window in Washington in 1861 set down some of her thoughts on paper. "She wrote about a fiery gospel writ in burnished rows of steel, of the trampling out of the winepress of the Almighty, of the terrible swift sword which was flashing a fateful lightning and it seemed to her that God was on the march." Bruce Catton, *Terrible Swift Sword*, p. 126.
2. Wiley, p. 498.

Units continued to be organized in Monongalia County, or in nearby counties with Monongalia County men.

*Company D, Third West Virginia Cavalry.*[3] This company was formed at Morgantown in August 1862, and proceeded to Wheeling where it was mustered in October 21 and sent to New Creek. In about a month of scouting through the mountains near Petersburg they captured a number of the enemy equal to their own and without any loss.

Officers

James R. Utt, captain, killed in action at Piedmont Station, Fauquier County, May 16, 1863.

George W. McVicker, captain, commissioned July 18, 1863.

McGill Clark, first lieutenant

Joseph Robbins, second lieutenant

Jacob Sturgeon, sergeant

Nelson Snodgrass, commanding sergeant, taken prisoner and recaptured October 14, 1864.

Charles E. Morris, quartermaster sergeant, prisoner since July 28, 1863.

John C. Reppert, sergeant

Neely Mahanah, sergeant

John W. Conwell, sergeant, prisoner of war since June 9, 1864.

Thomas H. Lough, sergeant

William Rogers, sergeant

Albert G. Everly, corporal

Joseph Doherty, corporal

William E. Garlow, corporal

Joseph F. Halfin, corporal

W. R. Richard, corporal

O. B. Lawless, corporal

David E. Cordery, corporal

Joseph Hartley, corporal

James Boord, bugler

Allison S. Dilliner, bugler

William Irvin, farrier

Jacob Lemons, blacksmith

Charles Johnson, blacksmith

W. A. Lewellan, teamster

George W. Snider, teamster

Privates

Amos C. Anderson

Thomas Boice

Isaac Boice

John F. Brand

Jonathan Brown

John P. Burbridge

William H. Bixler

Jacob Barracman

James B. Craig

Christoper Core

E. J. Clayton

John Clark[4]

Silas Henderson

Elza Hall

3. *Ann. Rpt. Adj. Gen.*, pp. 549-51, 567-70.
4. Committed suicide at Camp Chase, Ohio, April 5, 1863.

Marion Hawkins
William Harris[5]
John O. Johnson[6]
John W. Jester[7]
James M. Jones
John Keefover
George S. Laydly
Bernard F. Leonard
Elza T. Lough[8]
Elijah Lawson
Nimrod Cole
John Core
Benjamin Core
James A. Downey
Isaac N. Furman
Stephen G. Hess
James R. Hall
James Hayes
Asa Henderson
John S. Nuzum
Jacob Piles
Joseph Pride
Albert Plum
William Phillips
George W. Robinson
James Rogers
Uriah Rider
Edgar F. Reece
Oric Rinehart[9]
Riley H. Smith[10]

George C. Shaffer
Washington Martin
Silas McGraw
Azel McCurdy
James E. Myers
Warren Murphy[11]
Calvin Vandegraft
George W. Wilson[12]
George W. Weekly[13]
Levi Weekly
Peter J. Winieg
George W. West
Thomas Watton
John Wright
Samuel Gardner[14]
Joseph Bowers, trans.
Joseph Skentz, trans.
Isaiah Riggs, trans.
Dennis M. Shaffer
Alpheus Springer
John J. Stewart
David Stanton
James D. Springer
W. Thompson
Chris. Toothman
Ezra Tennant[15]
Jacob K. Kennedy,
    Hospital Steward
Josephus Muldrew
William S. Glasscock

5. Discharged for disability at Grafton, August 1863.
6. Died at Winchester, May 26, 1863.
7. Deserted at Winchester, March 9, 1863.
8. Died of fever at Winchester, May 27, 1863.
9. Killed near Moorefield, January 19, 1863.
10. Discharged at Gallipolis, July 16, 1864.
11. Captured five rebels and a negro in the charge at Winchester, September 19, 1864.
12. Deserted at Winchester, March 9, 1863.
13. Prisoner of war since November 2, 1864.
14. Died of smallpox, July 20, 1863.
15. Killed by bushwhackers near Martinsburg, October 14, 1864.

Isaac T. Lyon[16]
Perry Arnett
Barnett Haney
John B. Grey

James M. Henry
William P. Lazzel
David Weedman
Charles H. McLane

Aggregate, 109 men.

*Company C, Fourteenth West Virginia Infantry.* This company, mustered in August 25, 1862, at Wheeling, was later stationed at Camp Russell.[17]

Officers

Oliver P. Jolliffe, captain
John W. Bishop, first lieutenant, promoted at Burlington March 17, 1864.
Isaac N. Holland, second lieutenant, promoted August 17, 1863.
Henry Baker, first sergeant, promoted March 15, 1864.
Henry Howell, sergeant
William Craig, sergeant
James F. Jolliffe, sergeant, promoted August 17, 1863.

John A. Holland, sergeant, promoted March 15, 1864.
Eugenus Lanham, corporal
Rawley C. McKee, corporal
Ashabel G. Devault, corporal
William H. Snowden, corporal
William W. Hess, corporal
Elza L. Morgan, corporal
James T. Darnell, corporal
William H. Austin, corporal
J. B. Williamson, fifer
Samuel McElroy, drummer

Privates

Daniel F. Ashcraft
Henry Austin
Joseph Austin
John Boyd
William Carroll
Garrett Conn
Lindsey Cox
Edward G. Eaglen
David C. Fetty
Benjamin F. Fletcher
Jacob Fredericks
Samuel B. Frum
John Grim
Morgan B. Hale
Thomas D. Harden

Henry W. Hardman
Charles G. Howell
John H. Howell
Jacob Jacobs
Eugenius Jenkins
Alpheus Jolliffe
John M. Jolliffe, Jr.
John M. Jolliffe, Sr.
William R. Jolliffe
Nathan Kerns
Franklin C. Kidwell
George W. King
Henry H. King
Jefferson Kisner
Joseph F. Lemons

William L. McClarman
Nathaniel McCosh
Daniel McElroy
Ezekiel Marple
Michael Price
Richard W. Prickett
William H. Prickett
Christopher Russler
James H. Smell

16. "Prisoner of war since September 27, 1864."
17. *Ann. Rpt. Adj. Gen.*, pp. 378-80, 398-400.

Fig. 87. Tenting on the old camp ground. (Library of Congress.)

| James A. Smith | Asa D. Springer | George W. Watkins |
|---|---|---|
| Thomas H. Smith | Alpheus Steele | Thomas W. Watkins |
| Caleb D. Spencer | Caleb Tarleton | James S. Watson |
| Thomas P. Spencer | Caleb Watkins | James W. Watson |

Discharged

Granville Brown, first lieutenant, by order Secretary of War, April 4, 1863.

Henry Bell, second lieutenant, by order Secretary of War, April 4, 1863, at New Creek.

George W. Grubb, private, for disability, at New Creek, January 8, 1863, by order of General Wright.

Joseph A. Kincade, private, for disability, at Grafton, November 13, 1863, by order of General Wright.

Transferred

George W. Jolliffe, first sergeant, by promotion to sergeant major, at Burlington, March 15, 1864.

Died

George H. Hardman, first lieutenant, killed in action near Burlington, November 10, 1863.

Solomon Holland, corporal, of dropsy, at home, Monongalia, March 20, 1863.

John W. Mouser, of typhoid fever, at Romney, August 24, 1863.

William Gardner, killed at Burlington, November 15, 1863.

William Kisner, killed at Cloyd Mountain, May 9, 1864.

Isaac B. Powell, wounded at Cloyd Mountain, May 9, 1864, died in enemy's hands, May 16, 1864.

Milton F. Walls, of typhoid fever, at Charleston, May 16, 1864.

John J. Trickett, wounded at Cloyd Mountain, May 9, 1864, died in enemy's hands, June 3, 1864.

John W. Miller, drowned in Kanawha River, July 9, 1864, having fallen from Victor No. 1.

Nelson Steele, drowned in Kanawha River, July 9, 1864, having fallen from Victor No. 1.

Harrison Austin, corporal, wounded at Carter's Farm, July 20, 1864, and died of wounds, July 24, 1864.

William H. Smith, killed at Cedar Creek, October 13, 1864.

Joseph Rumble, captured between Martinsburg, Virginia, and

Williamsport, Maryland, paroled and sent to Annapolis, Maryland, where he died October 23, 1864.

Arche C. McBee, wounded July 20, 1864, near Winchester, and died November 14, 1864, at Claryville, Hospital, Maryland.

David Mellon, captured at Cloyd Mountain, May 15, 1864, and taken to Andersonville, Georgia. Died September 22, 1864.

Jacob T. Mouser, captured at Cloyd Mountain, May 15, 1864, and taken to Andersonville, Georgia. Died September 23, 1864.

Aggregate, 91 men.

*Company I, Fourteenth West Virginia Infantry.*[18] This company was organized at Wheeling September 11, 1862, sent to Clarksburg and then to New Creek. The regiment was involved in many bloody engagements, including Greenland Gap, Cloyd Mountain, Carter's Farm, Kearneystown, Winchester, etc.

Officers

Elias C. Finnell, captain.

James B. Fogle, first lieutenant, promoted November 10, 1864.

Joseph R. Peck, second lieutenant.

Silas W. Hare, first lieutenant.

Rezon Holland, sergeant, wounded at Carter's Farm, July 20, 1864.

Thomas B. Wells, sergeant.

Frederick Breakiron, sergeant.

Cyrus Courtney, sergeant, wounded at Winchester, September 19, 1864.

Jacob S. Shisler, sergeant.

Jackson R. Stoker, corporal.

George W. Dawson, corporal.

Frederick A. Wells, corporal.

W. J. F. Martin, corporal, wounded at Carter's Farm, July 24, 1864, leg amputated.

William L. Anderson, corporal.

John W. Martin, corporal.

Joseph J. Weaver, corporal, wounded at Carter's Farm, July 24, 1864.

18. *Ann. Rpt. Adj. Gen.*, pp. 393-95, 398-400.

John Saunders, corporal, wounded at Lynchburg, June 17, 1864.

## Privates

| | | |
|---|---|---|
| William L. Abel | Francis M. Fetty | William A. Morris |
| Robert Brooks | John P. Fetty[24] | Charles H. Madera |
| Marshall Brand | Samuel Gould | George Nuce |
| William Beaty | Isaac McGallagher | Abram Nuce[31] |
| John Beaty | William B. Heix | Jonah T. Summers |
| G. Barrickman | John Hunter | Marion N. Shanes |
| Levi Bolinger[19] | James F. Porter[25] | Felix Scott[32] |
| Eugenius Bell[20] | William L. Pool | Imlah Scott |
| James A. Barnes | Robert Powell | James L. Shroyer |
| D. W. Breakiron[21] | Michael Rice[26] | William A. Stewart[33] |
| Lawrence S. Blaney | Robert B. Reed | George T. Turner |
| William S. Hoard | Henry Roby[27] | Napoleon B. Tibbs |
| John W. Haney | Joshua W. Keener | Lebbens C. |
| Daniel W. Jones | Aaron B. Lewellen | Weltner[34] |
| Daniel R. Jackson | Draper Lawless | Lewis A. Sisley |
| George W. Kelly[22] | Alpheus D. Lyons[28] | John M. Weltner |
| Joseph S. Kelly | Benson Mollisey | George W. Castle |
| Mortimer Cade | Arthur Murray[29] | William Dawson |
| John S. Cole | Perry McLane[30] | William A. Friend |
| Francis O. Chalfant | Alex. McCauley | A. D. Fundenburg |
| Benjamin F. Childers | John S. McMillen | Thomas P. Knox |
| Zacquill Dunn[23] | Pevid Murphy | David B. McIlwain |

## Died

Uriah Griffith, first lieutenant, wounded at Cloyd Mountain, May 9, 1864, died May 16, 1864.

19. Captured at Cloyd Mountain, May 9, 1864.
20. Wounded at Fisher's Hill, September 22, 1864.
21. Captured at Cloyd Mountain, May 9, 1864.
22. Captured at Winchester, July 24, 1864.
23. Captured at Cloyd Mountain, May 9, 1864.
24. Wounded at Lynchburg, June 17, 1864.
25. Wounded at Lynchburg, June 17, 1864.
26. Captured at Cloyd Mountain, May 9, 1864.
27. Wounded at Carter's Farm, July 27, 1864.
28. Wounded at Carter's Farm, July 20, 1864.
29. Wounded and captured at Cloyd Mountain, May 9, 1864.
30. Wounded at Carter's Farm, July 20, 1864.
31. Wounded at Carter's Farm, July 20, 1864.
32. Wounded at Cedar Creek, October 19, 1864.
33. Captured at Cloyd Mountain, May 9, 1864.
34. Captured at Cloyd Mountain, May 9, 1864.

William S. Morrison, second lieutenant, wounded at Cedar Creek, October 19, 1864, died October 25, 1864.

George C. Bowers, died at Clarksburg, November 1862, of rubeola.

Beth Boice, died at Grafton, April 1864, pneumonia.

William D. Bougher, wounded at Winchester, September 19, 1864, died September 20.

Nicholas V. Flum, corporal, died at Parkersburg, October 16, 1862, of typhus fever.

James W. Heix, died at Grafton, August 2, 1864, of typhus fever.

Robert C. Jackson, killed at Cedar Creek, October 13, 1864.

Elias Martin, killed at Myerstown, November 18, 1864.

Josephus Neighbors, died at Petersburg, December, 1863, of fever.

Abraham Piles, died in Monongalia County, 1862, of disease.

Israel Phillips, died in Grafton hospital, 1864, of consumption.

Nickolin Sayers, died in Confederate prison, March 12, 1864.

William Scott, wounded at Cloyd Mountain, May 9, 1864, died May 16, 1864.

Henry C. Thorn, wounded at Carter's Farm, July 20, 1864, died August 12, 1864.

Francis Thomas, died of fever at Grafton hospital, April 13, 1864.

Alpheus B. Fear, died of fever at Meadow Bluff, May 25, 1864.

Aggregate, 100 men.

**The Restored Government.** The legislature of the Restored Government, meeting in Wheeling, had for one of its purposes the preservation of the state of Virginia for the Union. But there was more to it than that. The representatives, all from the northwestern counties, realized that they could not speak for the people on the other side of the mountains, who had seceded from the Union.

For decades the rift had widened between eastern and western Virginia. The more realistic way of looking at the situation was that *western* Virginia had restored the state government— the government did not truly represent Virginia at all. For a long time the westerners had talked of forming a new state. The time now seemed at hand.

Governor Pierpont had called for a constitutional convention to meet at Wheeling on November 26, 1861, to draft the constitution for the proposed new state. Working under considerable difficulty in the stress of war, the convention completed its work and adjourned on February 18, 1862.[35] A vote of the people, on April 18, gave approval, by 14,199 to 368.

On May 13, 1862, the legislature of the Restored Government passed an act giving the formal consent of Virginia to the erection of a new state out of her territory. Forty-eight counties were included at the time, and provision was made for including three more, Jefferson, Berkeley, and Frederick, if they should vote to come in. The first two subsequently voted in favor of the proposition; Frederick never voted.

On May 29, 1862, Monongalia's United States Senator, Waitman T. Willey, presented the constitution of the proposed new state, to be known as West Virginia,[36] to the Senate of the United States, with a memorial from the general assembly requesting its admission to the Union. We may well imagine him filled with pride mingled with anxiety. His address, in part, follows:

"And now it only remains for Congress to give its assent. Ought that assent to be given? Before I answer this question, I desire to correct a misapprehension which I find is prevalent, not only throughout the country, but likewise here. It seems to be supposed that this movement for a new State has been conceived since the breaking out of the rebellion, and was a consequence of it; that it grew alone out of the abhorrence with which the loyal citizens of West Virginia regarded the traitorous proceedings of the conspirators east of the Alleghenies, and that

35. See *Debates and Proceedings of the first Constitutional Convention of West Virginia (1861-1863)*. Eds. Charles H. Ambler, Frances Haney Atwood, and William B. Mathews (1939?).

36. The name Kanawha, at first proposed, was rejected, along with numerous other suggestions, as Allegheny, Augusta, Columbia, and Potomac. "According to a delegate from Monongalia County, 'Kanawha' should be rejected because it was too difficult to spell. This caused laughter at the convention because the residents of Monongalia County had experienced difficulty" in spelling the name of their own county. Conley and Doherty, *West Virginia History*, p. 274.

the effort was prompted simply by a desire to dissolve the connection between the loyal and disloyal sections of the State. Not so, sir. The question of dividing the State of Virginia, either by the Blue Ridge mountain, or by the Alleghanies, has been mooted for fifty years. It has frequently been agitated with such vehemence as to threaten seriously the public peace. It has been a matter of constant strife and bitterness in the Legislature of the State. The animosity existing at this time between the North and the South is hardly greater than what has at times distinguished the relations between East and West Virginia, arising from a diversity of interests and geographical antagonisms. Indeed, so incompatible was the union of the territory lying west of the Alleghany mountains with the territory lying east thereof, under one and the same State municipality, that as long ago as 1781, several of the States insisted that Virginia should include in her act of session all her trans-Alleghany territory, making the Alleghany mountains her western, as they were her natural, boundary."

Mr. Willey concluded with an eloquent appeal to the Senate:

"Sir, these counties of Western Virginia, knocking for admission into the Union as a new State, contain, in rich abundance, all the elements of a great Commonwealth. Why have they remained undeveloped in the oldest State in the American Union? Why are our mines unworked? Why are our water-falls forever wasting away, unappreciated by the skill of man, chafing and foaming in their channels, as if in conscious rage at the long neglect? The answer to these questions is an irrefutable argument in favor of the division desired. Unless the State is divided, the natural resources of wealth and power will forever remain undeveloped. Is this just to the people there? Is it just to the country at large?

"Thus, sir, we present our claims for this new State. We pray you to grant your assent. It will send a thrill of joy through three hundred thousand hearts, and it will do no injustice to any. Then, sir, will our invaluable virgin mines invite the espousal of your surplus capital, and our perennial streams will lend their exhaustless power to your manufacturing skill. Then shall we soon be able to say, in the jubilant language of the Psalmist: 'The pastures are clothed with flocks; the valleys also are covered over with corn; they shout for joy; they also sing.'

Virginia—East Virginia,—restored from her temporary aberration; West Virginia, like a newly discovered star—East Virginia and West Virginia, twin stars, shall henceforth shine with ever-brightening lustre in the republican zodiac of States encircling our western hemisphere."

After considerable debate, the bill passed the Senate on July 14, 1862, and the House of Representatives early in the next session of Congress.

**School Commissioners.** The last board of school commissioners under the old school system was appointed October 29, 1862, as follows:

East Side. No. 1, John Bowers; No. 2, Thomas M. Jarrett; No. 3, Jacob Miller, No. 4, John Mills; No. 5, William Anderson; No. 6, A. S. Vance; No. 7, Charles Watts; No. 8, Robert Mayfield; No. 9, Caleb Beall; No. 10, Moses Steel; No. 11, Isaac Reed; No. 12, William Holland; No. 13, Henry Watson; No. 14, Thomas Tarleton.

West Side. No. 1, Waitman Davis; No. 2, M. L. Boyers; No. 3, Peter Fogle; No. 4, John N. Waters; No. 5, Dudley E. Miller; No. 6, Michael Core; No. 7, William Price; No. 8, David Lemley; No. 9, R. S. Thomas; No. 10, Alexander Wade; No. 11, James G. White; No. 12, Milton Wilson.

J. Marshall Hagans was appointed county superintendent, succeeding Waitman T. Willey, who had served since 1848.

**John Bowers and Laurel Iron Works.** John Bowers, son of Joseph and Barbara Ann (Everly) Bowers, opened a grocery and general store in Cheat Neck, in 1862. He was born January 27, 1819, in Fayette County, Pennsylvania, and purchased a farm in the Cheat Neck section in 1835, making a specialty of grazing and stock-raising, especially of thoroughbred Shorthorn cattle. He was married on February 16, 1843, to Harriet, daughter of John N. Baker, and they had ten children, including George, Margaret Ann, Susannah G., John, Joseph, William D., Harriet E., and H. Coleman.

A post office was established in the community, called Ices Ferry, June 9, 1841, with Evan T. Ellicott the first postmaster. John Bowers succeeded him August 22, 1845, and served until 1853. The name was changed to Laurel Iron Works in 1865.[37]

37. *Cyclopedia of Monongalia County*, p. 205; Wiley, p. 690.

**Thomas Mapel Settles in Cass.** Of French descent, Thomas Mapel, son of the Reverend Thomas and Elizabeth (Schroyer) Mapel, settled near Cassville in 1862. His father was a local preacher, in Greene County, Pennsylvania. Thomas was born June 4, 1816, and married Susannah, daughter of Peter and Barbara (Miller) Pickenpaugh, on March 1, 1857.[38]

**County and Borough Government.** John Brand was elected sheriff. John Pierpont was elected commissioner of the revenue for the Eastern District.

John G. Gay was elected mayor of Morgantown, James Johnson, sergeant, and Manliff Hayes was reelected recorder. S. Pickenpaugh, William A. Hanway, Robert P. Hennen, Frederick A. Dering, and Jacob Kiger were elected councilmen.

**Miscellany.** In 1862: The Woodgrove Furnace was destroyed by fire (Wiley, p. 256). . . . James Nimon built a steam foundry in Durbannah (Wiley, p. 262). . . . E. S. Bland, B. F. Martin, S. A. Morgan, and W. W. Peck were admitted to the county bar (Wiley, p. 318). . . . The *West Virginia Herald* was projected as a new county newspaper, by Joseph H. Powell and W. T. Mathers, but only a few issues were published (Wiley, pp. 427, 437). . . . The *Virginia Weekly Star* was a war casualty, the last issue appearing on January 4 (Wiley, p. 436). . . . A charter was procured January 10 for a bank to be known as the Farmers' and Drovers' Bank of Morgantown (Wiley, p. 464). . . . Births numbered 285, marriages 58, deaths 76 (Wiley, p. 470). . . . F. K. O'Kelley was a Morgantown tailor (Wiley, p. 602). . . . Dr. James Way was appointed postmaster of Cassville (Wiley, p. 701). . . . The old National Hotel property was sold by John Wallace to James C. Wallace (Callahan, p. 114). . . . Alexander Hayes turned over management of the Washington Hotel to his son, Lewis S. Hayes (Callahan, pp. 118, 312). . . . Jesse J. Fitch conveyed Lot 96 to Parnisse Gilmer for one thousand dollars (Callahan, p. 323).

38. *Cyclopedia of Monongalia County*, p. 178.

# CHAPTER EIGHTY-SEVEN

# 1863

The most exciting event of the war, so far as Monongalia County was concerned (and one of the most memorable in the whole history of the county) was the Confederate raid of April 1863. Brigadier General William Ezra ("Grumble") Jones and General John D. Imboden made a raid into Northwestern Virginia for the purpose of destroying the Baltimore and Ohio Railroad and securing as many horses as possible. They entered Preston County in two divisions. General Jones came by way of the Northwestern Turnpike and attacked Rowlesburg, but was repulsed by Federal forces under Major John H. Showalter. He then marched to Independence, where he was joined by the other division, which had come by Cranberry Summit and Kingwood.[1]

**Jones's Raid on Morgantown.** A Morgantown newspaper[2] gave a thrilling account of the local phase of the raid:

"On Monday morning, the 27th ult., several citizens of Kingwood arrived at our place, and reported that the rebels were encamped a short distance beyond Kingwood, and that they numbered about 5,000, as they had counted about 500 campfires. It was court day, and by 10 o'clock some 500 people were in town. As soon as the news from Kingwood was circulated, Mr. [George M.] Hagans, the president, and Mr. [William] Wagner, the cashier of the M. and M. Bank here, left with the

1. Stutler, *West Virginia in the Civil War*, pp. 204-14; Gen. C. E. Evans, ed., *Confederate Military History* (West Virginia), vol. 2, pp. 72-77; Stan Cohen, *The Civil War in West Virginia*, pp. 104-6.
2. *Morgantown Monitor*, May 6, 1863.

funds of the bank. Senator Willey[3] and other prominent citizens also left. A meeting was called at the courthouse, and it was determined to send out scouts on different roads to ascertain the number of the rebels, and if there were not over 100 of them, it was the determination of our citizens to resist and defend the town. Col. James Evans proposed to be one of ten men to go out and reconnoitre, and discover, if possible, how large a force was coming. . . .

"After nearly an hour by Col. Evans in trying to get men to volunteer to go with him, he got six besides himself. . . . They were Col. Evans, J. J. Jenkins, Kinsey Fife, Evans D. Fogle, John Holland, Peter Hess, and Sylvanus Pierpont, who mounted and started to reconnoitre the Kingwood turnpike. Holland and Hess were sent up the Forge Road, and Col. Evans and his party continued on the pike, Jenkins being sent a short distance ahead of the rest of the party. . . .

"Just as Col. Evans and his party were going up a rising piece of ground, the rebel cavalry advance came in sight over the hill, with Jenkins as a prisoner between them. Jenkins, by raising his hat, gave our party a sign by which they knew the character of the company he was in. It was but the work of a second to 'bout face', run, and down the hill they came like a thundergust, closely pursued by the rebels, who were soon within seventy yards of them: but they were at the bottom of the hill, and on rising ground our party left them far in rear. They were pursued about two miles, Fogle and Pierpont leaving Evans and Fife behind, owing to the superior fleetness of their horses. Evans and Fife dismounted and led their horses into the brush on the road-side, and watched the advance pass them, and then entered the woods and took to the river, which they crossed some distance above Morgantown. During the chase after this party, Jenkins escaped, took to the woods, and succeeded in gaining town before the cavalry, as did, also, Fogle and Pierpont, and reported that they had been chased by the rebels,

3. Moreland (*Anecdotes*, p. 48) tells a story of how a Confederate officer, Lieutenant Colonel O'Ferrel, encountered a young lady in Morgantown and told her they were looking for the "U. S. Senator from Virginia," W. T. Willey. She told him that the senator was too smart for them and had escaped, then revealed the fact that she was Julia Willey, daughter of the senator.

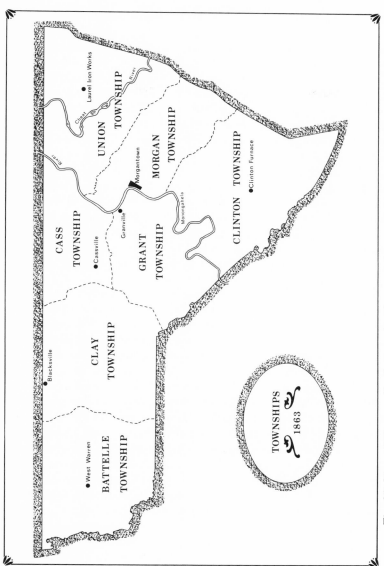

Fig. 88. Map of Monongalia County showing townships, 1863. (Drawn by Diane Lenhart.)

541

who were numberless, and that they were at the farm of G. W. Dorsey, only two miles from town.

"The citizens nearly all commenced leaving; those who had horses on the roads, and those on foot fled to the hills. About 1 o'clock two rebels came to town, with a flag of truce, and were informed that the town was surrendered to them. They returned to their main force, and in about half an hour, some eighty of their men came to town. . . . They called at the different houses and taverns for something to eat. Some were engaged in squads scouring the country for horses—others were trying to get into the stores, which were all closed. Some of them got in and purchased some few goods; others forced their way into Captain William Lazier's, Charles Watts', and Frank Demain's stores. . . . They got all the boots and men's shoes from the stores; and all the hats. Our citizens, especially the ladies, talked freely with them and gave them to eat with as good a grace as possible. Shortly before night the whole force left on the Independence Road."

This force bivouaced on the Independence Road, about ten miles south of Morgantown, then in the morning met the main force of General Jones and they all set out in the direction of town.

"At Morgantown many of the citizens had returned, and several people from the country had come into town, and were standing around the streets in small crowds discussing the events of the day previous until about 10 o'clock, when about sixty rebel cavalry came into the two main streets of the town on a charge at their highest speed, yelling like devils, with their cocked pistols in their hands, and commenced gathering the horses. The most of the people got off the streets in a hurry, supposing that the rebels were intending to shoot, burn, conscript, etc. In a few minutes it was discovered that they were after horses. They canvassed every street, searched every stable, and at the sound of the bugle, assembled in front of the bank, and left town within fifteen minutes after they had come in, with about thirty or forty horses.

"Soon after, the whole force commenced coming in. They occupied the town and surrounding country, during the day, and they conducted themselves very much as on the day previous, only on a more extended scale. The General put guards over the drug store and bars, which were kept there as long as he remained in town. Toward evening he left, and some 200 who stayed behind succeeded in getting whiskey, and some of them got quite merry. One soldier, about half-seas over (a private in a Jefferson County company by the name of Bushrod Washington and a son of Lewis Washington, one of the witnesses against John Brown), apologized to the ladies for drinking so much, by stating that the whiskey they got here was so much better than they got in the confederacy, that they could not restrain themselves. On Tuesday evening the rebels left in the direction of Fairmont on the west side of the river. . . . The whole force numbered about 2,000 men. They also set fire to the suspension bridge on that day, but were prevailed upon to put out the fire."[4]

According to local tradition, the Confederate soldiers who set fire to the bridge promptly extinguished the fire by direction of their commanding officer, Lt. William L. Wilson, who in 1882 would be elected president of West Virginia University.[5]

During the raid, as the Confederates advanced along the pike from Kingwood, there occurred the only two casualties in Monongalia County. The raiders were fired upon from ambush; giving quick chase, they captured Lloyd Beall and Andrew Johnson, both of Clinton Township, and shot them dead. The tombstone of the latter was inscribed thus: "To the memory of Andrew Johnson, killed by rebels under Gen. Jones, on their raid through this county, April 30, 1863, aged 31 years, 4 months." Albert Robey was also shot and left for dead, but survived.[6]

**The War Goes On.** On many fronts, the war went on, growing in intensity, in bloodshed, reaching a climax at Gettysburg early in July.

4. It probably didn't seem at all funny at the time, but seven years later the editor of the *Morgantown Post* (April 30, 1870) could see the humorous side: "We reckon there was a leetle the liveliest 'skedaddling' in and around Morgantown that ever took place within the memory of that 'old inhabitant'. There was a universal desire to 'snuff the mountain air' and view the enemy from afar, and we expect faster 'gittin' was never heard of before, as the rebs came in and *we* went out."

5. Callahan, *Making of Morgantown*, p. 205.

6. Wiley, pp. 624, 625; Festus P. Summers, "The Jones-Imboden Raid," *West Virginia History* 1:15-29.

A war that seemed in 1861 to promise only glory, with speeches and music and flags, had settled down into a war of suffering, of bitterness, of despair; on the rude campgrounds many hearts were weary every night, wishing for the war to cease, hoping soon to see the dawn of peace.

**More Raids.** Several times during the remainder of the year the people were frightened by rumors of rebel raids, enumerated as the "Dusenberry," the "Weaver," the "Granny," and the "Cartwright" raids.[7]

**The New Dominion.** The bill providing for the admission to the Union of the new state of West Virginia passed the United States Senate on July 14, 1862, and the House of Representatives on December 9. It was then sent to President Abraham Lincoln, who signed it on December 31, 1862. Thus was finally accomplished what had been discussed for so many years. From the Old Dominion there emerged a New Dominion in the west.

But the bill for admission of the new state provided for the gradual elimination of slavery, a stipulation not included in the constitution that had been adopted by the Wheeling convention on February 18, 1862. This required another meeting of the constitutional convention and it reassembled early in February 1863.

Monongalia's representative at this convention, Waitman T. Willey, spoke on the thirteenth of February, a speech thus noted by the Wheeling *Intelligencer*:[8]

"Mr. Van Winkle[9] moved that Mr. Willey be now invited to address the convention, and that gentleman accepting the invitation, in an address of some two hours, of such breadth and power that it is but faint praise to say that he exhausted the whole new State question, and left nothing for others to say."

Going back of the immediate purpose of the convention, that is, to consider the slavery amendment, Mr. Willey examined carefully the legal and political objections that had been proposed to the admission of the state into the Union. A portion of his speech follows:

"I hardly suppose it is necessary to controvert the idea before

7. Wiley, p. 157, 157 note.
8. Quoted by Wiley, p. 199.
9. Peter G. Van Winkle.

the people of West Virginia, that the Richmond Legislature since the 17th day of April, 1861, was the true and rightful Legislature of Virginia. Traitors may think so, but loyal men cannot think so. Those who believe in the doctrine that a State has a right to secede from the Union, may be excused for entertaining such an opinion, but those who believe that Virginia is still in the Union, and one of the United States, cannot tolerate such a political heresy. Why, sir, those men at Richmond were rebels. They had abjured their allegiance to the United States and sworn to support the constitution of the so-called Confederate States. They had levied war against the United States. Shall they be recognized as the rightful Legislature of Virginia? Not by me, sir, while God spares my life! Not by me while the old flag of my fathers floats over one foot of ground between the Atlantic and Pacific oceans."

Some had objected that Congress was exercising its power in an oppressive and unconstitutional manner, by requiring a clause on the subject of slavery in the constitution of the new state. Willey admitted that this amendment was not acceptable to everyone, and he himself, he said, would have preferred to have had the state admitted under the constitution as originally framed. Yet he could not hesitate, because the advantages of admission, even with this change, were so overwhelming that there need be no hesitation. Furthermore, there were numerous earlier instances wherein Congress had provided restrictions and qualifications governing the admission of states. The ordinance of 1787, for example, had forbidden slavery in the Northwest Territory, and, therefore, in the states created from the territory. The admission of Missouri was contingent upon a provision relative to slavery. Michigan and Wisconsin had also been admitted with conditions imposed by Congress. The same was true of Texas, finally of Kansas.

Furthermore, Willey continued, it was well known that slavery was not adapted to the soil or climate of West Virginia, and slave labor should not be brought into competition with the white labor in the new state.

The separation, he said, could not injure Virginia in the least, and would derange no mutual interest, because "in the East the tone of society is aristocratic; in the West it is democratic." This he enforced in the following words:

"It was when speaking of what he called the 'peasantry' of the West, that Benjamin Watkins Leigh, in the constitutional convention of 1829, said that in political economy slaves fill exactly the same place as the white laborers of the West. 'What real share,' said this illustrious representative of the aristocratic sentiment of Eastern Virginia, 'what real share, so far as mind is concerned, does any man suppose the peasantry of the West . . . can or will take in the affairs of State? Yes, sir, this was the sentiment of the Tidewater and Piedmont districts of the State at that time—an assumption of social and political superiority based on slave labor and slave property. Nor has this sentiment at all abated. It was at the bottom of the present rebellion."

As is well known, the Wheeling convention approved the amendment unanimously on February 17, 1863, and set March 26 as the date for a vote by the people, who ratified it by 27,749 to 572.

The results of the voting were sent to President Lincoln on April 16 and on April 20 the president issued a proclamation admitting West Virginia to the Union sixty days later. On June 20, 1863, West Virginia became the thirty-fifth state admitted to the Union.

On the assembling of the first legislature, Waitman T. Willey was elected, on August 4, 1863, as one of the first United States Senators to represent the New Dominion.[10]

**A New Slack Water Effort.** In the midst of the struggles of the war, slack water was not forgotten. On October 19, 1863, the Marion and Monongahela Navigation Company was incorporated by the new state government, for the purpose of slacking the Monongahela from the Pennsylvania line to Fairmont. The capital stock was set at two hundred thousand dollars, with shares at twenty dollars each. Henry Dering, D. H. Chadwick, Alfred Yeager, Samuel Sears, and George M. Hagans were designated to receive subscriptions. The company was authorized to start work as soon as enough money was subscribed to build one lock and dam and to continue until the whole work was completed.[11]

10. Wiley, pp. 197-202.
11. Wiley, p. 129.

**Townships.** In its provisions for local government, the new state constitution showed a drastic departure from the provisions of earlier Virginia constitutions. The pioneer county court system (*Monongalia Story*, vol. 2, pp. 362, 363), although much improved by the constitution of 1851, was still objectionable to many people of western Virginia. The framers of the new constitution, therefore, adopted the "Yankee institution" of townships as sub-divisions of the counties, with provision for regular township meetings. Various officers were to be elected for each township: a supervisor, a clerk, surveyor of the roads and an overseer of the poor, annually; one or more constables biennially, and one or more justices quadrenially.

The legislature, on July 31, 1863, appointed William Price, Reuben Finnell, James T. McClaskey, Thomas Tarleton, Philemon L. Rice, Jesse Mercer, and Jesse J. Fitch as commissioners to divide Monongalia County into townships and to designate them by names. Rice and Fitch did not serve, and Michael White and Harvey Staggers were appointed in their places.

The commissioners marked off the first township and ran its lines with but slight deviation from the existing boundaries of the old First Magisterial District and named it Clinton Township. The remainder of the county was laid off in a similar way, making each magisterial district a township with but little variation of its boundaries. The Second District thus became the second township, named Morgan; the Third District the third township, named Union; the Fourth District became Cass Township; the Fifth District became Grant Township; the Sixth District Clay Township; and the Seventh District Battelle Township.[12]

**Andrew Coleman Baker.** A farmer of Union Township, A. C. Baker, died June 14, 1863. He was a son of John N. and Nancy (Norris) Baker and a grandson of George and Elizabeth (Norris) Baker, pioneer settlers in the Cheat Neck area. Andrew was born January 20, 1832, and married Hannah A., daughter of Addison S. Vance. Among their children was George C. Baker, prominent Morgantown attorney. "He was a man of attainments and high Christian character and possessed many worthy

12. Wiley, pp. 156, 157.

traits. During the Civil War he served for a time in the State Militia, and died while that struggle was in progress."[13]

**Abraham Ice.** Abraham Ice, son of Andrew and Mary (Bayles) Ice, died in Marion County September 22, 1863. He was a descendant of the pioneer Ice family of Ice's Ferry.

Abraham Ice was born on Buffalo Creek, Monongalia County, in 1785. He was a successful farmer and miller of that area. He married Phebe, a daughter of Adam Ice, and to this union were born Serilda, Elvira, David M., Andrew S., and Luther S.[14]

**Nicholas Johnston.** Nicholas Johnston died at Blacksville in May 1863, aged eighty-two years. The son of John Johnston, he was born on Muddy Creek, Greene County, Pennsylvania, removing to the Dunkard Creek section of Monongalia County upon reaching manhood; he served in the War of 1812.[15]

**Abraham DeVault.** Abraham DeVault died April 29, 1863, at the mouth of White Day Creek. A son of Jacob and Mary De-Vault, he was born April 14, 1791. He was a carpenter by trade, but followed farming, his essential trade. "Liberal in his support of worthy enterprises, generous and accommodating as a neighbor, he possessed, in a high degree, the admiration of all who were thrown into either business or social relations with him."[16]

**The Hermit of Allsop's Island.** On September 8, 1863, twenty-eight-year-old Philip Shuttlesworth, son of John and Susan Shuttlesworth, was shot and killed by a mysterious hermit, Doctor Bonaparte Allsop, living in a lean-to hut near Uffington. He had appeared in the area years before, his origin unknown. Each year he planted corn and vegetables on a nearby island in the river, known by the neighbors as Allsop's Island. It is said that Shuttlesworth was killed because he had been taking vegetables from the garden. On February 16, 1864, he was found guilty in the circuit court of second degree murder and sentenced to twelve years in the penitentiary. After his release he

13. Callahan, *History of West Virginia*, vol. 2, p. 59; *Cyclopedia of Monongalia County*, p. 79.
14. *Cyclopedia of Marion County*, p. 93.
15. *Cyclopedia of Monongalia County*, p. 124.
16. *Cyclopedia of Monongalia County*, p. 125.

Fig. 89. The Hermit of Allsop's Island. (*Fairmont Times*, December 11, 1937.)

returned to Uffington to live, but became mentally upset and was taken to the Weston Hospital.[17]

**The Morgantown Monitor.** A new weekly newspaper, the *Morgantown Monitor*, was started in 1863 by George C. Sturgiss and William P. Willey as a conservative paper. It was undertaken at the request of prominent citizens of the county who gave assurances of financial aid. The two young men[18] promised to give the project a trial for one year and at the end of that time, the assistance having proved insufficient, publication ceased. Another reason for its failure may have been that its conservative policy had no hope of winning popular favor after Lincoln's Emancipation Proclamation. Judge Berkshire referred to the paper as "a gun boat that shot blank cartridges."[19]

**"Frissbang" Church and School.** About 1863 John Fetty made land available near the head of Indian Creek for the erection of a building to be used for both church and school purposes. The double-purpose structure had a built-in blackboard which was recessed into the wall on Friday evening, and the pulpit brought out, converting the school into a church. Doubtless for this reason it was known locally as the Frissbang Church and School.[20]

**The Battle Ground Church.** Michael and Sarah Shively, on December 8, 1863, deeded a lot on a branch of Scotts Run to "Disciple Church trustees," named as William Jones, Solomon Huffman, Robert Birtcher, Solomon Berry, and Thomas Lalas. A Disciple congregation (see p. 125) thereupon built a structure known as the Scotts Run Church. Popularly, however, it came

17. The above account appears to include the essentials of a story that has become so overladen with myth and tradition that it is virtually impossible to separate truth from fiction. That he was a relative of Napoleon Bonaparte, a schoolmate of James G. Blaine, a graduate of Jefferson Medical College, the actual inventor of Dr. McLane's liver pills, are some of the stories told of him. See Circuit Court Order Book No. 4, pp. 27, 31, 32, 39. See numerous pieces about him by E. E. Meredith ("Do You Remember?") in the *Fairmont Times*, including December 11, 1937, December 20, 1937, and December 31, 1937. See also Dennis Rasche, "The Emperor's Kinsman," *Tableland Trails* 2 (3) (1958):123-28.

18. They were not old enough to vote.

19. Wiley, pp. 347, 427, 437; Callahan, *Making of Morgantown*, p. 206.

20. Dodds and Dodds, *Churches of Monongalia County*, p. 126. The church and school were later called Point Pleasant.

to be referred to as the Battle Ground Church, from the general name of the community in which it was located, so-called, tradition stated, because the early settlers "used to go there to settle their differences."[21]

**Free Schools.** The first legislature of the new state, on December 20, 1863, passed a long act establishing a system of free schools. The voters of each township were to elect a board of education, consisting of three commissioners, and the voters of the county were to elect a superintendent of free schools.

The township board of education had control and management of the school property; were to take the annual enumeration of youth between the ages of six and twenty-one years; divide the township into sub-districts; cause a sufficient number of schools to be taught to accommodate all those of proper age in the township; direct what books should be used; buy lots and erect, buy or rent schoolhouses, and supply them with fuel, etc.; appoint the teachers and fix their wages; visit the schools, etc.

The county superintendent was to examine all candidates for the profession of teacher and grant certificates to those found competent; visit the schools at least three times during each six-month term; encourage the formation of county associations of teachers, and teachers' institutes; use all proper means to create and foster among the people an interest in free schools; and to secure, as far as practicable, uniformity in the textbooks used in the schools throughout the county. He was to receive an annual salary of from one hundred dollars to five hundred dollars, the amount to be fixed by the board of supervisors.[22]

**New Congressional Districts.** On January 30, 1863, the legislature of the Reorganized Government ordered that the Eleventh Congressional District consist of Monongalia, Taylor, Marion, Preston, Tucker, Lewis, Barbour, Upshur, Webster, Pocahontas, Randolph, Pendleton, Hardy, Hampshire, and Morgan counties.

Under the new state, on September 24, 1863, the Second District was formed of the counties of Monongalia, Taylor,

21. Core, *Morgantown Disciples*, p. 18.
22. Wiley, pp. 365, 366; Ambler, *History of Education in West Virginia*, pp. 134-39.

Fig. 90. Col. James Evans. (From Wiley's *History of Monongalia County.*)

Fig. 91. Francis H. Pierpont.

Fig. 92. Dr. Fielding H. Youst. (Photo courtesy J. Paul Yost, Pontiac, Illinois.)

Fig. 93. Augustus Haymond. (From Wiley's *History of Monongalia County.*)

Marion, Preston, Tucker, Barbour, Upshur, Webster, Pocahontas, Randolph, Pendleton, Hardy, Hampshire, Berkeley, and Morgan.

**County, Township, and Borough Government.** County officers retained by the new constitution included the sheriff, elected for four years, ineligible for the succeeding term, and a prosecuting attorney, a surveyor of land, a recorder, and an assessor, all elected for two years. Officers whose terms had not expired were mostly kept in office.

Township clerks were E. H. Coombs (Morgan), F. A. Coombs (Union), E. J. Arnett (Cass), M. Shanks (Grant), Alpheus Garrison (Clay), and E. Harker (Battelle).

William Price was elected county surveyor. James B. Price was elected assessor of the Eastern District and Benjamin McCurdy of the Western District; this office, under the Virginia government had been called commissioner of revenue.

The old county court was abolished under the new state government and replaced by a county board of supervisors, consisting of one member from each of the seven townships. A. W. Brown was the first president, E. H. Coombs the first clerk, and A. L. Wade the first recorder of the board.

The first supervisors were F. R. Sinclair for Morgan; George V. Coombs for Union; Samuel Hackney for Cass; Matthew Lough for Grant; A. W. Brown for Clay; and A. D. Haines for Battelle.

Township constables were Harvey Staggers, Kinsey Fife, for Morgan; Joseph Hartman, E. C. Donaldson, for Union; J. B. Dusenberry, G. W. Sample, for Cass; R. B. Fogle, C. W. Miller, for Grant; R. C. Shriver, A. J. Statler, for Clay; and A. S. Core, A. Harker, for Battelle.

John G. Gay was reelected mayor of Morgantown, and Manliff Hayes was reelected recorder. James F. Snyder and F. K. O'Kelly were sergeants.

**Miscellany.** In 1863: John Kelley was operating the Anna Furnace (Wiley, p. 257). . . . James Kern and his son, W. T. Kern, were operating a steam buggy factory at the east end of the suspension bridge (Wiley, pp. 260, 261). . . . Cane mills, for crushing sorghum to squeeze out the juice, were being made at a foundry on Foundry Street operated by George M. Reay

(Wiley, p. 262). . . . Monongalia County, in the new state, was included in the Second Judicial Circuit, composed of the counties of Preston, Tucker, and Taylor, in addition to Monongalia, and John A. Dille was elected judge succeeding Ralph L. Berkshire,[23] who in June was elected judge of the State Supreme Court (Wiley, pp. 309, 324). . . . Augustus Haymond was sworn in as clerk of the circuit court, on June 20 (Wiley, pp. 312, 353). . . . W. P. Willey, A. B. Woods, and F. M. Woods were teachers in Monongalia Academy (Wiley, p. 396). . . . The Presbyterian churches of Monongalia County on October 6, 1863, became part of the Presbytery of West Virginia, Wheeling Synod (Wiley, p. 446). . . . Dr. Fielding H. Youst began the practice of medicine in Morgantown (Wiley, pp. 468, 584). . . . Vital statistics for the county included 202 births, 49 marriages, 185 deaths (Wiley, p. 470). . . . Charles M. Chalfant was a Morgantown tailor (Wiley, p. 602). . . . Hadley Johnson, of Clinton Township, died on July 31, aged eighty-three years (Wiley, p. 617). . . . James Hoard was running Ice's Ferry (Wiley, p. 680). . . . Smyth and Chess (B. F. Smyth, Sr., and David Chess) acquired the Laurel Iron Works on December 23 (Wiley, p. 682). . . . H. Clay Miller opened a store at Laurel Point (Wiley, p. 724). . . . C. W. Finnell began an insurance business in Morgantown (Callahan, p. 214).

23. Judge Berkshire's biography appears in *The Hagans Reports*, pp. 83-86; see p. 667 note 6.

# CHAPTER EIGHTY-EIGHT

# 1864

While it could scarcely be said that any battles of the Civil War were actually fought on the soil of Monongalia County, there was some difference of opinion among the people. The sentiment was overwhelmingly in favor of the Union; after the war was fully under way, it was dangerous to speak out in favor of the South, so most Confederate sympathizers worked under cover.[1]

**Monongalians in Confederate Service.** Three Monongalia County men, Dudley Evans, J. M. Hock, and Lowrie Wilson, were colonels in Confederate armies. D. Boston Stewart was a major on the staff of Gen. W. L. Jackson, Rawley Stewart was captain of Company A, Thirty-first Virginia Infantry, and was killed. Laben Exeline[2] was captain of Company A, Twenty-fifth Virginia Infantry, and Orlando Shay was quartermaster.

Several Monongalians were in the First Brigade of the Second Division of Gen. Thomas J. ("Stonewall") Jackson's corps, and fought in all the battles of the Army of Northern Virginia from 1861 to 1865. Among them were:

Company A, Twentieth Virginia Cavalry

Officers

| | |
|---|---|
| David M. Camp, captain | P. L. Jamison, sergeant |
| Stephen Franks, sergeant | George W. Wilson, corporal |

1. Some of the agony felt on the border is expressed in H. M. Calhoun, *'Twixt North and South* (Parsons, W.Va.: McClain Printing Company, 1974), 280 pp.
2. Laben Exeline, with his arm shattered, led two charges at South Mountain.

Privates

Alfred Ammon, killed  L. B. Camp         Elsworth Stewart
Rezin Ammon           V. S. Camp         William Stewart
Zimri Ammon           A. J. Camp         G. W. Smith
Edgar Barker          Van Coombs         George Shay
John T. Bell          George Garrison    Edward Trickett
Edward Bell           William Garvis     A. O. Wilson[3]
David Bussey          J. W. Jamison

Company B, Twentieth Virginia Cavalry
Officers

A. J. Jones, sergeant              Henry Wilson, corporal
Frank Jones, sergeant

Privates

Calvin Arnett      William Fisher    John Wilson
Edward Boer        Andrew Tennant    George Wilson[4]
Miller Clark

Twenty-sixth Battalion Cavalry
Officers

H. A. Ferrel, captain              Asbury Toothman, sergeant,
                                       killed

Privates

Charles Malot      James Hurry       Zack West
Jesse Thomas       William Malot     Joseph Wiseman
Ed Arnett

**Brown's Mills Destroyed.** The fire that destroyed Brown's Mills, on October 1, 1864, was believed to have been the work of Southern sympathizers who had a strong dislike for the owner, Andrew Brown, because of his intense loyalty to the Union:

"On Saturday night (October 1, 1864) the large and valuable Mills of Andrew Brown, Esq., on Dunkard, this county, were destroyed by fire, and are now a heap of smouldering ruins. These Mills were the most extensive in the county, consisting of water and steam power, and contained six run of stones, carding machines, and saw mill. The property was almost new—having been completed but a few years since. A considerable quantity

3. After the war, Wilson went to Bates County, Missouri, where he was elected constable and was killed by one of the Jesse James band of robbers.
4. George Wilson carried a dispatch around Fort Lincoln, near Washington, D.C., after twelve men had been killed in the attempt.

of grain, flour, flaxseed, and wool, were consumed. Mr. Brown has been making additions to this valuable property for years, and, at present values, the loss will be from $20,000 to $25,000. The fire was discovered about 9 o'clock at night, in a part of the Mill that leaves no doubt that it was the hellish work of an incendiary. Threats have been made by Greene County copperheads for a year past to burn these Mills, owing to the open expression of Union sentiment by Mr. Brown. The recent draft in that county maddened the parties making these threats, some of them having been drafted. The absence of Mr. Brown in Marion County on business and of most of his employees under the last military call of the Governor was regarded as a favorable time for the so-called 'Sons of Liberty' to consummate their fiendish purpose."[5]

Fig. 94. Core's Mill on Dunkard Creek, operated by Isaac Core until 1871. (Photo courtesy Sara I. Scott.)

The burning of the mills was a disaster, not only to Andrew Brown, but to the entire community for miles around, dependent upon the mills for various services, most of all for the grinding of grain. Before the end of the month reconstruction was

5. The *Morgantown Post*, October 8, 1864.

under way. The *Post*, a few days later, reported "that Mr. Andrew Brown, of this county, whose extensive mill property was burned some few weeks since, is now engaged in putting up new mills on the old site. Mr. Brown is one of the most enterprising men in the county, and the mills are indispensable to the people."[6] The new building for the gristmill was constructed thirty-four by seventy-three feet and the machinery was driven by a forty-horsepower engine.

Andrew Brown was a son of Adam Brown, who came in 1796 from Fayette County, Pennsylvania, to locate along Dunkard Creek near the site of Brown's Mills. Adam in turn was a son of Wendell Brown; Thomas Brown, another son of Wendell's, laid out the town of Brownsville, Pennsylvania.

Andrew Brown was born March 9, 1796, and succeeded his father as operator of the mills. In 1840 he refitted the complex, making extensive improvements. Besides the important gristmill, he ran a large sawmill and a carding machine to prepare wool for clothing. A few years later he installed a steam engine. The neighbors never tired of telling how John Foley, who built the eighty-foot high chimney, stood on its summit when he had laid the last brick and drank a half-pint of whiskey before coming down.

In addition to being an outstanding businessman, Andrew Brown was a civic leader and took a prominent part in politics, being an ardent Whig. On the outbreak of the Civil War he took a strong stand against secession, and during the struggle was a firm and uncompromising supporter of the Union, which explains the antagonism against him in some quarters, resulting in the burning of his establishment.

**Company E, Seventeenth West Virginia Infantry.**[7] This company was recruited in Monongalia County in August 1864 and mustered into service at Wheeling September 3. Soon after its organization it was sent to Bulltown, Braxton County, where its members engaged in scouting and skirmishing until April 1865, when they were ordered to Clarksburg and later to Wheeling, where they were mustered out June 30.

6. The *Morgantown Post*, October 29, 1864.
7. *Ann. Rpt. Adj. Gen.*, pp. 435, 436, 439; Wiley, pp. 508, 509.

## Officers

Frank L. Hicks, captain
Harvey Staggars, first
　lieutenant
Alpheus Garrison, second
　lieutenant
Harmon Tricket, sergeant
Granville Brown, sergeant
Clark Kelly, sergeant
Nathan Jones, sergeant
Thomas A. Ryan, sergeant
Leonard Selby, corporal

Edgar McRa, corporal
William J. Vandivert,
　corporal
John Brown, corporal
J. Milton Hartley, corporal
James N. Davis, corporal
Isaac N. Litman, corporal
George C. Hayes, corporal
Nimrod Protzman, musician
William N. Arnett, teamster

## Privates

Simeon Austin
Robert M. Altman
Henry Bell
John W. Carrico
Samuel Albright
William B. Brown
Daniel Brown
Henry H. Burgoine
Horatio Britten
John W. Britten
R. D. Brookover
Thomas D. Field
Leonard Fisher
James Freeman
Martin V. B. Funk
Joseph Gwyn
Jeremiah Hare
Samuel W. Harden
William R. Hopkins
Erastus Kirkpatrick
Marshall Knox
Jacob Lyons
Thomas Lanham
Alex. H. Lindsey
Adam Moore

Gilbert M. Moore
Waitman Mercer
P. D. McKenney
Oliver P. McRa
Zadoc McBee
George W. Male
Ammi Orr
Asa S. O'Kelly
John Cole
Henry Conaway
Rush W. Dorsey
Solomon Dorton
James T. Eberhart
William A. Eberhart
Thomas Flumm
James K. Phillips
William H. Phillips
Alpheus Pew
Henry F. Pew
William W. Pixler
Francis M. Powell
Elza Plum
Alexander Rumble
Isaiah Robe
John Rice

Isaac H. Smith
Benjamin F. Selby
Peter Shafer
Columbus Summers
Hiram Springer
Adam Staggers
Jesse S. Severe
John A. Thompson
William M. Tennant
Zimary Tennant
Simon P. Tennant
Andrew Tennant
C. Puffenberger
Marion Protzman
Enoch Tennant
Joseph E. Watts
George W. Watson
Alpheus West
James Williams
Amon J. Tennant
Jacob P. Tennant
Michael P. Williams
Jeremiah Wright
Lewis Walter

Aggregate, 92 men

**Other Monongalians in the Union Army.**[8] In addition to the Personnel of the various outfits that have been discussed above, several Monongalia County men served in other organizations, including the following:

Battery F, First West Virginia Light Artillery: John W. Mason, Samuel Fetty, Jonathan Fast, Elisha C. Allender, Capell Holland, Albert B. Mason, Robert Robes.

Company A, Third West Virginia Infantry: John C. Davis, John E. Carrothers, William H. Shriver, Charles Martin, F. M. Burns, Marshall Scott, Henry L. Scott, Charles B. Schisler, Solomon Wright.

Company B, Third West Virginia Infantry: John Bell.

Company B, Sixth West Virginia Infantry: James H. Arnett.

Company N, Sixth West Virginia Infantry: James Pettatal.

Company K, Seventh West Virginia Infantry: John M. Jones.

Company F, Twelfth West Virginia Infantry: Jonathan Arnett.

Company E, Fourteenth West Virginia Infantry: William J. Stewart.

Company K, Fourteenth West Virginia Infantry: S. W. Gilmore, David C. Furman.

Company B, Fifteenth West Virginia Infantry: Joseph Jenkins.

Company D, Seventeenth West Virginia Infantry: Isaac Gallagher.

Company B, First West Virginia Cavalry: David Shaw.

Company G, First West Virginia Cavalry: Jacob Eaglen, Nimrod Neely, Thomas Minear, Richard B. Berry.

Company H, Second West Virginia Cavalry: Thomas Warman.

Company A, Third West Virginia Cavalry: Thomas H. McBee.

Company B, Third West Virginia Cavalry: William I. Ervin, T. J. Woody, William L. Simpson.

Company E, Third West Virginia Cavalry: E. W. Snyder.

Company B, Fourth West Virginia Cavalry: Sylvanus Reppert, Samuel G. Walls.

Company M, Fourth West Virginia Cavalry: W. H. Phillips.

Company A, Sixth West Virginia Cavalry: Garrett T. Fogle.

8. Wiley, pp. 509, 510.

Company E, Sixth West Virginia Cavalry: S. W. Fleming, James A. Mayfield.

Company G, Sixth West Virginia Cavalry: John Bean.

Company H, Seventh West Virginia Cavalry: Isaac Smith.

Company C, Sixty-first Pennsylvania: George W. Smith.

Company B, Sixty-second Pennsylvania: Josiah Frankenberry.

Company ——, Sixteenth Ohio: William Simpson.

Company G, United States Regiment: Samuel N. Stewart.

Company F, Sixth West Virginia Cavalry veteran: Richard W. Blue, W. W. Hickman, Jacob M. Widdows, W. R. Batson, B. Jennewine, James McGraw, Henry Shisler, John Dancer, John A. Doty, Oliver P. Widdows, William S. Cobun, William Doty, John E. Price, John P. Shively, Luther Sheets.

Company ——, Twenty-fifth Ohio Volunteers, William Fogle.

Company ——, Forty-fifth Illinois Volunteers, Bruce Fogle.

Seventh West Virginia Infantry: Enoch Plummer Fitch, died.

In the United States Navy Thomas J. Meeks served on the *Cricket* No. 6 and French Ensor Chadwick graduated from the Naval Academy in November 1864 and was attached to the flagship *Susquehanna.*

**The B&O in the Civil War.**[9] The Baltimore and Ohio Railroad played a prominent role in the history of the Civil War. In the first place, it "profited from the traffic windfall of the storm years. . . . But the company did not enjoy the full fruits of war prosperity because a large part of its main line lay on debatable ground. Although United States troops endeavored to keep the road open, it was repeatedly cut by the Confederates. Advance and retreat in the contest for control furnish interesting side-lights on the conduct of the war."[10]

Furthermore, it "was the first railroad to play a leading part in the drama of war; no other railway rendered more important service to the United States during the Civil War. The founders spoke prophetically when they dedicated it to the nation's use.

9. Festus P. Summers, *The Baltimore and Ohio in the Civil War* (1939), 304 pp.
10. Summers, p. vii.

The Baltimore and Ohio did 'contribute to the permanence of the union of the United States.' "[11]

**John Rogers.** In the closing months of the bitter Civil War, John Rogers passed away, his life perhaps shortened by the sadness of the times. For nearly half a century he had been one of Morgantown's best known businessmen.

John Rogers was born in November 1786, in Fayette County, Pennsylvania, the son of Thomas and Ann McKinnon Rogers. George Rogers Clark was a relative of the family.

In April 1816 John Rogers and his brother-in-law, Zadoc Walker, purchased most of the old Michael Kerns tract of seven hundred acres, in the area of the sections later known as South Morgantown, South Park, Greenmont, Marilla, Woodburn, and Sabraton. On this tract, says Callahan, "he began the raising of sheep at a time when South Park was not yet free from wolves."[12]

Fig. 95. The Calmese twins (born May 6, 1786), Isabella, wife of John Rogers, and Mary, wife of John Hoye. (Photos by David Goff of original portraits, courtesy B. B. Laidley.)

11. Summers, pp. 224, 225.
12. *Making of Morgantown*, p. 95.

He was married December 16, 1819, in Cumberland, Maryland, to Isabella Calmese, the ceremony being performed by the Reverend Ashbel G. Fairchild, popular Morgantown minister.

Along Deckers Creek at the "Hogback" he built and operated a paper mill, the water being supplied by a tunnel through the ridge at that point. The principal user of the paper produced was the local newspaper, saving the long haul by wagon across the mountains. At the site of Kerns' old mill, by the covered bridge across Deckers Creek, he operated a water-powered gristmill to grind the farmers' grain.

Still further downstream, at the foot of High Street, he erected in 1826 a sawmill, also operated by water power. With one of his mills he also operated a wool carding machine and his records for 1819 show that his mill carded 3,732 pounds of wool for 230 different customers.

Meanwhile he was busily acquiring more property, in the borough of Morgantown. He secured four lots along Deckers Creek east of High Street and the property south of Plum Alley (later Foundry Street) from High Street to the road crossing Deckers Creek at the lower covered bridge (built in 1830). North of Plum Alley, between High Street and Long Alley (later Chestnut Street) he purchased several lots. One of these was conveyed in 1852 to the trustees of the Morgantown Female Academy and here the seminary building was erected shortly afterwards. The section of Plum Alley east of High Street was disannulled and ceded to him in exchange for a strip of land used by the borough for widening Plum Alley into a street.

In 1839 he completed a new paper mill (the "Live Oak") at the foot of High Street. It was a stone building, four stories high, and cost about six thousand dollars. Here, on September 2, 1839, Tillton and Crowl began the manufacture of paper. They were succeeded by Rogers and Tillton and by various others, who operated the plant until 1855, when it burned down.[13]

Through all the years of his busy commercial life he found plenty of time for religious and civic affairs. He was a member

13. Many years later, after the death of Rogers, the stones were given by the executors of his estate to the new West Virginia University, and were used for the foundation and trimming of Martin Hall, the first building constructed by the university.

and trustee of the Protestant Episcopal Church and worked with the Presbyterians in 1819 in building a church used jointly by the two bodies.

He was interested in education and was a member of the board of trustees of Monongalia Academy, which moved into its new building at the corner of Walnut and Spruce streets in 1831. He was the contractor for construction of a new building for the Morgantown Female Academy in 1832, at Bumbo Lane (later Fayette Street) and Long Alley.

In 1837 he was president of the Morgantown Central Temperance Society, an organization that was very active at the time, and he was secretary of the Monongalia County Bible Society in 1823.

He was a member of the board of directors of the Morgantown Bridge Company, which worked for several years to raise money for construction of a suspension bridge across the river, a project finally completed in 1854.

John Rogers lived, until about 1840, in a stone house near Deckers Creek, at the foot of High Street. In 1840 he built a new house on Foundry Street.[14]

It was in this house that John Rogers died, in 1864, a few years after his wife. In accordance with his wish he was buried in the Calmese vault at Cumberland, where she was also buried. John and Isabella Calmese Rogers had no children and much of his property ultimately passed to his nephew, Thomas.

**James Robertson Moore.** One of the most distinguished of Morgantown's educational leaders, Prof. J. R. Moore, died December 12, 1864.

Professor Moore was born in Columbiana County, Ohio, August 20, 1823, the son of William and Susana (Maxwell) Moore. His grandfather, Augustine Moore, who married Verlinda Dawson, had settled near Beesontown before 1767, supposing he was settling in Monongalia County.

James R. Moore graduated at Washington College in 1847 and then spent about three years teaching at Linsly Institute. He next qualified himself for the ministry in the Presbyterian church, entering Princeton Theological Seminary in 1849 and

14. Now (1979) the location of Dering's Funeral Home. See pp. 196, 203.

Fig. 96. James Robertson
Moore.

Fig. 97. Elizabeth I. Moore.
(Courtesy West Virginia
University Library.)

studying there for three years. An affliction of his throat compelled him to quit public speaking, and he then turned to teaching, becoming principal of Monongalia Academy, a position he
held until his death. In 1853 he married Miss Elizabeth I.
Moore, of Wheeling.

Under his direction the Monongalia Academy attained its
greatest prosperity and became widely known. It made Morgantown an educational center to which students came from many
states, as far away as Louisiana. In one' year it had 176 students,
representing fourteen states.

He also conducted, as superintendent, the Woodburn Female
Seminary, which had sixty-eight students in 1864.

"Mr. Moore was a man of rather striking appearance and
grave countenance—a man whose decision of character, great
executive ability, and remarkable knowledge of human nature,
won for him the respect and esteem of all who came in contact
with him. Under his administration Monongalia Academy became an educational power, and students crowded its halls from
many States of the Union."[15]

**Ashbel Green Fairchild.** The Reverend A. G. Fairchild (*Monongalia Story*, vol. 2, p. 500), one of the best known Presbyterian
leaders of western Pennsylvania and northern West Virginia,
died near Fairchance, Pennsylvania, June 30, 1864. He married

15. Wiley, pp. 401, 402. On October 4, 1865, the Reverend H. W.
Biggs delivered a commemorative address which, with a poem read at the
Woodburn Female Seminary reunion at the same time, was published in
pamphlet form. A monument was placed over his grave in 1868 by students of Monongalia Academy, who contributed most of the money to
purchase it.

Eliza, daughter of Hugh McDougal, and left a daughter, Anna, married to Morgantown attorney Lycurgus S. Hough, and a son, Col. Ashbel Fairchild, a wagon manufacturer of Morgantown.

He was born May 1, 1795, in Hanover, New Jersey, and named for Dr. Ashbel Green, a Presbyterian minister of Philadelphia, later president of Princeton College, where young Fairchild graduated in 1817. After some time in missionary work in North Carolina, and preaching in New Jersey, he came to Morgantown as the first pastor of the Presbyterian Church, spending one-third time here, one-third at Georges Creek, one-third at Greensboro. He was principal of Monongalia Academy between 1822 and 1827. During his stay here the first Presbyterian church was built (*Monongalia Story*, vol. 2, pp. 447-49). In 1827 he resigned the Morgantown pastorate to devote his time to the Pennsylvania charges. He was a man of broad education and knew eight languages. "He impressed himself on the whole region, as no other one has done.

"In person Dr. Fairchild stood over six feet in height, very erect, with a countenance marked with intellectuality, beauty and loveliness. His manners were of the most dignified, graceful and winning type, such as attract special notice in any assembly. . . . His life was very beautiful, full of industry and usefulness. An admirer and student of nature, he delighted in horticulture, selecting the finest fruits and flowers for his orchard and garden."[16]

He wrote several books on Presbyterian doctrine, the best known of which was *The Great Supper*.[17] Others included *Scripture Baptism*, *Unpopular Doctrines of the Bible*, and *What Presbyterians Believe*.

**Henry Weed Biggs.** The Reverend H. W. Biggs (Fig. 49), Presbyterian minister in Morgantown, resigned in 1864 to accept a call to Chillicothe, Ohio. He was born at Frankfort, Pennsylvania, May 15, 1828. He graduated from the University of Cincinnati in 1845 and from Princeton Theological Seminary in 1851.

16. Aaron Moore Buchanan, quoted by Moreland, *The First Presbyterian Church*, where the Reverend Mr. Fairchild's biography appears on pp. 45-48; see also *Cyclopedia of Monongalia County*, p. 116; and Clara Hough in *Woman's Edition of the New Dominion*, December 30, 1896.

17. *The Great Supper: or an Illustration and Defence of the Leading Doctrines of Grace; in Three Discourses, on Luke XIV 16-24* (Philadelphia, 1847), 180 pp.

After serving as a missionary at Lebanon, Indiana, and as stated supply at Princeton, he came to Morgantown in 1855. He was greatly beloved by Morgantown people.[18]

**David W. Jones.** David W. Jones died in Clinton Township November 8, 1864. He was a son of David and Mary Jones and was born in Wales June 16, 1797. He located at Smithtown about 1810 and later on Indian Creek. He married Mary Caruthers in 1825 and they moved to the Smithtown area. They had six children, Mary Ellen (married Z. M. Clelland), John C., Rebecca A. (married Oliver Travis), Andrew J., David W., and Thomas G.[19]

**Robert Anderson.** Robert Anderson, a son of James Anderson, who settled in the Dunkard Creek section in pioneer times, died January 21, 1864. He was born February 7, 1814, and reared on the farm, following farming, stock-raising, and stock-dealing all his life. "He located in the woods when but a young man, and before he was married became the owner of a large tract of uncleared land, about seven hundred acres. . . . He was a man of many good business qualities and possessed a thoroughgoing and frugal spirit." He married Sarah, daughter of Return and Elizabeth Temple, and they had nine children including Eliza Jane, William L., Hester A., John W., Martin L., and Sanford R.[20]

**Benjamin Thomas.** Benjamin Thomas, born in Monongalia County in 1799, died in 1864. He learned the trade of carpenter and was eminently successful. He served in the War of 1812 and was in the storming of the city of Norfolk. He was twice married, first to a Miss Shively, and upon her death to Elizabeth Casady. Children of the first marriage were Mary, John, Philip, and James; of the second marriage, Jane, Caroline, Marion, and Benjamin F.[21]

**Josiah Jackson.** A person closely associated with the history of the Cheat Neck iron industry, Josiah Jackson, died in 1864. He

18. Moreland, *The First Presbyterian Church*, p. 51. He died March 8, 1906.
19. *Cyclopedia of Monongalia County*, p. 146.
20. *Cyclopedia of Monongalia County*, pp. 197, 198.
21. *Cyclopedia of Marion County*, p. 82.

was a son of Samuel (1749-1818) and Rebecca (Dixon) Jackson, and a grandson of Joseph (1699-1760) and Susanna (Miller) Jackson (1712-1767).

Josiah Jackson was born in 1785 and was a college graduate who practiced medicine in Fayette County, Pennsylvania, before going into the iron smelting business at Ice's Ferry, where he owned fifteen thousand acres of land and three furnaces. He was married twice; by his first wife, Sarah McCartney, he had eighteen children, and by his second wife, Virlinda Robey Fleming, eleven more.[22]

**Last Sale of Slaves.** Very few slaves were ever sold in Monongalia County and the last sale in the county was on April 11, 1864. Two slaves, Stephen and Elizabeth Trimble—brother and sister—the property of A. C. Dorsey, deceased, were sold to liquidate a debt. The sale took place on the public square. The man was sold to William A. Hanway for $326, the woman was purchased by Dorsey's widow for $71. They were of an age that left them slaves for life by the state constitution. Able-bodied male slaves up to the time of the war generally sold for fifteen hundred to two thousand dollars, but the unsettled state of affairs caused a low price to be realized on them.[23]

**The Morgantown Weekly Post.** The *Morgantown Post*, destined to be the longest-lived paper in the county's history, was established March 12, 1864, by Henry M. Morgan, a son of Enos D. Morgan, who had been a successful publisher for many years. The paper, a four-page sheet, twenty-six by thirty-two inches in size, with six columns to the page, was dedicated to the principles of the Republican party. Its motto was "The Union right or wrong; right we'll defend it, and wrong we'll right it."

Beginning with Henry M. Morgan, a new era for county papers was initiated. The earlier papers were published on the "trust" system, often $1.50 a year if paid in advance and $2.00 if not paid until the end of the year. The papers generally died

22. See Jesse Calvin Cross, *A History of Ephraim Jackson, First Ancestor to come to America, and His Descendants, 1684-1960, 1961.*
23. Wiley, p. 543; all slaves in the county (and elsewhere in the country) were freed by the Thirteenth Amendment to the United States Constitution, proclaimed December 18, 1865.

by having too many "trust" subscribers. Morgan's price was $2.00 per year, in advance.[24]

Morgan's announcement, on his first issue, reads:

"The subscriber takes this mode to announce to the people of Monongalia and the adjoining Counties that he has succeeded the proprietors of the 'Morgantown Monitor,' and will continue the publication of a Newspaper, to be called

The Morgantown Weekly Post.

The great advantages that accrue to every community, to every sphere of business, and to every family, from a well-conducted HOME PAPER, is sufficient to recommend our enterprise, and we trust, draw for it a hearty support from the public.

Henry M. Morgan
Editor and Proprietor."

It is noteworthy that, while about two dozen newspapers had risen and fallen between 1803, when the county's first paper was started, and 1864, when the *Weekly Post* began, the enterprise Henry Morgan founded is still in good health, 115 years later.

**John A. Dille Moves to Morgantown.** John A. Dille (Fig. 139), an attorney of Kingwood (see p. 315), moved to Morgantown in the fall of 1864 to provide his children with an opportunity to obtain a good education. Dille was a member of the Constitutional Convention which met in Wheeling November 26, 1861, and upon the creation of the new state was elected, without opposition, judge of the Second Judicial Circuit.

His first wife had died in 1852 and he married Linnie S., daughter of Thomas Brown, of Kingwood; they had two children, Clarence B. and Mary.[25]

**John J. Brown Moves to Morgantown.** John James Brown (Fig. 50), nephew of William G. Brown (see p. 315), also moved from Kingwood to Morgantown in the fall of 1864. He was born in Kingwood November 19, 1825, the son of Robert and Annie Brown. He was educated at Monongalia Academy under classical scholar Thomas Martin and at Washington College.

24. Wiley, pp. 437, 439.
25. Wiley, pp. 324-31.

Upon graduation in 1845 he returned to Kingwood and studied law under his uncle, with whom he formed a partnership in 1849. "This firm soon won a reputation second to none in the State, which was owing perhaps not more to the ability and experience of the uncle, than to the industry, activity, and ability of the nephew."

He was a member of the Wheeling convention of June 1861, and of the Constitutional Convention of November 1861. At the first general election under the constitution of West Virginia he was elected to the state senate, where it was said of him: "He speaks not very often, but well and very short. He is one of the most pointed and logical debaters in the Senate; does not say a word too much or too little, and nothing that is not right to the point; his gestures are natural and forceful, and his enunciation is exceedingly clear and striking."[26]

He was commissioned a major in the 148th Regiment of Virginia Militia in June 1858.

**Another Confederate Raid?** In August 1864, the militia were called out and went into camp for four days on the Runner farm, about five miles from Morgantown, in apprehension of a Confederate raid. But no Confederates appeared. A gang of rebels early on May 6 seized the county jail and released Van Cicero Amos. In November, someone entered the courthouse one night and tore up or otherwise injured valuable public records.[27]

"The war was in its fourth year, death and agony were familiar shapes, casualty lists were reaching out to every city and village in the land, day after heartbreaking day, all spring and all summer, and it was hard to see that victory was any nearer now than it had been in the spring."[28]

**Mr. Willey in the Senate.** Waitman T. Willey, with his colleague, Peter G. Van Winkle, of Parkersburg, took his seat in the United States Senate on December 7, 1863. On drawing the lot usual under such circumstances, Mr. Willey drew the short term of two years.

On March 22, 1864, he made a speech in the Senate in favor

26. Wiley, pp. 283-87.
27. Wiley, pp. 157, 517; *Morgantown Post*, numerous issues.
28. Bruce Catton, *Never Call Retreat* (1965), p. 379.

of the constitutional amendment abolishing slavery. "In entire harmony with his character he is always found upon the side of order and precedent. He argued for the passage of the amendment, because it then became a part of the organic law, which defied the turbulence of the times or the sophistries of the demagogue. Nothing, he maintained, could justify a violent step outside of the obligations of the National Constitution."[29]

**Francis Madera.** Morgantown's postmaster, Francis Madera, died February 11, 1864, at the age of fifty-three. He was a son of Nicholas B. Madera, who had also served as postmaster. Francis married Julia Ann Watts, daughter of Capt. John Watts. He served as borough trustee in 1840, 1841, 1845, 1854, 1855, and 1858 and became postmaster in 1861. His children included John W. and Mary B. (married Col. M. A. McCallum).[30]

**County, Township, and Borough Government.** Col. George Price was elected surveyor for the Eastern District and Joseph McCallum for the Western District. A. W. Brown was reelected president of the county board of supervisors. Members of the board of supervisors were O. B. Johnson, from Clinton Township; F. R. Sinclair, from Morgan; James Hare, from Union; Samuel Hackney, from Cass; Reuben Finnell, from Grant; A. W. Brown, from Clay; and J. S. Lemley, from Battelle.

Township clerks were T. P. Selby (Clinton), E. H. Coombs (Morgan), F. A. Coombs (Union), E. J. Arnett (Cass), and M. Shanks (Grant).

The state levy was set at forty cents and the county levy at twenty-eight cents.

John G. Gay and J. J. Fitch served as mayors of Morgantown, Manliff Hayes was recorder and James F. Snyder sergeant. Councilmen were James C. Wallace, F. S. Dawson, F. M. Durbin, Henry M. Morgan, and George W. Johnson. For the first time, a borough officer was allowed to receive a salary: on March 5, 1864, it was ordered that the sergeant receive a salary of fifty dollars a year, in addition to his fees, if he completed his term, nothing if he resigned.

A gutter was built along Bumbo Lane from top to bottom

29. Wiley, pp. 203-6. Long excerpts from his speech are given.
30. Callahan, *Making of Morgantown,* p. 88.

and a sewer from Long Alley to Front Street. Sidewalks in general were rickety and streets filthy: "Walks at the lower end of Front Street are in dangerous condition";[31] "the gutters are filled with old rags, boots, stones, corncobs, and all manner of dirt and filth";[32] "the streets are in a filthy condition."[33]

Perhaps because of an increase in rowdyism and street fights, a new liquor law was adopted, effective May 1, 1864, whereby bars in hotels were closed.

Miscellany. In 1864: George C. Sturgiss was admitted to the county bar on May 11, William P. Willey on May 12, and John J. Brown on November 9 (Wiley, p. 317). . . . The first election of school officers occurred on the fourth Thursday in April, in. pursuance of an act passed by the legislature of that year; H. W. Biggs was elected the first county superintendent but he removed from the county and never served; on September 22 George C. Sturgiss was appointed by the board of supervisors to the vacant office (Wiley, pp. 366, 370, 371, 386). . . . Rev. W. W. Laverty[34] was appointed principal of Monongalia Academy (Wiley, p. 395). . . . A. L. Nye was master of the Masonic lodge (Wiley, p. 548). . . . Frederick A. Dering was appointed Morgantown postmaster on February 11. . . . James Gallagher, of Grant Township, died, age sixty-six; he was born in Uniontown, Pennsylvania, in 1797 and moved to Monongalia County about 1839 (Wiley, p. 737). . . . C. W. Finnell purchased the old National Hotel from Alexander Hayes (Callahan, p. 114). . . . Jerry J. Hutchinson, Smithtown merchant, was brutally murdered in his store on November 4 (*Morgantown Post*, November 12, 1864).

31. *Morgantown Post*, March 12, 1864.
32. *Morgantown Post*, March 12, 1864.
33. *Morgantown Post*, August 20, 1864.
34. He died October 27, 1865; see *Morgantown Post*, November 4, 1865.

# CHAPTER EIGHTY-NINE

# 1865

On April 9, 1865, General Robert E. Lee surrendered the forces of the Confederate States of America to General U. S. Grant, commander of the Union army, and the war was over.

"All over, finished forever," says Bruce Catton,[1] in the third volume of his centennial history of the Civil War, "ready to be done up in veterans' reunion music and oratory and lilacs-on-gravestones in a thousand village cemeteries, as if it had been nothing more than tragedy and shared agony...."

**Triumph and Tragedy.** Then at half-past ten in the evening of April 14 John Wilkes Booth came on the stage of Ford's Theater in Washington and shot President Lincoln to death. Catton comments:

"Booth pulled the trigger, and the mind that held in cloudy solution the elements that might some day have crystallized into an answer for the nation's most profound riddle disintegrated under the impact of a one-ounce pellet of lead; the heaviest bullet, all things considered, ever fired in America. Thinking to destroy a tyrant, Booth managed to destroy a man who was trying to create a broader freedom for all men; with him, he destroyed also the chance for a transcendent peace made without malice and with charity for all...."[2]

"Something had been won; but it was nothing more, and at the same time nothing less, than a chance to make a new approach toward a goal that had to be reached if the war and the nation that had endured it had final meaning. The ship was moving through Lincoln's dream, toward a dark indefinite shore, it had a long way to go, and the sky contained no stars

1. *Never Call Retreat*, p. 469.
2. *Never Call Retreat*, p. 462.

the ordinary mortal could see. All that was certain was that the voyage was under way."[3]

"For the full four years of the war," says Boyd B. Stutler,[4] "West Virginia was, for the most part, an armed camp. But of more particular concern to the citizens of that part of the Old Dominion west of the Alleghenies, out of the series of conventions at Wheeling came a new state, the thirty-fifth in the American Union."

Monongalia County had done its part in the conflict. From the beginning of hostilities until December 31, 1864, the county had provided 1,550 men for service in the Union army. From January 1, 1865, to August 31, of the same year, another 155 men were provided, for a total of 1,705. Several men from the county enlisted in companies in other counties, even in other states. Wiley estimated the total at more than 2,000, not bad for a total population of only 13,000.[5]

Up until March 14, 1864, no quotas were assigned to the different counties of the state. Monongalia's quota under the call of that date was 65 men; under the next call, July 18, it was 263 men. By December 31 these two quotas were filled and the county had a surplus of 7 men. Under the call of December 19 the county's quota was 164 men and by August 1865 this quota was filled except for 2 men. Had not the war already come to a close, this call would likely have resulted in a surplus also.

West Virginia was a border state and the war found sympathies divided. Since all spoke the same language, it was difficult to distinguish friend from foe. Relatives debated and fought against relatives, and the end of the war left much bitterness.

Reconstruction. Monongalia County entered the Civil War, in April 1861, as a part of the state of Virginia and emerged, in April 1865, as a part of the state of West Virginia. Not only was the county forced to transfer its political allegiance from one government to another, but the change was made under the stress and agony of war. It is really remarkable that the functions of government continued uninterrupted through all this period and that the lapse of public affairs that has so often accompanied such a political revolution in world history did not at all take place.

3. *Never Call Retreat*, p. 469.
4. *West Virginia in the Civil War*, p. v.
5. *History of Monongalia County*, pp. 511, 512.

By the new state constitution, in 1863, Monongalia was included in the Second Judicial Circuit, along with Preston, Tucker, and Taylor and John A. Dille was elected judge.

The Virginia constitution of 1851 provided for a state senate of fifty members. Monongalia, Preston, and Taylor composed the Forty-ninth District and Jonathan Huddleson was the senator just before the Civil War began. Beginning in 1863, the district of which Monongalia was a part, was represented by John J. Brown and E. C. Bunker.

After 1852 Monongalia County had two members in the House of Delegates, serving two year terms. John Wallace and Andrew Brown were Monongalia's delegates from 1859 until 1861. Delegates to the legislature of the Reorganized Government of Virginia, in 1861, were LeeRoy Kramer and Joseph Snider. For the new state legislature, the first delegates, in 1863, were LeeRoy Kramer and John B. Lough.

Winston Churchill[6] expresses his amazement that the due processes of law were not suspended during the war. Describing the 1864 presidential campaign he says:

"It was astonishing that in the height of ruthless civil war all the process of election should be rigidly maintained. Lincoln's first term was expiring, and he must now submit himself to the popular vote of such parts of the American Union as were under his control. Nothing shows the strength of the institutions which he defended better than this incongruous episode."

The citizens of Monongalia County were no exception. They believed the purpose of government was to serve the people and, come what may, they were determined to uphold it.

**The Monongahela and Lewisburg Railway.** Before the war was hardly over efforts were renewed to secure a railroad for the county. On March 6, 1865, the Monongahela and Lewisburg Railway Company was incorporated by the legislature, the object being the building of a road from a point on the Pennsylvania line, near Morgantown, to or near Lewisburg, Greenbrier County. Capital stock was set at $5 million, with shares at fifty dollars each. A period of four years was allowed to receive subscriptions and to begin construction work. A large meeting

6. *History of the English-Speaking Peoples*, vol. 4, p. 256.

Fig. 98. Charles W. Finnell. (From
the *New Dominion*, May 10,
1906.)

Fig. 99. Rev. Peter T. Laishley.
(From Wiley's *History of Monongalia County.*)

Fig. 100. William Sanford Cobun.
(From Wiley's *History of Monongalia County.*)

Fig. 101. Dr. George W. John.
(From Wiley's *History of Monongalia County.*)

was held at Fairmont on November 4, but the enterprise, like its predecessors, turned out to be only a paper railway.

Among the stockholders were James Evans, William Lazier, Henry Dering, D. H. Chadwick, B. F. Smith, George M. Hagans, William Wagner, William A. Hanway, Samuel Sears, Alfred Yeager, S. S. Yeager, Amos Courtney, E. C. Bunker, W. T. Willey, and James McClaskey.[7]

**Oil Fever.** The oil excitement, which had been felt in the county in the spring of 1861 and which had been suspended during the war, broke out again in 1865. Oil companies were organized, including the Baltimore and Dunkard, incorporated March 3, authorized capital $150,000; Dolls Run and Dunkard Creek Petroleum, March 3, $300,000; Cheat River Oil and Mining, March 4, $500,000; Laurel Run Oil, April 7, $500,000; Maidsville Oil and Mining, April 8, $1 million; Monongalia Oil and Mining, April 24, $1 million; Hawthorne Petroleum and Lumbering, May 6, $100,000; and Woodgrove Oil, August 30, $500,000.

Several wells were drilled, down a few hundred feet, but very little oil was obtained. Brine was struck at the conglomerate sandstone in some wells and at the mouth of Pedlar Run a well yielded sulphur water, which flowed freely for local use. Another sulphur vein was struck at Clinton Furnace. Something resembling gold quartz was found at 519 feet near New Brownsville and at 343 feet on Deckers Creek and considerable excitement prevailed, but the quartz did not turn out to be gold.

Other outfits operating in the county in 1865 included the Essex Petroleum, the Teutonia, the Deckers Creek Petroleum, and the Keyser Oil companies.[8]

**Joseph L. Fry.** Judge Joseph L. Fry, of the Circuit Superior Court of Law, Twentieth Circuit, Tenth Judicial District, from 1831 until 1852, died in Wheeling June 10, 1865, aged seventy-one years. He was a native of Orange County, then practiced law in Kanawha County until he was elected judge. He was a man of fine literary tastes and had an excellent library.[9]

7. Wiley, pp. 109, 110, 124.
8. Wiley, pp. 263, 264, 620, 621; *Chronicles of Core*, p. 100.
9. Wiley, p. 322.

**John Liming.** John Liming, a farmer of Licking County, Ohio, but formerly of Monongalia County, died in 1865, aged about eighty years. He had been a farmer in the vicinity of Cassville in the early part of his life and moved to Ohio about 1850. He married Susanna Lemley, and they had seven children.[10]

**Rev. Edward Pople.** A native of Wales, the Reverend Edward Pople, died in Monongalia County in March 1865, at the age of eighty-six years. He migrated to the United States in 1842 and later settled in this county, where he followed coal mining and was a local minister of the Methodist Church. He had ten children, including John, an expert in coal mining.[11]

**Richard Fast.** Richard Fast, a farmer, miller, and politician of Marion County, died in 1865. He was a son of Adam and Elizabeth Rex Fast, who had located on White Day Creek in pioneer times. Richard was born in 1813 and married Mrs. Litha (Farrell) Jacobs. He was elected justice of the peace and served for several years in that position.

He was elected a member of the general assembly just before the outbreak of the Civil War. He was known as a war Democrat, one who believed in the preservation of the Union at any cost, and was one of the signers of the Original Declaration of the Restored Government of Virginia.[12]

**James D. Watson.** A prominent citizen of Smithtown, James D. Watson, died November 2, 1865. A son of James G. Watson (see p. 112), he was born July 10, 1794, and grew up on his father's farm. In 1825 he married Ann Maria, a daughter of William and Cynthia Haymond, and they settled on Bunners Run, remaining there until 1834, when he bought the farm of John Caruthers, of Smithtown, and moved there. "In his chosen pursuits, farming and grazing, he was in advance of the average man of his day."

James and Ann Maria had four children, Helen, William E., James G. H., and Thomas F. Mrs. Watson died January 14,

10. *Cyclopedia of Monongalia County*, p. 169.
11. *Cyclopedia of Marion County*, p. 55.
12. *Cyclopedia of Monongalia County*, pp. 221, 222. A son was Richard E. Fast, later clerk of the circuit court and mayor of Morgantown (see vol. 2, p. 72).

1844, and James married Minerva, daughter of John S. Barnes, who also preceded him in death.[13]

**John Keck.** A farmer of western Monongalia County, John Keck, died in 1865. He was born in Pennsylvania in 1788, and married Catharine Creichbaum. They came to Monongalia County in 1823 and "proceeded to convert a portion of the wilderness into a farm and a home, a fit place for the dwelling of man." One of their thirteen children was Philip H. Keck, who came to Morgantown, read law in the offices of Guy R. C. Allen and R. L. Berkshire, and was admitted to the bar in October 1844.[14]

**The Strosnider Store.** Arthur Inghram Strosnider, after "the Civil War was over and the smoke of battle had cleared away," came to Blacksville, it is said, for a two-week visit, but instead settled for life, at first entering the boot and shoe business, then expanding it into a general mercantile business, one of the largest in the county.

Fig. 102. Shop and residence of A. I. Strosnider in Blacksville. (From Caldwell's *Illustrated Centennial Atlas of Greene County*, 1876.)

13. *Cyclopedia of Monongalia County*, p. 172; Wiley, p. 614.
14. *Cyclopedia of Monongalia County*, p. 45.

A son of Reason and Jane Strosnider, he was born September 9, 1842, at Waynesburg, Greene County, Pennsylvania. He learned the cobbler's trade, but did not follow it very long, being among the first volunteers to respond to Lincoln's call for troops at the beginning of the Civil War. He took place in thirty-one battles, but was never seriously wounded.[15]

**The Strosnider Mill.** Another member of the Strosnider family was at the same time locating near Blacksville to begin the milling business. Jasper (Gasper) F. Strosnider was a son of Moses and Mary Thompson Strosnider and was born August 3, 1839, in Greene County, Pennsylvania.

He located in 1865 along Dunkard Creek, a few miles east of Blacksville, and built a gristmill in Blacksville, furnishing it with new and modern machinery for flour manufacture, including the roller process, and soon built up a flourishing business. He also owned a farm of 117 acres, and another mill property, the old Minor mill, along Dunkard Creek near the mouth of Days Run.[16]

He married Susan Virginia, daughter of Elias Marsh, and their children were: Moses Elias; Mary Belle, married Corbley Orndorff II; Emma Maude; Samuel Thompson; Laura Dell; Frank Marsh; Victoria Ann; Sarah Myrtle, drowned in the mill pond; Homer Pierce; Edna Blanche; Ana Marie; and Pansie Ocha.[17]

**Free Schools.** Honorably discharged Union soldiers in 1865 were admitted to the privileges of attending the new free schools, which went into operation this year. Township levies for schools were limited to a maximum of twenty-five cents on each one hundred dollar valuation for the building fund and to twenty cents for the teachers' fund. Monongalia County received $4,330.72 from the state fund.

It was enacted that the state superintendent "may prescribe a series of class books to be used." Another 1865 enactment required the county superintendent to visit each school at least once, rather than three times during each term. A Teachers'

15. *Cyclopedia of Monongalia County,* p. 214.
16. *Cyclopedia of Monongalia County,* pp. 179, 180; pers. comm., Ruth Strosnider.
17. Pers. comm., Ruth Strosnider.

Association was organized by Superintendent George C. Sturgiss December 27, 1865.[18]

**Monongalia and Preston County Gazette.** The Morgantown *Post* completed its first volume March 25, 1865, and then suspended until May 20, Editor Henry M. Morgan having associated with him Nelson Nimrod Hoffman. The above title was added to the original name of the paper.[19]

Nelson Hoffman, born in 1827, was a son of Philip and Alethe (Summers) Hoffman, and grandson of John and Sarah Hoffman, who settled near Smithtown in 1796. He learned the "art preservative of all arts" with Enos D. Morgan. He was a soldier in the Mexican War and a captain in the Civil War.[20]

**Merchants' National Bank.** The Merchants' National Bank of West Virginia at Morgantown was organized October 1, 1865, under the new federal banking system, succeeding the old Merchants' and Mechanics' Bank of Wheeling, Morgantown branch, which went out of business the same day. The capital stock was $110,000. The bank contained a fireproof vault, in which was a double burglar-proof safe, the whole secured by combination locks and a time lock. The first president of the new bank was George M. Hagans. William Wagner, who had been cashier of the old bank since 1838, became cashier of the new one. He was born August 21, 1813, in Cumberland County, Pennsylvania, and had worked in various banks before coming to Morgantown in 1838.[21]

**Oak Grove Cemetery.** "Between the Evansville and Fairmont pikes, a few minutes' walk from Morgantown," beautiful Oak Grove Cemetery was laid out in 1865. The certificate of incorporation was filed in the county clerk's office on August 1; incorporators were Martin Callendine, W. T. Willey, John J. Brown, E. C. Bunker, Richard B. Carry, J. V. Boughner, Jacob P. Shafer, H. W. Brock, and George M. Hagans. On August 5 they bought eight and one half acres of land from W. T. Willey

18. Wiley, pp. 367, 380, 385, 386.
19. But the extra title was dropped June 2, 1866.
20. Wiley, pp. 437, 438, 533, 534.
21. Wiley, pp. 462, 463.

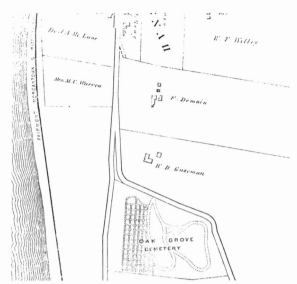

Fig. 103. Map showing location of Oak Grove Cemetery. (From *Atlas of Marion and Monongalia
Counties*, 1886.)

for nine hundred dollars and neatly laid out the ample grounds
for the sleep of the dead.[22]

**Grant Methodist Church.** On a dead-end road in the big bend of
the Monongahela River in Grant Township, Margaret O'Neill,
about 1865, gave the ground for a school building, with the
stipulation that the grounds and building be used for church
purposes as well. At first the Southern Methodists had charge
and the Reverend Mr. White ("Daddy White"), a Civil War veteran, held meetings for a number of years.[23]

**County, Township, and Borough Government.** A. W. Brown was
reelected president of the board of supervisors, Joseph Grubb,
Jr., was elected supervisor for Clinton Township, George V.
Coombs for Union, Allen Dilliner for Cass, Daniel Glasscock for
Grant, A. W. Brown for Clay, and S. H. Shriver for Battelle. The
state levy was forty cents and the county levy one dollar.

22. Wiley, pp. 656, 657; *Morgantown Post*, August 5, 1865.
23. Dodds and Dodds, *Churches of Monongalia County*, p. 101.

Township clerks were T. P. Selby (Clinton), E. H. Coombs (Morgan), F. A. Coombs (Union), James Dean (Cass), D. C. Shaffer (Grant), Titus Lemley (Clay), and William Kinney (Battelle).

William Lazier was mayor of Morgantown, Manliff Hayes recorder, and N. S. Evans sergeant. Councilmen were George M. Hagans, William H. Staggers, Alexander Hayes, Jacob Kiger, and Henry D. McGeorge. Several citizens were ordered to place sidewalks in front of their properties, and the borough laid stone walks or stepping stones at several street crossings.

**Miscellany.** In 1865: The Reverend G. W. Arnold was appointed principal of Morgantown Female Academy (Wiley, p. 399). . . . J. P. Barron and Adam Staggers were teachers at Monongalia Academy (Wiley, p. 396). . . . There were 216 recorded births, 62 marriages, and 137 deaths (Wiley, p. 470). . . . E. C. Bunker and E. H. Coombs were masters of the Masonic lodge (Wiley, p. 548). . . . Henry Robertsen was representing the Aetna Insurance Company, of Hartford, Connecticut, in Morgantown (Wiley, p. 553). . . . L. S. Layton opened a store in the Shisler building (Wiley, p. 581). . . . Hanway and Lorentz opened a store in the Wallace building (Wiley, p. 582). . . . F. L. Hix and Henry Reed opened grocery stores in Morgantown (Wiley, p. 583). . . . E. E. Cobun was a physician in Morgantown (Wiley, p. 584). . . . Rufus E. Weaver was running Ice's Ferry (Wiley, p. 680). . . . A post office called Andy, for Andrew Brown, was opened January 10, with Alpheus W. Brown as postmaster. . . . Levi Lowe's mill at Lowesville burned Sunday night, June 4, and his young son died in the fire (*Morgantown Post*, June 10, 1865).

# CHAPTER NINETY

# 1866

At first glance, a reader of the educational history of what is now West Virginia may wonder why it was that antebellum Virginia, dominated by "tidewater aristocrats," lacked a state-wide system of public schools, while the relatively unlettered mountaineers who founded West Virginia, wrote it into their first constitution.

**Free Public Schools.** "The patriotic men who," says Wiley,[1] in 1883, "in the troublous days of sixty and sixty-one, refusing to follow the State in secession, stood steadfast by the Union, and who were driven by the stern logic of events to advocate the formation of a new State, and who were chosen by their fellow-citizens to frame a Constitution for it, had seen the beneficial workings of a uniform system of free schools in the adjoining States of Pennsylvania and Ohio as well as in other States of the Union." As a result of this, Wiley concludes, they put into the first constitution this injunction:

"The Legislature shall provide, as soon as practicable, for the establishment of a thorough and efficient system of free schools. They shall provide for the support of such schools by appropriating thereto the interest of the invested school fund, the net proceeds of all forfeitures, confiscations and fines accruing to this State under the laws thereof; and by general taxation on persons or property, or otherwise. They shall also provide for raising, in each township, by the authority of the people thereof, such a proportion of the amount required for the support of free schools therein as shall be prescribed by general laws."

1. *History of Monongalia County,* pp. 364, 365.

But the incentive for this movement is perhaps more accurately stated by Ambler[2] writing in 1951, after the heats and passions of the Civil War had subsided. The founders of the new state had wanted to improve on conditions existing in the Old Dominion, and one way to do this was to model after the Northern States. Nevertheless, a strong approach to universal free education had been made in Virginia before the Civil War, and educational leaders of the new state, at least unconsciously, were more influenced by these advances, which were well known to them, than they were by the teachings of Northern leaders, who were too remote to be effective.

Ambler points out that by 1860 several counties of Virginia, including Kanawha, Jefferson, and Ohio, were already operating free schools, and several others had approved them by majorities of the voters, as provided by state law. Indeed, Virginia was, in 1860, "on the eve of accepting the free school idea in its fullest."

Regardless of what the incentives may have been, West Virginia did emerge from the Civil War with a system of free schools, at least on paper. Among persons who had assisted in setting it up were some individuals well known in Monongalia County, including the Reverend Gordon Battelle, chairman of the constitutional convention's committee on education and his friend, the Reverend Alexander Martin, who prepared for the committee "An Outline for a System of General Education for the New State."

The first legislature of the new state of West Virginia, on December 20, 1863, passed a long act establishing the free school system. The voters of each township were to elect a board of education consisting of three commissioners and the voters of the county were to elect a county superintendent of free schools. Among other duties, the boards of education were to have control and management of the school property of the township; to take the annual enumeration of youth between the ages of six and twenty-one years; divide the township into sub-districts; cause a sufficient number of schools to be taught to accommodate all of the proper age in the township; direct what books should be used; buy lots and erect, buy, or rent

2. *History of Education in West Virginia*, pp. 130-34.

schoolhouses, and supply them with fuel, etc.; appoint the teachers and fix their wages; visit the schools, etc.

Fig. 104. An early public school.

The state superintendent of schools was elected by joint ballot of both houses of the legislature, for a term of two years. The first election was on February 16, 1864, when the Reverend William Ryland White was elected. He served (through reelections) from June 1, 1864, to March 3, 1869. At the time of his election he was serving as principal of the Fairmont Male and Female Seminary.

The first election in the state for county school officers was held in Monongalia County on April 28, 1864, and the first county superintendent to be elected was the Reverend H. W. Biggs, minister of the Morgantown Presbyterian Church. But he removed from the county before his term of office started and on September 22, George C. Sturgiss was appointed by the board of supervisors to the vacant office. The superintendent's salary was four hundred dollars a year.

From the state fund Monongalia County revised $4,330.72 in 1865 and $4,052.02 in 1866.

The first school commissioners for the various townships appear as follows:

Clinton—Thomas McBee, Jr., William Holland, and James A. Johnson.

Morgan—John Mills, Lewis W. Runner, and William Lazier.

Union—W. S. Swindler, Jacob Miller, and Robert Beatty.

Cass—Lorenzo Davis, George Alexander, and S. S. Lemley.

Grant—G. F. C. Conn, Eugenius Shafer, and D. E. Miller.

Clay—William Price, Christopher Core, and Emrod Tennant.

Battelle—S. H. Shriver, Jacob Wiley, and J. G. White.

The free school system went into effect in Monongalia County in 1865, Grant Township being the first to open free schools, followed by Cass and Clinton.

**The First Telegraph.** The year 1866 was a great year in the history of Monongalia County. The Civil War was over, the agony and uncertainty of conflict had ended, reconstruction was under way, the wounds were slowly beginning to heal.

But the year is remembered especially as the year the first telegraph line reached Morgantown.

The telegraph was the first of man's inventions to increase the speed of communication. Until its invention, men had to depend chiefly upon messengers to communicate with each other at a distance. For example, a special convention in Richmond, on April 17, 1861, passed an ordinance of secession for the state of Virginia. A large meeting of citizens assembled in Morgantown that same evening to take counteraction. They could only assume the ordinance had passed—they had no way of knowing for sure. Waitman T. Willey, a member of the convention, did not arrive home until April 24, although the news had reached here before that time.

The telegraph, already in use between large cities in the country before the Civil War, changed all man's ideas about communication. The Pony Express, opened in 1860 between the end of the railroad at Saint Joseph, Missouri, and Sacramento, California, furnished the fastest movement of mail to the West Coast that America had as yet seen, but it quickly went out of date when a telegraph line spanned the entire three thousand miles between New York and San Francisco in the fall of 1861.

Although Samuel F. B. Morse gets most of the credit, in the

popular mind, for the development of the telegraph, a great many people really contributed[3]—actually Morse did not make any of the basic inventions. He did, however, put them together in a practical form, invent a code for telegraphers, and persuade Congress to finance the first line, opened between Washington and Baltimore in 1844.

The story began with the development of the electric battery in 1799 and the development of the electromagnet a few years later. Hans Oersted, in 1820, found that an electric current flowing along a wire would cause a compass needle to turn. In 1837 Sir Charles Wheatstone and his partner, Sir William Cooke, took out a patent in England for a system of sending messages over wires, depending upon the ability of an electric current to turn a needle to send signals. This system was used in England for several years for sending commercial messages.

Joseph Henry, later the first secretary of the Smithsonian Institution, improved over earlier crude electromagnets by making many turns of insulated wire upon the coil. In this way, even a feeble electric current would produce a considerable magnetic effect.

In 1832 Samuel Finley Breese Morse (1791-1872), an American artist, traveling on the packet ship *Sully*, heard a fellow traveler describing Henry's experiments. When he returned home he set to work in New York City to make a practical telegraph. He found a financial backer in Stephen Vail, of Morristown, New Jersey, and Stephen's son, Alfred, worked with him on the experiments.

Morse finally secured a patent for his invention in 1840, after his first claim had been overthrown by a decision of the United States Supreme Court on the ground that it was not possible for any man to patent a law of nature.

But he found it difficult to interest wealthy men in his invention. The country was just emerging from a financial depression and private investors were cautious. In 1843, however, when Morse was on the verge of starvation, Congress appropriated thirty thousand dollars to build a test line between Washington and Baltimore. On May 24, 1844, with a sending device in the Supreme Court chambers in Washington, Morse

3. For contribution of Israel T. Nicklin, see *The Monongalia Story*, vol. 2, p. 326 note. See also John Alexander George, "Dr. I. T. Nicklin— Inventor of the First Telegraph," *West Virginia Review*, July, 1924.

tapped out the message, "What hath God wrought!" (Numbers 23:23). Vail was at the receiving end in Baltimore and returned the message.

The telegraph was a complete success and Morse became famous overnight. One of the first important uses of the new facility came when James K. Polk was nominated for president at the Democratic convention in Baltimore. A few hours later the report was printed in a Washington newspaper under the heading "Telegraphic News." A new era had begun.

Fig. 105. Telegraph line to Morgantown. (Sketch by Diane Lenhart.)

A telegraph line had been constructed along the Baltimore and Ohio Railroad to Fairmont, but until 1866 Morgantown had no telegraphic communication with the outside world. In that year the Pacific and Atlantic Telegraph Company, with headquarters in Pittsburgh, built a line from Pittsburgh via Carmichaels and Greensboro to Morgantown. A considerable amount of the company's stock was sold in this county.

Alexander L. Wade was the first telegraph operator in Morgantown and being also county recorder, he established the telegraph office in the courthouse.[4]

4. Wiley, pp. 554, 555.

**Highland Methodist Church.** A group of residents of the Miracle Run section, in Battelle Township, gathered in the early sixties in a home at Flyblow[5] for a religious meeting. A short time later they moved to a log school building near the Marion County line, on a hill overlooking the headwaters of Miracle, Harvey and Sugar runs, while plans were made for erection of a church building. A deed dated November 7, 1866, transferred an adjacent lot from Isaac Moore to Robert Harvey, John Whetzel, Ezra Wallace, Samuel Moore, and Merryman Price, trustees, and a frame building was constructed that year.[6]

**Rev. Joseph Grubb.** A well-known local Methodist Episcopal minister, Joseph Grubb, Sr., died March 23, 1866, aged seventy-three years. He came from Pennsylvania in 1812 and settled in what later became Clinton Township, where he married Sarah May. Their son, Joseph, Jr., born in 1820 was also a local minister.[7]

**Elijah South.** Elijah South, a farmer of Cass Township, died in 1866. He was a son of Dissaway and Ruhanah (Eakin) South and was born near Greensboro, Pennsylvania, in 1809. He married Mary A., daughter of Nicholas Livengood, and they moved to Monongalia County in 1843. They had seven children—six sons and one daughter. Educational facilities in the neighborhood were very rude and Mr. South employed a private tutor for his children, allowing his neighbors to send their children, providing they paid a tuition fee. Only two families availed themselves of this opportunity and it is said others criticized him, predicting his financial ruin and the ruin of his children through giving them "book l'arnin'."[8]

**Alexander Hayes.** One of Morgantown's best known businessmen, Alexander Hayes, died September 14, 1866. He was born at Dover, Delaware, in 1799, the son of Curtis and Mary (Willey) Hayes. The family located on Robinson Run about 1812, engaging in agricultural pursuits. His father died in 1820, aged fifty years, and his mother, a first cousin of W. T. Willey's father, died in 1849, at the age of ninety-three.

5. The name Flyblow was applied during the oil boom, much later.
6. Dodds and Dodds, *Churches of Monongalia County*, p. 133.
7. Wiley, p. 641.
8. *Cyclopedia of Monongalia County*, pp. 93, 94.

Alexander moved to a location across the river from Morgantown in 1831 and moved into Morgantown in 1841. He ran a variety of businesses, including a ferry, a stage line, and hotel-keeping.

He married Phoebe, daughter of Rev. John Davis, and their children were Nancy, Elizabeth, John A., Hester, Malinda, Lewis S., James C., Henry S., George C., L. S. Manliff, Catherine, Jane V., and Louisa.[9]

**William Berkshire.** William Berkshire, father of Judge Ralph L. Berkshire, died in 1866. He was a son of John A. Berkshire, one of Monongalia County's early settlers, locating on the west side of the river not far from Morgantown. William Berkshire was a farmer, a man of limited education, but of good judgment and had a rare mechanical genius. He was married three times; his first union, with Ruth Bradget, resulted in ten children, including Ralph L.; the second, with Nancy Martin, resulted in three children; and the third, to Mrs. Mary (Steen) Brown, resulted in one child.[10]

**Michael Barrickman Killed by Lightning.** Standing in the doorway of his home on Dunkard Ridge "on Friday, May 11th, 1866, during the prevalence of a heavy thunderstorm, Michael Barrickman was killed by lightning. He had been out gunning, and after returning with his gun, was standing in his door cleaning squirrels, when the lightning struck him—commencing at his left temple and following down his left side to the middle of his foot, then square across the top of his foot to the floor—killing him instantly. The family were on the porch on the opposite side of the house, but none of them were injured."[11] The son of Jacob and Jane Barrickman, he was thirty-eight years old.

**James Robison, Jr.** A farmer of Grant Township, James Robison, Jr., died May 4, 1866; he was born June 2, 1782, the son of James, Sr., and Agnes (McCrea) Robison. He married Rachel McKelvey and their children were Arrah, Ann, Rebecca, William, James, John, Rachel, Sarah Jane, Margaret (married John

9. *Cyclopedia of Monongalia County*, pp. 216, 217; Wiley, p. 604; *Morgantown Post*, September 22, 1866.
10. *Cyclopedia of Monongalia County*, p. 42.
11. *Morgantown Weekly Post*, May 19, 1866.

Barbe; Waitman T. Barbe was a son), Ruhamah, and George
Rezeau.[12]

**County, Township, and Borough Government.** George W. Mc-
Vicker was elected sheriff. David Wiedman was elected county
surveyor. Assessors elected were E. Trickett for the Eastern
District and A. Garrison for the Western District. William
Donaldson was president of the board of supervisors and A. L.
Wade recorder. The state levy was forty cents and the county
levy fifty cents. Members of the board of supervisors were: O.
B. Johnson for Clinton; Manliff Hayes for Morgan; William
Donaldson for Union; Samuel Hackney for Cass; Reuben
Finnell for Grant; Emrod Tennant for Clay; and S. H. Shriver
for Battelle.

Township clerks were F. D. Hardman (Clinton), E. H.
Coombs (Morgan), J. N. Dawson (Union), E. J. Arnett (Cass),
John Johnson (Grant), John E. Price (Clay), and George
Keefover (Battelle).

Morgantown borough councilmen were Henry M. Morgan,
George C. Sturgiss, N. B. Madera, L. S. Hayes, and John C.
Wagner. J. M. Hagans was mayor, Manliff Hayes recorder, and
James M. Shank sergeant. Salaries of the mayor and town ser-
geant were reduced one-half; the recorder received forty dollars.

**Miscellany.** In 1866: Dr. John W. Scott was principal of Monongalia Academy (Wiley, p. 395). . . . The nineteenth session of
the West Virginia Methodist Episcopal Session was held at Morgantown, beginning March 21, presided over by Bishop Clark
(Wiley, p. 446). . . . Jane Lough died, aged ninety-six, and Susan
Mayfield, aged ninety (Wiley, p. 472). . . . Steamboats arriving
at the Port of Morgantown included the *Elector*, the *Fayette*,
and the *Chieftain* (Wiley, p. 542). . . . Monongalia Lodge No. 62
Independent Order of Odd Fellows of Virginia became Monongalia Lodge No. 10 of West Virginia and held its first meeting
February 17 (Wiley, p. 549). . . . Dr. Henry B. Lazier opened a
book and drug store facing the courthouse square (Wiley, p.
583, Callahan, p. 211). . . . N. N. Hoffman was keeping the

---

12. Gordon C. Baker, "A Brief History of the Robison Family of Monongalia County," *Monongalia Chronicle*, April, 1975. The name is mis-
spelled Robinson in *The Monongalia Story*, vol. 2, pp. 328, 487.

Saint Clair House, on the northwest corner of Front and Walnut streets (Callahan, p. 117). . . . H. H. Hayes was keeping a grocery on Walnut Street (Callahan, p. 210).

# CHAPTER NINETY-ONE

# 1867

On October 3, 1863, the legislature of the new state of West Virginia accepted the conditions of the Land Grant (Morrill) Act, passed by Congress on July 2, 1862, for the benefit of schools of agriculture and mechanic arts, and asked Congress to extend these rights to it. On April 19, 1864, Congress granted this request and land scrip was issued for 150,000 acres, mostly in Iowa and Minnesota. The state was given until July 2, 1867, to establish the land-grant college thus subsidized.

**West Virginia Agricultural College.** The trustees of Monongalia Academy, on January 9, 1866, in conformity with an arrangement worked out among residents of Morgantown, offered to give the state all its property, including the site and other property of Woodburn Female Seminary, valued at about $51,000, on condition that the proposed agricultural college "be located permanently at or near Morgantown." The senate agreed to accept this offer, but the house, instead, passed a bill locating the proposed college in Charleston. The conference committee could not work out an agreement and in consequence both bills were lost.

The deadline for the establishment of the proposed land-grant college was rapidly approaching. Governor Arthur I. Boreman, therefore, sold the land scrip allotted to West Virginia to a jobber, realizing $88,000. He urged the 1867 legislature to take definite action for the establishment of the college. A house of delegates resolution, in January, asked Congress to donate additional land scrip and to extend by one year the time for establishing the proposed college, on the grounds that West Virginia itself contained no public lands and was thus at a disadvantage in comparison with other states. But the senate refused to approve the resolution and action became necessary at once, if the consequences were to be avoided.

Ambler tells the story of the final decision:

"Thus the matter resolved itself largely to the choice of a site. From the outset Morgantown, Monongalia County, was a favorite, but Morgantown was sometimes behind Frankford, Greenbrier County, in the balloting in the house. Other proposed locations were Bethany, Brooke County; Point Pleasant, Mason County; Greenwood, Doddridge County; Harrisville, Ritchie County; and Martinsburg, Berkeley County. The chief objection to both Bethany and Morgantown was that they were too close to Pennsylvania. The final vote in the house was Morgantown, 32; Frankford, 7; Harrisville, 7; Bethany, 4; and Greenwood, 3. The victory of the Morgantown proponents may have been influenced somewhat by understandings, extending over a year or more, between persons eager to maintain their city as an educational center and residents of Moundsville trying to make sure of a market for farm and garden products. However that may be, tradition insists that Moundsville preferred the state penitentiary to the state land-grant college."[1]

On February 7, 1867, the legislature passed an act accepting the offer of Monongalia Academy and establishing the Agricultural College of West Virginia. Its management and control was vested in a board of visitors[2] composed of one member from each of the eleven senatorial districts. This board met on April 3 and appointed an executive committee, composed of residents of Morgantown, charged with care of the buildings and grounds of the newly established college. George M. Hagans, a local merchant, was later made chairman of this committee, which, in turn, made him the first superintendent of buildings and grounds.

The visitors at their first meeting also elected the Reverend Alexander Martin president of the college and professor of mental and moral science, at an annual salary of sixteen hundred dollars. He was born at Nairn, Scotland, January 24,

1. *History of Education in West Virginia,* p. 187.
2. The first members of the board were T. H. Logan, D. B. Dorsey, G. M. Hagans, Samuel Billingsley, W. E. Stevenson, J. Loomis Gould, W. W. Harper, Mark Poor, Samuel Young, Joseph T. Hoke, and James Carskadon.

1822, and migrated with his parents to Jefferson County, Ohio, in 1836. He graduated from Allegheny College, Meadville, Pennsylvania, in 1847; previously he had served for one year as principal of Kingwood Academy. He married Carrie C. Hursey, of Clarksburg.

Fig. 106. Alexander Martin. (Courtesy West Virginia University Library.)

Fig. 107. Dr. Marmaduke Dent. (From Wiley's *History of Monongalia County*.)

Following his graduation from college he was for two years associated with the Reverend Gordon Battelle as a teacher in Northwestern Virginia Academy at Clarksburg. After a period as a minister in Charleston he succeeded the Reverend Mr. Battelle as principal of Northwestern Virginia Academy in 1851. This was followed by a two-year ministry at Moundsville and in 1856 he returned to his alma mater as professor of Greek. During the war he came back to West Virginia, working in hospitals and with the Christian Commission.

On June 27, 1867, six days ahead of the deadline, the college was formally established, with the inauguration of the president. Ambler says that his address occupied "upwards of an hour on an excessively warm day," but was listened to with marked attention, and was used to inform the public that he intended to establish a college that would meet the general educational needs of the state.[3]

Other members of the original faculty were the Reverend J. W. Scott, vice-president and professor of languages; F. S. Lyon, professor of English and principal of the preparatory department; Col. J. R. Weaver, professor of mathematics and military tactics; and S. G. Stevens, professor of natural sciences.

The first term opened on September 2, with 122 students in attendance; only 6 were in the college proper, the others being preparatory and primary students.

**Community Centers.** In the years just after the Civil War life in Monongalia County was striving to get back to normal after the long interruption, but everyone realized that for a long time to come events would be dated as "before" and "after" the war.

The county seat was growing slowly but because of the relatively long traveling time required to reach it from most sections, small villages or hamlets developed throughout the county. These were especially important in the western end of the county, where distances were greatest. A visit to the county seat usually involved at least two days.

The community centers normally included a post office, a general store, a school, a church, and possibly a gristmill or sawmill. A few dwelling houses, widely scattered, surrounded these facilities.

*Center.* One of these community centers had a post office by the name of Center, established July 3, 1854, with William Case as postmaster, succeeded on April 16, 1855, by Alphaeus Lemasters. Benjamin McCurdy became postmaster July 8, 1857,

3. President Martin said, in part: "In West Virginia the cultivation of the soil is certainly as everywhere, a commanding interest; but so also are its grazing, mineral, and manufacturing interests; while the greatest of all—the proper education of its youth, and the means and appliances thereto—is perhaps the most backward of all.

"Notwithstanding past experience and contributions of long ages, it is the humiliating truth that unhappy and illiberal legislatures across the mountains have left us here in West Virginia an inheritance of hundreds and thousands and tens of thousands of our fellow citizens in such a state of brutish and besotted ignorance as to be absolutely unable to read or write their names or read God's word.

"Until this reproach is wiped out it would be folly to restrict the course of instruction in the state college to the cultivation of the earth, or the profession of arms—especially as both the congressional and state acts relating thereto contemplate more than this."

and by most people the village gradually became known as McCurdysville.

The community was on the old "State Road," a horseback trail built soon after the Revolution to connect Morgantown with the Ohio River at New Martinsville. But, since it crossed many hills, when wagon roads came to be built, they were on courses quite different from the early route, with the result that Center was no longer on the main route. It is on the headwaters of Little Paw Paw Creek and it was (and still is) much easier for the residents to reach Fairmont, the county seat of Marion County, than to reach their own county seat.

*Jobe.* A post office named Jobe was established July 25, 1867, to serve the agricultural community on Miracle Run; George Keefover was the first postmaster.

The name of the post office was from the name of a pioneer family. William Jobe and his wife Alcy were among the early settlers in this section made famous by Robin Darrah and "The Road to Morgantown" (p. 75). William Jobe died June 13, 1851, at the age of eighty-eight, while his wife passed away February 21, 1853, also at the age of eighty-eight.

Their daughter Eleanor married Alexander Eddy, also an early settler, who, according to tradition, moved all his earthly possessions, including a tea kettle, a skillet, a lid, a few pewter plates, a small amount of cutlery, and a cream pitcher, into the area on a one horse sled. The cream pitcher is said to have been preserved by descendants to this day. Eleanor Eddy died on June 15, 1867, only fifty-seven years of age.[4]

The first school in the community was known as Darrah School, from the Darrah family, and was started about 1845. George Keefover, the first postmaster, was one of the teachers in this school.

The first church in the community was organized in 1861, and a building erected later, on land given by R. S. Thomas and was named the Philadelphia Baptist Church. Later the name was changed to the Bula Baptist Church.

A branch of Miracle Run nearby has the unusual name of Mahogany Run, said to have been so called for a rare tree, the

4. One of their six children was Elias J., the second postmaster at Jobe, appointed March 1, 1870.

Kentucky mahogany or Kentucky Coffeetree (*Gymnocladus dioica*) which stood there in early times.

Fig. 108. Nineteenth century farm scene. (Drawn by Diane Lenhart.)

"Union County." On January 21, 1867, a petition was presented to the legislature, signed by eight hundred citizens, for the formation of a new county to be called Union. It would include parts of Wetzel, Harrison, and Marion counties, and that part of Monongalia west of a line beginning at the corner of "Battelle and Clay townships on the Monongalia and Marion county lines, and with said lines to the pictured rocks at the head of Bennefields Fork of Pawpaw; thence with the dividing ridge between Miracle and Days Run to the Union School-house on the head of Kings Run; thence with the county road to a bridge across Dunkard Creek at or near Blacksville, including the same; thence a straight line to the nearest point on the Pennsylvania line." Mannington would be the county seat.

Since the state constitution provided that no county of the state should be reduced in area to less than four hundred square miles, and as Monongalia did not contain as many as this minimum, the proposal was clearly unconstitutional. It was, however, favored by residents of the western end of the county, 285 of whom signed the petition, since the proposed new county seat would have been much closer to them.[5]

**Marion and Monongalia Navigation Company.** In the midst of the Civil War, on October 19, 1863, the Marion and Monongalia Navigation Company was chartered by the state legislature, for the purpose of slacking the Monongahela River from the Pennsylvania line to Fairmont (p. 546). But nothing more was done until after the end of the war.

On January 9, 1867, the project was revived, when the borough of Morgantown voted twenty thousand dollars to the capital stock of the company. On February 21 the charter was amended so that tolls could be collected both ways as soon as a lock and dam were completed; previously it was specified that all crafts or lumber passing down went free of toll.

David H. Chadwick, Alfred Yeager, Samuel Sears, James Evans, William P. Willey, James Lazzell, George M. Hagans, William A. Hanway, and Francis Thompson were authorized to receive subscriptions in Monongalia. Presently they accumulated twenty-five thousand dollars in subscriptions and James Evans, W. T. Willey, and R. B. Carr were sent to Pittsburgh to solicit aid. As with so many projects previously, however, this one also proved fruitless.[6]

**Edward C. Bunker.** A prominent attorney who resided several years in Morgantown, Judge Bunker, died on November 24, 1867, in Piedmont and was buried in Kingwood. He was born in New York City October 9, 1830, and came to Kingwood when he was about six years old to live with his uncle and guardian, Israel Baldwin.

He entered Washington College in 1844 but had to withdraw because of poor health. He studied law in 1849 with Guy R. C. Allen, of Morgantown, and was admitted to the Preston County bar in 1850. He married Delia, daughter of Harrison Hagans, and moved to Morgantown in 1857, associating with W. T. Willey in the practice of law. He was prosecuting attorney for Monongalia County from 1861 until 1863, when he was elected to the state senate, and was a member of that body until 1865,

5. Wiley, pp. 101, 102.
6. Wiley, pp. 129, 130.

when he was appointed judge of the Eleventh Judicial Circuit. He then removed to Piedmont, where he spent the remainder of his life.

A high tribute of respect was paid him by the bar of his district, "bearing testimony to his pure, uncorrupted sense of justice and right," as being "a citizen of tried public and private virtues," and "a faithful, upright, and efficient judge."[7]

**Educational Development.** In 1867 a legislative act fixed a maximum levy which might be laid by the townships for school purposes. Up until that time the law had provided that school terms should be six months in length. This act was a virtual repeal of that provision, since most townships could not raise sufficient funds. In the same year it was enacted that schools should be open at least four months, and that no township which failed to lay a school levy should be eligible for state funds.[8] It was provided that persons over twenty-one years of age might be admitted upon payment of tuition fees.

Henry L. Cox, on October 24, was elected county superintendent.[9]

**Temperance Societies.** The last of several local temperance organizations in the county was the Independent Order of Good Templars, which formed Redemption Lodge No. 14 in Morgantown in January 1867. The lodge had nearly two hundred members.

The vote of the county in 1867 on the question of granting license to sell intoxicating liquor was for license, 847; against, 285.[10]

**End of the County Militia.** On February 26, 1867, the militia law was repealed by the legislature and so the county militia,[11] which dated back to 1776, came to an end.

The militia had been reorganized by the Reorganized Government of Virginia in 1861 and again by the West Virginia Legislature in 1863. In March 1864 Monongalia County was in the

7. Wiley, p. 343.
8. Monongalia County's share of the state funds, in 1867, was $5,187.10.
9. Wiley, pp. 367, 368, 370, 371.
10. Wiley, p. 453.
11. *The Monongalia Story*, vol. 2, pp. 496, 497.

Third Brigade, First Division, commanded by Gen. Edward C. Bunker. The Fourteenth Regiment was commanded by Col. Franklin R. Sinclair; the Fifteenth by Col. Reuben Finnell; and the Sixteenth by Col. George Price.

The Monongalia militia was called out twice in 1864, to repel threatened invasions, on August 14 and on September 30, but was not attacked.[12]

**Washington A. Hooper.** The Reverend W. A. Hooper, Morgantown Presbyterian pastor, resigned in 1867 to go to Ellicott City, Maryland. He was born November 10, 1834, at Springville, Ohio, the son of John and Jane Rice Hooper, and graduated from Western Theological Seminary in 1861. He served at Tyrone and Birmingham, Pennsylvania, before coming to Morgantown in 1864.[13]

**Isaac Thrall.** Son of pioneer Kings Run settler Richard Thrall, Isaac Thrall died on Dunkard Creek about a mile from Blacksville on September 5, 1867. He was born February 1, 1799. He married Elizabeth Johnson, a daughter of John William and Catherine (Fries) Johnson. This union resulted in the birth of ten children, including Catherine, who married Jacob Minor.[14]

**Harrison Hagans.** The father of Morgantown attorney John M. Hagans, Harrison Hagans, died May 7, 1867, at his home in Preston County. He had been a member of the Wheeling Convention of 1861. "He was a man of great natural ability, was a mathematician and mechanic of superior business qualifications, wonderfully energetic and quick of perception, liberal to a fault, kind to the poor, generous to the cause of education, and a large contributor to the church. His life was one long round of usefulness, and his name is indelibly stamped on the history of the county [Preston] for all time."

He married Jane McCollum, daughter of Capt. Daniel McCollum, and they had ten children.[15]

12. Wiley, pp. 516, 517.
13. Moreland, *The First Presbyterian Church*, pp. 51, 52.
14. *Cyclopedia of Monongalia County*, pp. 140, 141.
15. *Cyclopedia of Monongalia County*, pp. 156, 157; Wiley, *History of Preston County*, pp. 383, 384; Reardon Stuart Cuppett, *Harrison Hagans and His Times*, M.A. thesis, West Virginia University, 1935, 133 pp.

**Thomas Lazzelle, Jr.** A farmer of Cass District, Thomas Lazzelle, Jr., son of pioneer settlers Thomas and Hannah (Beck) Lazzelle (or Lazzlele; *Monongalia Story*, vol. 2, p. 510), died July 20, 1867; he was born May 3, 1787. Thomas, Jr., married Rebecca, daughter of James and Lydia Bowlby, and, for his second wife, Rebecca, daughter of John and Rebecca Courtney. His children included James, Thomas, William, Polly, John W., Samuel C., Lydia, Joseph S., Cornelius, Nancy, and Matilda.[16]

**Rev. Asby Poole.** The Reverend Asby Poole, whose name has appeared on many earlier pages of this work, died in 1867. He was born in Hampshire County in 1787 and became an itinerant minister of the Methodist Episcopal Church in 1810. He transferred to the Methodist Protestant Church in 1830. He and his wife Christina had three sons who were ministers, W. L., of the Methodist Protestant Church; George A., who became a Presbyterian; and John, a Baptist.[17]

**County, Township, and Borough Government.** In 1867 Samuel Hackney, of Cass Township, was president of the board of supervisors; other members were Thomas Tarleton, for Clinton Township; James Evans for Morgan; William Donaldson for Union; J. E. Arnett for Grant; A. W. Tennant for Clay; and A. J. Moore for Battelle.

Township clerks were T. B. Harden (Clinton), E. H. Coombs (Morgan), F. A. Coombs (Union), David Simpson (Cass), George Barb (Grant), and S. J. Kennedy (Clay).

The state levy was forty cents and the county levy was also forty cents.

John C. Wagner was mayor of Morgantown, Manliff Hayes recorder and John W. Madera sergeant. Councilmen were Frank W. Thompson, Jacob Kiger, Daniel Fordyce, James A. Davis, and James M. Shank.

**Miscellany.** In 1867: Loyd and Lawson Company was operating Anna Furnace (Wiley, p. 257). . . . Newton B. Jones was admitted to the Monongalia County bar (Wiley, p. 318). . . . The motto

16. *175th Anniversary of Monongalia County*, p. 428; *Cyclopedia of Monongalia County*, pp. 112, 150, 151; pers. comm., Don Lazzelle, Jr.
17. Wiley, p. 593 note. His name was variously spelled as Asby, Ashby, and Asbury. His death is recorded in the Monongalia County courthouse as occurring in January 1866, and in other records as August 1866.

of the *Morgantown Post* was changed to "Firmness in the right, as God gives us to see the right" (Wiley, p. 437); the paper began to establish a corps of regular local correspondents in various parts of the county (Wiley, p. 439). . . . Catharine Workman died at the age of ninety-two (Wiley, p. 472). . . . The corner-stone of a soldier's monument was laid in Oak Grove Cemetery by the Masonic lodge; Dr. Alexander Martin addressed a large assemblage of people present (Wiley, p. 520). . . . Steamboats calling at the Port of Morgantown included the *Franklin*, *Tidioute*, and the *Active* (Wiley, p. 542). . . . Gill Commandery No. 4, of the Masonic fraternity, was organized (Wiley, p. 547). . . . The old John Rogers Mill ("Morgantown Mills") was bought by H. N. Mackey (Wiley, p. 579). . . . H. H. Hayes moved his grocery store to a site facing the courthouse square (Wiley, p. 583). . . . The Morgantown Lecture Association was formed in December (Wiley, p. 589). . . . Nelson W. Protzman opened a marble cutting shop in Morgantown (Wiley, p. 603). . . . James Allender bought the mill of Michael Kern, Jr., below Morgantown (Wiley, p. 653). . . . Loyd and Lawson rented the furnace of the Laurel Iron Works (Wiley, p. 682). . . . John W. Tucker became postmaster at Cassville (Wiley, pp. 701, 702). . . . Dr. Charles H. McLane, son of Dr. Joseph McLane, opened an office for the practice of medicine in Cassville (Wiley, p. 702). . . . Joseph R. Everly sold his tannery at Cassville to James Sanders (Wiley, p. 707). . . . Sarah Dering, widow of William Musser Dering, died at the age of seventy-one (Callahan, p. 86). . . . The telegraph line was extended from Morgantown to Fairmont via the Fairmont Pike (Callahan, p. 219).

# CHAPTER NINETY-TWO

# 1868

By an act of the legislature of West Virginia passed December 4, 1868, the name of the "Agricultural College of West Virginia" was changed to "West Virginia University" and the name of the governing board from visitors to regents. The change in the name of the school had been urged by President Alexander Martin as being helpful in adapting the institution to the "special wants of this young commonwealth," and also in keeping with the spirit and intent of the Morrill Act of 1862. The change was also justified on the ground that the act established the Agricultural College in terms really broader than implied by that term, since it had authorized six distinct fields or departments of study, namely, preparatory, literary, scientific, agricultural, military and normal.

**West Virginia University.** In a private letter from President Martin to Governor Arthur I. Boreman (in which the chief executive was addressed as "Dear Sir and Bro."), the president indicated that the word "Agricultural," as used in the name of the institution, was a misnomer, as each of the authorizing acts contemplated instruction in scientific, classical, military, agricultural, and mechanical subjects. Since all the people of the state were to have common rights and privileges in the institution and since the use of the word "Agricultural" caused "some to think it is *only* a Farmers' school," President Martin suggested that the name be changed to "West Virginia College," as more appropriate.

The change to West Virginia University was influenced largely by the example of the midwestern states, which were then establishing several state "Universities," and by the fact that there was, in 1868, a West Virginia College at nearby Flemington, which was being confused with the Agricultural College in the distribution of mail.

By an act of March 3, 1868, the legislature had appropriated $6,000 for the general use of the college, and $10,000 to supplement the permanent endowment. A later act, on June 25, 1868, authorized the sale of the Monongalia Academy and an adjoining dwelling and the application of the proceeds to construction of another building on the college grounds. In July the academy building was sold to the local board of education (see p. 610) for $13,500 and the house and lot adjoining for $1,500. Soon thereafter, in the presence of a large assemblage, the cornerstone of a new university hall was laid.[1]

For the first year of its operation the enrollment had totaled 184, of which only 6 were in the college proper. Enrollment in the preparatory department was 115 and there were 63 in the "primary" department, which had been retained temporarily as an accommodation to public schools in the new state, then in the process of being established.

Ambler describes the first commencement exercises, in June 1868:[2]

"With the openly conducted finals occupying 'the central point', the year ended on Thursday, June 18, 1868. On the preceding Sunday President Martin had delivered 'a masterly address' on 'The Self-Evidencing Power of Revelation.' The examinations began the next morning and were continued during the afternoon and the next two days through a range of courses consisting largely of elementary and secondary subjects. The performances were witnessed by friends and patrons and were impressive because of the results and the manner of determining them.

"The regents met in one of the literary society halls on Wednesday to hear the first annual reports of the president, the treasurer, and the executive committee. The exercises of that day were closed with an address before the literary societies by the Hon. J. T. Hoke, the newly elected president of the visitors and a Radical state senator from the Martinsburg district. Thursday was devoted to military review and drill, and, in the eve-

1. Callahan, *Making of Morgantown*, p. 226; Ambler, *History of Education in West Virginia*, p. 191.
2. *History of Education in West Virginia*, p. 189.

ning, the exercises closed in a "reunion of citizens and strangers with President Martin and his gracious wife presiding."

The citizens of Morgantown and of all Monongalia County were indeed greatly interested in the establishment of the new institution and proud of the town's reputation as an educational center. For many years local newspapers, along with announcements from the three local academies, had pointed out the advantages of the community as a place for young people to live while in school,—quiet, protected, free from unwholesome influences.

One of the first roads across the mountains to the Monongahela extended from Cumberland to Morgantown (*Monongalia Story*, vol. 2, p. 247). Over it thousands of immigrants plodded wearily, then at Morgantown took flatboats for the voyage downstream. George Washington, in his visit here in 1784, referred to it as the "new road." But when the National Road was completed to the Ohio in 1818, it passed to the north of Morgantown, through Uniontown and Brownsville to Washington and Wheeling. Monongalia County citizens were greatly disappointed to have been left to one side (p. 2).

Then, in 1852, the Baltimore and Ohio Railroad, replacing in importance the National Road, was completed to the Ohio and it, too, missed Morgantown, passing to the south, by way of Evansville and Fairmont to Wheeling. Once again our citizens were greatly disappointed.

But, while the communities through which passed the National Road, and later, the railroad, were rapidly growing into busy commercial and industrial centers, the county seat of Monongalia County was growing very slowly and life proceeded at a quiet pace. Without all the distractions of centers of trade Morgantown was indeed a good place for academic development (pp. 59, 400).

We might now conclude that these developments were blessings in disguise and that if Morgantown had been on one of the main communication lines, it would not today be the home of West Virginia University.

**End of the Iron Works.** About 1868 the once flourishing iron works of Monongalia County came to an end, when David Chess made the last iron.

It is not at all strange that the manufacture of iron was one of the earliest industries to be developed in Monongalia County. Iron implements for use in agriculture and in construction were much in demand by the pioneers and they were difficult to procure. Except for the smaller articles, it was not practical to attempt their transportation across the mountains.

Fortunately, iron carbonate and hematite ores were quickly discovered by the settlers as shale interbeds between the Pottsville sandstones outcropping on the slopes of Chestnut Ridge. The horizons were often recognized by the deep red color of the outcrop. The ore could be extracted from shallow hand-dug trenches, mostly occurring in three main beds within an interval of thirty feet.

The early blast furnaces, for removing the iron from the ore, were built of native stone, about thirty to forty feet high, along a bank or hill so that a broad platform could be built across to the top of the furnace. Measured quantities of iron ore, charcoal, and limestone were introduced at the top of the furnace.

The charcoal used for fuel was produced from the abundant forests of the mountain slopes. Beech trees were preferred. The limestone was also available locally, a happy combination of all three raw materials, of great importance in a day when transportation was chiefly by ox team.

The Jacksons were among the leaders in the development of the iron industry in the county. Samuel Jackson, of Fayette County, Pennsylvania, built his first forge before 1809 and soon thereafter a furnace to supply it. Woodgrove Furnace, three miles from Ice's Ferry, on the road to Uniontown, was built by Josiah Jackson about 1825. The Henry Clay Furnace, on a branch of Quarry Run, was built about 1835.

The Jacksons eventually failed, about 1835, and the Cheat iron works were operated by various other concerns, as related on earlier pages of this volume. But the industry continued to decline and owner after owner failed. Finally, in 1863, Smyth and Chess acquired the works and it was David Chess who made the last iron, in 1868.[3]

3. James R. Moreland has written the classical history of the Monongalia County iron industry. His typescript book (see bibliography), of 340 pages, is now available in local libraries. Moreland was an attorney and had

Callahan writes the conclusion: "The one-time industries of Cheat are silent now. Even the places where they stood are grown over with trees and underbrush. One can scarcely believe that they cover the site of a once busy and populous community. Only the ore pits, the cinders, an occasional bar of metal, and the disintegrating and half buried furnaces, remain to tell the story of the struggle, and the final failure of the pioneer iron masters of Cheat river."[4]

**The Constitution.** The first number of a new county paper, the *Constitution*, was issued on Saturday, April 4, 1868. It was a folio, twenty-five by thirty-two inches, with twenty-four columns; the price was two dollars. Its motto was "Eternal Vigilance is the price of Liberty." It was published by the Democratic and Conservative County Club and was edited by Joseph H. Powell. On September 12 E. Shisler became editor and proprietor.[5]

**County Superintendent's Report.** H. L. Cox, county superintendent of schools, in his 1868 report, said, "We are making much progress." Fifteen school buildings were constructed during the year—"excellent houses, 26 x 30 feet." The Monongalia Academy building was purchased, at a cost of $13,500. "Heretofore there has been a large opposition to the system, and, indeed, there are many yet who oppose it, but I am happy to say that such feelings are giving away, and a more liberal and

ready access to documents concerning the legal aspects of the industry. More recently, Dr. Kenneth Carvell, of West Virginia University's Division of Forestry, has made an extensive study of the Cheat area and has located many of the old workings, tramways, excavations, and towns, publishing his findings in various magazine and newspaper articles. Some of them are in "Henry Clay Furnace," *Wonderful West Virginia* 39 (9) (1973):18-21; "Stand composition—effects of the past on the present," *West Virginia Forestry Notes* 1 (1973):3-5; "Heartstone of Coopers Rock Forest," *Wonderful West Virginia* 39 (1) (1975):26, 27; "Heritage of Cheat Lake," *Wonderful West Virginia* 39 (11) (1975):8-11; "Ice's Ferry," *Cheat Area News* 1 (3) (1975):13; "Camp Rhododendron," *Cheat Area News* 1 (4) (1976):13; "Of streams and names in the Cheat area," *Cheat Area News* 1 (5) (1976):9, 22; "The original Mont Chateau," *Cheat Area News* 1 (6) (1976):11; "Early post offices in the Cheat area," *Cheat Area News* 1 (7) (1977):11; (with B. W. White) "The Henry Clay Furnace—Coopers Rock State Forest," pamphlet published by W.Va. Dept. Nat. Res., 1976, 6 pp.
    4. *Making of Morgantown*, p. 133.
    5. Wiley, pp. 427, 438. The West Virginia University Library has scattered issues, the last one for March 25, 1871.

appreciative spirit is manifest." The number of teaching certificates granted was twenty-four, of which four were number one.[6]

**Morgantown School District.** On February 24, 1868, the legislature passed an act creating the Morgantown School District, with boundaries as follows:

"Beginning at the mouth of Falling run, and up said run with its meanderings to the northeastern line of the lands of the Kiger heirs; thence with said line to the old road; thence across the hill to and including the house now occupied by B. H. Sear; thence in a straight line to the Deckers Creek bridge, near the old paper mill; thence to and including the Guseman property on the Kingwood Pike; thence to the Morgantown and Beverly road, including the property now owned by L. H. Jenkins; thence with said road to and including the county poor-house; thence to the Monongahela River, and down the same to the southern line of the property of Joseph Kinkaid, on the west side of the river; thence with said line to its western terminus; thence in a straight line to the first mile-post on the Fairmont Pike; thence down an old road to the river, and up the same to the place of beginning."[7]

At first an effort was made to build a large public school building, but this was abandoned and the old Monongalia Academy was bought instead. This school was thereafter known as the Morgantown Graded School. The first principal was Adam Staggers, at a monthly salary of seventy-five dollars, and there were two assistant teachers.

Members of the first board of this district were D. H. Chadwick, A. Fairchild, William A. Hanway, Samuel Sears, and Manliff Hayes.

**A New Presbyterian Church.** A second church building was constructed in 1868 on the High Street lot which had been the subject of much controversy between the Presbyterians and the Episcopalians. Either by purchase or by arbitration, the title of the Presbyterian congregation to the property had been quieted and a court decision confirmed it.

6. Wiley, pp. 386, 387, 397.
7. Wiley, p. 596; Callahan, *Making of Morgantown*, p. 222.

Fig. 109. Morgantown Presbyterian Church, corner of High Street and Kirk Alley, constructed in 1868. (From the church bulletin, 1978.)

The new building was a commodious brick structure, with a Sunday school room in the basement, which, except in front, was practically above ground. Broad steps led up to the main church entrance from High Street. The cost was ten thousand dollars.

It is interesting to note that the new building was constructed at a time when the congregation was without a pastor. Prof. Samuel G. Stevens, of West Virginia University, was clerk of the session at the time. There is evidence to indicate that Prof. Samuel J. Wilson, of Western Theological Seminary, delivered the dedicatory sermon on November 8, 1868.[8]

**Monongahela Valley Railroad Company.** The legislature, on March 3, 1868, passed an act authorizing the Monongahela Valley Railroad Company, of Pennsylvania, to construct a railway from the state line along the Monongahela River by Morgan-

8. Moreland, *The First Presbyterian Church*, pp. 36-38; Dodds and Dodds, *Churches of Monongalia County*, p. 94; Wiley, p. 592.

town to a point on the Baltimore and Ohio Railroad at or near Fairmont. The work was to commence in three years and to be completed in ten years. But nothing was ever done.[9]

**Steamboat Whistle.** "An event that always broke the routine of community life . . . , when the river was at the right stage for boats to run, was the whistle of an approaching steamboat. When its welcome noise broke the stillness of the listening town, men left their business, women dropped their household tasks, and children quit their play, and all joined in a general scurry to the wharf. In 1868, Ash Fairchild, appreciating the excitement produced by the whistle of a steamboat, adjusted the whistle of his machine shop so that at will of the operator it could imitate the sound of the steamboat whistle. One evening in early October when the river had reached the proper stage to justify expectations of boat arrivals, a blast from the shop whistle was followed by a general rush to the wharf, at which no boat appeared. The incident typified the alternating expectancy and disappointment produced by frequent promises of slack water and a regular steamboat service. . . ."[10]

**Leander S. Laidley.** Leander Laidley, son of Thomas and Sarah Laidley (*Monongalia Story*, vol. 2, pp. 98-100), died in Marion County September 10, 1868. He was born in Morgantown February 20, 1798, and lived here until 1809, when the family moved to a new home on Buffalo Creek, where his father had taken up a large tract of land, eventually owning several thousand acres. Leander devoted most of his life to the interests of agriculture, besides engaging in mercantile pursuits.

He married Elizabeth, daughter of Joseph Morgan (*Monongalia Story*, vol. 2, p. 367) and they had eleven children, namely, Cordelia, Serena E., Malissa A., Valina E., Louisa, Napoleon D., Helen M., Narcissa M., George L., Martha L., and Agnes H.[11]

**Leven Howell.** A pioneer settler near Morgantown, Leven Howell, died May 9, 1868. He was born in 1806, the son of Samuel and P. Howell, and came to Monongalia County about

9. Wiley, pp. 110, 124.
10. Callahan, *Making of Morgantown*, p. 230.
11. *Cyclopedia of Marion County*, pp. 210, 211.

1820, locating three miles south of the county seat. He was a farmer, plasterer, and bricklayer, as well as a lay minister in the Baptist church. He was a forceful and logical speaker, and rode one year as a missionary. He was married first to Ann King, by whom he had nine children, then to Mary E. Elliott, by whom he had three children.[12]

**M. J. Garrison, Merchant.** Morris J. Garrison, a farmer of Greene County, Pennsylvania, located at Wadestown, in Battelle Township in 1868 and thereafter for many years, adding merchandizing to his farming interests, was one of the most prominent citizens of the area. He was born August 24, 1843, at Jollytown, Pennsylvania, the son of Abner and Hannah (Morris) Garrison. In 1868 he married Adelaide V., a daughter of William Jolly, and they had six children, Kate, Maude, Frank, Blanche, Nell, and Harry.[13]

His merchandise shipments arrived by railroad boxcar at Burton, six miles away in Wetzel County, and were transported to Wadestown by wagon. In addition to retail sales, he also supplied other stores in Battelle Township by wholesale.

**County, Township, and Borough Government.** New county officers elected in 1868 included John E. Price, surveyor, and John I. Swindler, assessor for the Eastern District, and Silas W. Hare, for the Western District. The state levy was thirty cents, the county levy forty-eight cents.

President of the board of supervisors was Samuel Hackney (of Grant Township). Other members of the board were Oliver P. Jolliffe, for Clinton Township; F. R. Sinclair, for Morgan; G. D. Ridgeway, Union; J. H. Bowlby, Cass; William Fear, Grant; E. Morris, Clay; and James McKee, Battelle.

Township clerks were T. D. Harden (Clinton), E. H. Coombs (Morgan), F. A. Coombs (Union), A. G. Halfin (Cass), George Barb (Grant), and C. E. Johnson (Clay).

F. W. Thompson was mayor of Morgantown, James A. Davis recorder, Alpheus Jenkins, sergeant, and T. F. Pickenpaugh the first treasurer. Members of council were Frederick A. Dering,

12. *Cyclopedia of Monongalia County*, p. 145.
13. *Cyclopedia of Monongalia County*, p. 219; pers. comm., Virginia Garrison Cole Ayers. See Fig. 74, p. 420.

William N. Jarrett, John Protzman, Robert P. Hennen, and Thornton Pickenpaugh.

**Miscellany.** In 1868: Alfred Gallatin Sturgiss was sworn in as prosecuting attorney of the Circuit Court (Wiley, p. 311). . . . New members admitted to the Monongalia County bar were John W. Mason (on February 3), H. Clay Showalter (on February 15), John E. Kern (on May 4), and A. G. Sturgiss (on May 13) (Wiley, pp. 317, 318). . . . Hoffman and Company (J. H. Hoffman and Charles W. Finnell) opened a banking business in Morgantown[14] (Wiley, p. 463). . . . The steamboat *Alena May* was among those calling at the Port of Morgantown (Wiley, p. 542). . . . Thornton Pickenpaugh opened a store on the corner of High Street and Maiden Alley (Wiley, p. 581). . . . G. W. McVicker opened a grocery store in Morgantown (Wiley, p. 583). . . . Dr. Luther S. Brock opened an office for the practice of medicine at Arnettsville (Wiley, p. 585). . . . Mary G., daughter of James G. Watson, died near Smithtown (Wiley, p. 635). . . . Owen John died on April 15, aged eighty years (Wiley, p. 675). . . . Janette (Smith) Ray, widow of Thomas P. Ray, died (Callahan, p. 91). . . . A housing shortage was reported in Morgantown (Callahan, p. 208).

14. The business closed in 1874.

# CHAPTER NINETY-THREE

# 1869

The close of the Civil War did not at once end the problems that had caused it nor the difficulties it had brought about. In addition there were many new problems which the people had to solve. A new state had been formed, new political problems had been raised. Industry, in many cases, had to be rebuilt, or new industries developed.

Monongalia County had much less readjustment to make than some of the other counties in West Virginia, farther south, where the county government completely broke down during the war, and disorder reigned. Here, despite the rigors of war, elections were held on schedule, taxes collected, laws enforced.

**Post-Bellum Days.** The town of Morgantown was still governed under its charter of 1860, providing for a mayor and council of five persons, elected every two years, assembling monthly.

Early town ordinances, after 1860, required property owners to guard against fires, provided for weighing of coal by the town weighmaster on the town scales, and regulated burial of the dead. Morgantown had no police force, no fire department, no street lights, no sewers. Occasional arrests were made by the sheriff or the town sergeant. Usually good order was maintained, occasional exceptions "were the animated arguments between students and town boys which were sometimes punctuated by physical blows for emphasis."[1]

Fires were rather frequent due to the large number of old buildings and especially from the defective flues and chimneys or from the fall of burning coals from the open grate to the floor. Another cause of fires was the burning of trash along the streets; storekeepers were especially guilty of this. The need for

1. Callahan, *Making of Morgantown*, p. 217.

better fire-fighting equipment was much discussed, especially shortly after fires.

A primitive waterworks was provided by wagon, hauling barrels of water from the river, at ten cents a barrel, for use by housewives on wash days.

To improve sanitation the council took steps to abolish privies and also to clean up filth along Deckers Creek. Horse racks around the courthouse were abolished and the courthouse janitor was forbidden to clean the public spittoons at the town pump.

James Bell, proprietor of a livery stable, kept for hire good carriage and saddle horses, single or double teams, buggies, carriages, and sleighs, and also carried "passengers to and from all points at reasonable rates," according to a newspaper advertisement.[2]

Oyster saloons and ice cream saloons were popular social centers. Fresh oysters in season were received daily from Baltimore and kept on ice cut from the river or from Deckers Creek in the winter. Ice cream was made locally, using ice from the same sources, and fresh fruit was served in season.

Most county stores were general stores, selling both groceries and dry goods, but in Morgantown several merchants, by 1869, were beginning to specialize in certain particular lines. Nye and Chadwick handled only dry goods and men's articles. Mrs. Christie Hayes kept a shop for women's wear. Coombs and Dering kept a hardware store, with "a complete line of goods." J. W. Conars dealt in grain and livestock, exchanging supplies for chickens brought in from the surrounding community.

**B.&O. Reopened.** The B.&O. line to Wheeling, often closed and badly damaged during the war, was gradually being put in shape, and advertised for travelers:

"In addition to the unequalled attractions of natural scenery heretofore conceded to this route, the recent troubles upon the border have associated numerous points on the Road, between the Ohio River and Harper's Ferry, with painful but instructive interest." "Cars and Machinery destroyed are replaced by new

2. *Morgantown Post,* various issues.

Running Stock, with all recent improvements;" "bridges and track are again in good condition."[3]

**Another Railroad Effort.** The year opened with still another attempt to get a railroad through the county. On February 18, 1869, the legislature passed an act empowering the townships east of the Monongahela, severally or jointly, to subscribe stock, by vote of the people, not exceeding two hundred thousand dollars, to the Uniontown and West Virginia Railroad, a Pennsylvania corporation. An election was held in Union and Morgan townships on May 17, but the proposal was turned down. The enterprise, however, was not abandoned, and another meeting on behalf of the project was held at Morgantown on December 26.[4]

**Base Ball.** "A match game of Base Ball was played on the Fair grounds on Saturday between the Stewarttown Club of this county and the 'Lazy Club' of our town, which resulted in the defeat of our boys.—Score: 30-50.

"After the game was over both clubs repaired to Finnell's Hotel, where a nice supper was given them by our boys."[5]

**The University.** From its very beginning the university had literary, scientific, agricultural, and military departments.

In the second and third years the curriculum was expanded and several changes were made in the faculty personnel. For example, A. C. Alcott began to offer instruction in elocution, H. M. Harman was elected to the chair of languages, formerly held by John W. Scott and John J. Stevenson[6] was elected to the chair of chemistry and natural history in place of S. G. Stevens, who was assigned to astronomy and physics.

In 1869 a department of engineering was added, and F. W. Wood was named to the chair of languages, succeeding H. M. Harman. A library with 247 volumes and two thousand relics "inherited from the parent institutions" was increased by an

3. *Morgantown Weekly Post,* October 30, 1869.
4. Wiley, pp. 110, 124, 685.
5. *Morgantown Weekly Post,* September 4, 1869.
6. See his "Geological Examination of Monongalia County, West Virginia," published as an appendix to the *Third Annual Report of the Board of Regents of West Virginia University, for the year 1870.*

accession of government documents; Capt. H. H. Pierce, commandant of cadets, was the librarian.

On October 2, 1869, a "lurid, red glare of flaming fire in the direction of the State University" was noted and "the cry of 'the College's on fire!' was sounded far and near. The Court House and M. E. Church bells rang out the alarm, and people rushed frantically from their houses." On reaching the campus, it was discovered that one of the outhouses was in flames, "and the agreeably disappointed crowd . . . sloshed back through the mud and rain to their homes, some swearing, others laughing, but all thankful that the University was safe and sound."[7]

**Morgantown Female Seminary.** On June 22, 1869, the trustees of the Monongalia Academy met for the last time, to sell the property of the Morgantown Female Collegiate Institute, as provided by an act of the legislature on March 14, 1868. W. T. Willey was president, William Wagner secretary, and the other members were R. L. Berkshire, John J. Brown, George M. Hagans, and A. L. Wade. The High Street building was transferred to Mrs. Elizabeth I. Moore for five thousand dollars. In this building she had already opened, on April 14, 1869, a new girls school called the Morgantown Female Seminary. The university was now doing the work, for boys, that had formerly been done by the Monongalia Academy and here Mrs. Moore, an able, efficient, and experienced principal, proposed "to perform the other part of the work mapped out by that historic old academy—the thorough, elevated and refined education of the daughters of Western Virginia."[8]

The history of the distinguished Monongalia Academy was at its end. "There are many men, and these of the number of our most distinguished citizens throughout our State, and also in other States of the Union, in whose patriotic hearts the name of the old Monongalia academy lies enshrined as sacred today as it was in the years of long ago, and anything purporting to be even a sketch of West Virginia University would be very incomplete indeed did it not mention this, the Mother of our present institution. For over a half century the Monongalia academy sowed the seeds of progress in our valleys, and at last, when its work

7. *Morgantown Weekly Post,* October 9, 1869.
8. Wiley, pp. 398, 399, 400.

was done, it laid down its duties to be taken up by its child and successor."[9]

**Progress of Free Schools.** In his 1869 report Superintendent Henry L. Cox said Battelle Township is divided into thirteen sub-districts, "in nine of which new school-houses have been built," the average length of terms was a "little over three months to each district." "Insufficient salaries of teachers" was one of the "great barriers" in that township, where 502 pupils attended.

In Clay Township there were twelve schools taught, with an average length of 3 3/4 months. Seven new houses had been built, and the attendance was 436.

"Cass Township," he said, "is deserving of much praise for having supplied each of the school districts with a good house." Numbers of Pennsylvania teachers were employed and the attendance was 387.

In Grant Township, "the people in general are much attached to the school cause." Eight new schoolhouses had been built; twelve schools were taught, of an average length of over five months, attended by 557 youths.

In Clinton "the people seemed anxious to embrace the opportunity to educate their children," although the levies were "quite burdensome" on the people in the mountainous part of the township, "the wealth being mainly in a narrow strip on one side."

In Morgan there were seven school districts and six new houses; the attendance was three hundred.

The Morgantown Independent District should have had a very superior school but suffered for the want of efficient and faithful teachers. Nevertheless, the school was in session ten months, with an average daily attendance of 151 pupils.

Union is "perhaps the banner township in the county in school matters. Each of its nine districts have been supplied with an excellent house." School terms had an average length of four months and the attendance was 594.

The state superintendent attended a meeting of the county teachers association on October 16, with forty-two teachers present.[10]

9. *Monticola*, 1896 (West Virginia University annual).
10. Wiley, pp. 380, 387, 389.

**Churches in the 1860s.** Ministers of the Morgantown Station of the Methodist Episcopal Church were: 1859-61, G. Martin; 1861-63, J. B. Blakeney; 1863-64, D. T. Daugherty; 1864-67, Benjamin Ison;[11] 1867-68, J. D. Onins; 1868-70, E. T. Pitcher. Superintendents of the Sunday school were: 1859-61, William Lazier; 1862, Thomas Daugherty; 1863, William Wagner; 1864-67, William Lazier; 1867, John J. Brown; 1868-70, G. C. Sturgiss.[12]

Henry Weed Biggs was minister of the Morgantown Presbyterian Church from 1855 until 1865. He was succeeded by W. A. Hooper (1865-68), John Creath (stated supply, 1868), and Robert White (1869-71). Among ruling elders were Jesse Duncan, John Hare, William K. Fear, and S. G. Stevens.[13]

Ministers of the Morgantown Methodist Protestant Church included Samuel Young (1861), William Wragg, Daniel Davis (1864-65), etc.[14]

Pastors of the Morgantown Baptist Church were G. W. Hertzog (1861-64), A. B. Pendleton (1864-67), and J. M. Purinton (1867-69).[15]

The Smithtown Circuit of the Methodist Episcopal Church was organized in 1866, embracing nine appointments, with the parsonage located near the Pisgah church.[16] Early ministers serving the circuit were W. D. Carrico (1866-68) and J. W. Hess (1868-71).[17]

Ministers serving the Monongalia Circuit included: 1860, G. W. Arnold; 1861, D. O. Stewart; 1862, D. O. Stewart, J. B. Pinchen; 1863, J. B. Feather, A. Stephens; 1864, J. B. Feather,

11. Benjamin Ison was born in Shropshire, England, November 12, 1824, and died in Washington, D.C., May 12, 1901. He married Ellen E. Robinson, daughter of Joshua Robinson, of Taylor County. Wilding, *Promoted Pioneer Preachers*, pp. 78, 79.
12. Wiley, pp. 590, 591.
13. Wiley, pp. 592, 593.
14. Wiley, p. 594.
15. Wiley, p. 595.
16. Wiley, p. 626.
17. For biography of John W. Hess, see Wilding, *Promoted Pioneer Preachers*, pp. 50, 51. He died October 13, 1889, aged fifty-six years. "He had a pleasant voice, was fluent and correct in the use of language, and wonderfully pathetic in prayer and exhortation."

G. W. Metheny;[18] 1865, J. W. Webb, J. W. Swartz; 1866, J. W. Webb, T. F. Bracken; 1867, J. W. Webb; 1868-69, J. J. Dolliver,[19] J. D. Hunter.

Ministers serving the Forks of Cheat Baptist Church included A. B. Pendleton (1864) and D. W. Rogers (1867).[20]

Ministers serving the Avery Methodist Protestant Circuit included D. R. Helmick (1860), J. B. McCormack (1860-62), G. G. Westfall (1862-64), William Blake (1865), J. L. Simpson (1868-69), and P. T. Laishley (1869-70).[21]

**Monongalia Salt Works.** In borings for oil, brine was often struck, and at Stumptown, on Scotts Run, in 1869, an abandoned oil well was converted into a salt well. Thursby, Kidd and Company started the Monongalia Salt Works, at which about fifteen barrels of good salt was made per day. It was a very white product, but coarse because of proper machinery to treat it, and the enterprise was soon abandoned.[22]

**County Fair.** The Monongahela Valley Agricultural and Mechanical Society was incorporated on January 7, 1869, the purpose being to hold annual county fairs. The authorized capital was ten thousand dollars, in shares of twenty-five dollars. Incorporators were J. H. Hoffman, William Wagner, Samuel Howell, Manliff Hayes, J. P. Shafer, W. T. Willey, E. C. Lazier, W. A. Hanway, W. P. Willey, J. M. Hagans, J. K. Durr, J. C. Wallace, L. S. Layton, A. L. Wade, and J. H. Hoffman and Company. William Wagner was elected president and Manliff Hayes vice-president.[23] The fairgrounds were across Deckers Creek from Morgantown, near the site of old Fort Kerns.

Morgantown's first "daily" newspaper was published in 1869,

18. G. W. Metheny was born in Preston County February 4, 1838, and died in Buckhannon October 18, 1899. He served in the Union army from July 1863 to April 1864. He married Elizabeth High. Wilding, *Promoted Pioneer Preachers*, pp. 74, 75.

19. James J. Dolliver, father of U.S. Senator J. P. Dolliver, was born in New York in 1816. For biography, see Wilding, *Promoted Pioneer Preachers*, pp. 92-96.

20. Wiley, p. 686.

21. Wiley, p. 689.

22. Wiley, p. 264.

23. Wiley, p. 248. The society held nine fairs, the last being in 1878.

when the Morgantown *Post* issued an edition for two consecutive days during the county fair.[24]

**Prices of Farm Products.** During the 1860s prices of farm products varied tremendously, under the influence of the war.[25]

**West Virginia Historical Society.** In acceptance of invitations issued by the faculty of West Virginia University, a preliminary meeting for the purpose of organizing a West Virginia Historical Society was held in the hall of the Columbian Literary Society on September 30, 1869, with W. T. Willey as chairman and John J. Brown secretary. Committees were appointed on Founders, Constitution, and Charter, which reported at a meeting held at Grafton on December 30, 1869, when a permanent organization was effected. The regents gave the society a room in the university where its library and collections were to be kept. Two regular meetings were to be held annually, one at a designated point in the state, the other at Morgantown. Dr. Thomas H. Logan was the first president.[26]

**Joseph Moreland.** Joseph Moreland was admitted to the county bar on February 10, 1869. He was the son of John and Priscilla (Rogers) Moreland, one of the first coke producers, and was born near Connellsville, Pennsylvania, May 26, 1842. He attended Monongalia Academy and graduated from Washington and Jefferson College in 1866. He read law with Brown and Hagans, in Morgantown.[27]

**William Meredith.** William Meredith, son of early Smithtown settler Thomas Meredith (p. 386), died February 13, 1869. William was born in Wales, and was only three years old when his parents came to America. "He was reared a witness to many of the struggles characteristic to an early pioneer life in Monongalia County. He took up agricultural pursuits first on a farm which he cleared for cultivation on the Monongahela River," below Smithtown, but later located on a three-hundred-acre farm on Pricketts Creek, where he passed the remainder of his life.

24. Wiley, p. 439.
25. Wiley, p. 249. Wheat was the highest in the summer of 1867, when it reached $3.25 per bushel.
26. Wiley, pp. 424, 425; Callahan, *Making of Morgantown*, p. 234.
27. Wiley, pp. 317, 356, 357. He married Mary E., daughter of Thomas Brown, of Kingwood, October 26, 1875. He was named to the University Board of Regents in 1882.

Fig. 110. Joseph Moreland. (Cour-    Fig. 111. A. W. Lorentz. (From *The*
tesy William A. Moreland.)    *Monticola*, vol. 1, 1896.)

He married Hannah, daughter of John Powell, and they had twelve children, including Thomas, Mary, William, Catharine, John Q. A., D. Clifford, Louisa, Amanda, Marquis Lafayette, and Francis M.[28]

**Samuel Lemley.** George Lemley was a pioneer settler of Greene County, Pennsylvania, locating on "Lemley's Plain," along Whiteley Creek in 1784 and at his "Shiver-de-Frise" plantation along Dunkard Creek, just north of the Mason-Dixon Line, in 1794. He married Catharine Yoho, and many of their descendants moved south to become prominent citizens of Monongalia County.[29]

28. *Cyclopedia of Marion County*, pp. 143-48.
29. See Alvah John Washington Headlee, *George Lemley and wife Catharine Yoho and their Descendants for Two Centuries* (1975).

Samuel Lemley, a son of George and Catherine, was born in 1784 and died on November 2, 1869. He married Rebecca, daughter of Rudolph Snider, and they lived along Dunkard Creek just south of the state line in a red brick house built in 1837 by B. Mahanna, of local clay. Samuel was a farmer and stock-raiser and drove cattle across the mountains to eastern markets.

His marriage resulted in the birth of seven children, namely, John, Elizabeth, Jacob, Asa, Sarah, Mary, and Samuel S.[30]

**Adam Tennant.** The Tennant family, descendants of Richard and Elizabeth (Haught) Tennant (*Monongalia Story*, vol. 2, p. 464), became during the nineteenth century one of the best known in western Monongalia County.[31]

One of the thirteen children of Richard Tennant was Adam Tennant, born in 1818, near Blacksville. He was a cabinetmaker and undertaker by trade, and also followed to some extent the art of photography, running for several years a gallery in Blacksville. He died there July 9, 1869, his death coming "as a result of injuries received at the hands of a band of ruffians, who beat him at a political meeting in Morgantown."

He married Elizabeth, daughter of William Haines, and they had four children, namely, Lee Van Doran, Irvin, Sanford M., and Mary Ellen.[32]

**Jesse Martin Purinton.** The Reverend J. M. Purinton, D.D., pastor of the Morgantown Baptist Church, died June 17, 1869. "A man of fine personal appearance; calm, grave and dignified, he always retained on acquaintanceship the respect which his appearance involuntarily commanded. . . . His death was a severe loss to the church of which he was so useful a servant and so bright an ornament." The degree of Doctor of Divinity was conferred by Burritt College, Tennessee.

He was born at Colrain, Massachusetts, August 12, 1809, the son of the Reverend Thomas and Sabrina (Boardman) Purinton. He was educated at Madison University, New York, and entered the Baptist ministry in 1829. His early pastorates were near

30. *Cyclopedia of Monongalia County*, pp. 96, 192, 193.
31. For genealogical material on the family, see J. Ross Tennant, *Memories* I (1942), II (1945), III (1946), and IV (1948).
32. *Cyclopedia of Monongalia County*, pp. 206, 207, 210, 211.

Lake Erie, and he came south to Preston County in 1848, founding the Buffalo Creek church, near Rowlesburg. He was pastor of the Mount Moriah Church, at Smithfield, Pennsylvania, in 1852-55 and again in 1862-67, removing to Morgantown in 1867.

Dr. Purinton was married to Miss Roxea Buell in 1833. She died in 1845 and in 1846 he married Miss Nancy A. Lyon. They had four children, Edward, Daniel Boardman, Aaron L., and G. Dana.[33]

**County and Borough Government.** F. R. Sinclair (Morgan Township) was president of the board of supervisors. Other members were S. T. Shuttleworth (Clinton), G. D. Ridgeway (Union), N. L. South (Cass), William Fear (Grant), David Lemley (Clay) and James McKee (Battelle).

Township clerks were L. C. Beals (Clinton), E. H. Coombs (Morgan), A. C. Rude (Union), A. G. Halfin (Cass), George Barb (Grant), —— (Clay), and George Anderson (Battelle).

The state levy was thirty cents and the county levy was fifty cents.

J. M. Hagans was mayor of Morgantown, G. W. McVicker recorder, Alonzo Finnell and Joseph Dawson sergeants, and William N. Jarrett treasurer. Councilmen were Jacob Kiger, Lewis S. Hayes, James Shanks, William N. Jarrett, and James C. Wallace.

**Miscellany.** In 1869: Henry L. Cox was elected to his second term as county superintendent of schools (Wiley, p. 370). . . . George Hayes and Robert Powell opened grocery stores in Morgantown (Wiley, pp. 582, 583). . . . Lewis Hagedorn and Peter J. Weinig bought the old Guseman Mill on Deckers Creek (Wiley, p. 654). . . . David Chess built a log dam at the mill in Union Township; with repairs to the mill, it cost $22,023.08 (Wiley, p. 679). . . . The old Hanway "Mansion House" (the Washington Hotel), on Lot 19, Morgantown, became the residence of Alexander Martin (Callahan, pp. 100, 118, 188). . . . In February the Morgantown borough trustees issued an ordinance against throwing ashes in the street (Callahan, p. 197).

33. Wiley, pp. 454, 455.

# CHAPTER NINETY-FOUR

# 1870

Monongalia County, in 1870, the first census year since West Virginia had become a separate state, showed a very small increase over ten years earlier. The total population was 13,547, an increase of 499 over the census of 1860, a gain of only about 4 percent.

**The Census of 1870.** Of the total population of the county in 1870, the report showed 11,731 were natives of the Virginias, 1,390 natives of Pennsylvania, 61 of Ohio, 178 of Maryland, 8 of Kentucky, and 16 of New York. Of the foreign population, 37 were natives of England and Wales, 29 of Ireland, 6 of Scotland, 16 of Germany, and 2 of France.

The number of male citizens twenty-one years of age and over was 2,929.

The population of Morgantown was given as 797, up from 741 in 1860.

For the first time, population was given for the areas into which the county was divided:

|  | Total Population | Colored | Foreign Born |
|---|---|---|---|
| Battelle Township | 1,856 | 15 | 6 |
| Cass Township | 1,449 | 1 | 7 |
| Clay Township | 1,972 | 9 | 1 |
| Clinton Township | 1,900 | 30 | 20 |
| Grant Township | 2,216 | 30 | 14 |
| Morgan Township | 2,536 | 139 | 24 |
| Union Township | 1,618 | 7 | 20 |

The total number of farms in the county in 1870 was 1,555, classified as follows: under ten acres, 69; ten to twenty acres, 134; twenty to fifty acres, 481; fifty to one hundred acres, 509; one hundred to five hundred acres, 353; five hundred to one thousand acres, 7; over one thousand acres, 2.

Agricultural production was given as follows:

*Lands, Stock, Etc.*

| | |
|---|---:|
| Acres in improved farms | 112,045 |
| Acres in unimproved farms | 80,662 |
| Cash value of farms | $4,724,358 |
| Value of farm implements | 83,187 |
| Number of Horses | 4,238 |
| Number of Mules and Asses | 36 |
| Number of Milch Cows | 4,606 |
| Number of Working Oxen | 761 |
| Number of Other Cattle | 7,743 |
| Number of Sheep | 17,371 |
| Number of Swine | 7,324 |
| Value of Live Stock | $871,260 |

*Grain and Produce*

| | |
|---|---:|
| Wheat, bu. | 111,805 |
| Rye, bu. | 5,130 |
| Corn, bu. | 301,328 |
| Oats, bu. | 148,072 |
| Tobacco, lbs. | 2,733 |
| Wool, lbs. | 55,856 |
| Peas and beans, bu. | 25 |
| Irish potatoes, bu. | 23,772 |
| Sweet potatoes, bu. | 435 |
| Barley, bu. | 80 |
| Buckwheat, bu. | 1,575 |
| Orchard products, value | $37,427 |
| Wine, gallons | 3 |
| Market garden products, value | $470 |
| Butter, lbs. | 345,573 |
| Cheese, lbs. | 1,030 |
| Hay, tons | 12,030 |
| Clover and grass seed, bu. | 309 |
| Hops, lbs. | 13 |
| Flax, lbs. | 540 |
| Maple Sugar, lbs. | 24,274 |
| Maple molasses, gallons | 733 |
| Sorghum molasses, gallons | 36,504 |
| Beeswax, lbs. | 32 |
| Honey, lbs. | 10,710 |
| Home-made manufactures, value | $12,928 |
| Animals slaughtered | 304,006 |
| Estimated value of all farm products | $1,141,914 |

The number of steam engines in the county in 1870 was reported as seventeen, their total horsepower 361. The number of water wheels was twenty-seven, their total horsepower 440.

In 1870 there were two "bituminous coal establishments" in the county, employing three hands, with $1,200 capital invested, paying $700 in wages, using $200 worth of raw material, producing 2,400 tons of coal worth $2,400.

Major industrial statistics for 1870 were summarized as shown on page 629.

Statistics for religious organizations show that there were a total of thirty-six Methodist church bodies, with 5,750 sittings; ten Baptist groups with 3,000 sittings; two Presbyterian groups with 400 sittings; and one Christian, with 500 sittings. From other information available on church groups in 1870, it is obvious that numerous bodies did not report.

The county was slowly recovering from the agony of the Civil War. Almost every family had lost a member or at least a close relative, and for a while there had been a general despair; incentives for improvements were mostly lacking. But now carpenters were busy, erecting new homes or repairing and enlarging old ones. Contractors were building, plastering, laying bricks, papering. After a decade in which there had been more destruction than construction in the country, the prospects for the future at last appeared a little brighter.

**Terrific Tornado.** "On Wednesday, 27th ult., our town and surrounding vicinity was visited by one of the most terrible hurricanes, accompanied by rain, thunder and lightning, that has visited this section for ten or twelve years past."

On the university grounds, the top was blown off one of the chimneys of the old building and several windows were smashed in the new building. The new bridge at Granville, across Dents Run, was lifted from its fastenings and dashed into the stream.

"The Suspension bridge was severely tested, and several times rose and fell ten feet, swaying to and fro, while the timbers creaked and trembled, and every wire seemed strained to its utmost."[1]

1. *Morgantown Weekly Post,* August 6, 1870.

| | Number of Establishments | Number of Hands | Annual Wages | Cost of Raw Material | Capital Invested | Annual value of Products |
|---|---|---|---|---|---|---|
| Carriages, Wagons | 3 | 14 | $16,336 | $ 4,250 | $ 12,350 | $ 19,600 |
| Flouring-mill Products | 7 | 11 | 3,200 | 77,235 | 39,300 | 80,700 |
| Leather | 8 | 11 | 1,950 | 23,325 | 11,400 | 29,065 |
| Lumber, Sawed | 3 | 9 | 1,500 | 7,400 | 3,350 | 15,625 |
| Wool, Carded | 2 | 3 | | 8,940 | 2,200 | 11,000 |
| Totals | 115 | 178 | $28,273 | $208,091 | $148,750 | $329,714 |

**Daring Robbery at McCurdysville.** "On Monday night of last week a very bold robbery occurred at McCurdysville, this county. About 11 o'clock the proprietor of the store—Mr. Geo. W. Swisher—had just closed his store, preparatory to leaving for his dwelling. As he was locking the door, he was approached by three men in disguise, who demanded his keys."[2]

The men carried off boots, clothing, dry goods, etc., but only two dollars in money. Deputy Sheriff Emrod Tennant, the following Wednesday, arrested two men named Raver, on Pedlar Run, on suspicion of being engaged in the robbery.

**Water Wagons.** "Wm. I. Protzman has refitted up his water wagon, with a large *fifty gallon barrel*—which is ten gallons more than the ordinary barrel—and is prepared to deliver water to any point in town or suburbs, on short notice, and will haul water any day, to order. Look out for the *bells* and the *old gray horse.*"[3]

Fig. 112. A water wagon on Walnut Street. (Courtesy Morgantown Public Library.)

2. *Morgantown Weekly Post,* August 20, 1870.
3. *Morgantown Weekly Post,* July 16, 1870.

**New Railroad Proposals.** Four different railroad companies involving Monongalia County were incorporated during 1870 by the legislature. The first, on February 15, was for the West Virginia Central Railway Company and was really only a renewal and amendment of an earlier charter. This railroad was to begin on the Pennsylvania line in Preston County and extend thence to Charleston, in Kanawha County. The amendment gave it the right to run by the best route through Preston *or* Monongalia County.

On February 25 an act was passed granting to the Pittsburgh, Virginia, and Charleston Railroad Company the privilege of extending its line across West Virginia. The work of constructing the road was to be commenced within three years, and to be finished within ten years. But nothing was ever done.

All hope of the extension of the Uniontown and West Virginia Railway through Monongalia County having been abandoned, the legislature, on March 2, 1870, passed an act incorporating the Pennsylvania and West Virginia Railway Company, to begin near where Rubles Run crosses the state line and pass by Morgantown to intersect the B.&O. at or east of Grafton. Capital stock was set at $1.5 million but not enough was sold to start construction.

Another company, the Northern and Southern West Virginia Railroad, was incorporated on February 26. It was to run from the Pennsylvania line by way of Morgantown, Fairmont, Clarksburg, and Charleston, to some point in Wayne County on the Kentucky line. Capital stock was authorized at $5 million.[4]

**Hotel Accommodations.** The progress of the borough of Morgantown was being reflected in the improvement of hotel accommodations. In 1870 the Hayes Hotel, on Front Street, and the Wallace House, on High Street, were the chief places accommodating travelers.

Another place, at the northwest corner of Front and Walnut streets, was the Virginia House, which had been opened and kept by J. W. Saer, who was succeeded by David F. Campbell, John J. Pierpont, John Devore, Samuel Darnell, N. N. Hoffman (1866-69), and Stephen Snyder.

The Franklin House, at the corner of Walnut Street and Long

4. Wiley, pp. 111-13, 124, 685.

Alley, had been managed for a long time (before 1853) by Alex Hayes and after 1855 was run by C. W. Finnell.

The old National Hotel, on High Street opposite the courthouse, had been managed successfully by Addison S. Vance (to 1853), John Wallace, George C. Hayes (1869), and J. P. St. Clair (after 1870).[5]

**School for Black Children.** The 1863 legislature provided for the education of "free colored children" and in 1866 amended the law so as to make it apply to "colored children" of school age. The first public free school for black children was opened in Parkersburg in 1866 and the second one in Clarksburg in 1867.

The 1870 census showed only 231 black people in Monongalia County, most of them in or near Morgantown. The number of black children, therefore, was not very great but a school for them was established in 1870, conducted in the African Methodist Episcopal Church.[6]

**The University.** The cornerstone of a new West Virginia University building, University Hall[7] was laid June 16, 1869, and completed in 1870. The building was ninety-eight by fifty-four feet in size, of four stories, with projections and verandas on the north and south fronts, "the corners of which, with the corners of the building, are quoins of neatly cut sandstone." The first story was sixteen feet high, of stone, the second thirteen feet and the third seventeen feet, of brick, with "openings recessed and arches trimmed with keys and blocks of cut stone," the fourth story ten feet, mansard, covered with alternate belts of blue and green slate. The total cost, including furnishings, was over sixty-three thousand dollars.[8]

The new building was described as "a model of architectural beauty and convenient arrangement" which will increase "the facilities for carrying out the noble designs for which the University was established." Its completion made possible the trans-

5. Callahan, pp. 113-18, 212.
6. Wiley, p. 596; Ambler, *History of Education in West Virginia,* pp. 161-63.
7. Later recalled Preparatory Hall, and still later Martin Hall.
8. Wiley, pp. 405, 406. Ambler (*History of Education in West Virginia,* p. 191) says $22,855. A long description appears in the *Morgantown Weekly Post,* January 15, 1870.

Fig. 113. University Hall (later Preparatory Building), completed in 1870. (Courtesy West Virginia University Library.)

fer of all classes to the new building, and the old Woodburn Seminary structure was thereafter used as a dormitory and dining room.[9]

The primary department was discontinued in 1870. This department, retained temporarily when the institution was established as an accommodation to local schools, then undergoing reorganization, had enrolled sixty-three students during the first year of operation. University professors were reluctant to teach elementary and secondary subjects and this hastened the abolition of the department.

Marmaduke H. Dent, son of Marshall Dent, became the first alumnus of the university, receiving his bachelor's degree at the 1870 commencement; see John Philip Reid, *An American Judge, Marmaduke Dent of West Virginia.* University of London Press. 1968.

**Second Annual Fair.** The second annual county fair was held October 4, 5, 6, 1870, with a long list of exhibits and activities.

9. Ambler, *History of Education in West Virginia*, p. 191.

"At any early hour on Wednesday the mountains, hills, and valleys began to pour out their inhabitants, and a constant stream of human beings, horses, and vehicles of every description were wending their way toward the Fair grounds."[10]

**U.S. Mail Service.** According to an announcement covering more than a full page in the local newspaper[11] concerning West Virginia mail routes, the following service was provided in Monongalia County.

4221. From Barracksville by Gray's Flat and Basnettsville to Blacksville and return, by Andy, Jakes Run, Mooresville, Statler Run, Center, and Hoodsville, twenty miles and back, once a week.

4223. From Fairmont, by Rivesville, Arnettsville, and Laurel Point, to Morgantown, nineteen miles and back, three times a week each way.

4224. From Fairmont, by Palatine, Meredith's Tavern, White Day, and Pleasant Valley, to Morgantown, 19½ miles and back, three times a week each way.

4226. From Morgantown, by Easton, Laurel Iron Works, Springhill Furnace, and Smithfield, to Uniontown, 26½ miles and back, three times a week each way.

4227. From Morgantown, by Stewarttown, Morris Cross Roads, and Smithfield, to Uniontown, twenty-six miles and back, three times a week each way.

4228. From Morgantown, by Granville, Randall, Maidsville, and Rosedale, to Dunkard, 11¾ miles and back, twice a week.

4229. From Morgantown by Granville, Randall, Cassville, Mount Morris, Andy, Blacksville, Jobe, Miracle Run, and Wadestown, to Burton, 40½ miles and back, once a week.

**George B. Morris, Dentist.** Dr. George B. Morris set up business as a dentist in Morgantown in 1861. He was born at Woodgrove Furnace in 1832 and married Frances E., daughter of John N. and Nancy Baker. Wiley, writing in 1883, said: "He is the first dental graduate in the State (1866), and is one of only thirteen now in the State. He now travels over 200 square miles of

10. *Morgantown Weekly Post,* October 15, 1870.
11. *Morgantown Weekly Post,* December 3, 1870.

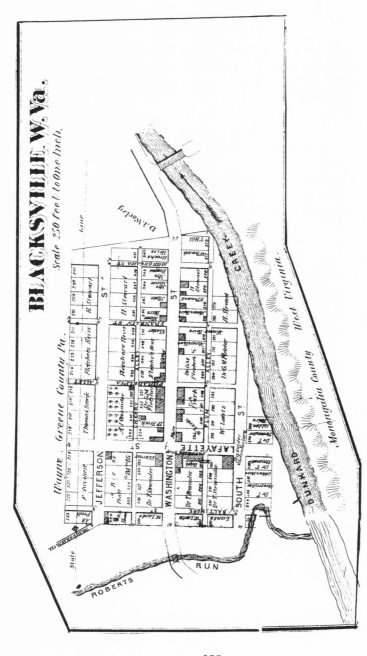

Fig. 114. Map of Blacksville, 1870. (From Caldwell's *Illustrated Centennial Atlas of Greene County*, 1876.)

635

territory and visits eight towns. He first made an obdurator (or artificial palate) for Elias Courtwright, of Marshall County."[12]

J. M. Lazier and A. M. Jarrett were other peripatetic (visiting) dentists of the day. Some of them were quite rude in their methods of competition and occasionally carried their quarrels and denunciations into the newspapers.[13]

**William Clark McGrew.** W. C. McGrew, son of James C. McGrew, and a descendant of the pioneer James Clark family, of Bruceton Mills (*Monongalia Story*, vol. 1, pp. 314, 315), moved to Morgantown in 1870. He was born in Kingwood April 21, 1842, and received an academic education. In 1864 he was married to Julia E., daughter of W. T. Willey. For several years prior to 1870 he was engaged in the mercantile business in Kingwood, and opened a store in Morgantown upon his arrival here.[14]

**James Evans.** The son of Col. John and Ann (Martin) Evans, James Evans died March 9, 1870. He was born April 30, 1782, read law, and was admitted to the Monongalia County bar July 11, 1803. He moved to Missouri in 1807 and was elected judge of a circuit court there and served for many years. He resided for a while on a farm near Louisville, Kentucky, and moved back to Monongalia County towards the end of the Civil War.[15]

**County, Township, and Borough Government.** Alpheus Garrison was sworn in as sheriff, Thomas R. Evans as surveyor, John I. Swindler as assessor for the Eastern District, and Silas W. Hare for the Western District.

Members of the board of supervisors were J. A. Faulkner (Clinton), S. B. McVicker (Morgan), W. I. Vandervort (Union), N. L. South (Cass), William Fear (Grant), A. W. Brown (Clay), and S. H. Shriver (Battelle).

Township clerks were H. Stansberry (Clinton), E. H. Coombs (Morgan), A. C. Rude (Union), A. G. Halfin (Cass), Garrett Conn (Grant), —— (Clay), and S. White (Battelle).

12. Wiley, p. 602.
13. Callahan, *Making of Morgantown*, p. 215.
14. Wiley, pp. 289, 290, 582.
15. Wiley, p. 332. Not to be confused with Col. James Evans, son of John Evans, Jr.

J. M. Hagans was mayor of Morgantown, F. A. Dering recorder, Jacob S. Shisler and John Watts sergeants, and F. M. Durbin treasurer. Councilmen were Frank W. Thompson, L. S. Hough, J. J. Fitch, George C. Sturgiss, and F. M. Durbin. The borough poll tax was thirty cents per male citizen over twenty-one years of age. The salary of the mayor was one hundred dollars a year, the recorder seventy-five dollars, and the sergeant seventy-five dollars.

**Street Lights.** Lighting of Morgantown streets was long delayed. On May 16, 1870, a committee was appointed, composed of George C. Sturgiss, L. S. Hough, and J. M. Hagans, to purchase and erect lighting fixtures. They bought twenty-five kerosene lamps and placed them on poles, mostly along High Street and Front Street. Amos Harris, "colored," was employed at two hundred dollars a year to "light the lamps and blow them out"; the time for "blowing out" was fixed at 11 p.m., by which time most people should be in bed. But soon it was complained that "the lamps are so dirty that they are of but little use." They were also in danger from stones thrown by small boys.

Fig. 115. The lamp lighter. (Sketch by Diane Lenhart.)

The lamp posts were also a source of trouble. Boys began to carve them, country people used them for hitching posts, merchants for billboards. The council then made it a finable offense to destroy any lamp or deface or destroy any lamp post, to hitch an animal to it, or to fasten an advertisement on it.

To prevent carving, the posts were sanded, which only made it easier for boys to climb them. In June 1870 four university students were arrested and brought before the mayor for breaking one of the lamps the night before. Just as he was about to fine them, Walter Hayes appeared in the mayor's court and reported that he had accidentally broken the lamp when he climbed the pole to light his cigar. The students were released and Hayes replaced the lamp.[16]

**Miscellany.** In 1870: J. M. Hagans was sworn in as prosecuting attorney of the circuit court (Wiley, p. 311). . . . The number of persons ten years old and over who cannot read was reported as 679; those unable to write were 1,554 (Wiley, p. 382). . . . A branch of the World's Evangelical Alliance was formed at Morgantown July 15 (Wiley, p. 451). . . . Cheat River was declared a public highway by the legislature on March 3 (Wiley, p. 540). . . . Under the jurisdiction of West Virginia, Orphan Friend Encampment No. 23 Independent Order of Odd Fellows, became No. 14 on April 27; its officers were James A. Davis, C.P.; David H. Stine, H.P.; Henry Reese, S.W.; John C. Davis, J.W.; Manliff Hayes, scribe; and Daniel Fordyce, treasurer (Wiley, p. 549). . . . Prof. A. W. Lorentz began a fire and marine insurance business, representing national firms (Wiley, p. 554). . . . Luther S. Brock began the practice of medicine in Morgantown (Wiley, pp. 584, 585). . . . James Watson, of Clinton Township, died January 10, aged sixty-four years; his wife, Christianne, had died December 5, 1836, aged twenty-three years (Wiley, p. 618). . . . Lucy Ann Evans Goff died; she was a daughter of John Evans, Jr., was born in 1808 and married Nathan Goff, Sr. (Callahan, p. 79). . . . George C. Hayes and Company had a jewelry and grocery store at the corner of Walnut Street and Long Alley (Callahan, p. 210). . . . A second building for the Liming Church of Christ was constructed to replace an earlier one destroyed by fire (Dodds and Dodds, p.

16. Callahan, *Making of Morgantown*, pp. 197, 198, 217.

132). . . . The Miracle Run Methodist congregation moved into a new church built on land given by Hamilton Parks (Dodds and Dodds, p. 133). . . . Rev. E. F. Westfall became the first pastor of the Bakers Ridge Methodist Protestant Church, which had been organized in 1867 (Dodds and Dodds, pp. 149, 150).

# CHAPTER NINETY-FIVE

# 1871

The Civil War had resulted in much waste and destruction of property in some sections of West Virginia and in arrested development even in sections like Monongalia County, where there had been almost no fighting. Now that the war was over, the people in the next few years turned to an economic and political reconstruction of the state.

**Towards a New Constitution.** Many people felt that a new state constitution was necessary to get the people on the way to recovery. The constitution of 1862-63, they pointed out, was adopted without the consent of the whole people; many were in the Confederate army, and others, refusing to recognize the reorganized state authority, had not participated in the election. The legislature on February 23, 1871, passed a convention bill and on August 24, 1871, the people determined the question in favor of a new constitutional convention by a vote of 30,220 to 27,638. The vote in Monongalia County was, for the convention, 688; against, 1,214.

All advocates of the convention were emphatic in expressing their wish to abolish the township system, which they said was a new and expensive importation from the northern states. They desired to restore the old county court system. Some hinted that too many people were voting and that some property qualification should be adopted to disenfranchise the negro population and some of the poor whites.

In October members of the convention were elected, sixty-six of the seventy-eight members being Democrats, only twelve Republicans, these humorously called the "twelve apostles."

The so-called "Flick amendment" (from being proposed by Delegate W. H. H. Flick), to the old constitution, restoring the privileges of those who had been disfranchised through identification with the secessionists, had been ratified by a vote of the people early in 1871 and proclaimed by the governor in April. The vote in Monongalia County was 786 for the amendment; 200 against.

**The Dunkard Valley Turnpike.** As a kind of revival of the old "Turnpike Days," the legislature incorporated, on February 23, 1871, the Dunkard Valley Turnpike Company, to construct a turnpike-road from the Morgantown and Fairmont road, one mile west of Morgantown, by way of Granville, Hamilton (Jimtown), Cassville, and the valley of Dunkard Creek to its source in western Monongalia County, thence across the divide to Burton. This important road was designed to provide Dunkard Valley residents with easier access to the county seat, as well as to the railroad at Burton; it would also constitute a through highway from Morgantown to the railroad. Books of subscription were to be opened at Cassville, Blacksville, and West Warren, under the direction of Morgan L. Boyers, John W. Tucker, Dr. A. W. Brown, Abraham Hair, and Charles W. Edwards. The capital stock was to be formed of shares of twenty dollars each.[1]

**Dunkard Creek Bridge.** "The bridge across Dunkard Creek, at South's Ford, was completed on Thursday last, 17th inst. The contractors for the woodwork, were Messrs. Wm. Dann, Wm. A. Watts, and Wm. Jackson; and the stonework was done under the superintendence of Wm. Utt."

The "four Bills" constructed the imposing covered bridge and submitted a fifth bill to the county supervisors![2]

1. Wiley, pp. 125, 126, 539.
2. *Morgantown Weekly Post*, August 26, 1871. A familiar type of covered bridge was designed by Lemuel Chenoweth (1811-1884), of Beverly, who built many bridges in the Monongahela Valley during this period; the bridge across the Tygart Valley River at Philippi (built 1852) is one of these. See Emory L. Kemp and John Hall "Case Study of Burr Truss Covered Bridge," *Engineering Issues* 101 (1975):391-412.

Fig. 116. A Monongalia County covered bridge. (Sketch by Mary Louise
Adams.)

**The Iron Valley Railroad.** On February 28, 1871, an act was
passed authorizing the extension of the Iron Valley Railroad
from Irondale, Preston County, by Morgantown to the state
line, but no work was done.[3]

**The Northern and Southern West Virginia Railroad.** The charter
of this company which had been incorporated in 1870 (see p.
631), was amended on February 28, 1871, and the capital stock
raised to $10 million. Numerous meetings were held and the
company was organized at Clarksburg on October 31, by which
time three hundred thousand dollars of the stock had been
subscribed. Officers of the company were elected on December 2. The Pennsylvania Central Railroad had surveyed the
route from the Pennsylvania line to Morgantown and this company surveyed it north to Weston.[4]

3. Wiley, pp. 113, 116, 124.
4. Wiley, pp. 112, 113.

**Free Schools.** Henry L. Cox was reelected county superintendent. In his report for the year, he indicated that he felt the free school system was gaining favor with the people, although "it is true that there is on the part of some a strong opposition to the main features of the free school law, and there are others, no doubt, who seek its entire overthrow, yet in general the opposition manifested is less violent than at first, while the friends of the system are daily becoming more firm and earnest in its support."

Superintendent Cox continued: "When we take into account the radical difference between the present system and that which preceded it, as well as the extremely unfavorable condition of public affairs at the time of its introduction, it is, indeed, a matter of surprise that so much has been done."

He expressed some fears that an attempt would be made in the approaching constitutional convention to abolish the system.

**Steamboat Transportation.** Morgantown continued to feel its isolation, resulting from inadequate transportation facilities. In 1870 some freight arrived by irregular steamers and especially by Captain Province's flatboats. County produce and manufactured articles, such as buggies and other carriages, were shipped out by these boats. In the autumn of 1870 J. C. Cooper started a tri-weekly stagecoach line from Morgantown to New Geneva to connect with steam packets to Pittsburgh. The fare was two dollars to New Geneva, five dollars to Pittsburgh.

Early in 1871 several Morgantown businessmen interested themselves in an enterprise of Captain P. Donaldson to provide regular river services to Morgantown, by steamer when the water was high enough, by flatboats when the water level was low.

On Easter Sunday, in 1871, Captain Donaldson's new boat, the *West Virginia*, made its first appearance at Morgantown.[5] It carried both passengers and freight and thereafter made trips twice a week when water conditions were favorable. S. R. Patterson was the local agent to collect ahd receive consignments of freight.[6]

5. *Morgantown Weekly Post*, April 15, 1871.
6. Callahan, pp. 219, 220.

**Front Street Prosperity.** "Five or six years ago Front Street did not present the appearance, in a business point of view, that it does today. From Walnut Street to the mouth of Deckers Creek we have now no less than three steam engines in full blast, and just opposite, across the creek, we are, morning, noon, and night, greeted with the shrill voice of the steam whistle at Fairchild, Lawhead & Co.'s steam Manufactory."[7]

R. P. Hennen and Son were turning out furniture, J. M. Kern and Son had a wagonmaker's shop on the Bridge corner, and Thompson Brothers were running their pottery and corn mill by steam.

**The Wallace House.** "This is the name of the new hotel just opened in this place by Mr. Jas. C. Wallace, whose name and reputation is so well established as a landlord. The Wallace House is the large and commodious three-story brick, situated on Main Street, and has just been refitted with new beds, bed-

Fig. 117. The Wallace House, on High Street. (Courtesy West Virginia University Library.)

7. *Morgantown Weekly Post*, February 25, 1871.

ding, carpets, furniture, etc., etc., and now presents what we may well term *a city air* of neatness and comfort."[8]

**Real Estate Agency.** The county's first real estate agency was managed by George M. Hagans, an industrial promoter who offered for sale not only town lots, but also suburban property, timber land, coal mines, and farms. The sale of real estate was stimulated by hopes of railroad connections in the near future. In May 1871 J. M. Hagans divided into lots his land adjoining that of W. T. Willey south of Deckers Creek.[9]

**Mount Calvary Church.** The Mount Calvary Methodist Protestant Church, six miles south of Morgantown, on the Evansville Pike, was dedicated October 29, 1871, under the pastorate of the Reverends Daniel Helmick, Sr., and P. T. Conway. Reverend P. T. Laishley preached the dedicatory sermon.[10]

During the Civil War, it is said, Captain O. P. Jolliffe night after night vowed in his prayer to God that if his life was spared so that he might return to his wife and family, he would establish a church and be a faithful member of it. He did return safely and donated the land for a church building, the stone for the foundation, and the timber for the framework. In May 1869 he employed Paul Bayles to build the foundation and Jonna and David Summers to erect the building. Throughout the construction Mrs. Jolliffe boarded the men without charge. Other leaders in the congregation were Nicholas Vandervort, Albert Roby, William Boyd, and their families.[11]

**The University.** In efforts to enforce the "Code of Laws and Resolutions" prescribed by the regents and approved by the faculty, much attention was given to student discipline. Each student was required to be in his place for all stated university exercises, the six o'clock cannon shot was the rising command and the nine o'clock curfew bell was the retiring signal, students were required to refrain from the use of intoxicants, tobacco, and profanity; and they were forbidden to dance, to visit billiard rooms, and to attend circuses.

8. *Morgantown Weekly Post*, April 8, 1871.
9. Callahan, p. 211.
10. *Morgantown Weekly Post*, October 21, 1871.
11. Wiley, p. 627; Dodds and Dodds, *Churches of Monongalia County*, pp. 143, 144; Barnes, *M. P. Church*, pp. 146, 147.

Among numerous incidents associated with violations of the "Laws" was that of 1871 in which the later distinguished Philander C. Knox refused to desist from playing billiards and was ordered to leave the campus at once. He did so and enrolled in Mount Union College, Alliance, Ohio, where he graduated in due time.[12]

Professor F. S. Lyon resigned in 1870 and Prof. S. G. Stevens was made vice-president. J. H. McMechan, a Protestant Episcopal rector, was appointed to the chair of English literature and made principal of the preparatory department. He resigned in December 1870, and was succeeded by the Reverend J. B. Solomon, who soon thereafter was made secretary to the faculty to succeed Vice-President Stevens. G. N. Glover was appointed professor of history, political science, and belles-lettres in 1871.

**Noah Morris.** A farmer of Clay Township, Noah Morris, son of Levi and Elizabeth Morris, died July 8, 1871, from inflammation of the windpipe, aged fifty-nine years. He married Eunice Cannon and their children were Minerva, Eliza J., John Calvin, and Anne.[13]

**William S. Fletcher.** A Blacksville iron mechanic, William S. Fletcher, died February 22, 1871. He was born in Caroline County and moved to Blacksville in 1838. He became especially noted as the manufacturer of the Fletcher axe, widely known and used throughout the area. He married Alice Henkins and one of their children was Dr. George M. Fletcher, who located in Blacksville in 1869 and developed a large medical practice.[14]

**Joseph Thomas.** One of the pioneer settlers of Flat Run, Monongalia County, was Joseph Thomas, who acquired a tract of more than a thousand acres there, living on it the remainder of his life. He died in 1870, at the age of one hundred years. He was of Welsh ancestry and was born in Fayette County, Pennsylvania. He married Nancy Riggs and they became the parents of ten children, five sons and five daughters.[15]

12. Ambler, *History of Education in West Virginia*, pp. 191, 192.
13. Core, *Chronicles of Core*, p. 104.
14. *Cyclopedia of Monongalia County*, p. 218.
15. *Cyclopedia of Marion County*, p. 197.

**Other Deaths.** John Core died near Clarksburg on December 2, 1870, in the eighty-second year of his age. For many years he resided and kept hotel in a house which stood on Lot No. 100, Front Street, known as "The Boat," from the fact that in building it he had used two boat gunnels for sills, seventy feet long, ten by twenty-two inches. He left Morgantown in 1839.[16]

**Samuel Vance.** A former resident of Morgantown, Samuel Vance, died at his home in Fayette County, Indiana, on February 3, 1871, aged eighty-five years. He was a brother of Mrs. J. J. Thompson.[17]

**William Fisher.** A farmer of Flaggy Meadow Run, William Fisher, died November 23, 1871. He was born about 1800, the son of John and Christine Fisher. He married Elizabeth, daughter of William and Mary Barbe, and they had five children, Alpheus, Silas, Elizabeth, John Wesley, and Rachel.[18]

**County and Borough Government.** A. W. Brown was chosen as president of the board of supervisors. Other members included Henry S. Coombs (Union), James Sanders (Cass), J. M. Taylor (Grant), S. Barrickman (Clay), and E. J. Eddy (Battelle).

Township clerks were H. Stansberry (Clinton), E. H. Coombs (Morgan), A. C. Rude (Union), A. E. Cushman (Cass), Garrett Conn (Grant), —— (Clay), and J. M. John (Battelle).

John H. Hoffman was mayor of Morgantown, F. A. Dering recorder, Jacob Kiger and James Odbert sergeants, and F. M. Durbin treasurer. Members of the council were Frank W. Thompson, L. S. Hough, F. M. Durbin, Henry M. Morgan, and David H. Chadwick.

The council placed the care of the new street lamps in the hands of the town sergeant, for which extra service they paid him an additional salary, usually about $200, but up to $150 more if he furnished the oil and other supplies.

**Miscellany.** In 1871: During the summer a survey was made of the Monongahela River from New Geneva to Morgantown with regard to slacking the river; the survey was authorized by a

16. *Morgantown Weekly Post*, January 7, 1871.
17. *Morgantown Weekly Post*, February 18, 1871.
18. Gordon C. Baker, "Notes on the Fisher Family," *Monongalia Chronicle*, April, 1975.

United States Congress bill introduced by Representative James C. McGrew (Wiley, p. 130). . . . Dr. George W. John opened a store and an office for the practice of medicine in Morgantown (Wiley, pp. 478, 584). . . . Bowman and Basnett were operating a store in Morgantown (Wiley, p. 583). . . . Dr. Melville L. Casselberry associated with Dr. Elisha H. Coombs for the practice of medicine in Morgantown (Wiley, p. 585). . . . Jacob Conn was running the Line Ferry on Cheat River (Wiley, p. 681). . . . Kern's New Steam Wagon Factory was established on Front Street (Callahan, p. 208). . . . Kern's Ice Cream Saloon was opened, furnishing not only ice cream but also cakes, and fresh fruit in season (Callahan, p. 213).

# CHAPTER NINETY-SIX

# 1872

An important change in county and state government and in the judicial system came in 1872, as a result of the adoption of the new state constitution. Monongalia County up until that time had existed under the first constitution of Virginia, adopted June 29, 1776, under the Virginia constitution of 1829-30 and under that of 1850, as well as under the 1861-63 constitution of the new state of West Virginia.

**The Constitution of 1872.** The convention assembled in Charleston on January 16, 1872. The document as finally submitted to the voters on August 22, 1872, was ratified by a majority of 4,567 in a total vote of 80,121. The vote in Monongalia County was 895 for ratification, 1,470 against.

The new constitution divided the state into twelve senatorial districts, with two senators from each district, as compared with the 1863 constitution, which had only nine districts. Monongalia and Preston counties constituted the Tenth District. Monongalia had two members in the House of Delegates, as had been the case since 1852.

The state judicial circuits were rearranged and Monongalia, with Wetzel, Marion, Taylor, Doddridge, and Harrison constituted the Second Judicial Circuit.

The old county court was reestablished, in place of the county board of supervisors, which had operated since 1863. The court was to be composed of two justices from each county subdivision.

The township system was abolished by the new constitution and the subdivisions were reconstituted as magisterial districts, with the same names as before.

County and district officers, in general, were to be elected for

649

four-year terms, but current terms were shortened by new elections.

**Fielding H. Youst.** A man who had served as a Morgantown physician and who had acquired a wide national fame, Dr. Fielding Hamilton Youst, died May 13, 1872, in Fairview, Marion County, only forty-five years of age.

The Youst family had settled on Indian Creek, Monongalia County, as early as 1783. John Youst migrated from Bavaria to New York in 1773. Shortly after his arrival in America he met a young English-Dutch girl, Miss Katie Snuiche (Snook), a girl who was a fine scholar, well read in English, Dutch, and German.

They were married in New Jersey and spent the years of the Revolutionary War there, where he served in the Continental army. Their first three children, Henry, Elizabeth, and John, were born there.

After the war the family moved across the mountains with the frontier tide of migration, being among the forerunners of civilization in the Monongahela Valley. Their settlement on Indian Creek was not far from the government fort called Old Station (or Paw Paw Station), on Paw Paw Creek, at one time under command of Levi Morgan, the noted frontier Indian fighter. The two older Youst boys, Henry and John, later served with Morgan.

Five other children were born on Indian Creek, Aaron, William, Peter, Niers, and David. From these seven sons came all the descendants of the Youst name that spread the family throughout northwestern Virginia.

David Youst was born September 3, 1788, and, about 1808 located on a homestead of over one thousand acres on Paw Paw Creek, Monongalia County.[1] Here he married Rebecca Fluharty, of Morgantown, in 1810. Eleven children were born to this union, among them Jehu D. Youst and Nicholas B. Youst, who became noted physicians.

Fielding H. Youst was one of the children of David and Rebecca Youst and was born August 4, 1827, on Paw Paw Creek, Monongalia County (Marion County, after 1842).

1. The site of the later town of Fairview was on this tract; it was named by Mrs. Fielding Youst.

He received a good elementary education in the subscription schools in the neighborhood, and then in 1846 completed his collegiate course at Rector College, then a well-known school at Pruntytown, county seat of Taylor County (which had just been formed, in 1844).

Fielding then took up the study of medicine under his older brothers, Jehu and Nicholas, reading widely on the reform systems of medicine, and later graduated at the Eclectic Medical Institute, in Cincinnati.

After his graduation he returned to Marion County, where he had already established a reputation for special fitness for the medical profession. He turned down an offer of a position on the staff of his alma mater, and also a chair in the Georgia Botanical Medical College.

Eclectic medicine was at that time a reform system, breaking away from the old system of medicine, many of whose practitioners thought bleeding was a cure for almost everything. The new system made more use of botanical remedies and tried to select a specific remedy for the disease.

At the outbreak of the Civil War his sympathies were with Virginia and he enlisted in the Confederate army, serving under Stonewall Jackson. He was appointed surgeon by the General Assembly of Virginia shortly after secession. He was on General Lee's staff in his early campaigns in western Virginia and was for a while in charge of the Confederate hospital at Monterey.

In 1863, after having been a "Citizen Prisoner" at Camp Chase, near Wheeling, he was released and located in Morgantown for the practice of general medicine. He remained neutral throughout the remainder of the war, and apparently his neutrality was respected by both Northerners and Southerners.

Failing health caused him to attempt to retire from active work and he left Morgantown in 1867, returning to his Marion County home to live the remainder of his life, associating with a relative, Dr. Jorier Yost, in general practice. His fame, however, made it difficult for him to really retire and he died at an early age.

He was a gifted speaker, an eloquent lecturer, and took part in public affairs and movements for civic improvement in the various communities in which he lived. He was a Sunday school teacher and an active member of the Methodist Episcopal Church South.

Fielding Youst married Malinda A. Jones, daughter of John Jones, of Pleasant Valley, and they had eight children, Galen B., DeLaniel L., Zoath Freeman, Larnard H., Lucian M., Martha, Zoa L., and Maria A. ("Allie").[2]

**William Lazier.** The Lazier family was among the Monongalia County's most prominent, through most of the nineteenth century in commercial and civic affairs. William Lazier, the best known representative of the family, died May 1, 1872, aged seventy-five years. His wife had died September 22, 1866, aged sixty-eight.

William and Henry Lazier came to Morgantown, Wiley says,[3] "some time after the War of 1812." Henry Lazier was running a store in Morgantown before 1815. William migrated from Bedford, Pennsylvania, first to Wheeling and then, in company with Eli B. Swearingen, located in Morgantown. He married Mary Ann McClure, and they bought lots 54 and 55, on Spruce Street, in 1831, and built their beautiful home in 1832. Their children were Mary (married Joseph A. McLane), Ann, Julia (married John F. Fleming), Henry B. (p. 654), Sarah J., Frances, John (a dentist), and Louise R.

William Lazier was running some of the Cheat Iron Works before 1830. From 1829 to 1831 advertisements of William Lazier and Company appear in local newspapers. In 1837, 1838, and 1839 he was in business simply as William Lazier. In 1849 the business was known as William Lazier and Company.

He was sworn in as justice of the peace (member of the county court) on March 28, 1832, resigning May 26, 1834.

William Lazier, throughout his life, was interested in education. When the Virginia General Assembly, in 1839, incorporated the Morgantown Female Collegiate Institute, he was named the first president of the board of trustees.

The foundry which gave Foundry Street its name, started by

2. *Cyclopedia of Marion County*, p. 252; pers. comm., J. Paul Yost, Pontiac, Ill., son of Zoath Freeman. The family name was originally spelled Youst and was changed to Yost by some of Dr. Fielding's children. Fielding Harris ("Hurry-Up") Yost, was a grandson of Nicholas.

3. *History of Monongalia County*, p. 601; see also Dr. Eldon B. Tucker, Jr., *West Virginia Hillbilly*, February 10, 1973.

Henry Daugherty in 1844, was operated by Lazier for several years; he installed a steam engine in the works in 1848. From 1856 until 1859 he operated the plant in association with James Nimon, and they sold it to George M. Reay, who continued its operation for many years. Around 1850 Lazier began the production of coke in the county, at first merely by burning coal in ricks on the ground, then in a brick oven at a foundry across Deckers Creek in Durbannah.

The county's first insurance company, The Monongalia County Mutual Insurance Company, was incorporated by the general assembly on March 29, 1851. William Lazier was named in the charter as a member of the board of directors, along with Elza C. Lazier. The organization, however, never got under way.

The completion of the Baltimore and Ohio Railroad to Fairmont and Wheeling in 1852, led Morgantown civic leaders to long-continued efforts to secure a line through the county and Lazier was an active worker in such endeavors. The Morgantown and Independence Railroad Company was incorporated by the general assembly November 30, 1852; it was provided that books of subscription be opened at Morgantown by various persons, one of whom was William Lazier. But the necessary amount of subscriptions could not be obtained.

Another enterprise, the Monongahela and Lewisburg Railway Company, was incorporated March 6, 1865, by the legislature of the new state of West Virginia and William Lazier was named as one of the stockholders. But this project, also, failed because sufficient subscriptions could not be obtained.

Lazier was in the forefront of the movement to resist secession and to form a new state. On April 17, 1861, the day the special convention at Richmond voted for secession, a mass meeting of citizens was held in the courthouse in Morgantown and William Lazier was elected president. On May 4 he was named as one of the delegates to meet in Wheeling to consider further concerted action. When the convention, on June 19, passed "an ordinance for the reorganization of the State Government," he was named a member of Governor Francis H. Pierpont's Council.

William Lazier's store in Morgantown suffered considerable losses in Jones's raid on Morgantown, on April 27, 1863 (p. 542). A local newspaper reported that all the stores in town were closed as the Confederate forces approached, but that some of the invaders forced their way into some of the stores, including Lazier's. The paper also reported that Lazier's farm-house, one mile from town, was burned by the rebels.

As the war drew towards its close, and in the years immediately following the close, Lazier continued his public service. He was Morgan Township treasurer in 1864 and was an unsuccessful candidate for the state senate the same year. He served as mayor of the borough of Morgantown in 1865, and was a Morgan Township school commissioner in that year.[4]

Doctor Henry Bayard Lazier, son of William and Mary Lazier, was born January 26, 1831, attended Monongalia Academy, and graduated from Jefferson Medical College. When the Civil War began, he raised Company E, Seventh West Virginia Infantry, and was captain of the company. The company fought at Malvern Hill and at Antietam. In the latter battle, Captain Lazier commanded the left wing of the regiment and was severely wounded. He resigned his commission in February 1863 and was commissioned assistant surgeon in the Sixteenth Army Corps, serving in that capacity until the end of the war.

After the war he ran a book and drug store facing the Courthouse Square, and, like his father, was a promoter of railroad projects and a leader in education and civic affairs.

**Abraham Barnes.** Abraham Barnes died near Fairmont July 25, 1872, at the age of eighty-eight years. He was born in New Jersey October 13, 1784, and came to Monongalia County at an early age with his parents, Mr. and Mrs. William Barnes. He learned the trade of millwright with his father and followed this, along with farming, most of his life. He married Mary, daughter of Jordan and Nancy (Neil) Hall, and they had nine children.[5]

**John Jamison.** A farmer and stock-dealer of Grant District, John Jamison, died in 1872. He was a son of John Jamison and was born in 1814 in Greene County, Pennsylvania. He married Cinderella, daughter of Pierce Lynch, and in 1835 they located on a farm near Laurel Point. He engaged in farming and in cattle

4. Wiley, p. 601.
5. *Cyclopedia of Marion County*, p. 257; Lough, *Now and Long Ago*, p. 383.

dealing, driving cattle across the mountains to market in Baltimore.

John and Cinderella Jamison had ten children, including, Ellen, Pierce L., John W., Jarrett L., William C., Margaret I. (married C. W. Arnett), Lucinda (married William H. John), Jesse A., and David L. William and Jesse were physicians at Bruceton Mills.[6]

**William Arnett.** A prosperous farmer and well-known citizen of Marion County, William Arnett, died in 1872. He was born in 1796, the son of John Arnett, of German nativity, who, with his brother Andrew, settled in the vicinity of the later village of Arnettsville in 1785. The family later moved to Paw Paw Creek, where they engaged in agriculture. "William Arnett was a great leader and exceptionally well posted in the political history of the country. In that crisis which arose threatening the destruction of the country and the dismemberment of the Union, he was a strong Union man, energetic and prudent."

He married Eleanor, daughter of Davis Meredith, and they had ten children, namely, Rebecca, Dorcas, Lavina, Ever, Riley, Franklin, Melissa, Elbert, Sallie, and C. W., a Fairmont banker.[7]

**Joseph Tennant.** The third son of Richard and Elizabeth Tennant, Joseph Tennant, a farmer of Statler Run, died December 24, 1872. He was born in Fayette County, Pennsylvania, in 1782, and served 5½ months in the War of 1812.

He married Catherine, a daughter of Peter Haught, and they had twelve children, Ezra, Tobias, Lucy, Eliab, Silas, Walter, Joseph, Denney, Seth, Rachel, Jerusha, and Enoch.[8]

**Northern and Southern West Virginia Railroad.** On February 20 this company was authorized to increase its stock to $12 million. At a meeting held in Charleston in March Col. Thomas Scott of the Pennsylvania Central proposed that his company would construct the road if West Virginia would raise $1 mil-

6. *Cyclopedia of Monongalia County*, p. 115; Wiley, p. 736.
7. *Cyclopedia of Marion County*, pp. 32, 33.
8. *Cyclopedia of Monongalia County*, pp. 207, 210; a photograph of Joseph and Catherine Tennant's log cabin appears in *The Monongalia Story*, vol. 2, p. 491.

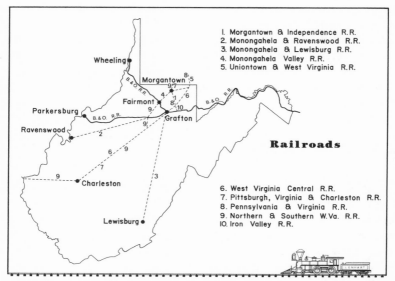

Fig. 118. Map showing routes of proposed railroads passing through or near Monongalia County. (Drawn by Diane Lenhart.)

lion. A division of this amount among the counties concerned was made and Monongalia's share was $175,000.[9]

**Slack Water Is Approved.** On February 12, 1872, Congressman James C. McGrew introduced a bill appropriating funds, and $25,000 was voted by the second session of the forty-second Congress to begin the work of slacking the river from New Geneva to Morgantown. Meanwhile, a board of trade was organized in Morgantown and R. L. Berkshire and George C. Sturgiss were sent to Washington on behalf of the project. The next session of Congress appropriated an additional $66,000.

Later in the year the contract for construction of a stone lock (No. 9) was let to Smith, Hawkins and Davis for $54,641.75, theirs being the lowest of twelve bids.[10]

**Free Schools.** The Free School System was retained in the Constitution of 1872, which enjoined upon the legislature to "pro-

9. Wiley, pp. 113, 124.
10. Wiley, p. 130.

vide, by general law, for a thorough and efficient system of free schools." The first legislature which met after the ratification of the constitution provided for the election of a board of education in each district, composed of the president and two commissioners, and the election of one trustee for each subdistrict, at a poll held therein. The board determined the length of the school term, the number of teachers to be employed, and fixed their wages according to the grades of certificate.[11]

"The year ending August 31, 1872" wrote Superintendent H. L. Cox, "was one of unusual success in the free schools" of Monongalia County. He noted better attendance, more enthusiasm among the pupils, and a growing appreciation on the part of the people.[12]

**The University.** The total college enrollment for the 1872-73 academic year was sixty-two and President Martin described the curriculum as "quite equal to the average of our *best* American colleges." While some persons had been "watchful for mistakes, and perhaps anxious to produce them," words of cheer and acts of kindness had fallen "like a benediction."[13] Professor Stevenson resigned in 1872 and William M. Fontaine was elected to the chair of agriculture, chemistry, and natural history.

A telescope was purchased and mounted "to look at the stars":

"The Telescope, made expressly for this Institution, by John Byrne, of New York, has been unpacked, and in a few days will be fully adjusted to its work. It is a very fine instrument, 7 feet focal length, 5½ inches aperture, with right ascension and declension circles, and eye pieces from 45 to 300 diameters."[14]

**New Mode of Transporting the Mail.** "For the benefit of future historians we chronicle the fact that, in consequence of the epizootic having attacked all the horses in this section, Mr. Bright, the mail route contractor between this place and Fairmont, has been reduced to the extremity of hiring men to walk and carry the mail."[15] W. R. Batsen carried the letter mail-bag

11. Wiley, pp. 368, 369.
12. Wiley, p. 390.
13. Ambler, *History of Education in West Virginia*, p. 193.
14. *Morgantown Weekly Post*, August 31, 1872; H. W. Gould, "Astronomy's Might-Have-Been Years," *West Virginia University Magazine* 3(2): 18-23, 1971.
15. *Morgantown Weekly Post*, December 7, 1872.

to Fairmont on Thanksgiving Day, November 28, and the next day James Turner did the same thing.

**The First Dairy.** "Morgantown can now boast of a well established first class Dairy. It may be understood now to be a permanent institution. We will never be without a dairy again. We are learning to live like other people. . : . A few, of course, will always refuse to learn. With them, ignorance is bliss, but to the really wise there is no bliss, comfort, or money in an old cow about the house."[16]

**County Fair.** The Fourth Annual Fair was held September 25, 26, and 27, 1872, with, as usual, good attendance. "A monster balloon" was scheduled "to ascend on the last day—one of the greatest novelties ever undertaken at a Fair."[17] It wouldn't hold air, however, and required patching, finally going up and away the following Monday evening.[18]

Fig. 119. Artist's concept of the county fair, Greenmont. (Sketch by Diane Lenhart.)

16. *Morgantown Weekly Post*, September 21, 1872.
17. *Morgantown Weekly Post*, September 28, 1872.
18. *Morgantown Weekly Post*, October 5, 1872.

There was plenty of entertainment, however, with exhibitions, pacing, and trotting matches, and concerts by a brass band.

**Another Good Citizen Gone.** "Mr. Caleb Beall, one of the old landmarks of Monongalia, died at his home three miles from town, on Saturday last, after a lingering illness, aged about 65 years."[19]

**Enterprise Building Association.** Morgantown's first building and loan company, the Enterprise Building Association, was formed in March 1872. A. W. Lorentz, J. A. Davis, W. C. McGrew, W. P. Willey, and W. W. Dering were charter members. The shares were one hundred dollars each, and by the terms of its charter it was to "expire in seven years from the date of incorporation, or when a sufficient amount had been received by the association to make each share of stock worth one hundred dollars."[20]

**Rev. Thomas Martin.** A former principal of Monongalia Academy, the Reverend Thomas Martin, died April 18, 1872, at Petersburg, Indiana. He was born December 16, 1804, at Rathfriland, County Down, Ireland, and graduated from Belfast College and Princeton Theological Seminary. In 1833 he came to Morgantown as principal of the academy and served as stated supply of the Presbyterian church. He married Jane Isabella, only child of Jonathan Prentis, a distinguished Morgantown citizen. After leaving Morgantown he served at Brownsville, Pennsylvania, until 1852, when he retired to live in Morgantown again, but left in 1856 to serve as pastor of the Petersburg Church.[21]

**Jones African Methodist Episcopal Church.** A story is told that a Negro slave was sent from Morgantown to eastern Virginia to bring home for burial the body of a white person who had died there. When he was asked what reward he would like, he asked that his brother and sister might be brought here to live. The request was granted; he was the ancestor of the later prominent Edwards family.

19. *Morgantown Weekly Post*, April 27, 1872.
20. Wiley, p. 555.
21. Moreland, *The First Presbyterian Church*, p. 50.

Fig. 120. The Jones African Methodist Episcopal Church. (Photo Dr. and Mrs. Gideon S. Dodds.)

Other black people followed and a church group was formed, worshiping at first in the Methodist Episcopal Church on Pleasant Street. The bishop finally told them this could not continue, and the Jones African Methodist Episcopal Church was formed. George and Mary Kiger in 1869 deeded a lot on Long Alley to the congregation. About 1871 a difference arose among the members, and part of the group organized the Saint Paul's A.M.E. Church, which constructed a building near the river, just north of the borough line, securing a lot from John Huffman, Sr. The deed was recorded in 1872 by trustees John Edwards, Sr., Robert Johnson, Robert Hamilton, and Preston Hedricks. The Reverend Mr. McKnight was the pastor.[22]

**Rock Forge Methodist Church.** A new building was constructed by the Rock Forge congregation on ground used for the earlier church. It was made of hand-hewn lumber, oak and poplar

22. Dodds and Dodds, *Churches of Monongalia County*, pp. 91, 92; Wiley, p. 596. The church at first faced on Water Street but when Beechurst Avenue was built it was remodeled to face on that thoroughfare.

being donated by James Henry, and other lumber given by Samuel Bell. The carpenters were William Jackson and Lein Shoemaker.[23]

**County, Township, and Borough Government.** George W. McVicker was sworn in as sheriff, Thomas R. Evans, surveyor, Henry C. Baker assessor for the Eastern District and George Barb for the Western District. Manliff Hayes was president of the county court. Justices (members of the county court) were J. A. Holland and Moses Steele (for Clinton District), James A. Davis and Harvey Staggers (Morgan), John N. Dawson and Albert C. Rude (Union), John K. Barrickman and John W. Tucker (Cass), E. W. Brand and Shelby P. Barker (Grant), Simon P. Tennant and Coverdille Williams (Clay), and P. A. Tennant and Perry Hennen (Battelle).

Township clerks, the last to be elected, were E. H. Coombs (Morgan), A. C. Rude (Union), A. E. Cushman (Cass), and Garrett Conn (Grant).

Joseph Moreland was mayor of Morgantown, Charles McLane recorder, and James Odbert sergeant. Members of the council were David H. Chadwick, L. S. Hough, F. M. Durbin, Frank W. Thompson, and William N. Jarrett.

**Miscellany.** In 1872: Oliver H. Dille was admitted to the county bar on September 9 and Marmaduke H. Dent on September 13 (Wiley, pp. 317, 318). . . . The Goshen Baptist Sunday School Convention was organized on December 25, at Morgantown, with Prof. D. B. Purinton president (Wiley, p. 450). . . . Henry H. Hayes opened a grocery and jewelry store in Morgantown (Wiley, pp. 581, 583). . . . A brick house, perhaps the oldest in Morgantown, constructed by John Davis on Lot 89 about 1803, was sold by the heirs of William Dering to Fielding O'Kelley (Callahan, p. 188). . . . In March a small mutual insurance association for men only, called the Aid Society, was organized by J. C. Wagner with William Wagner president (Callahan, p. 214). . . . An Englishman, traveling in Monongalia County, wrote a long description of the "Cheat River View," which, he said, "has more than repaid me for crossing the Atlantic" (*Morgantown Weekly Post*, June 22, 1872).

23. Dodds and Dodds, *Churches of Monongalia County,* p. 85.

CHAPTER NINETY-SEVEN

# 1873

In the area later to become Grant Township the construction of the Brandonville and Fishing Creek Turnpike, about 1838, stimulated the growth of several small community centers, including Laurel Point, Georgetown, and Arnettsville. The road left Morgantown by a river ferry (later over the suspension bridge) and followed the route of the old state road as far as the crossing of Dents Run.[1] Despite the fact that it was called a "Turnpike," it scarcely operated as such; locally it became known as the Fairmont Pike. Over it ran for a half century or more various stagecoach lines, including the famous "Uncle Caney" Bright coaches, making connection at Fairmont after 1852, with Baltimore and Ohio trains to the east and the west.

**The Village of Georgetown.**[2] Where the pike crossed a small stream called Sniders Run a small village began to grow up in mid-nineteenth century times.

John Snider (or Snyder) was the original owner of the land on which the village developed. An early tradition pointed out an oak tree under which he is said to have slept as a boy when returning home after having been stolen by the Indians.

A log church was built here at an early date, known locally only as Snider's Church. Later, about 1846, a second log church was built; it received the name of Sniderville Meeting House, the neighbors being hopeful that a village would develop there. David Snider and his wife, Elizabeth Cotton Snider, made a deed on March 5, 1846, giving the land to the church, Eugenus Wilson Snider and Asbury Snider built the church, described in

1. *The Monongalia Story*, vol. 2, p. 237.
2. The name Georgetown was not actually applied until 1881. The first post office, established May 8, 1876, with William N. Stewart the first postmaster, was called Cedar Valley.

the deed as standing near the Turnpike on the Snider plantation. The building was said to be "for the Episcopal Methodists
to preach in and for the proper use and benefit of the people."
Later the church came to be called Snider's Temple.

Another pioneer settler was Joseph Barker, who came in
1775 to Monongalia County with his brothers, John and James.
Joseph married Catharine Carpenter and their children included
Aaron, David, Joseph, James, Moses, and Catharine (who married James Scott).

Aaron Barker married Sarah, daughter of Jacob Scott, and
their children were Jacob, Joseph, Drusilla (married Gen. E. S.
Pindall), Benjamin H., and Alfred C.

Benjamin H. Barker married Rebecca, daughter of Zackwell
Morgan (son of David Morgan), and their children were Cath-
arine (married Ira Hall), Shelby P., Zackwell M., Sarah, Drusilla,
Aaron, and Linah.

Shelby Pindall Barker, born July 8, 1835, became one of the
prominent businessmen and developers of the growing community. He traveled through the West, returning in 1859 and
marrying Mary, daughter of Philip Lowe. Their children were
Rebecca, Ida J., Laura C., Charles, Lulu M., Sarah, Aaron, Benjamin H., and Hugh M. He enlisted in the Union army in 1861
and was in several battles, including the second battle of Bull
Run, where he was captured and spent some time in Confederate prisons before he was paroled and exchanged.

He served two terms as school commissioner, one term as
justice of the peace, and two terms as county commissioner.

The blacksmith shop was an important service center for
rural communities in those days and Emory Hill and R. S. Michael were early blacksmiths at Georgetown. Their services to
farmers in the surrounding country kept them both busy.

Another important service rendered in those days was the
cobbler or cordwainer; Thomas Wells was the Georgetown shoemaker of that time.

On nearby Stewarts Run Samuel Calvin Stewart was a prominent farmer and public citizen. He was born July 1, 1832, the
son of William and Elizabeth Stewart, a descendant of Stewartstown pioneers. He applied himself to the study of surveying and
had an extensive practice in preparing deeds. He served as a
member of the board of education and in other public offices.

Fig. 121. Capt. George Washington McVicker. (From Wiley's *History of Monongalia County*.)

Fig. 122. Shelby Pindall Barker. (From Wiley's *History of Monongalia County*.)

Fig. 123. Alpha Ralphsynder. (From Wiley's *History of Monongalia County*.)

Fig. 124. John H. Bowlby. (From Wiley's *History of Monongalia County*.)

John M. Ralphsnyder, of German ancestry, was another of the pioneer settlers in the Georgetown area. He married Elizabeth Riffle and became one of the most extensive farmers in the section. They had four sons and four daughters, namely, Aaron, William, Alpha, Franklin, Jemima, Elizabeth, Catharine and Mary Ann.

Alpha Ralphsnyder, born April 26, 1821, continued his father's reputation as a good farmer, in later years turning his attention largely to stock raising. He married Christena, daughter of Isaac Cox, and their children included John M., Marion A., Richard L., Isaac Cox, George M., and William.

**Saint Cloud.** A post office was established August 5, 1873, at Saint Cloud, with John Hagan Six as the first postmaster. The little village was the westernmost in the county, standing on a ridge above the headwaters of Dunkard Creek, almost on the Wetzel County line. Only a few miles east of Hundred, on the B.&O. line, Saint Cloud was closer to the railroad than any other community in the county. Handsucker Knob (elevation, 1,652 feet), where the Handsucker family was murdered by Wyandotte Indians in 1791 (*Monongalia Story*, vol. 2, pp. 188, 189), is nearby, and is the highest elevation in the area.

Early settlers in the area included the White family, the Stiles family, and two families of Dutch ancestry, Pethtel and Six. A member of the Six family found the skeleton of Mr. Handsucker, many years after his murder, and gave it a decent burial. The first school in the community was the Oak Grove School, named for a grove of oak trees in which it stood.

**"Osageville."** This "is a new town, laid off at Jacob Rice's Mills, on the waters of Scotts Run, one mile from the river and four miles from Morgantown. Osageville and suburbs contain a population of perhaps 25 souls, but the prospects are the place will shortly be a thriving little village. . . . We already have a good steam grist mill, a sawmill and carding machine, and—and—some of the prettiest girls in the county."[3]

**Another Boundary Change Proposed.** Notwithstanding the provision of the state constitution to which reference was made in

3. *Morgantown Weekly Post*, April 12, 1873.

the account of the proposed Union County (p. 599), a new attempt at a boundary change was made in 1873.

On December 2, W. S. Laidley, of Kanawha County, as chairman of the committee on counties, districts, and municipal corporations, submitted a report to the House of Delegates, that the said committee, "to whom was referred the petition of W. H. McCans and two hundred and twenty-five others of Monongalia County, 'asking that the county line of Monongalia and Marion counties, be so changed as to annex the district of Battelle to the county of Marion,' beg leave to report the same back with recommendation that the prayer of said petitioners be granted, and report therefore House Bill No. 249."

The bill was ordered to its second reading on December 4. Then, on December 8, it was laid on the table. An effort to take it up on December 10 failed, but a similar motion on the next day prevailed. On the sixteenth a motion to indefinitely postpone the measure was made, superseded by a motion to table, which was adopted. There the measure died.[4]

**The Hagans Reports.** John Marshall Hagans was born August 13, 1838, at Brandonville, Preston County, and was educated in Monongalia Academy. "At the instance of many friends who saw in him that peculiar diversity of talent which seldom fails to win distinction at the bar, he commenced the study of the law in the office of the Hon. Waitman T. Willey, and afterward pursued his studies at the law school of Harvard University." He was admitted to the bar in 1859 and began the practice of law in Morgantown.

He was elected prosecuting attorney for Monongalia County in 1862, at the first election under the new constitution, and was reelected in 1863, in 1864, and again in 1870. He served three terms as mayor of Morgantown and was a delegate to the 1871 convention to revise the constitution of the state.[5]

In January 1864 he was appointed reporter of the West Virginia Supreme Court of Appeals, which position he held until March 1873. During this time five volumes of the leading cases decided by the court were published, known as "Hagans' West Virginia Reports." The first volume contains an accurate and

4. Wiley, p. 102.
5. See characterization of him in the *Baptist Record*, April 10, 1872.

well-written account of the formation of the new state of West Virginia.[6]

**The University.** Robert C. Berkeley, a graduate of the University of Virginia (1861), was in 1873 elected professor of ancient languages and literature at West Virginia University. He had previously taught at Washington College, Maryland (1867-73).[7]

Franklin S. Lyon returned to the university in 1873, succeeding J. B. Solomon as principal of the preparatory department. Professor Lyon was born in Massachusetts in 1819 and graduated at the University of Rochester in 1852. He taught in Albion Academy, New York, and in the Male Seminary, Indian Territory, before coming to Morgantown as principal of the preparatory department in 1867. In 1871 he resigned, was principal of Fenton Seminary, Michigan, and then United States Indian Agent for the Creek Nation, Indian Territory, before coming back to the university.[8]

D. Boardman Purinton became assistant teacher in the preparatory department in 1873. He was born in Preston County in 1850, the son of the Reverend J. M. Purinton (p. 624). In 1866 he taught in Georges Creek Academy, Smithfield, Pennsylvania, then entered the preparatory department in 1867 and graduated from the university in 1873.[9]

The old Woodburn Seminary buildings, on the campus of West Virginia University, was destroyed by fire on Saturday evening, January 25, 1873.[10]

A four-column story in a local newspaper[11] gave a detailed account of the fire, headed by such phrases as "Total Destruction of University Dining Hall," "Narrow Escape of Some of the Inmates," "Old 'Woodburn' in Ashes!" "Fearfully Sublime Spectacle!", etc.

"Saturday night, Jan'y 25th, at 20 minutes to ten o'clock, the usual quiet of our town was broken by the sudden, piercing cries of 'fire!' and the rapid ringing of bells. The streets were

6. Wiley, pp. 277-79. The historical account constitutes ninety-six pages of vol. 1 of the *West Virginia Supreme Court Reports* (1866). This section was reprinted separately by Butler Printing Co., Charleston, in 1891, and by Jonathan Sheppard Enterprises, Albany, N.Y., in 1978.
7. Wiley, p. 417.
8. Wiley, p. 418.
9. Wiley, p. 419.
10. Wiley, pp. 400, 403, 406.
11. *Morgantown Weekly Post*, February 1, 1873.

Fig. 125. Ruins of the old Woodburn seminary, at right, following the fire of January 25, 1873. University Hall to the left. (Courtesy West Virginia University Library.)

soon thronged with an excited crowd of men, women and children—some of whom had been aroused from their slumbers by the wild cries, and rushed out of their abodes, in some instances, scarcely half clothed.

"The scene of the conflagration was University Dining Hall, owned by the State, situated about 100 feet from the State University and occupied by Mr. Kinsey Fife and family, who had in their charge nearly forty students of the University as boarders. The building, large and commodious (two stories and a basement) is of brick—a part of which was built by Thos. P. Ray, dec'd. It is . . . less than one-fourth of a mile outside the borough limits."

The fire apparently started in room 23, occupied by a young man named Hinkle, from Buckhannon, and it was supposed that it was caused by the explosion of a lamp, or from hot coals falling on the floor. The building, with its contents, was totally destroyed, except for the walls, "which remain, in many places, to all appearances, almost as substantial as ever."

"The building was insured in the Aetna, of Hartford, Conn.,

for $4,000, and Peabody, of Wheeling, for $2,500—in all $6,500. The property was valued at about $15,000 or $20,000."

"The destruction of the old Thomas P. Ray residence removes one of the grandest buildings, in its time, ever erected in or near Morgantown."

**Morgantown Female Seminary.** "The annual catalogue of this Institution has just been issued from the Post Job Printing office, and we find in it evidences of greatly increased popularity of the above named school.—Mrs. J. R. Moore, the very estimable and accomplished Principal, has been conducting the Institution with great success for three years, and now has the proud satisfaction of seeing it rank second to none in the State."[12]

**Free Schools.** In his report for 1873, Superintendent Henry L. Cox reported "that there is no longer a question as to whether the people desire schools." An epidemic of measles (and other diseases) during the year, however, resulted in low attendance and short terms in schools in many sections of the county. Forty-eight teachers were granted certificates, eight receiving No. 1, thirty-three No. 2, six No. 3, and one No. 4.[13]

**Arnettsville Methodist Episcopal Church.** William Arnett and his wife Drusella in 1873 deeded to Stephen G. West, John H. Coogle, and William Arnett, trustees of the Arnettsville Methodist Episcopal congregation, a plot of ground along the Fairmont Pike ten miles south of Morgantown as the site of a new church building.[14]

**Halleck Church is Dedicated.** On a beautiful day in August 1873, a new frame building was dedicated by the Halleck Methodist Episcopal congregation. The program was conducted by Dr. J. Wesley Webb, presiding elder, and Rev. J. W. Hess, pastor. Dr. Alexander Martin, president of West Virginia University, delivered the morning sermon, and Dr. Webb spoke in the afternoon.

The first building on the site, a hewed log structure, was built in 1854. The ground was deeded June 9, 1856, by Mr. and Mrs.

12. *Morgantown Weekly Post*, May 17, 1873.
13. Wiley, p. 390.
14. Dodds and Dodds, *Churches of Monongalia County*, p. 101.

Joseph Smith to the church's trustees, Oliver P. McRae, Hugh Austin, Joseph Smith, John Stevens, Thomas Miller, Samuel Stevens, and Jacob Cartwright.[15]

**Burning of the Methodist Church.** On Wednesday night, November 12, 1873, "about nine o'clock, flames were discovered issuing from the roof of the Methodist . . . Protestant or 'Reform' Church of this place, and the alarm of fire was sounded. A stiff gale was blowing, and by the time fifty people arrived on the ground the entire roof was wrapped in fire and all hope of saving the building abandoned. An effort was made to save the movable articles inside the Church, which was partially successful—the clock, a few chairs, the pastor's Bible, and some of the lamps being secured, while the Library was consumed, together with most of the carpet on the floor.

"There had been prayer meeting in the Church that evening, and a defective chimney was the cause of the fire. . . .

"Fortunately the wind was blowing *from* instead of towards the heart of the town, and the vast sheet of flame threw up and scattered the immense volume of sparks far over the edge of the town. . . . Brave men . . . stood up manfully and defended their neighbors' property from destruction.

". . . Some idea of the heat may be formed when search was made for the bell which hung in the cupola. Only two small pieces of it could be found, and they were melted into odd shapes!"[16]

**The Eureka Mills.** The first gristmill within the borough limits of Morgantown, a steam flouring mill, was started by Col. Francis Thompson in the fall of 1873 at the wharf at the foot of Walnut Street. Known as the Eureka Mills, it was run by an engine of fifty-six horsepower and its grinding capacity was nine bushels of grain per hour. Up until that time Morgantown had

15. Dodds and Dodds, *Churches of Monongalia County*, p. 142. See also Elijah McRae, *History of Halleck Community*, typescript in West Virginia University Library (no date) 10 pp. The name Halleck honors the Union general in the Civil War, Henry Wagner Halleck (1815-1872).

16. *Morgantown Weekly Post*, November 22, 1873. See also various historical pamphlets published by the Spruce Street United Methodist Church, the present name of the congregation, courtesy of Rev. Marvan G. Frame and C. Roy Moyers.

depended on the Kerns-Rogers mill for grinding (*Monongalia Story*, vol. 2, pp. 121, 123, 148, 331, 429).

Colonel Thompson had been engaged in the Oregon War (p. 419) and in 1861 raised the first company in the county for the Federal service. He was in the battle of Droop Mountain, where his outfit was distinguished for heroism. He was commissioned colonel April 21, 1864.[17]

**Hugh Evans.** The original proprietor of Evansville, Hugh Evans, died in the town his son James founded, in 1873, aged 104 years. He was born in 1769 in what was later to be Monongalia County and moved about 1800 to the area later to be Evansville. "He became an active, successful and prominent farmer and a man of influence in the business and political circles" of Preston County, serving a number of years as justice of the peace and one term as sheriff.

He married Sarah Thomas and they had seven children, namely, Hugh, Samuel, William, Rawley, James, Sarah, and Nancy.[18]

**Samuel Snyder.** A prosperous and well-to-do farmer of Georgetown, Samuel Snyder, died March 31, 1873. He was a son of David and Elizabeth Snyder, and was fifty-seven years of age.

Samuel Snyder was married to Lydia A. Thorn and they had seven children. She died in 1847, at the age of thirty-five years and he married as his second wife Hulda Waters. His third marriage was with Elizabeth Summers and they had seven children, including Ashville S. Snyder, a farmer of Indian Creek.[19]

**Robert Painter Hennen.** One of Morgantown's first expert cabinetmakers, Robert P. Hennen, died October 30, 1873, and was buried in the new Oak Grove Cemetery, alongside his wife, Elizabeth (Wilkins), who had died October 24, 1871. Mr. Hennen, the son of Matthew, Jr., and Nancy Hennen, was born in Greene County, Pennsylvania, December 22, 1805. He and Elizabeth were married in Monongalia County by Dr. Charles McLane and resided throughout their married life in Morgantown.

17. Wiley, pp. 529-31, 579; Callahan, *Making of Morgantown*, pp. 203, 209.

18. *Cyclopedia of Taylor County*, p. 87; Morton, *History of Preston County*, vol. 1, pp. 343, 427.

19. *Cyclopedia of Monongalia County*, pp. 202, 203.

His first land purchase was a lot on Front Street, in 1831, where he began the manufacture of high grade furniture, about 1840. His son, Matthew, joined him in the business in 1865 and after Robert's death, Matthew's brother, Frederick, became associated, the business being known as Hennen Brothers, adding the manufacture of caskets and coffins to items previously made.

Robert and Elizabeth had eight children, Valinda Ann, Nancy Catherine, Helen Samantha, Matthew, Samuel E., Sarah Isabel, Frederick Augustus, and Emily F.[20]

**Jacob Sine.** A farmer of Dolls Run, Jacob Sine, son of William and Margaret (Christy) Sine, died November 23, 1873. He was born September 12, 1796. He was twice married, the first time to Rebecca Piles, by whom he had five children, namely, Elizabeth (married Joseph Piles), William, Amelia (married John West), Margaret (married Asbury T. Hough), and Jacob, Jr. By his second wife, Hannah Piles, he had one son, Jackson.

**Eli Morris.** A farmer of Clay Township, Eli Morris, died October 30, 1873. He was born May 12, 1823, the son of Barton and Comfort Morris. He married Delila Fetty and they were the parents of Mary Elizabeth, John Calvin, David Franklin, Louisa, and Luther.[21]

**Jacob Statler.** A farmer of Clay Township, Jacob Statler, died November 20, 1873. The son of John and Eve Statler (*Monongalia Story*, vol. 2, p. 344, etc.), he was born June 30, 1805. He married Elizabeth Walker and they were the parents of Susanna, Sarah, Plezzy Ann, Catherine, and John.

**Road Conditions.** Roads, while much improved in a half century, were still unsurfaced, dusty in summer, muddy in winter. Only a few were "macadamized," most of these poorly done. In summer traveling was easy and pleasant:

"Thursday of last week we made a flying trip to Fairmont, with our neighbor, Mr. J. C. Wallace, who drove us up to the 'mountain city' behind a pair of his horses in exactly *two hours and three quarters.*"[22]

20. Dorothy T. Hennen, *Hennen's Choice*, vol. 1, pp. 54, 55.
21. Core, *Chronicles of Core*, p. 109.
22. *Morgantown Weekly Post*, September 20, 1873.

But in winter it was quite different:

"The roads of this county are in a worse condition at the present time than they have been for the past ten years. It is almost impossible for four horses to haul a carriage or hack containing four passengers twenty miles on the Fairmont or Uniontown roads. How gladly we would pay a road tax if one large enough were imposed to *thoroughly* McAdamize our turnpikes."[23]

**Pedlar Run.** A store was started on Pedlar Run October 27, 1873, by Alphaeus Garrison and on June 22, 1874, a post office called Pedlars Run was opened in the store, with the storekeeper as postmaster. A correspondent noted: "I suppose you are not much acquainted with our little city. . . . We have one store, kept by Captain Garrison, . . . one church, one school house, chair factory, photograph gallery, and we are to have a blacksmith next week. Some day if you should happen to be with us you would think the war had broke out again, so many covered wagons passing—hucksters from Pittsburgh. . . . We have a singing school going on at Core's frame—Sampson Lough, teacher."[24]

**County and Borough Government.** George C. Sturgiss became prosecuting attorney of the county court and W. S. Cobun clerk.

District levies in 1873 were as follows:

|  | Road | School | Building |
|---|---|---|---|
| Clinton | . . . | $0.20 | $0.05 |
| Morgan | . . . | .05 | .02½ |
| Union | . . . | .10 | .02 |
| Cass | . . . | .10 | . . . |
| Grant | . . . | .16 | .04 |
| Clay | . . . | .10 | .05 |
| Battelle | . . . | .03 | . . . |
| Morgantown | . . . | .20 | .35 |

23. *Morgantown Weekly Post*, December 27, 1873.
24. *Morgantown Weekly Post*, March 28, 1874.

Joseph Moreland was mayor of Morgantown, Charles McLane recorder, and James Odbert sergeant. Members of council were David H. Chadwick, L. S. Hough, William N. Jarrett, Ed Shisler, and George W. McVicker.

**Miscellany.** In 1873: Susanna Piles died at the age of ninety and George P. Wilson at the age of ninety-six (Wiley, p. 472). . . . F. H. St. Clair opened the St. Clair House, on Lot 23, in Morgantown (Wiley, p. 587). . . . Charles J. Johnson opened a wagon-making and blacksmith shop at Rock Forge (Wiley, p. 655). . . . Capt. Alphaeus Garrison opened a store on Pedlar Run (Wiley, p. 755). . . . Nimrod, son of Col. Dudley Evans, died (Callahan, p. 79). . . . Hennen Brothers succeeded Robert Hennen and Son as manufacturers of high grade furniture in Morgantown (Callahan, p. 136). . . . The Morgantown council began a policy of annual macadamizing of the principal streets (Callahan, p. 197). . . . A proposal to use gas for street lights met with "conscientious" objection (Callahan, p. 198). . . . The financial crisis of 1873 only temporarily postponed the construction of new houses in Morgantown (Callahan, p. 207). . . . The council established a "chain-gang" to enable jail inmates to pay their fines by working on the streets (Callahan, p. 216). . . . The Mount Union Methodist Church building was repaired (Dodds and Dodds, p. 152). . . . The *Pittsburgh Gazette* carried a two-and-one-half column description of the Cheat River Valley (reprinted in the *Morgantown Weekly Post*, March 22, 1873). . . . Peter A. Layton, pioneer Cassville merchant, died September 6, aged eighty years (*Chronicle of Core*, p. 109).

# CHAPTER NINETY-EIGHT

# 1874

The Civil War had placed a large strain on the credit of the national government, and Congress had to devise some new system of banking, a unified and safe system that would operate the same way in all parts of the country. A new banking law, providing for the establishment of national banks, was passed in February 1863 and revised June 3, 1864. The minimum capital for a national bank in a city of less than six thousand people was fixed at fifty thousand dollars. The Merchants' National Bank (see p. 581) was the first national bank in Monongalia County.

State banks continued to exist, under banking methods somewhat similar to national banks, but they could be chartered with much less capital. A state bank was organized in Morgantown in 1874.

**The Morgantown Bank.** The commercial concern known as Hoffman and Company (see p. 614) was succeeded by the Morgantown Bank, chartered March 23, 1874. Among its organizers were J. H. Hoffman, William Price, George B. Morris, William M. Jones, John Sutton, and William Lyons. William Price was elected the first president and J. H. Hoffman cashier.

J. H. Hoffman was born in Frederick, Maryland, February 3, 1819. He engaged in business in Baltimore and moved to Frostburg in 1836, then in 1846 to Bruceton Mills, a place he named for his stepfather, George Bruce. He engaged in a large milling and mercantile business there and moved to Morgantown in 1860.[1]

**Free Schools.** The county school enumeration for 1874 was 4,948, of whom 3,443 attended school; the average daily at-

1. Wiley, pp. 463, 464; Callahan, *Making of Morgantown*, p. 213.

tendance was 2,337. Superintendent H. L. Cox pointed out in his report that the daily attendance was less than 50 percent of the enumeration, and declared that "here lies the great obstacle to our success." Alexander L. Wade was employed to visit the schools and held thirty-one educational meetings, which were well attended. The county superintendent's salary was $169.[2]

**The University.** The cornerstone of a new building on the university campus, called New Hall, later simply "University Building,"[3] was laid June 18, 1874, on the site of the old Woodburn Seminary. The dimensions of the building to be constructed were given as 104 feet long by 61 feet wide, and 96 feet high, with four stories.[4]

A vocal music department was added, with D. B. Purinton as instructor.[5]

William ("Doctor") Danser was made janitor, replacing William Pastorius. As an appointee of the board of regents, Danser was free from control either by the president or the superintendent of grounds and buildings and this would lead to some interesting developments.[6]

The graduating class was composed of seven young men. The total enrollment in the 1873-74 term was 138 men.

A monthly paper, the *University Bulletin*, was started by William L. Jacobs and Julian E. Fleming.[7] It was composed of sixteen pages, six by nine, printed in brevier type and sold for fifty cents a year.

Student housing was beginning to be scarce, and in 1874 William Dunn built a large two-story boarding house at the corner of Front and Hough streets.

**County Poor House.** A new home for the indigent was constructed in 1874 on Scotts Run a half-mile below Cassville, replacing an earlier home just south of Morgantown on the Clarksburg road. The property, and a dwelling-house on it, cost $2,000. A building committee composed of Emrod Tennant,

2. Wiley, pp. 390, 391.
3. Still later called Woodburn Hall; it was completed in 1876, at a total cost of $41,500.
4. Wiley, p. 406.
5. Wiley, pp. 405, 410. Purinton was author of "College Songs for West Virginia University" (1875).
6. Ambler, *History of Education in West Virginia*, p. 193.
7. It lasted only two years, expiring in 1876.

Fig. 126. The county poor house at Cassville, constructed 1874. (Photo courtesy Mrs. John F. Morris and Mrs. Elizabeth Bish.)

Alpheus Yeager, and Barton Core awarded the contract for construction of the new building to —— Haines for $4,200. The structure was a two-story brick building, thirty by forty feet in dimension. Mrs. Alice Carothers was employed as the first caretaker.[8]

The earlier poor house, which it replaced, stood along the Evansville Pike just south of Morgantown.

**Andrew Brown.** One of the best known citizens of Monongalia County, Andrew Brown, died at Browns Mill on October 11, 1874. He was born March 9, 1796, the son of Adam and Christina (Statler) Brown. He was raised on a farm on Dunkard Creek.

He married Martha, daughter of David Worley, July 5, 1821, and their children were Dr. Aphaeus W., Louisa J. (married Dr. J. V. Boughner), Melissa A., Albert, and Lee Roy J. He was a farmer and a miller, and took an active interest in public affairs. He was appointed justice of the peace in 1832 and served until

8. Wiley, p. 708.

Fig. 127. Dr. Absalom Morris Jarrett. (From Wiley's *History of Monongalia County*.)

Fig. 128. William Edmund Watson. (From Wiley's *History of Monongalia County*.)

Fig. 129. Samuel Calvin Stewart. (From Wiley's *History of Monongalia County*.)

Fig. 130. Andrew Brown. (From Wiley's *History of Monongalia County*.)

1851. In 1846 he was nominated by the Whig party as a candidate for the house of delegates and, although the county was strongly Democratic, he was elected. He was again nominated in 1859 and again elected.

When the Civil War broke out he took a strong stand against secession and throughout the war was a firm and uncompromising supporter of the Union (see p. 556).

"He was a man of great industry and energy, and accumulated a considerable fortune. Of strict integrity, possessing much natural talent and strong common-sense, always taking an active part in public questions and enterprises, a reader and thinker, one of the leading men of his neighborhood, he was an eminently useful man to the community and the county."[9]

**Thomas Atha.** A farmer of Lincoln District, Marion County, Thomas Atha, died in 1874. He was a son of Jacob Atha, who settled in Monongalia County, on Dunkard Mill Run, about 1820. Thomas Atha married Nancy Sutton and they had seven sons and one daughter. "As a farmer he manifested great enterprise, and was possessed of considerable financial ability."[10]

**George Dent Martin.** A mechanic and cabinetmaker, George Dent Martin, died in Doddridge County in 1874. He was born near Jimtown in 1801, the son of Col. Rawley Evans and Margaret Dent Martin. He had a training as a mechanic and migrated to Indiana in 1838, remaining there until 1848, when he returned to Virginia and located in Marion County.

He married Charlotte, daughter of Boaz Basnett, of Cassville, and they had ten children, including, Matilda, John D., Nimrod (an early mail carrier from Morgantown to Wheeling), William, Zephaniah (a merchant of Amos), Marmaduke D., Mary (married Marion Stevens), and Julia (married Albert Ammons).[11]

**"What a Country!"** On Wednesday morning, the thirty-first of December, 1873, "the thermometer stood at 10 degrees below zero—the coldest day of the season, and on Sunday following, the mercury was up to 75°, doors and windows were thrown open throughout the town, and Dr. Morris came out in his

9. Wiley, pp. 753, 754; *Cyclopedia of Monongalia County*, p. 185.
10. *Cyclopedia of Marion County*, p. 206.
11. *Cyclopedia of Marion County*, pp. 71, 72.

white linen! One week it's cold enough to freeze ice four inches thick—the next we have regular 'fourth of July' weather. What a country!"[12]

**Borough Government.** Joseph Moreland was serving his third year as mayor of Morgantown. C. W. Finnell, Jr., was recorder, Jacob Kiger, sergeant, and E. Shisler, treasurer. Members of council were David H. Chadwick, L. S. Hough, Matthew Hennen, Ed Shisler, and H. W. Brock.

**Miscellany.** In 1874: Moses Strosnider built a woolen mill on Dunkard Creek at Strosnider's Mill (Wiley, p. 259). . . . W. L. Boughner was admitted to the county bar on September 10 (Wiley, p. 318). . . . White Day Grange No. 331 was organized at Smithtown by Patrons of Husbandry (Wiley, pp. 550, 551). . . . W. C. McGrew, Thornton Pickenpaugh, and T. J. Meeks and Company opened stores in Morgantown (Wiley, pp. 581, 582, 583). . . . Benjamin Ryan was operating the National Hotel (Wiley, p. 586). . . . Henry Koontz built a mill at Easton (Wiley, p. 676). . . . Harriet, wife of Joseph Lowry, died; she was born in 1789, the daughter of Henry and Rebecca Dering (Callahan, p. 85). . . . Margaret, widow of Mathew Gay, died; she was born in 1798, the daughter of Alexander and Volinder Smith (Callahan, p. 91). . . . Dr. H. N. Mackey began the practice of medicine in Morgantown, giving special attention to surgery and to eye and ear troubles (Callahan, p. 214). . . . The steamboat *West Virginia*, which had been operating on a fairly regular schedule between Morgantown and New Geneva since 1871, was sold to a company which thereafter used it between New Geneva and Pittsburgh (Callahan, p. 220). . . . Morgantown Episcopalians held services once a month in the old Monongalia Academy building under the direction of Rev. G. A. Gibbons, rector of the Fairmont Church (Dodds and Dodds, p. 75). . . . Mr. Enoch Evans, the oldest man in the county, died February 22; he was ninety-seven years old in December (*Morgantown Weekly Post*, February 28, 1874). . . . Mrs. Nackey Clark, mother of Jacob Blue, died January 18, 1874, aged eighty years. She was formerly the property of Larkin H. Dorsey and was familiarly known as "Aunt Nackey." (*Morgantown Weekly Post*, January 24, 1874).

12. *Morgantown Weekly Post*, January 10, 1874.

# CHAPTER NINETY-NINE

# 1875

For those beginning the study of the culture of different places or different times, one of the first questions that comes to mind is, "What did they do to pass the time away?" In the 1870s, of course, automobiles, telephones, radio, television were as yet unheard of. Even so, people of that day in Monongalia County had few problems in keeping themselves entertained.

**Social Life in the Seventies.** Parties of various kinds were frequent, especially among the young people, including fishing parties, masquerade parties, and ice-cream parties. The ice cream was made by hand, using ice cut from the rivers or creeks and stored in sawdust bins. A relatively new game, called baseball, invented by Abner Doubleday at Cooperstown, New York, in 1839, was already popular in Monongalia County. There were skating parties, both on ice and on roller skates, band concerts at the fairgrounds, riding and driving on the racetrack or on county roads, festivals and circuses.

Among community events contributing to social life were patriotic celebrations and great political rallies, along with humorous post-election stunts to pay pre-election bets, such as pushing a victor down High Street in a wheelbarrow.

Concerts were well attended and there were three popular local bands, the Comet Band, the Home Band, and Walter A. Mestrezat's Band.

The annual county fair, managed by a local committee, was an occasion of social importance. At the fairgrounds, in a new section called Greenmont, being developed by Morgantown's first real estate agent, ample space was provided for exhibits, and there was a racetrack.

Fig. 131. Skating on the Monongahela River. (Sketch by Diane Lenhart.)

Spelling matches were popular throughout the county, usually held in schoolhouses, at which people of the local communities gathered for pleasure and entertainment. Through contests
much community spirit was aroused. Now that there were free
schools, there were many more buildings and much more use
made of them.

Hunting was another popular activity in which men and boys
participated. Rabbits and squirrels were the chief targets; there
were scarcely any deer in the county in those days. Men's fishing parties often ended with the arrival of the ladies, bringing
food.

At church there were many opportunities for social enjoyment, especially at Thanksgiving, Christmas, and Easter, and at
special programs for raising money, such as the prettiest girl
contest. At Christmas, usually on Christmas Eve, a program was
given, a Christmas tree was revealed, and Santa Claus distributed
presents for everyone. Halloween was another "religious" holi-
day, with parades on High Street and much amusement, such as
placing the privy on the barn roof.

Buggy riding was one of the most popular and accepted ways of courting or "sparking." When a young man took out a girl for a Sunday afternoon buggy ride, much interest was displayed by local gossips, who predicted possible wedding dates.

Young men students at the university and young women students at the seminary contributed immensely to the social life of Morgantown, and especially to its courtships, which always attracted much attention on the part of others, who frequently published their observations in the newspapers.

"The girls of that day," says Callahan[1] "were reminded how much better were the girls of former days when their mothers were girls. By the older set they were criticized for their less breeding and refinement, for their loud and ostentatious dress and manners, for their freedom and lack of restraint, and for their lack of appreciation of advice and counsel."

At the university, social events were planned by the faculty and students. For example, in February 1871, the students, dressed in linen coats and chip hats, armed with bean poles or broom handles, marched downtown in a parade led by a martial band.

University students upon entrance were required to sign an agreement to obey the rules of the institution and to conduct themselves with propriety. The rules prohibited intoxication, smoking, betting, profanity, the carrying of concealed weapons, etc.

At the seminary many literary exercises and other entertainments were open to the public. Festivals and fairs, presented by the young ladies under the direction of Mrs. Elizabeth Moore, always attracted good crowds. Occasionally, theatrical productions were presented in the auditorium of the old academy building (corner of Spruce and Walnut streets), which was used as a theater. There was no theater building in the town.

A daily social activity was standing in front of the post office waiting for the mail to be sorted, following the arrival of the mail hack from Fairmont. This provided opportunity for neighborhood gossip and political discussions. In winter it was less pleasant, however, and a newspaper editor proposed to reduce the crowd by eliminating about seventy-five men who

1. Callahan, *Making of Morgantown*, p. 233.

monopolized the delivery window while a dozen or so chilled businessmen were losing time from their business.[2]

**Slack Water Progress.** The work on the stone lock at Hoards Rocks (see p. 656) having been suspended because the money ran out, J. Marshall Hagans, member of Congress from Morgantown, in 1875 secured an appropriation of $22,000 to continue work on the lock. He also secured the passage of an act authorizing a survey of the Monongahela River from Morgantown to Fairmont. This survey was made under the direction of Capt. T. P. Roberts, whose report gave the distance as twenty-eight miles, with a fall of fifty-five feet in the river, which would require six dams.[3]

**A Graduating System for Country Schools.** Alexander L. Wade, on August 13, 1875, was elected county superintendent of schools. The son of George and Anna Wade (see p. 283), he was born near Rushville, Indiana, February 1, 1832, and came with his parents to Monongalia County in 1839. His father died in 1846 and Alexander, the eldest of five children, had to aid his mother in supporting the family. "He had early imbibed a love for reading and an earnest desire to be a scholar. But schools were inferior and books were scarce, and his time was divided between labor and study, while his earnings went to buy bread for the family and books for the library."[4]

In 1848, being but sixteen years of age, he began teaching school, in a subscription school on Pedlar Run. He continued teaching until the beginning of the Civil War, working on the farm during the summer. "During all these years he was an earnest student, mastering, one by one, without an instructor, most of the English branches."

In 1861 he was elected clerk of the county court and in 1863 he was elected county recorder, a position he held until 1871, when he was named principal of the Morgantown public school. Superintendent Cox, in 1873, engaged him to study all the county schools and make recommendations. This continued until his election as county superintendent.

2. *Morgantown Weekly Post,* December 20, 1873.
3. Wiley, p. 130.
4. Wiley, pp. 371, 372. See also Mary I. Barbe, "The Life of Alexander L. Wade," *West Virginia History* 9 (1948):240-95.

"He had long entertained the belief that there is entirely too much waste in country school work; and, while County Superintendent, he saw this fact in a still clearer light. He saw that average students in academies and colleges complete more branches in a single year, than average pupils in country schools complete in the entire school period. After much careful study he became satisfied that the chief cause of difference is found in the fact, that in all higher schools there is a definite work to do, a definite time in which it ought to be done, and a test as to whether it is well done; while in country schools no such provisions exist. He, therefore, determined to introduce into the country schools of his county, a system of graduation, similar to that of academies and colleges."[5]

In 1874 he had begun to organize a program by grades, with a definite time for graduation, and he continued this program after he became county superintendent.

**The University.** The progress of the university was being hindered by conflicting plans and purposes of two parties, the pro-Southerners, or "Virginians," on the one hand, and the Northerners, or "Puritans" on the other. The differences involved such matters as coeducation, first proposed in 1871, the relation of the preparatory department to the university, questions of student discipline, and the nature of the curriculum. The Northerners generally favored coeducation, retention of the preparatory department, and rigid discipline in both social and educational matters, the Southerners were generally opposed to coeducation and retention of the preparatory department, and they resented the Puritan conceived "Code of Laws and Regulations" as an infringement upon liberties guaranteed in the Bill of Rights.

Political advantages were increasingly with the "Virginians." An act of April 12, 1873, reduced the number of regents from eleven to nine and the result was to place the Democrats in control. Colonel D. D. Johnson became president of the board, replacing Dr. T. H. Logan, Republican, who had served since 1869. At the same time George M. Hagans, Republican, gave way to L. S. Hough as chairman of the executive committee.

5. Wiley, pp. 373, 374. See also Ambler, *History of Education in West Virginia*, p. 163.

Numerous changes in faculty assignments were made, often not happily received. The situation was increasingly trying to President Alexander Martin and his trials were complicated by the Panic of 1873, which reduced college enrollments throughout the country. The enrollment at West Virginia University gradually decreased from 166 in the 1870-71 term; there were 159 in 1871-72, 144 in 1872-73, 138 in 1873-74, 125 in 1874-75, only 96 in the 1875-76 term.

President Martin signified his intention to resign and the regents hastened his decision through a secret meeting held at Martinsburg on August 11-12, at which time all university professorships and tutorships were declared vacant. The regents then reelected those of the faculty "deemed worthy." Vice-President John W. Scott, a Presbyterian minister, was made acting president effective September 6 and the regents placed advertisements in newspapers inviting applicants for vacant positions.[6]

John W. Scott was born in York County, Pennsylvania, in 1807, and graduated at Jefferson College in 1827. He also graduated from Princeton, served in the ministry, then was president of Washington College for twelve years. He was principal of Woodburn Seminary and was the last principal of Monongalia Academy.[7]

**Western Union Telegraph Company.** On July 1, 1875, the Pacific and Atlantic Telegraph Company, which had constructed the first telegraph line into the county, leased the line to the Western Union Telegraph Company for twenty years, the latter assuming the payment of 4 percent per annum on the $2 million stock of the former.

The first operator in Morgantown, Alexander L. Wade, had been succeeded in 1870 by H. R. Dering, who moved the office to his hardware store. T. P. Reay was the third operator.[8]

**Valley Chapel Methodist Church.** A group of Methodists met in 1875 in the Henderson Schoolhouse for worship. Later they decided to build a church and selected a site along the Dunkard Creek Turnpike two miles west of Wadestown. The lot was

6. Ambler, *History of Education in West Virginia*, pp. 193, 194.
7. Wiley, pp. 417, 418.
8. Wiley, pp. 554, 555.

donated by J. V. Mapel to the first trustees, Moses Lough, W. S. Hillery, and Henry Whisler. The people furnished money, materials, and labor for construction of the church, which was called Valley Chapel.[9]

**Joshua Hunt.** A farmer of Maidsville, Joshua Hunt, died July 23, 1875, aged eighty-nine years and sixteen days. He was a native of New Jersey and lived successively in Fayette and Greene counties, Pennsylvania, before settling in 1819 at the place later called Maidsville. He married Sallie Robbins, who died February 29, 1865, aged seventy-nine years, and they had thirteen children, including Jesse Hunt, a Mannington merchant.[10]

**David Henderson.** A farmer of the Pedlar Run section of Clay District, David Henderson, died March 12, 1875. He was born April 18, 1806, in the same area, the son of James Henderson (see p. 85).

He married Elizabeth, a daughter of Levi Morris, and they had eight children, namely, Charlotte (married Alphaeus Garrison), Alphaeus (married Drusilla Core), Noah (married Narcissus Barrickman), Prudence (married A. J. Statler), Asa (married Delilah Barrickman), Silas (married Melinda Chisler), Michael, and William.[11]

**John Franklin Dering.** A son of pioneer settlers Henry and Rebecca Dering (*Monongalia Story*, vol. 2, pp. 350, 351), J. F. Dering, died May 1, 1875; he was born May 5, 1799. He was a farmer and owned land along the Monongahela River just south of Morgantown. He married Priscilla, daughter of George Dorsey, and their children were John S., George R., and Edmund W. S.[12]

**Fighting Fires.** The need for better fire-fighting equipment and methods in Morgantown was evident, although little was done about it between fires. A fire at the home of Mrs. Chadwick on High Street in 1875 was thus described:

9. Dodds and Dodds, *Churches of Monongalia County*, p. 135.
10. *Cyclopedia of Marion County*, p. 97.
11. *Cyclopedia of Monongalia County*, pp. 195, 196; *Chronicles of Core*, p. 112.
12. *175th Anniversary of Monongalia County*, p. 407.

Fig. 132. Bucket Brigade. (Sketch by Diane Lenhart.)

"Fire wagons, containing ladders and buckets, were hurried to the scene. Eager and excited men rushed into the building, hunting for the fire, with buckets of water. The smoke was so thick that the flames were unable to be found. Windows were smashed and plaster was knocked off. The fire was finally found in one room rented to students where a live coal had fallen from the open grate upon the floor. The fire, after once found, was quickly extinguished. Damages amounted to $150."[13]

**Borough Government.** E. Shisler was mayor of Morgantown in 1875, W. W. Dering recorder, Uriah Rider sergeant, and George C. Sturgiss treasurer. Members of council were L. S. Hough, E. H. Coombs, W. A. Robison, George C. Sturgiss and H. W. Brock.

**Miscellany.** In 1875: Another unsuccessful attempt was made to annex Battelle District to Marion County (Wiley, p. 102). . . . There was considerable agitation of a project to build a railroad from Mannington through western Monongalia

13. Callahan, *Making of Morgantown*, p. 217.

County to Waynesburg, Pennsylvania (Wiley, p. 113). . . . William C. McGrew succeeded E. H. Coombs as president of the county fair organization (Wiley, p. 248). . . . T. P. Jacobs was admitted to the county bar on September 16 (Wiley, p. 318). . . . H. G. West succeeded Prof. D. B. Purinton as president of the Goshen Baptist Sunday School Convention (Wiley, p. 450). . . . Samuel Johnson died April 9, aged seventy-four, his wife Mary, June 2, aged sixty-five (Wiley, p. 633). . . . The old Walnut Hill homestead of Col. John Evans (*Monongalia Story*, vol. 2, pp. 253-55) was purchased by O. H. Dille (Callahan, p. 79). . . . Hauling of heavy timbers over Morgantown streets in wet weather was prohibited by council (Callahan, p. 197). . . . W. F. Baker opened a music store, where organs, violins, sheet music, and medical supplies were offered for sale (Callahan, p. 210). . . . Fitch and Moreland opened a real estate office in Morgantown (Callahan, p. 211). . . . A survey was made by Pittsburgh men to see if there was a need for gas works in Morgantown (Callahan, p. 217). . . . An ordinance proposing to drive cows from Morgantown streets was defeated by a vote of ninety-one to thirty-five (Callahan, p. 218). . . . A new hack line to Fairmont, for passengers only, was established by Edward W. Shurtleff (Callahan, p. 219). . . . Extensive repairs were made to the Forks of Cheat Baptist Church (Dodds and Dodds, p. 148). . . . Rev. C. H. Conaway was pastor of the Miracle Run Methodist Church (Dodds and Dodds, p. 134).

# 1876

The year 1876 marked Monongalia County's centennial anniversary, as well as that of the nation, and plans were begun early for an appropriate celebration. W. T. Willey was chairman of the arrangements committee and Henry M. Morgan secretary. The celebration was held on the Fourth of July.

"No event," said a Morgantown newspaper,[1] "that has transpired in our town for time immemorial was so generally observed as the Centennial Celebration here on the 4th. Early in the morning immense crowds poured into town from every direction, in every conceivable means of conveyance. The rich and the poor, the high and the low, in carriages, wagon, on horseback and on foot, without regard to past or present, political or religious distinction, they assembled for a day of genuine pleasure, enjoyment and hearty patriotic demonstration. . . . The reverence which we feel for our noble fathers, who so earnestly labored to give us pure and independent government, was brilliantly manifested. . . . Though after the exercises had been concluded, a heavy rain commenced to fall, which made it extremely unpleasant for all those going home that evening, still they did the best they could to protect themselves, and departed for their homes with a feeling of serene satisfaction and supreme contentment over the manner in which the day had been passed, and with renewed zeal for the perpetual and enduring prosperity and Union."

**The Centennial Celebration.** Another newspaper[2] provided further details: "The celebration in Monongalia County, West Virginia, on Tuesday, July 4th, 1876, of the one hundredth anni-

1. The *New Dominion*, July 8, 1876.
2. *Morgantown Weekly Post*, July 8, 1876.

versary of American Independence and the one hundredth anniversary of the organization of Monongalia County, will long be remembered by our children after the present generation has passed away. . . .

"At 3.30 o'clock Tuesday morning, the signal was given for a general ringing of bells. The clear notes of the old bell in the cupola of the court-house, immediately under the statue of Patrick Henry, one of Virginia's patriotic sons, rang out on the still air of that balmy July morning with music sweet to the American heart. Then followed the ponderous strokes of the sledgehammer upon the big bell at the University, and the ringing of the old Monongalia Academy bell, and all the church bells in town."

An impressive parade marched down the streets. "The attractive feature at the head of the procession was a splendid representation of 'Brother Jonathan'; personated by John Guseman. John was on horseback, decked out in the stars and stripes. His horse was covered with a blanket of stars and stripes, and he wore a suit of the same. The short breeches, strapped to the bottoms of his boots, the gaunt figure, the hatchet-faced visage, the keen Yankee *contour* in every respect, was a real 'Uncle Sam' in costume and figure. . . . The day indeed was a glorious one, in which we will all recur in the future with patriotic pride and joyful recollection."

Following "Brother Jonathan," the procession was headed by the artillery under command of Col. Frank W. Thompson. Next came two martial bands, one from Fayette County, Pennsylvania, composed of Henry, John, and Ulysses Scott, and Philip and Ad. Lyons, the other the Monongalia band, "headed by Silas Sinclair, fifer, and the irrepressible Riley Walker on the tenor drum." Then came citizens, then "Indians" (boys decked out in full Indian costume). A brass band from Morris Cross Roads, Pennsylvania, came next, composed of Thomas F. Protzman, leader, Martin Hope, Ira Conn, Paton B. Protzman, George Hertzog, Hugh Scott, Amody Gans, Samuel Conn, James Frankenberry, "Abe" B. Hall, Jr., and A. Jackson Herdman. Black citizens closed the procession. After marching through the streets, the parade filed to the fairgrounds, where a national salute of thirty-eight guns was fired.

At the fairgrounds, after music by the band and a prayer by

Rev. A. A. Jimeson, a choir sang "1876," a patriotic ode. J. S. Boyers read the Declaration of Independence. The "Star Spangled Banner" (solo, duet, and chorus) was sung by T. P. Reay and J. M. Lazier, the chorus by all the people. John J. Brown gave a local historical oration, followed by Carl Reden's "Centennial Hymn" by the choir, and music by the band. The general historical oration was delivered by W. T. Willey and following music by the band came a recess for dinner. During the recess a centennial salute of one hundred guns was fired.

In the afternoon, the black citizens had an hour for the presentation of a program of their own making. Then came music by the band and at two o'clock an oration by Rev. J. R. Thompson; music by the choir followed, then "Old Hundred" by all the people, led by Dr. J. M. Lazier. The benediction was then pronounced and the "vast concourse" of people dismissed about four o'clock. The heavy rainstorm set in before all of them reached town.

In the evening came a balloon ascension, fireworks from the suspension bridge, and a pyrotechnic display at Robert L. Demain's on the hill south of town.

"It was one of the largest popular demonstrations ever witnessed in the county, participated in by nearly three thousand people, and not marred by the arrest of a single person by the police."[3]

**John J. Brown's Oration.** John J. Brown's oration was regarded as a masterly effort and the text was preserved.[4] His opening remarks follow:

"The voiceless tomb holds in eternal silence the unrecorded 'thoughts that breathed and words that burned' a hundred years ago. The patriots who then rallied around the unfurled standard of freedom, erected by their invincible courage, burning zeal, and patient and prolonged sufferings, this grand temple of liberty, under whose shadow we this day gather. More than forty millions of freemen are met to-day at the shrine of patriotism to worship, and to learn from tradition, from history, from eloquence, from poetry and song, the events of other years; and to renew at a common altar their pledges of fidelity to their coun-

3. See Wiley, pp. 157-62.
4. See Wiley, pp. 161, 162.

try, and to be baptized with the spirit of a hundred years ago. Those brave men who would have gathered around Washington in the mountains of West Augusta, had the cause of their country gone down amid the shock of battle on the eastern slopes of the Alleghenies, are now forever speechless and silent.

"The recorded events of the distant past alone remain to us. And, as the years go by, even these are yielding to those seen and unseen agencies, before whose power the solid brass and the enduring marble perish. Other generations will live when the record of those I address today has been made up, and they in turn make room for others.

'So the multitude goes, like the flowers or the weed
That withers away to let others succeed.
So the multitude comes, even those we behold,
To repeat every tale that has often been told.'

"As distance lends enchantment to the view, so time softens the asperities and hallows the memories of the past. History written amidst passing events is fraught with the angular harshness, the prejudices and excitements of the hour. As the azure hue covers and hides from our vision the huge rocks and deep ravines on the mountain-side, so may the record of this day conceal beneath the mantle of charity the imperfections of all, and breathe naught but the spirit of kindness."

Mr. Brown then went on, in the same eloquent terms, to tell of the early settlements, the formation and extent of the county, its participation in past wars, its courts of law, its county seat, its newspapers, banks, and post offices, its honored sons and daughters, its educational institutions and influences.

**The Philadelphia Exposition.** Over three hundred citizens of Monongalia County attended the exhibit of arts and industries at the Centennial Exposition in Philadelphia. Among exhibits from Monongalia County were sample boards of red cedar, spruce, white walnut, black walnut, white oak, hickory, yellow poplar, black locust, black cherry, white ash, sugar maple, linden, and chestnut, from Fairchild, Lawhead and Company, and curly walnut boards from Walter Mestrezatt.[5]

Among other entries were a "Pencil Drawing of H. W. Beech-

5. Wiley, pp. 162, 265.

er," by Perry Morris, and a "Pencil Drawing of H. L. Cox," by W. C. Shaffer, both from the "Free School, Morgantown."[6]

**Hoards Rocks Dam.** In another step towards providing slack water navigation for Morgantown, a contract was awarded in March 1876 for construction of the dam across the Mononga-hela River at Hoards Rocks. The contract went to Smith and Hawkins, of Cincinnati, for fifty thousand dollars. The work was to be completed by November 15, but was suspended in October because of exhaustion of the funds and the failure of Congress to provide further appropriations.[7]

**Lumbering Operations.** Monongalia County at the time of its first settlement was mostly covered with heavy forests of large timber, chiefly oak, beech, maple, walnut, and chestnut.[8] Trees at first were mostly a nuisance, since they had to be removed before agricultural crops could be grown. Often the logs were simply rolled into heaps and burned.

Later the lumber became more valuable and water-powered sawmills were located in many communities. Hundreds of water mills operated in western Virginia during the first half of the nineteenth century and as late as 1860, seven-eighths of the lumber sawed in the area was by waterpower.[9]

Little by little, however, steam engines were being harnessed to sawmills and came steadily to be of more importance.

As the lumber industry grew it became necessary to transport the logs greater distances in order to get them to the mill. Along the rivers, such as the Monongahela or Cheat, the logs were dragged down to the water and made into rafts, an average raft carrying about seventy logs and about twenty-five thousand feet of lumber. In 1876 it was estimated that fifty thousand dollars worth of timber in logs was floated down the Monongahela by Morgantown.[10]

On the "Big Survey," a large tract of land lying between the Kingwood Pike and the Evansville Pike, southeast of Morgan-

6. Wiley, p. 381.
7. Wiley, pp. 130, 131.
8. See *The Monongalia Story*, vol. 1, pp. 50-53, 59-65, 69-73.
9. J. H. Diss Debar, *The West Virginia Handbook and Immigrants Guide* (1870), p. 112.
10. Roy B. Clarkson, *Tumult on the Mountains* (1964), pp. 19-22, 48, 49; Wiley, p. 238.

Fig. 133. Logs floating on the Monongahela River at Morgantown, from a broken boom upstream. (Photo by W. E. Rumsey.)

town, Griffith, Brewster and Company operated a large steam sawmill which did a considerable business for some years.

**The New Dominion.** A Democratic weekly newspaper, the *New Dominion*, in competition with the Republican *Morgantown Weekly Post*, was established April 11, 1876, by William L. Jacobs and Julian E. Fleming, issued as a quarto, twenty-six by forty inches, forty columns, two dollars a year. Fleming became the sole proprietor in October.

Fig. 134. Capt. Alphaeus Garrison. (From Wiley's *History of Monongalia County*.)

Fig. 135. Capt. Oliver P. Jolliffe. (From Wiley's *History of Monongalia County*.)

The year before, in Kansas City, Jacobs and Fleming has discussed the project of starting a Democratic paper in Morgantown; "and, in faith of a great future for West Virginia, selected as the name of their paper the title of 'New Dominion', reasoning as Virginia was the 'Old Dominion', why should not West Virginia become the New Dominion."[11]

Julian E. Fleming[12] was born in Morgantown October 14, 1852, the son of George W. and Sarah J. (Evans) Fleming. He

11. Wiley, pp. 427, 438, 439.
12. *Cyclopedia of Monongalia County*, pp. 131-33.

attended West Virginia University and from 1874 to 1876 engaged in publishing the *University Bulletin* (p. 676).

In 1876 the *Dominion* (thirteen by twenty inches, four pages, twenty columns) was issued daily during Commencement Week.

**Thomas J. West.** A Monongalia County native, Thomas J. West, son of Nathaniel West, in 1876 was elected state treasurer. He was born in this county in 1830, educated at Smithfield, Pennsylvania, and then settled in Harrison County. He was elected to the legislature in 1870.[13]

**Free Schools.** The first common school diplomas, under A. L. Wade's new "Graduating System," were granted in the spring of 1876. The first common school catalog was published in autumn of the same year. The system was exciting the attention of educators all over the country.[14]

The first annual examination was held, beginning February 25, and one each day thereafter until March 11. The examiners were A. L. Wade, H. L. Cox, Prof. F. S. Lyon, of West Virginia University, and W. R. White, former state superintendent. Of 261 advanced students who entered the class, 196 completed the course and received diplomas.[15]

Mr. Wade visited every school in the county and held forty-three educational meetings at night, assisted by "representative men, professors in the University, teachers, ministers, physicians, farmers and mechanics." Three new schoolhouses were built, one burned down. The superintendent's salary was $298.50.[16]

**The University.** The resignation of President Alexander Martin, hastened by the action of the board of regents (p. 686) caused considerable dissension. Although he had been criticized because of his alleged mercenary interest in Morgantown and because of his "uncompromising and tactless puritanism," the

13. Wiley, p. 296.
14. Wiley, p. 374.
15. Wiley, p. 378.
16. Wiley, p. 391.

general public felt that the action of the regents against him was "nasty" and unfortunate.[17]

Fig. 136. The New Hall (later University Hall), completed in 1876. (Courtesy West Virginia University Library.)

Under the acting presidency of Vice-President John W. Scott the university became "a rapidly disappearing quantity," with only ninety-three students enrolled. The Reverend Mr. Scott agitated admission of females as a means of increasing the enrollment, but, while this caused considerable heated debate, it did not improve the situation. The regents offered the presidency to W. T. Willey, a "Northern Methodist" and a Republican, but two Democrats on the board held out against him, and Willey declined, saying, "I, being a Republican and a member of the M. E. Church, as was Dr. Martin, would be obnoxious to the same objections."[18]

There were nine graduates in 1876.[19]

17. The Reverend Mr. Martin, meanwhile, had become president of Indiana Asbury University, Greencastle, Ind., an institution which he developed into DePauw University. He died there December 16, 1893. Wilding, *Promoted Pioneer Preachers*, pp. 121, 122.

18. Ambler, *History of Education in West Virginia*, pp. 194-96.

19. Wiley, p. 423.

**Churches in the Seventies.** Ministers of the Morgantown Station, Methodist Episcopal Church were: 1868-70, E. T. Pitcher; 1870-73, W. M. Mullenix; 1873-76, E. W. Ryan; 1876, J. R. Thompson.[20] Presiding elders were: 1866-70, J. B. Blakeney; 1870-74, J. W. Webb; 1874-77, Samuel Steele. Sunday school superintendents were: 1868-70, G. C. Sturgiss; 1870, Adam W. Lorentz; 1871-74, G. M. Hagans; 1875-78, G. C. Sturgiss.[21]

Ministers in charge at the Morgantown Presbyterian Church were: 1869-71, Robert White; 1871-78, A. A. Jimeson. Among ruling elders were: 1870, Isaac J. Newkirk; 1872, John A. Dille.[22] The Sugar Grove Church, in Grant District, was under the care of these pastors.[23]

Morgantown Methodist Protestants were also worshipping in the Monongalia Academy, following the destruction of their church on Long Alley in 1872. John Cowan was minister in 1876.[24]

Ministers serving the Smithtown Circuit of the Methodist Episcopal Church were: 1868-71, J. W. Hess; 1871-72, J. F. Snodgrass; 1872-73, W. C. Snodgrass; 1873-76, F. G. W. Ford; 1876-78, N. B. Johnson.

Ministers at the Forks of Cheat Baptist Church were: 1871, William Fourtney; 1872, John A. Simpson; 1874, D. W. Rogers and S. N. Rogers; 1876, Robert Miller.

At the Avery Methodist Church ministers were: 1869-70, P. T. Laishley; 1871, Peter T. Conway; 1872, John G. McCarty; 1873, Leonard Warman; 1874-75, William West; 1875-76, Eli J. Wilson.

Ministers serving the Monongalia Circuit (p. 302) were: 1870, J. J. Dolliver; 1871, J. M. Warden, C. J. Trippett;[25] 1872, J. M. Warden, J. W. Huggans; 1873, J. M. Warden, David Tasker;

20. For biography of John Rhey Thompson, see Wilding, *Promoted Pioneer Preachers*, p. 124.
21. Wiley, pp. 590, 591.
22. Wiley, p. 592.
23. Wiley, p. 729.
24. Wiley, pp. 594, 595; Barnes, *The Methodist Protestant Church in West Virginia*, pp. 116, 117.
25. Caleb J. Trippett was born near Morgantown May 14, 1845, and died at Ravenswood August 7, 1898. He married Ophelia A. Riggs, "who shared with him the trials and triumphs of an itinerant life." Wilding, *Promoted Pioneer Preachers*, p. 70.

1874, J. A. Fullerton, J. W. Satterfield; 1875, J. F. Snodgrass, W. N. Stewart; 1876, J. F. Snodgrass.

**Trinity Parish.** Trinity Parish, Protestant Episcopal Church, composed of Morgan, Grant, and Union districts, was organized February 12, 1876, at the house of Thomas Rogers. The parish was received into the Diocese of Virginia in May. Services were held in the old Monongalia Academy.[26]

**Mellon's Chapel.** A Methodist church was built in 1876 near Rock Forge, on land donated by Thomas Mellon, father of Andrew Mellon. He owned considerable land in the area because of the deposits of iron ore it contained. In earlier times some of this ore had been smelted and made into pig iron at a furnace not far from the site of the church.

The first trustees were Frederick Breakiron, William Peterson, John E. Clark, Michael Nuce, and Henry Nuce. Sylvester Lowther was the first minister. The lumber used was hand-dressed in the churchyard, and the pews and pulpit were also made on the grounds.[27]

**Catholics and Mormons.** As the first century of Monongalia's history drew to its close, religious institutions of the citizens, who were almost wholly Anglo-Saxon in origin, remained almost wholly Protestant.

A Catholic priest had preached in Morgantown on Sunday, January 13, 1822, and scattered services were held in the county, but no organization had been effected except for a small one near Stewartstown.

"Nearly half a century ago a Mormon preached once or twice in the courthouse. He was so derisively received that he soon quitted the country, and neither he nor any of his brethren ever visited Monongalia afterward."[28]

26. Wiley, pp. 447, 593.
27. Dodds and Dodds, *Churches of Monongalia County*, p. 83.
28. Wiley (writing in 1883), p. 448.

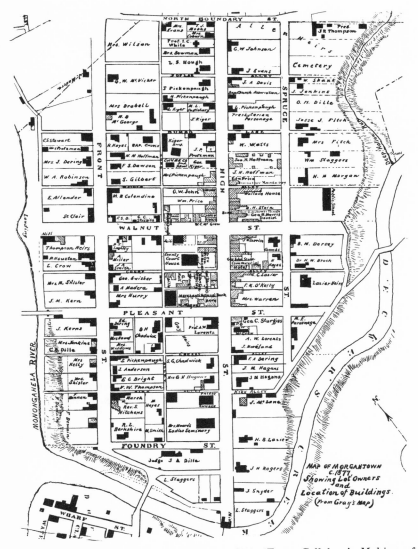

Fig. 137. Map of Morgantown, about 1876. (From Callahan's *Making of Morgantown*.)

**Wealth of the County.** Information concerning the real and personal wealth of the county for the first hundred years of its history is mostly fragmentary. Records for the first twenty years were burned (*Monongalia Story*, vol. 2, p. 253) and from 1796 to 1852 the land assessment books of the commissioners of the revenue lack summaries. The books from 1852 to 1863 are somewhat better, but few accurate totals are available. From 1863 to 1872 part of the books are missing. Only from 1873 on are summaries available and these are given in the table on page 703.[29]

**Josiah Yost.** Dr. Josiah Yost died March 28, 1876. He was born along Paw Paw Creek, Monongalia County, June 11, 1834, a son of Aaron and Sarah Pitzer Yost, who were pioneers in the Glovers Gap section. Josiah Yost was educated in the neighborhood public schools and studied medicine under Dr. Fielding H. Yost. He married Harriet Neptune and they had three children, H. Sanford, Rosa D., and Franklin Josiah.[30]

**Real Estate Developments.** The population of Morgantown was gradually expanding beyond the borough boundaries, which had not been changed since its incorporation in 1785. In 1876 the "lot of land known as Greenmont," situated on an eminence across Deckers Creek from the town, near the fairgrounds, was divided into town lots which were sold at prices ranging from $70 to $226 each. In March 1876, Joseph Keener purchased from Alexander Martin for $2,000 two lots comprising eighteen acres, situated north of the university and extending from the P.B.&M. Turnpike down to the river.[31]

**"Ponetown."** A small community was growing up around the headwaters of Days Run, popularly known as Ponetown. The name originated, it is said, when a tramp passing through stopped at a house to get something to eat. The lady of the house gave him a piece of corn bread ("pone"), which he apparently did not greatly relish. As he left the house, and started up the road he began yelling "Ponetown! Ponetown!"

Early settlers included John Shriver, who built the first mill,

29. Wiley, pp. 557, 558.
30. *Cyclopedia of Marion County*, pp. 120, 121, 160, 161.
31. Callahan, *Making of Morgantown*, p. 212.

## County Assessment

| | Clinton | Morgan | Morgantown | Union | Cass | Grant | Clay | Battelle | Total for County |
|---|---|---|---|---|---|---|---|---|---|
| **REAL ESTATE** | | | | | | | | | |
| 1873 | $337,273 | $396,073 | $205,427 | $369,364 | $372,612 | $549,453 | $404,901 | $305,091 | |
| 1874 | 340,304 | 404,773 | 205,327 | 372,082 | 372,891 | 551,413 | 404,778 | 305,326 | |
| 1875 | 367,865 | 399,380 | 221,653 | 384,013 | 432,371 | 624,744 | 510,533 | 397,627 | |
| 1876 | 368,073 | 398,878 | 222,053 | 384,341 | 432,709 | 626,699 | 511,679 | 397,670 | |
| **PERSONAL** | | | | | | | | | |
| 1873 | 172,178 | 176,280 | 250,198 | 171,528 | 191,281 | 244,390 | 242,528 | 173,251 | |
| 1874 | 165,216 | 167,520 | 316,073 | 176,081 | 159,988 | 227,220 | 248,093 | 180,756 | |
| 1875 | 166,391 | 162,857 | 274,749 | 165,608 | 153,221 | 231,123 | 241,485 | 167,116 | |
| 1876 | 142,897 | 160,239 | 297,944 | 135,656 | 156,575 | 208,261 | 193,029 | 148,255 | |
| **TOTALS** | | | | | | | | | |
| 1873 | 509,451 | 572,353 | 455,625 | 540,892 | 563,893 | 793,843 | 647,429 | 478,342 | $4,561,828 |
| 1874 | 505,520 | 572,303 | 521,400 | 548,163 | 532,879 | 778,633 | 652,871 | 486,082 | 4,597,851 |
| 1875 | 534,256 | 562,237 | 496,402 | 549,621 | 485,592 | 855,867 | 752,018 | 564,743 | 4,800,736 |
| 1876 | 510,970 | 559,117 | 519,997 | 519,997 | 589,284 | 834,960 | 704,708 | 545,925 | 4,784,958 |

Stephen Wilson, Charles Dowd, and James Dowd. Abraham Lemley opened the first store.

The first post office was called Jakes Run (p. 295); it had been started on the stream by that name, with Richard D. Tennant the first postmaster. Solomon Wagner succeeded him July 2, 1861, and since he lived on Days Run, the Jakes Run post office was moved to Days Run. Later the name Daybrook was generally applied, as being a more accurate and respectable name for a community on Days Run, but the name of the post office was not changed for many years.

A new post office on Jakes Run was established September 29, 1876, with Nimrod Tennant as postmaster. Since there was already a Jakes Run post office, the new office was named Statlers Run, another name for the stream (Jake Statlers Run, *Monongalia Story*, vol. 1, p. 184).

**County and Borough Government.** Samuel Hackney was elected sheriff, James M. Stewart, surveyor, Henry C. Baker assessor for the Eastern District, and George Barb for the Western District. Manliff Hayes was president of the county court; other members were John Howell and William C. Wilson (Clinton); F. W. Thompson and Harvey Staggers (Morgan); Albert C. Rude and Oliver Bayles (Union); J. Alexander and F. R. Sinclair (Cass); E. W. Brand and James E. Dent (Grant); Simon P. Tennant and Coverdille Williams (Clay); and Peter A. Tennant and Silas Haught (Battelle).

W. C. McGrew[32] was mayor of Morgantown, W. W. Dering recorder, Charles Chalfant, sergeant, and Joseph Moreland, treasurer. Councilmen were L. S. Hough, W. A. Robison, Frank W. Thompson, Joseph Moreland, and H. W. Brock.

**Liquor Licenses.** A considerable amount of debate transpired in the borough council on the subject of temperance. Since 1870, the council, recognizing the strength of anti-saloon forces, had refused to approve applications for liquor licenses. On

32. According to the charter of 1860, officers of the borough were required to be freeholders. In the election of May 8, 1876, this requirement was overlooked; McGrew, who was not a freeholder, was elected mayor with only one dissenting vote. When the oversight was discovered, the office was declared vacant. He later became a freeholder, however, and on May 16, 1876, the council appointed him mayor for the year (*Journal of the Proceedings of the Council*, May 16, 1876).

Fig. 138. John Marshall Hagans. (From Wiley's *History of Monongalia County*.)

Fig. 139. John A. Dille. (From Wiley's *History of Monongalia County*.)

Fig. 140. Waitman Thomas Willey. (From Wiley's *History of Monongalia County*.)

Fig. 141. William Price. (From Wiley's *History of Monongalia County*.)

December 20, 1873, at an irregular session, three wet members of council, G. W. McVicker, W. N. Jarrett, and D. H. Chadwick, during absence of two dry members, approved an order granting permission to Ben F. Ryan. This action, however, aroused the anti-license citizens, and the action was rescinded three days later when Joseph Moreland cast the deciding vote to sustain the three dry members, Charles McLane, E. Shisler, and L. S. Hough. In May 1875, and again in May 1876, the anti-license ticket was elected to council.[33]

**Miscellany.** In 1876: E. C. Lazier was president of the Monongahela Valley Agricultural and Mechanical Society, which held the annual fairs (Wiley, p. 248). . . . Edgar W. Wilson was admitted to the county bar on September 15 (Wiley, p. 318). . . . Martha Brand died, aged ninety-two (Wiley, p. 472). . . . Thomas H. Price opened an office in Morgantown for the practice of medicine (Wiley, p. 584). . . . James Hopkins opened the Franklin House on Walnut Street (Wiley, p. 587). . . . I. Scott Reed, son of Henry Reed, Morgantown's first coppersmith, opened a tin shop providing tin roofing and spouting (Wiley, p. 603). . . . Asaph C. Fletcher, of Clinton District, died November 28; his wife was Mary A. Campbell and their children were Polly, John, Nancy, Nimrod, Hannah, David, Anson, Rebecca, Benjamin, and Isaac C. (Wiley, p. 644). . . . E. M. Snyder and E. W. St. Clair opened a store at Stewarttown (Wiley, p. 673). . . . John N. Dawson became superintendent of the Laurel Iron Works; although no iron was being made, various other activities continued to be carried on (Wiley, pp. 682, 683). . . . Capt. Francis M. Arnett was keeping Arnett House in Morgantown (Wiley, p. 723). . . . The Grangers organized a lodge and established a store at Flickersville (Wiley, pp. 724, 725). . . . Shelby P. Barker built a flouring mill along the Fairmont Pike in Grant District, naming it the Wagner Mill, for William Wagner, of Morgantown (Wiley, pp. 726, 727, 732, 733). . . . D. T. Miller succeeded Dr. A. W. Brown as storekeeper at Browns Mills (Wiley, p. 747). . . . Chadwick and Son advertised "City-made," or "ready-made" suits and clothing (Callahan, p. 210). . . . In April the large courtroom in the courthouse was repaired; it had been withdrawn from use for social gatherings since 1874 because of its poor condition. In July the front

33. Callahan, *Making of Morgantown*, p. 216.

portico, about to fall to pieces, was also repaired (Callahan, p. 215).

**Summary.** It had been a fruitful half century. The sturdy pioneers who had cleared the first fields and organized the county, often protecting it in bloody warfare with the aborigines, were now all gone, and their sons and daughters occupied the stage, along with newcomers from outside.

> "Time, like an ever-rolling stream,
> Bears all its sons away."—Isaac Watts.

It had been a period of steady growth, interrupted for what seemed like an interminable period, by the violence and anguish of the Civil War. But by 1876 the roads were much better, the social and economic institutions much stronger, than they had been in 1826. A firm foundation had been laid for the remarkable developments to come in the next half century.

\* \* \* \* \*

*Michael Core had a strange dream. He thought he saw curiously designed carriages, not drawn by horses, proceeding smoothly at incredible speeds along the Dunkard Creek Turnpike in front of his house.*

# Appendix A

## UNITED STATES POST OFFICES IN MONONGALIA COUNTY[1] 1826-1876

The dates following names of postmasters indicate times of their appointments. Under each post office, the first date usually indicates also the time of establishment of the post office.

### Andy

Alpheus W. Brown, January 10, 1865

### Arnettsville

James Arnett, July 12, 1851
George B. Snider, October 30, 1851
Eugenius W. Snider, November 11, 1851
    Discontinued May 12, 1852
    Reestablished January 27, 1853
George G. Gregg, January 27, 1853
Robinson Layton, January 18, 1856
James M. Price, January 23, 1857
Arnett Glasscock, March 25, 1857
Alpheus N. Millan, March 27, 1858
James Arnett, August 15, 1861
Francis M. Arnett, September 13, 1861
Sarah Emeline Cox, July 13, 186—
Joseph H. Coogle, December 11, 1865
Calvin W. Miller, January 15, 1875

### Barnes Mills

Thomas Barnes, Jr., ——
R. Martin, July 13, 1829
    Discontinued March 2, 1833

1. Data courtesy the National Archives, Washington, D.C.

## Blacksville

Fletcher Brock, ——
L. Wilson, July 5, 1832
Anthony Conrad, May 30, 1835
Elijah ——, June ——, 1835
Eagon B. Taggard, March 29, 1839
Thomas Brock, April 9, 1849
Robert S. Fletcher, August 21, 1850
Nathaniel F. Keighy, May 30, 1853
Abraham B. Pratt, August 31, 1865
William Lantz, September 4, 1866

## Cassville

Peter A. Layton, September 20, 1847
James Way, July 22, 1861
John W. Tucker, March 21, 1867

## Cedar Valley

William N. Stewart, March 8, 1876

## Center

William Case, July 3, 1854
Alpheus Lemasters, April 16, 1855
Benjamin McCurdy, July 8, 1857
    Discontinued October 17, 1860
    Reestablished July 2, 1861
Benjamin McCurdy, July 2, 1861

## Clinton Furnace

George Hardman, July 9, 1857
Omer B. Johnson, May 24, 1858
    Reappointed July 25, 1867

## Dents Mills

Nimrod Dent, October 4, 1839
    Discontinued May 24, 1843

## Dornicktown

William Hale, January 14, 1851
David Rich, January 27, 1851
Joseph Snider, June 26, 1852
Changed to Fort Martin, May 16, 1854

## Dunkard

Thomas Reynolds, ——
    Discontinued June 11, 1834

## Easton

Charles Lewellen, July 9, 1860
Thomas W. Anderson, June 3, 1867

## Fort Martin

Joseph Snider, Jr., May 16, 1854
Charles A. Kramer, February 15, 1851
George Reppert, June 3, 1862
Barnett Friby, May 25, 1865
George Reppert, June 21, 1865
Daniel Rich, September 13, 1865
William P. Williams, April 9, 1867

## Granville

Melford P. Massie, ——
Marmaduke Dent, March 2, 1833
Alexander Menifee, June 19, 1861
Felix J. Dent, November 21, 1863
William Carothers, December 3, 1864
Marmaduke Dent, May 28, 1873

## Ice's Ferry

Evan T. Ellicott, June 9, 1841
John Bowers, August 22, 1845
Calvin Holmes, December 20, 1849
Cornelius McShane, November 27, 1850
Anthony Loftis, December 23, 1850
Thomas J. Duvall, January 15, 1853
    Reappointed August 1, 1854
Nathaniel H. Tripplett, June 16, 1856
    Reappointed July 20, 1861
Charles H. Burgess, January 21, 1862
Changed to Laurel Iron Works, December 28, 1864

## Jakes Run

Richard D. Tennant, May 23, 1844
Solomon Wagner, July 2, 1861
Robert Berry, March 13, 1866
Benjamin Wilson, March 19, 1868

## Jobe

George Keefover, July 25, 1867
Elias J. Eddy, March 1, 1870
Peter R. Core, December 6, 1872
Elias J. Eddy, June 16, 1874
Remembrance Thomas, July 16, 1874

## Jimtown

William Pendleton Williams, February 18, 1850
Purnel Simpson, February 26, 1851
Jesse H. Hull, May 20, 1851
    Discontinued October 30, 1851

## Kings Ferry

Job Springer, ——
M. Jefferies, ——
I. Rodgers, May 24, 1826

## Knottsville

Absalom Knotts, ——
I. Knotts, N. Boggess, January 4, 1832
Rawley Gandy, July 14, 1834

## Lakeville

George Lake, ——
    Discontinued January 19, 1833

## Laurel Iron Works

John H. Conn, May 25, 1865
Nathaniel H. Triplett, March 11, 1868

## Laurel Point

John Jamison, July 20, 1848
Edward G. Brooke, October 5, 1848
Benjamin C. Fear, ——, 1851
Asa C. Frey, June 17, 1853
William Fear, March 27, 1858
    Discontinued July 9, 1863
    Reestablished August 13, 1863
William Fear, August 13, 1863
Benjamin F. Swisher, September 21, 186—
Jane Fleming, August 31, 1865
William M. Jones, January 8, 1867
S. W. Fleming, March 25, 1870
J. Milton Taylor, July 7, 1870
Henry C. Miller, February 8, 1876
Thomas L. Miller, May 26, 1873

## Lowesville

Levi Lowe, February 13, 1856
    Discontinued December 6, 1858
John Hood, December 16, 1874

## Maidsville

Adonijah E. Cushman, January 24, 1857
William W. Lazzell, February 19, 1859
James Sanders, July 12, 1861
Adonijah E. Cushman, February 13, 1866
Lorenzo Davis, August 7, 1871
John Sanders, May 13, 1873
Lorenzo Davis, December 8, 1874

## Miracle Run

Adam B. Tennant, June 6, 1854
   Discontinued July 2, 1861
   Reestablished February 19, 1862
John Anderson, February 19, 1862
William Tuttle, Jr., January 19, 1863

## Mooresville

Isaac N. Litman, July 25, 1867
Simon G. Tennant, February 2, 1870

## Morgantown

Nicholas B. Madera
James Shay, April 6, 1853
Charles Wallace, June 16, 1860
Frederick A. Dering, February 11, 1864

## Mount Linus

Gouldin Arnett, January 4, 1831
L. Shaidley, Clement Morgan, February 29, 1833
Joseph Morgan, January 19, 1833

## Palatine Hill

William Haymond, ——

## Park

Thomas Johnson, December 30, 1833
Thomas Steel, Peter Johnstone, February 6, 1834
   Discontinued October 11, 1834

## Pawpaw

George Wilson, February 25, 1837
   Discontinued February 3, 1842

## Pedlars Run

Alpheus Garrison, June 22, 1874

## Pentress

Cyrenius Cox, August 23, 1847
John M. Wilson, June 9, 1853
Cyrenius Cox, April 13, 1854
Eagan B. Tygard, February 14, 1855
Abraham W. Tennant, March 13, 1865
Nicholas B. Johnson, August 1, 1865
    Discontinued July 10, 1867
    Reestablished January 21, 1873
John Ruse, January 21, 1873
Titus Lemley, June 23, 1875

## Pleasant Valley

Elisha C. Allender, July 29, 1867
Moses Steele, February 2, 1870
    Discontinued January 16, 1876
    Reestablished January 24, 1876
Charles H. Holland, January 24, 1876

## Polsleys

Ebenezer Newcomb, ——

## Pridevale

Nathaniel H. Triplett, December 8, 1854
Duncan J. Perry, January 8, 1856
Thomas Collingwood, April 29, 1856
Zadock Walker, April 2, 1860
    Discontinued June 30, 1860

## Randall

Samuel S. Yeager, November 25, 1867
Isaac N. Furman, April 13, 1874

## Rivesville

Elisha Snodgrass, February 25, 1837

## Saint Cloud

John H. Six, August 5, 1873

## Scotts Run

Peter A. Layton, August 1, 1843
    Discontinued July 26, 1844

## Snidersville

David Snider, June 13, 1840
    Discontinued January 17, 1843

## Statlers Run

Nimrod Tennant, September 29, 1876

## Stewartstown

Owen John, January 8, 1850
Samuel Witherow, January 22, 1850
David D. Wade, February 16, 1852
Samuel O. Robison, May 8, 1857
Owen John, September 27, 1858
George W. John, November 13, 1858
Nicholas Blosser, May 10, 1861
Miss Amanda John, October 22, 1861
Edgar W. St. Clair, October 7, 1868
John G. Conn, June 22, 1874

## Three Forks

Joseph Barrill, March 6, 1840

## Uffington

William D. Smith, July 8, 1850
Charles M. Kern, October 22, 1858
Alexander H. Osborn, September 4, 1861
Miss Virginia Kern, April 13, 1864
    Discontinued May 16, 1864
    Reestablished July 8, 1873
James S. Watson, July 8, 1873

## Wadestown

William Kinney, October 14, 1847
John McCarl, December 29, 1854
Miss Pleasant Santee, May 7, 1862
Mark G. Lester, June 24, 1867

## White Day

James D. Watson, May 18, 1841
Joseph Jolliffe, July 21, 1845
William C. Wilson, January 16, 1867

# Appendix B

## MONONGALIA COUNTY'S REPRESENTATION IN THE GENERAL ASSEMBLY OF VIRGINIA AND LEGISLATURE OF WEST VIRGINIA

(From Earl G. Swem and John W. Williams, *Register of the General Assembly of Virginia, 1776-1918* 1918; Wiley, pp. 272-74, 281, 282.)

### Senate

December 4, 1826-March 9, 1827 (Ohio, Tyler, Brooke, Preston, and Monongalia). Charles S. Morgan.

December 3, 1827-March 1, 1828. Charles S. Morgan.

December 1, 1828-February 17, 1829. Charles S. Morgan.

December 7, 1829-February 23, 1830. Charles S. Morgan.

December 6, 1830-April 19, 1831 (Monongalia, Preston, and Randolph). Charles S. Morgan.

December 5, 1831-March 21, 1832. Charles S. Morgan.

December 3, 1832-March 9, 1833. Richard Watts.

December 2, 1833-March 14, 1834. Richard Watts.

December 1, 1834-March 12, 1835. Richard Watts.

December 7, 1835-March 24, 1936. Francis Billingsly.

December 5, 1836-March 31, 1837. Francis Billingsly.

January 1-April 9, 1838. Francis Billingsly.

January 7-April 10, 1939. Francis Billingsly.

December 2, 1839-March 19, 1840. William J. Willey.

December 1, 1840-March 22, 1841. William J. Willey.

December 6, 1841-March 26, 1842. William J. Willey.

December 5, 1842-March 28, 1843 (Monongalia, Preston, Randolph, and Marion). William J. Willey.

December 4, 1843-February 15, 1844 (Monongalia, Preston, Randolph, Barbour and Marion). William J. Willey.

December 2, 1844-February 22, 1845 (Monongalia, Preston, Randolph, Barbour, Marion and Taylor). William J. Willey.

December 1, 1845-March 6, 1846. William J. Willey.

December 7, 1846-March 23, 1847. William J. Willey.

December 6, 1847-April 5, 1848. John S. Carlile.

December 4, 1848-March 19, 1849; May 28-June 4, 1849; June 11-August 17, 1849. John S. Carlile.

December 3, 1849-March 22, 1850. John S. Carlile.

December 2, 1850-March 31, 1851. John S. Carlile.

January 12-June 7, 1852; November 22, 1852-April 11, 1853 (Monongalia, Preston, and Taylor). Alexander Wade, Jr.

December 5, 1853-March 4, 1854. Alexander Wade, Jr.

December 3, 1855-March 19, 1856. Jonathan Huddleson.

December 7, 1857-April 8, 1858. Jonathan Huddleson.

December 5, 1859-April 2, 1860; January 7, 1861-April 4, 1861. Charles W. Newlon.

## State of West Virginia
### (Sessions held annually)

1863. John J. Brown, E. C. Bunker

1864. E. C. Bunker, John J. Brown

1865. John J. Brown, William Price

1866. John S. Burdett, William Price

1867. William B. Zinn, John S. Burdett

1868. William Price, William B. Zinn

1869. Jesse H. Cather, William Price

1870. William B. Crane, Jesse H. Cather

1871. William Price, William B. Crane

1872. Jesse H. Cather, William Price

### (Sessions held biennially)

1873. C. M. Bishop, Ralph L. Berkshire

1875. C. M. Bishop, Ralph L. Berkshire

## House of Delegates
### State of Virginia

1826. Richard Watts, Francis Billingsly

1827. Richard Watts, Francis Billingsly

1828. Richard Watts, Edgar C. Wilson

1829. Richard Watts, Francis Billingsly

1830. Richard Watts, Francis Billingsly

1831. Francis Billingsly, William G. Henry

1832. William J. Willey, William G. Henry

1833. Francis Billingsly, Isaac Cooper

1834. William J. Willey, Stephen H. Morgan

1835. William J. Willey, Stephen H. Morgan

1836. William J. Willey, Isaac Cooper
1837. Thomas S. Haymond, Stephen H. Morgan
1838. Thomas S. Haymond, John Clayton
1839. John Clayton, James Evans
1840. John Clayton, Caleb Tanzey
1841. William S. Morgan, Joseph F. Harrison
1842. Caleb Tanzey
1843. John H. Bowlby
1844. Alexander Wade, Jr.
1845. Alexander Wade, Jr.
1846. Andrew Brown
1847. Caleb Tanzey
1848. Caleb Tanzey
1849. Francis Warman
1850. Francis Warman
1851. Andrew McDonald
1852. Andrew McDonald, John S. Lemley
(After this year sessions were held biennially; prior to 1852, they were held annually.)
1853. John B. Lough, Henry S. Coombs
1855. William Lantz, Robert C. Carothers
1857. Alfred M. Barbour, Albert G. Davis
1859. John Wallace, Andrew Brown

## Reorganized Government of Virginia
(Sessions held annually)

1861. LeeRoy Kramer, Joseph Snider
1862. LeeRoy Kramer, Joseph Snider

## State of West Virginia
(Sessions held annually)

1863. LeeRoy Kramer, John B. Lough
1864. LeeRoy Kramer, John B. Lough
1865. Alpheus W. Brown, Henry S. Coombs
1866. Alpheus W. Brown, Nelson N. Hoffman
1867. James T. McClaskey, James V. Boughner
1868. James T. McClaskey, Alpheus Garrison
1869. William Price, George C. Sturgiss
1870. John B. Lough, George C. Sturgiss
1871. George C. Sturgiss, John B. Lough

(Sessions held biennially)

1873. William Price, Joseph Snider
1875. John B. Lough, Joseph Snider

# Selected Bibliography

Ambler, Charles H., Frances Haney Atwood, and William B. Mathews, eds. *Debates and Proceedings of the First Constitutional Convention of West Virginia* (1861-1863). 1939?

Ambler, Charles H. *Francis H. Pierpont* (see p. 508). 1937.

Ambler, Charles H. *History of Education in West Virginia.* 1951.

Ambler, Charles H. *Waitman Thomas Willey* (inc. *The Wesley Methodist Church*). 1954.

Anonymous. *Biographical and Portrait Cyclopedia of Monongalia, Marion, and Taylor Counties, West Virginia.* Philadelphia. 1895.

Aspinall, Rowland, and Charles W. Evans, eds. *Minutes of the Western Virginia Conference,* 1848 to 1857. 1939.

Baker, Gordon C. *Daniel and Rebecca Stewart.* 1977.

Baker, Ira. *History of Drummond Chapel.* Typescript, n.d.

Balderson, W. L. *Fort Prickett Frontier and Marion County* [1977].

Baldwin, Leland D. *The Keelboat Age on the Western Waters.* 1941.

Barnes, I. A. *The Methodist Protestant Church in West Virginia.* 1926.

Bartlett, Paul C., ed. *Historical Anecdotes of Taylor County,* n.d.

Bartlett, Richard A. *The New Country. A Social History of the American Frontier.* 1974.

Bauer, K. Jack. *The Mexican War, 1846-1848.* 1974.

Boette, Marie, ed. *Singa Hipsy Doodle and other Folk Songs of West Virginia.* 1971.

Brand, Franklin Marion. *The Brand Family.* 1922.

Brand, Franklin Marion. *The Fleming Family.* 1941.

Brand, Franklin Marion. *The Wade Family.* 1927.

Brandon, Ruth. *A Capitalist Romance. Singer and the Sewing Machine.* 1977.

Brinkman, Charles. *History of Taylor County* (in installments in the *Grafton Sentinel*). 1939.

Brown, George. *Recollections of Itinerant Life.* 1858.

Butcher, Bernard L. (and others), eds. *Genealogical and Personal History of the Upper Monongahela Valley.* 1912.

Calhoun, H. M. *'Twixt North and South.* 1974.

Callahan, James Morton. *Semi-Centennial History of West Virginia.* 1913.

Callahan, James Morton. *History of the Making of Morgantown.* 1926.

Catton, Bruce. *The Coming Fury.* 1961.

Catton, Bruce. *Terrible Swift Sword.* 1963.

Catton, Bruce. *Never Call Retreat.* 1965.

Chadwick, French Ensor. *Causes of the Civil War.* 1906.

Clarkson, Roy B. *Tumult in the Mountains.* 1964.

Cohen, Stan. *The Civil War in West Virginia.* A Pictorial History. 1976.

Conley, Phil, and William Thomas Doherty. *West Virginia History.* 1974.

Core, Earl L. *Morgantown Disciples.* 1960.

Core, Earl L. *Chronicles of Core.* 3d ed. 1975.

Davis, Dorothy. *History of Harrison County.* 1970.

DeVault, Belva Mae, and Clara DeVault. *History of Uffington.* Typescript, n.d.

Dodds, Dr. and Mrs. Gideon S. *The Churches of Monongalia County* (in *175th Anniversary . . . of Monongalia County*). 1954.

Dunnington, George A. *A History and Progress of the County of Marion, West Virginia.* 1880.

Eskew, Roderick Koinig. *History of the Quarrier, Laidley, Bickers, Eskew, and Allied Families.* 1971.

Evans, Clement A. *Confederate Military History.* Vol. 2, *Maryland and West Virginia,* n.d.

Flowers, Manford Grover. *The Western Virginia Conference of the Methodist Episcopal Church.* 1947.

Gainer, Patrick W. *Folk Songs from the West Virginia Hills.* 1975.

Gluck, Joseph C. (and others). *Forks of Cheat Baptist Church.* 1975.

Greenwood, Isaac J. *The Circus, Its Origin and Growth Prior to 1835.* 1898.

Hagans, John Marshall. *West Virginia Supreme Court Reports.* 1866.

Hasting, Lynn. *School and Local History.* (typescript). 10 vols. 1960.

Haymond, Henry. *History of Harrison County.* 1910.

Headlee, Alvah J. W. *George Lemley and wife Catharine Yoho and Their Descendants for Two Centuries.* 1975.

Headlee, Alvah J. W. *Greene County in 1865.* 1977.

Hedman, Kathryn Pierpont. *The Pierpoint-Pierpont Family.* 2d ed. 1973.

Hennen, Dorothy T. *Hennen's Choice.* Vol. 1, 1970. Vol. 2. 1972.

Hoard, Clifford B. *House of Hoard.* 1965.

Hungerford, Edward. *The Story of the Baltimore and Ohio Railroad.* 2 vols. 1928.

Johnston, Ross B. *West Virginians in the American Revolution.* 1959.

Kenny, Hamill. *West Virginia Place Names.* 1945.

Kenton, Edna. *Simon Kenton, His Life and Period.* 1930.

Lee, Howard B. *The Burning Springs and Other Tales of the Little Kanawha.* 1968.

Lough, Glenn D. *Now and Long Ago.* 1969.

McRae, Elijah. *History of Halleck Community.* Typescript, n.d.

Martin, Joseph. *Gazetteer of Virginia* (see p. 120). 1935.

Millspaugh, Charles F. *American Medicinal Plants* (see p. 212). 1892.

Monongalia Historical Society. *The 175th Anniversary of the Formation of Monongalia County, West Virginia, and other Relative Historical Data.* 1954.

Moreland, James R. *The Early Cheat Iron Works* (for full title see p. 144). Typescript, 1940.

Moreland, James R. *The First Presbyterian Church of Morgantown.* 1938.

Moreland, James R. *Anecdotes, . . .* , etc. Typescript. 2 vols. 1940.

Moreland, Joseph. *Morgantown, Its Practical Jokes and Jokers.* 1885.

Morgan, French. *History . . . of the Family of Col. Morgan Morgan.* 1950.

Morton, Oren F. *History of Preston County.* 2 vols. 1914.

Music, Ruth Ann. *Ballads, Folk Songs and Folk Tales from West Virginia.* 1960.

Newhall, Beaumont. *The Daguerreotype in America.* 1961.

Newman, Dora Lee, ed. *Marion County in the Making.* 1917.

Owens, Ivan C. *Easton-Avery Community History.* 1964.

Pierpoint, Francis P. *Annual Report of the Adjutant General of the State of West Virginia for the Year ending December 31, 1864.* 1865.

Reeder, Benjamin Garnet. *Book of Reeder.* Typescript, n.d.

Reynolds, Grafton T. *Manual of the Pittsburgh Conference of the Methodist Episcopal Church.* 1928.

Rice, Otis K. *The Allegheny Frontier.* 1970.

Robinson, Felix G., ed. *Monongalia County Issue, Tableland Trails.* Vol 2. No. 3, 197 pp. Summer, 1958.

Rowland, Ralph Shearer and Star Wilson Rowland. *Wilsons and Burchells and Related Families.* 1976.

Searight, Thomas B. *The Old Pike.* 1894. New ed. by Joseph E. Morse and R. Duff Green. 1971.

Shinn, Josiah H. *The History of the Shinn Family in Europe and America.* 1903.

Shively, Norman B. *Index to Samuel T. Wiley's History of Monongalia County, West Virginia (1883).* McClain. 1976.

Sims, Edgar B. *Index to Land Grants in West Virginia.* 1952.

Stegmaier, Harry, Jr., David Dean, Gordon Kershaw, and John Wiseman. *Allegany County: A History.* 1976.

Stutler, Boyd B. *West Virginia in the Civil War.* 1963.

Summers, Festus P. *The Baltimore and Ohio in the Civil War.* 1939.

Swetnam, George, and Helene Smith. *Guidebook to Historic Western Pennsylvania.* 1976.

Tennant, J. Ross. *Memories.* 1, 1942; 2, 1945; 3, 1946; 4, 1948.

Thoenen, Eugene D. *History of the Oil and Gas Industry in West Virginia.* 1964.

Tucker, William E., and Lester G. McAllister. *Journey in Faith. A History of the Christian Church (Disciples of Christ).* 1975.

Tunis, Edwin. *Wheels.* 1955.

Welter, Rush. *The Mind of America, 1820-1860.* 1975.

Weltner, Fred Hamilton, and Harry Leroy Jeffries, Sr. *The Stewartstown Story.* 1971.

Wilcox, William. *How Our Marion County Churches Began.* 1976.

Wilding, George Cleaton. *Promoted Pioneer Preachers of the West Virginia Conference of the Methodist Episcopal Church, and a Sketch of Her Early Ministers who were transferred to other Fields.* 1927.

Wiley, Richard T. *Monongahela. The River and Its Region.* 1937.

Wiley, Samuel T. *History of Monongalia County.* 1883.

Wiley, Samuel T. *History of Preston County.* 1882.

Willey, Waitman T. *A Sketch of the Life of Philip Doddridge.* 1875.

# Index

The spelling of proper names in the earlier part of this period still varied considerably and in this work the orthography, in general, reflects that of the sources, even though a given person's name may appear in various forms on different pages.

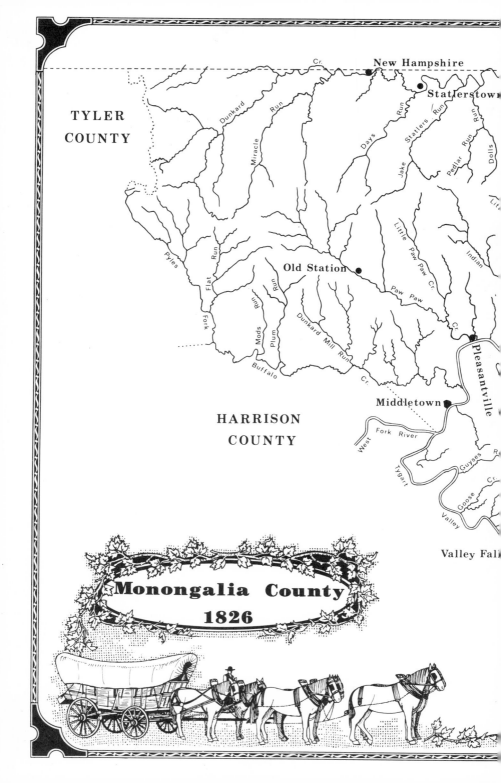

TYLER
COUNTY

HARRISON
COUNTY

New Hampshire

Statlerstown

Old Station

Pleasantville

Middletown

Valley Falls

Monongalia County
1826